S0-BBR-990

in real life

Boxed Applications

Indicates global example

MICROECONOMICS
SECOND EDITION in MODULES

MICROECONOMICS
SECOND EDITION in MODULES

Paul Krugman | Robin Wells
Princeton University

with

Margaret Ray and David Anderson
University of Mary
Washington

Centre College

Worth Publishers

Cover photo credits

Senior Publisher: Catherine Woods
Executive Editor: Charles Linsmeier
Senior Media Development Editor: Marie McHale
Development Editors: Barbara Brooks, Sharon Balbos
Senior Consultant: Andreas Bentz
Editorial Assistant: Mary Walsh
Executive Marketing Manager: Scott Guile
Art Director: Babs Reingold
Cover Designer: Kevin Kall
Interior Designer: TSI Graphics
Photo Editor: Cecilia Varas
Photo Researcher: Dena Digilio Betz
Associate Managing Editor: Tracey Kuehn
Production Manager: Barbara Anne Seixas
Composition: TSI Graphics
Printing and Binding: RR Donnelley

Library of Congress Control Number: 2011924408

ISBN-13: 978-1-4292-8730-2
ISBN-10: 1-4292-8730-6

Printed in the United States of America

First printing, 2011

Worth Publishers
41 Madison Avenue
New York, NY 10010
www.wortheconomics.com

To beginning students everywhere,
which we all were at one time.

About the Authors

Paul Krugman, recipient of the 2008 Nobel Memorial Prize in Economic Sciences, is Professor of Economics at Princeton University, where he regularly teaches the principles course. He received his BA from Yale and his PhD from MIT. Prior to his current position, he taught at Yale, Stanford, and MIT. He also spent a year on the staff of the Council of Economic Advisers in 1982–1983. His research is mainly in the area of international trade, where he is one of the founders of the "new trade theory," which focuses on increasing returns and imperfect competition. He also works in international finance, with a concentration in currency crises. In 1991, Krugman received the American Economic Association's John Bates Clark medal. In addition to his teaching and academic research, Krugman writes extensively for nontechnical audiences. Krugman is a regular op-ed columnist for the *New York Times.* His latest trade books, both best sellers, include *The Return of Depression Economics and the Crisis of 2008,* a history of recent economic troubles and their implications for economic policy, and *The Conscience of a Liberal,* a study of the political economy of economic inequality and its relationship with political polarization from the Gilded Age to the present. His earlier books, *Peddling Prosperity* and *The Age of Diminished Expectations,* have become modern classics.

Robin Wells was a Lecturer and Researcher in Economics at Princeton University. She received her BA from the University of Chicago and her PhD from the University of California at Berkeley; she then did postdoctoral work at MIT. She has taught at the University of Michigan, the University of Southampton (United Kingdom), Stanford, and MIT. The subject of her teaching and research is the theory of organizations and incentives.

Contributors to This Edition

Margaret Ray is Professor of Economics at the University of Mary Washington, where she specializes in teaching introductory economics. She received her BS in Economics from Oklahoma State University and her PhD in Economics from the University of Tennessee. Prior to her current position, she taught at Western Illinois University, Mississippi State University, Texas Christian University, the University of Texas—Arlington, and the University of Arizona. She also worked as an Economist at the Federal Reserve Bank of Richmond for three years. She won the Council on Economic Education Excellence in Economic Education Award in 1991. Her research is primarily in the areas of economic education and equine industry economics.

David Anderson is the Paul G. Blazer Professor of Economics at Centre College. He received his BA in Economics from the University of Michigan and his MA and PhD in Economics from Duke University. Anderson has authored dozens of scholarly articles and ten books, including *Favorite Ways to Learn Economics*, *Environmental Economics and Natural Resource Management*, *Contemporary Economics for Managers*, *Treading Lightly*, and *Economics by Example*. His research is primarily on economic education, environmental economics, law and economics, and labor economics. Anderson teaches courses in each of these fields and loves teaching introductory economics.

Brief Contents

Contents

Contents

Contents

Contents

Preface

"If you want to be listened to, you should put in time listening." —Marge Piercy

FROM PAUL AND ROBIN

We both believe that a successful second edition is an exercise in listening. Writing a successful first edition is largely a matter of capitalizing on one's strengths, but writing a successful second edition means listening to those who used the first edition and using that to address one's oversights and misjudgments. In many ways, writing a second edition can be as challenging as writing a first edition.

We've been fortunate to have a devoted group of adopters and reviewers to help guide us in this revision. Although the first edition of *Microeconomics* received an overwhelmingly positive reception, it also generated many helpful suggestions for improvement. We planned from the beginning to make significant revisions to incorporate those suggestions.

The world has changed a lot since the first edition of *Microeconomics,* and we've tried hard to include those changes in this new edition.

That said, the fundamental principles of microeconomics remain the same. Most of the changes we've made in this edition are in an effort to respond to the suggestions of adopters and reviewers about how to teach those principles more effectively. With that, let's talk about those changes, including this new modular format.

Why a Modular Book?

We have also listened to those of you who have long been eager to use our book but wanted a shorter, more accessible version of it. So, for those of you who like our current and lively examples, our international focus, and the fluid friendly writing of *Microeconomics,* we present to you a modularized version of the text that offers all of these benefits and more.

> **Modules mean greater accessibility and happier students.** The main benefit of this modular book is that chapters are divided into short, digestible chapters (the modules). Based on feedback from the instructors who have urged us to devise a more streamlined text, we know that shorter chapters make for happier students. Instead of tackling 21 chapters at about 30 to 40 pages each, students will encounter 5- to 10-page modules designed to be read in a single sitting. Our goal was to make each module informative and thorough, but short enough to keep students reading and engaged. At the end of the text, we also offer a more substantial module on international trade, for those who wish to explore this topic in depth (Module 45).

> **Modules offer greater flexibility for instructors.** We have often heard that time limits during the semester can make it impossible to teach every chapter in a textbook or some of the chapters in their entirety. Happily, the modular format addresses this issue by allowing instructors the flexibility to assign the topics they do teach, without having to break chapters into bits and pieces. Even better, because the modules are so short, instructors may find the time to cover some of the more compelling and interesting material that too often gets cut from the course when using a book with longer chapters.

> **Modules (and sections) mean more opportunity for structured learning and assessment.** Students benefit because each module concentrates on a specific topic using a learning-objectives approach and concludes with three separate types of self-assessment questions. Instructors benefit because—while students navigate more easily from topic to topic within the modular structure—assessment across interrelated modules still occurs at the end of each section.

Each brief module includes "Check Your Understanding" questions that do just that, five multiple-choice questions that encourage reflection, as well as some thought-provoking critical-thinking questions. Answers for all of these questions appear at the back of the book, so students can truly test their understanding.

Then, each major section ends with our highly praised collection of problems that test related concepts across the modules in that section. Problems can be assigned for practice and for student assessment. We have heard from users and reviewers that our problems are among the best they've ever seen in a principles text.

Highlights from the Second Edition of Microeconomics in Modules

In preparing this new modular edition, every single module was carefully evaluated and revised, many of them significantly, to clarify explanations, streamline when necessary, and update. As always, we've made a concerted effort to update our examples and applications to keep up with a fast-changing world. We hope that these revisions lead to a more successful teaching experience for you. We look forward to your comments about the revisions and this new format.

An Impressive Collection of New Examples and Applications Throughout

In both the second edition and the modular edition of *Microeconomics,* we integrate theory with practice through the extensive use of real-world examples. Each section begins with an opening story taken from real life; that opening story is often woven into the exposition throughout the various modules. There are also many examples and applications integrated right into the narrative. In truth, we have included far more new examples than we had originally anticipated. But current events intervened and every day would bring new example possibilities that we just *had* to incorporate. The end result is, we believe, a fresh, current, and cutting-edge microeconomics book.

New Boxed Feature: "In Real Life"

Once or twice in most modules, some of our examples appear as "In Real Life" boxed features. There are 41 of these boxes throughout the book. The "In Real Life" boxes offer real-world applications of the major concepts explored in each module. Some take a closer look at real data and use it to illustrate international comparisons. In all instances, these boxes examine real-world events and issues.

Our goal in these boxes is to generate a sense of the power and breadth of economics and clarify its relevance to everyday life. We also use the boxes to infuse the modules with our distinctive voice. But, above all, we also wish to use these boxes to show students that economics can be fun despite being labeled the "dismal science."

A vast majority of the integrated and boxed examples in this edition are new. Many are global in focus. Globally oriented "In Real Life" boxes are marked with this globe icon.

Advantages of This Book

Although a lot is new in this second edition, our basic approach to textbook writing remains the same:

> **Modules build intuition through realistic examples.** In every module, we use real-world examples, stories, applications, and case studies to teach the core concepts and motivate student learning. The best way to introduce concepts and reinforce them is through real-world examples; students simply relate more easily to them.

> **Pedagogical features reinforce learning.** We've crafted what we believe are a genuinely helpful set of features that are illustrated and described in the section, "Tools for Learning" on pages xxii–xxv of this preface.

> **Modules are accessible and entertaining.** We use a fluid and friendly writing style to make concepts accessible. Whenever possible, we use examples that are familiar to students.

> **Although easy to understand, the book also prepares students for further coursework.** Too often, instructors find that selecting a textbook means choosing between two unappealing alternatives: a textbook that is "easy to teach" but leaves major gaps in students' understanding, or a textbook that is "hard to teach" but adequately prepares students for future coursework. We offer an easy-to-understand textbook that offers the best of both worlds.

The Organization of This Book and How to Use It

The organization of this book is inspired by our goal of adapting our chapter-based book into a unique modular format for increased flexibility in teaching and learning. The sequence of sections and modules conforms to a sequence of material that has been found to be pedagogically effective. The sections and modules are grouped into building blocks in which conceptual material learned at one stage is built upon and then integrated into the conceptual material covered in the next stage. However, instructors can also chart their own paths through the material, skipping or including modules, based on their students' mastery of the concepts. Following is a walkthrough of the sections in the book:

Section 1: Basic Economic Concepts

The first section initiates students into the study of economics, including scarcity, choice and opportunity cost. Module 1 provides students with definitions of basic terms in economics. Module 2 looks at how models are used by economists and examines one simplified version of reality, the circular-flow diagram. Modules 3 and 4 present the production possibility frontier model and use it to explain comparative and absolute advantage, specialization and exchange. The Appendix explains how graphs are constructed, interpreted, and used in economics.

Section 2: Supply and Demand

Section 2 begins with an opening story that uses the market for coffee beans to illustrate supply and demand, market equilibrium, and surplus and shortage. Modules 5, 6, and 7 introduce the important parts of the supply and demand model; demand, supply, and equilibrium. Module 8 and 9 teach students how to use the model to analyze price and quantity in markets.

Section 3: Behind the Demand Curve: Consumer Choice

This section looks more closely at topics related to the demand curve. Module 10 explains how the income and substitution effects relate to a downward sloping demand curve and presents the concept of elasticity. Module 11 is devoted to developing price elasticity while Module 12 explains three additional elasticity measures important in economics. Consumer and producer surplus are presented in Modules 13 and 14 and are used to explain deadweight loss. Finally, Module 15 presents consumer theory and utility maximization.

Section 4: Behind the Supply Curve: Profit, Production, and Costs

Section 4 shifts to a more detailed discussion of the supply curve. This section introduces the production and cost concepts used throughout the following sections. The section begins with a discussion of profit and profit maximization in Modules 16 and 17. Module 18 develops the production function. Modules 19 and 20 introduce cost concepts, both short-run and long-run. The last module provides an introduction to the market structures covered in Sections 5 and 6.

Section 5: Market Structures: Perfect Competition and Monopoly

Section 5 presents the perfect competition and monopoly market structures. Modules 22-24 present perfect competition. Modules 22 and 23 develop the perfect competition model and graphs. Module 24 presents the long-run outcomes under perfect competition. Modules 25–27 present the monopoly market structure. Module 25 develops the basic monopoly model. Module 26 presents public policies toward monopoly and Module 27 explains the practice of price discrimination.

Section 6: Market Structures: Imperfect Competition

This section introduces the imperfectly competitive market structures: oligopoly and monopolistic competition. Module 28 introduces oligopoly and Module 30 discusses oligopoly market structures in the real world. Game theory as it relates to oligopoly is given special attention in Module 29. Module 31 explains monopolistic competition. Module 32 covers product differentiation under monopolistic competition with special focus on the role of advertising.

Section 7: Factor Markets

This section begins with Module 33, an introduction to factor markets and factor demand. Modules 34 and 35 present the markets for land, capital, and labor. Module 36 explains how to find the cost-minimizing combination of inputs. The last module in the section discusses the marginal productivity theory of income distribution and various sources of wage differentials.

Section 8: Market Failure and the Role of Government

This section focuses on the conditions under which markets fail and explains public and private approaches to market failure. Modules 38 and 39 discuss externalities and the public policies and private remedies available to address them. Module 40 covers public goods. Module 41 presents the use of antitrust law and government regulation to promote competition. Module 42 explains theories of income distribution and income inequality.

Section 9: Appendix

This end-of-book appendix provides coverage of interesting but often optional topics. Module 43 presents the economics of information, including adverse selection and moral hazard. Module 44 discusses indifference curves and consumer choice, an extension of the material in Module 15. Lastly, Module 45 covers the intricacies of international trade for those who wish to move beyond coverage of comparative advantage and the PPF.

Supplements and Media

Worth Publishers is pleased to offer an enhanced and completely revised supplements and media package to accompany this textbook. The package has been crafted to help instructors teach their principles course and to give students the tools to develop their skills in economics.

For Instructors

Instructor's Resource Manual with Solutions Manual

The Instructor's Resource Manual is a resource meant to provide materials and tips to enhance the classroom experience. The Instructor's Resource Manual provides the following:

- Learning objectives
- Outlines
- Teaching tips and ideas that include: Hints on how to create student interest and tips on presenting the material in class
- Discussion of the examples used in the text, including points to emphasize with your students
- Activities that can be conducted in or out of the classroom
- Hints for dealing with common misunderstandings that are typical among students
- Web resources
- Solutions manual with detailed solutions to all of the Problems from the textbook

Printed Test Bank

The Test Bank provides a wide range of questions appropriate for assessing your students' comprehension, interpretation, analysis, and synthesis skills. The Test Bank offers multiple-choice, true/false, and short-answer questions designed for comprehensive coverage of the text concepts.

("Supplements" continued, p. xxviii)

Tools for Learning...Getting the Most from This Book

Each section and its modules are structured around a common set of features designed to help students learn while keeping them engaged.

The **section outline** offers a quick preview of the modules that comprise the section.

section 2

Module 5	Supply and Demand: Introduction and Demand
Module 6	Supply and Demand: Supply and Equilibrium
Module 7	Supply and Demand: Changes in Supply and Demand
Module 8	Supply and Demand: Price Controls (Ceilings and Floors)
Module 9	Supply and Demand: Quantity Controls

Supply and Demand

For those who need a cappuccino, mocha latte, or Frappuccino to get through the day, coffee drinking can become an expensive habit. And on October 6, 2006, the habit got a little more expensive. On that day, Starbucks raised its drink prices for the first time in six years. The average price of coffee beverages at the world's leading chain of coffeehouses rose about 11 cents per cup.

Starbucks had kept its prices unchanged for six years. So what compelled them to finally raise their prices in the fall of 2006? Mainly the fact that the cost of a major ingredient—coffee beans—had gone up significantly. In fact, coffee bean prices doubled between 2002 and 2006.

Who decided to raise the prices of coffee beans? Nobody: prices went up because of events outside anyone's control. Specifically, the main cause of rising bean prices was a significant decrease in the supply of coffee beans from the world's two leading coffee exporters: Brazil and Vietnam. In Brazil, the decrease in supply was a delayed reaction to low prices earlier in the decade, which led coffee growers to cut back on planting. In Vietnam, the problem was weather: a prolonged drought sharply reduced coffee harvests.

And a lower supply of coffee beans from Vietnam or Brazil inevitably translates into a higher price of coffee on Main Street. It's just a matter of supply and demand.

What do we mean by that? Many people use "supply and demand" as a sort of catchphrase to mean "the laws of the marketplace at work." To economists, however, the concept of supply and demand has a precise meaning: it is a *model* of how a market behaves.

In this section, we lay out the pieces that make up the *supply and demand model*, put them together, and show how this model can be used to understand how many—but not all—markets behave.

Opening Story Each section opens with a compelling story that often extends through the modules. The opening stories are designed to illustrate important concepts, to build intuition with realistic examples, and then to encourage students to read on and learn more.

47

What You Will Learn in This Module

What You Will Learn in This Module Each module has an easy-to-review bulleted list format that alerts students to critical concepts and module objectives.

Module 1
The Study of Economics

Individual Choice: The Core of Economics

Economics is the study of scarcity and choice. Every economic issue involves, at its most basic level, **individual choice**—decisions by individuals about what to do and what *not* to do. In fact, you might say that it isn't economics if it isn't about choice.

Step into a big store such as Walmart or Target. There are thousands of different products available, and it is extremely unlikely that you—or anyone else—could afford to buy everything you might want to have. And anyway, there's only so much space in your home. Given the limitations on your budget and your living space, you must choose which products to buy and which to leave on the shelf.

The fact that those products are on the shelf in the first place involves choice—the store manager chose to put them there, and the manufacturers of the products chose to produce them. The **economy** is a system that coordinates choices about production with choices about consumption, and distributes goods and services to the people who want them. The United States has a **market economy,** in which production and consumption are the result of decentralized decisions by many firms and individuals. There is no central authority telling people what to produce or where to ship it. Each individual producer makes what he or she thinks will be most profitable, and each consumer buys what he or she chooses.

All economic activities involve individual choice. Let's take a closer look at what this means for the study of economics.

Resources Are Scarce

You can't always get what you want. Almost everyone would like to have a beautiful house in a great location (and help with the housecleaning), two or three luxury cars, ... even in a rich country like the United States, ... must make choices—whether to go to ... er to make do with a small backyard or ... nd is cheaper.

Key Terms Every key term is defined in the text and then again in the margin, making it easier for students to study and review important vocabulary.

Economics is the study of scarcity and choice.

Individual choice is decisions by individuals about what to do, which necessarily involve decisions about what not to do.

An **economy** is a system for coordinating a society's productive and consumptive activities.

In a **market economy,** the decisions of individual producers and consumers largely determine what, how, and for whom to produce, with little government involvement in ...

The Great Tortilla Crisis

"Thousands in Mexico City protest rising food prices." So read a recent headline in the *New York Times.* Specifically, the demonstrators were protesting a sharp rise in the price of tortillas, a staple food of Mexico's poor, which had gone from 25 cents a pound to between 35 and 45 cents a pound in just a few months.

Why were tortilla prices soaring? It was a classic example of what happens to equilibrium prices when supply falls. Tortillas are made from corn; much of Mexico's corn is imported from the United States, with the price of corn in both countries basically set in the U.S. corn market. And U.S. corn prices were rising rapidly thanks to surging demand in a new market: the market for ethanol.

Ethanol's big break came with the Energy Policy Act of 2005, which mandated the use of a large quantity of "renewable" fuels starting in 2006, and rising steadily thereafter. In practice, that meant increased use of ethanol. Ethanol producers rushed to build new production facilities and quickly began buying lots of corn. The result was a rightward shift of the demand curve for corn, leading to a sharp rise in the price of corn. And since corn is an input in the production of tortillas, a sharp rise in the price of corn led to a fall in the supply of tortillas and higher prices for tortilla consumers.

The increase in the price of corn was good news in Iowa, where farmers began planting

A cook prepares tortillas made with four different types of corn in a restaurant in Mexico City.

more corn than ever before. But it was bad news for Mexican consumers, who found themselves paying more for their tortillas.

In Real Life The IRL feature provides a short but compelling application of the major concept just covered in a module. Students experience an immediate payoff when they can apply concepts they've just read about to real phenomena. For example, we use the tortilla crisis of 2007 to illustrate how changes in supply impact consumers as bread-and-butter (and tortilla) issues.

Each module concludes with a unique set of review questions.

Module ① Review

Solutions appear at the back of the book.

Check Your Understanding

1. What are the four categories of resources? Give an example of a resource from each category.

2. What type of resource is each of the following?
   a. time spent flipping hamburgers at a restaurant
   b. a bulldozer
   c. a river

3. You make $45,000 per year at your current job with Whiz Kids Consultants. You are considering a job offer from Brainiacs, Inc., which would pay you $50,000 per year. Which of the following are elements of the opportunity cost of accepting the new job at Brainiacs, Inc.? Answer yes or no, and explain your answer.

   a. the increased time spent commuting to your new job
   b. the $45,000 salary from your old job
   c. the more spacious office at your new job

4. Identify each of the following statements as positive or normative, and explain your answer.
   a. Society should take measures to prevent people from engaging in dangerous personal behavior.
   b. People who engage in dangerous personal behavior impose higher costs on society through higher medical costs.

> **Check Your Understanding** review questions allow students to immediately test their understanding of a module. By checking their answers with those found in the back of the book, students will know when they need to reread the module before moving on.

Multiple-Choice Questions

1. Which of the following is an example of a resource?
   - I. petroleum
   - II. a factory
   - III. a cheeseburger dinner
   a. I only
   b. II only
   c. III only
   d. I and II only
   e. I, II, and III

2. Which of the following situations represent(s) resource scarcity?
   - I. Rapidly growing economies experience increasing levels of water pollution.
   - II. There is a finite amount of petroleum in the physical environment.
   - III. Cassette tapes are no longer being produced.
   a. I only
   b. II only
   c. III only
   d. I and II only
   e. I, II, and III

3. Suppose that you prefer reading a book you already own to watching TV and that you prefer watching TV to listening to music. If these are your only three choices, what is the opportunity cost of reading?

   a. watching TV and listening to music
   b. watching TV
   c. listening to music
   d. sleeping
   e. the price of the book

4. Which of the following statements is/are normative?
   - I. The price of gasoline is rising.
   - II. The price of gasoline is too high.
   - III. Gas prices are expected to fall in the near future.
   a. I only
   b. II only
   c. III only
   d. I and III only
   e. I, II, and III

5. Which of the following questions is studied in microeconomics?
   a. Should I go to college or get a job after I graduate?
   b. What government policies should be adopted to promote employment in the economy?
   c. How many people are employed in the economy this year?
   d. Has the overall level of prices in the economy increased or decreased this year?
   e. What determines the overall salary levels paid to workers in a given year?

> **Multiple-Choice Questions** offer students additional opportunity to practice what they've learned via five questions in a multiple-choice format. Solutions to these questions can be found at the back of the book.

Critical-Thinking Question

In what type of economic analysis do questions have a "right" or "wrong" answer? In what type of economic analysis do questions not necessarily have a "right" answer? On what type of economic analysis do economists tend to disagree most frequently? Why might economists disagree? Explain.

> In addition, concluding **Critical-Thinking Questions** are provided to offer students the opportunity to think more deeply about content in the module.

Each section ends with a comprehensive review and problem set.

Section 2 Review

Summary

Introduction and Demand

1. The **supply and demand model** illustrates how a **competitive market,** one with many buyers and sellers of the same product, works.

2. The **demand schedule** shows the **quantity demanded** at each price and is represented graphically by a **demand curve.** The **law of demand** says that demand curves slope downward, meaning that as price decreases, the quantity demanded increases.

3. A **movement along the demand curve** occurs when the price changes and causes a change in the quantity demanded. When economists talk of **changes in demand,** they mean shifts of the demand curve—a change in the quantity demanded at any given price. An increase in demand causes a rightward shift

- A change in income: when income rises, the demand for **normal goods** increases and the demand for **inferior goods** decreases
- A change in tastes
- A change in expectations
- A change in the number of consumers

Supply and Equilibrium

5. The **supply schedule** shows the **quantity supplied** at each price and is represented graphically by a **supply curve.** Supply curves usually slope upward.

6. A **movement along the supply curve** occurs when the price changes and causes a change in the quantity supplied. When economists talk of **changes in supply,** they ... ge in the quan... ... ase in supply ... rve. A decrease

Key Terms

Competitive market, p. 48
Supply and demand model, p. 48
Demand schedule, p. 49
Quantity demanded, p. 49
Demand curve, p. 49
Law of demand, p. 50
Change in demand, p. 51
Movement along the demand curve, p. 51

Supply curve, p. 59
Law of supply, p. 60
Change in supply, p. 60
Movement along the supply curve, p. 60
Input, p. 62
Individual supply curve, p. 63
Equilibrium, p. 66
Equilibrium price, p. 66

Inefficient allocation to consumers, p. 80
Wasted resources, p. 80
Inefficiently low quality, p. 81
Black markets, p. 81
Minimum wage, p. 82
Inefficient allocation of sales among sellers, p. 84
Inefficiently high quality, p. 85
Quantity control or quota, p. 88

Problems

1. A survey indicated that chocolate ice cream is America's favorite ice-cream flavor. For each of the following, indicate the possible effects on the demand and/or supply, equilibrium price, and equilibrium quantity of chocolate ice cream.

   a. A severe drought in the Midwest causes dairy farmers to reduce the number of milk-producing cows in their herds by a third. These dairy farmers supply cream that is used to manufacture chocolate ice cream.

   b. A new report by the American Medical Association reveals that chocolate does, in fact, have significant health benefits.

   c. The discovery of cheaper synthetic vanilla flavoring lowers the price of vanilla ice cream.

   d. New technology for mixing and freezing ice cream lowers manufacturers' costs of producing chocolate ice cream.

2. In a supply and demand diagram, draw the change in demand for hamburgers in your hometown due to the following events. In each case show the effect on equilibrium price and quantity.

   a. The price of tacos increases.

   b. All hamburger sellers raise the price of their french fries.

   c. Income falls in town. Assume that hamburgers are a normal good for most people.

   d. Income falls in town. Assume that hamburgers are an inferior good for most people.

   e. Hot dog stands cut the price of hot dogs.

   b. The price of a Christmas tree is lower after Christmas than before and fewer trees are sold.

   c. The price of a round-trip ticket to Paris on Air France falls by more than $200 after the end of school vacation in September. This happens despite the fact that generally worsening weather increases the cost of operating flights to Paris, and Air France therefore reduces the number of flights to Paris at any given price.

4. Show in a diagram the effect on the demand curve, the supply curve, the equilibrium price, and the equilibrium quantity of each of the following events on the designated market.

   a. the market for newspapers in your town
      Case 1:   The salaries of journalists go up.
      Case 2:   There is a big news event in your town, which is ... reported in the newspapers, and residents want ... learn more about it.

   b. the market for St. Louis Rams cotton T-shirts
      Case 1:   The Rams win the national championship.
      Case 2:   The price of cotton increases.

   c. the market for bagels
      Case 1:   People realize how fattening bagels are.
      Case 2:   People have less time to make themselves a cook... breakfast.

5. Find the flaws in reasoning in the following statements, p... ing particular attention to the distinction between chang...

End-of-Section Review and Problems In addition to the opportunities for review at the end of every module, each section ends with a brief but complete Summary of the key concepts, a list of key terms, and a comprehensive set of end-of-chapter problems.

Questions have been checked for continuity with the text content, overall usability, and accuracy.

To aid instructors in building tests, each question has been categorized according to its general *degree of difficulty*. The three levels are: *easy, moderate,* and *difficult*.

➤ *Easy* questions require students to recognize concepts and definitions. These are questions that can be answered by direct reference to the textbook.

➤ *Moderate* questions require some analysis on the student's part.

➤ *Difficult* questions usually require more detailed analysis by the student.

Each question has also been categorized according to a *skill descriptor*. These include: *Fact-Based, Definitional, Concept-Based, Critical-Thinking,* and *Analytical-Thinking*.

➤ *Fact-Based Questions* require students to identify facts presented in the text.

➤ *Definitional Questions* require students to define an economic term or concept.

➤ *Concept-Based Questions* require a straightforward knowledge of basic concepts.

➤ *Critical-Thinking Questions* require the student to apply a concept to a particular situation.

➤ *Analytical-Thinking Questions* require another level of analysis to answer the question. Students must be able to apply a concept and use this knowledge for further analysis of a situation or scenario.

To further aid instructors in building tests, each question is conveniently cross-referenced to the appropriate topic heading in the textbook. Questions are presented in the order in which concepts are presented in the text.

The Test Bank includes questions with tables that students must analyze to solve for numerical answers. It contains questions based on the graphs that appear in the book. These questions ask students to use the graphical models developed in the textbook and to interpret the information presented in the graph. Selected questions are paired with scenarios to reinforce comprehension.

Diploma 6 Computerized Test Bank

The printed Test Banks are also available in CD-ROM format for both Windows and Macintosh users. WebCT and Blackboard-formatted versions of the Test Bank are also available on the CDROM. With Diploma, you can easily write and edit questions as well as create and print tests. You can sort questions according to various information fields and scramble questions to create different versions of your tests. You can preview and reformat tests before printing them. Tests can be printed in a wide range of formats. The software's unique synthesis of flexible word-processing and database features creates a program that is extremely intuitive and capable.

Lecture PowerPoint Presentation

The PowerPoint presentation slides are designed to assist you with lecture preparation and presentations. The slides are organized by topic and contain graphs, data tables, and bulleted lists of key concepts suitable for lecture presentation. Key figures from the text are replicated and animated to demonstrate how they build. These slides can be customized to suit your individual needs. These files may be accessed on the instructor's side of the website.

For Students

Study Guide

The Study Guide reinforces the topics and key concepts covered in the text. For each module, the Study Guide provides the following:

➤ Summary: an opening paragraph that provides a brief overview of the module.

➤ Objectives: a numbered list outlining and describing the material that the student should have learned in the module. These objectives can be easily used as a study tool for students.

➤ Key Terms: a list of boldface key terms with their definitions—including room for note-taking.

➤ Tips: numbered list of learning tips with graphical analysis.

➤ Problems and Exercises: a set of 10–15 comprehensive problems.

➤ Module Review Questions: a set of 30 multiple-choice questions that focus on the key concepts from the text students should grasp after reading the module. These questions are designed for student exam preparation. A parallel set of these questions is also available to instructors in the Test Bank.

➤ Answers to Problems and Exercises: detailed solutions to the Problems and Exercises in the Study Guide.

➤ Answers to Module Review Questions: solutions to the multiple-choice questions in the Study Guide—along with thorough explanations.

Online Offerings

Companion Website for Students and Instructors

www.worthpublishers.com/krugmanwells

The companion website for the text offers valuable tools for both the instructor and students.

For instructors, the site gives you the ability to track students' interaction with the site and gives you access to additional instructor resources.

The following instructor resources are available:

➤ **Quiz Gradebook:** The site gives you the ability to track students' work by accessing an online gradebook.

➤ Instructors also have the option to have student results e-mailed directly to them. All student answers to the Self-Test Quizzes are saved in this online database.

- **Lecture PowerPoint Presentations:** Instructors have access to helpful lecture material in PowerPoint® format.
- **Illustration PowerPoint Slides:** A complete set of figures and tables from the textbook in PowerPoint format is available.
- **Images from the Textbook:** Instructors have access to a complete set of figures and tables from the textbook in high-res and low-res JPEG formats. The textbook art has been processed for "high-resolution" (150 dpi). These figures and photographs have been especially formatted for maximum readability in large lecture halls and follow standards that were set and tested in a real university auditorium.
- **Instructor's Resource Manual:** Instructors have access to the files for the Instructor's Resource Manual.
- **Solutions Manual:** Instructors have access to the files for the detailed solutions.

For students, the site offers many opportunities for self-testing and review.

The following resources are available for students:

- **Self-Test Quizzes:** This quizzing engine provides a set of multiple-choice questions per module. Immediate and appropriate feedback is provided to students along with topic references for further review. The questions as well as the answer choices are randomized to give students a different quiz with every refresh of the screen.
- **Key Term Flashcards:** Students can test themselves on the key terms with these pop-up electronic flashcards.
- **Web Links:** Links allow students to easily and effectively locate outside resources and readings that relate to topics covered in the textbook. They list web addresses that hotlink to relevant websites; each URL is accompanied by a detailed description of the site and its relevance to each topic. This allows students to conduct research and explore related readings on specific topics with ease. Also hotlinked are relevant articles by Paul Krugman.

EconPortal

EconPortal is designed to enrich your course, help you organize and better utilize resources, and improve your students' understanding of economics. EconPortal provides a powerful, easy-to-use, completely customizable teaching and learning management system. EconPortal organizes pre-loaded assignments (based on a comprehensive course outline) and provides the flexibility for you to add your own assignments. The system enables you to create assignments from a variety of question types and to prepare self-graded homework, quizzes, or tests. You can select your preferred policies for scheduling, maximum attempts, time limitations, feedback, and more. A setup wizard will guide you through assignment creation. Assignments may be created from the following pools of questions:

- *Test Bank Questions*
- *End-of-Chapter Problems:* The end-of-chapter problems from the text are available in a self-graded format—perfect for quick quizzes or homework assignments.
- *Graphing Questions:* EconPortal includes electronically gradable graphing problems. Students draw their response to a question and the software grades that response. These graphing exercises replicate the pencil-and-paper experience for students of drawing graphs—with the added bonus that you don't have to hand-grade each assignment.

You can assign and track any aspect of your students' EconPortal. The Gradebook will capture your students' results and allow you to easily export reports.

Enhanced E-Pack and Course Cartridge

To further save time and to provide additional support, the E-Pack and Course Cartridge includes student AND instructor resources in one place. Course management solutions are available for WebCT, Blackboard, Desire2Learn, and Angel.

Additional Offerings

i>clicker

Developed by a team of University of Illinois physicists, i>clicker is the most flexible and most reliable classroom response system available. It is the only solution created *for educators, by educators,* with continuous product improvements made through direct classroom testing and faculty feedback. You'll love i>clicker no matter your level of technical expertise because the focus is on *your* teaching, *not the technology.* To learn more about packaging i>clicker with this textbook, please contact your local sales rep or visit www.iclicker.com.

Financial Times Edition

For adopters of the Krugman/Wells text, Worth Publishers and the *Financial Times* are offering a 15-week subscription to students at a tremendous savings. Professors also receive their own free *Financial Times* subscription for one year. Students and professors may access research and archived information at www.ft.com.

Dismal Scientist

A high-powered business database and analysis service comes to the classroom! Dismal Scientist offers real-time monitoring of the global economy, produced locally by economists and professionals at Economy.com's London, Sydney, and West Chester offices. Dismal Scientist is *free* when packaged with the Krugman/Wells text. Please contact your local sales rep for more information or go to www.economy.com.

Acknowledgments

Our deep appreciation and heartfelt thanks go out to Margaret Ray, University of Mary Washington, and Dave Anderson, Centre College, for all of their hard work reshaping Krugman and Wells, *Economics,* second edition, to create this modularized version of the book. Margaret and Dave worked with us to make the all-important decisions about content to keep and cut. They then worked hard at weaving together all the coverage that remained in a way that flows seamlessly and retains our style. Thank you, Margaret and Dave, for doing such an exceptional job. The more we look at this modular book, the more we like it.

We would also like to thank the following instructors who helped us and the editorial staff at Worth fine-tune this text through their thoughtful commentary and insights:

Miki Brunyer Anderson, *Pikes Peak Community College*

Giuliana Campanelli Andreopoulos, *William Paterson University*

Myra L. Moore, *University of Georgia*

Elizabeth Sawyer-Kelly, *University of Wisconsin, Madison*

Nora Underwood, *University of Central Florida*

We are also indebted to the following reviewers, focus-group participants, and other consultants for their suggestions and advice on the second edition.

Carlos Aguilar, *El Paso Community College*

Terence Alexander, *Iowa State University*

Morris Altman, *University of Saskatchewan*

Farhad Ameen, *State University of New York, Westchester Community College*

Christopher P. Ball, *Quinnipiac University*

Sue Bartlett, *University of South Florida*

Scott Beaulier, *Mercer University*

David Bernotas, *University of Georgia*

Marc Bilodeau, *Indiana University and Purdue University, Indianapolis*

Kelly Blanchard, *Purdue University*

Anne Bresnock, *California State Polytechnic University*

Douglas M. Brown, *Georgetown University*

Joseph Calhoun, *Florida State University*

Douglas Campbell, *University of Memphis*

Kevin Carlson, *University of Massachusetts, Boston*

Andrew J. Cassey, *Washington State University*

Shirley Cassing, *University of Pittsburgh*

Sewin Chan, *New York University*

Mitchell M. Charkiewicz, *Central Connecticut State University*

Joni S. Charles, *Texas State University, San Marcos*

Adhip Chaudhuri, *Georgetown University*

Eric P. Chiang, *Florida Atlantic University*

Hayley H. Chouinard, *Washington State University*

Kenny Christianson, *Binghamton University*

Lisa Citron, *Cascadia Community College*

Steven L. Cobb, *University of North Texas*

Barbara Z. Connolly, *Westchester Community College*

Stephen Conroy, *University of San Diego*

Thomas E. Cooper, *Georgetown University*

Cesar Corredor, *Texas A&M University and University of Texas, Tyler*

Jim F. Couch, *University of Northern Alabama*

Daniel Daly, *Regis University*

H. Evren Damar, *Pacific Lutheran University*

Antony Davies, *Duquesne University*

Greg Delemeester, *Marietta College*

Patrick Dolenc, *Keene State College*

Christine Doyle-Burke, *Framingham State College*

Ding Du, *South Dakota State University*

Jerry Dunn, *Southwestern Oklahoma State University*

Robert R. Dunn, *Washington and Jefferson College*

Ann Eike, *University of Kentucky*

Tisha L. N. Emerson, *Baylor University*

Hadi Salehi Esfahani, *University of Illinois*

William Feipel, *Illinois Central College*

Rudy Fichtenbaum, *Wright State University*

David W. Findlay, *Colby College*

Mary Flannery, *University of California, Santa Cruz*

Robert Francis, *Shoreline Community College*

Shelby Frost, *Georgia State University*

Frank Gallant, *George Fox University*

Robert Gazzale, *Williams College*

Robert Godby, *University of Wyoming*

Michael Goode, *Central Piedmont Community College*

Douglas E. Goodman, *University of Puget Sound*

Marvin Gordon, *University of Illinois at Chicago*

Kathryn Graddy, *Brandeis University*

Alan Day Haight, *State University of New York, Cortland*

Mehdi Haririan, *Bloomsburg University*

Clyde A. Haulman, *College of William and Mary*

Richard R. Hawkins, *University of West Florida*

Mickey A. Hepner, *University of Central Oklahoma*

Michael Hilmer, *San Diego State University*

Tia Hilmer, *San Diego State University*

Jane Himarios, *University of Texas, Arlington*

Jim Holcomb, *University of Texas, El Paso*

Don Holley, *Boise State University*

Alexander Holmes, *University of Oklahoma*

Julie Holzner, *Los Angeles City College*

Robert N. Horn, *James Madison University*

Steven Husted, *University of Pittsburgh*

John O. Ifediora, *University of Wisconsin, Platteville*

Hiro Ito, *Portland State University*

Mike Javanmard, *Rio Hondo Community College*

Robert T. Jerome, *James Madison University*

Shirley Johnson-Lans, *Vassar College*

David Kalist, *Shippensburg University*

Lillian Kamal, *Northwestern University*

Roger T. Kaufman, *Smith College*

Herb Kessel, *St. Michael's College*

Rehim Kiliç, *Georgia Institute of Technology*

Grace Kim, *University of Michigan, Dearborn*

Michael Kimmitt, *University of Hawaii, Manoa*

Robert Kling, *Colorado State University*

Sherrie Kossoudji, *University of Michigan*

Charles Kroncke, *College of Mount Saint Joseph*

Reuben Kyle, *Middle Tennessee State University (retired)*

Katherine Lande-Schmeiser, *University of Minnesota, Twin Cities*

David Lehr, *Longwood College*

Mary Jane Lenon, *Providence College*

Mary H. Lesser, *Iona College*

Solina Lindahl, *California Polytechnic State University, San Luis Obispo*

Haiyong Liu, *East Carolina University*

Jane S. Lopus, *California State University, East Bay*

María José Luengo-Prado, *Northeastern University*

Rotua Lumbantobing, *North Carolina State University*

Ed Lyell, *Adams State College*

John Marangos, *Colorado State University*

Ralph D. May, *Southwestern Oklahoma State University*

Wayne McCaffery, *University of Wisconsin, Madison*

Bill McLean, *Oklahoma State University*

Larry McRae, *Appalachian State University*

Mary Ruth J. McRae, *Appalachian State University*

Ellen E. Meade, *American University*

Meghan Millea, *Mississippi State University*

Norman C. Miller, *Miami University (of Ohio)*

Khan A. Mohabbat, *Northern Illinois University*

Myra L. Moore, *University of Georgia*

Jay Morris, *Champlain College in Burlington*

Akira Motomura, *Stonehill College*

Kevin J. Murphy, *Oakland University*

Robert Murphy, *Boston College*

Ranganath Murthy, *Bucknell University*

Anthony Myatt, *University of New Brunswick, Canada*

Randy A. Nelson, *Colby College*

Charles Newton, *Houston Community College*

Daniel X. Nguyen, *Purdue University*

Dmitri Nizovtsev, *Washburn University*

Thomas A. Odegaard, *Baylor University*

Constantin Oglobin, *Georgia Southern University*

Charles C. Okeke, *College of Southern Nevada*

Terry Olson, *Truman State University*

Una Okonkwo Osili, *Indiana University and Purdue University, Indianapolis*

Maxwell Oteng, *University of California, Davis*

P. Marcelo Oviedo, *Iowa State University*

Jeff Owen, *Gustavus Adolphus College*

James Palmieri, *Simpson College*

Walter G. Park, *American University*

Elliott Parker, *University of Nevada, Reno*

Michael Perelman, *California State University, Chico*

Nathan Perry, *Utah State University*

Dean Peterson, *Seattle University*

Ken Peterson, *Furman University*

Paul Pieper, *University of Illinois at Chicago*

Dennis L. Placone, *Clemson University*

Michael Polcen, *Northern Virginia Community College*

Raymond A. Polchow, *Zane State College*

Linnea Polgreen, *University of Iowa*

Michael A. Quinn, *Bentley University*

Eileen Rabach, *Santa Monica College*

Matthew Rafferty, *Quinnipiac University*

Jaishankar Raman, *Valparaiso University*

Margaret Ray, *Mary Washington College*

Helen Roberts, *University of Illinois, Chicago*

Jeffrey Rubin, *Rutgers University, New Brunswick*

Rose M. Rubin, *University of Memphis*

Lynda Rush, *California State Polytechnic University, Pomona*

Michael Ryan, *Western Michigan University*

Sara Saderion, *Houston Community College*

Djavad Salehi-Isfahani, *Virginia Tech*

Elizabeth Sawyer-Kelly, *University of Wisconsin, Madison*

Jesse A. Schwartz, *Kennesaw State University*

Chad Settle, *University of Tulsa*

Steve Shapiro, *University of North Florida*

Robert L. Shoffner III, *Central Piedmont Community College*

Joseph Sicilian, *University of Kansas*

Judy Smrha, *Baker University*

John Solow, *University of Iowa*

John Somers, *Portland Community College*

Stephen Stageberg, *University of Mary Washington*

Monty Stanford, *DeVry University*

Rebecca Stein, *University of Pennsylvania*

William K. Tabb, *Queens College, City University of New York (retired)*

Sarinda Taengnoi, *University of Wisconsin, Oshkosh*

Henry Terrell, *University of Maryland*

Rebecca Achée Thornton, *University of Houston*

Michael Toma, *Armstrong Atlantic State University*

Brian Trinque, *University of Texas, Austin*

Boone A. Turchi, *University of North Carolina, Chapel Hill*

Nora Underwood, *University of Central Florida*

J. S. Uppal, *State University of New York, Albany*

John Vahaly, *University of Louisville*

Jose J. Vazquez-Cognet, *University of Illinois at Urbana-Champaign*

Daniel Vazzana, *Georgetown College*

Roger H. von Haefen, *North Carolina State University*

Andreas Waldkirch, *Colby College*

Christopher Waller, *University of Notre Dame*

Gregory Wassall, *Northeastern University*

Robert Whaples, *Wake Forest University*

Thomas White, *Assumption College*

Jennifer P. Wissink, *Cornell University*

Mark Witte, *Northwestern University*

Kristen M. Wolfe, *St. Johns River Community College*

Larry Wolfenbarger, *Macon State College*

Louise B. Wolitz, *University of Texas, Austin*

Gavin Wright, *Stanford University*

Bill Yang, *Georgia Southern University*

Jason Zimmerman, *South Dakota State University*

We want to thank the many people at Worth Publishers for their assistance. As always, the keen insights offered by Elizabeth Widdicombe, President of Freeman and Worth, Craig Bleyer, Director of High School, and Catherine Woods, Publisher at Worth, helped us to better understand our audience and point us in the right direction in terms of revision strategy. We are indebted to them for all of their contributions over the years to each of our books, including this one, and now, to our growing franchise.

We had a talented team working with us and we thank them all. Andreas Bentz did yeoman's work, granting us the ability to focus on larger issues because we could trust him to focus on the details. We had two development editors working with us: Sharon Balbos and Barbara Brooks read and commented on every module. And, Mary Walsh, editorial assistant extraordinaire, did hands-on manuscript work that helped us move the project along more quickly.

Many thanks go to Eric P. Chiang, Florida Atlantic University, for his invaluable contributions in accuracy checking. Eric also brought us James Watson, who assisted with extremely quick and thorough data research for the many updates in this edition. Special thanks must go to Bill McLean, Oklahoma State University, for his enthusiastic support of the modular format. And, of course, thank you Kathryn Graddy, Brandeis University, for your helpful contributions.

For their essential roles, our thanks to executive editor Ann Heath, assistant editor Dora Figueiredo, and of course, Marie McHale for her work coordinating supplements and media.

We have had an incredible production and design team on this book, people whose hard work, creativity, and dedication continue to amaze us. Thank you, Tracey Kuehn, Director of Print and Digital Development, Laura McGinn, Project Editor, and Lisa Kinne, Associate Managing Editor, for producing this book; Kevin Kall, Lissi Sigillo, and TSI Graphics for their beautiful interior design (and to Kevin for his original new cover); Barbara Seixas, who worked her magic once again on the manufacturing end; Cecilia Varas and Dena Dibiglio Betz for photo research; Stacey Alexander, Jenny Chiu, and Edgar Bonilla for coordinating the production on all supplemental materials.

Lastly, we owe a special debt of gratitude to Scott Guile, Executive Marketing Manager for Economics, without whose inspiration and persistence this book may never have come into existence. From his travels and conversations with instructors, Scott sensed the interest in and enthusiasm for a streamlined and modularized version of our main principles text. We can't thank you enough, Scott, for the idea of creating this book and for your tireless advocacy in marketing all variations of it. Chuck Linsmeier, Executive Editor in Economics, worked closely with Scott to bring this book to fruition. Although new to his position, Chuck jumped right in, convincing us of the value of a modular book and then coordinating the people and pieces that would make it happen. Welcome, Chuck, and thank you.

Paul Krugman   Robin Wells

MICROECONOMICS
SECOND EDITION in MODULES

Basic Economic Concepts

COMMON GROUND

The annual meeting of the American Economic Association draws thousands of economists, young and old, famous and obscure. There are booksellers, business meetings, and quite a few job interviews. But mainly the economists gather to talk and listen. During the busiest times, 60 or more presentations may be taking place simultaneously, on questions that range from the future of the stock market to who does the cooking in two-earner families.

What do these people have in common? An expert on the stock market probably knows very little about the economics of housework, and vice versa. Yet an economist who wanders into the wrong seminar and ends up listening to presentations on some unfamiliar topic is nonetheless likely to hear much that is familiar. The reason is that all economic analysis is based on a set of common principles that apply to many different issues.

Some of these principles involve *individual choice*—for economics is, first of all, about the choices that individuals make. Do you choose to eat breakfast at home or pick it up on the way? Do you buy a new CD or go to a movie? These decisions involve *making a choice* from among a limited number of alternatives—limited because no one can have everything that he or she wants. Every question in economics at its most basic level involves individuals making choices.

But to understand how an economy works, you need to understand more than how individ-

uals make choices. None of us lives like Robinson Crusoe, alone on an island—we must make decisions in an environment that is shaped by the decisions of others. Indeed, in our global economy even the simplest decisions you make—say, what to have for breakfast—are shaped by the decisions of thousands of other people, from the banana grower in Costa Rica who decided to grow the fruit you eat to the farmer in Iowa who provided the corn in your cornflakes.

And because each of us depends on so many others—and they, in turn, depend on us—our choices interact. So although all economics at a basic level is about individual choice, in order to understand behavior within an economy we must also understand economic *interaction*—how my choices affect your choices, and vice versa.

Many important economic interactions can be understood by looking at the markets for individual goods—for example, the market for corn. But we must also understand economy-wide interactions in order to understand how they can lead to the ups and downs we see in the economy as a whole.

In this section we discuss the study of economics and the difference between microeconomics and macroeconomics. We also introduce the major topics within macroeconomics and the use of models to study the macroeconomy. Finally, we present the production possibility frontier model and use it to understand basic economic activity, including trade between two economies. Because the study of economics relies on graphical models, an appendix on the use of graphs follows the end of this section.

One must choose!

1

What you will learn in this **Module:**

- How scarcity and choice are central to the study of economics

- The importance of opportunity cost in individual choice and decision making

- The difference between positive economics and normative economics

- When economists agree and why they sometimes disagree

- What makes macroeconomics different from microeconomics

Module 1
The Study of Economics

Individual Choice: The Core of Economics

Economics is the study of scarcity and choice. Every economic issue involves, at its most basic level, **individual choice**—decisions by individuals about what to do and what *not* to do. In fact, you might say that it isn't economics if it isn't about choice.

Step into a big store such as Walmart or Target. There are thousands of different products available, and it is extremely unlikely that you—or anyone else—could afford to buy everything you might want to have. And anyway, there's only so much space in your home. Given the limitations on your budget and your living space, you must choose which products to buy and which to leave on the shelf.

The fact that those products are on the shelf in the first place involves choice—the store manager chose to put them there, and the manufacturers of the products chose to produce them. The **economy** is a system that coordinates choices about production with choices about consumption, and distributes goods and services to the people who want them. The United States has a **market economy,** in which production and consumption are the result of decentralized decisions by many firms and individuals. There is no central authority telling people what to produce or where to ship it. Each individual producer makes what he or she thinks will be most profitable, and each consumer buys what he or she chooses.

All economic activities involve individual choice. Let's take a closer look at what this means for the study of economics.

Resources Are Scarce

You can't always get what you want. Almost everyone would like to have a beautiful house in a great location (and help with the housecleaning), two or three luxury cars, and frequent vacations in fancy hotels. But even in a rich country like the United States, not many families can afford all of that. So they must make choices—whether to go to Disney World this year or buy a better car, whether to make do with a small backyard or accept a longer commute in order to live where land is cheaper.

Economics is the study of scarcity and choice.

Individual choice is decisions by individuals about what to do, which necessarily involve decisions about what not to do.

An **economy** is a system for coordinating a society's productive and consumptive activities.

In a **market economy,** the decisions of individual producers and consumers largely determine what, how, and for whom to produce, with little government involvement in the decisions.

Limited income isn't the only thing that keeps people from having everything they want. Time is also in limited supply: there are only 24 hours in a day. And because the time we have is limited, choosing to spend time on one activity also means choosing not to spend time on a different activity—spending time studying for an exam means forgoing a night at the movies. Indeed, many people feel so limited by the number of hours in the day that they are willing to trade money for time. For example, convenience stores usually charge higher prices than larger supermarkets. But they fulfill a valuable role by catering to customers who would rather pay more than spend the time traveling farther to a supermarket where they might also have to wait in longer lines.

Why do individuals have to make choices? The ultimate reason is that *resources are scarce*. A **resource** is anything that can be used to produce something else. The economy's resources, sometimes called *factors of production,* can be classified into four categories: **land** (including timber, water, minerals, and all other resources that come from nature), **labor** (the effort of workers), **capital** (machinery, buildings, tools, and all other manufactured goods used to make other goods and services), and **entrepreneurship** (risk taking, innovation, and the organization of resources for production).

A resource is **scarce** when there is not enough of it available to satisfy the various ways a society wants to use it. For example, there are limited supplies of oil and coal, which currently provide most of the energy used to produce and deliver everything we buy. And in a growing world economy with a rapidly increasing human population, even clean air and water have become scarce resources.

Just as individuals must make choices, the scarcity of resources means that society as a whole must make choices. One way for a society to make choices is simply to allow them to emerge as the result of many individual choices. For example, there are only so many hours in a week, and Americans must decide how to spend their time. How many hours will they spend going to supermarkets to get lower prices rather than saving time by shopping at convenience stores? The answer is the sum of individual decisions: each of the millions of individuals in the economy makes his or her own choice about where to shop, and society's choice is simply the sum of those individual decisions.

For various reasons, there are some decisions that a society decides are best not left to individual choice. For example, two of the authors live in an area that until recently was mainly farmland but is now being rapidly built up. Most local residents feel that the community would be a more pleasant place to live if some of the land were left undeveloped. But no individual has an incentive to keep his or her land as open space, rather than sell it to a developer. So a trend has emerged in many communities across the United States of local governments purchasing undeveloped land and preserving it as open space. Decisions about how to use scarce resources are often best left to individuals but sometimes should be made at a higher, community-wide, level.

Opportunity Cost: The Real Cost of Something Is What You Must Give Up to Get It

Think back to when you decided to attend college. What was the cost of making that decision? Of course, there are the obvious costs in dollars. As a college student, you have to pay for tuition, books, and housing (or, for travel to campus). But, there is also another cost to consider: the cost of what you gave up to become a student. Had you decided not to go to college, you probably would have gone to work. You would have found a job that paid a salary. The salary that you gave up to go to school is also a cost. It is the foregone opportunity of your next best alternative. Economists call the value of what you must give up when you make a particular choice an **opportunity cost.**

A **resource** is anything that can be used to produce something else.

Land refers to all resources that come from nature, such as minerals, timber and petroleum.

Labor is the effort of workers.

Capital refers to manufactured goods used to make other goods and services.

Entrepreneurship describes the efforts of entrepreneurs in organizing resources for production, taking risks to create new enterprises, and innovating to develop new products and production processes.

A **scarce** resource is not available in sufficient quantities to satisfy all the various ways a society wants to use it.

The real cost of an item is its **opportunity cost:** what you must give up in order to get it.

Charles D. Winters

Opportunity costs are crucial to individual choice because, in the end, all costs are opportunity costs. That's because with every choice, an alternative is forgone—money or time spent on one thing can't be spent on another. If you spend $15 on a pizza, you forgo the opportunity to spend that $15 on a steak. If you spend Saturday afternoon at the park, you can't spend Saturday afternoon doing homework. And if you attend one school, you can't attend another.

The park and school examples show that economists are concerned with more than just costs paid in dollars and cents. The forgone opportunity to do homework has no direct monetary cost, but it is an opportunity cost nonetheless. And if the local college and the state university have the same tuition and fees, the cost of choosing one school over the other has nothing to do with payments and everything to do with forgone opportunities.

Now suppose tuition and fees at the state university are $5,000 less than at the local college. In that case, what you give up to attend the local college is the ability to attend the state university *plus* the enjoyment you could have gained from spending $5,000 on other things. So the opportunity cost of a choice includes all the costs, whether or not they are monetary costs, of making that choice.

The choice to go to college *at all* provides an important final example of opportunity costs. High school graduates can either go to college or seek immediate employment. Even with a full scholarship that would make college "free" in terms of monetary costs, going to college would still be an expensive proposition because most young people, if they were not in college, would have a job. By going to college, students forgo the income they could have earned if they had gone straight to work instead. Therefore, the opportunity cost of attending college is the value of all necessary monetary payments for tuition and fees *plus* the forgone income from the best available job that could take the place of going to college.

For most people the value of a college degree far exceeds the value of alternative earnings, with notable exceptions. The opportunity cost of going to college is high for people who could earn a lot during what would otherwise be their college years. Basketball star LeBron James bypassed college because the opportunity cost would have included his $13 million contract with the Cleveland Cavaliers and even more from corporate sponsors Nike and Coca-Cola. Golfer Tiger Woods, Microsoft co-founder Bill Gates, and actor Matt Damon are among the high achievers who decided the opportunity cost of completing college was too much to swallow.

LeBron James understood the concept of opportunity cost, both when he signed with Cleveland and then with Miami.

Got a Penny?

At many cash registers there is a little basket full of pennies. People are encouraged to use the basket to round their purchases up or down. If an item costs $5.02, you give the cashier $5.00 and take two pennies from the basket to give to the cashier. If an item costs $4.99, you pay $5.00 and the cashier throws a penny into the basket. It makes everyone's life a bit easier. Of course, it would be easier still if we just abolished the penny, a step that some economists have urged.

But why do we have pennies in the first place? If it's too small a sum to worry about, why calculate prices that precisely?

The answer is that a penny wasn't always such a negligible sum: the purchasing power of a penny has been greatly reduced by *inflation,* a general rise in the prices of all goods and services over time. Forty years ago, a penny had more purchasing power than a nickel does today.

Why does this matter? Well, remember the saying "A penny saved is a penny earned"? Of course, there are other ways to earn money, so you must decide whether saving a penny is a productive use of your time. Could you earn more by devoting that time to other uses?

Sixty years ago, the average wage was about $1.20 an hour. A penny was equivalent to 30 seconds' worth of work, so it was worth saving a penny if doing so took less than 30 seconds. But wages have risen along with overall prices,

so that the average worker is now paid more than $18 per hour. A penny is therefore equivalent to just a little under 2 seconds of work, so it's not worth the opportunity cost of the time it takes to worry about a penny more or less.

In short, the rising opportunity cost of time in terms of money has turned a penny from a useful coin into a nuisance.

Microeconomics Versus Macroeconomics

We have presented economics as the study of choices and described how, at its most basic level, economics is about individual choice. The branch of economics concerned with how individuals make decisions and how these decisions interact is called **microeconomics.** Microeconomics focuses on choices made by individuals, households, or firms—the smaller parts that make up the economy as a whole.

Macroeconomics focuses on the bigger picture—the overall ups and downs of the economy. When you study macroeconomics, you learn how economists explain these fluctuations and how governments can use economic policy to minimize the damage they cause. Macroeconomics focuses on **economic aggregates**—economic measures such as the unemployment rate, the inflation rate, and gross domestic product—that summarize data across many different markets.

Table 1.1 lists some typical questions that involve economics. A microeconomic version of the question appears on the left, paired with a similar macroeconomic question on the right. By comparing the questions, you can begin to get a sense of the difference between microeconomics and macroeconomics.

Microeconomics is the study of how people make decisions and how those decisions interact.

Macroeconomics is concerned with the overall ups and downs in the economy.

Economic aggregates are economic measures that summarize data across many different markets.

table **1.1**

Microeconomic Versus Macroeconomic Questions

Microeconomic Questions	Macroeconomic Questions
Should I go to college or get a job?	How many people are employed in the economy as a whole this year?
What determines the salary that Citibank offers to a new college graduate?	What determines the overall salary levels paid to workers in a given year?
What determines the cost to a college of offering a new course?	What determines the overall level of prices in the economy as a whole?
What government policies should be adopted to make it easier for low-income students to afford college?	What government policies should be adopted to promote employment and growth in the economy as a whole?
What determines the number of iPhones exported to France?	What determines the overall trade in goods, services, and financial assets between the United States and the rest of the world?

As these questions illustrate, microeconomics focuses on how individuals and firms make decisions, and the consequences of those decisions. For example, a school will use microeconomics to determine how much it would cost to offer a new course, which includes the instructor's salary, the cost of class materials, and so on. By weighing the costs and benefits, the school can then decide whether or not to offer the course. Macroeconomics, in contrast, examines the *overall* behavior of the economy—how the actions of all of the individuals and firms in the economy interact to produce a particular economy-wide level of economic performance. For example, macroeconomics is concerned with the general level of prices in the economy and how high or low they are relative to prices last year, rather than with the price of a particular good or service.

Positive Versus Normative Economics

Economic analysis, as we will see throughout this book, draws on a set of basic economic principles. But how are these principles applied? That depends on the purpose of the analysis. Economic analysis that is used to answer questions about the way the world works, questions that have definite right and wrong answers, is known as **positive economics.** In contrast, economic analysis that involves saying how the world *should* work is known as **normative economics.**

Imagine that you are an economic adviser to the governor of your state and the governor is considering a change to the toll charged along the state turnpike. Below are three questions the governor might ask you.

1. How much revenue will the tolls yield next year?

2. How much would that revenue increase if the toll were raised from $1.00 to $1.50?

3. Should the toll be raised, bearing in mind that a toll increase would likely reduce traffic and air pollution near the road but impose some financial hardship on frequent commuters?

There is a big difference between the first two questions and the third one. The first two are questions about facts. Your forecast of next year's toll revenue without any increase will be proved right or wrong when the numbers actually come in. Your estimate of the impact of a change in the toll is a little harder to check—the increase in revenue depends on other factors besides the toll, and it may be hard to disentangle the causes of any change in revenue. Still, in principle there is only one right answer.

But the question of whether or not tolls should be raised may not have a "right" answer—two people who agree on the effects of a higher toll could still disagree about whether raising the toll is a good idea. For example, someone who lives near the turnpike but doesn't commute on it will care a lot about noise and air pollution but not so much about commuting costs. A regular commuter who doesn't live near the turnpike will have the opposite priorities.

Should the toll be raised?

This example highlights a key distinction between the two roles of economic analysis and presents another way to think about the distinction between positive and normative analysis: positive economics is about description, and normative economics is about prescription. Positive economics occupies most of the time and effort of the economics profession.

Looking back at the three questions the governor might ask, it is worth noting a subtle but important difference between questions 1 and 2. Question 1 asks for a simple prediction about next year's revenue—a forecast. Question 2 is a "what if" question, asking how revenue would change if the toll were to change. Economists are often called upon to answer both types of questions. Economic *models*, which provide simplified representations of reality such as graphs or equations, are especially useful for answering "what if" questions.

The answers to such questions often serve as a guide to policy, but they are still predictions, not prescriptions. That is, they tell you what will happen if a policy is changed, but they don't tell you whether or not that result is good. Suppose that your economic model tells you that the governor's proposed increase in highway tolls will raise property values in communities near the road but will tax or inconvenience people who currently use the turnpike to get to work. Does that information make this proposed toll increase a good idea or a bad one? It depends on whom you ask. As we've just seen, someone who is very concerned with the communities near the road will support the increase, but someone who is very concerned with the welfare of drivers will feel differently. That's a value judgment—it's not a question of positive economic analysis.

Still, economists often do engage in normative economics and give policy advice. How can they do this when there may be no "right" answer? One answer is that economists are also citizens, and we all have our opinions. But economic analysis can often be used to show that some policies are clearly better than others, regardless of individual opinions.

Suppose that policies A and B achieve the same goal, but policy A makes everyone better off than policy B—or at least makes some people better off without making other people worse off. Then A is clearly more efficient than B. That's not a value judgment: we're talking about how best to achieve a goal, not about the goal itself.

For example, two different policies have been used to help low-income families obtain housing: rent control, which limits the rents landlords are allowed to charge, and rent subsidies, which provide families with additional money with which to pay rent. Almost all economists agree that subsidies are the more efficient policy. (In a later module we'll see why this is so.) And so the great majority of economists, whatever their personal politics, favor subsidies over rent control.

When policies can be clearly ranked in this way, then economists generally agree. But it is no secret that economists sometimes disagree.

When and Why Economists Disagree

Economists have a reputation for arguing with each other. Where does this reputation come from?

One important answer is that media coverage tends to exaggerate the real differences in views among economists. If nearly all economists agree on an issue—for example, the proposition that rent controls lead to housing shortages—reporters and editors are likely to conclude that there is no story worth covering, and so the professional consensus tends to go unreported. But when there is some issue on which prominent economists take opposing sides—for example, whether cutting taxes right now would help the economy—that does make a good news story. So you hear much more about the areas of disagreement among economists than you do about the many areas of agreement.

It is also worth remembering that economics is, unavoidably, often tied up in politics. On a number of issues, powerful interest groups know what opinions they want to hear. Therefore, they have an incentive to find and promote economists who profess those opinions, which gives these economists a prominence and visibility out of proportion to their support among their colleagues.

Although the appearance of disagreement among economists exceeds the reality, it remains true that economists often *do* disagree about important things. For example, some highly respected economists argue vehemently that the U.S. government should replace the income tax with a *value-added tax* (a national sales tax, which is the main source of government revenue in many European countries). Other equally respected economists disagree. What are the sources of this difference of opinion?

One important source of differences is in values: as in any diverse group of individuals, reasonable people can differ. In comparison to an income tax, a value-added tax typically falls more heavily on people with low incomes. So an economist who values a society with more social and income equality will likely oppose a value-added tax. An economist with different values will be less likely to oppose it.

A second important source of differences arises from the way economists conduct economic analysis. Economists base their conclusions on models formed by making simplifying assumptions about reality. Two economists can legitimately disagree about which simplifications are appropriate—and therefore arrive at different conclusions.

Suppose that the U.S. government was considering a value-added tax. Economist A may rely on a simplification of reality that focuses on the administrative costs of tax systems—that is, the costs of monitoring compliance, processing tax forms, collecting the tax, and so on. This economist might then point to the well-known high costs of administering a value-added tax and argue against the change. But economist B may think that the right way to approach the question is to ignore the administrative

When Economists Agree

"If all the economists in the world were laid end to end, they still couldn't reach a conclusion." So goes one popular economist joke. But do economists really disagree that much?

Not according to a classic survey of members of the American Economic Association, reported in the May 1992 issue of the *American Economic Review.* The authors asked respondents to agree or disagree with a number of statements about the economy; what they found was a high level of agreement among professional economists on many of the statements. At the top of the list, with more than 90% of the economists agreeing, were the statements "Tariffs and import quotas usually reduce general economic welfare" and "A ceiling on rents reduces the quantity and quality of housing available." What's striking about these two statements is that many noneconomists disagree: tariffs and import quotas to keep out foreign-produced goods are favored by many voters, and proposals to do away with rent control in cities like New York and San Francisco have met fierce political opposition.

So is the stereotype of quarreling economists a myth? Not entirely. Economists do disagree quite a lot on some issues, especially in macroeconomics, but they also find a great deal of common ground.

costs and focus on how the proposed law would change individual savings behavior. This economist might point to studies suggesting that value-added taxes promote higher consumer saving, a desirable result. Because the economists have made different simplifying assumptions, they arrive at different conclusions. And so the two economists may find themselves on different sides of the issue.

Most such disputes are eventually resolved by the accumulation of evidence that shows which of the various simplifying assumptions made by economists does a better job of fitting the facts. However, in economics, as in any science, it can take a long time before research settles important disputes—decades, in some cases. And since the economy is always changing in ways that make old approaches invalid or raise new policy questions, there are always new issues on which economists disagree. The policy maker must then decide which economist to believe.

Module 1 Review

Solutions appear at the back of the book.

Check Your Understanding

1. What are the four categories of resources? Give an example of a resource from each category.

2. What type of resource is each of the following?
   a. time spent flipping hamburgers at a restaurant
   b. a bulldozer
   c. a river

3. You make $45,000 per year at your current job with Whiz Kids Consultants. You are considering a job offer from Brainiacs, Inc., which would pay you $50,000 per year. Which of the following are elements of the opportunity cost of accepting the new job at Brainiacs, Inc.? Answer yes or no, and explain your answer.

   a. the increased time spent commuting to your new job
   b. the $45,000 salary from your old job
   c. the more spacious office at your new job

4. Identify each of the following statements as positive or normative, and explain your answer.
   a. Society should take measures to prevent people from engaging in dangerous personal behavior.
   b. People who engage in dangerous personal behavior impose higher costs on society through higher medical costs.

Multiple-Choice Questions

1. Which of the following is an example of a resource?
   - I. petroleum
   - II. a factory
   - III. a cheeseburger dinner
   - a. I only
   - b. II only
   - c. III only
   - d. I and II only
   - e. I, II, and III

2. Which of the following situations represent(s) resource scarcity?
   - I. Rapidly growing economies experience increasing levels of water pollution.
   - II. There is a finite amount of petroleum in the physical environment.
   - III. Cassette tapes are no longer being produced.
   - a. I only
   - b. II only
   - c. III only
   - d. I and II only
   - e. I, II, and III

3. Suppose that you prefer reading a book you already own to watching TV and that you prefer watching TV to listening to music. If these are your only three choices, what is the opportunity cost of reading?
   - a. watching TV and listening to music
   - b. watching TV
   - c. listening to music
   - d. sleeping
   - e. the price of the book

4. Which of the following statements is/are normative?
   - I. The price of gasoline is rising.
   - II. The price of gasoline is too high.
   - III. Gas prices are expected to fall in the near future.
   - a. I only
   - b. II only
   - c. III only
   - d. I and III only
   - e. I, II, and III

5. Which of the following questions is studied in microeconomics?
   - a. Should I go to college or get a job after I graduate?
   - b. What government policies should be adopted to promote employment in the economy?
   - c. How many people are employed in the economy this year?
   - d. Has the overall level of prices in the economy increased or decreased this year?
   - e. What determines the overall salary levels paid to workers in a given year?

Critical-Thinking Question

In what type of economic analysis do questions have a "right" or "wrong" answer? In what type of economic analysis do questions not necessarily have a "right" answer? On what type of economic analysis do economists tend to disagree most frequently? Why might economists disagree? Explain.

Landov Photos

Module 2
Models and the Circular Flow

In 1901 Wilbur and Orville Wright built something that would change the world. No, not the airplane—their successful flight at Kitty Hawk (pictured above) would come two years later. What made the Wright brothers true visionaries was their wind tunnel, an apparatus that let them experiment with many different designs for wings and control surfaces. These experiments gave them the knowledge that would make heavier-than-air flight possible.

A miniature airplane sitting motionless in a wind tunnel isn't the same thing as an actual aircraft in flight. But it is a very useful model of a flying plane—a simplified representation of the real thing that can be used to answer crucial questions, such as how much lift a given wing shape will generate at a given airspeed.

Needless to say, testing an airplane design in a wind tunnel is cheaper and safer than building a full-scale version and hoping it will fly. More generally, models play a crucial role in almost all scientific research—economics very much included.

In fact, you could say that economic theory consists mainly of a collection of models, a series of simplified representations of economic reality that allow us to understand a variety of economic issues. In this module, we will look at why models are so useful to economists. We'll also examine one important simplified representation of economic reality—the circular-flow diagram.

Models Take Flight in Economics

A **model** is any simplified version of reality that is used to better understand real-life situations. But how do we create a simplified representation of an economic situation?

One possibility—an economist's equivalent of a wind tunnel—is to find or create a real but simplified economy. For example, economists interested in the economic role of money have studied the system of exchange that developed in World War II prison camps, in which cigarettes became a universally accepted form of payment, even among prisoners who didn't smoke.

A **model** is a simplified representation used to better understand a real-life situation.

Another possibility is to simulate the workings of the economy on a computer. For example, when changes in tax law are proposed, government officials use *tax models*—large mathematical computer programs—to assess how the proposed changes would affect different groups of people.

Models are important because their simplicity allows economists to focus on the effects of only one change at a time. That is, they allow us to hold everything else constant and to study how one change affects the overall economic outcome. So when building economic models, an important assumption is the **other things equal assumption,** which means that all other relevant factors remain unchanged. Sometimes the Latin phrase *ceteris paribus,* which means "other things equal," is used.

But it isn't always possible to find or create a small-scale version of the whole economy, and a computer program is only as good as the data it uses. (Programmers have a saying: garbage in, garbage out.) For many purposes, the most effective form of economic modeling is the construction of "thought experiments": simplified, hypothetical versions of real-life situations. And as you will see throughout this book, economists' models are often in the form of a graph. In Module 3 we will look at graphs of the *production possibilities frontier,* a model that helps economists think about the choices made in every economy. Models can also be represented in diagrams. In this module we will use the circular-flow diagram to better understand the workings of the economy.

> The **other things equal assumption** means that all other relevant factors remain unchanged. This is also known as the *ceteris paribus* assumption.

Models for Money

What's an economic model worth, anyway? In some cases, quite a lot of money.

Although many economic models are developed for purely scientific purposes, others are developed to help governments make economic policies. And there is a growing business in developing economic models to help corporations make decisions.

Who models for money? There are dozens of consulting firms that use models to predict future trends, offer advice based on their models, or develop custom models for business and government clients. A notable example is Global Insight, the world's biggest economic consulting firm. It was created by a merger between Data Resources, Inc., founded by professors from Harvard and MIT, and Wharton Economic Forecasting Associates, founded by professors at the University of Pennsylvania.

One particularly lucrative branch of economics is finance theory, which helps investors figure out what assets, such as shares in a company, are worth. Finance theorists often become highly paid "rocket scientists" at big Wall Street firms because financial models demand a high level of technical expertise.

Unfortunately, the most famous business application of finance theory came spectacularly to grief. In 1994 a group of Wall Street traders teamed up with famous finance theorists—including two Nobel Prize winners—to form Long-Term Capital Management (LTCM), a fund that used sophisticated financial models to invest the money of wealthy clients. At first, the fund did very well. But in 1998 bad economic news from all over the world—with countries as disparate as Russia, Japan, and Brazil in financial trouble at the same time—inflicted huge losses on LTCM's investments. For a few anxious days, many people feared not only that the fund would collapse but also that it would bring many other companies down with it. Thanks in part to a rescue operation organized by government officials, this did not happen; but LTCM was closed a few months later, having lost millions of dollars and with some of its investors losing most of the money they had put in.

What went wrong? Partly it was bad luck. But experienced hands also faulted the economists at LTCM for taking too many risks. Although

If shoppers decide to spend more, the income of other groups will rise.

LTCM's models indicated that a run of bad news like the one that actually happened was extremely unlikely, a sensible economist knows that sometimes even the best model misses important possibilities.

Interestingly, a similar phenomenon occurred in the summer of 2007, when problems in the financial market for home mortgage loans caused severe losses for several investment funds. It turns out that these funds had made the same mistake as LTCM—omitting from their models the possibility of a severe downturn in the home mortgage loan market.

The Circular-Flow Diagram

The U.S. economy is a vastly complex entity, with more than 150 million workers employed by more than 25 million companies, producing millions of different goods and services. Yet you can learn some very important things about the economy by considering the simple graphic shown in Figure 2.1. This **circular-flow diagram** is a simplified representation of the way money, goods and services, and factors of production flow through the economy. The yellow arrows show how goods, services, labor, and raw materials flow in one direction, and the green arrows show how the money that pays for these things flows in the opposite direction. The underlying principle is that the flow of money into each market or sector is equal to the flow of money coming out of that market or sector.

This simple model illustrates an economy that contains only two types of participants: households and firms. A **household** consists of either an individual or a group of people (typically a family) who share their income. A **firm** is an organization (typically a corporation) that produces goods or services for sale—and that employs members of households.

As shown in Figure 2.1, there are two kinds of markets in this simple economy. On the left side are markets for goods and services, also known as **product markets,** in which households buy the goods and services they want from firms. This produces a flow of goods and services to households and a return flow of money to firms.

On the right side are **factor markets** in which firms buy the resources they need to produce goods and services. Recall from the preceding module that the factors of production are land, labor, capital, and entrepreneurship.

The best known factor market is the *labor market,* in which workers are paid for their time and effort. Besides labor, we can think of households as owning the other factors of production as well, and selling them to firms. For example, when a corporation pays dividends to its stockholders, who are members of households, it is in effect paying them for the use of the machines and buildings that belong to those investors.

In the interest of simplicity, the circular-flow diagram in Figure 2.1 does not include a number of real-world complications. A few examples:

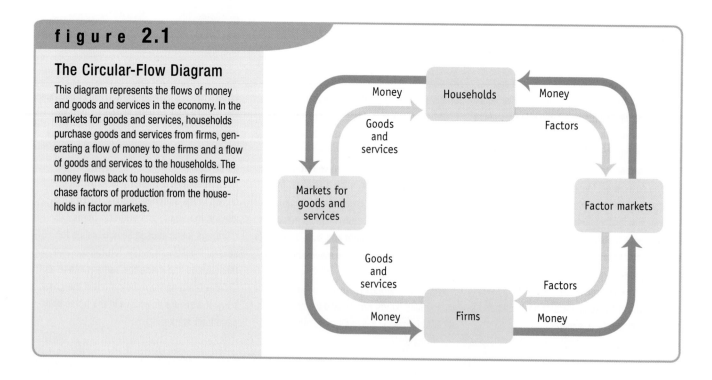

figure 2.1

The Circular-Flow Diagram

This diagram represents the flows of money and goods and services in the economy. In the markets for goods and services, households purchase goods and services from firms, generating a flow of money to the firms and a flow of goods and services to the households. The money flows back to households as firms purchase factors of production from the households in factor markets.

- In reality, exports and imports bring the rest of the world into the picture with interactions between our economy and the economies of our trading partners.

- A more complete picture would include the sale of goods by firms to other firms; for example, steel companies sell mainly to other companies such as auto manufacturers, not to households.

- The diagram doesn't show the government, which takes money out of the circular flow in the form of taxes and injects it back into the flow as spending.

- Also absent are financial markets, which accept money out of the circular flow as private savings and stock purchases and send it back in as loans and payments for stock issues.

Figure 2.1, in other words, is by no means a complete picture of the economy's participants and the flows that take place among them. But despite its simplicity, the circular-flow diagram is a useful guide to how the economy works and how the participants are interconnected. Next we'll take a closer look at the relationship between individual decision-making and broader economic outcomes.

One Person's Spending is Another Person's Income

The circular-flow diagram shows that what goes around comes around. The circularity of spending magnifies the importance of individual and firm behavior at every level. And it helps to explain why conservative spending by one segment of the economy can lead to problems for almost everyone in the economy.

Consider Wichita, Kansas, known as the "Air Capital of the World" because so many airplanes are made there. In 2010, even as the economy recovered from the recession of 2007–2009, several corporations that had been buying a lot of airplanes decided to cut back on their purchases. These cuts bruised the Wichita economy, and spending dropped off at the city's retail stores. A similar problem occurred at the national level in 2001 and 2008, when cuts in business investment spending fueled a sharp downfall in retail sales.

But why should cuts in spending on airplanes by businesses mean empty stores in the shopping malls? After all, malls are places where families, not businesses, go to shop. The answer is that lower business spending led to lower incomes throughout the economy, because people who had been making those airplanes lost their jobs or were forced to take pay cuts. Between 2008 and 2010, Wichita's aviation industry lost about 13,000 jobs. As incomes evaporated in the aviation industry, so did spending by consumers who worked in the aviation industry. And then incomes and spending in industries supported by aviation workers—retail sales, day care, home construction, and so on—fell, and the domino effect of falling consumption and falling incomes continued.

This story illustrates a general principle: *One person's spending is another person's income*. In a market economy, people make a living selling things—including their labor—to other people. If some group in the economy decides, for whatever reason, to spend more, the income of other groups will rise. If some group decides to spend less, the income of other groups will fall.

Because one person's spending is another person's income, a chain reaction of changes in spending behavior occurs. Spending cuts lead to reduced family incomes; families respond by reducing consumer spending, which leads to more conservative hiring by firms, and another round of income cuts; and so on.

Through these repercussions, individual and firm decisions send ripple effects throughout the economy. Although the remainder of this book is about the "micro" side of economics, keep in mind that behavior on the micro level can have macro consequences.

Tasos Katopodis/Getty Images

Solutions appear at the back of the book.

Check Your Understanding

1. Use the circular-flow diagram to explain how an increase in the amount of money spent by households results in an increase in the number of jobs in the economy.

2. Oil companies are investing heavily in projects that will extract oil from the "oil sands" of Canada. Near these projects, in Edmonton, Alberta, restaurants and other consumer businesses are booming. Explain why on the basis of a principle you learned about in this Module.

Multiple-Choice Questions

1. The other things equal assumption allows economists to
   a. avoid making assumptions about reality.
   b. focus on the effects of only one change at a time.
   c. oversimplify.
   d. allow nothing to change in their model.
   e. reflect all aspects of the real world in their model.

2. Which of the following is true? The simple circular-flow diagram
      I. includes only the product markets.
      II. includes only the factor markets.
      III. is a simplified representation of the macroeconomy.
   a. I only
   b. II only
   c. III only
   d. I and III only
   e. none of the above

3. A firm is necessarily
   a. an employer of lawyers or accountants.
   b. a service provider.
   c. an organization.
   d. a corporation.
   e. manufacturer of goods.

4. In the United States, we can think of the factors of production as being owned by
   a. firms.
   b. the government.
   c. factor markets.
   d. households.
   e. economists.

5. Economists are drawn to models by their
   a. good looks
   b. realism
   c. high level of detail
   d. snap-on parts
   e. simplicity

Critical-Thinking Questions

The inhabitants of the fictional economy of Atlantis use money in the form of cowry shells. Draw a circular-flow diagram showing households and firms. Firms produce potatoes and fish, and households buy potatoes and fish. Households also provide the land and labor to firms. Identify where, within the flows of cowry shells, goods and services, or resources, each of the following impacts would occur. Describe how this impact spreads around the circle.

a. A devastating hurricane floods many of the potato fields.
b. A productive fishing season yields an especially large number of fish.
c. The inhabitants of Atlantis discover the music of singer Shakira and spend several days a month at dancing festivals.

- The importance of trade-offs in economic analysis

- What the production possibilities curve model tells us about efficiency, opportunity cost, and economic growth

- The two sources of economic growth—increases in the availability of resources and improvements in technology

Module 3
The Production Possibility Frontier Model

A good economic model can be a tremendous aid to understanding. In this module, we look at the *production possibility frontier,* a model that helps economists think about the *trade-offs* every economy faces. The production possibility frontier helps us understand three important aspects of the real economy: efficiency, opportunity cost, and economic growth.

Trade-offs: The Production Possibility Frontier

The 2000 hit movie *Cast Away,* starring Tom Hanks, was an update of the classic story of Robinson Crusoe, the hero of Daniel Defoe's eighteenth-century novel. Hanks played the role of a sole survivor of a plane crash who was stranded on a remote island. As in the original story of Robinson Crusoe, the Hanks character had limited resources: the natural resources of the island, a few items he managed to salvage from the plane, and, of course, his own time and effort. With only these resources, he had to make a life. In effect, he became a one-man economy.

One of the important principles of economics we introduced in Module 1 was that resources are scarce. As a result, any economy—whether it contains one person or millions of people—faces trade-offs. You make a **trade-off** when you give up something in order to have something else. For example, if a castaway devotes more resources to catching fish, he benefits by catching more fish, but he cannot use those same resources to gather coconuts, so the trade-off is that he has fewer coconuts.

To think about the trade-offs necessary in any economy, economists often use the **production possibility frontier** model. The idea behind this model is to improve our understanding of trade-offs by considering a simplified economy that produces only two goods. This simplification enables us to show the trade-offs graphically.

Figure 3.1 shows a hypothetical production possibility frontier for Tom, a castaway alone on an island, who must make a trade-off between fish production and coconut

You make a **trade-off** when you give up something in order to have something else.

The **production possibility frontier (PPF)** illustrates the trade-offs facing an economy that produces only two goods. It shows the maximum quantity of one good that can be produced for each possible quantity of the other good produced.

figure 3.1

The Production Possibility Frontier

The PPF illustrates the trade-offs facing an economy that produces two goods. It shows the maximum quantity of one good that can be produced, given the quantity of the other good produced. Here, the maximum quantity of coconuts that Tom can gather depends on the quantity of fish he catches, and vice versa. His feasible production is shown by the area *inside* or *on* the curve. Production at point *C* is feasible but not efficient. Points *A* and *B* are feasible and efficient in production, but point *D* is not feasible.

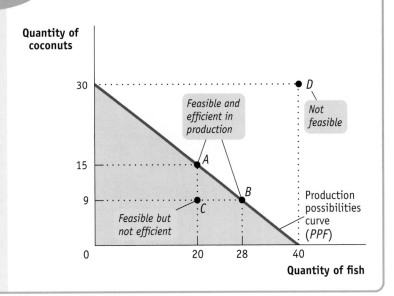

production. The curve shows the maximum quantity of fish Tom can catch during a week *given* the quantity of coconuts he gathers, and vice versa. That is, it answers questions of the form, "What is the maximum quantity of fish Tom can catch if he also gathers 9 (or 15, or 30) coconuts?"

There is a crucial distinction between points *inside* or *on* the production possibility frontier (the shaded area) and points *outside* the PPF. If a production point lies inside or on the curve—like point *C*, at which Tom catches 20 fish and gathers 9 coconuts—it is feasible. After all, the curve tells us that if Tom catches 20 fish, he could also gather a maximum of 15 coconuts, so he could certainly gather 9 coconuts. However, a production point that lies outside the curve—such as point *D*, which would have Tom catching 40 fish and gathering 30 coconuts—isn't feasible.

In Figure 3.1 the production possibility frontier intersects the horizontal axis at 40 fish. This means that if Tom devoted all his resources to catching fish, he would catch 40 fish per week but would have no resources left over to gather coconuts. The PPF intersects the vertical axis at 30 coconuts. This means that if Tom devoted all his resources to gathering coconuts, he could gather 30 coconuts per week but would have no resources left over to catch fish. Thus, if Tom wants 30 coconuts, the trade-off is that he can't have any fish.

The curve also shows less extreme trade-offs. For example, if Tom decides to catch 20 fish, he would be able to gather at most 15 coconuts; this production choice is illustrated by point *A*. If Tom decides to catch 28 fish, he could gather at most 9 coconuts, as shown by point *B*.

Thinking in terms of a production possibility frontier simplifies the complexities of reality. The real-world economy produces millions of different goods. Even a castaway on an island would produce more than two different items (for example, he would need clothing and housing as well as food). But in this model we imagine an economy that produces only two goods, because in a model with many goods, it would be much harder to study trade-offs, efficiency, and economic growth.

Efficiency

The production possibility frontier is useful for illustrating the general economic concept of efficiency. An economy is **efficient** if there are no missed opportunities—meaning that there is no way to make some people better off without making other people worse off. For example, suppose a course you are taking meets in a lecture hall or classroom that is

An economy is **efficient** if there is no way to make anyone better off without making at least one person worse off.

Crowded classrooms reflect inefficiency if switching to a larger space would make some students better off without making anyone worse off.

too small for the number of students—some may be forced to sit on the floor or stand—despite the fact that a larger space nearby is empty during the same period. Economists would say that this is an *inefficient* use of resources because there is a way to make some people better off without making anyone worse off—after all, the larger space is empty. The school is not using its resources efficiently.

When an economy is using all of its resources efficiently, the only way one person can be made better off is by rearranging the use of resources in such a way that the change makes someone else worse off. So in our classroom example, if all larger classrooms or lecture halls were already fully occupied, we could say that the school was run in an efficient way; your classmates could be made better off only by making people in the larger classroom worse off—by moving them to the room that is too small.

Returning to our castaway example, as long as Tom produces a combination of coconuts and fish that is on the production possibility frontier, his production is efficient. At point *A*, the 15 coconuts he gathers are the maximum quantity he can get *given* that he has chosen to catch 20 fish; at point *B*, the 9 coconuts he gathers are the maximum he can get *given* his choice to catch 28 fish; and so on. If an economy is producing at a point on its production possibility frontier, we say that the economy is *efficient in production*.

But suppose that for some reason Tom was at point *C*, producing 20 fish and 9 coconuts. Then this one-person economy would definitely not be efficient in production, and would therefore be *inefficient*: it is missing the opportunity to produce more of both goods.

Another example of inefficiency in production occurs when people in an economy are involuntarily unemployed: they want to work but are unable to find jobs. When that happens, the economy is not efficient in production because it could produce more output if those people were employed. The production possibility frontier shows the amount that can *possibly* be produced if all resources are fully employed. In other words, changes in unemployment move the economy closer to, or further away from, the PPF. But the curve itself is determined by what would be possible if there were full employment in the economy. Greater unemployment is represented by points farther below the PPF—the economy is not reaching its possibilities if it is not using all of its resources. Lower unemployment is represented by points closer to the PPF—as unemployment decreases, the economy moves closer to reaching its possibilities.

Although the production possibility frontier helps clarify what it means for an economy to be efficient in production, it's important to understand that efficiency in production is only *part* of what's required for the economy as a whole to be efficient. Efficiency also requires that the economy allocate its resources so that consumers are as well off as possible. If an economy does this, we say that it is *efficient in allocation*.

To see why efficiency in allocation is as important as efficiency in production, notice that points *A* and *B* in Figure 3.1 both represent situations in which the economy is efficient in production, because in each case it can't produce more of one good without producing less of the other. But these two situations may not be equally desirable. Suppose that Tom prefers point *B* to point *A*—that is, he would rather consume 28 fish and 9 coconuts than 20 fish and 15 coconuts. Then point *A* is inefficient from the point of view of the economy as a whole: it's possible to make Tom better off without making anyone else worse off. (Of course, in this castaway economy there isn't anyone else; Tom is all alone.)

This example shows that efficiency for the economy as a whole requires *both* efficiency in production and efficiency in allocation. To be efficient, an economy must produce as much of each good as it can, given the production of other goods, and it must also produce the mix of goods that people want to consume.

Opportunity Cost

The production possibility frontier is a useful reminder that the true cost of any good is not only its price but also everything else in addition to money that must be given up in order to get that good—the *opportunity cost*. If, for example, Tom decides to go from point *A* to point *B* on the PPF in Figure 3.1, he will produce 8 more fish but 6 fewer coconuts. So the opportunity cost of those 8 fish is the 6 coconuts not gathered. Since 8 extra fish have an opportunity cost of 6 coconuts, 1 fish has an opportunity cost of $^6\!/_8 = ^3\!/_4$ of a coconut.

Is the opportunity cost of an extra fish in terms of coconuts always the same, no matter how many fish Tom catches? In the example illustrated by Figure 3.1, the answer is yes. If Tom increases his catch from 28 to 40 fish, an increase of 12, the number of coconuts he gathers falls from 9 to zero. So his opportunity cost per additional fish is $^9\!/_{12} = ^3\!/_4$ of a coconut, the same as it was when his catch went from 20 fish to 28.

However, the fact that in this example the opportunity cost of an additional fish in terms of coconuts is always the same is a result of an assumption we've made, an assumption that's reflected in the way Figure 3.1 is drawn. Specifically, whenever we assume that the opportunity cost of an additional unit of a good doesn't change regardless of the output mix, the production possibilities curve is a straight line.

Moreover, as you might have already guessed, the slope of a straight-line production possibilities curve is equal to the opportunity cost—specifically, the opportunity cost for the good measured on the horizontal axis in terms of the good measured on the vertical axis. In Figure 3.1, the production possibility frontier has a *constant slope* of $-^3\!/_4$, implying that Tom faces a *constant opportunity cost* per fish equal to $^3\!/_4$ of a coconut. (The Section I Appendix reviews how to calculate the slope of a straight line.) This is the simplest case, but the production possibility frontier model can also be used to examine situations in which opportunity costs change as the mix of output changes.

Figure 3.2 illustrates a different assumption, a case in which Tom faces *increasing opportunity cost*. Here, the more fish he catches, the more coconuts he has to give up to catch an additional fish, and vice versa. For example, to go from producing zero fish to producing 20 fish, he has to give up 5 coconuts. That is, the opportunity cost of those 20 fish is 5 coconuts. But to increase his fish production from 20 to 40—that is, to produce an additional 20 fish—he must give up 25 more coconuts, a much higher opportunity cost. As you can see in Figure 3.2, when opportunity costs are increasing rather

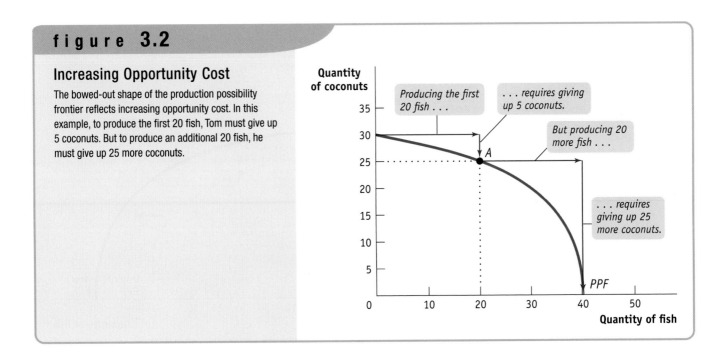

figure 3.2

Increasing Opportunity Cost

The bowed-out shape of the production possibility frontier reflects increasing opportunity cost. In this example, to produce the first 20 fish, Tom must give up 5 coconuts. But to produce an additional 20 fish, he must give up 25 more coconuts.

Producing the first 20 fish . . .

. . . requires giving up 5 coconuts.

But producing 20 more fish . . .

. . . requires giving up 25 more coconuts.

than constant, the production possibility frontier is a bowed-out curve rather than a straight line.

Although it's often useful to work with the simple assumption that the production possibility frontier is a straight line, economists believe that in reality, opportunity costs are typically increasing. When only a small amount of a good is produced, the opportunity cost of producing that good is relatively low because the economy needs to use only those resources that are especially well suited for its production. For example, if an economy grows only a small amount of corn, that corn can be grown in places where the soil and climate are perfect for growing corn but less suitable for growing anything else, such as wheat.

So growing that corn involves giving up only a small amount of potential wheat output. Once the economy grows a lot of corn, however, land that is well suited for wheat but isn't so great for corn must be used to produce corn anyway. As a result, the additional corn production involves sacrificing considerably more wheat production. In other words, as more of a good is produced, its opportunity cost typically rises because well-suited inputs are used up and less adaptable inputs must be used instead.

Economic Growth

Finally, the production possibility frontier helps us understand what it means to talk about *economic growth*. We introduced the concept of economic growth in Module 2, saying that it allows *a sustained rise in aggregate output*. We learned that economic growth is one of the fundamental features of the economy. But are we really justified in saying that the economy has grown over time? After all, although the U.S. economy produces more of many things than it did a century ago, it produces less of other things—for example, horse-drawn carriages. In other words, production of many goods is actually down. So how can we say for sure that the economy as a whole has grown?

The answer, illustrated in Figure 3.3, is that economic growth means an *expansion of the economy's production possibilities:* the economy *can* produce more of everything. For example, if Tom's production is initially at point *A* (20 fish and 25 coconuts), economic growth means that he could move to point *E* (25 fish and 30 coconuts). Point *E* lies outside the original curve, so in the production possibility frontier model, growth is shown as an outward shift of the curve. Unless the PPF shifts outward, the points beyond the PPF are unattainable. Those points beyond a given PPF are beyond the economy's possibilities.

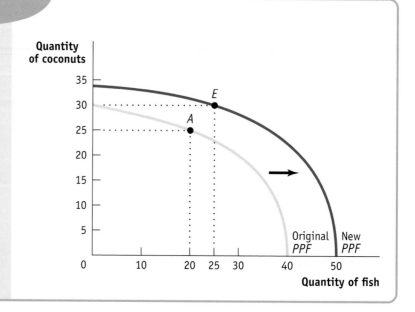

figure 3.3

Economic Growth

Economic growth results in an *outward shift* of the production possibility frontier because production possibilities are expanded. The economy can now produce more of everything. For example, if production is initially at point *A* (20 fish and 25 coconuts), it could move to point *E* (25 fish and 30 coconuts).

What can cause the production possibility frontier to shift outward? There are two general sources of economic growth. One is an increase in the resources used to produce goods and services: labor, land, capital, and entrepreneurship. To see how adding to an economy's resources leads to economic growth, suppose that Tom finds a fishing net washed ashore on the beach. The fishing net is a resource he can use to produce more fish in the course of a day spent fishing.

We can't say how many more fish Tom will catch; that depends on how much time he decides to spend fishing now that he has the net. But because the net makes his fishing more productive, he can catch more fish without reducing the number of coconuts he gathers, or he can gather more coconuts without reducing his fish catch. So his possibility frontier shifts outward.

The other source of economic growth is progress in **technology,** the technical means for the production of goods and services. Suppose Tom figures out a better way either to catch fish or to gather coconuts—say, by inventing a fishing hook or a wagon for transporting coconuts. Either invention would shift his production possibility frontier outward. However, the shift would not be a simple outward expansion of every point along the PPF. Technology specific to the production of only one good has no effect if all resources are devoted to the other good: a fishing hook will be of no use if Tom produces nothing but coconuts. So the point on the PPF that represents the number of coconuts that can be produced if there is no fishing will not change.

In real-world economies, innovations in the techniques we use to produce goods and services have been a crucial force behind economic growth. Again, economic growth means an increase in what the economy *can* produce. What the economy actually produces depends on the choices people make. After his production possibilities expand, Tom might not choose to produce both more fish and more coconuts; he might choose to increase production of only one good, or he might even choose to produce less of one good. For example, if he gets better at catching fish, he might decide to go on an all-fish diet and skip the coconuts, just as the introduction of motor vehicles led most people to give up horse-drawn carriages.

But even if, for some reason, he chooses to produce either fewer coconuts or fewer fish than before, we would still say that his economy has grown, because he *could* have produced more of everything. If an economy's PPF shifts inward, the economy has become smaller. This could happen if the economy loses resources or technology (for example, if it experiences war or a natural disaster).

The production possibility frontier is a very simplified model of an economy, yet it teaches us important lessons about real-life economies. The PPF gives us our first clear sense of what constitutes economic efficiency, it illustrates the concept of opportunity cost, and it makes clear what economic growth is all about.

Technology is the technical means for producing goods and services.

Module 3 Review

Solutions appear at the back of the book.

Check Your Understanding

1. True or false? Explain your answer.
   a. An increase in the amount of resources available to Tom for use in producing coconuts and fish does not change his production possibility frontier.
   b. A technological change that allows Tom to catch more fish relative to any amount of coconuts gathered results in a change in his production possibility frontier.
   c. Points inside a production possibility frontier are efficient and points outside a PPF are inefficient.

Multiple-Choice Questions

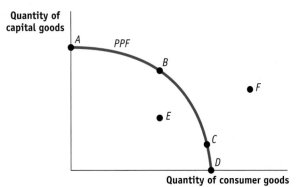

Quantity of capital goods / Quantity of consumer goods / PPF

Refer to the graph above to answer the following questions.

1. Which point(s) on the graph represent efficiency in production?
   a. *B* and *C*
   b. *A* and *D*
   c. *A, B, C,* and *D*
   d. *A, B, C, D,* and *E*
   e. *A, B, C, D, E,* and *F*

2. For this economy, an increase in the quantity of capital goods produced without a corresponding decrease in the quantity of consumer goods produced
   a. cannot happen because there is always an opportunity cost.
   b. is represented by a movement from point *E* to point *A*.
   c. is represented by a movement from point *C* to point *B*.
   d. is represented by a movement from point *E* to point *B*.
   e. is only possible with an increase in resources or technology.

3. An increase in unemployment could be represented by a movement from point
   a. *D* to point *C*.
   b. *B* to point *A*.
   c. *C* to point *F*.
   d. *B* to point *E*.
   e. *E* to point *B*.

4. Which of the following might allow this economy to move from point *B* to point *F*?
   a. more workers
   b. discovery of new resources
   c. building new factories
   d. technological advances
   e. all of the above

5. This production possibility frontier shows the trade-off between consumer goods and capital goods. Since capital goods are a resource, an increase in the production of capital goods today will increase the economy's production possibilities in the future. Therefore, all other things equal (*ceteris paribus*), producing at which point today will result in the largest outward shift of the PPF in the future?
   a. *A*
   b. *B*
   c. *C*
   d. *D*
   e. *E*

Critical-Thinking Question

Assume that an economy can choose between producing food and producing shelter at a constant opportunity cost. Draw a correctly labeled production possibility frontier for the economy. On your graph:
a. Use the letter *E* to label one of the points that is efficient in production.

b. Use the letter *U* to label one of the points at which there might be unemployment.
c. Use the letter *I* to label one of the points that is not feasible.

Module 4
Comparative Advantage and Trade

What you will learn in this Module:

- How trade leads to gains for an individual or an economy
- The difference between absolute advantage and comparative advantage
- How comparative advantage leads to gains from trade in the global marketplace

Gains from Trade

A family could try to take care of all its own needs—growing its own food, sewing its own clothing, providing itself with entertainment, and writing its own economics textbooks. But trying to live that way would be very hard. The key to a much better standard of living for everyone is **trade,** in which people divide tasks among themselves and each person provides a good or service that other people want in return for different goods and services that he or she wants.

The reason we have an economy is that there are **gains from trade:** by dividing tasks and trading, two people (or 7 billion people) can each get more of what they want than they could get by being self-sufficient. Gains from trade arise, in particular, from this division of tasks, which economists call **specialization:** each person engages in a different task that he or she is good at performing.

The advantages of specialization, and the resulting gains from trade, were the starting point for Adam Smith's 1776 book *The Wealth of Nations,* which many regard as the beginning of economics as a discipline. Smith's book begins with a description of an eighteenth-century pin factory where, rather than each of the 10 workers making a pin from start to finish, each worker specialized in one of the many steps in pin-making:

> One man draws out the wire, another straights it, a third cuts it, a fourth points it, a fifth grinds it at the top for receiving the head; to make the head requires two or three distinct operations; to put it on, is a particular business, to whiten the pins is another; it is even a trade by itself to put them into the paper; and the important business of making a pin is, in this manner, divided into about eighteen distinct operations. . . . Those ten persons, therefore, could make among them upwards of forty-eight thousand pins in a day. But if they had all wrought separately and independently, and without any of them having been educated to this particular business, they certainly could not each of them have made twenty, perhaps not one pin a day. . . .

The same principle applies when we look at how people divide tasks among themselves and trade in an economy. The economy, as a whole, can produce more when each person *specializes* in a task and *trades* with others.

In a market economy, individuals engage in **trade:** they provide goods and services to others and receive goods and services in return.

There are **gains from trade:** people can get more of what they want through trade than they could if they tried to be self-sufficient. This increase in output is due to **specialization:** each person engages in the task that he or she is good at performing.

The benefits of specialization are the reason a person typically focuses on the production of only one type of good or service. It takes many years of study and experience to become a doctor; it also takes many years of study and experience to become a commercial airline pilot. Many doctors might have the potential to become excellent pilots, and vice versa, but it is very unlikely that anyone who decided to pursue both careers would be as good a pilot or as good a doctor as someone who specialized in only one of those professions. So it is to everyone's advantage when individuals specialize in their career choices.

Markets are what allow a doctor and a pilot to specialize in their respective fields. Because markets for commercial flights and for doctors' services exist, a doctor is assured that she can find a flight and a pilot is assured that he can find a doctor. As long as individuals know that they can find the goods and services that they want in the market, they are willing to forgo self-sufficiency and are willing to specialize.

Comparative Advantage and Gains from Trade

The production possibility frontier model is particularly useful for illustrating gains from trade—trade based on *comparative advantage*. Let's stick with Tom stranded on his island, but now let's suppose that a second castaway, who just happens to be named Hank, is washed ashore. Can they benefit from trading with each other?

It's obvious that there will be potential gains from trade if the two castaways do different things particularly well. For example, if Tom is a skilled fisherman and Hank is very good at climbing trees, clearly it makes sense for Tom to catch fish and Hank to gather coconuts—and for the two men to trade the products of their efforts.

But one of the most important insights in all of economics is that there are gains from trade even if one of the trading parties isn't especially good at anything. Suppose, for example, that Hank is less well suited to primitive life than Tom; he's not nearly as good at catching fish, and compared to Tom, even his coconut-gathering leaves something to be desired. Nonetheless, what we'll see is that both Tom and Hank can live better by trading with each other than either could alone.

For the purposes of this example, let's go back to the simple case of straight-line production possibility frontiers. Tom's production possibilities are represented by the PPF in panel (a) of Figure 4.1, which is the same as the production possibility

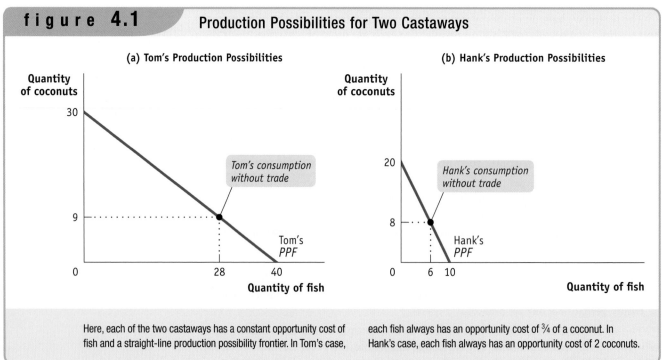

figure 4.1   **Production Possibilities for Two Castaways**

Here, each of the two castaways has a constant opportunity cost of fish and a straight-line production possibility frontier. In Tom's case, each fish always has an opportunity cost of ¾ of a coconut. In Hank's case, each fish always has an opportunity cost of 2 coconuts.

frontier in Figure 3.1 (page 17). According to this PPF, Tom could catch 40 fish, but only if he gathered no coconuts, and he could gather 30 coconuts, but only if he caught no fish. Recall that this means that the slope of his production possibility frontier is −¾: his opportunity cost of 1 fish is ¾ of a coconut.

Panel (b) of Figure 4.1 shows Hank's production possibilities. Like Tom's, Hank's production possibility frontier is a straight line, implying a constant opportunity cost of fish in terms of coconuts. His production possibility frontier has a constant slope of −2. Hank is less productive all around: at most he can produce 10 fish or 20 coconuts. But he is particularly bad at fishing: whereas Tom sacrifices ¾ of a coconut per fish caught, for Hank the opportunity cost of a fish is 2 whole coconuts. Table 4.1 summarizes the two castaways' opportunity costs of fish and coconuts.

table **4.1**

Tom's and Hank's Opportunity Costs of Fish and Coconuts

	Tom's Opportunity Cost	Hank's Opportunity Cost
One fish	3/4 coconut	2 coconuts
One coconut	4/3 fish	1/2 fish

Now, Tom and Hank could go their separate ways, each living on his own side of the island, catching his own fish and gathering his own coconuts. Let's suppose that they start out that way and make the consumption choices shown in Figure 4.1: in the absence of trade, Tom consumes 28 fish and 9 coconuts per week, while Hank consumes 6 fish and 8 coconuts.

But is this the best they can do? No, it isn't. Given that the two castaways have different opportunity costs, they can strike a deal that makes both of them better off.

Table 4.2 shows how such a deal works: Tom specializes in the production of fish, catching 40 per week, and gives 10 to Hank. Meanwhile, Hank specializes in the production of coconuts, gathering 20 per week, and gives 10 to Tom. The result is shown in Figure 4.2 on the next page. Tom now consumes more of both goods than before: instead of 28 fish and 9 coconuts, he consumes 30 fish and 10 coconuts. Hank also consumes more, going from 6 fish and 8 coconuts to 10 fish and 10 coconuts. As Table 4.2 also shows, both Tom and Hank experience gains from trade: Tom's consumption of fish increases by two, and his consumption of coconuts increases by one. Hank's consumption of fish increases by four, and his consumption of coconuts increases by two.

table **4.2**

How the Castaways Gain from Trade

		Without Trade		With Trade		Gains from Trade
		Production	Consumption	Production	Consumption	
Tom	Fish	28	28	40	30	+2
	Coconuts	9	9	0	10	+1
Hank	Fish	6	6	0	10	+4
	Coconuts	8	8	20	10	+2

So both castaways are better off when they each specialize in what they are good at and trade with each other. It's a good idea for Tom to catch the fish for both of them, because his opportunity cost of a fish is only ¾ of a coconut not gathered versus 2 coconuts for Hank. Correspondingly, it's a good idea for Hank to gather coconuts for both of them.

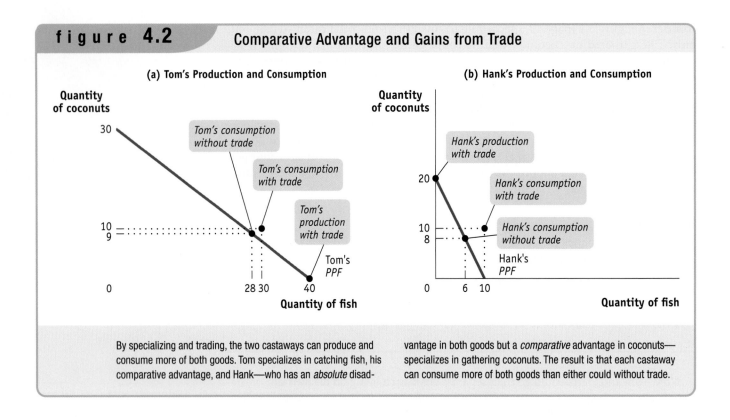

figure 4.2 **Comparative Advantage and Gains from Trade**

(a) Tom's Production and Consumption

Quantity
of coconuts

- Tom's consumption without trade
- Tom's consumption with trade
- Tom's production with trade

Tom's PPF

Quantity of fish

(b) Hank's Production and Consumption

Quantity
of coconuts

- Hank's production with trade
- Hank's consumption with trade
- Hank's consumption without trade

Hank's PPF

Quantity of fish

By specializing and trading, the two castaways can produce and consume more of both goods. Tom specializes in catching fish, his comparative advantage, and Hank—who has an *absolute* disadvantage in both goods but a *comparative* advantage in coconuts—specializes in gathering coconuts. The result is that each castaway can consume more of both goods than either could without trade.

Or we could describe the situation in a different way. Because Tom is so good at catching fish, his opportunity cost of gathering coconuts is high: ⁴⁄₃ of a fish not caught for every coconut gathered. Because Hank is a pretty poor fisherman, his opportunity cost of gathering coconuts is much less, only ½ of a fish per coconut.

An individual has a **comparative advantage** in producing something if the opportunity cost of that production is lower for that individual than for other people. In other words, Hank has a comparative advantage over Tom in producing a particular good or service if Hank's opportunity cost of producing that good or service is lower than Tom's. In this case, Hank has a comparative advantage in gathering coconuts and Tom has a comparative advantage in catching fish.

One point of clarification needs to be made before we proceed further. You may have wondered why Tom and Hank traded 10 fish for 10 coconuts. Why not some other deal, like trading 15 coconuts for 5 fish? The answer to that question has two parts. First, there may indeed be deals other than 10 fish for 10 coconuts that Tom and Hank are willing to agree to. Second, there are some deals that we can, however, safely rule out—such as 15 coconuts for 5 fish.

To understand why, reexamine Table 4.1 and consider Hank first. When Hank works on his own without trading with Tom, his opportunity cost of 1 fish is 2 coconuts. Therefore, it's clear that Hank will not accept any deal with Tom in which he must give up more than 2 coconuts per fish—otherwise, he's better off not trading at all. So we can rule out a deal that requires Hank to pay 3 coconuts per fish—such as trading 15 coconuts for 5 fish.

But Hank will accept a trade in which he pays less than 2 coconuts per fish—such as paying 1 coconut for 1 fish. Likewise, Tom will reject a deal that requires him to give up more than ⁴⁄₃ of a fish per coconut. For example, Tom would refuse a trade that required him to give up 10 fish for 6 coconuts. But he will accept a deal where he pays less than ⁴⁄₃ of a fish per coconut—and 1 fish for 1 coconut works. You can check for yourself why a trade of 1 fish for 1½ coconuts would also be acceptable to both Tom and Hank.

So the point to remember is that Tom and Hank will be willing to engage in a trade only if the "price" of the good each person is obtaining from the trade is less than his own opportunity cost of producing the good himself. Moreover, that's a general statement that is true whenever two parties trade voluntarily.

The story of Tom and Hank clearly simplifies reality. Yet it teaches us two important lessons that also apply to the real economy.

1. The PPF model provides a clear illustration of the gains from trade. By agreeing to specialize and provide goods to each other, Tom and Hank can produce more; therefore, both are better off than if each tried to be self-sufficient.

2. The PPF model demonstrates an important point often overlooked in real-world arguments: as long as people have different opportunity costs, *everyone has a comparative advantage in something, and everyone has a comparative disadvantage in something.*

Notice that in our example Tom is actually better than Hank at producing both goods: Tom can catch more fish in a week, and he can also gather more coconuts. That is, Tom has an **absolute advantage** in both activities: he can produce more output with a given amount of input (in this case, his time) than Hank can. You might therefore be tempted to think that Tom has nothing to gain from trading with the less-competent Hank.

But we've just seen that Tom can indeed benefit from a deal with Hank, because *comparative,* not *absolute,* advantage is the basis for mutual gain. It doesn't matter that it takes Hank more time to gather a coconut; what matters is that for him the opportunity cost of that coconut in terms of fish is lower. So Hank, despite his absolute disadvantage, even in coconuts, has a comparative advantage in coconut-gathering. Meanwhile Tom, who can use his time better by catching fish, has a comparative disadvantage in coconut-gathering.

If comparative advantage were relevant only to castaways, it might not be that interesting. However, the idea of comparative advantage applies to many activities in the

> An individual has an **absolute advantage** in producing a good or service if he or she can make more of it with a given amount of time and resources than anyone else can. Having an absolute advantage is not the same thing as having a comparative advantage.

Rich Nation, Poor Nation

Try taking off your clothes—at a suitable time and in a suitable place, of course—and take a look at the labels inside that say where the clothes were made. It's a very good bet that much, if not most, of your clothing was manufactured overseas, in a country that is much poorer than the United States is—say, in El Salvador, Sri Lanka, or Bangladesh.

Why are these countries so much poorer than the United States? The immediate reason is that their economies are much less *productive*—firms in these countries are just not able to produce as much from a given quantity of resources as comparable firms in the United States or other wealthy countries. Why countries differ so much in productivity is a deep question—indeed, one of the main questions that preoccupy economists. But in any case, the difference in productivity is a fact.

But if the economies of these countries are so much less productive than ours, how is it that they make so much of our clothing? Why don't we do it for ourselves?

The answer is "comparative advantage." Just about every industry in Bangladesh is much less productive than the corresponding industry in the United States. But the productivity difference between rich and poor countries varies across goods; there is a very great difference in the production of sophisticated goods such as aircraft but not as great a difference in the production of simpler goods such as clothing. So Bangladesh's position with regard to clothing production is like Hank's position with respect to coconut gathering: he's not as good at it as his fellow castaway is, but it's the thing he does comparatively well.

Although Bangladesh is at an absolute disadvantage compared with the United States in almost everything, it has a comparative advantage

Although less productive than American workers, Bangladeshi workers have a comparative advantage in clothing production.

in clothing production. This means that both the United States and Bangladesh are able to consume more because they specialize in producing different things, with Bangladesh supplying our clothing and the United States supplying Bangladesh with more sophisticated goods.

economy. Perhaps its most important application is in trade—not between individuals, but between countries. So let's look briefly at how the model of comparative advantage helps in understanding both the causes and the effects of international trade.

Comparative Advantage and International Trade

Look at the label on a manufactured good sold in the United States, and there's a good chance you will find that it was produced in some other country—in China or Japan or even in Canada. On the other hand, many U.S. industries sell a large portion of their output overseas. (This is particularly true for the agriculture, high technology, and entertainment industries.)

Should we celebrate this international exchange of goods and services, or should it cause us concern? Politicians and the public often question the desirability of international trade, arguing that the nation should produce goods for itself rather than buy them from foreigners. Industries around the world demand protection from foreign competition: Japanese farmers want to keep out American rice, and American steelworkers want to keep out European steel. These demands are often supported by public opinion.

Economists, however, have a very positive view of international trade. Why? Because they view it in terms of comparative advantage.

Figure 4.3 shows, with a simple example, how international trade can be interpreted in terms of comparative advantage. Although the example is hypothetical, it is based on an actual pattern of international trade: American exports of pork to Canada and Canadian exports of aircraft to the United States. Panels (a) and (b) illustrate hypothetical production possibility frontier for the United States and Canada, with pork measured on the horizontal axis and aircraft measured on the vertical axis. The U.S. production possibility frontier is flatter than the Canadian PPF, implying that producing one more ton of pork costs fewer aircraft in the United States than it does

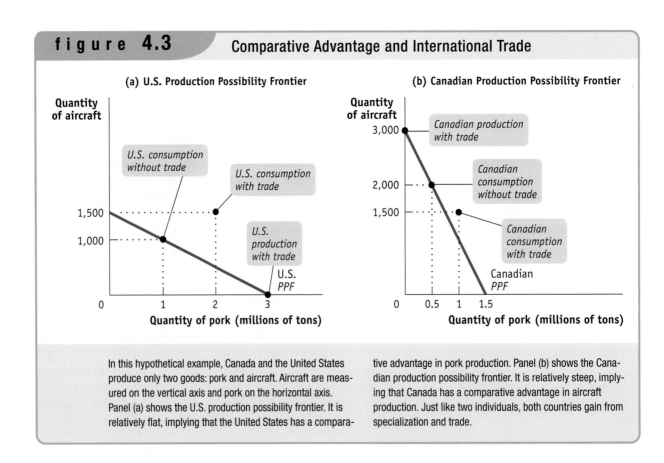

figure 4.3 **Comparative Advantage and International Trade**

In this hypothetical example, Canada and the United States produce only two goods: pork and aircraft. Aircraft are measured on the vertical axis and pork on the horizontal axis. Panel (a) shows the U.S. production possibility frontier. It is relatively flat, implying that the United States has a compara-tive advantage in pork production. Panel (b) shows the Canadian production possibility frontier. It is relatively steep, imply-ing that Canada has a comparative advantage in aircraft production. Just like two individuals, both countries gain from specialization and trade.

in Canada. This means that the United States has a comparative advantage in pork and Canada has a comparative advantage in aircraft.

Although the consumption points in Figure 4.3 are hypothetical, they illustrate a general principle: just like the example of Tom and Hank, the United States and Canada can both achieve mutual gains from trade. If the United States concentrates on producing pork and ships some of its output to Canada, while Canada concentrates on aircraft and ships some of its output to the United States, both countries can consume more than if they insisted on being self-sufficient.

Moreover, these mutual gains don't depend on each country's being better at producing one kind of good. Even if one country has, say, higher output per person-hour in both industries—that is, even if one country has an absolute advantage in both industries—there are still mutual gains from trade.

Module 4 Review

Solutions appear at the back of the book.

Check Your Understanding

1. In Italy, an automobile can be produced by 8 workers in one day and a washing machine by 3 workers in one day. In the United States, an automobile can be produced by 6 workers in one day, and a washing machine by 2 workers in one day.
   a. Which country has an absolute advantage in the production of automobiles? In washing machines?
   b. Which country has a comparative advantage in the production of washing machines? In automobiles?
   c. What type of specialization results in the greatest gains from trade between the two countries?

2. Refer to the story of Tom and Hank illustrated by Figure 4.1 in the text. Explain why Tom and Hank are willing to engage in a trade of 1 fish for 1½ coconuts.

Multiple-Choice Questions

Refer to the graph below to answer the following questions.

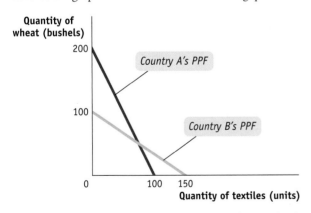

1. Use the graph to determine which country has an absolute advantage in producing each good.

Absolute advantage in wheat production	Absolute advantage in textile production
a. Country A	Country B
b. Country A	Country A
c. Country B	Country A
d. Country B	Country B
e. Country A	Neither Country

2. For country A, the opportunity cost of a bushel of wheat is
   a. ½ units of textiles
   b. ⅔ units of textiles
   c. 1⅓ units of textiles
   d. 1½ units of textiles
   e. 2 units of textiles

3. Use the graph to determine which country has a comparative advantage in producing each good.

Comparative advantage in wheat production	Comparative advantage in textile production
a. Country A	Country B
b. Country A	Country A
c. Country B	Country A
d. Country B	Country B
e. Country A	Neither Country

4. If the two countries specialize and trade, which of the choices below describes the countries' imports?

Import Wheat	Import Textiles
a. Country A	Country A
b. Country A	Country B
c. Country B	Country B
d. Country B	Country A
e. Neither Country	Country B

5. What is the highest price Country B is willing to pay to buy wheat from Country A?
   a. ½ units of textiles
   b. ⅔ units of textiles
   c. 1 unit of textiles
   d. 1½ units of textiles
   e. 2 units of textiles

Critical-Thinking Questions

Refer to the table below to answer the following questions. These two countries are producing textiles and wheat using equal amounts of resources.

| | Weekly output per worker | |
	Country A	Country B
Bushels of Wheat	15	10
Units of Textiles	60	60

a. What is the opportunity cost of producing a bushel of wheat for each country?
b. Which country has the absolute advantage in wheat production?
c. Which country has the comparative advantage in textile production? Explain.

Section I Review

Summary

The Study of Economics

1. Everyone has to make choices about what to do and what *not* to do. **Individual choice** is the basis of economics—if it doesn't involve choice, it isn't economics. The **economy** is a system that coordinates choices about production and consumption. In a **market economy**, these choices are made by many firms and individuals.

2. The reason choices must be made is that **resources**—anything that can be used to produce something else—are **scarce.** The four categories of resources are **land, labor, capital** and **entrepreneurship.** Individuals are limited in their choices by money and time; economies are limited by their supplies of resources.

3. Because you must choose among limited alternatives, the true cost of anything is what you must give up to get it—all costs are **opportunity costs.**

4. Economists use economic models for both **positive economics,** which describes how the economy works, and for **normative economics,** which prescribes how the economy *should* work. Positive economics often involves making forecasts. Economics can determine correct answers for positive questions, but typically not for normative questions, which involve value judgments. Exceptions occur when policies designed to achieve a certain prescription can be clearly ranked in terms of efficiency.

5. There are two main reasons economists disagree. One, they may disagree about which simplifications to make in a model. Two, economists may disagree—like everyone else—about values.

6. **Microeconomics** is the branch of economics that studies how people make decisions and how those decisions interact. **Macroeconomics** is concerned with the overall ups and downs of the economy, and focuses on **economic aggregates** such as the unemployment rate and gross domestic product, that summarize data across many different markets.

Introduction to Macroeconomics

7. Economies experience ups and downs in economic activity. This pattern is called the **business cycle.**

8. With respect to the business cycle, economists are interested in the levels of **aggregate output, unemployment** and **inflation.**

9. Over longer periods of time, economists focus on **economic growth.**

10. Almost all economics is based on **models,** "thought experiments" or simplified versions of reality, many of which use analytical tools such as mathematics and graphs. An important assumption in economic models is the **other things equal (*ceteris paribus*) assumption,** which allows analysis of the effect of change in one factor by holding all other relevant factors unchanged.

The Production Possibility Frontier

11. One important economic model is the **production possibility frontier,** which illustrates the **trade-offs** facing an economy that produces only two goods. The PPF illustrates three elements: opportunity cost (showing how much less of one good must be produced if more of the other good is produced), **efficiency** (an economy is efficient in production if it produces on the production possibility frontier and efficient in allocation if it produces the mix of goods and services that people want to consume), and economic growth (an outward shift of the production possibility frontier).

12. There are two basic sources of growth in the production possibility frontier model: an increase in resources and improved **technology.**

13. There are **gains from trade:** by engaging in the **trade** of goods and services with one another, the members of an economy can all be made better off. Underlying gains from trade are the advantages of **specialization,** of having individuals specialize in the tasks they are comparatively good at.

Comparative Advantage and Trade

14. **Comparative advantage** explains the source of gains from trade between individuals and countries. Everyone has a comparative advantage in something—some good or service in which that person has a lower opportunity cost than everyone else. But it is often confused with **absolute advantage,** an ability to produce more of a particular good or service than anyone else. This confusion leads some to erroneously conclude that there are no gains from trade between people or countries.

Key Terms

Problems

1. Imagine a firm that manufactures textiles (pants and shirts). List the four categories of resources, and for each category, give an example of a specific resource that the firm might use to manufacture textiles.

2. Describe some of the opportunity costs of the following choices.

   a. Attend college instead of taking a job.

   b. Watch a movie instead of studying for an exam.

   c. Ride the bus instead of driving your car.

3. Use the concept of opportunity cost to explain the following situations.

   a. More people choose to get graduate degrees when the job market is poor.

   b. More people choose to do their own home repairs when the economy is slow and hourly wages are down.

   c. There are more parks in suburban areas than in urban areas.

   d. Convenience stores, which have higher prices than supermarkets, cater to busy people.

4. A representative of the U.S. clothing industry recently made this statement: "Workers in Asia often work in sweatshop conditions earning only pennies an hour. American workers are more productive and, as a result, earn higher wages. In order to preserve the dignity of the American workplace, the government should enact legislation banning imports of low-wage Asian clothing."

   a. Which parts of this quotation are positive statements? Which parts are normative statements?

   b. Is the policy that is being advocated consistent with the statement about the wages and productivities of American and Asian workers?

   c. Would such a policy make some Americans better off without making any other Americans worse off? That is, would this policy be efficient from the viewpoint of all Americans?

   d. Would low-wage Asian workers benefit from or be hurt by such a policy?

5. Are the following statements true or false? Explain your answers.

   a. "When people must pay higher taxes on their wage earnings, it reduces their incentive to work" is a positive statement.

   b. "We should lower taxes to encourage more work" is a positive statement.

   c. Economics cannot always be used to determine what society ought to do.

   d. "The system of public education in this country generates greater benefits to society than the cost of running the system" is a normative statement.

   e. All disagreements among economists are generated by the media.

6. Why do we consider a business-cycle expansion to be different from economic growth?

7. Evaluate this statement: "It is easier to build an economic model that accurately reflects events that have already occurred than to build an economic model to forecast future events." Do you think that this is true or not? Why? What does this imply about the difficulties of building good economic models?

8. Suppose Atlantis is a small, isolated island in the South Atlantic. The inhabitants grow potatoes and catch fish. The accompanying table shows the maximum annual output combinations of potatoes and fish that can be produced. Obviously, given their limited resources and available technology, as they use more of their resources for potato production, there are fewer resources available for catching fish.

Maximum annual output options	Quantity of potatoes (pounds)	Quantity of fish (pounds)
A	1,000	0
B	800	300
C	600	500
D	400	600
E	200	650
F	0	675

   a. Draw a production possibility frontier with potatoes on the horizontal axis and fish on the vertical axis, and illustrate these options, showing points A–F.

   b. Can Atlantis produce 500 pounds of fish and 800 pounds of potatoes? Explain. Where would this point lie relative to the production possibility frontier?

   c. What is the opportunity cost of increasing the annual output of potatoes from 600 to 800 pounds?

d. What is the opportunity cost of increasing the annual output of potatoes from 200 to 400 pounds?

e. Explain why the answers to parts c and d are not the same. What does this imply about the slope of the production possibilities curve?

9. Two important industries on the island of Bermuda are fishing and tourism. According to data from the World Resources Institute and the Bermuda Department of Statistics, in the year 2000 the 307 registered fishermen in Bermuda caught 286 metric tons of marine fish. And the 3,409 people employed by hotels produced 538,000 hotel stays (measured by the number of visitor arrivals). Suppose that this production point is efficient in production. Assume also that the opportunity cost of one additional metric ton of fish is 2,000 hotel stays and that this opportunity cost is constant (the opportunity cost does not change).

a. If all 307 registered fishermen were to be employed by hotels (in addition to the 3,409 people already working in hotels), how many hotel stays could Bermuda produce?

b. If all 3,409 hotel employees were to become fishermen (in addition to the 307 fishermen already working in the fishing industry), how many metric tons of fish could Bermuda produce?

c. Draw a production possibility frontier for Bermuda, with fish on the horizontal axis and hotel stays on the vertical axis, and label Bermuda's actual production point for the year 2000.

10. In the ancient country of Roma, only two goods, spaghetti and meatballs, are produced. There are two tribes in Roma, the Tivoli and the Frivoli. By themselves, the Tivoli each month can produce either 30 pounds of spaghetti and no meatballs, or 50 pounds of meatballs and no spaghetti, or any combination in between. The Frivoli, by themselves, each month can produce 40 pounds of spaghetti and no meatballs, or 30 pounds of meatballs and no spaghetti, or any combination in between.

a. Assume that all production possibility frontiers are straight lines. Draw one diagram showing the monthly production possibility frontier for the Tivoli and another showing the monthly production possibility frontier for the Frivoli.

b. Which tribe has the comparative advantage in spaghetti production? In meatball production?

In A.D. 100, the Frivoli discovered a new technique for making meatballs that doubled the quantity of meatballs they could produce each month.

c. Draw the new monthly production possibility frontier for the Frivoli.

d. After the innovation, which tribe had an absolute advantage in producing meatballs? In producing spaghetti? Which had the comparative advantage in meatball production? In spaghetti production?

11. According to data from the U.S. Department of Agriculture's National Agricultural Statistics Service, 124 million acres of land in the United States were used for wheat or corn farming in 2004. Of those 124 million acres, farmers used 50 million acres to grow 2.158 billion bushels of wheat, and 74 million acres of land to grow 11.807 billion bushels of corn. Suppose that U.S. wheat and corn farming is efficient in production. At that production point, the opportunity cost of producing one additional bushel of wheat is 1.7 fewer bushels of corn. However, farmers have increasing opportunity costs, so additional bushels of wheat have an opportunity cost greater than 1.7 bushels of corn. For each of the production points described below, decide whether that production point is (i) feasible and efficient in production, (ii) feasible but not efficient in production, (iii) not feasible, or (iv) uncertain as to whether or not it is feasible.

a. From their original production point, farmers use 40 million acres of land to produce 1.8 billion bushels of wheat, and they use 60 million acres of land to produce 9 billion bushels of corn. The remaining 24 million acres are left unused.

b. From their original production point, farmers transfer 40 million acres of land from corn to wheat production. They now produce 3.158 billion bushels of wheat and 10.107 billion bushels of corn.

c. From their original production point, farmers reduce their production of wheat to 2 billion bushels and increase their production of corn to 12.044 billion bushels. Along the production possibilities curve, the opportunity cost of going from 11.807 billion bushels of corn to 12.044 billion bushels of corn is 0.666 bushel of wheat per bushel of corn.

12. The Hatfield family lives on the east side of the Hatatoochie River, and the McCoy family lives on the west side. Each family's diet consists of fried chicken and corn-on-the-cob, and each is self-sufficient, raising their own chickens and growing their own corn. Explain the conditions under which each of the following statements would be true.

a. The two families are made better off when the Hatfields specialize in raising chickens, the McCoys specialize in growing corn, and the two families trade.

b. The two families are made better off when the McCoys specialize in raising chickens, the Hatfields specialize in growing corn, and the two families trade.

13. According to the U.S. Census Bureau, in July 2006 the United States exported aircraft worth $1 billion to China and imported aircraft worth only $19,000 from China. During the same month, however, the United States imported $83 million worth of men's trousers, slacks, and jeans from China but exported only $8,000 worth of trousers, slacks, and jeans to China. Using what you have learned about how trade is determined by comparative advantage, answer the following questions.

a. Which country has the comparative advantage in aircraft production? In production of trousers, slacks, and jeans?

b. Can you determine which country has the absolute advantage in aircraft production? In production of trousers, slacks, and jeans?

14. Peter Pundit, an economics reporter, states that the European Union (EU) is increasing its productivity very rapidly in all industries. He claims that this productivity advance is so rapid that output from the EU in these industries will soon exceed that of the United States and, as a result, the United States will no longer benefit from trade with the EU.

a. Do you think Peter Pundit is correct or not? If not, what do you think is the source of his mistake?

b. If the EU and the United States continue to trade, what do you think will characterize the goods that the EU exports to the United States and the goods that the United States exports to the EU?

Section ①Appendix
Graphs in Economics

Getting the Picture

Whether you're reading about economics in the *Wall Street Journal* or in your economics textbook, you will see many graphs. Visual presentations can make it much easier to understand verbal descriptions, numerical information, or ideas. In economics, graphs are the type of visual presentation used to facilitate understanding. To fully understand the ideas and information being discussed, you need to know how to interpret these visual aids. This module explains how graphs are constructed and interpreted and how they are used in economics.

Graphs, Variables, and Economic Models

One reason to attend college is that a bachelor's degree provides access to higher-paying jobs. Additional degrees, such as MBAs or law degrees, increase earnings even more. If you were to read an article about the relationship between educational attainment and income, you would probably see a graph showing the income levels for workers with different levels of education. This graph would depict the idea that, in general, having more education increases a person's income. This graph, like most graphs in economics, would depict the relationship between two economic variables. A **variable** is a quantity that can take on more than one value, such as the number of years of education a person has, the price of a can of soda, or a household's income.

As you learned in this Section, economic analysis relies heavily on *models,* simplified descriptions of real situations. Most economic models describe the relationship between two variables, simplified by holding constant other variables that may affect the relationship. For example, an economic model might describe the relationship between the price of a can of soda and the number of cans of soda that consumers will buy, assuming that everything else that affects consumers' purchases of soda stays constant. This type of model can be described mathematically or verbally, but illustrating the relationship in a graph makes it easier to understand. Next we show how graphs that depict economic models are constructed and interpreted.

How Graphs Work

Most graphs in economics are based on a grid built around two perpendicular lines that show the values of two variables, helping you visualize the relationship between them. So a first step in understanding the use of such graphs is to see how this system works.

Two-Variable Graphs

Figure A.1 shows a typical two-variable graph. It illustrates the data in the accompanying table on outside temperature and the number of sodas a typical vendor can expect to sell at a baseball stadium during one game. The first column shows the values of outside temperature (the first variable) and the second column shows the values of the number of sodas sold (the second variable). Five combinations or pairs of the two variables are shown, denoted by points *A* through *E* in the third column.

Now let's turn to graphing the data in this table. In any two-variable graph, one variable is called the *x*-variable and the other is called the *y*-variable. Here we have made

figure A.1   Plotting Points on a Two-Variable Graph

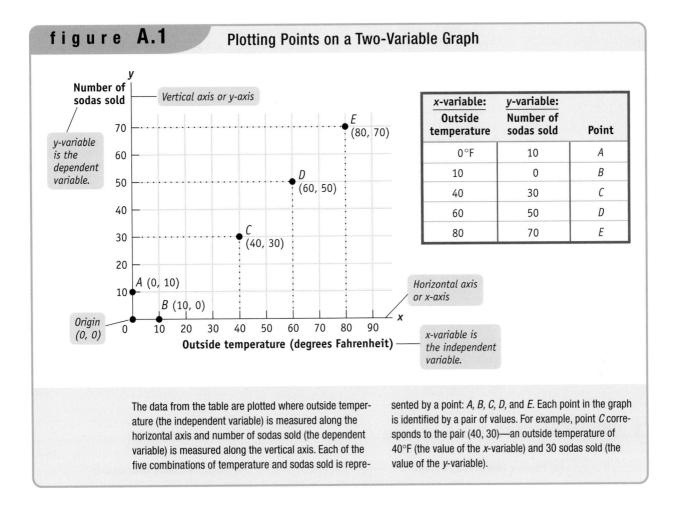

x-variable: Outside temperature	y-variable: Number of sodas sold	Point
0°F	10	A
10	0	B
40	30	C
60	50	D
80	70	E

The data from the table are plotted where outside temperature (the independent variable) is measured along the horizontal axis and number of sodas sold (the dependent variable) is measured along the vertical axis. Each of the five combinations of temperature and sodas sold is represented by a point: A, B, C, D, and E. Each point in the graph is identified by a pair of values. For example, point C corresponds to the pair (40, 30)—an outside temperature of 40°F (the value of the x-variable) and 30 sodas sold (the value of the y-variable).

outside temperature the x-variable and number of sodas sold the y-variable. The solid horizontal line in the graph is called the **horizontal axis** or **x-axis,** and values of the x-variable—outside temperature—are measured along it. Similarly, the solid vertical line in the graph is called the **vertical axis** or **y-axis,** and values of the y-variable—number of sodas sold—are measured along it. At the **origin,** the point where the two axes meet, each variable is equal to zero. As you move rightward from the origin along the x-axis, values of the x-variable are positive and increasing. As you move up from the origin along the y-axis, values of the y-variable are positive and increasing.

You can plot each of the five points A through E on this graph by using a pair of numbers—the values that the x-variable and the y-variable take on for a given point. In Figure A.1, at point C, the x-variable takes on the value 40 and the y-variable takes on the value 30. You plot point C by drawing a line straight up from 40 on the x-axis and a horizontal line across from 30 on the y-axis. We write point C as (40, 30). We write the origin as (0, 0).

Looking at point A and point B in Figure A.1, you can see that when one of the variables for a point has a value of zero, it will lie on one of the axes. If the value of the x-variable is zero, the point will lie on the vertical axis, like point A. If the value of the y-variable is zero, the point will lie on the horizontal axis, like point B.

Most graphs that depict relationships between two economic variables represent a **causal relationship,** a relationship in which the value taken by one variable directly influences or determines the value taken by the other variable. In a causal relationship, the determining variable is called the **independent variable;** the variable it determines is called the **dependent variable.** In our example of soda sales, the outside temperature is the independent variable. It directly influences the number of sodas that are sold, which is the dependent variable in this case.

By convention, we put the independent variable on the horizontal axis and the dependent variable on the vertical axis. Figure A.1 is constructed consistent with this convention: the independent variable (outside temperature) is on the horizontal axis and the dependent variable (number of sodas sold) is on the vertical axis. An important exception to this convention is in graphs showing the economic relationship between the price of a product and quantity of the product: although price is generally the independent variable that determines quantity, it is always measured on the vertical axis.

Curves on a Graph

Panel (a) of Figure A.2 contains some of the same information as Figure A.1, with a line drawn through the points *B, C, D,* and *E.* Such a line on a graph is called a **curve,** regardless of whether it is a straight line or a curved line. If the curve that shows the relationship between two variables is a straight line, or linear, the variables have a **linear relationship.** When the curve is not a straight line, or nonlinear, the variables have a **nonlinear relationship.**

A point on a curve indicates the value of the *y*-variable for a specific value of the *x*-variable. For example, point *D* indicates that at a temperature of 60°F, a vendor can expect to sell 50 sodas. The shape and orientation of a curve reveal the general nature of the relationship between the two variables. The upward tilt of the curve in panel (a) of Figure A.2 suggests that vendors can expect to sell more sodas at higher outside temperatures.

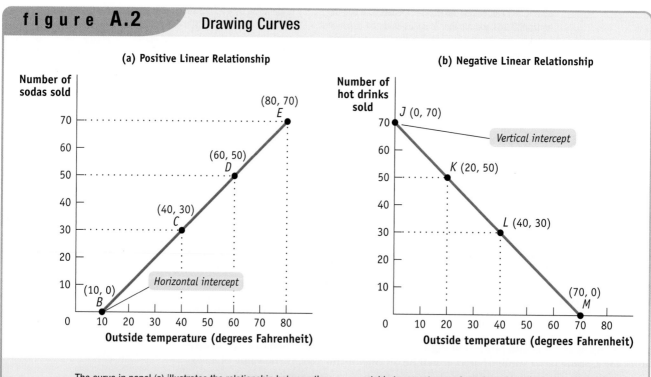

figure A.2 — Drawing Curves

(a) Positive Linear Relationship

(b) Negative Linear Relationship

The curve in panel (a) illustrates the relationship between the two variables, outside temperature and number of sodas sold. The two variables have a positive linear relationship: positive because the curve has an upward tilt, and linear because it is a straight line. The curve implies that an increase in the *x*-variable (outside temperature) leads to an increase in the *y*-variable (number of sodas sold). The curve in panel (b) is also a straight line, but it tilts downward. The two variables here, outside temperature and number of hot drinks sold, have a negative linear relationship: an increase in the *x*-variable (outside temperature) leads to a decrease in the *y*-variable (number of hot drinks sold). The curve in panel (a) has a horizontal intercept at point *B,* where it hits the horizontal axis. The curve in panel (b) has a vertical intercept at point *J,* where it hits the vertical axis, and a horizontal intercept at point *M,* where it hits the horizontal axis.

When variables are related in this way—that is, when an increase in one variable is associated with an increase in the other variable—the variables are said to have a **positive relationship.** It is illustrated by a curve that slopes upward from left to right. Because this curve is also linear, the relationship between outside temperature and number of sodas sold illustrated by the curve in panel (a) of Figure A.2 is a positive linear relationship.

When an increase in one variable is associated with a decrease in the other variable, the two variables are said to have a **negative relationship.** It is illustrated by a curve that slopes downward from left to right, like the curve in panel (b) of Figure A.2. Because this curve is also linear, the relationship it depicts is a negative linear relationship. Two variables that might have such a relationship are the outside temperature and the number of hot drinks a vendor can expect to sell at a baseball stadium.

Return for a moment to the curve in panel (a) of Figure A.2, and you can see that it hits the horizontal axis at point B. This point, known as the **horizontal intercept,** shows the value of the x-variable when the value of the y-variable is zero. In panel (b) of Figure A.2, the curve hits the vertical axis at point J. This point, called the **vertical intercept,** indicates the value of the y-variable when the value of the x-variable is zero.

A Key Concept: The Slope of a Curve

The **slope** of a curve is a measure of how steep it is; the slope indicates how sensitive the y-variable is to a change in the x-variable. In our example of outside temperature and the number of cans of soda a vendor can expect to sell, the slope of the curve would indicate how many more cans of soda the vendor could expect to sell with each $1°$ increase in temperature. Interpreted this way, the slope gives meaningful information. Even without numbers for x and y, it is possible to arrive at important conclusions about the relationship between the two variables by examining the slope of a curve at various points.

The Slope of a Linear Curve

Along a linear curve the slope, or steepness, is measured by dividing the "rise" between two points on the curve by the "run" between those same two points. The rise is the amount that y changes, and the run is the amount that x changes. Here is the formula:

$$\frac{\text{Change in } y}{\text{Change in } x} = \frac{\Delta y}{\Delta x} = \text{Slope}$$

In the formula, the symbol Δ (the Greek uppercase delta) stands for "change in." When a variable increases, the change in that variable is positive; when a variable decreases, the change in that variable is negative.

The slope of a curve is positive when the rise (the change in the y-variable) has the same sign as the run (the change in the x-variable). That's because when two numbers have the same sign, the ratio of those two numbers is positive. The curve in panel (a) of Figure A.2 has a positive slope: along the curve, both the y-variable and the x-variable increase. The slope of a curve is negative when the rise and the run have different signs. That's because when two numbers have different signs, the ratio of those two numbers is negative. The curve in panel (b) of Figure A.2 has a negative slope: along the curve, an increase in the x-variable is associated with a decrease in the y-variable.

Figure A.3 illustrates how to calculate the slope of a linear curve. Let's focus first on panel (a). From point A to point B the value of the y-variable changes from 25 to 20 and the value of the x-variable changes from 10 to 20. So the slope of the line between these two points is

$$\frac{\text{Change in } y}{\text{Change in } x} = \frac{\Delta y}{\Delta x} = \frac{-5}{10} = -\frac{1}{2} = -0.5$$

Because a straight line is equally steep at all points, the slope of a straight line is the same at all points. In other words, a straight line has a constant slope. You can check

figure A.3   Calculating the Slope

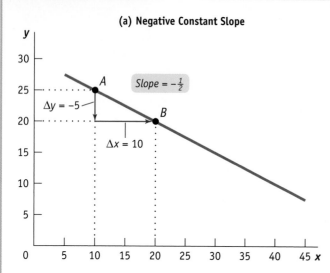

(a) Negative Constant Slope

Slope = $-\frac{1}{2}$

$\Delta y = -5$

$\Delta x = 10$

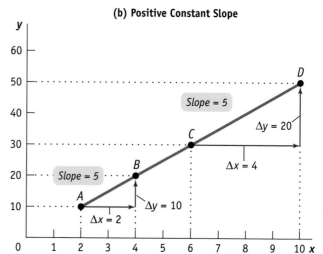

(b) Positive Constant Slope

Slope = 5

Slope = 5

$\Delta y = 20$

$\Delta x = 4$

$\Delta y = 10$

$\Delta x = 2$

Panels (a) and (b) show two linear curves. Between points A and B on the curve in panel (a), the change in y (the rise) is -5 and the change in x (the run) is 10. So the slope from A to B is $\frac{\Delta y}{\Delta x} = \frac{-5}{10} = -\frac{1}{2} = -0.5$, where the negative sign indicates that the curve is downward sloping. In panel (b), the curve has a slope from A to B of $\frac{\Delta y}{\Delta x} = \frac{10}{2} = 5$. The slope from C to D is $\frac{\Delta y}{\Delta x} = \frac{20}{4} = 5$. The slope is positive, indicating that the curve is upward sloping. Furthermore, the slope between A and B is the same as the slope between C and D, making this a linear curve. The slope of a linear curve is constant: it is the same regardless of where it is calculated along the curve.

this by calculating the slope of the linear curve between points A and B and between points C and D in panel (b) of Figure A.3.

$$\frac{\Delta y}{\Delta x} = \frac{10}{2} = 5$$

$$\frac{\Delta y}{\Delta x} = \frac{20}{4} = 5$$

Horizontal and Vertical Curves and Their Slopes

When a curve is horizontal, the value of y along that curve never changes—it is constant. Everywhere along the curve, the change in y is zero. Now, zero divided by any number is zero. So regardless of the value of the change in x, the slope of a horizontal curve is always zero.

If a curve is vertical, the value of x along the curve never changes—it is constant. Everywhere along the curve, the change in x is zero. This means that the slope of a vertical line is a ratio with zero in the denominator. A ratio with zero in the denominator is equal to infinity—that is, an infinitely large number. So the slope of a vertical line is equal to infinity.

A vertical or a horizontal curve has a special implication: it means that the x-variable and the y-variable are unrelated. Two variables are unrelated when a change in one variable (the independent variable) has no effect on the other variable (the dependent variable). To put it a slightly different way, two variables are unrelated when the dependent variable is constant regardless of the value of the independent variable. If, as is usual, the y-variable is the dependent variable, the curve is horizontal. If the dependent variable is the x-variable, the curve is vertical.

The Slope of a Nonlinear Curve

A **nonlinear curve** is one in which the slope changes as you move along it. Panels (a), (b), (c), and (d) of Figure A.4 show various nonlinear curves. Panels (a) and (b) show nonlinear curves whose slopes change as you follow the line's progression, but the slopes always remain positive. Although both curves tilt upward, the curve in panel (a) gets steeper as the line moves from left to right in contrast to the curve in panel (b),

figure A.4   **Nonlinear Curves**

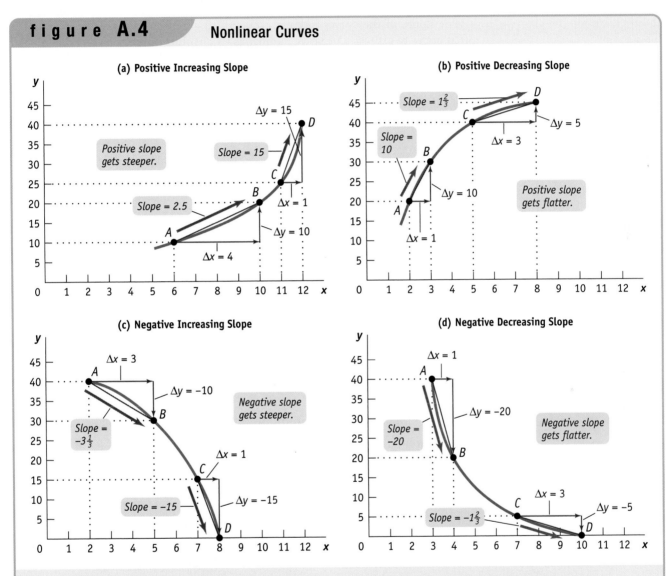

In panel (a) the slope of the curve from A to B is $\frac{\Delta y}{\Delta x} = \frac{10}{4} = 2.5$, and from C to D it is $\frac{\Delta y}{\Delta x} = \frac{15}{1} = 15$. The slope is positive and increasing; it gets steeper as it moves to the right. In panel (b) the slope of the curve from A to B is $\frac{\Delta y}{\Delta x} = \frac{10}{1} = 10$, and from C to D it is $\frac{\Delta y}{\Delta x} = \frac{5}{3} = 1\frac{2}{3}$. The slope is positive and decreasing; it gets flatter as it moves to the right. In panel (c) the slope from A to B is $\frac{\Delta y}{\Delta x} = \frac{-10}{3} = -3\frac{1}{3}$, and from C to D it is $\frac{\Delta y}{\Delta x} = \frac{-15}{1} = -15$. The slope is negative and increasing; it gets steeper as it moves to the right.

And in panel (d) the slope from A to B is $\frac{\Delta y}{\Delta x} = \frac{-20}{1} = -20$, and from C to D it is $\frac{\Delta y}{\Delta x} = \frac{-5}{3} = -1\frac{2}{3}$. The slope is negative and decreasing; it gets flatter as it moves to the right.

The slope in each case has been calculated by using the *arc method*—that is, by drawing a straight line connecting two points along a curve. The average slope between those two points is equal to the slope of the straight line between those two points.

which gets flatter. A curve that is upward sloping and gets steeper, as in panel (a), is said to have *positive increasing* slope. A curve that is upward sloping but gets flatter, as in panel (b), is said to have *positive decreasing* slope.

When we calculate the slope along these nonlinear curves, we obtain different values for the slope at different points. How the slope changes along the curve determines the curve's shape. For example, in panel (a) of Figure A.4, the slope of the curve is a positive number that steadily increases as the line moves from left to right, whereas in panel (b), the slope is a positive number that steadily decreases.

The slopes of the curves in panels (c) and (d) are negative numbers. Economists often prefer to express a negative number as its **absolute value,** which is the value of the negative number without the minus sign. In general, we denote the absolute value of a number by two parallel bars around the number; for example, the absolute value of −4 is written as |−4| = 4. In panel (c), the absolute value of the slope steadily increases as the line moves from left to right. The curve therefore has *negative increasing* slope. And in panel (d), the absolute value of the slope of the curve steadily decreases along the curve. This curve therefore has *negative decreasing* slope.

Maximum and Minimum Points

The slope of a nonlinear curve can change from positive to negative or vice versa. When the slope of a curve changes from positive to negative, it creates what is called a *maximum* point of the curve. When the slope of a curve changes from negative to positive, it creates a *minimum* point.

Panel (a) of Figure A.5 illustrates a curve in which the slope changes from positive to negative as the line moves from left to right. When x is between 0 and 50, the slope of the curve is positive. At x equal to 50, the curve attains its highest point—the largest value of y along the curve. This point is called the **maximum** of the curve. When x exceeds 50, the slope becomes negative as the curve turns downward. Many important curves in economics, such as the curve that represents how the profit of a firm changes as it produces more output, are hill-shaped like this one.

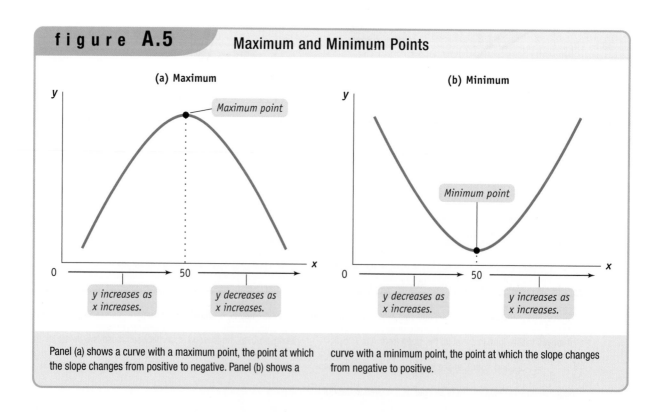

figure A.5 Maximum and Minimum Points

Panel (a) shows a curve with a maximum point, the point at which the slope changes from positive to negative. Panel (b) shows a curve with a minimum point, the point at which the slope changes from negative to positive.

In contrast, the curve shown in panel (b) of Figure A.5 is U-shaped: it has a slope that changes from negative to positive. At *x* equal to 50, the curve reaches its lowest point—the smallest value of *y* along the curve. This point is called the **minimum** of the curve. Various important curves in economics, such as the curve that represents how a firm's cost per unit changes as output increases, are U-shaped like this one.

Calculating the Area Below or Above a Curve

Sometimes it is useful to be able to measure the size of the area below or above a curve. To keep things simple, we'll only calculate the area below or above a linear curve.

How large is the shaded area below the linear curve in panel (a) of Figure A.6? First, note that this area has the shape of a right triangle. A right triangle is a triangle in which two adjacent sides form a 90° angle. We will refer to one of these sides as the *height* of the triangle and the other side as the *base* of the triangle. For our purposes, it doesn't matter which of these two sides we refer to as the base and which as the height. Calculating the area of a right triangle is straightforward: multiply the height of the triangle by the base of the triangle, and divide the result by 2. The height of the triangle in panel (a) of Figure A.6 is 10 − 4 = 6. And the base of the triangle is 3 − 0 = 3. So the area of that triangle is

$$\frac{6 \times 3}{2} = 9$$

How about the shaded area above the linear curve in panel (b) of Figure A.6? We can use the same formula to calculate the area of this right triangle. The height of the triangle is 8 − 2 = 6. And the base of the triangle is 4 − 0 = 4. So the area of that triangle is

$$\frac{6 \times 4}{2} = 12$$

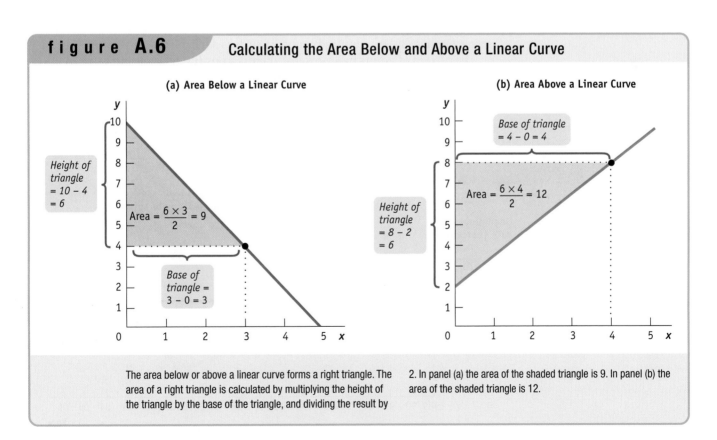

figure A.6 Calculating the Area Below and Above a Linear Curve

(a) Area Below a Linear Curve

Height of triangle = 10 − 4 = 6

Area = $\frac{6 \times 3}{2}$ = 9

Base of triangle = 3 − 0 = 3

(b) Area Above a Linear Curve

Base of triangle = 4 − 0 = 4

Area = $\frac{6 \times 4}{2}$ = 12

Height of triangle = 8 − 2 = 6

The area below or above a linear curve forms a right triangle. The area of a right triangle is calculated by multiplying the height of the triangle by the base of the triangle, and dividing the result by

2. In panel (a) the area of the shaded triangle is 9. In panel (b) the area of the shaded triangle is 12.

Graphs That Depict Numerical Information

Graphs offer a convenient way to summarize and display data without assuming some underlying causal relationship. Graphs that simply display numerical information are called *numerical graphs*. Here we will consider four types of numerical graphs: *time-series graphs, scatter diagrams, pie charts,* and *bar graphs*. These are widely used to display real empirical data about different economic variables, because they often help economists and policy makers identify patterns or trends in the economy.

Types of Numerical Graphs

You have probably seen graphs in newspapers that show what has happened over time to economic variables such as the unemployment rate or stock prices. A **time-series graph** has successive dates on the horizontal axis and the values of a variable that occurred on those dates on the vertical axis. For example, Figure A.7 shows the unemployment rate in the United States from 1989 to late 2006. A line connecting the points that correspond to the unemployment rate for each month during those years gives a clear idea of the overall trend in unemployment during that period. Note the two short diagonal lines toward the bottom of the *y*-axis in Figure A.7. This *truncation sign* indicates that a piece of the axis—here, unemployment rates below 4%—was cut to save space.

Figure A.8 is an example of a different kind of numerical graph. It represents information from a sample of 158 countries on average life expectancy and gross national product (GNP) per capita—a rough measure of a country's standard of living. Each point in the graph indicates an average resident's life expectancy and the log of GNP per capita for a given country. (Economists have found that the log of GNP rather than the simple level of GNP is more closely tied to average life expectancy.)

The points lying in the upper right of the graph, which show combinations of high life expectancy and high log of GNP per capita, represent economically advanced countries such as the United States. Points lying in the bottom left of the graph, which show combinations of low life expectancy and low log of GNP per capita, represent economically less advanced countries such as Afghanistan and Sierra Leone.

The pattern of points indicates that there is a positive relationship between life expectancy and log of GNP per capita: on the whole, people live longer in countries with a higher standard of living. This type of graph is called a **scatter diagram,** a diagram in which each point corresponds to an actual observation of the *x*-variable and

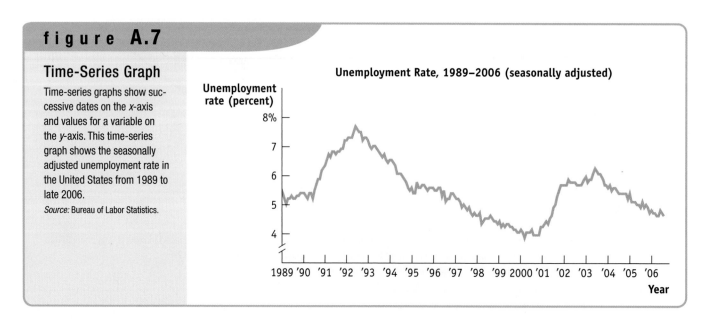

figure A.7

Time-Series Graph

Time-series graphs show successive dates on the *x*-axis and values for a variable on the *y*-axis. This time-series graph shows the seasonally adjusted unemployment rate in the United States from 1989 to late 2006.

Source: Bureau of Labor Statistics.

Unemployment Rate, 1989–2006 (seasonally adjusted)

figure A.8

Scatter Diagram

In a scatter diagram, each point represents the corresponding values of the *x*- and *y*-variables for a given observation. Here, each point indicates the observed average life expectancy and the log of GNP per capita of a given country for a sample of 158 countries. The upward-sloping fitted line here is the best approximation of the general relationship between the two variables.

Source: Eduard Bos et al., *Health, Nutrition, and Population Indicators: A Statistical Handbook* (Washington, DC: World Bank, 1999).

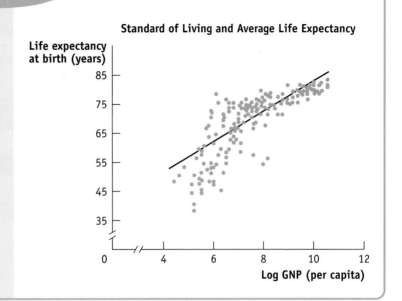

Standard of Living and Average Life Expectancy

the *y*-variable. In scatter diagrams, a curve is typically fitted to the scatter of points; that is, a curve is drawn that approximates as closely as possible the general relationship between the variables. As you can see, the fitted curve in Figure A.8 is upward-sloping, indicating the underlying positive relationship between the two variables. Scatter diagrams are often used to show how a general relationship can be inferred from a set of data.

A **pie chart** shows the share of a total amount that is accounted for by various components, usually expressed in percentages. For example, Figure A.9 is a pie chart that depicts the various sources of revenue for the U.S. government budget in 2005, expressed in percentages of the total revenue amount, $2,153.9 billion. As you can see, social insurance receipts (the revenues collected to fund Social Security, Medicare, and unemployment insurance) accounted for 37% of total government revenue, and individual income tax receipts accounted for 43%.

figure A.9

Pie Chart

A pie chart shows the percentages of a total amount that can be attributed to various components. This pie chart shows the percentages of total federal revenues received from each source.

Source: Office of Management and Budget.

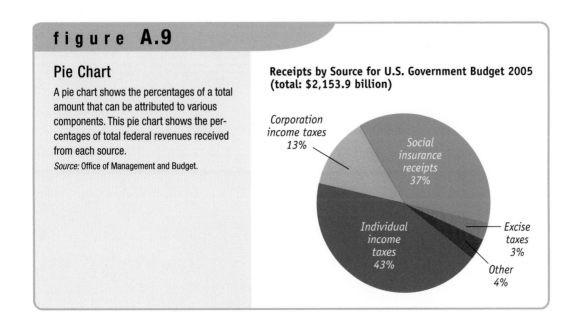

Receipts by Source for U.S. Government Budget 2005 (total: $2,153.9 billion)

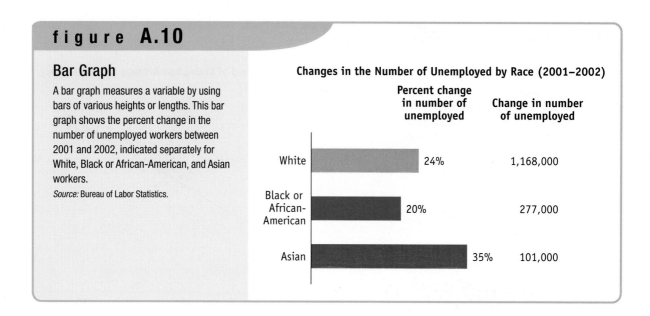

figure A.10

Bar Graph

A bar graph measures a variable by using bars of various heights or lengths. This bar graph shows the percent change in the number of unemployed workers between 2001 and 2002, indicated separately for White, Black or African-American, and Asian workers.

Source: Bureau of Labor Statistics.

Changes in the Number of Unemployed by Race (2001–2002)

	Percent change in number of unemployed	Change in number of unemployed
White	24%	1,168,000
Black or African-American	20%	277,000
Asian	35%	101,000

Bar graphs use bars of various heights or lengths and colors to indicate relative values of a variable. In the bar graph in Figure A.10, the bars show the percent change in the number of unemployed workers in the United States from 2001 to 2002. Exact values of the variable that is being measured may be written at the end of the bar, as in this figure. (For instance, the number of unemployed Asian workers in the United States increased by 35% between 2001 and 2002.) But even without the precise values, comparing the heights or lengths of the bars for each group—White, Black or African-American, and Asian workers can give useful insight into the relative magnitudes of the different values of the variable.

Solutions appear at the back of the book.

Check Your Understanding

1. Study the four accompanying diagrams. Consider the following statements and indicate which diagram matches each statement. For each statement, tell which variable would appear on the horizontal axis and which on the vertical. In each of these statements, is the slope positive, negative, zero, or infinity?

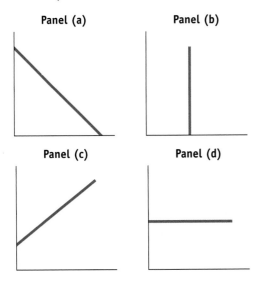

Panel (a)   **Panel (b)**

Panel (c)   **Panel (d)**

   a. If the price of movies increases, fewer consumers go to see movies.
   b. Workers with more experience typically have higher incomes than less experienced workers.
   c. Regardless of the temperature outside, Americans consume the same number of hot dogs per day.
   d. Consumers buy more frozen yogurt when the price of ice cream goes up.
   e. Research finds no relationship between the number of diet books purchased and the number of pounds lost by the average dieter.
   f. Regardless of its price, there is no change in the quantity of salt that Americans buy.

2. During the Reagan administration, economist Arthur Laffer argued in favor of lowering income tax rates in order to increase tax revenues. Like most economists, he believed that at tax rates above a certain level, tax revenue would fall (because high taxes would discourage some people from working) and that people would refuse to work at all if they received no income after paying taxes. This relationship between tax rates and tax revenue is graphically summarized in what is widely known as the Laffer curve. Plot the Laffer curve relationship, assuming that it has the shape of a nonlinear curve. The following questions will help you construct the graph.
   a. Which is the independent variable? Which is the dependent variable? On which axis do you therefore measure the income tax rate? On which axis do you measure income tax revenue?
   b. What would tax revenue be at a 0% income tax rate?
   c. The maximum possible income tax rate is 100%. What would tax revenue be at a 100% income tax rate?
   d. Estimates now show that the maximum point on the Laffer curve is (approximately) at a tax rate of 80%. For tax rates less than 80%, how would you describe the relationship between the tax rate and tax revenue, and how is this relationship reflected in the slope? For tax rates higher than 80%, how would you describe the relationship between the tax rate and tax revenue, and how is this relationship reflected in the slope?

section 2

Supply and Demand

For those who need a cappuccino, mocha latte, or Frappuccino to get through the day, coffee drinking can become an expensive habit. And on October 6, 2006, the habit got a little more expensive. On that day, Starbucks raised its drink prices for the first time in six years. The average price of coffee beverages at the world's leading chain of coffeehouses rose about 11 cents per cup.

Starbucks had kept its prices unchanged for six years. So what compelled them to finally raise their prices in the fall of 2006? Mainly the fact that the cost of a major ingredient—coffee beans—had gone up significantly. In fact, coffee bean prices doubled between 2002 and 2006.

Who decided to raise the prices of coffee beans? Nobody: prices went up because of events outside anyone's control. Specifically, the main cause of rising bean prices was a significant decrease in the supply of coffee beans from the world's two leading coffee exporters: Brazil and Vietnam. In Brazil, the decrease in supply was a delayed reaction to low prices earlier in the decade, which led coffee growers to cut back on planting. In Vietnam, the problem was weather: a prolonged drought sharply reduced coffee harvests.

And a lower supply of coffee beans from Vietnam or Brazil inevitably translates into a higher price of coffee on Main Street. It's just a matter of supply and demand.

What do we mean by that? Many people use "supply and demand" as a sort of catchphrase to mean "the laws of the marketplace at work." To economists, however, the concept of supply and demand has a precise meaning: it is a *model* of how a market behaves.

In this section, we lay out the pieces that make up the *supply and demand model,* put them together, and show how this model can be used to understand how many—but not all—markets behave.

Jed Jacobsohn/Getty Images

Module 5
Supply and Demand: Introduction and Demand

Supply and Demand: A Model of a Competitive Market

Coffee bean sellers and coffee bean buyers constitute a *market*—a group of producers and consumers who exchange a good or service for payment. In this section, we'll focus on a particular type of market known as a *competitive market*. Roughly, a **competitive market** is a market in which there are many buyers and sellers of the same good or service. More precisely, the key feature of a competitive market is that no individual's actions have a noticeable effect on the price at which the good or service is sold. It's important to understand, however, that this is not an accurate description of every market. For example, it's not an accurate description of the market for cola beverages. That's because in the market for cola beverages, Coca-Cola and Pepsi account for such a large proportion of total sales that they are able to influence the price at which cola beverages are bought and sold. But it *is* an accurate description of the market for coffee beans. The global marketplace for coffee beans is so huge that even a coffee retailer as large as Starbucks accounts for only a tiny fraction of transactions, making it unable to influence the price at which coffee beans are bought and sold.

It's a little hard to explain why competitive markets are different from other markets until we've seen how a competitive market works. For now, let's just say that it's easier to model competitive markets than other markets. When taking an exam, it's always a good strategy to begin by answering the easier questions. In this book, we're going to do the same thing. So we will start with competitive markets.

When a market is competitive, its behavior is well described by the **supply and demand model.** Because many markets *are* competitive, the supply and demand model is a very useful one indeed.

A **competitive market** is a market in which there are many buyers and sellers of the same good or service, none of whom can influence the price at which the good or service is sold.

The **supply and demand model** is a model of how a competitive market works.

There are five key elements in this model:

- The *demand curve*
- The *supply curve*
- The set of factors that cause the demand curve to shift and the set of factors that cause the supply curve to shift
- The *market equilibrium,* which includes the *equilibrium price* and *equilibrium quantity*
- The way the market equilibrium changes when the supply curve or demand curve shifts

To explain the supply and demand model, we will examine each of these elements in turn. In this module we begin with demand.

The Demand Curve

How many pounds of coffee beans do consumers around the world want to buy in a given year? You might at first think that we can answer this question by multiplying the number of cups of coffee drunk around the world each day by the weight of the coffee beans it takes to brew a cup, and then multiplying by 365. But that's not enough to answer the question because how many pounds of coffee beans consumers want to buy—and therefore how much coffee people want to drink—depends on the price of coffee beans. When the price of coffee rises, as it did in 2006, some people drink less, perhaps switching completely to other caffeinated beverages, such as tea or Coca-Cola. (Yes, there are people who drink Coke in the morning.) In general, the quantity of coffee beans, or of any good or service that people want to buy (taking "want" to mean they are willing and able to buy it), depends on the price. The higher the price, the less of the good or service people want to purchase; alternatively, the lower the price, the more they want to purchase.

So the answer to the question "How many pounds of coffee beans do consumers want to buy?" depends on the price of coffee beans. If you don't yet know what the price will be, you can start by making a table of how many pounds of coffee beans people would want to buy at a number of different prices. Such a table is known as a *demand schedule*. This, in turn, can be used to draw a *demand curve,* which is one of the key elements of the supply and demand model.

The Demand Schedule and the Demand Curve

A **demand schedule** is a table showing how much of a good or service consumers will want to buy at different prices. On the right side of Figure 5.1 on the next page, we show a hypothetical demand schedule for coffee beans. It's hypothetical in that it doesn't use actual data on the world demand for coffee beans and it assumes that all coffee beans are of equal quality (with our apologies to coffee connoisseurs).

According to the table, if coffee beans cost $1 a pound, consumers around the world will want to purchase 10 billion pounds of coffee beans over the course of a year. If the price is $1.25 a pound, they will want to buy only 8.9 billion pounds; if the price is only $0.75 a pound, they will want to buy 11.5 billion pounds; and so on. So the higher the price, the fewer pounds of coffee beans consumers will want to purchase. In other words, as the price rises, the **quantity demanded** of coffee beans—the actual amount consumers are willing to buy at some specific price—falls.

The graph in Figure 5.1 is a visual representation of the information in the table. The vertical axis shows the price of a pound of coffee beans and the horizontal axis shows the quantity of coffee beans. Each point on the graph corresponds to one of the entries in the table. The curve that connects these points is a **demand curve.** A demand curve is a graphical representation of the demand schedule, another way of showing the relationship between the quantity demanded and the price.

Note that the demand curve shown in Figure 5.1 slopes downward. This reflects the general proposition that a higher price reduces the quantity demanded. For example, some people who drink two cups of coffee a day when beans are $1 per pound will cut down to

A **demand schedule** shows how much of a good or service consumers will be willing and able to buy at different prices.

The **quantity demanded** is the actual amount of a good or service consumers are willing and able to buy at some specific price.

A **demand curve** is a graphical representation of the demand schedule. It shows the relationship between quantity demanded and price.

figure **5.1** The Demand Schedule and the Demand Curve

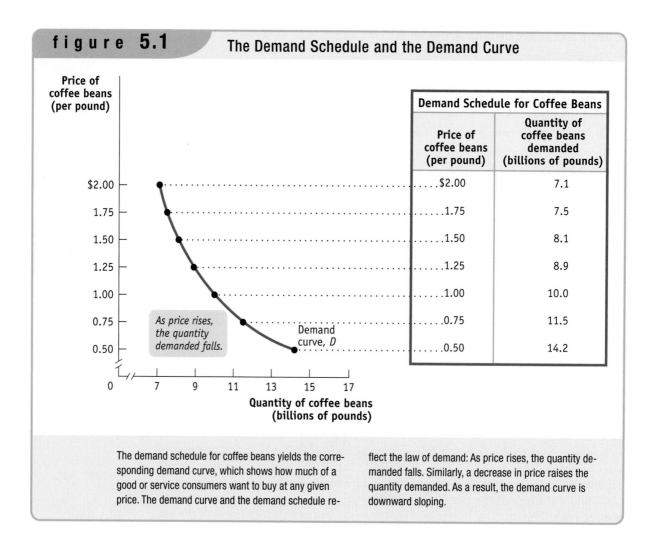

The demand schedule for coffee beans yields the corresponding demand curve, which shows how much of a good or service consumers want to buy at any given price. The demand curve and the demand schedule reflect the law of demand: As price rises, the quantity demanded falls. Similarly, a decrease in price raises the quantity demanded. As a result, the demand curve is downward sloping.

The **law of demand** says that a higher price for a good or service, all other things being equal, leads people to demand a smaller quantity of that good or service.

one cup when beans are $2 per pound. Similarly, some who drink one cup when beans are $1 a pound will drink tea instead if the price doubles to $2 per pound and so on. In the real world, demand curves almost always slope downward. (The exceptions are so rare that for practical purposes we can ignore them.) Generally, the proposition that a higher price for a good, all other things being equal, leads people to demand a smaller quantity of that good is so reliable that economists are willing to call it a "law"—the **law of demand.**

Shifts of the Demand Curve

Even though coffee prices were a lot higher in 2006 than they had been in 2002, total world consumption of coffee was higher in 2006. How can we reconcile this fact with the law of demand, which says that a higher price reduces the quantity demanded, all other things being equal?

The answer lies in the crucial phrase *all other things being equal*. In this case, all other things weren't equal: the world had changed between 2002 and 2006, in ways that increased the quantity of coffee demanded at any given price. For one thing, the world's population, and therefore the number of potential coffee drinkers, increased. In addition, the growing popularity of different types of coffee beverages, like lattes and cappuccinos, led to an increase in the quantity demanded at any given price. Figure 5.2 illustrates this phenomenon using the demand schedule and demand curve for coffee beans. (As before, the numbers in Figure 5.2 are hypothetical.)

The table in Figure 5.2 shows two demand schedules. The first is a demand schedule for 2002, the same one shown in Figure 5.1. The second is a demand schedule for 2006.

figure 5.2   An Increase in Demand

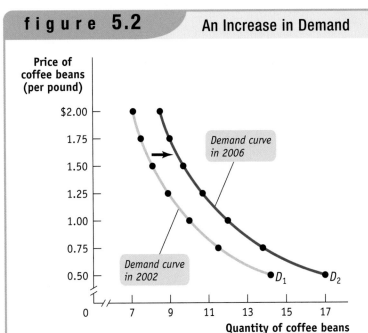

Demand Schedules for Coffee Beans		
Price of coffee beans (per pound)	Quantity of coffee beans demanded (billions of pounds)	
	in 2002	in 2006
$2.00	7.1	8.5
1.75	7.5	9.0
1.50	8.1	9.7
1.25	8.9	10.7
1.00	10.0	12.0
0.75	11.5	13.8
0.50	14.2	17.0

An increase in the population and other factors generate an increase in demand—a rise in the quantity demanded at any given price. This is represented by the two demand schedules—one showing demand in 2002, before the rise in population, the other showing demand in 2006, after the rise in population—and their corresponding demand curves. The increase in demand shifts the demand curve to the right.

It differs from the 2002 demand schedule due to factors such as a larger population and the greater popularity of lattes, factors that led to an increase in the quantity of coffee beans demanded at any given price. So at each price, the 2006 schedule shows a larger quantity demanded than the 2002 schedule. For example, the quantity of coffee beans consumers wanted to buy at a price of $1 per pound increased from 10 billion to 12 billion pounds per year, the quantity demanded at $1.25 per pound went from 8.9 billion to 10.7 billion pounds, and so on.

What is clear from this example is that the changes that occurred between 2002 and 2006 generated a *new* demand schedule, one in which the quantity demanded was greater at any given price than in the original demand schedule. The two curves in Figure 5.2 show the same information graphically. As you can see, the demand schedule for 2006 corresponds to a new demand curve, D_2, that is to the right of the demand curve for 2002, D_1. This **change in demand** shows the increase in the quantity demanded at any given price, represented by the shift in position of the original demand curve, D_1, to its new location at D_2.

It's crucial to make the distinction between such changes in demand and **movements along the demand curve,** changes in the quantity demanded of a good that result from a change in that good's price. Figure 5.3 on the next page illustrates the difference.

The movement from point A to point B is a movement along the demand curve: the quantity demanded rises due to a fall in price as you move down D_1. Here, a fall in the price of coffee beans from $1.50 to $1 per pound generates a rise in the quantity demanded from 8.1 billion to 10 billion pounds per year. But the quantity demanded can also rise when the price is unchanged if there is an *increase in demand*—a rightward shift of the demand curve. This is illustrated in Figure 5.3 by the shift of the demand curve from D_1 to D_2. Holding the price constant at $1.50 a pound, the quantity demanded rises from 8.1 billion pounds at point A on D_1 to 9.7 billion pounds at point C on D_2.

A **change in demand** is a shift of the demand curve, which changes the quantity demanded at any given price.

A **movement along the demand curve** is a change in the quantity demanded of a good that is the result of a change in that good's price.

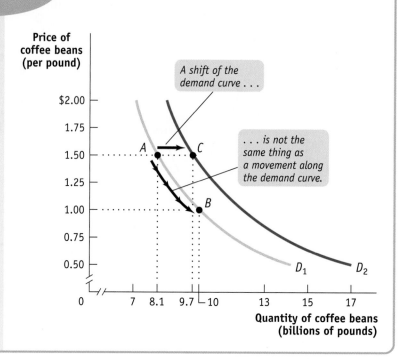

figure 5.3

A Movement Along the Demand Curve Versus a Shift of the Demand Curve

The rise in the quantity demanded when going from point *A* to point *B* reflects a movement along the demand curve: it is the result of a fall in the price of the good. The rise in the quantity demanded when going from point *A* to point *C* reflects a change in demand: this shift to the right is the result of a rise in the quantity demanded at any given price.

When economists talk about a "change in demand," saying "the demand for *X* increased" or "the demand for *Y* decreased," they mean that the demand curve for *X* or *Y* shifted—*not* that the quantity demanded rose or fell because of a change in the price.

Understanding Shifts of the Demand Curve

Figure 5.4 illustrates the two basic ways in which demand curves can shift. When economists talk about an "increase in demand," they mean a *rightward* shift of the demand curve: at any given price, consumers demand a larger quantity of the good or service than

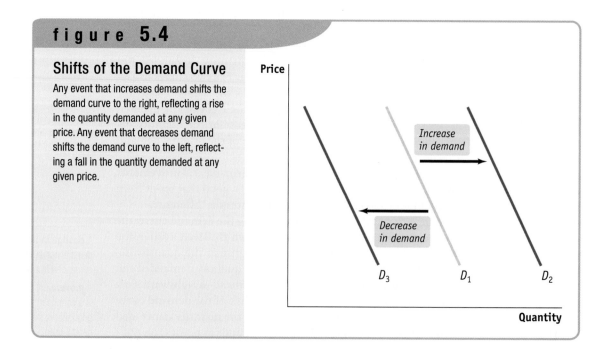

figure 5.4

Shifts of the Demand Curve

Any event that increases demand shifts the demand curve to the right, reflecting a rise in the quantity demanded at any given price. Any event that decreases demand shifts the demand curve to the left, reflecting a fall in the quantity demanded at any given price.

before. This is shown by the rightward shift of the original demand curve D_1 to D_2. And when economists talk about a "decrease in demand," they mean a *leftward* shift of the demand curve: at any given price, consumers demand a smaller quantity of the good or service than before. This is shown in Figure 5.4 by the leftward shift of the original demand curve D_1 to D_3.

What caused the demand curve for coffee beans to shift? We have already mentioned two reasons: changes in population and a change in the popularity of coffee beverages. If you think about it, you can come up with other things that would be likely to shift the demand curve for coffee beans. For example, suppose that the price of tea rises. This will induce some people who previously drank tea to drink coffee instead, increasing the demand for coffee beans.

Economists believe that there are five principal factors that shift the demand curve for a good or service:

- Changes in the prices of related goods or services
- Changes in income
- Changes in tastes
- Changes in expectations
- Changes in the number of consumers

Although this is not an exhaustive list, it contains the five most important factors that can shift demand curves. So when we say that the quantity of a good or service demanded falls as its price rises, all other things being equal, we are in fact stating that the factors that shift demand are remaining unchanged. Let's now explore, in more detail, how those factors shift the demand curve.

Changes in the Prices of Related Goods or Services While there's nothing quite like a good cup of coffee to start your day, a cup or two of strong tea isn't a bad alternative. Tea is what economists call a *substitute* for coffee. A pair of goods are **substitutes** if a rise in the price of one good (coffee) makes consumers more willing to buy the other good (tea). Substitutes are usually goods that in some way serve a similar function: concerts and theater plays, muffins and doughnuts, train rides and air flights. A rise in the price of the alternative good induces some consumers to purchase the original good *instead* of it, shifting demand for the original good to the right.

But sometimes a fall in the price of one good makes consumers *more* willing to buy another good. Such pairs of goods are known as **complements.** Complements are usually goods that in some sense are consumed together: computers and software, cappuccinos and croissants, cars and gasoline. Because consumers like to consume a good and its complement together, a change in the price of one of the goods will affect the demand for its complement. In particular, when the price of one good rises, the demand for its complement decreases, shifting the demand curve for the complement to the left. So the October 2006 rise in Starbucks's cappuccino prices is likely to have precipitated a leftward shift of the demand curve for croissants, as people consumed fewer cappuccinos and croissants. Likewise, when the price of one good falls, the quantity demanded of its complement rises, shifting the demand curve for the complement to the right. This means that if, for some reason, the price of cappuccinos falls, we should see a rightward shift of the demand curve for croissants as people consume more cappuccinos *and* croissants.

Changes in Income When individuals have more income, they are normally more likely to purchase a good at any given price. For example, if a family's income rises, it is more likely to take that summer trip to Disney World—and therefore also more likely to buy plane tickets. So a rise in consumer incomes will cause the demand curves for most goods to shift to the right.

Why do we say "most goods," not "all goods"? Most goods are **normal goods**—the demand for them increases when consumer income rises. However, the demand for

Two goods are **substitutes** if a rise in the price of one of the goods leads to an increase in the demand for the other good.

Two goods are **complements** if a rise in the price of one of the goods leads to a decrease in the demand for the other good.

When a rise in income increases the demand for a good—the normal case—it is a **normal good.**

some products falls when income rises. Goods for which demand decreases when income rises are known as **inferior goods.** Usually an inferior good is one that is considered less desirable than more expensive alternatives—such as a bus ride versus a taxi ride. When they can afford to, people stop buying an inferior good and switch their consumption to the preferred, more expensive alternative. So when a good is inferior, a rise in income shifts the demand curve to the left. And, not surprisingly, a fall in income shifts the demand curve to the right.

One example of the distinction between normal and inferior goods that has drawn considerable attention in the business press is the difference between so-called casual-dining restaurants such as Applebee's and Olive Garden and fast-food chains such as McDonald's and KFC. When their incomes rise, Americans tend to eat out more at casual-dining restaurants. However, some of this increased dining out comes at the expense of fast-food venues—to some extent, people visit McDonald's less once they can afford to move upscale. So casual dining is a normal good, while fast-food appears to be an inferior good.

Changes in Tastes Why do people want what they want? Fortunately, we don't need to answer that question—we just need to acknowledge that people have certain preferences, or tastes, that determine what they choose to consume and that these tastes can change. Economists usually lump together changes in demand due to fads, beliefs, cultural shifts, and so on under the heading of changes in *tastes,* or *preferences.*

For example, once upon a time men wore hats. Up until around World War II, a respectable man wasn't fully dressed unless he wore a dignified hat along with his suit. But the returning GIs adopted a more informal style, perhaps due to the rigors of the war. And President Eisenhower, who had been supreme commander of Allied Forces before becoming president, often went hatless. After World War II, it was clear that the demand curve for hats had shifted leftward, reflecting a decrease in the demand for hats.

We've already mentioned one way in which changing tastes played a role in the increase in the demand for coffee beans from 2002 to 2006: the increase in the popularity of coffee beverages such as lattes and cappuccinos. In addition, there was another route by which changing tastes increased worldwide demand for coffee beans: the switch by consumers in traditionally tea-drinking countries to coffee. "In 1999," reported *Roast* magazine, "the ratio of Russian tea drinkers to coffee drinkers was five to one. In 2005, the ratio is roughly two to one."

Economists have little to say about the forces that influence consumers' tastes. (Marketers and advertisers, however, have plenty to say about them!) However, a *change* in tastes has a predictable impact on demand. When tastes change in favor of a good, more people want to buy it at any given price, so the demand curve shifts to the right. When tastes change against a good, fewer people want to buy it at any given price, so the demand curve shifts to the left.

Changes in Expectations When consumers have some choice about when to make a purchase, current demand for a good is often affected by expectations about its future price. For example, savvy shoppers often wait for seasonal sales—say, buying next year's holiday gifts during the post-holiday markdowns. In this case, expectations of a future drop in price lead to a decrease in demand today. Alternatively, expectations of a future rise in price are likely to cause an increase in demand today. For example, savvy shoppers, knowing that Starbucks was going to increase the price of its coffee

Photodisc

beans on October 6, 2006, would stock up on Starbucks coffee beans before that date.

Expected changes in future income can also lead to changes in demand: if you expect your income to rise in the future, you will typically borrow today and increase your demand for certain goods; and if you expect your income to fall in the future, you are likely to save today and reduce your demand for some goods.

Changes in the Number of Consumers As we've already noted, one of the reasons for rising coffee demand between 2002 and 2006 was a growing world population. Because of population growth, overall demand for coffee would have risen even if each individual coffee-drinker's demand for coffee had remained unchanged.

Let's introduce a new concept: the **individual demand curve,** which shows the relationship between quantity demanded and price for an individual consumer. For example, suppose that Darla is a consumer of coffee beans and that panel (a) of Figure 5.5 shows how many pounds of coffee beans she will buy per year at any given price per pound. Then D_{Darla} is Darla's individual demand curve.

An **individual demand curve** illustrates the relationship between quantity demanded and price for an individual consumer.

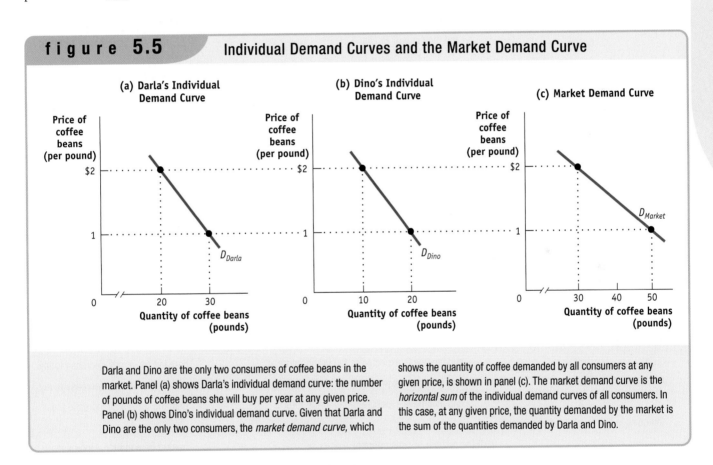

figure 5.5   **Individual Demand Curves and the Market Demand Curve**

Darla and Dino are the only two consumers of coffee beans in the market. Panel (a) shows Darla's individual demand curve: the number of pounds of coffee beans she will buy per year at any given price. Panel (b) shows Dino's individual demand curve. Given that Darla and Dino are the only two consumers, the *market demand curve,* which shows the quantity of coffee demanded by all consumers at any given price, is shown in panel (c). The market demand curve is the *horizontal sum* of the individual demand curves of all consumers. In this case, at any given price, the quantity demanded by the market is the sum of the quantities demanded by Darla and Dino.

The *market demand curve* shows how the combined quantity demanded by all consumers depends on the market price of that good. (Most of the time, when economists refer to the demand curve, they mean the market demand curve.) The market demand curve is the *horizontal sum* of the individual demand curves of all consumers in that market. To see what we mean by the term *horizontal sum,* assume for a moment that there are only two consumers of coffee, Darla and Dino. Dino's individual demand curve, D_{Dino}, is shown in panel (b). Panel (c) shows the market demand curve. At any given price, the quantity demanded by the market is the sum of the quantities demanded by Darla and Dino. For example, at a price of $2 per pound, Darla demands

20 pounds of coffee beans per year and Dino demands 10 pounds per year. So the quantity demanded by the market is 30 pounds per year.

Clearly, the quantity demanded by the market at any given price is larger with Dino present than it would be if Darla were the only consumer. The quantity demanded at any given price would be even larger if we added a third consumer, then a fourth, and so on. So an increase in the number of consumers leads to an increase in demand.

For an overview of the factors that shift demand, see Table 5.1.

table 5.1

Factors That Shift Demand

Changes in the prices of related goods or services		
If *A* and *B* are **substitutes** . . .	. . . and the price of *B* rises, . . .	. . . demand for *A* increases (shifts to the right).
	. . . and the price of *B* falls, . . .	. . . demand for *A* decreases (shifts to the left).
If A and *B* are **complements** . . .	. . . and the price of *B* rises, . . .	. . . demand for *A* decreases.
	. . . and the price of *B* falls, . . .	. . . demand for *A* increases.
Changes in income		
If *A* is a **normal good** . . .	. . . and income rises, . . .	. . . demand for *A* increases.
	. . . and income falls, . . .	. . . demand for *A* decreases.
If *A* is an **inferior good** . . .	. . . and income rises, . . .	. . . demand for *A* decreases.
	. . . and income falls, . . .	. . . demand for *A* increases.
Changes in tastes		
	If tastes change in favor of *A*, . . .	. . . demand for *A* increases.
	If tastes change against *A*, . . .	. . . demand for *A* decreases.
Changes in expectations		
	If the price of *A* is expected to rise in the future, . . .	. . . demand for *A* increases today.
	If the price of *A* is expected to fall in the future, . . .	. . . demand for *A* decreases today.
If A is a **normal good** . . .	. . . and income is expected to rise in the future, . . .	. . . demand for *A* may increase today.
	. . . and income is expected to fall in the future, . . .	. . . demand for *A* may decrease today.
If A is an **inferior good** . . .	. . . and income is expected to rise in the future, . . .	. . . demand for *A* may decrease today.
	. . . and income is expected to fall in the future, . . .	. . . demand for *A* may increase today.
Changes in the number of consumers		
	If the number of consumers of *A* rises, . . .	. . . market demand for *A* increases.
	If the number of consumers of *A* falls, . . .	. . . market demand for *A* decreases.

Beating the Traffic

All big cities have traffic problems, and many local authorities try to discourage driving in the crowded city center. If we think of an auto trip to the city center as a good that people consume, we can use the economics of demand to analyze anti-traffic policies.

One common strategy of local governments is to reduce the demand for auto trips by lowering the prices of substitutes. Many metropolitan areas subsidize bus and rail service, hoping to lure commuters out of their cars.

An alternative strategy is to raise the price of complements: several major U.S. cities impose high taxes on commercial parking garages, both to raise revenue and to discourage people from driving into the city. Short time limits on parking meters, combined with vigilant parking enforcement, is a related tactic.

However, few cities have been willing to adopt the politically controversial direct ap-proach: reducing congestion by raising the price of driving. So it was a shock when, in 2003, London imposed a "congestion charge" on all cars entering the city center during business hours—currently £8 (about $13) for drivers who pay on the same day they travel.

Compliance is monitored with automatic cameras that photograph license plates. People can either pay the charge in advance or pay it by midnight of the day they have driven. If they pay on the day after they have driven, the charge increases to £10 (about $16). And if they don't pay and are caught, a fine of £120 (about $192) is imposed for each transgression. (A full description of the rules can be found at www.cclondon.com.)

Not surprisingly, the result of the new policy confirms the law of demand: three years after the charge was put in place, traffic in central London was about 10 percent lower than before the

London's bold policy to charge cars a fee to enter the city center proved effective in reducing traffic congestion.

charge. In February 2007, the British government doubled the area of London covered by the congestion charge, and it suggested that it might institute congestion charging across the country by 2015. Several American and European municipalities, having seen the success of London's congestion charge, have said that they are seriously considering adopting a congestion charge as well.

Module 5 Review

Solutions appear at the back of the book.

Check Your Understanding

1. Explain whether each of the following events represents (i) a *change in demand* (a *shift of* the demand curve) or (ii) a *movement along* the demand curve (a *change in the quantity demanded*).
   a. A store owner finds that customers are willing to pay more for umbrellas on rainy days.
   b. When XYZ Telecom, a long-distance telephone service provider, offered reduced rates on weekends, its volume of weekend calling increased sharply.
   c. People buy more long-stem roses the week of Valentine's Day, even though the prices are higher than at other times during the year.
   d. A sharp rise in the price of gasoline leads many commuters to join carpools in order to reduce their gasoline purchases.

Multiple-Choice Questions

1. Which of the following would increase demand for a normal good? A decrease in
   a. price.
   b. income.
   c. the price of a substitute.
   d. consumer taste for a good.
   e. the price of a complement.

2. A decrease in the price of butter would most likely decrease the demand for
   a. margarine.
   b. bagels.
   c. jelly.
   d. milk.
   e. syrup.

3. If an increase in income leads to a decrease in demand, the good is
   a. a complement.
   b. a substitute.
   c. inferior.
   d. abnormal.
   e. normal.

4. Which of the following will occur if consumers expect the price of a good to fall in the coming months?
   a. The quantity demanded will rise today.
   b. The quantity demanded will remain the same today.
   c. Demand will increase today.
   d. Demand will decrease today.
   e. No change will occur today.

5. Which of the following will increase the demand for disposable diapers?
   a. a new "baby boom"
   b. concern over the environmental effect of landfills
   c. a decrease in the price of cloth diapers
   d. a move toward earlier potty training of children
   e. a decrease in the price of disposable diapers

Critical-Thinking Question

Draw a correctly labeled graph showing the demand for apples. On your graph, illustrate what happens to the demand for apples if a new report from the Surgeon General finds that an apple a day really *does* keep the doctor away.

Module 6
Supply and Demand: Supply and Equilibrium

What you will learn in this Module:

- What the supply curve is
- The difference between movements along the supply curve and changes in supply
- The factors that shift the supply curve
- How supply and demand curves determine a market's equilibrium price and equilibrium quantity
- In the case of a shortage or surplus, how price moves the market back to equilibrium

The Supply Curve

Some parts of the world are especially well suited to growing coffee beans, which is why, as the lyrics of an old song put it, "There's an awful lot of coffee in Brazil." But even in Brazil, some land is better suited to growing coffee than other land. Whether Brazilian farmers restrict their coffee-growing to only the most ideal locations or expand it to less suitable land depends on the price they expect to get for their beans. Moreover, there are many other areas in the world where coffee beans could be grown—such as Madagascar and Vietnam. Whether farmers there actually grow coffee depends, again, on the price.

So just as the quantity of coffee beans that consumers want to buy depends on the price they have to pay, the quantity that producers are willing to produce and sell—the **quantity supplied**—depends on the price they are offered.

The Supply Schedule and the Supply Curve

The table in Figure 6.1 on the next page shows how the quantity of coffee beans made available varies with the price—that is, it shows a hypothetical **supply schedule** for coffee beans.

A supply schedule works the same way as the demand schedule shown in Figure 5.1: in this case, the table shows the quantity of coffee beans farmers are willing to sell at different prices. At a price of $0.50 per pound, farmers are willing to sell only 8 billion pounds of coffee beans per year. At $0.75 per pound, they're willing to sell 9.1 billion pounds. At $1, they're willing to sell 10 billion pounds, and so on.

In the same way that a demand schedule can be represented graphically by a demand curve, a supply schedule can be represented by a **supply curve,** as shown in Figure 6.1. Each point on the curve represents an entry from the table.

Suppose that the price of coffee beans rises from $1 to $1.25; we can see that the quantity of coffee beans farmers are willing to sell rises from 10 billion to 10.7 billion pounds. This is the normal situation for a supply curve, reflecting the general proposition that a higher price leads to a higher quantity supplied. Some economists refer to

The **quantity supplied** is the actual amount of a good or service producers are willing to sell at some specific price.

A **supply schedule** shows how much of a good or service producers will supply at different prices.

A **supply curve** shows the relationship between quantity supplied and price.

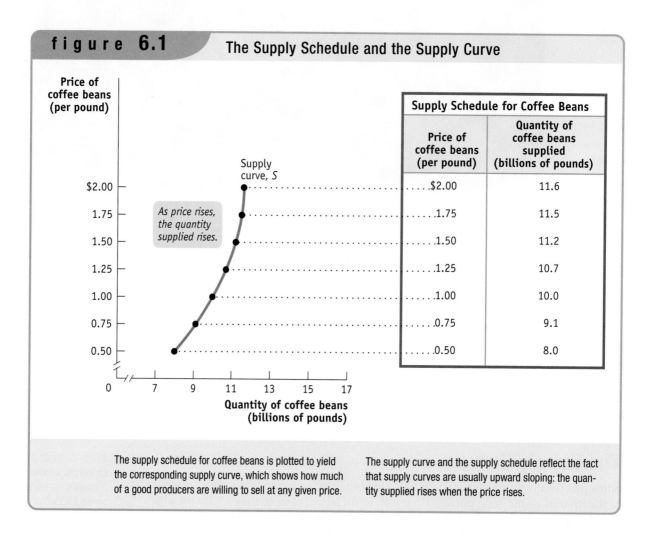

figure 6.1 The Supply Schedule and the Supply Curve

Price of coffee beans (per pound)

Supply curve, S

As price rises, the quantity supplied rises.

$2.00 —
1.75 —
1.50 —
1.25 —
1.00 —
0.75 —
0.50 —

0   7   9   11   13   15   17

Quantity of coffee beans (billions of pounds)

Supply Schedule for Coffee Beans	
Price of coffee beans (per pound)	Quantity of coffee beans supplied (billions of pounds)
$2.00	11.6
1.75	11.5
1.50	11.2
1.25	10.7
1.00	10.0
0.75	9.1
0.50	8.0

The supply schedule for coffee beans is plotted to yield the corresponding supply curve, which shows how much of a good producers are willing to sell at any given price.

The supply curve and the supply schedule reflect the fact that supply curves are usually upward sloping: the quantity supplied rises when the price rises.

this relationship as the **law of supply.** Generally, the price and quantity supplied are positively related. So just as demand curves normally slope downward, supply curves normally slope upward: the higher the price being offered, the more of any good or service producers are willing to sell.

Shifts of the Supply Curve

Compared to earlier trends, coffee beans were unusually cheap in the early years of the twenty-first century. One reason was the emergence of new coffee bean–producing countries, which began competing with the traditional sources in Latin America. Vietnam, in particular, emerged as a big new source of coffee beans. Figure 6.2 illustrates this event in terms of the supply schedule and the supply curve for coffee beans.

The table in Figure 6.2 shows two supply schedules. The schedule before new producers such as Vietnam arrived on the scene is the same one as in Figure 6.1. The second schedule shows the supply of coffee beans *after* the entry of new producers. Just as a change in the demand schedule leads to a shift of the demand curve, a change in the supply schedule leads to a shift of the supply curve—a **change in supply.** This is shown in Figure 6.2 by the shift of the supply curve before the entry of the new producers, S_1, to its new position after the entry of the new producers, S_2. Notice that S_2 lies to the right of S_1, a reflection of the fact that the quantity supplied increases at any given price.

As in the analysis of demand, it's crucial to draw a distinction between such changes in supply and **movements along the supply curve**—changes in the quantity supplied that result from a change in price. We can see this difference in

The **law of supply** says that, other things being equal, the price and quantity supplied of a good are positively related.

A **change in supply** is a shift of the supply curve, which changes the quantity supplied at any given price.

A **movement along the supply curve** is a change in the quantity supplied of a good that is the result of a change in that good's price.

figure 6.2 An Increase in Supply

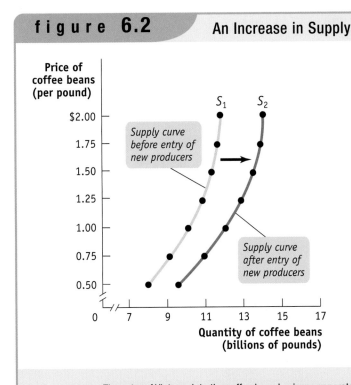

Supply Schedules for Coffee Beans		
Price of coffee beans (per pound)	Quantity of coffee beans supplied (billions of pounds)	
	Before entry	After entry
$2.00	11.6	13.9
1.75	11.5	13.8
1.50	11.2	13.4
1.25	10.7	12.8
1.00	10.0	12.0
0.75	9.1	10.9
0.50	8.0	9.6

The entry of Vietnam into the coffee bean business generated an increase in supply—a rise in the quantity supplied at any given price. This event is represented by the two supply schedules—one showing supply before Vietnam's entry, the other showing supply after Vietnam came in—and their corresponding supply curves. The increase in supply shifts the supply curve to the right.

Figure 6.3 on the next page. The movement from point *A* to point *B* is a movement along the supply curve: the quantity supplied rises along S_1 due to a rise in price. Here, a rise in price from $1 to $1.50 leads to a rise in the quantity supplied from 10 billion to 11.2 billion pounds of coffee beans. But the quantity supplied can also rise when the price is unchanged if there is an increase in supply—a rightward shift of the supply curve. This is shown by the rightward shift of the supply curve from S_1 to S_2. Holding price constant at $1, the quantity supplied rises from 10 billion pounds at point *A* on S_1 to 12 billion pounds at point *C* on S_2.

Understanding Shifts of the Supply Curve

Figure 6.4 on the next page illustrates the two basic ways in which supply curves can shift. When economists talk about an "increase in supply," they mean a *rightward* shift of the supply curve: at any given price, producers supply a larger quantity of the good than before. This is shown in Figure 6.4 by the rightward shift of the original supply curve S_1 to S_2. And when economists talk about a "decrease in supply," they mean a *leftward* shift of the supply curve: at any given price, producers supply a smaller quantity of the good than before. This is represented by the leftward shift of S_1 to S_3.

Economists believe that shifts of the supply curve for a good or service are mainly the result of five factors (though, as in the case of demand, there are other possible causes):

- Changes in input prices
- Changes in the prices of related goods or services
- Changes in technology
- Changes in expectations
- Changes in the number of producers

figure **6.3**

Movement Along the Supply Curve Versus Shift of the Supply Curve

The increase in quantity supplied when going from point *A* to point *B* reflects a movement along the supply curve: it is the result of a rise in the price of the good. The increase in quantity supplied when going from point *A* to point *C* reflects a change in supply: this shift to the right is the result of an increase in the quantity supplied at any given price.

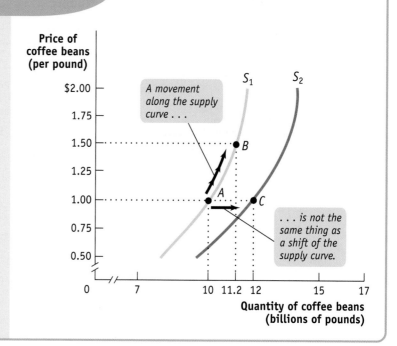

Changes in Input Prices To produce output, you need inputs. For example, to make vanilla ice cream, you need vanilla beans, cream, sugar, and so on. An **input** is anything used to produce a good or service. Inputs, like output, have prices. And an increase in the price of an input makes the production of the final good more costly for those who produce and sell it. So producers are less willing to supply the final good at any given price, and the supply curve shifts to the left. For example, newspaper publishers buy large quantities of newsprint (the paper on which newspapers are printed). When newsprint prices rose sharply in 1994–1995, the supply of newspapers fell: several newspapers went out of business and a number of new publishing ventures were canceled.

An **input** is anything that is used to produce a good or service.

---

figure **6.4**

Shifts of the Supply Curve

Any event that increases supply shifts the supply curve to the right, reflecting a rise in the quantity supplied at any given price. Any event that decreases supply shifts the supply curve to the left, reflecting a fall in the quantity supplied at any given price.

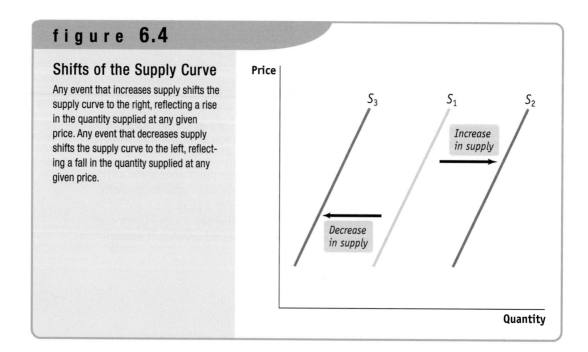

Similarly, a fall in the price of an input makes the production of the final good less costly for sellers. They are more willing to supply the good at any given price, and the supply curve shifts to the right.

Changes in the Prices of Related Goods or Services A single producer often produces a mix of goods rather than a single product. For example, an oil refinery produces gasoline from crude oil, but it also produces heating oil and other products from the same raw material. When a producer sells several products, the quantity of any one good it is willing to supply at any given price depends on the prices of its other co-produced goods. This effect can run in either direction. An oil refinery will supply less gasoline at any given price when the price of heating oil rises, shifting the supply curve for gasoline to the left. But it will supply more gasoline at any given price when the price of heating oil falls, shifting the supply curve for gasoline to the right. This means that gasoline and other co-produced oil products are *substitutes in production* for refiners. In contrast, due to the nature of the production process, other goods can be *complements in production*. For example, producers of crude oil— oil-well drillers—often find that oil wells also produce natural gas as a byproduct of oil extraction. The higher the price at which drillers can sell natural gas, the more oil wells they will drill and the more oil they will supply at any given price for oil. As a result, natural gas is a complement in production for crude oil.

istockphoto

Changes in Technology When economists talk about "technology," they don't necessarily mean high technology—they mean all the methods people can use to turn inputs into useful goods and services. In that sense, the whole complex sequence of activities that turn corn from an Iowa farm into cornflakes on your breakfast table is technology. And when better technology becomes available, reducing the cost of production—that is, letting a producer spend less on inputs yet produce the same output—supply increases, and the supply curve shifts to the right. For example, an improved strain of corn that is more resistant to disease makes farmers willing to supply more corn at any given price.

Changes in Expectations Just as changes in expectations can shift the demand curve, they can also shift the supply curve. When suppliers have some choice about when they put their good up for sale, changes in the expected future price of the good can lead a supplier to supply less or more of the good today. For example, consider the fact that gasoline and other oil products are often stored for significant periods of time at oil refineries before being sold to consumers. In fact, storage is normally part of producers' business strategy. Knowing that the demand for gasoline peaks in the summer, oil refiners normally store some of their gasoline produced during the spring for summer sale. Similarly, knowing that the demand for heating oil peaks in the winter, they normally store some of their heating oil produced during the fall for winter sale. In each case, there's a decision to be made between selling the product now versus storing it for later sale. Which choice a producer makes depends on a comparison of the current price versus the expected future price, among other factors. This example illustrates how changes in expectations can alter supply: an increase in the anticipated future price of a good or service reduces supply today, a leftward shift of the supply curve. But a fall in the anticipated future price increases supply today, a rightward shift of the supply curve.

Changes in the Number of Producers Just as changes in the number of consumers affect the demand curve, changes in the number of producers affect the supply curve. Let's examine the **individual supply curve,** which shows the relationship between

An **individual supply curve** illustrates the relationship between quantity supplied and price for an individual producer.

A farmer in Brazil sorts coffee beans by tossing them into the air. With advances in technology, more beans can be sorted in less time, and the supply curve shifts to the right.

quantity supplied and price for an individual producer. For example, suppose that Mr. Figueroa is a Brazilian coffee farmer and that panel (a) of Figure 6.5 shows how many pounds of beans he will supply per year at any given price. Then $S_{Figueroa}$ is his individual supply curve.

The *market supply curve* shows how the combined total quantity supplied by all individual producers in the market depends on the market price of that good. Just as the market demand curve is the horizontal sum of the individual demand curves of all consumers, the market supply curve is the horizontal sum of the individual supply curves of all producers. Assume for a moment that there are only two producers of coffee beans, Mr. Figueroa and Mr. Bien Pho, a Vietnamese coffee farmer. Mr. Bien Pho's individual supply curve is shown in panel (b). Panel (c) shows the market supply curve. At any given price, the quantity supplied to the market is the sum of the quantities supplied by Mr. Figueroa and Mr. Bien Pho. For example, at a price of $2 per pound, Mr. Figueroa supplies 3,000 pounds of coffee beans per year and Mr. Bien Pho supplies 2,000 pounds per year, making the quantity supplied to the market 5,000 pounds.

Clearly, the quantity supplied to the market at any given price is larger with Mr. Bien Pho present than it would be if Mr. Figueroa were the only supplier. The quantity supplied at a given price would be even larger if we added a third producer, then a fourth, and so on. So an increase in the number of producers leads to an increase in supply and a rightward shift of the supply curve.

For an overview of the factors that shift supply, see Table 6.1.

figure 6.5   The Individual Supply Curve and the Market Supply Curve

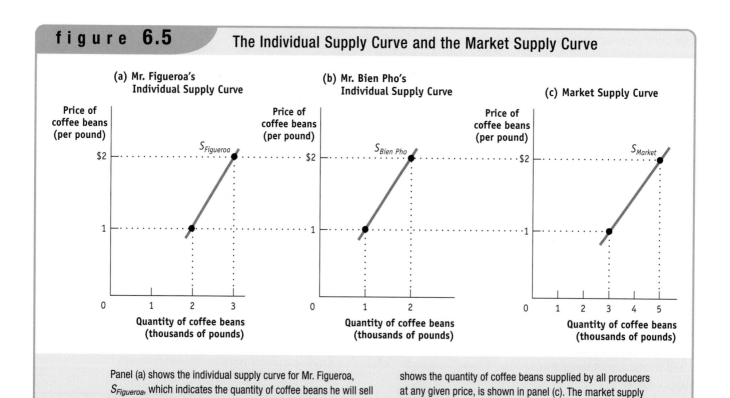

Panel (a) shows the individual supply curve for Mr. Figueroa, $S_{Figueroa}$, which indicates the quantity of coffee beans he will sell at any given price. Panel (b) shows the individual supply curve for Mr. Bien Pho, $S_{Bien\ Pho}$. The market supply curve, which shows the quantity of coffee beans supplied by all producers at any given price, is shown in panel (c). The market supply curve is the horizontal sum of the individual supply curves of all producers.

table **6.1**

Factors That Shift Supply

Changes in input prices		
	If the price of an input used to produce *A* rises, . . .	. . . supply of *A* decreases (shifts to the left).
	If the price of an input used to produce *A* falls, . . .	. . . supply of *A* increases (shifts to the right).

Changes in the prices of related goods or services		
If A and *B* are substitutes in production . . .	. . . and the price of *B* rises, . . .	. . . supply of *A* decreases.
	. . . and the price of *B* falls, . . .	. . . supply of *A* increases.
If A and *B* are complements in production . . .	. . . and the price of *B* rises, . . .	. . . supply of *A* increases.
	. . . and the price of *B* falls, . . .	. . . supply of *A* decreases.

Changes in technology		
	If the technology used to produce *A* improves, . . .	. . . supply of *A* increases.

Changes in expectations		
	If the price of *A* is expected to rise in the future, . . .	. . . supply of *A* decreases today.
	If the price of *A* is expected to fall in the future, . . .	. . . supply of *A* increases today.

Changes in the number of producers		
	If the number of producers of *A* rises, . . .	. . . market supply of *A* increases.
	If the number of producers of *A* falls, . . .	. . . market supply of *A* decreases.

in real life

Only Creatures Small and Pampered

During the 1970s, British television featured a popular show titled *All Creatures Great and Small*. It chronicled the real life of James Herriot, a country veterinarian who tended to cows, pigs, sheep, horses, and the occasional house pet, often under arduous conditions, in rural England during the 1930s. The show made it clear that in those days the local vet was a critical member of farming communities, saving valuable farm animals and helping farmers survive financially. And it was also clear that Mr. Herriot considered his life's work well spent.

But that was then and this is now. According to a 2007 article in the *New York Times,* the United States has experienced a severe decline in the number of farm veterinarians over the past two decades. The source of the problem is competition. As the number of household pets has increased and the incomes of pet owners have grown, the demand for pet veterinarians has increased sharply. As a result, vets are being drawn away from the business of caring for farm animals into the more lucrative business of caring for pets. As one vet stated, she began her career caring for farm animals but changed her mind after "doing a C-section on a cow and it's 50 bucks. Do a C-section on a Chihuahua and you get $300. It's the money. I hate to say that."

How can we translate this into supply and demand curves? Farm veterinary services and pet veterinary services are like gasoline and fuel oil: they're related goods that are substitutes in production. A veterinarian typically specializes in one type of practice or the other, and that decision often depends on the going price for the service. America's growing pet population, combined with the increased willingness of doting owners to spend on their companions' care, has driven up the price of pet veterinary services. As a result, fewer and fewer veterinarians have gone into farm animal practice. So the supply curve of farm veterinarians has shifted leftward—fewer farm veterinarians are offering their services at any given price.

In the end, farmers understand that it is all a matter of dollars and cents—that they get fewer veterinarians because they are unwilling to pay more. As one farmer, who had recently lost an expensive cow due to the unavailability of a veterinarian, stated, "The fact that there's nothing you can do, you accept it as a business expense now. You didn't used to. If you have livestock, sooner or later you're going to have deadstock." (Although we should note that this farmer *could* have chosen to pay more for a vet who would have then saved his cow.)

Supply, Demand, and Equilibrium

We have now covered the first three key elements in the supply and demand model: the demand curve, the supply curve, and the set of factors that shift each curve. The next step is to put these elements together to show how they can be used to predict the actual price at which the good is bought and sold, as well as the actual quantity transacted.

In competitive markets this interaction of supply and demand tends to move toward what economists call *equilibrium.* Imagine a busy afternoon at your local supermarket; there are long lines at the checkout counters. Then one of the previously closed registers opens. The first thing that happens is a rush to the newly opened register. But soon enough things settle down and shoppers have rearranged themselves so that the line at the newly opened register is about as long as all the others. This situation—all the checkout lines are now the same length, and none of the shoppers can be better off by doing something different—is what economists call **equilibrium.**

The concept of equilibrium helps us understand the price at which a good or service is bought and sold as well as the quantity transacted of the good or service. A competitive market is in equilibrium when the price has moved to a level at which the quantity of a good demanded equals the quantity of that good supplied. At that price, no individual seller could make herself better off by offering to sell either more or less of the good and no individual buyer could make himself better off by offering to buy more or less of the good. Recall the shoppers at the supermarket who cannot make themselves better off (cannot save time) by changing lines. Similarly, at the market equilibrium, the price has moved to a level that exactly matches the quantity demanded by consumers to the quantity supplied by sellers.

The price that matches the quantity supplied and the quantity demanded is the **equilibrium price;** the quantity bought and sold at that price is the **equilibrium quantity.** The equilibrium price is also known as the **market-clearing price:** it is the price that "clears the market" by ensuring that every buyer willing to pay that price finds a seller willing to sell at that price, and vice versa. So how do we find the equilibrium price and quantity?

Finding the Equilibrium Price and Quantity

The easiest way to determine the equilibrium price and quantity in a market is by putting the supply curve and the demand curve on the same diagram. Since the supply curve shows the quantity supplied at any given price and the demand curve shows the quantity demanded at any given price, the price at which the two curves cross is the equilibrium price: the price at which quantity supplied equals quantity demanded.

Figure 6.6 combines the demand curve from Figure 5.1 and the supply curve from Figure 6.1. They *intersect* at point *E,* which is the equilibrium of this market; that is, $1 is the equilibrium price and 10 billion pounds is the equilibrium quantity.

Let's confirm that point *E* fits our definition of equilibrium. At a price of $1 per pound, coffee bean producers are willing to sell 10 billion pounds a year and coffee bean consumers want to buy 10 billion pounds a year. So at the price of $1 a pound, the quantity of coffee beans supplied equals the quantity demanded. Notice that at any other price the market would not clear: some willing buyers would not be able to find a willing seller, or vice versa. More specifically, if the price were more than $1, the quantity supplied would exceed the quantity demanded; if the price were less than $1, the quantity demanded would exceed the quantity supplied.

The model of supply and demand, then, predicts that given the curves shown in Figure 6.6, 10 billion pounds of coffee beans would change hands at a price of $1 per pound. But how can we be sure that the market will arrive at the equilibrium price? We begin by answering three simple questions:

YEAH, I KNOW IT'S PRICEY, BUT I ONLY GOTTA SELL *ONE* GLASS AND I'M SET FOR LIFE.

Lemonade $1,000,000 a glass

figure **6.6**

Market Equilibrium

Market equilibrium occurs at point *E*, where the supply curve and the demand curve intersect. In equilibrium, the quantity demanded is equal to the quantity supplied. In this market, the equilibrium price is $1 per pound and the equilibrium quantity is 10 billion pounds per year.

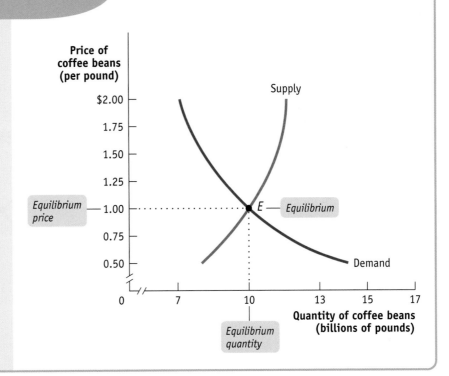

1. Why do all sales and purchases in a market take place at the same price?
2. Why does the market price fall if it is above the equilibrium price?
3. Why does the market price rise if it is below the equilibrium price?

Why Do All Sales and Purchases in a Market Take Place at the Same Price?

There are some markets in which the same good can sell for many different prices, depending on who is selling or who is buying. For example, have you ever bought a souvenir in a "tourist trap" and then seen the same item on sale somewhere else (perhaps even in the shop next door) for a lower price? Because tourists don't know which shops offer the best deals and don't have time for comparison shopping, sellers in tourist areas can charge different prices for the same good.

But in any market where the buyers and sellers have both been around for some time, sales and purchases tend to converge at a generally uniform price, so that we can safely talk about *the* market price. It's easy to see why. Suppose a seller offered a potential buyer a price noticeably above what the buyer knew other people to be paying. The buyer would clearly be better off shopping elsewhere—unless the seller was prepared to offer a better deal. Conversely, a seller would not be willing to sell for significantly less than the amount he knew most buyers were paying; he would be better off waiting to get a more reasonable customer. So in any well-established, ongoing market, all sellers receive and all buyers pay approximately the same price. This is what we call the *market price*.

Why Does the Market Price Fall If It Is Above the Equilibrium Price?

Suppose the supply and demand curves are as shown in Figure 6.6 but the market price is above the equilibrium level of $1—say, $1.50. This situation is illustrated in Figure 6.7 on the next page. Why can't the price stay there?

figure **6.7**

Price Above Its Equilibrium Level Creates a Surplus

The market price of $1.50 is above the equilibrium price of $1. This creates a surplus: at a price of $1.50, producers would like to sell 11.2 billion pounds but consumers want to buy only 8.1 billion pounds, so there is a surplus of 3.1 billion pounds. This surplus will push the price down until it reaches the equilibrium price of $1.

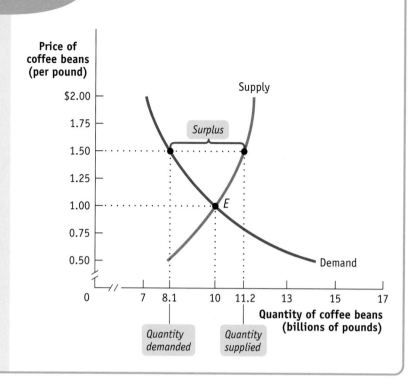

There is a **surplus** of a good when the quantity supplied exceeds the quantity demanded. Surpluses occur when the price is above its equilibrium level.

There is a **shortage** of a good when the quantity demanded exceeds the quantity supplied. Shortages occur when the price is below its equilibrium level.

As the figure shows, at a price of $1.50 there would be more coffee beans available than consumers wanted to buy: 11.2 billion pounds, versus 8.1 billion pounds. The difference of 3.1 billion pounds is the **surplus**—also known as the *excess supply*—of coffee beans at $1.50.

This surplus means that some coffee producers are frustrated: at the current price, they cannot find consumers who want to buy their coffee beans. The surplus offers an incentive for those frustrated would-be sellers to offer a lower price in order to poach business from other producers and entice more consumers to buy. The result of this price cutting will be to push the prevailing price down until it reaches the equilibrium price. So the price of a good will fall whenever there is a surplus—that is, whenever the market price is above its equilibrium level.

Why Does the Market Price Rise If It Is Below the Equilibrium Price?

Now suppose the price is below its equilibrium level—say, at $0.75 per pound, as shown in Figure 6.8. In this case, the quantity demanded, 11.5 billion pounds, exceeds the quantity supplied, 9.1 billion pounds, implying that there are would-be buyers who cannot find coffee beans: there is a **shortage**—also known as an *excess demand*—of 2.4 billion pounds.

When there is a shortage, there are frustrated would-be buyers—people who want to purchase coffee beans but cannot find willing sellers at the current price. In this situation, either buyers will offer more than the prevailing price or sellers will realize that they can charge higher prices. Either way, the result is to drive up the prevailing price. This bidding up of prices happens whenever there are shortages—and there will be shortages whenever the price is below its equilibrium level. So the market price will always rise if it is below the equilibrium level.

figure 6.8

Price Below Its Equilibrium Level Creates a Shortage

The market price of $0.75 is below the equilibrium price of $1. This creates a shortage: consumers want to buy 11.5 billion pounds, but only 9.1 billion pounds are for sale, so there is a shortage of 2.4 billion pounds. This shortage will push the price up until it reaches the equilibrium price of $1.

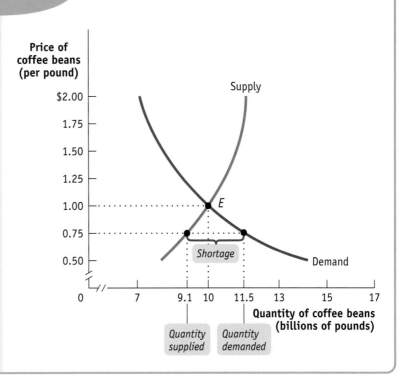

Using Equilibrium to Describe Markets

We have now seen that a market tends to have a single price, the equilibrium price. If the market price is above the equilibrium level, the ensuing surplus leads buyers and sellers to take actions that lower the price. And if the market price is below the equilibrium level, the ensuing shortage leads buyers and sellers to take actions that raise the price. So the market price always *moves toward* the equilibrium price, the price at which there is neither surplus nor shortage.

M o d u l e ⑥ R e v i e w

Solutions appear at the back of the book.

Check Your Understanding

1. Explain whether each of the following events represents (i) a *change in* supply or (ii) a *movement along* the supply curve.
   a. During a real estate boom that causes house prices to rise, more homeowners put their houses up for sale.
   b. Many strawberry farmers open temporary roadside stands during harvest season, even though prices are usually low at that time.
   c. Immediately after the school year begins, fewer young people are available to work. Fast-food chains must raise wages, which represent the price of labor, to attract workers.
   d. Many construction workers temporarily move to areas that have suffered hurricane damage, lured by higher wages.
   e. Since new technologies have made it possible to build larger cruise ships (which are cheaper to run per passenger), Caribbean cruise lines have offered more cabins, at lower prices, than before.

2. In the following three situations, the market is initially in equilibrium. After each event described below, does a surplus or shortage exist at the original equilibrium price? What will happen to the equilibrium price as a result?
   a. In 2010 there was a bumper crop of wine grapes.
   b. After a hurricane, Florida hoteliers often find that many people cancel their upcoming vacations, leaving them with empty hotel rooms.
   c. After a heavy snowfall, many people want to buy second-hand snowblowers at the local tool shop.

Multiple-Choice Questions

1. Which of the following will decrease the supply of good "X"?
   a. There is a technological advance that affects the production of *all* goods.
   b. The price of good "X" falls.
   c. The price of good "Y" (which consumers regard as a substitute for good "X") decreases.
   d. The wages of workers producing good "X" increase.
   e. The demand for good "X" decreases.

2. An increase in the demand for steak will lead to an increase in which of the following?
   a. the supply of steak
   b. the supply of hamburger (a substitute in production)
   c. the supply of chicken (a substitute in consumption)
   d. the supply of leather (a complement in production)
   e. the demand for leather

3. A technological advance in textbook production will lead to which of the following?
   a. a decrease in textbook supply
   b. an increase in textbook demand
   c. an increase in textbook supply
   d. a movement along the supply curve for textbooks
   e. an increase in textbook prices

4. Which of the following is true at equilibrium?
   a. The supply schedule is identical to the demand schedule at every price.
   b. The quantity demanded is the same as the quantity supplied.
   c. The quantity is zero.
   d. Every consumer who enjoys the good can consume it.
   e. Producers could not make any more of the product regardless of the price.

5. The market price of a good will tend to rise if
   a. demand decreases.
   b. supply increases.
   c. it is above the equilibrium price.
   d. it is below the equilibrium price.
   e. demand shifts to the left.

Critical-Thinking Question

Draw a correctly labeled graph showing the market for oranges in equilibrium. Show on your graph how a hurricane that destroys large numbers of orange groves in Florida will affect supply and demand, if at all.

Module 7
Supply and Demand: Changes in Equilibrium

Changes in Supply and Demand

The emergence of Vietnam as a major coffee-producing country came as a surprise, but the subsequent fall in the price of coffee beans was no surprise at all. Suddenly, the quantity of coffee beans available at any given price rose—that is, there was an increase in supply. Predictably, the increase in supply lowered the equilibrium price.

The entry of Vietnamese producers into the coffee bean business was an example of an event that shifted the supply curve for a good without affecting the demand curve. There are many such events. There are also events that shift the demand curve without shifting the supply curve. For example, a medical report that chocolate is good for you increases the demand for chocolate but does not affect the supply. That is, events often shift either the supply curve or the demand curve, but not both; it is therefore useful to ask what happens in each case.

We have seen that when a curve shifts, the equilibrium price and quantity change. We will now concentrate on exactly how the shift of a curve alters the equilibrium price and quantity.

What Happens When the Demand Curve Shifts

Coffee and tea are substitutes: if the price of tea rises, the demand for coffee will increase, and if the price of tea falls, the demand for coffee will decrease. But how does the price of tea affect the *market equilibrium* for coffee?

Figure 7.1 on the next page shows the effect of a rise in the price of tea on the market for coffee. The rise in the price of tea increases the demand for coffee. Point E_1 shows the original equilibrium, with P_1 the equilibrium price and Q_1 the equilibrium quantity bought and sold.

An increase in demand is indicated by a *rightward* shift of the demand curve from D_1 to D_2. At the original market price, P_1, this market is no longer in equilibrium: a shortage occurs because the quantity demanded exceeds the quantity supplied. So the price of coffee rises and generates an increase in the quantity supplied, an upward

figure **7.1**

Equilibrium and Shifts of the Demand Curve

The original equilibrium in the market for coffee is at E_1, at the intersection of the supply curve and the original demand curve, D_1. A rise in the price of tea, a substitute, shifts the demand curve rightward to D_2. A shortage exists at the original price, P_1, causing both the price and quantity supplied to rise, a movement along the supply curve. A new equilibrium is reached at E_2, with a higher equilibrium price, P_2, and a higher equilibrium quantity, Q_2. When demand for a good or service increases, the equilibrium price and the equilibrium quantity of the good or service both rise.

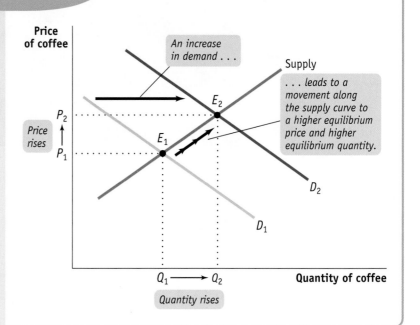

movement along the supply curve. A new equilibrium is established at point E_2, with a higher equilibrium price, P_2, and higher equilibrium quantity, Q_2. This sequence of events reflects a general principle: *When demand for a good or service increases, the equilibrium price and the equilibrium quantity of the good or service both rise.*

What would happen in the reverse case, a fall in the price of tea? A fall in the price of tea reduces the demand for coffee, shifting the demand curve to the *left*. At the original price, a surplus occurs as quantity supplied exceeds quantity demanded. The price falls and leads to a decrease in the quantity supplied, resulting in a lower equilibrium price and a lower equilibrium quantity. This illustrates another general principle: *When demand for a good or service decreases, the equilibrium price and the equilibrium quantity of the good or service both fall.*

To summarize how a market responds to a change in demand: *An increase in demand leads to a rise in both the equilibrium price and the equilibrium quantity. A decrease in demand leads to a fall in both the equilibrium price and the equilibrium quantity.*

What Happens When the Supply Curve Shifts

In the real world, it is a bit easier to predict changes in supply than changes in demand. Physical factors that affect supply, like the availability of inputs, are easier to get a handle on than the fickle tastes that affect demand. Still, with supply as with demand, what we can best predict are the *effects* of shifts of the supply curve.

As we mentioned earlier, a prolonged drought in Vietnam sharply reduced its production of coffee beans. Figure 7.2 shows how this shift affected the market equilibrium. The original equilibrium is at E_1, the point of intersection of the original supply curve, S_1, and the demand curve, with an equilibrium price, P_1, and equilibrium quantity, Q_1. As a result of the drought, supply falls and S_1 shifts *leftward* to S_2. At the original price, P_1, a shortage of coffee beans now exists and the market is no longer in equilibrium. The shortage causes a rise in price and a fall in quantity demanded, an upward movement along the demand curve. The new equilibrium is at E_2, with an equilibrium price, P_2, and an equilibrium quantity, Q_2. In the new equilibrium, E_2, the price

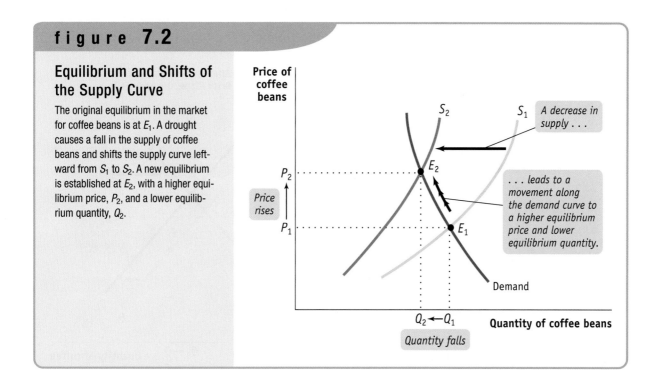

figure 7.2

Equilibrium and Shifts of the Supply Curve

The original equilibrium in the market for coffee beans is at E_1. A drought causes a fall in the supply of coffee beans and shifts the supply curve leftward from S_1 to S_2. A new equilibrium is established at E_2, with a higher equilibrium price, P_2, and a lower equilibrium quantity, Q_2.

is higher and the equilibrium quantity is lower than before. This may be stated as a general principle: *When supply of a good or service decreases, the equilibrium price of the good or service rises and the equilibrium quantity of the good or service falls.*

What happens to the market when supply increases? An increase in supply leads to a *rightward* shift of the supply curve. At the original price, a surplus now exists; as a result, the equilibrium price falls and the quantity demanded rises. This describes what happened to the market for coffee beans when Vietnam entered the field. We can formulate a general principle: *When supply of a good or service increases, the equilibrium price of the good or service falls and the equilibrium quantity of the good or service rises.*

To summarize how a market responds to a change in supply: *An increase in supply leads to a fall in the equilibrium price and a rise in the equilibrium quantity. A decrease in supply leads to a rise in the equilibrium price and a fall in the equilibrium quantity.*

Simultaneous Shifts of Supply and Demand Curves

Finally, it sometimes happens that events shift *both* the demand and supply curves at the same time. This is not unusual; in real life, supply curves and demand curves for many goods and services typically shift quite often because the economic environment continually changes. Figure 7.3 on the next page illustrates two examples of simultaneous shifts. In both panels there is an increase in demand—that is, a rightward shift of the demand curve, from D_1 to D_2—say, for example, representing the increase in the demand for coffee due to changing tastes. Notice that the rightward shift in panel (a) is larger than the one in panel (b): we can suppose that panel (a) represents a year in which many more people than usual choose to drink double lattes and panel (b) represents a year with only a small increase in coffee demand. Both panels also show a decrease in supply—that is, a leftward shift of the supply curve from S_1 to S_2. Also notice that the leftward shift in panel (b) is large relative to the one in panel (a); we can suppose that panel (b) represents the effect of a particularly extreme drought in Vietnam and panel (a) represents the effect of a much less severe weather event.

In both cases, the equilibrium price rises from P_1 to P_2 as the equilibrium moves from E_1 to E_2. But what happens to the equilibrium quantity, the quantity of coffee bought and sold? In panel (a), the increase in demand is large relative to the decrease in supply,

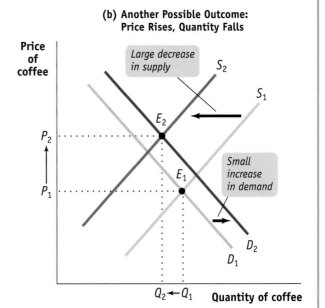

**(a) One Possible Outcome:
Price Rises, Quantity Rises**

**(b) Another Possible Outcome:
Price Rises, Quantity Falls**

In panel (a) there is a simultaneous rightward shift of the demand curve and leftward shift of the supply curve. Here the increase in demand is larger than the decrease in supply, so the equilibrium price and equilibrium quantity both rise. In panel (b) there is also a simultaneous rightward shift of the demand curve and leftward shift of the supply curve. Here the decrease in supply is larger than the increase in demand, so the equilibrium price rises and the equilibrium quantity falls.

and the equilibrium quantity rises as a result. In panel (b), the decrease in supply is large relative to the increase in demand, and the equilibrium quantity falls as a result. That is, when demand increases and supply decreases, the actual quantity bought and sold can go either way, depending on *how much* the demand and supply curves have shifted.

In general, when supply and demand shift in opposite directions, we can't predict what the ultimate effect will be on the quantity bought and sold. What we can say is that a curve that shifts a disproportionately greater distance than the other curve will have a disproportionately greater effect on the quantity bought and sold. That said, we can make the following prediction about the outcome when the supply and demand curves shift in opposite directions:

■ When demand increases and supply decreases, the equilibrium price rises but the change in the equilibrium quantity is ambiguous.

■ When demand decreases and supply increases, the equilibrium price falls but the change in the equilibrium quantity is ambiguous.

But suppose that the demand and supply curves shift in the same direction. This was the case in the global market for coffee beans, in which both supply and demand increased over the past decade. Can we safely make any predictions about the changes in price and quantity? In this situation, the change in quantity bought and sold can be predicted but the change in price is ambiguous. The two possible outcomes when the supply and demand curves shift in the same direction (which you should check for yourself) are as follows:

■ When both demand and supply increase, the equilibrium quantity increases but the change in equilibrium price is ambiguous.

■ When both demand and supply decrease, the equilibrium quantity decreases but the change in equilibrium price is ambiguous.

The Great Tortilla Crisis

"Thousands in Mexico City protest rising food prices." So read a recent headline in the *New York Times*. Specifically, the demonstrators were protesting a sharp rise in the price of tortillas, a staple food of Mexico's poor, which had gone from 25 cents a pound to between 35 and 45 cents a pound in just a few months.

Why were tortilla prices soaring? It was a classic example of what happens to equilibrium prices when supply falls. Tortillas are made from corn; much of Mexico's corn is imported from the United States, with the price of corn in both countries basically set in the U.S. corn market. And U.S. corn prices were rising rapidly thanks to surging demand in a new market: the market for ethanol.

Ethanol's big break came with the Energy Policy Act of 2005, which mandated the use of a large quantity of "renewable" fuels starting in 2006, and rising steadily thereafter. In practice, that meant increased use of ethanol. Ethanol producers rushed to build new production facilities and quickly began buying lots of corn. The result was a rightward shift of the demand curve for corn, leading to a sharp rise in the price of corn. And since corn is an input in the production of tortillas, a sharp rise in the price of corn led to a fall in the supply of tortillas and higher prices for tortilla consumers.

The increase in the price of corn was good news in Iowa, where farmers began planting

A cook prepares tortillas made with four different types of corn in a restaurant in Mexico City.

more corn than ever before. But it was bad news for Mexican consumers, who found themselves paying more for their tortillas.

Module 7 Review

Solutions appear at the back of the book.

Check Your Understanding

1. For each of the following examples, explain how the indicated change affects supply or demand for the good in question and how the shift you describe affects equilibrium price and quantity.
   a. As the price of gasoline fell in the United States during the 1990s, more people bought large cars.
   b. As technological innovation has lowered the cost of recycling used paper, fresh paper made from recycled stock is used more frequently.
   c. When a local cable company offers cheaper pay-per-view films, local movie theaters have more unfilled seats.

2. Periodically, a computer chip maker like Intel introduces a new chip that is faster than the previous one. In response, demand for computers using the earlier chip decreases as customers put off purchases in anticipation of machines containing the new chip. Simultaneously, computer makers increase their production of computers containing the earlier chip in order to clear out their stocks of those chips.

    Draw two diagrams of the market for computers containing the earlier chip: (a) one in which the equilibrium quantity falls in response to these events and (b) one in which the equilibrium quantity rises. What happens to the equilibrium price in each diagram?

Multiple-Choice Questions

1. Which of the following describes what will happen in the market for tomatoes if a salmonella outbreak is attributed to tainted tomatoes?
   a. Supply will decrease and price will increase.
   b. Supply will decrease and price will decrease.
   c. Demand will decrease and price will increase.
   d. Demand will decrease and price will decrease.
   e. Supply and demand will both decrease.

2. Which of the following will lead to an increase in the equilibrium price of product "X"? A(n)
   a. increase in consumer incomes if product "X" is an inferior good
   b. increase in the price of machinery used to produce product "X"
   c. technological advance in the production of good "X"
   d. decrease in the price of good "Y" (a substitute for good "X")
   e. expectation by consumers that the price of good "X" is going to fall

3. The equilibrium price will rise, but equilibrium quantity may increase, decrease, or stay the same if
   a. demand increases and supply decreases.
   b. demand increases and supply increases.
   c. demand decreases and supply increases.
   d. demand decreases and supply decreases.
   e. demand increases and supply does not change.

4. An increase in the number of buyers and a technological advance will cause
   a. demand to increase and supply to increase.
   b. demand to increase and supply to decrease.
   c. demand to decrease and supply to increase.
   d. demand to decrease and supply to decrease.
   e. no change in demand and an increase in supply.

5. Which of the following is certainly true if demand and supply increase at the same time?
   a. The equilibrium price will increase.
   b. The equilibrium price will decrease.
   c. The equilibrium quantity will increase.
   d. The equilibrium quantity will decrease.
   e. The equilibrium quantity may increase, decrease, or stay the same.

Critical-Thinking Question

Draw a correctly labeled graph showing the market for cups of coffee in equilibrium. On your graph, show the effect of a decrease in the price of coffee beans on equilibrium price and equilibrium quantity in the market for cups of coffee.

Module 8
Supply and Demand: Price Controls (Ceilings and Floors)

What you will learn in this Module:

- The meaning of price controls, one way government intervenes in markets

- How price controls can create problems and make a market inefficient

- Why economists are often deeply skeptical of attempts to intervene in markets

- Who benefits and who loses from price controls, and why they are used despite their well-known problems

Why Governments Control Prices

You learned in Module 6 that a market moves to equilibrium—that is, the market price moves to the level at which the quantity supplied equals the quantity demanded. But this equilibrium price does not necessarily please either buyers or sellers.

After all, buyers would always like to pay less if they could, and sometimes they can make a strong moral or political case that they should pay lower prices. For example, what if the equilibrium between supply and demand for apartments in a major city leads to rental rates that an average working person can't afford? In that case, a government might well be under pressure to impose limits on the rents landlords can charge.

Sellers, however, would always like to get more money for what they sell, and sometimes they can make a strong moral or political case that they should receive higher prices. For example, consider the labor market: the price for an hour of a worker's time is the wage rate. What if the equilibrium between supply and demand for less skilled workers leads to wage rates that yield an income below the poverty level? In that case, a government might well be pressured to require employers to pay a rate no lower than some specified minimum wage.

In other words, there is often a strong political demand for governments to intervene in markets. And powerful interests can make a compelling case that a market intervention favoring them is "fair." When a government intervenes to regulate prices, we say that it imposes **price controls.** These controls typically take the form of either an upper limit, a **price ceiling,** or a lower limit, a **price floor.**

Unfortunately, it's not that easy to tell a market what to do. As we will now see, when a government tries to legislate prices—whether it legislates them *down* by imposing a price ceiling or *up* by imposing a price floor—there are certain predictable and unpleasant side effects.

Price controls are legal restrictions on how high or low a market price may go. They can take two forms: a **price ceiling,** a maximum price sellers are allowed to charge for a good or service, or a **price floor,** a minimum price buyers are required to pay for a good or service.

We make an important assumption in this module: the markets in question are efficient before price controls are imposed. Markets can sometimes be inefficient—for example, a market dominated by a monopolist, a single seller who has the power to influence the market price. When markets are inefficient, price controls don't necessarily cause problems and can potentially move the market closer to efficiency. In practice, however, price controls often *are* imposed on efficient markets—like the New York City apartment market. And so the analysis in this module applies to many important real-world situations.

Price Ceilings

Aside from rent control, there are not many price ceilings in the United States today. But at times they have been widespread. Price ceilings are typically imposed during crises— wars, harvest failures, natural disasters—because these events often lead to sudden price increases that hurt many people but produce big gains for a lucky few. The U.S. government imposed ceilings on many prices during World War II: the war sharply increased demand for raw materials, such as aluminum and steel, and price controls prevented those with access to these raw materials from earning huge profits. Price controls on oil were imposed in 1973, when an embargo by Arab oil-exporting countries seemed likely to generate huge profits for U.S. oil companies. Price controls were imposed on California's wholesale electricity market in 2001, when a shortage created big profits for a few power-generating companies but led to higher electricity bills for consumers.

Rent control in New York is, believe it or not, a legacy of World War II: it was imposed because wartime production created an economic boom, which increased demand for apartments at a time when the labor and raw materials that might have been used to build them were being used to win the war instead. Although most price controls were removed soon after the war ended, New York's rent limits were retained and gradually extended to buildings not previously covered, leading to some very strange situations.

You can rent a one-bedroom apartment in Manhattan on fairly short notice—if you are able and willing to pay several thousand dollars a month and live in a less-than-desirable area. Yet some people pay only a small fraction of this for comparable apartments, and others pay hardly more for bigger apartments in better locations.

Aside from producing great deals for some renters, however, what are the broader consequences of New York's rent-control system? To answer this question, we turn to the supply and demand model.

Modeling a Price Ceiling

To see what can go wrong when a government imposes a price ceiling on an efficient market, consider Figure 8.1, which shows a simplified model of the market for apartments in New York. For the sake of simplicity, we imagine that all apartments are exactly the same and so would rent for the same price in an unregulated market. The table in the figure shows the demand and supply schedules; the demand and supply curves are shown on the left. We show the quantity of apartments on the horizontal axis and the monthly rent per apartment on the vertical axis. You can see that in an unregulated market the equilibrium would be at point *E*: 2 million apartments would be rented for $1,000 each per month.

Now suppose that the government imposes a price ceiling, limiting rents to a price below the equilibrium price—say, no more than $800.

Figure 8.2 shows the effect of the price ceiling, represented by the line at $800. At the enforced rental rate of $800, landlords have less incentive to offer apartments, so they won't be willing to supply as many as they would at the equilibrium rate of $1,000. They will choose point *A* on the supply curve, offering only 1.8 million apartments for rent, 200,000 fewer than in the unregulated market. At the same time, more people will want to rent apartments at a price of $800 than at the equilibrium price of $1,000; as shown at point *B* on the demand curve, at a monthly rent of $800 the quantity of apartments

figure 8.1 The Market for Apartments in the Absence of Government Controls

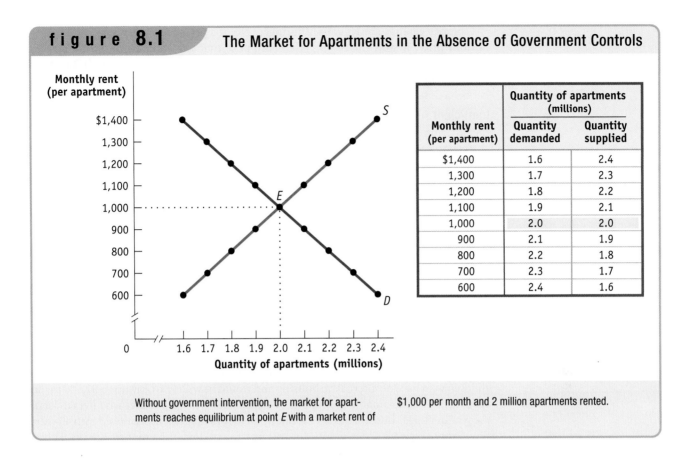

Monthly rent (per apartment)	Quantity of apartments (millions)	
	Quantity demanded	Quantity supplied
$1,400	1.6	2.4
1,300	1.7	2.3
1,200	1.8	2.2
1,100	1.9	2.1
1,000	2.0	2.0
900	2.1	1.9
800	2.2	1.8
700	2.3	1.7
600	2.4	1.6

Without government intervention, the market for apartments reaches equilibrium at point *E* with a market rent of $1,000 per month and 2 million apartments rented.

demanded rises to 2.2 million, 200,000 more than in the unregulated market and 400,000 more than are actually available at the price of $800. So there is now a persistent shortage of rental housing: at that price, 400,000 more people want to rent than are able to find apartments.

figure 8.2

The Effects of a Price Ceiling

The black horizontal line represents the government-imposed price ceiling on rents of $800 per month. This price ceiling reduces the quantity of apartments supplied to 1.8 million, point *A*, and increases the quantity demanded to 2.2 million, point *B*. This creates a persistent shortage of 400,000 units: 400,000 people who want apartments at the legal rent of $800 but cannot get them.

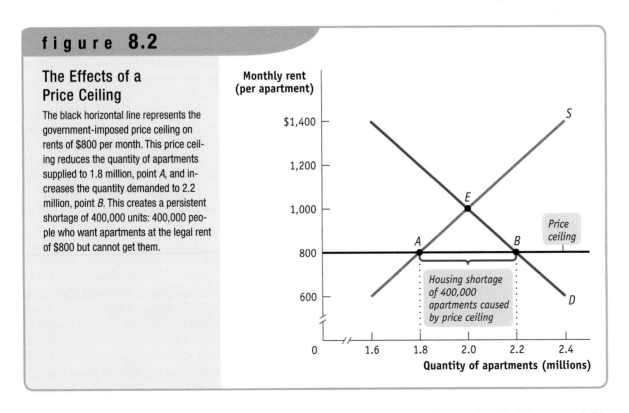

Do price ceilings always cause shortages? No. If a price ceiling is set above the equilibrium price, it won't have any effect. Suppose that the equilibrium rental rate on apartments is $1,000 per month and the city government sets a ceiling of $1,200. Who cares? In this case, the price ceiling won't be binding—it won't actually constrain market behavior—and it will have no effect.

Inefficient Allocation to Consumers Rent control doesn't just lead to too few apartments being available. It can also lead to misallocation of the apartments that are available: people who badly need a place to live may not be able to find an apartment, while some apartments may be occupied by people with much less urgent needs.

In the case shown in Figure 8.2, 2.2 million people would like to rent an apartment at $800 per month, but only 1.8 million apartments are available. Of those 2.2 million who are seeking an apartment, some want an apartment badly and are willing to pay a high price to get one. Others have a less urgent need and are only willing to pay a low price, perhaps because they have alternative housing. An efficient allocation of apartments would reflect these differences: people who really want an apartment will get one and people who aren't all that eager to find an apartment won't. In an inefficient distribution of apartments, the opposite will happen: some people who are not especially eager to find an apartment will get one and others who are very eager to find an apartment won't. Because people usually get apartments through luck or personal connections under rent control, it generally results in an **inefficient allocation to consumers** of the few apartments available.

To see the inefficiency involved, consider the plight of the Lees, a family with young children who have no alternative housing and would be willing to pay up to $1,500 for an apartment—but are unable to find one. Also consider George, a retiree who lives most of the year in Florida but still has a lease on the New York apartment he moved into 40 years ago. George pays $800 per month for this apartment, but if the rent were even slightly more—say, $850—he would give it up and stay with his children when he is in New York.

This allocation of apartments—George has one and the Lees do not—is a missed opportunity: there is a way to make the Lees and George both better off at no additional cost. The Lees would be happy to pay George, say, $1,200 a month to sublease his apartment, which he would happily accept since the apartment is worth no more than $849 a month to him. George would prefer the money he gets from the Lees to keeping his apartment; the Lees would prefer to have the apartment rather than the money. So both would be made better off by this transaction—and nobody else would be made worse off.

Generally, if people who really want apartments could sublease them from people who are less eager to live there, both those who gain apartments and those who trade their occupancy for money would be better off. However, subletting is illegal under rent control because it would occur at prices above the price ceiling. The fact that subletting is illegal doesn't mean it never happens. In fact, chasing down illegal subletting is a major business for New York private investigators. A 2007 report in the *New York Times* described how private investigators use hidden cameras and other tricks to prove that the legal tenants in rent-controlled apartments actually live in the suburbs, or even in other states, and have sublet their apartments at two or three times the controlled rent. This subletting is a kind of illegal activity, which we will discuss shortly. For now, just notice that the aggressive pursuit of illegal subletting surely discourages the practice, so there isn't enough subletting to eliminate the inefficient allocation of apartments.

Wasted Resources Another reason a price ceiling causes inefficiency is that it leads to **wasted resources**: people expend money, effort, and time to cope with the shortages caused by the price ceiling. Back in 1979, U.S. price controls on gasoline led to shortages that forced millions of Americans to spend hours each week waiting in lines at gas stations. The opportunity cost of the time spent in gas lines—the wages not earned, the leisure time not enjoyed—constituted wasted resources from the point of view of consumers and of the economy as a whole. Because of rent control, the Lees will spend all their spare time for several months searching for an apartment, time they would rather have spent working or engaged in family activities. That is, there is an opportunity cost to the Lees' prolonged search for an apartment—the leisure or income

Price ceilings often lead to inefficiency in the form of **inefficient allocation to consumers**: people who want the good badly and are willing to pay a high price don't get it, and those who care relatively little about the good and are only willing to pay a relatively low price do get it.

Price ceilings typically lead to inefficiency in the form of **wasted resources**: people expend money, effort, and time to cope with the shortages caused by the price ceiling.

they had to forgo. If the market for apartments worked freely, the Lees would quickly find an apartment at the equilibrium rent of $1,000, leaving them time to earn more or to enjoy themselves—an outcome that would make them better off without making anyone else worse off. Again, rent control creates missed opportunities.

Inefficiently Low Quality Yet another way a price ceiling causes inefficiency is by causing goods to be of inefficiently low quality. **Inefficiently low quality** means that sellers offer low-quality goods at a low price even though buyers would rather have higher quality and are willing to pay a higher price for it.

Signs advertising apartments to rent or sublet are common in New York City.

Again, consider rent control. Landlords have no incentive to provide better conditions because they cannot raise rents to cover their repair costs but are able to find tenants easily. In many cases, tenants would be willing to pay much more for improved conditions than it would cost for the landlord to provide them—for example, the upgrade of an antiquated electrical system that cannot safely run air conditioners or computers. But any additional payment for such improvements would be legally considered a rent increase, which is prohibited. Indeed, rent-controlled apartments are notoriously badly maintained, rarely painted, subject to frequent electrical and plumbing problems, sometimes even hazardous to inhabit. As one former manager of Manhattan buildings explained, "At unregulated apartments we'd do most things that the tenants requested. But on the rent-regulated units, we did absolutely only what the law required. . . . We had a perverse incentive to make those tenants unhappy. With regulated apartments, the ultimate objective is to get people out of the building [because rents can be raised for new tenants]."

This whole situation is a missed opportunity—some tenants would be happy to pay for better conditions, and landlords would be happy to provide them for payment. But such an exchange would occur only if the market were allowed to operate freely.

Black Markets And that leads us to a last aspect of price ceilings: the incentive they provide for illegal activities, specifically the emergence of **black markets.** We have already described one kind of black market activity—illegal subletting by tenants. But it does not stop there. Clearly, there is a temptation for a landlord to say to a potential tenant, "Look, you can have the place if you slip me an extra few hundred in cash each month"—and for the tenant to agree, if he or she is one of those people who would be willing to pay much more than the maximum legal rent.

What's wrong with black markets? In general, it's a bad thing if people break *any* law because it encourages disrespect for the law in general. Worse yet, in this case illegal activity worsens the position of those who try to be honest. If the Lees are scrupulous about upholding the rent-control law but other people—who may need an apartment less than the Lees—are willing to bribe landlords, the Lees may *never* find an apartment.

So Why Are There Price Ceilings?

We have seen three common results of price ceilings:

- a persistent shortage of the good
- inefficiency arising from this persistent shortage in the form of inefficiently low quantity, inefficient allocation of the good to consumers, resources wasted in searching for the good, and the inefficiently low quality of the good offered for sale
- the emergence of illegal, black market activity

Given these unpleasant consequences, why do governments still sometimes impose price ceilings? Why does rent control, in particular, persist in New York?

One answer is that although price ceilings may have adverse effects, they do benefit some people. In practice, New York's rent-control rules—which are more complex than our

Price ceilings often lead to inefficiency in that the goods being offered are of **inefficiently low quality:** sellers offer low quality goods at a low price even though buyers would prefer a higher quality at a higher price.

A **black market** is a market in which goods or services are bought and sold illegally— either because it is illegal to sell them at all or because the prices charged are legally prohibited by a price ceiling.

The **minimum wage** is a legal floor on the wage rate, which is the market price of labor.

simple model—hurt most residents but give a small minority of renters much cheaper housing than they would get in an unregulated market. And those who benefit from the controls may be better organized and more vocal than those who are harmed by them.

Also, when price ceilings have been in effect for a long time, buyers may not have a realistic idea of what would happen without them. In our previous example, the rental rate in an unregulated market (Figure 8.1) would be only 25% higher than in the regulated market (Figure 8.2): $1,000 instead of $800. But how would renters know that? Indeed, they might have heard about black market transactions at much higher prices—the Lees or some other family paying George $1,200 or more—and would not realize that these black market prices are much higher than the price that would prevail in a fully unregulated market.

A last answer is that government officials often do not understand supply and demand analysis! It is a great mistake to suppose that economic policies in the real world are always sensible or well informed.

Price Floors

Sometimes governments intervene to push market prices up instead of down. *Price floors* have been widely legislated for agricultural products, such as wheat and milk, as a way to support the incomes of farmers. Historically, there were also price floors on such services as trucking and air travel, although these were phased out by the U.S. government in the 1970s. If you have ever worked in a fast-food restaurant, you are likely to have encountered a price floor: governments in the United States and many other countries maintain a lower limit on the hourly wage rate of a worker's labor—that is, a floor on the price of labor—called the **minimum wage.**

Just like price ceilings, price floors are intended to help some people but generate predictable and undesirable side effects. Figure 8.3 shows hypothetical supply and demand

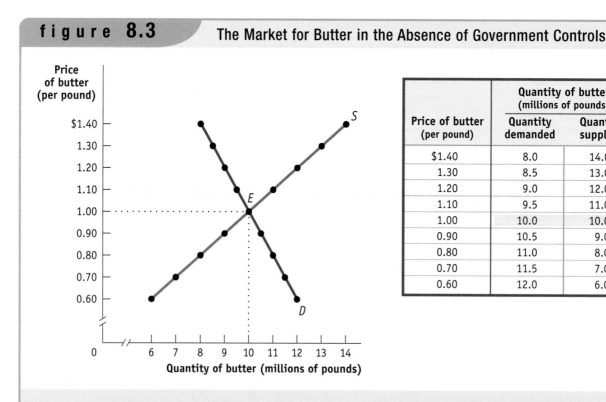

figure 8.3 **The Market for Butter in the Absence of Government Controls**

Price of butter (per pound)	Quantity of butter (millions of pounds)	
	Quantity demanded	Quantity supplied
$1.40	8.0	14.0
1.30	8.5	13.0
1.20	9.0	12.0
1.10	9.5	11.0
1.00	10.0	10.0
0.90	10.5	9.0
0.80	11.0	8.0
0.70	11.5	7.0
0.60	12.0	6.0

Without government intervention, the market for butter reaches equilibrium at a price of $1 per pound with 10 million pounds of butter bought and sold.

curves for butter. Left to itself, the market would move to equilibrium at point *E,* with 10 million pounds of butter bought and sold at a price of $1 per pound.

Now suppose that the government, in order to help dairy farmers, imposes a price floor on butter of $1.20 per pound. Its effects are shown in Figure 8.4, where the line at $1.20 represents the price floor. At a price of $1.20 per pound, producers would want to supply 12 million pounds (point *B* on the supply curve) but consumers would want to buy only 9 million pounds (point *A* on the demand curve). So the price floor leads to a persistent surplus of 3 million pounds of butter.

Does a price floor always lead to an unwanted surplus? No. Just as in the case of a price ceiling, the floor may not be binding—that is, it may be irrelevant. If the equilibrium price of butter is $1 per pound but the floor is set at only $0.80, the floor has no effect.

But suppose that a price floor *is* binding: what happens to the unwanted surplus? The answer depends on government policy. In the case of agricultural price floors, governments buy up unwanted surplus. As a result, the U.S. government has at times found itself warehousing thousands of tons of butter, cheese, and other farm products. (The European Commission, which administers price floors for a number of European countries, once found itself the owner of a so-called butter mountain, equal in weight to the entire population of Austria.) The government then has to find a way to dispose of these unwanted goods.

Some countries pay exporters to sell products at a loss overseas; this is standard procedure for the European Union. The United States gives surplus food away to schools, which use the products in school lunches. In some cases, governments have actually destroyed the surplus production. To avoid the problem of dealing with the unwanted surplus, the U.S. government typically pays farmers not to produce the products at all.

When the government is not prepared to purchase the unwanted surplus, a price floor means that would-be sellers cannot find buyers. This is what happens when there is a price floor on the wage rate paid for an hour of labor, the *minimum wage:* when the minimum wage is above the equilibrium wage rate, some people who are willing to work—that is, sell labor—cannot find buyers—that is, employers—willing to give them jobs.

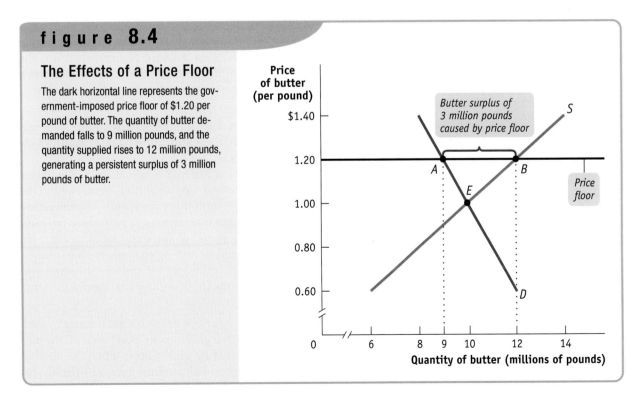

figure 8.4

The Effects of a Price Floor

The dark horizontal line represents the government-imposed price floor of $1.20 per pound of butter. The quantity of butter demanded falls to 9 million pounds, and the quantity supplied rises to 12 million pounds, generating a persistent surplus of 3 million pounds of butter.

Price Floors and School Lunches

When you were in grade school, did your school offer free or very cheap lunches? If so, you were probably a beneficiary of price floors.

Where did all the cheap food come from? During the 1930s, when the U.S. economy was going through the Great Depression, a prolonged economic slump, prices were low and farmers were suffering severely. In an effort to help rural Americans, the U.S. government imposed price floors on a number of agricultural products. The system of agricultural price floors—officially called price support programs—continues to this day. Among the products subject to price support are sugar and various dairy products; at times grains, beef, and pork have also had a minimum price.

The big problem with any attempt to impose a price floor is that it creates a surplus. To some extent the U.S. Department of Agriculture

has tried to head off surpluses by taking steps to reduce supply; for example, by paying farmers *not* to grow crops. As a last resort, however, the U.S. government has been willing to buy up the surplus, taking the excess supply off the market.

But then what? The government has to find a way to get rid of the agricultural products it has bought. It can't just sell them: that would depress market prices, forcing the government to buy the stuff right back. So it has to give it away in ways that don't depress market prices. One of the ways it does this is by giving surplus food, free, to school lunch programs. These gifts are known as "bonus foods." Along with financial aid, bonus foods are what allow many school districts to provide free or very cheap lunches to their students. Is this a story with a happy ending?

istockphoto

Not really. Nutritionists, concerned about growing child obesity in the United States, place part of the blame on those bonus foods. Schools get whatever the government has too much of—and that has tended to include a lot of dairy products, beef, and corn, and not much in the way of fresh vegetables or fruit. As a result, school lunches that make extensive use of bonus foods tend to be very high in fat and calories. So this is a case in which there is such a thing as a free lunch—but this lunch may be bad for your health.

How a Price Floor Causes Inefficiency

The persistent surplus that results from a price floor creates missed opportunities—inefficiencies—that resemble those created by the shortage that results from a price ceiling.

Inefficiently Low Quantity Because a price floor raises the price of a good to consumers, it reduces the quantity of that good demanded; because sellers can't sell more units of a good than buyers are willing to buy, a price floor reduces the quantity of a good bought and sold below the market equilibrium quantity. Notice that this is the *same* effect as a price ceiling. You might be tempted to think that a price floor and a price ceiling have opposite effects, but both have the effect of reducing the quantity of a good bought and sold.

Inefficient Allocation of Sales Among Sellers Like a price ceiling, a price floor can lead to *inefficient allocation*—but in this case **inefficient allocation of sales among sellers** rather than inefficient allocation to consumers.

An episode from the Belgian movie *Rosetta,* a realistic fictional story, illustrates the problem of inefficient allocation of selling opportunities quite well. Like many European countries, Belgium has a high minimum wage, and jobs for young people are scarce. At one point Rosetta, a young woman who is very eager to work, loses her job at a fast-food stand because the owner of the stand replaces her with his son—a very reluctant worker. Rosetta would be willing to work for less money, and with the money he would save, the owner could give his son an allowance and let him do something else. But to hire Rosetta for less than the minimum wage would be illegal.

Wasted Resources Also like a price ceiling, a price floor generates inefficiency by *wasting resources*. The most graphic examples involve government purchases of the unwanted surpluses of agricultural products caused by price floors. When the surplus production is simply destroyed, and when the stored produce goes, as officials euphemistically put it, "out of condition" and must be thrown away, it is pure waste.

Price floors lead to **inefficient allocation of sales among sellers:** those who would be willing to sell the good at the lowest price are not always those who manage to sell it.

Price floors also lead to wasted time and effort. Consider the minimum wage. Would-be workers who spend many hours searching for jobs, or waiting in line in the hope of getting jobs, play the same role in the case of price floors as hapless families searching for apartments in the case of price ceilings.

Inefficiently High Quality Again like price ceilings, price floors lead to inefficiency in the quality of goods produced.

We've seen that when there is a price ceiling, suppliers produce goods that are of inefficiently low quality: buyers prefer higher-quality products and are willing to pay for them, but sellers refuse to improve the quality of their products because the price ceiling prevents their being compensated for doing so. This same logic applies to price floors, but in reverse: suppliers offer goods of **inefficiently high quality.**

Price floors often lead to inefficiency in that goods of **inefficiently high quality** are offered: sellers offer high-quality goods at a high price, even though buyers would prefer a lower quality at a lower price.

How can this be? Isn't high quality a good thing? Yes, but only if it is worth the cost. Suppose that suppliers spend a lot to make goods of very high quality but that this quality isn't worth much to consumers, who would rather receive the money spent on that quality in the form of a lower price. This represents a missed opportunity: suppliers and buyers could make a mutually beneficial deal in which buyers got goods of lower quality for a much lower price.

A good example of the inefficiency of excessive quality comes from the days when transatlantic airfares were set artificially high by international treaty. Forbidden to compete for customers by offering lower ticket prices, airlines instead offered expensive services, like lavish in-flight meals that went largely uneaten. At one point the regulators tried to restrict this practice by defining maximum service standards—for example, that snack service should consist of no more than a sandwich. One airline then introduced what it called a "Scandinavian Sandwich," a towering affair that forced the convening of another conference to define *sandwich*. All of this was wasteful, especially considering that what passengers really wanted was less food and lower airfares.

istockphoto

Since the deregulation of U.S. airlines in the 1970s, American passengers have experienced a large decrease in ticket prices accompanied by a decrease in the quality of in-flight service—smaller seats, lower-quality food, and so on. Everyone complains about the service—but thanks to lower fares, the number of people flying on U.S. carriers has grown several hundred percent since airline deregulation.

Illegal Activity Finally, like price ceilings, price floors provide incentives for illegal activity. For example, in countries where the minimum wage is far above the equilibrium wage rate, workers desperate for jobs sometimes agree to work off the books for employers who conceal their employment from the government—or bribe the government inspectors. This practice, known in Europe as "black labor," is especially common in southern European countries such as Italy and Spain.

So Why Are There Price Floors?

To sum up, a price floor creates various negative side effects:

- a persistent surplus of the good
- inefficiency arising from the persistent surplus in the form of inefficiently low quantity, inefficient allocation of sales among sellers, wasted resources, and an inefficiently high level of quality offered by suppliers
- the temptation to engage in illegal activity, particularly bribery and corruption of government officials

So why do governments impose price floors when they have so many negative side effects? The reasons are similar to those for imposing price ceilings. Government officials often disregard warnings about the consequences of price floors either because they believe that the relevant market is poorly described by the supply and demand model or, more often, because they do not understand the model. Above all, just as price ceilings are often imposed because they benefit some influential buyers of a good, price floors are often imposed because they benefit some influential sellers.

Check Your Understanding

1. On game days, homeowners near Middletown University's stadium used to rent parking spaces in their driveways to fans at a going rate of $11. A new town ordinance now sets a maximum parking fee of $7. Use the accompanying supply and demand diagram to explain how each of the following can result from the price ceiling.

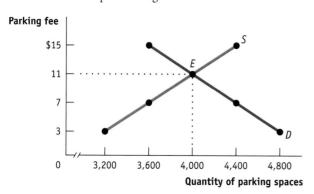

a. Some homeowners now think it's not worth the hassle to rent out spaces.
b. Some fans who used to carpool to the game now drive alone.
c. Some fans can't find parking and leave without seeing the game.

Explain how each of the following adverse effects arises from the price ceiling.

d. Some fans now arrive several hours early to find parking.
e. Friends of homeowners near the stadium regularly attend games, even if they aren't big fans. But some serious fans have given up because of the parking situation.
f. Some homeowners rent spaces for more than $7 but pretend that the buyers are nonpaying friends or family.

2. True or false? Explain your answer. A price ceiling below the equilibrium price in an otherwise efficient market does the following:
a. increases quantity supplied
b. makes some people who want to consume the good worse off
c. makes all producers worse off

3. The state legislature mandates a price floor for gasoline of P_F per gallon. Assess the following statements and illustrate your answer using the figure provided.

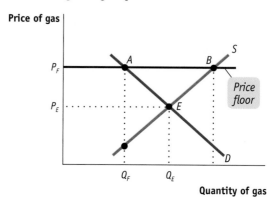

a. Proponents of the law claim it will increase the income of gas station owners. Opponents claim it will hurt gas station owners because they will lose customers.
b. Proponents claim consumers will be better off because gas stations will provide better service. Opponents claim consumers will be generally worse off because they prefer to buy gas at cheaper prices.
c. Proponents claim that they are helping gas station owners without hurting anyone else. Opponents claim that consumers are hurt and will end up doing things like buying gas in a nearby state or on the black market.

Multiple-Choice Questions

1. To be effective, a price ceiling must be set
    I. above the equilibrium price.
    II. in the housing market.
    III. to achieve the equilibrium market quantity.
a. I
b. II
c. III
d. I, II, and III
e. None of the above

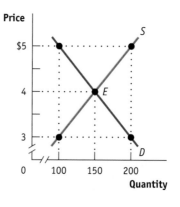

2. Refer to the graph provided. A price floor set at $5 will result in
   a. a shortage of 100 units.
   b. a surplus of 100 units.
   c. a shortage of 200 units.
   d. a surplus of 200 units.
   e. a surplus of 50 units.

3. Effective price ceilings are inefficient because they
   a. create shortages.
   b. lead to wasted resources.
   c. decrease quality.
   d. create black markets.
   e. do all of the above.

4. Refer to the graph provided. If the government establishes a minimum wage at $10, how many workers will benefit from the higher wage?

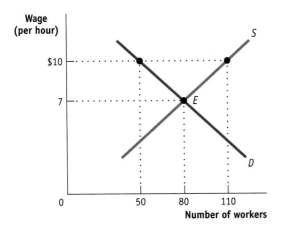

   a. 30
   b. 50
   c. 60
   d. 80
   e. 110

5. Refer to the graph for question 4. With a minimum wage of $10, how many workers are unemployed (would like to work, but are unable to find a job)?
   a. 30
   b. 50
   c. 60
   d. 80
   e. 110

Critical-Thinking Question

Draw a correctly labeled graph of a housing market in equilibrium. On your graph, illustrate an effective legal limit (ceiling) on rent. Identify the quantity of housing demanded, the quantity of housing supplied, and the size of the resulting surplus or shortage.

What you will learn in this Module:

- The meaning of quantity controls, another way government intervenes in markets

- How quantity controls create problems and can make a market inefficient

- Who benefits and who loses from quantity controls, and why they are used despite their well-known problems

Module 9
Supply and Demand: Quantity Controls

Controlling Quantities

In the 1930s, New York City instituted a system of licensing for taxicabs: only taxis with a "medallion" were allowed to pick up passengers. Because this system was intended to ensure quality, medallion owners were supposed to maintain certain standards, including safety and cleanliness. A total of 11,787 medallions were issued, with taxi owners paying $10 for each medallion.

In 1995, there were still only 11,787 licensed taxicabs in New York, even though the city had meanwhile become the financial capital of the world, a place where hundreds of thousands of people in a hurry tried to hail a cab every day. (An additional 400 medallions were issued in 1995, and after several rounds of sales of additional medallions, today there are 13,257 medallions.)

The result of this restriction on the number of taxis was that a New York City taxi medallion became very valuable: if you wanted to operate a taxi in New York, you had to lease a medallion from someone else or buy one for a going price of several hundred thousand dollars.

It turns out that this story is not unique; other cities introduced similar medallion systems in the 1930s and, like New York, have issued few new medallions since. In San Francisco and Boston, as in New York, taxi medallions trade for six-figure prices.

A taxi medallion system is a form of **quantity control,** or **quota,** by which the government regulates the quantity of a good that can be bought and sold rather than regulating the price. Typically, the government limits quantity in a market by issuing **licenses;** only people with a license can legally supply the good. A taxi medallion is just such a license. The government of New York City limits the number of taxi rides that can be sold by limiting the number of taxis to only those who hold medallions. There are many other cases of quantity controls, ranging from limits on how much foreign currency (for instance, British pounds or Mexican pesos) people are allowed to buy to the quantity of clams New Jersey fishing boats are allowed to catch.

A **quantity control,** or **quota,** is an upper limit on the quantity of some good that can be bought or sold.

A **license** gives its owner the right to supply a good or service.

Some attempts to control quantities are undertaken for good economic reasons, some for bad ones. In many cases, as we will see, quantity controls introduced to address a temporary problem become politically hard to remove later because the beneficiaries don't want them abolished, even after the original reason for their existence is long gone. But whatever the reasons for such controls, they have certain predictable—and usually undesirable—economic consequences.

The **demand price** of a given quantity is the price at which consumers will demand that quantity.

The Anatomy of Quantity Controls

To understand why a New York taxi medallion is worth so much money, we consider a simplified version of the market for taxi rides, shown in Figure 9.1. Just as we assumed in the analysis of rent control that all apartments were the same, we now suppose that all taxi rides are the same—ignoring the real-world complication that some taxi rides are longer, and so more expensive, than others. The table in the figure shows supply and demand schedules. The equilibrium—indicated by point *E* in the figure and by the shaded entries in the table—is a fare of $5 per ride, with 10 million rides taken per year. (You'll see in a minute why we present the equilibrium this way.)

The New York medallion system limits the number of taxis, but each taxi driver can offer as many rides as he or she can manage. (Now you know why New York taxi drivers are so aggressive!) To simplify our analysis, however, we will assume that a medallion system limits the number of taxi rides that can legally be given to 8 million per year.

Until now, we have derived the demand curve by answering questions of the form: "How many taxi rides will passengers want to take if the price is $5 per ride?" But it is possible to reverse the question and ask instead: "At what price will consumers want to buy 10 million rides per year?" The price at which consumers want to buy a given quantity—in this case, 10 million rides at $5 per ride—is the **demand price** of that

---

figure 9.1 — The Market for Taxi Rides in the Absence of Government Controls

Fare (per ride)	Quantity of rides (millions per year)	
	Quantity demanded	Quantity supplied
$7.00	6	14
6.50	7	13
6.00	8	12
5.50	9	11
5.00	10	10
4.50	11	9
4.00	12	8
3.50	13	7
3.00	14	6

Without government intervention, the market reaches equilibrium with 10 million rides taken per year at a fare of $5 per ride.

quantity. You can see from the demand schedule in Figure 9.1 that the demand price of 6 million rides is $7 per ride, the demand price of 7 million rides is $6.50 per ride, and so on.

Similarly, the supply curve represents the answer to questions of the form: "How many taxi rides would taxi drivers supply at a price of $5 each?" But we can also reverse this question to ask: "At what price will producers be willing to supply 10 million rides per year?" The price at which producers will supply a given quantity—in this case, 10 million rides at $5 per ride—is the **supply price** of that quantity. We can see from the supply schedule in Figure 9.1 that the supply price of 6 million rides is $3 per ride, the supply price of 7 million rides is $3.50 per ride, and so on.

Now we are ready to analyze a quota. We have assumed that the city government limits the quantity of taxi rides to 8 million per year. Medallions, each of which carries the right to provide a certain number of taxi rides per year, are made available to selected people in such a way that a total of 8 million rides will be provided. Medallion holders may then either drive their own taxis or rent their medallions to others for a fee.

Figure 9.2 shows the resulting market for taxi rides, with the black vertical line at 8 million rides per year representing the quota. Because the quantity of rides is limited to 8 million, consumers must be at point *A* on the demand curve, corresponding to the shaded entry in the demand schedule: the demand price of 8 million rides is $6 per ride. Meanwhile, taxi drivers must be at point *B* on the supply curve, corresponding to the shaded entry in the supply schedule: the supply price of 8 million rides is $4 per ride.

But how can the price received by taxi drivers be $4 when the price paid by taxi riders is $6? The answer is that in addition to the market in taxi rides, there is also a market in medallions. Medallion-holders may not always want to drive their taxis: they

figure 9.2   Effect of a Quota on the Market for Taxi Rides

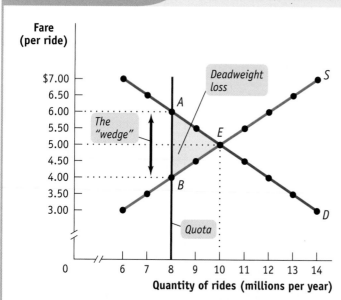

Fare (per ride)	Quantity of rides (millions per year)	
	Quantity demanded	Quantity supplied
$7.00	6	14
6.50	7	13
6.00	8	12
5.50	9	11
5.00	10	10
4.50	11	9
4.00	12	8
3.50	13	7
3.00	14	6

The table shows the demand price and the supply price corresponding to each quantity: the price at which that quantity would be demanded and supplied, respectively. The city government imposes a quota of 8 million rides by selling enough medallions for only 8 million rides, represented by the black vertical line. The price paid by consumers rises to $6 per ride, the demand price of 8 million rides, shown by point *A*. The sup-

ply price of 8 million rides is only $4 per ride, shown by point *B*. The difference between these two prices is the quota rent per ride, the earnings that accrue to the owner of a medallion. The quota rent drives a wedge between the demand price and the supply price. Because the quota discourages mutually beneficial transactions, it creates a deadweight loss equal to the shaded triangle.

may be ill or on vacation. Those who do not want to drive their own taxis will sell the right to use the medallion to someone else. So we need to consider two sets of transactions here, and so two prices: (1) the transactions in taxi rides and the price at which these will occur and (2) the transactions in medallions and the price at which these will occur. It turns out that since we are looking at two markets, the $4 and $6 prices will both be right.

To see how this all works, consider two imaginary New York taxi drivers, Sunil and Harriet. Sunil has a medallion but can't use it because he's recovering from a severely sprained wrist. So he's looking to rent his medallion out to someone else. Harriet doesn't have a medallion but would like to rent one. Furthermore, at any point in time there are many other people like Harriet who would like to rent a medallion. Suppose Sunil agrees to rent his medallion to Harriet. To make things simple, assume that any driver can give only one ride per day and that Sunil is renting his medallion to Harriet for one day. What rental price will they agree on?

To answer this question, we need to look at the transactions from the viewpoints of both drivers. Once she has the medallion, Harriet knows she can make $6 per day—the demand price of a ride under the quota. And she is willing to rent the medallion only if she makes at least $4 per day—the supply price of a ride under the quota. So Sunil cannot demand a rent of more than $2—the difference between $6 and $4. And if Harriet offered Sunil less than $2—say, $1.50—there would be other eager drivers willing to offer him more, up to $2. So, in order to get the medallion, Harriet must offer Sunil at least $2. Since the rent can be no more than $2 and no less than $2, it must be exactly $2.

It is no coincidence that $2 is exactly the difference between $6, the demand price of 8 million rides, and $4, the supply price of 8 million rides. In every case in which the supply of a good is legally restricted, there is a **wedge** between the demand price of the quantity transacted and the supply price of the quantity transacted. This wedge, illustrated by the double-headed arrow in Figure 9.2, has a special name: the **quota rent.** It is the earnings that accrue to the medallion holder from ownership of a valuable commodity, the medallion. In the case of Sunil and Harriet, the quota rent of $2 goes to Sunil because he owns the medallion, and the remaining $4 from the total fare of $6 goes to Harriet.

So Figure 9.2 also illustrates the quota rent in the market for New York taxi rides. The quota limits the quantity of rides to 8 million per year, a quantity at which the demand price of $6 exceeds the supply price of $4. The wedge between these two prices, $2, is the quota rent that results from the restrictions placed on the quantity of taxi rides in this market.

But wait a second. What if Sunil doesn't rent out his medallion? What if he uses it himself? Doesn't this mean that he gets a price of $6? No, not really. Even if Sunil doesn't rent out his medallion, he could have rented it out, which means that the medallion has an *opportunity cost* of $2: if Sunil decides to use his own medallion and drive his own taxi rather than renting his medallion to Harriet, the $2 represents his opportunity cost of not renting out his medallion. That is, the $2 quota rent is now the rental income he forgoes by driving his own taxi. In effect, Sunil is in two businesses—the taxi-driving business and the medallion-renting business. He makes $4 per ride from driving his taxi and $2 per ride from renting out his medallion. It doesn't make any difference that in this particular case he has rented his medallion to himself! So regardless of whether the medallion owner uses the medallion himself or herself, or rents it to others, it is a valuable asset. And this is represented in the going price for a New York City taxi medallion. Notice, by the way, that quotas—like price ceilings and price floors—don't always have a real effect. If the quota were set at 12 million rides—that is, above the equilibrium quantity in an unregulated market—it would have no effect because it would not be binding.

A quantity control, or quota, drives a **wedge** between the demand price and the supply price of a good; that is, the price paid by buyers ends up being higher than that received by sellers. The difference between the demand and supply price at the quota amount is the **quota rent,** the earnings that accrue to the license-holder from ownership of the right to sell the good. It is equal to the market price of the license when the licenses are traded.

PNI Ltd./Picture Quest

New York City: An empty cab is hard to find.

The Costs of Quantity Controls

Like price controls, quantity controls can have some predictable and undesirable side effects. The first is the by-now-familiar problem of inefficiency due to missed opportunities: quantity controls prevent mutually beneficial transactions from occurring, transactions that would benefit both buyers and sellers. Looking back at Figure 9.2, you can see that starting at the quota of 8 million rides, New Yorkers would be willing to pay at least $5.50 per ride for an additional 1 million rides and that taxi drivers would be willing to provide those rides as long as they got at least $4.50 per ride. These are rides that would have taken place if there had been no quota. The same is true for the next 1 million rides: New Yorkers would be willing to pay at least $5 per ride when the quantity of rides is increased from 9 to 10 million, and taxi drivers would be willing to provide those rides as long as they got at least $5 per ride. Again, these rides would have occurred without the quota. Only when the market has reached the unregulated market equilibrium quantity of 10 million rides are there no "missed-opportunity rides"—the quota of 8 million rides has caused 2 million "missed-opportunity rides." A buyer would be willing to buy the good at a price that the seller would be willing to accept, but such a transaction does not occur because it is forbidden by the quota. Economists have a special term for the lost gains from missed opportunities such as these: **deadweight loss.** Generally, when the demand price exceeds the supply price, there is a deadweight loss. Figure 9.2 illustrates the deadweight loss with a shaded triangle between the demand and supply curves. This triangle represents the missed gains from taxi rides prevented by the quota, a loss that is experienced by both disappointed would-be riders and frustrated would-be drivers.

Because there are transactions that people would like to make but are not allowed to, quantity controls generate an incentive to evade them or even to break the law. New York's taxi industry again provides clear examples. Taxi regulation applies only to those drivers who are hailed by passengers on the street. A car service that makes prearranged pickups does not need a medallion. As a result, such hired cars provide much of the service that might otherwise be provided by taxis, as in other cities. In addition, there are substantial numbers of unlicensed cabs that simply defy the law by picking up passengers without a medallion. Because these cabs are illegal, their drivers are completely unregulated, and they generate a disproportionately large share of traffic accidents in New York City.

in real life

The Clams of New Jersey

Forget the refineries along the Jersey Turnpike; one industry that New Jersey *really* dominates is clam fishing. In 2005 the Garden State supplied 71% of the country's surf clams, whose tongues are used in fried-clam dinners, and 92% of the quahogs, which are used to make clam chowder.

In the 1980s, however, excessive fishing threatened to wipe out New Jersey's clam beds. To save the resource, the U.S. government introduced a clam quota, which sets an overall limit on the number of bushels of clams that may be caught and allocates licenses to owners of fishing boats based on their historical catches.

istockphoto

A fried clam feast is a favorite on the Jersey shore.

Notice, by the way, that this is an example of a quota that is probably justified by broader economic and environmental considerations—

unlike the New York taxicab quota, which has long since lost any economic rationale. Still, whatever its rationale, the New Jersey clam quota works the same way as any other quota.

Once the quota system was established, many boat owners stopped fishing for clams. They realized that rather than operate a boat part time, it was more profitable to sell or rent their licenses to someone else, who could then assemble enough licenses to operate a boat full time. Today, there are about 50 New Jersey boats fishing for clams; the license required to operate one is worth more than the boat itself.

In fact, in 2004 the hardships caused by the limited number of New York taxis led city leaders to authorize an increase in the number of licensed taxis. In a series of sales, the city sold more than 1,000 new medallions, to bring the total number up to the current 13,257 medallions—a move that certainly cheered New York riders. But those who already owned medallions were less happy with the increase; they understood that the nearly 1,000 new taxis would reduce or eliminate the shortage of taxis. As a result, taxi drivers anticipated a decline in their revenues as they would no longer always be assured of finding willing customers. And, in turn, the value of a medallion would fall. So to placate the medallion owners, city officials also raised taxi fares: by 25% in 2004, and again—by a smaller percentage—in 2006. Although taxis are now easier to find, a ride now costs more—and that price increase slightly diminished the newfound cheer of New York taxi riders.

Module 9 Review

Solutions appear at the back of the book.

Check Your Understanding

1. Suppose that the supply and demand for taxi rides is given by Figure 9.1 and a quota is set at 6 million rides. Replicate the graph from Figure 9.1, and identify each of the following on your graph:
   a. the price of a ride
   b. the quota rent
   c. the deadweight loss resulting from the quota

Suppose the quota on taxi rides is increased to 9 million.
   d. What happens to the quota rent and the deadweight loss?

2. Again replicate the graph from Figure 9.1. Suppose that the quota is 8 million rides and that demand decreases due to a decline in tourism. Show on your graph the smallest parallel leftward shift in demand that would result in the quota no longer having an effect on the market.

Multiple-Choice Questions

Refer to the graph provided for questions 1–3.

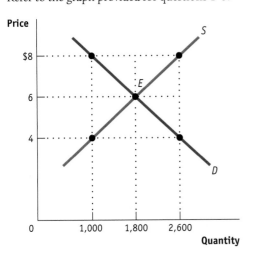

1. If the government established a quota of 1,000 in this market, the demand price would be
   a. less than $4.
   b. $4.
   c. $6.
   d. $8.
   e. more than $8.

2. If the government established a quota of 1,000 in this market, the supply price would be
   a. less than $4.
   b. $4.
   c. $6.
   d. $8.
   e. more than $8.

3. If the government established a quota of 1,000 in this market, the quota rent would be
   a. $2.
   b. $4.
   c. $6.
   d. $8.
   e. more than $8.

4. Quotas lead to which of the following?
   I. inefficiency due to missed opportunities
   II. incentives to evade or break the law
   III. a surplus in the market
   a. I
   b. II
   c. III
   d. I and II
   e. I, II, and III

5. Which of the following would decrease the effect of a quota on a market? A(n)
   a. decrease in demand
   b. increase in supply
   c. increase in demand
   d. price ceiling above the equilibrium price
   e. none of the above

Critical-Thinking Question

Draw a correctly labeled graph of the market for taxicab rides. On the graph, draw and label a vertical line showing the level of an effective quota. Label the demand price, the supply price, and the quota rent.

Section (2) Review

Summary

Introduction and Demand

1. The **supply and demand model** illustrates how a **competitive market,** one with many buyers and sellers of the same product, works.

2. The **demand schedule** shows the **quantity demanded** at each price and is represented graphically by a **demand curve.** The **law of demand** says that demand curves slope downward, meaning that as price decreases, the quantity demanded increases.

3. A **movement along the demand curve** occurs when the price changes and causes a change in the quantity demanded. When economists talk of **changes in demand,** they mean shifts of the demand curve—a change in the quantity demanded at any given price. An increase in demand causes a rightward shift of the demand curve. A decrease in demand causes a leftward shift.

4. There are five main factors that shift the demand curve:

- A change in the prices of related goods, such as **substitutes** or **complements**
- A change in income: when income rises, the demand for **normal goods** increases and the demand for **inferior goods** decreases
- A change in tastes
- A change in expectations
- A change in the number of consumers

Supply and Equilibrium

5. The **supply schedule** shows the **quantity supplied** at each price and is represented graphically by a **supply curve.** Supply curves usually slope upward.

6. A **movement along the supply curve** occurs when the price changes and causes a change in the quantity supplied. When economists talk of **changes in supply,** they mean shifts of the supply curve—a change in the quantity supplied at any given price. An increase in supply causes a rightward shift of the supply curve. A decrease in supply causes a leftward shift.

7. There are five main factors that shift the supply curve:

- A change in **input** prices
- A change in the prices of related goods and services
- A change in technology
- A change in expectations
- A change in the number of producers

8. The supply and demand model is based on the principle that the price in a market moves to its **equilibrium price,** or **market-clearing price,** the price at which the quantity demanded is equal to the quantity supplied. This quantity is the **equilibrium quantity.** When the price is above its market-clearing level, there is a **surplus** that pushes the price down. When the price is below its market-clearing level, there is a **shortage** that pushes the price up.

Changes in Equilibrium

9. An increase in demand increases both the equilibrium price and the equilibrium quantity; a decrease in demand has the opposite effect. An increase in supply reduces the equilibrium price and increases the equilibrium quantity; a decrease in supply has the opposite effect.

10. Shifts of the demand curve and the supply curve can happen simultaneously. When they shift in opposite directions, the change in price is predictable but the change in quantity is not. When they shift in the same direction, the change in quantity is predictable but the change in price is not. In general, the curve that shifts the greater distance has a greater effect on the changes in price and quantity.

Price Controls: Ceilings and Floors

11. Even when a market is efficient, governments often intervene to pursue greater fairness or to please a powerful interest group. Interventions can take the form of **price controls** or **quantity controls,** both of which generate predictable and undesirable side effects, consisting of various forms of inefficiency and illegal activity.

12. A **price ceiling,** a maximum market price below the equilibrium price, benefits successful buyers but creates persistent shortages. Because the price is maintained below the equilibrium price, the quantity demanded is increased and the quantity supplied is decreased compared to the equilibrium quantity. This leads to predictable problems including **inefficient allocation to consumers, wasted resources,** and **inefficiently low quality.** It also encourages illegal activity as people turn to **black markets** to get the good. Because of these problems, price ceilings have generally lost favor as an economic policy tool. But some governments continue to impose them either because they don't understand the effects or because the price ceilings benefit some influential group.

13. A **price floor,** a minimum market price above the equilibrium price, benefits successful sellers but creates a persistent surplus: because the price is maintained above the equilibrium price, the quantity demanded is decreased and the quantity supplied is increased compared to the equilibrium quantity. This leads to predictable problems: inefficiencies in the form of **inefficient allocation of sales among sellers,** wasted resources, and **inefficiently high quality.** It also encourages illegal activity and black markets. The most well known kind of price floor is the **minimum wage,** but price floors are also commonly applied to agricultural products.

Quantity Controls

14. Quantity controls, or **quotas,** limit the quantity of a good that can be bought or sold. The government issues **licenses** to individuals, the right to sell a given quantity of the good. The owner of a license earns a **quota rent,** earnings that accrue from ownership of the right to sell the good. It is equal to the difference between the **demand price** at the quota amount, what consumers are willing to pay for that amount, and the **supply price** at the quota amount, what suppliers are willing to accept for that amount. Economists say that a quota drives a **wedge** between the demand price and the supply price; this wedge is equal to the quota rent. By limiting mutually beneficial transactions, quantity controls generate inefficiency. Like price controls, quantity controls lead to **deadweight loss** and encourage illegal activity.

Key Terms

Competitive market, p. 48
Supply and demand model, p. 48
Demand schedule, p. 49
Quantity demanded, p. 49
Demand curve, p. 49
Law of demand, p. 50
Change in demand, p. 51
Movement along the demand curve, p. 51
Substitutes, p. 53
Complements, p. 53
Normal good, p. 53
Inferior good, p. 54
Individual demand curve, p. 55
Quantity supplied, p. 59
Supply schedule, p. 59

Supply curve, p. 59
Law of supply, p. 60
Change in supply, p. 60
Movement along the supply curve, p. 60
Input, p. 62
Individual supply curve, p. 63
Equilibrium, p. 66
Equilibrium price, p. 66
Market-clearing price, p. 66
Equilibrium quantity, p. 66
Surplus, p. 68
Shortage, p. 68
Price controls, p. 77
Price ceiling, p. 77
Price floor, p. 77

Inefficient allocation to consumers, p. 80
Wasted resources, p. 80
Inefficiently low quality, p. 81
Black markets, p. 81
Minimum wage, p. 82
Inefficient allocation of sales among sellers, p. 84
Inefficiently high quality, p. 85
Quantity control or quota, p. 88
License, p. 88
Demand price, p. 89
Supply price, p. 90
Wedge, p. 91
Quota rent, p. 91
Deadweight loss, p. 92

Problems

1. A survey indicated that chocolate ice cream is America's favorite ice-cream flavor. For each of the following, indicate the possible effects on the demand and/or supply, equilibrium price, and equilibrium quantity of chocolate ice cream.

   a. A severe drought in the Midwest causes dairy farmers to reduce the number of milk-producing cows in their herds by a third. These dairy farmers supply cream that is used to manufacture chocolate ice cream.

   b. A new report by the American Medical Association reveals that chocolate does, in fact, have significant health benefits.

   c. The discovery of cheaper synthetic vanilla flavoring lowers the price of vanilla ice cream.

   d. New technology for mixing and freezing ice cream lowers manufacturers' costs of producing chocolate ice cream.

2. In a supply and demand diagram, draw the change in demand for hamburgers in your hometown due to the following events. In each case show the effect on equilibrium price and quantity.

   a. The price of tacos increases.

   b. All hamburger sellers raise the price of their french fries.

   c. Income falls in town. Assume that hamburgers are a normal good for most people.

   d. Income falls in town. Assume that hamburgers are an inferior good for most people.

   e. Hot dog stands cut the price of hot dogs.

3. The market for many goods changes in predictable ways according to the time of year, in response to events such as holidays, vacation times, seasonal changes in production, and so on. Using supply and demand, explain the change in price in each of the following cases. Note that supply and demand may shift simultaneously.

   a. Lobster prices usually fall during the summer peak harvest season, despite the fact that people like to eat lobster during the summer months more than during any other time of year.

   b. The price of a Christmas tree is lower after Christmas than before and fewer trees are sold.

   c. The price of a round-trip ticket to Paris on Air France falls by more than $200 after the end of school vacation in September. This happens despite the fact that generally worsening weather increases the cost of operating flights to Paris, and Air France therefore reduces the number of flights to Paris at any given price.

4. Show in a diagram the effect on the demand curve, the supply curve, the equilibrium price, and the equilibrium quantity of each of the following events on the designated market.

   a. the market for newspapers in your town
      Case 1: The salaries of journalists go up.
      Case 2: There is a big news event in your town, which is reported in the newspapers, and residents want to learn more about it.

   b. the market for St. Louis Rams cotton T-shirts
      Case 1: The Rams win the national championship.
      Case 2: The price of cotton increases.

   c. the market for bagels
      Case 1: People realize how fattening bagels are.
      Case 2: People have less time to make themselves a cooked breakfast.

5. Find the flaws in reasoning in the following statements, paying particular attention to the distinction between changes in and movements along the supply and demand curves. Draw a diagram to illustrate what actually happens in each situation.

   a. "A technological innovation that lowers the cost of producing a good might seem at first to result in a reduction in the price of the good to consumers. But a fall in price will increase demand for the good, and higher demand will send the price up again. It is not certain, therefore, that an innovation will really reduce price in the end."

b. "A study shows that eating a clove of garlic a day can help prevent heart disease, causing many consumers to demand more garlic. This increase in demand results in a rise in the price of garlic. Consumers, seeing that the price of garlic has gone up, reduce their demand for garlic. This causes the demand for garlic to decrease and the price of garlic to fall. Therefore, the ultimate effect of the study on the price of garlic is uncertain."

6. In *Rolling Stone* magazine, several fans and rock stars, including Pearl Jam, were bemoaning the high price of concert tickets. One superstar argued, "It just isn't worth $75 to see me play. No one should have to pay that much to go to a concert." Assume this star sold out arenas around the country at an average ticket price of $75.

   a. How would you evaluate the arguments that ticket prices are too high?

   b. Suppose that due to this star's protests, ticket prices were lowered to $50. In what sense is this price too low? Draw a diagram using supply and demand curves to support your argument.

   c. Suppose Pearl Jam really wanted to bring down ticket prices. Since the band controls the supply of its services, what do you recommend they do? Explain using a supply and demand diagram.

   d. Suppose the band's next CD was a total dud. Do you think they would still have to worry about ticket prices being too high? Why or why not? Draw a supply and demand diagram to support your argument.

   e. Suppose the group announced their next tour was going to be their last. What effect would this likely have on the demand for and price of tickets? Illustrate with a supply and demand diagram.

7. After several years of decline, the market for handmade acoustic guitars is making a comeback. These guitars are usually made in small workshops employing relatively few highly skilled luthiers. Assess the impact on the equilibrium price and quantity of handmade acoustic guitars as a result of each of the following events. In your answers, indicate which curve(s) shift(s) and in which direction.

   a. Environmentalists succeed in having the use of Brazilian rosewood banned in the United States, forcing luthiers to seek out alternative, more costly woods.

   b. A foreign producer reengineers the guitar-making process and floods the market with identical guitars.

   c. Music featuring handmade acoustic guitars makes a comeback as audiences tire of heavy metal and grunge music.

   d. The country goes into a deep recession and the income of the average American falls sharply.

8. Will Shakespeare is a struggling playwright in sixteenth-century London. As the price he receives for writing a play increases, he is willing to write more plays. For the following situations, use a diagram to illustrate how each event affects the equilibrium price and quantity in the market for Shakespeare's plays.

   a. The playwright Christopher Marlowe, Shakespeare's chief rival, is killed in a bar brawl.

   b. The bubonic plague, a deadly infectious disease, breaks out in London.

   c. To celebrate the defeat of the Spanish Armada, Queen Elizabeth declares several weeks of festivities, which involves commissioning new plays.

9. The small town of Middling experiences a sudden doubling of the birth rate. After three years, the birth rate returns to normal. Use a diagram to illustrate the effect of these events on the following:

   a. the market for an hour of babysitting services in Middling today

   b. the market for an hour of babysitting services 14 years into the future, after the birth rate has returned to normal, by which time children born today are old enough to work as babysitters

   c. the market for an hour of babysitting services 30 years into the future, when children born today are likely to be having children of their own

10. Use a diagram to illustrate how each of the following events affects the equilibrium price and quantity of pizza.

    a. The price of mozzarella cheese rises.

    b. The health hazards of hamburgers are widely publicized.

    c. The price of tomato sauce falls.

    d. The incomes of consumers rise and pizza is an inferior good.

    e. Consumers expect the price of pizza to fall next week.

11. Although he was a prolific artist, Pablo Picasso painted only 1,000 canvases during his "Blue Period." Picasso is now dead, and all of his Blue Period works are currently on display in museums and private galleries throughout Europe and the United States.

    a. Draw a supply curve for Picasso Blue Period works. Why is this supply curve different from ones you have seen?

    b. Given the supply curve from part a, the price of a Picasso Blue Period work will be entirely dependent on what factor(s)? Draw a diagram showing how the equilibrium price of such a work is determined.

    c. Suppose that rich art collectors decide that it is essential to acquire Picasso Blue Period art for their collections. Show the impact of this on the market for these paintings.

12. Draw the appropriate curve in each of the following cases. Is it like or unlike the curves you have seen so far? Explain.

    a. the demand for cardiac bypass surgery, given that the government pays the full cost for any patient

    b. the demand for elective cosmetic plastic surgery, given that the patient pays the full cost

    c. the supply of Rembrandt paintings

    d. the supply of reproductions of Rembrandt paintings

13. Suppose it is decided that rent control in New York City will be abolished and that market rents will now prevail. Assume that all rental units are identical and are therefore offered at the same rent. To address the plight of residents who may be unable to pay the market rent, an income supplement will be paid to all low-income households equal to the difference between the old controlled rent and the new market rent.

    a. Use a diagram to show the effect on the rental market of the elimination of rent control. What will happen to the quality and quantity of rental housing supplied?

b. Now use a second diagram to show the additional effect of the income-supplement policy on the market. What effect does it have on the market rent and quantity of rental housing supplied in comparison to your answers to part a?

c. Are tenants better or worse off as a result of these policies? Are landlords better or worse off?

d. From a political standpoint, why do you think cities have been more likely to resort to rent control rather than a policy of income supplements to help low-income people pay for housing?

14. In the late eighteenth century, the price of bread in New York City was controlled, set at a predetermined price above the market price.

a. Draw a diagram showing the effect of the policy. Did the policy act as a price ceiling or a price floor?

b. What kinds of inefficiencies were likely to have arisen when the controlled price of bread was above the market price? Explain in detail.

One year during this period, a poor wheat harvest caused a leftward shift in the supply of bread and therefore an increase in its market price. New York bakers found that the controlled price of bread in New York was below the market price.

c. Draw a diagram showing the effect of the price control on the market for bread during this one-year period. Did the policy act as a price ceiling or a price floor?

d. What kinds of inefficiencies do you think occurred during this period? Explain in detail.

15. Suppose the U.S. government decides that the incomes of dairy farmers should be maintained at a level that allows the traditional family dairy farm to survive. It therefore implements a price floor of $1 per pint by buying surplus milk until the market price is $1 per pint. Use the accompanying diagram to answer the following questions.

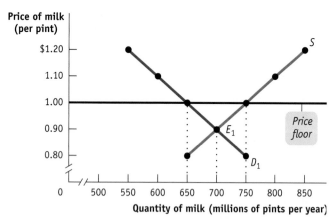

a. How much surplus milk will be produced as a result of this policy?

b. What will be the cost to the government of this policy?

c. Since milk is an important source of protein and calcium, the government decides to provide the surplus milk it purchases to elementary schools at a price of only $0.60 per pint. Assume that schools will buy any amount of milk available at this low price. But parents now reduce their purchases of milk at any price by 50 million pints per year because they

know their children are getting milk at school. How much will the dairy program now cost the government?

d. Give two examples of inefficiencies arising from wasted resources that are likely to result from this policy. What is the missed opportunity in each case?

16. As noted in the text, European governments tend to make greater use of price controls than does the U.S. government. For example, the French government sets minimum starting yearly wages for new hires who have completed *le bac*, certification roughly equivalent to a high school diploma. The demand schedule for new hires with *le bac* and the supply schedule for similarly credentialed new job seekers are given in the accompanying table. The price here—given in euros, the currency used in France—is the same as the yearly wage.

Wage (per year)	Quantity demanded (new job offers per year)	Quantity supplied (new job seekers per year)
€45,000	200,000	325,000
40,000	220,000	320,000
35,000	250,000	310,000
30,000	290,000	290,000
25,000	370,000	200,000

a. In the absence of government interference, what is the equilibrium wage and number of graduates hired per year? Illustrate with a diagram. Will there be anyone seeking a job at the equilibrium wage who is unable to find one—that is, will there be anyone who is involuntarily unemployed?

b. Suppose the French government sets a minimum yearly wage of 35,000 euros. Is there any involuntary unemployment at this wage? If so, how much? Illustrate with a diagram. What if the minimum wage is set at 40,000 euros? Also illustrate with a diagram.

c. Given your answer to part b and the information in the table, what do you think is the relationship between the level of involuntary unemployment and the level of the minimum wage? Who benefits from such a policy? Who loses? What is the missed opportunity here?

17. Until recently, the standard number of hours worked per week for a full-time job in France was 39 hours, similar to in the United States. But in response to social unrest over high levels of involuntary unemployment, the French government instituted a 35-hour workweek—a worker could not work more than 35 hours per week even if both the worker and employer wanted it. The motivation behind this policy was that if current employees worked fewer hours, employers would be forced to hire new workers. Assume that it is costly for employers to train new workers. French employers were greatly opposed to this policy and threatened to move their operations to neighboring countries that did not have such employment restrictions. Can you explain their attitude? Give an example of both an inefficiency and an illegal activity that are likely to arise from this policy.

18. For the last 70 years, the U.S. government has used price supports to provide income assistance to U.S. farmers. At times the government has used price floors, which it maintains by buying up the surplus farm products. At other times, it has used target prices, giving the farmer an amount equal to the difference between the market price and the target price for each unit sold. Use the accompanying diagram to answer the following questions.

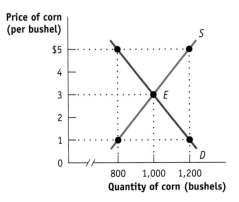

a. If the government sets a price floor of $5 per bushel, how many bushels of corn are produced? How many are purchased by consumers? by the government? How much does the program cost the government? How much revenue do corn farmers receive?

b. Suppose the government sets a target price of $5 per bushel for any quantity supplied up to 1,000 bushels. How many bushels of corn are purchased by consumers and at what price? by the government? How much does the program cost the government? How much revenue do corn farmers receive?

c. Which of these programs (in parts a and b) costs corn consumers more? Which program costs the government more? Explain.

d. What are the inefficiencies that arise in each of these cases (parts a and b)?

19. The waters off the north Atlantic coast were once teeming with fish. Now, due to overfishing by the commercial fishing industry, the stocks of fish are seriously depleted. In 1991, the National Marine Fishery Service of the U.S. government implemented a quota to allow fish stocks to recover. The quota limited the amount of swordfish caught per year by all U.S.-licensed fishing boats to 7 million pounds. As soon as the U.S. fishing fleet had met the quota, the swordfish catch was closed down for the rest of the year. The accompanying table gives the hypothetical demand and supply schedules for swordfish caught in the United States per year.

Price of swordfish (per pound)	Quantity of swordfish (millions of pounds per year)	
	Quantity demanded	Quantity supplied
$20	6	15
18	7	13
16	8	11
14	9	9
12	10	7

a. Use a diagram to show the effect of the quota on the market for swordfish in 1991.

b. How do you think fishermen will change how they fish in response to this policy?

Behind the Demand Curve: Consumer Choice

Panic was the only word to describe the situation at hospitals, clinics, and nursing homes across America in October 2004. Early that month, Chiron Corporation, one of only two suppliers of flu vaccine for the entire U.S. market, announced that contamination problems would force the closure of its manufacturing plant. With that closure, the U.S. supply of vaccine for the 2004–2005 flu season was suddenly cut in half, from 100 million to 50 million doses. Because making flu vaccine is a costly and time-consuming process, no more doses could be made to replace Chiron's lost output. And since every country jealously guards its supply of flu vaccine for its own citizens, none could be obtained from other countries.

If you've ever had a real case of the flu, you know just how unpleasant an experience it is. And it can be worse than unpleasant: every year the flu kills around 36,000 Americans and sends another 200,000 to the hospital. Victims are most commonly children, seniors, or those with compromised immune systems. In a normal flu season, this part of the population, along with health care workers, are immunized first.

But the flu vaccine shortfall of 2004 upended those plans. As news of it spread, there was a rush to get the shots. People lined up in the middle of the night at the few locations that had somehow obtained the vaccine and were offering it at a reasonable price: the crowds included seniors with oxygen tanks, parents with sleeping children, and others in wheelchairs. Meanwhile, some pharmaceutical distributors—the companies that obtain vaccine from manufacturers and then distribute it to hospitals and pharmacies—detected a profit-making opportunity in the frenzy. One company, Med-Stat, which normally charged $8.50 for a dose, began charging $90, more than 10 times the normal price.

A survey of pharmacists found that price-gouging was fairly widespread.

Although many people refused or were unable to pay such a high price for the vaccine, many others undoubtedly did. Med-Stat judged, correctly, that consumers of the vaccine were relatively *unresponsive* to price; that is, the large increase in the price of the vaccine left the quantity demanded by consumers relatively unchanged.

Clearly, the demand for flu vaccine is unusual in this respect. For many, getting vaccinated meant the difference between life and death. Let's consider a very different and less urgent scenario. Suppose, for example, that the supply of a particular type of breakfast cereal was halved due to manufacturing problems. It would be extremely unlikely, if not impossible, to find a consumer willing to pay 10 times the original price for a box of this particular cereal. In other words, consumers of breakfast cereal are much more responsive to price than consumers of flu vaccine. But how do we define *responsiveness*? Economists measure consumers' responsiveness to price with a particular number, called the *price elasticity of demand*.

In this section we take a closer look at the supply and demand model developed early in this book and present several economic concepts used to evaluate market results. We will see how the price elasticity of demand is calculated and why it is the best measure of how the quantity demanded responds to changes in price. We will then discover that the price elasticity of demand is only one of a family of related concepts, including the *income elasticity of demand* and the *price elasticity of supply*. We will look at how the price and the quantity bought and sold in a market affect consumer, producer, and overall welfare. And we will consider how consumers make choices to maximize their individual *utility*, the term economists use to describe "satisfaction."

AP Photo/Will Kincaid

Because consumers are relatively unresponsive to the price of flu vaccine, the price depends largely on availability.

101

© Joe Belanger/Alamy

What you will learn in this Module:

- How the income and substitution effects explain the law of demand

- The definition of elasticity, a measure of responsiveness to changes in prices or incomes

- The importance of the price elasticity of demand, which measures the responsiveness of the quantity demanded to changes in price

- How to calculate the price elasticity of demand

Module 10
Income Effects, Substitution Effects, and Elasticity

Explaining the Law of Demand

We introduced the demand curve and the law of demand in the earlier section on supply and demand. To this point, we have accepted that the demand curve has a negative slope. And we have drawn demand curves that are somewhere in the middle between flat and steep (with a negative slope). In this module, we present more detail about why demand curves slope downward and what the slope of the demand curve tells us. We begin with the *income* and *substitution effects,* which explain why the demand curve has a negative slope.

The Substitution Effect

When the price of a good increases, an individual will normally consume less of that good and more of other goods. Correspondingly, when the price of a good decreases, an individual will normally consume more of that good and less of other goods. This explains why the individual demand curve, which relates an individual's consumption of a good to the price of that good, normally slopes downward—that is, it obeys the law of demand.

An alternative way to think about why demand curves slope downward is to focus on opportunity costs. For simplicity, let's suppose there are only two goods between which to choose. When the price of one good decreases, an individual doesn't have to give up as many units of the other good in order to buy one more unit of the first good. That makes it attractive to buy more of the good whose price has gone down. Conversely, when the price of one good increases, one must give up more units of the other good to buy one more unit of the first good, so consuming that good becomes less attractive and the consumer buys fewer. The change in the quantity demanded as the good that has become relatively cheaper is substituted for the good that has become relatively more expensive is known as the **substitution effect.** When a good absorbs only a small share of the typical consumer's income, as with pillow cases and swim

The **substitution effect** of a change in the price of a good is the change in the quantity of that good demanded as the consumer substitutes the good that has become relatively cheaper for the good that has become relatively more expensive.

goggles, the substitution effect is essentially the sole explanation of why the market demand curve slopes downward. There are, however, some goods, like food and housing, that account for a substantial share of many consumers' incomes. In such cases another effect, called the *income effect,* also comes into play.

The Income Effect

Consider the case of a family that spends half of its income on rental housing. Now suppose that the price of housing increases everywhere. This will have a substitution effect on the family's demand: other things equal, the family will have an incentive to consume less housing—say, by moving to a smaller apartment—and more of other goods. But the family will also, in a real sense, be made poorer by that higher housing price—its income will buy less housing than before. When income is adjusted to reflect its true purchasing power, it is called *real income,* in contrast to *money income* or *nominal income,* which has not been adjusted. And this reduction in a consumer's real income will have an additional effect, beyond the substitution effect, on the family's consumption choices, including its consumption of housing. The **income effect** is the change in the quantity of a good demanded that results from a change in the overall purchasing power of the consumer's income due to a change in the price of that good.

It's possible to give more precise definitions of the substitution effect and the income effect of a price change, but for most purposes, there are only two things you need to know about the distinction between these two effects.

First, for the majority of goods and services, the income effect is not important and has no significant effect on individual consumption. Thus, most market demand curves slope downward solely because of the substitution effect—end of story.

Second, when it matters at all, the income effect usually reinforces the substitution effect. That is, when the price of a good that absorbs a substantial share of income rises, consumers of that good become a bit poorer because their purchasing power falls. And the vast majority of goods are *normal* goods, goods for which demand decreases when income falls. So this effective reduction in income leads to a reduction in the quantity demanded and reinforces the substitution effect.

The **income effect** of a change in the price of a good is the change in the quantity of that good demanded that results from a change in the consumer's purchasing power when the price of the good changes.

---

in real life

Giffen Goods

Two hundred years ago, when Ireland was under British rule and desperately poor, it was claimed that the Irish would eat *more* potatoes when the price of potatoes went up. That is, some observers claimed that Ireland's demand curve for potatoes sloped upward, not downward.

Can this happen? In theory, yes. If Irish demand for potatoes actually sloped upward, it would have been a real-life case of a "Giffen good," named after a nineteenth-century statistician who thought (probably wrongly) that he saw an upward-sloping demand curve in some data he was studying.

Here's the story. Suppose that there is some good that absorbs a large share of consumers'

budgets and that this good is also *inferior*—people demand less of it when their income rises. The classic supposed example was, as you might guess, potatoes in Ireland, back when potatoes were an inferior good—they were what poor people ate—and when the Irish were very poor.

Now suppose that the price of potatoes increases. This would, *other things equal,* cause people to substitute other goods for potatoes. But other things are not equal: given the higher price of potatoes, people are poorer. And this *increases* the demand for potatoes, because potatoes are an inferior good.

If this income effect outweighs the substitution effect, a rise in the price of potatoes would

increase the quantity demanded; the law of demand would not hold.

In a way the point of this story—which has never been validated in any real situation, nineteenth-century Ireland included—is how unlikely such an event is. The law of demand really is a law, with few exceptions.

However, in the case of an *inferior* good, a good for which demand increases when income falls, the income and substitution effects work in opposite directions. Although the substitution effect decreases the quantity of any good demanded as its price increases, the income effect of a price increase for an inferior good is an *increase* in the quantity demanded. This makes sense because the price increase lowers the real income of the consumer, and as real income falls, the demand for an inferior good increases.

If a good were so inferior that the income effect exceeded the substitution effect, a price increase would lead to an increase in the quantity demanded. There is controversy over whether such goods, known as "Giffen goods," exist at all. If they do, they are very rare. You can generally assume that the income effect for an inferior good is smaller than the substitution effect, and so a price increase will lead to a decrease in the quantity demanded.

Defining and Measuring Elasticity

As we saw in the Appendix, Graphs in Economics, *dependent variables* respond to changes in *independent variables*. For example, if two variables are negatively related and the independent variable increases, the dependent variable will respond by decreasing. But often the important question is not whether the variables are negatively or positively related, but how responsive the dependent variable is to changes in the independent variable (that is, **by how much** will the dependent variable change?). If price increases, we know that quantity demanded will decrease (that is the *law of demand*). The question in this context is *by how much* will quantity demanded decrease if price goes up?

Economists use the concept of *elasticity* to measure the responsiveness of one variable to changes in another. For example, *price elasticity of demand* measures the responsiveness of quantity demanded to changes in price—something a firm considering changing its price would certainly want to know! Elasticity can be used to measure responsiveness using any two related variables. We will start by looking at the price elasticity of demand and then move on to other examples of elasticities commonly used by economists.

Think back to the opening example of the 2004 flu shot panic. In order for Flunomics, a hypothetical flu vaccine distributor, to know whether it could raise its revenue by significantly raising the price of its flu vaccine during the 2004 flu vaccine panic, it would have to know whether the price increase would decrease the quantity demanded by a lot or a little. That is, it would have to know the price elasticity of demand for flu vaccinations.

Calculating the Price Elasticity of Demand

Figure 10.1 shows a hypothetical demand curve for flu vaccinations. At a price of $20 per vaccination, consumers would demand 10 million vaccinations per year (point *A*); at a price of $21, the quantity demanded would fall to 9.9 million vaccinations per year (point *B*).

Figure 10.1, then, tells us the change in the quantity demanded for a particular change in the price. But how can we turn this into a measure of price responsiveness? The answer is to calculate the price elasticity of demand. The **price elasticity of demand** compares the *percent change in quantity demanded* to the *percent change in price* as we move along the demand curve. As we'll see later, the reason economists use percent changes is to get a measure that doesn't depend on the units in which a good is measured (say, a child-size dose versus an adult-size dose of vaccine). But before we get to that, let's look at how elasticity is calculated.

To calculate the price elasticity of demand, we first calculate the *percent change in the quantity demanded* and the corresponding *percent change in the price* as we move along the demand curve. These are defined as follows:

The **price elasticity of demand** is the ratio of the percent change in the quantity demanded to the percent change in the price as we move along the demand curve (dropping the minus sign).

$$(10\text{-}1) \quad \% \text{ change in quantity demanded} = \frac{\text{Change in quantity demanded}}{\text{Initial quantity demanded}} \times 100$$

figure 10.1

The Demand for Vaccinations

At a price of $20 per vaccination, the quantity of vaccinations demanded is 10 million per year (point A). When price rises to $21 per vaccination, the quantity demanded falls to 9.9 million vaccinations per year (point B).

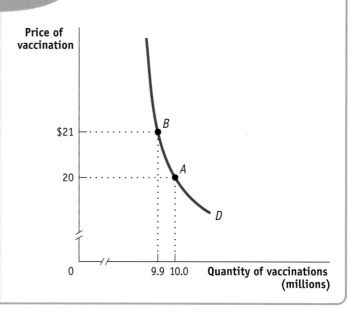

and

(10-2) $\% \text{ change in price} = \dfrac{\text{Change in price}}{\text{Initial price}} \times 100$

In Figure 10.1, we see that when the price rises from $20 to $21, the quantity demanded falls from 10 million to 9.9 million vaccinations, yielding a change in the quantity demanded of 0.1 million vaccinations. So the percent change in the quantity demanded is

$$\% \text{ change in quantity demanded} = \dfrac{-0.1 \text{ million vaccinations}}{10 \text{ million vaccinations}} \times 100 = -1\%$$

The initial price is $20 and the change in the price is $1, so the percent change in the price is

$$\% \text{ change in price} = \dfrac{\$1}{\$20} \times 100 = 5\%$$

To calculate the price elasticity of demand, we find the ratio of the percent change in the quantity demanded to the percent change in the price:

(10-3) $\text{Price elasticity of demand} = \dfrac{\% \text{ change in quantity demanded}}{\% \text{ change in price}}$

In Figure 10.1, the price elasticity of demand is therefore

$$\text{Price elasticity of demand} = \dfrac{1\%}{5\%} = 0.2$$

The *law of demand* says that demand curves slope downward, so price and quantity demanded always move in opposite directions. In other words, a positive percent change in price (a rise in price) leads to a negative percent change in the quantity demanded; a negative percent change in price (a fall in price) leads to a positive percent change in the quantity demanded. This means that the price elasticity of demand is, in strictly mathematical terms, a negative number. However, it is inconvenient to repeatedly write a minus sign. So when economists talk about the price elasticity of demand, they usually drop the minus sign and report the absolute value of the price elasticity of demand. In this case, for example, economists would usually say "the price elasticity of demand is 0.2," taking it for granted that you understand they mean *minus* 0.2. We follow this convention here.

The larger the price elasticity of demand, the more responsive the quantity demanded is to the price. When the price elasticity of demand is large—when consumers change their quantity demanded by a large percentage compared with the percent change in the price—economists say that demand is highly elastic.

As we'll see shortly, a price elasticity of 0.2 indicates a small response of quantity demanded to price. That is, the quantity demanded will fall by a relatively small amount when price rises. This is what economists call *inelastic* demand. And inelastic demand was exactly what Flunomics needed for its strategy to increase revenue by raising the price of its flu vaccines.

An Alternative Way to Calculate Elasticities: The Midpoint Method

We've seen that price elasticity of demand compares the *percent change in quantity demanded* with the *percent change in price*. When we look at some other elasticities, which we will do shortly, we'll see why it is important to focus on percent changes. But at this point we need to discuss a technical issue that arises when you calculate percent changes in variables and how economists deal with it.

The best way to understand the issue is with a real example. Suppose you were trying to estimate the price elasticity of demand for gasoline by comparing gasoline prices and consumption in different countries. Because of high taxes, gasoline usually costs about three times as much per gallon in Europe as it does in the United States. So what is the percent difference between American and European gas prices?

Well, it depends on which way you measure it. Because the price of gasoline in Europe is approximately three times higher than in the United States, it is 200 percent higher. Because the price of gasoline in the United States is one-third as high as in Europe, it is 66.7 percent lower.

This is a nuisance: we'd like to have a percent measure of the difference in prices that doesn't depend on which way you measure it. A good way to avoid computing different elasticities for rising and falling prices is to use the *midpoint method* (sometimes called the *arc method*).

The **midpoint method** replaces the usual definition of the percent change in a variable, X, with a slightly different definition:

$$(10\text{-}4) \quad \% \text{ change in } X = \frac{\text{Change in } X}{\text{Average value of } X} \times 100$$

where the average value of X is defined as

$$\text{Average value of } X = \frac{\text{Starting value of } X + \text{Final value of } X}{2}$$

When calculating the price elasticity of demand using the midpoint method, both the percent change in the price and the percent change in the quantity demanded are found using average values in this way. To see how this method works, suppose you have the following data for some good:

The **midpoint method** is a technique for calculating the percent change. In this approach, we calculate changes in a variable compared with the average, or midpoint, of the initial and final values.

	Price	Quantity demanded
Situation A	$0.90	1,100
Situation B	$1.10	900

To calculate the percent change in quantity going from situation A to situation B, we compare the change in the quantity demanded—a fall of 200 units—with the *average* of the quantity demanded in the two situations. So we calculate

$$\% \text{ change in quantity demanded} = \frac{-200}{(1,100 + 900)/2} \times 100 = \frac{-200}{1,000} \times 100 = -20\%$$

In the same way, we calculate the percentage change in price as

$$\% \text{ change in price} = \frac{\$0.20}{(\$0.90 + \$1.10)/2} \times 100 = \frac{\$0.20}{\$1.00} \times 100 = 20\%$$

So in this case we would calculate the price elasticity of demand to be

$$\text{Price elasticity of demand} = \frac{\% \text{ change in quantity demanded}}{\% \text{ change in price}} = \frac{20\%}{20\%} = 1$$

again dropping the minus sign.

The important point is that we would get the same result, a price elasticity of demand of 1, whether we went up the demand curve from situation A to situation B or down from situation B to situation A.

To arrive at a more general formula for price elasticity of demand, suppose that we have data for two points on a demand curve. At point 1 the quantity demanded and

in real life

Estimating Elasticities

You might think it's easy to estimate price elasticities of demand from real-world data: just compare percent changes in prices with percent changes in quantities demanded. Unfortunately, it's rarely that simple because changes in price aren't the only thing affecting changes in the quantity demanded: other factors—such as changes in income, changes in population, and changes in the prices of other goods—shift the demand curve, thereby changing the quantity demanded at any given price. To estimate price elasticities of demand, economists must use careful statistical analysis to separate the influence of these different factors, holding other things equal.

The most comprehensive effort to estimate price elasticities of demand was a mammoth study by the economists Hendrik S. Houthakker and Lester D. Taylor. Some of their results are summarized in Table 10.1. These estimates show a wide range of price elasticities. There are some goods, like eggs, for which demand hardly responds at all to changes in the price; there are other goods, most notably foreign travel, for which the quantity demanded is very sensitive to the price.

Notice that Table 10.1 is divided into two parts: inelastic and elastic demand. We'll explain in the next module the significance of that division.

table 10.1

Some Estimated Price Elasticities of Demand

Good	Price elasticity of demand
Inelastic demand	
Eggs	0.1
Beef	0.4
Stationery	0.5
Gasoline	0.5
Elastic demand	
Housing	1.2
Restaurant meals	2.3
Airline travel	2.4
Foreign travel	4.1

Source: Hendrick S. Houthakker and Lester D. Taylor, *Consumer Demand in the United States, 1929–1970* (Cambridge: Harvard University Press, 1970)

price are (Q_1, P_1); at point 2 they are (Q_2, P_2). Then the formula for calculating the price elasticity of demand is:

$$(10\text{-}5) \quad \text{Price elasticity of demand} = \dfrac{\dfrac{Q_2 - Q_1}{(Q_1 + Q_2)/2}}{\dfrac{P_2 - P_1}{(P_1 + P_2)/2}}$$

As before, when reporting a price elasticity of demand calculated by the midpoint method, we drop the minus sign and report the absolute value.

Module 10 Review

Solutions appear at the back of the book.

Check Your Understanding

1. In each of the following cases, state whether the income effect, the substitution effect, or both are significant. In which cases do they move in the same direction? In opposite directions? Why?

   a. Orange juice represents a small share of Clare's spending. She buys more lemonade and less orange juice when the price of orange juice goes up. She does not change her spending on other goods.

   b. Apartment rents have risen dramatically this year. Since rent absorbs a major part of her income, Delia moves to a smaller apartment. Assume that rental housing is a normal good.

   c. The cost of a semester-long meal ticket at the student cafeteria rises, representing a significant increase in living costs. As a result, many students have less money to spend on weekend meals at restaurants and eat in the cafeteria instead. Assume that cafeteria meals are an inferior good.

2. The price of strawberries falls from $1.50 to $1.00 per carton, and the quantity demanded goes from 100,000 to 200,000 cartons. Use the midpoint method to find the price elasticity of demand.

3. At the present level of consumption, 4,000 movie tickets, and at the current price, $5 per ticket, the price elasticity of demand for movie tickets is 1. Using the midpoint method, calculate the percentage by which the owners of movie theaters must reduce the price in order to sell 5,000 tickets.

4. The price elasticity of demand for ice-cream sandwiches is 1.2 at the current price of $0.50 per sandwich and the current consumption level of 100,000 sandwiches. Calculate the change in the quantity demanded when price rises by $0.05. Use Equations 10-1 and 10-2 to calculate percent changes and Equation 10-3 to relate price elasticity of demand to the percent changes.

Multiple-Choice Questions

1. Which of the following statements is true?

   I. When a good absorbs only a small share of consumer spending, the income effect explains the demand curve's negative slope.

   II. A change in consumption brought about by a change in purchasing power describes the income effect.

   III. In the case of an inferior good, the income and substitution effects work in opposite directions.

   a. I only
   b. II only
   c. III only
   d. II and III only
   e. I, II, and III

2. The income effect is most likely to come into play for which of the following goods?

   a. water
   b. clothing
   c. housing

   d. transportation
   e. entertainment

3. If a decrease in price from $2 to $1 causes an increase in quantity demanded from 100 to 120, using the midpoint method, price elasticity of demand equals

   a. 0.17.
   b. 0.27.
   c. 0.40.
   d. 2.5.
   e. 3.72.

4. Which of the following is likely to have the highest price elasticity of demand?

   a. eggs
   b. beef
   c. housing
   d. gasoline
   e. foreign travel

5. If a 2% change in the price of a good leads to a 10% change in the quantity demanded of a good, what is the value of price elasticity of demand?

   a. 0.02
   b. 0.2
   c. 5
   d. 10
   e. 20

Critical-Thinking Questions

Assume the price of an inferior good increases.

a. In what direction will the substitution effect change the quantity demanded? Explain.

b. In what direction will the income effect change the quantity demanded? Explain.

c. Given that the demand curve for the good slopes downward, what is true of the relative sizes of the income and substitution effects for the inferior good? Explain.

Module 11
Interpreting Price Elasticity of Demand

Interpreting the Price Elasticity of Demand

Med-Stat and other pharmaceutical distributors believed they could sharply drive up flu vaccine prices in the face of a shortage because the price elasticity of vaccine demand was low. But what does that mean? How low does a price elasticity have to be for us to classify it as low? How high does it have to be for us to consider it high? And what determines whether the price elasticity of demand is high or low, anyway? To answer these questions, we need to look more deeply at the price elasticity of demand.

How Elastic Is Elastic?

As a first step toward classifying price elasticities of demand, let's look at the extreme cases.

First, consider the demand for a good when people pay no attention to the price of, say, shoelaces. Suppose that consumers would buy 1 billion pairs of shoelaces per year regardless of the price. If that were true, the demand curve for shoelaces would look like the curve shown in panel (a) of Figure 11.1: it would be a vertical line at 1 billion pairs of shoelaces. Since the percent change in the quantity demanded is zero for *any* change in the price, the price elasticity of demand in this case is zero. The case of a zero price elasticity of demand is known as **perfectly inelastic** demand.

The opposite extreme occurs when even a tiny rise in the price will cause the quantity demanded to drop to zero or even a tiny fall in the price will cause the quantity demanded to get extremely large. Panel (b) of Figure 11.1 shows the case of pink tennis balls; we suppose that tennis players really don't care what color their balls are and that other colors, such as neon green and vivid yellow, are available at $5 per dozen balls. In this case, consumers will buy no pink balls if they cost more than $5 per dozen but will buy only pink balls if they cost less than $5. The demand curve will therefore be a horizontal line at a price of $5 per dozen balls. As you move back and forth along this line, there is a change in the quantity demanded but no change in the price. When you divide a number by zero, you get infinity, denoted by the symbol ∞.

Demand is **perfectly inelastic** when the quantity demanded does not respond at all to changes in the price. When demand is perfectly inelastic, the demand curve is a vertical line.

figure 11.1 — Two Extreme Cases of Price Elasticity of Demand

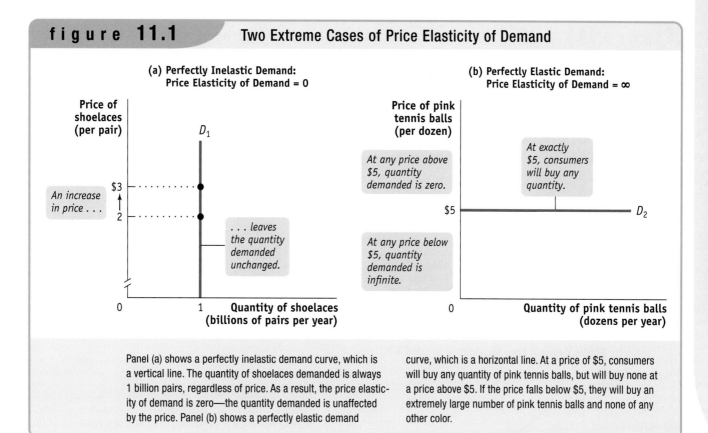

(a) Perfectly Inelastic Demand:
Price Elasticity of Demand = 0

Price of shoelaces (per pair)

D_1

An increase in price . . .

$3
2

. . . leaves the quantity demanded unchanged.

0   1   Quantity of shoelaces (billions of pairs per year)

(b) Perfectly Elastic Demand:
Price Elasticity of Demand = ∞

Price of pink tennis balls (per dozen)

At any price above $5, quantity demanded is zero.

At exactly $5, consumers will buy any quantity.

$5 D_2

At any price below $5, quantity demanded is infinite.

0   Quantity of pink tennis balls (dozens per year)

Panel (a) shows a perfectly inelastic demand curve, which is a vertical line. The quantity of shoelaces demanded is always 1 billion pairs, regardless of price. As a result, the price elasticity of demand is zero—the quantity demanded is unaffected by the price. Panel (b) shows a perfectly elastic demand curve, which is a horizontal line. At a price of $5, consumers will buy any quantity of pink tennis balls, but will buy none at a price above $5. If the price falls below $5, they will buy an extremely large number of pink tennis balls and none of any other color.

So a horizontal demand curve implies an infinite price elasticity of demand. When the price elasticity of demand is infinite, economists say that demand is **perfectly elastic.**

The price elasticity of demand for the vast majority of goods is somewhere between these two extreme cases. Economists use one main criterion for classifying these intermediate cases: they ask whether the price elasticity of demand is greater or less than 1. When the price elasticity of demand is greater than 1, economists say that demand is **elastic.** When the price elasticity of demand is less than 1, they say that demand is **inelastic.** The borderline case is **unit-elastic** demand, where the price elasticity of demand is—surprise—exactly 1.

To see why a price elasticity of demand equal to 1 is a useful dividing line, let's consider a hypothetical example: a toll bridge operated by the state highway department. Other things equal, the number of drivers who use the bridge depends on the toll, the price the highway department charges for crossing the bridge: the higher the toll, the fewer the drivers who use the bridge.

Figure 11.2 on the next page shows three hypothetical demand curves—one in which demand is unit-elastic, one in which it is inelastic, and one in which it is elastic. In each case, point *A* shows the quantity demanded if the toll is $0.90 and point *B* shows the quantity demanded if the toll is $1.10. An increase in the toll from $0.90 to $1.10 is an increase of 20% if we use the midpoint method to calculate percent changes.

Panel (a) shows what happens when the toll is raised from $0.90 to $1.10 and the demand curve is unit-elastic. Here the 20% price rise leads to a fall in the quantity of cars using the bridge each day from 1,100 to 900, which is a 20% decline (again using the midpoint method). So the price elasticity of demand is 20%/20% = 1.

Panel (b) shows a case of inelastic demand when the toll is raised from $0.90 to $1.10. The same 20% price rise reduces the quantity demanded from 1,050 to 950. That's only a 10% decline, so in this case the price elasticity of demand is 10%/20% = 0.5.

Demand is **perfectly elastic** when any price increase will cause the quantity demanded to drop to zero. When demand is perfectly elastic, the demand curve is a horizontal line.

Demand is **elastic** if the price elasticity of demand is greater than 1, **inelastic** if the price elasticity of demand is less than 1, and **unit-elastic** if the price elasticity of demand is exactly 1.

When the Bay Area Toll Authority deliberated a toll increase from $4 to $6 for San Francisco's Bay Bridge in 2010, at issue was the price elasticity of demand, which would determine the resulting drop in use.

figure **11.2**   Unit-Elastic Demand, Inelastic Demand, and Elastic Demand

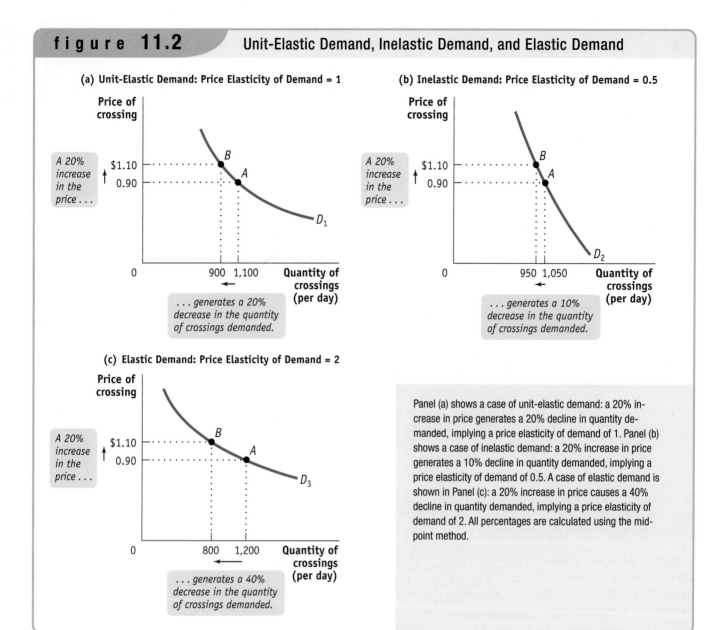

(a) Unit-Elastic Demand: Price Elasticity of Demand = 1

Price of crossing

A 20% increase in the price . . .

$1.10 •••••••••••• B
0.90 •••••••••••••• A

D_1

0   900 1,100   Quantity of crossings (per day)

. . . generates a 20% decrease in the quantity of crossings demanded.

(b) Inelastic Demand: Price Elasticity of Demand = 0.5

Price of crossing

A 20% increase in the price . . .

$1.10 •••••••••••• B
0.90 •••••••••••••• A

D_2

0   950 1,050   Quantity of crossings (per day)

. . . generates a 10% decrease in the quantity of crossings demanded.

(c) Elastic Demand: Price Elasticity of Demand = 2

Price of crossing

A 20% increase in the price . . .

$1.10 •••••••••••• B
0.90 •••••••••••••• A

D_3

0   800   1,200   Quantity of crossings (per day)

. . . generates a 40% decrease in the quantity of crossings demanded.

Panel (a) shows a case of unit-elastic demand: a 20% increase in price generates a 20% decline in quantity demanded, implying a price elasticity of demand of 1. Panel (b) shows a case of inelastic demand: a 20% increase in price generates a 10% decline in quantity demanded, implying a price elasticity of demand of 0.5. A case of elastic demand is shown in Panel (c): a 20% increase in price causes a 40% decline in quantity demanded, implying a price elasticity of demand of 2. All percentages are calculated using the midpoint method.

Panel (c) shows a case of elastic demand when the toll is raised from $0.90 to $1.10. The 20% price increase causes the quantity demanded to fall from 1,200 to 800, a 40% decline, so the price elasticity of demand is 40%/20% = 2.

Why does it matter whether demand is unit-elastic, inelastic, or elastic? Because this classification predicts how changes in the price of a good will affect the *total revenue* earned by producers from the sale of that good. In many real-life situations, such as the one faced by Med-Stat, it is crucial to know how price changes affect total revenue. **Total revenue** is defined as the total value of sales of a good or service: the price multiplied by the quantity sold.

(11-1)   Total revenue = Price × Quantity sold

Total revenue has a useful graphical representation that can help us understand why knowing the price elasticity of demand is crucial when we ask whether a price rise will increase or reduce total revenue. Panel (a) of Figure 11.3 shows the same demand curve as panel (a) of Figure 11.2. We see that 1,100 drivers will use the bridge if the toll

Total revenue is the total value of sales of a good or service. It is equal to the price multiplied by the quantity sold.

figure 11.3 — Total Revenue

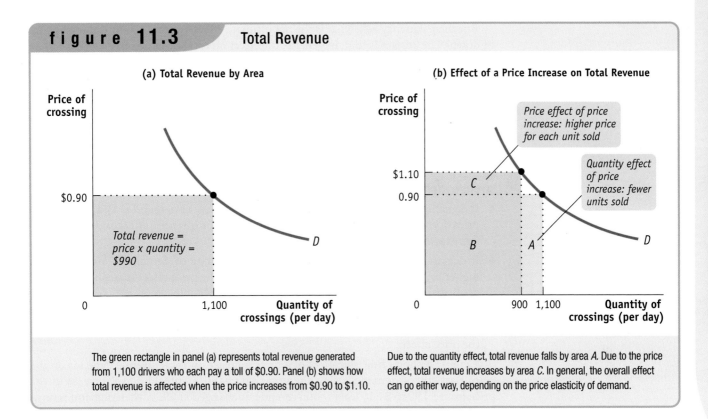

(a) Total Revenue by Area

Price of crossing

$0.90

Total revenue =
price x quantity =
$990

D

0   1,100   Quantity of crossings (per day)

(b) Effect of a Price Increase on Total Revenue

Price of crossing

Price effect of price increase: higher price for each unit sold

Quantity effect of price increase: fewer units sold

$1.10

0.90

C

B   A

D

0   900   1,100   Quantity of crossings (per day)

The green rectangle in panel (a) represents total revenue generated from 1,100 drivers who each pay a toll of $0.90. Panel (b) shows how total revenue is affected when the price increases from $0.90 to $1.10.

Due to the quantity effect, total revenue falls by area *A*. Due to the price effect, total revenue increases by area *C*. In general, the overall effect can go either way, depending on the price elasticity of demand.

---

is $0.90. So the total revenue at a price of $0.90 is $0.90 × 1,100 = $990. This value is equal to the area of the green rectangle, which is drawn with the bottom left corner at the point (0, 0) and the top right corner at (1,100, 0.90). In general, the total revenue at any given price is equal to the area of a rectangle whose height is the price and whose width is the quantity demanded at that price.

To get an idea of why total revenue is important, consider the following scenario. Suppose that the toll on the bridge is currently $0.90 but that the highway department must raise extra money for road repairs. One way to do this is to raise the toll on the bridge. But this plan might backfire, since a higher toll will reduce the number of drivers who use the bridge. And if traffic on the bridge dropped a lot, a higher toll would actually reduce total revenue instead of increasing it. So it's important for the highway department to know how drivers will respond to a toll increase.

We can see graphically how the toll increase affects total bridge revenue by examining panel (b) of Figure 11.3. At a toll of $0.90, total revenue is given by the sum of the areas *A* and *B*. After the toll is raised to $1.10, total revenue is given by the sum of areas *B* and *C*. So when the toll is raised, revenue represented by area *A* is lost but revenue represented by area *C* is gained. These two areas have important interpretations. Area *C* represents the revenue gain that comes from the additional $0.20 paid by drivers who continue to use the bridge. That is, the 900 who continue to use the bridge contribute an additional $0.20 × 900 = $180 per day to total revenue, represented by *C*. But 200 drivers who would have used the bridge at a price of $0.90 no longer do so, generating a loss to total revenue of $0.90 × 200 = $180 per day, represented by area *A*. (In this particular example, because demand is unit-elastic—the same as in panel (a) of Figure 11.2—the rise in the toll has no effect on total revenue; areas *A* and *B* are the same size.)

Except in the rare case of a good with perfectly elastic or perfectly inelastic demand, when a seller raises the price of a good, two countervailing effects are present:

- *A price effect.* After a price increase, each unit sold sells at a higher price, which tends to raise revenue.

- *A quantity effect.* After a price increase, fewer units are sold, which tends to lower revenue.

But then, you may ask, what is the net ultimate effect on total revenue: does it go up or down? The answer is that, in general, the effect on total revenue can go either way—a price rise may either increase total revenue or lower it. If the price effect, which tends to raise total revenue, is the stronger of the two effects, then total revenue goes up. If the quantity effect, which tends to reduce total revenue, is the stronger, then total revenue goes down. And if the strengths of the two effects are exactly equal—as in our toll bridge example, where a $180 gain offsets a $180 loss—total revenue is unchanged by the price increase.

The price elasticity of demand tells us what happens to total revenue when price changes: its size determines which effect—the price effect or the quantity effect—is stronger. Specifically:

- If demand for a good is *unit-elastic* (the price elasticity of demand is 1), an increase in price does not change total revenue. In this case, the quantity effect and the price effect exactly offset each other.

- If demand for a good is *inelastic* (the price elasticity of demand is less than 1), a higher price increases total revenue. In this case, the price effect is stronger than the quantity effect.

- If demand for a good is *elastic* (the price elasticity of demand is greater than 1), an increase in price reduces total revenue. In this case, the quantity effect is stronger than the price effect.

Table 11.1 shows how the effect of a price increase on total revenue depends on the price elasticity of demand, using the same data as in Figure 11.2. An increase in the price from $0.90 to $1.10 leaves total revenue unchanged at $990 when demand is unit-elastic. When demand is inelastic, the price effect dominates the quantity effect; the same price increase leads to an increase in total revenue from $945 to $1,045. And when demand is elastic, the quantity effect dominates the price effect; the price increase leads to a decline in total revenue from $1,080 to $880.

table **11.1**

Price Elasticity of Demand and Total Revenue

	Price of crossing = $0.90	Price of crossing = $1.10
Unit-elastic demand (price elasticity of demand = 1)		
Quantity demanded	1,100	900
Total revenue	$990	$990
Inelastic demand (price elasticity of demand = 0.5)		
Quantity demanded	1,050	950
Total revenue	$945	$1,045
Elastic demand (price elasticity of demand = 2)		
Quantity demanded	1,200	800
Total revenue	$1,080	$880

The price elasticity of demand also predicts the effect of a *fall* in price on total revenue. When the price falls, the same two countervailing effects are present, but they work in the opposite directions as compared to the case of a price rise. There is the price effect of a lower price per unit sold, which tends to lower revenue. This is countered by the quantity effect of more units sold, which tends to raise revenue. Which effect dominates depends on the price elasticity. Here is a quick summary:

- When demand is *unit-elastic,* the two effects exactly balance each other out; so a fall in price has no effect on total revenue.
- When demand is *inelastic,* the price effect dominates the quantity effect; so a fall in price reduces total revenue.
- When demand is *elastic,* the quantity effect dominates the price effect; so a fall in price increases total revenue.

Price Elasticity Along the Demand Curve

Suppose an economist says that "the price elasticity of demand for coffee is 0.25." What he or she means is that *at the current price* the elasticity is 0.25. In the previous discussion of the toll bridge, what we were really describing was the elasticity *at the price* of $0.90. Why this qualification? Because for the vast majority of demand curves, the price elasticity of demand at one point along the curve is different from the price elasticity of demand at other points along the same curve.

To see this, consider the table in Figure 11.4, which shows a hypothetical demand schedule. It also shows in the last column the total revenue generated at each price and quantity combination in the demand schedule. The upper panel of the graph in Figure

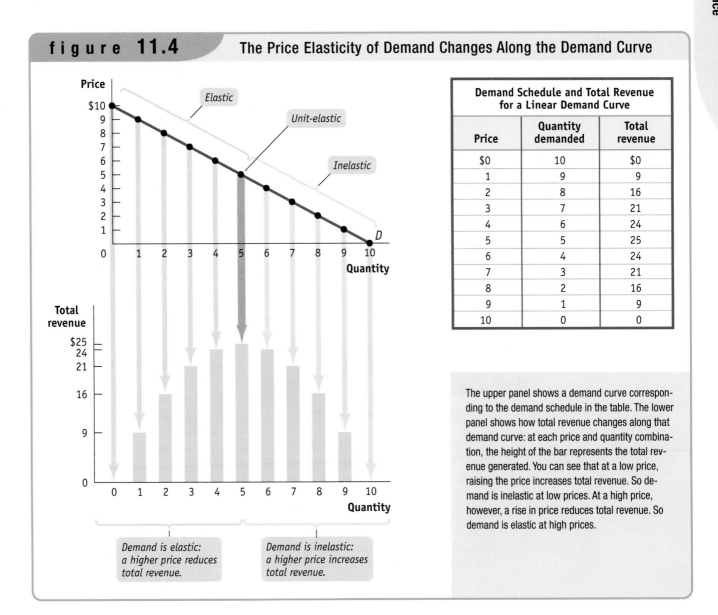

figure 11.4   The Price Elasticity of Demand Changes Along the Demand Curve

Demand Schedule and Total Revenue for a Linear Demand Curve		
Price	Quantity demanded	Total revenue
$0	10	$0
1	9	9
2	8	16
3	7	21
4	6	24
5	5	25
6	4	24
7	3	21
8	2	16
9	1	9
10	0	0

Demand is elastic: a higher price reduces total revenue.

Demand is inelastic: a higher price increases total revenue.

The upper panel shows a demand curve corresponding to the demand schedule in the table. The lower panel shows how total revenue changes along that demand curve: at each price and quantity combination, the height of the bar represents the total revenue generated. You can see that at a low price, raising the price increases total revenue. So demand is inelastic at low prices. At a high price, however, a rise in price reduces total revenue. So demand is elastic at high prices.

module 11   Interpreting Price Elasticity of Demand   **115**

11.4 shows the corresponding demand curve. The lower panel illustrates the same data on total revenue: the height of a bar at each quantity demanded—which corresponds to a particular price—measures the total revenue generated at that price.

In Figure 11.4, you can see that when the price is low, raising the price increases total revenue: starting at a price of $1, raising the price to $2 increases total revenue from $9 to $16. This means that when the price is low, demand is inelastic. Moreover, you can see that demand is inelastic on the entire section of the demand curve from a price of $0 to a price of $5.

When the price is high, however, raising it further reduces total revenue: starting at a price of $8, for example, raising the price to $9 reduces total revenue, from $16 to $9. This means that when the price is high, demand is elastic. Furthermore, you can see that demand is elastic over the section of the demand curve from a price of $5 to $10.

For the vast majority of goods, the price elasticity of demand changes along the demand curve. So whenever you measure a good's elasticity, you are really measuring it at a particular point or section of the good's demand curve.

What Factors Determine the Price Elasticity of Demand?

The flu vaccine shortfall of 2004–2005 allowed vaccine distributors to significantly raise their prices for two important reasons: there were no substitutes, and for many people the vaccine was a medical necessity. People responded in various ways. Some paid the high prices, and some traveled to Canada and other countries to get vaccinated. Some simply did without (and over time often changed their habits to avoid catching the flu, such as eating out less often and avoiding mass transit). This experience illustrates the four main factors that determine elasticity: whether close substitutes are available, whether the good is a necessity or a luxury, the share of income a consumer spends on the good, and how much time has elapsed since the price change. We'll briefly examine each of these factors.

Whether Close Substitutes Are Available The price elasticity of demand tends to be high if there are other goods that consumers regard as similar and would be willing to consume instead. The price elasticity of demand tends to be low if there are no close substitutes.

Whether the Good Is a Necessity or a Luxury The price elasticity of demand tends to be low if a good is something you must have, like a life-saving medicine. The price elasticity of demand tends to be high if the good is a luxury—something you can easily live without.

istockphoto

Share of Income Spent on the Good The price elasticity of demand tends to be low when spending on a good accounts for a small share of a consumer's income. In that case, a significant change in the price of the good has little impact on how much the consumer spends. In contrast, when a good accounts for a significant share of a consumer's spending, the consumer is likely to be very responsive to a change in price. In this case, the price elasticity of demand is high.

Time In general, the price elasticity of demand tends to increase as consumers have more time to adjust to a price change. This means that the long-run price elasticity of demand is often higher than the short-run elasticity.

A good illustration of the effect of time on the elasticity of demand is drawn from the 1970s, the first time gasoline prices increased dramatically in the United States. Initially, consumption fell very little because there were no close substitutes for gasoline and because driving their cars was necessary for people to carry out the ordinary tasks of life. Over time, however, Americans changed their habits in ways that enabled them to gradually reduce their gasoline consumption. The result was a steady decline in gasoline consumption over the next decade, even though the price of gasoline did not continue to rise, confirming that the long-run price elasticity of demand for gasoline was indeed much larger than the short-run elasticity.

Mike Thompson, Detroit Free Press. Reprinted by Permission.

Responding to Your Tuition Bill

College costs more than ever—and not just because of overall inflation. Tuition has been rising faster than the overall cost of living for years. But does rising tuition keep people from going to college? Two studies found that the answer depends on the type of college. Both studies assessed how responsive the decision to go to college is to a change in tuition.

A 1988 study found that a 3% increase in tuition led to an approximately 2% fall in the number of students enrolled at four-year institutions, giving a price elasticity of demand of 0.67 (2%/3%). In the case of two-year institutions, the study found a significantly higher response: a 3% increase in tuition led to a 2.7% fall in enrollments, giving a price elasticity of demand of 0.9. In other words, the enrollment decision for

students at two-year colleges was significantly more responsive to price than for students at four-year colleges. The result: students at two-year colleges are more likely to forgo getting a degree because of tuition costs than students at four-year colleges.

A 1999 study confirmed this pattern. In comparison to four-year colleges, it found that two-year college enrollment rates were significantly more responsive to changes in state financial aid (a decline in aid leading to a decline in enrollments), a predictable effect given these students' greater sensitivity to the cost of tuition. Another piece of evidence suggests that students at two-year colleges are more likely to be paying their own way and making a trade-off between attending college and working: the

study found that enrollments at two-year colleges are much more responsive to changes in the unemployment rate (an increase in the unemployment rate leading to an increase in enrollments) than enrollments at four-year colleges. So is the cost of tuition a barrier to getting a college degree in the United States? Yes, but more so at two-year colleges than at four-year colleges.

Interestingly, the 1999 study found that for both two-year and four-year colleges, price sensitivity of demand had fallen somewhat since the 1988 study. One possible explanation is that because the value of a college education has risen considerably over time, fewer people forgo college, even if tuition goes up. (See source note on copyright page.)

Module 11 Review

Solutions appear at the back of the book.

Check Your Understanding

1. For each case, choose the condition that characterizes demand: elastic demand, inelastic demand, or unit-elastic demand.
   a. Total revenue decreases when price increases.
   b. When price falls, the additional revenue generated by the increase in the quantity sold is exactly offset by the revenue lost from the fall in the price received per unit.
   c. Total revenue falls when output increases.

   d. Producers in an industry find they can increase their total revenues by working together to reduce industry output.

2. For the following goods, is demand elastic, inelastic, or unit-elastic? Explain. What is the shape of the demand curve?
   a. demand by a snake-bite victim for an antidote
   b. demand by students for blue pencils

Multiple-Choice Questions

1. A perfectly elastic demand curve is
   a. upward sloping.
   b. vertical.
   c. not a straight line.
   d. horizontal.
   e. downward sloping.

2. Which of the following would cause the demand for a good to be relatively inelastic?
   a. The good has a large number of close substitutes.
   b. Expenditures on the good represent a large share of consumer income.
   c. There is ample time to adjust to price changes.
   d. The good is a necessity.
   e. The price of the good is in the upper left section of a linear demand curve.

3. Which of the following is true if the price elasticity of demand for a good is zero?
   a. The slope of the demand curve is zero.
   b. The slope of the demand curve is one.
   c. The demand curve is vertical.
   d. The demand curve is horizontal.
   e. The price of the good is high.

4. Which of the following is correct for a price increase? When demand is _____, total revenue will _____.

Demand	Total Revenue
a. inelastic	decrease
b. elastic	decrease
c. unit-elastic	increase
d. unit-elastic	decrease
e. elastic	increase

5. Total revenue is maximized when demand is
   a. elastic.
   b. inelastic.
   c. unit-elastic.
   d. zero.
   e. infinite.

Critical-Thinking Questions

Draw a correctly labeled graph illustrating a demand curve that is a straight line and is neither perfectly elastic nor perfectly inelastic.
a. On your graph, indicate the half of the demand curve along which demand is elastic.
b. In the elastic range, how will an increase in price affect total revenue? Explain.

Module 12
Other Elasticities

Other Elasticities

We stated earlier that economists use the concept of *elasticity* to measure the responsiveness of one variable to changes in another. However, up to this point we have focused on the price elasticity of demand. Now that we have used elasticity to measure the responsiveness of quantity demanded to changes in price, we can go on to look at how elasticity is used to understand the relationship between other important variables in economics.

The quantity of a good demanded depends not only on the price of that good but also on other variables. In particular, demand curves shift because of changes in the prices of related goods and changes in consumers' incomes. It is often important to have a measure of these other effects, and the best measures are—you guessed it—elasticities. Specifically, we can best measure how the demand for a good is affected by prices of other goods using a measure called the *cross-price elasticity of demand,* and we can best measure how demand is affected by changes in income using the *income elasticity of demand.*

Finally, we can also use elasticity to measure supply responses. The *price elasticity of supply* measures the responsiveness of the quantity supplied to changes in price.

The Cross-Price Elasticity of Demand

The demand for a good is often affected by the prices of other, related goods—goods that are substitutes or complements. A change in the price of a related good shifts the demand curve of the original good, reflecting a change in the quantity demanded at any given price. The strength of such a "cross" effect on demand can be measured by the **cross-price elasticity of demand,** defined as the ratio of the percent change in the quantity demanded of one good to the percent change in the price of another.

(12-1)   Cross-price elasticity of demand between goods A and B

$$= \frac{\% \text{ change in quantity of A demanded}}{\% \text{ change in price of B}}$$

When two goods are substitutes, like hot dogs and hamburgers, the cross-price elasticity of demand is positive: a rise in the price of hot dogs increases the demand for hamburgers—that is, it causes a rightward shift of the demand curve for hamburgers. If the goods are close substitutes, the cross-price elasticity will be positive and large;

The **cross-price elasticity of demand** between two goods measures the effect of the change in one good's price on the quantity demanded of the other good. It is equal to the percent change in the quantity demanded of one good divided by the percent change in the other good's price.

if they are not close substitutes, the cross-price elasticity will be positive and small. So when the cross-price elasticity of demand is positive, its size is a measure of how closely substitutable the two goods are.

When two goods are complements, like hot dogs and hot dog buns, the cross-price elasticity is negative: a rise in the price of hot dogs decreases the demand for hot dog buns—that is, it causes a leftward shift of the demand curve for hot dog buns. As with substitutes, the size of the cross-price elasticity of demand between two complements tells us how strongly complementary they are: if the cross-price elasticity is only slightly below zero, they are weak complements; if it is very negative, they are strong complements.

Note that in the case of the cross-price elasticity of demand, the sign (plus or minus) is very important: it tells us whether the two goods are complements or substitutes. So we cannot drop the minus sign as we did for the price elasticity of demand.

Our discussion of the cross-price elasticity of demand is a useful place to return to a point we made earlier: elasticity is a *unit-free* measure—that is, it doesn't depend on the units in which goods are measured.

To see the potential problem, suppose someone told you that "if the price of hot dog buns rises by $0.30, Americans will buy 10 million fewer hot dogs this year." If you've ever bought hot dog buns, you'll immediately wonder: is that a $0.30 increase in the price *per bun,* or is it a $0.30 increase in the price *per package* of buns? It makes a big difference what units we are talking about! However, if someone says that the cross-price elasticity of demand between buns and hot dogs is −0.3, it doesn't matter whether buns are sold individually or by the package. So elasticity is defined as a ratio of percent changes, which avoids confusion over units.

The Income Elasticity of Demand

The **income elasticity of demand** measures how changes in income affect the demand for a good. It indicates whether a good is normal or inferior and specifies how responsive demand for the good is to changes in income. Having learned the price and cross-price elasticity formulas, the income elasticity formula will look familiar:

$$(12\text{-}2) \quad \text{Income elasticity of demand} = \frac{\%\ \text{change in quantity demanded}}{\%\ \text{change in income}}$$

Just as the cross-price elasticity of demand between two goods can be either positive or negative, depending on whether the goods are substitutes or complements, the income elasticity of demand for a good can also be either positive or negative. Recall that goods can be either *normal goods,* for which demand increases when income rises, or *inferior goods,* for which demand decreases when income rises. These definitions relate directly to the sign of the income elasticity of demand:

■ When the income elasticity of demand is positive, the good is a normal good—that is, the quantity demanded at any given price increases as income increases.

■ When the income elasticity of demand is negative, the good is an inferior good—that is, the quantity demanded at any given price decreases as income increases.

Economists often use estimates of the income elasticity of demand to predict which industries will grow most rapidly as the incomes of consumers grow over time. In doing this, they often find it useful to make a further distinction among normal goods, identifying which are *income-elastic* and which are *income-inelastic.*

The demand for a good is **income-elastic** if the income elasticity of demand for that good is greater than 1. When income rises, the demand for income-elastic goods rises *faster* than income. Luxury goods such as second homes and international travel tend to be income-elastic. The demand for a good is **income-inelastic** if the income elasticity of demand for that good is positive but less than 1. When income rises, the demand for income-inelastic goods rises, but more slowly than income. Necessities such as food and clothing tend to be income-inelastic.

The **income elasticity of demand** is the percent change in the quantity of a good demanded when a consumer's income changes divided by the percent change in the consumer's income.

The demand for a good is **income-elastic** if the income elasticity of demand for that good is greater than 1.

The demand for a good is **income-inelastic** if the income elasticity of demand for that good is positive but less than 1.

Where Have All the Farmers Gone?

What percentage of Americans live on farms? Sad to say, the U.S. government no longer publishes that number. In 1991 the official percentage was 1.9, but in that year the government decided it was no longer a meaningful indicator of the size of the agricultural sector because a large proportion of those who live on farms actually make their living doing something else. But in the days of the Founding Fathers, the great majority of Americans lived on farms. As recently as the 1940s, one American in six—or approximately 17%—still did.

Why do so few people now live and work on farms in the United States? There are two main reasons, both involving elasticities.

First, the income elasticity of demand for food is much less than 1—food demand is income-inelastic. As consumers grow richer, other things equal, spending on food rises less in proportion to income. As a result, as the U.S. economy has

grown, the share of income spent on food—and therefore the share of total U.S. income earned by farmers—has fallen.

Second, agriculture has been a technologically progressive sector for approximately 150 years in the United States, with steadily increasing yields over time. You might think that technological progress would be good for farmers. But competition among farmers means that technological progress leads to lower food prices. Meanwhile, the demand for food is price-inelastic, so falling prices of agricultural goods, other things equal, reduce the total revenue of farmers. That's right: progress in farming is good for consumers but bad for farmers.

The combination of these effects explains the relative decline of farming. Even if farming weren't such a technologically progressive sector, the low income elasticity of demand for food

Photodisc

would ensure that the income of farmers grows more slowly than the economy as a whole. The combination of rapid technological progress in farming with price-inelastic demand for farm products reinforces this effect, further reducing the growth of farm income. In short, the U.S. farm sector has been a victim of success—the U.S. economy's success as a whole (which reduces the importance of spending on food) and its own success in increasing yields.

The Price Elasticity of Supply

In the wake of the flu vaccine shortfall of 2004, attempts by vaccine distributors to drive up the price of vaccines would have been much less effective if a higher price had induced a large increase in the output of flu vaccines by flu vaccine manufacturers other than Chiron. In fact, if the rise in price had precipitated a significant increase in flu vaccine production, the price would have been pushed back down. But that didn't happen because, as we mentioned earlier, it would have been far too costly and technically difficult to produce more vaccine for the 2004–2005 flu season. (In reality, the production of flu vaccine is begun a year before it is to be distributed.) This was another critical element in the ability of some flu vaccine distributors, like Med-Stat, to get significantly higher prices for their product: a low responsiveness in the quantity of output supplied to the higher price of flu vaccine by flu vaccine producers. To measure the response of producers to price changes, we need a measure parallel to the price elasticity of demand—the *price elasticity of supply*.

Measuring the Price Elasticity of Supply

The **price elasticity of supply** is defined the same way as the price elasticity of demand (although there is no minus sign to be eliminated here):

$$\textbf{(12-3)} \quad \text{Price elasticity of supply} = \frac{\text{\% change in quantity supplied}}{\text{\% change in price}}$$

The only difference is that here we consider movements along the supply curve rather than movements along the demand curve.

Suppose that the price of tomatoes rises by 10%. If the quantity of tomatoes supplied also increases by 10% in response, the price elasticity of supply of tomatoes is

The **price elasticity of supply** is a measure of the responsiveness of the quantity of a good supplied to the price of that good. It is the ratio of the percent change in the quantity supplied to the percent change in the price as we move along the supply curve.

1 (10%/10%) and supply is unit-elastic. If the quantity supplied increases by 5%, the price elasticity of supply is 0.5 and supply is inelastic; if the quantity increases by 20%, the price elasticity of supply is 2 and supply is elastic.

As in the case of demand, the extreme values of the price elasticity of supply have a simple graphical representation. Panel (a) of Figure 12.1 shows the supply of cell phone frequencies, the portion of the radio spectrum that is suitable for sending and receiving cell phone signals. Governments own the right to sell the use of this part of the radio spectrum to cell phone operators inside their borders. But governments can't increase or decrease the number of cell phone frequencies they have to offer—for technical reasons, the quantity of frequencies suitable for cell phone operation is fixed. So the supply curve for cell phone frequencies is a vertical line, which we have assumed is set at the quantity of 100 frequencies. As you move up and down that curve, the change in the quantity supplied by the government is zero, whatever the change in price. So panel (a) illustrates a case of **perfectly inelastic supply,** meaning that the price elasticity of supply is zero.

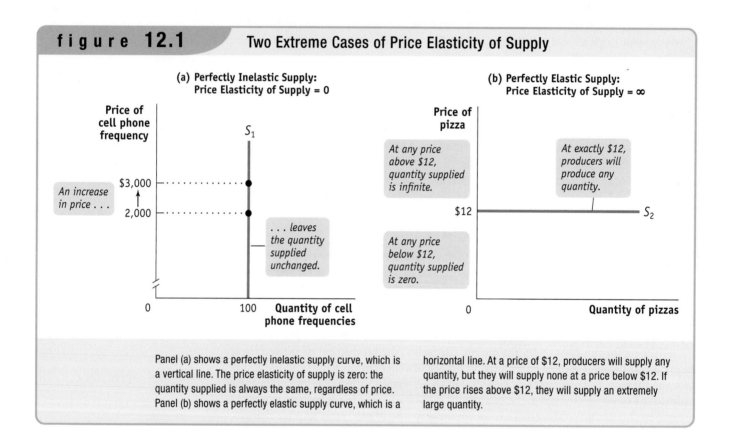

figure 12.1 — Two Extreme Cases of Price Elasticity of Supply

(a) Perfectly Inelastic Supply: Price Elasticity of Supply = 0

An increase in price . . . leaves the quantity supplied unchanged.

(b) Perfectly Elastic Supply: Price Elasticity of Supply = ∞

At any price above $12, quantity supplied is infinite.

At exactly $12, producers will produce any quantity.

At any price below $12, quantity supplied is zero.

Panel (a) shows a perfectly inelastic supply curve, which is a vertical line. The price elasticity of supply is zero: the quantity supplied is always the same, regardless of price. Panel (b) shows a perfectly elastic supply curve, which is a horizontal line. At a price of $12, producers will supply any quantity, but they will supply none at a price below $12. If the price rises above $12, they will supply an extremely large quantity.

Panel (b) shows the supply curve for pizza. We suppose that it costs $12 to produce a pizza, including all opportunity costs. At any price below $12, it would be unprofitable to produce pizza and all the pizza parlors would go out of business. At a price of $12 or more, there are many producers who could operate pizza parlors. The ingredients— flour, tomatoes, cheese—are plentiful. And if necessary, more tomatoes could be grown, more milk could be produced to make mozzarella cheese, and so on. So by allowing profits, any price above $12 would elicit the supply of an extremely large quantity of pizzas. The implied supply curve is therefore a horizontal line at $12. Since even a tiny increase in the price would lead to an enormous increase in the quantity supplied, the price elasticity of supply would be virtually infinite. A horizontal supply curve such as this represents a case of **perfectly elastic supply.**

As our cell phone frequencies and pizza examples suggest, real-world instances of both perfectly inelastic and perfectly elastic supply are easier to find than their counterparts in demand.

What Factors Determine the Price Elasticity of Supply? Our examples tell us the main determinant of the price elasticity of supply: the availability of inputs. In addition, as with the price elasticity of demand, time may also play a role in the price elasticity of supply. Here we briefly summarize the two factors.

The Availability of Inputs The price elasticity of supply tends to be large when inputs are readily available and can be shifted into and out of production at a relatively low cost. It tends to be small when inputs are available only in a more-or-less fixed quantity or can be shifted into and out of production only at a relatively high cost.

Time The price elasticity of supply tends to grow larger as producers have more time to respond to a price change. This means that the long-run price elasticity of supply is often higher than the short-run elasticity. In the case of the flu vaccine shortfall, time was the crucial element because flu vaccine must be grown in cultures over many months.

The price elasticity of pizza supply is very high because the inputs needed to make more pizza are readily available. The price elasticity of cell phone frequencies is zero because an essential input—the radio spectrum—cannot be increased at all.

Many industries are like pizza and have large price elasticities of supply: they can be readily expanded because they don't require any special or unique resources. On the other hand, the price elasticity of supply is usually substantially less than perfectly elastic for goods that involve limited natural resources: minerals like gold or copper, agricultural products like coffee that flourish only on certain types of land, and renewable resources like ocean fish that can be exploited only up to a point without destroying the resource.

istockphoto

But given enough time, producers are often able to significantly change the amount they produce in response to a price change, even when production involves a limited natural resource. For example, consider again the effects of a surge in flu vaccine prices, but this time focus on the supply response. If the price were to rise to $90 per vaccination and stay there for a number of years, there would almost certainly be a substantial increase in flu vaccine production. Producers such as Chiron would eventually respond by increasing the size of their manufacturing plants, hiring more lab technicians, and so on. But significantly enlarging the capacity of a biotech manufacturing lab takes several years, not weeks or months or even a single year.

For this reason, economists often make a distinction between the short-run elasticity of supply, usually referring to a few weeks or months, and the long-run elasticity of supply, usually referring to several years. In most industries, the long-run elasticity of supply is larger than the short-run elasticity.

An Elasticity Menagerie

We've just run through quite a few different types of elasticity. Keeping them all straight can be a challenge. So in Table 12.1 on the next page we provide a summary of all the types of elasticity we have discussed and their implications.

There is **perfectly elastic supply** if the quantity supplied is zero below some price and infinite above that price. A perfectly elastic supply curve is a horizontal line.

table **12.1**

An Elasticity Menagerie

Name	Possible values	Significance
Price elasticity of demand = $\dfrac{\text{\% change in quantity demanded}}{\text{\% change in price}}$ (dropping the minus sign)		
Perfectly inelastic demand	0	Price has no effect on quantity demanded (vertical demand curve).
Inelastic demand	Between 0 and 1	A rise in price increases total revenue.
Unit-elastic demand	Exactly 1	Changes in price have no effect on total revenue.
Elastic demand	Greater than 1, less than ∞	A rise in price reduces total revenue.
Perfectly elastic demand	∞	A rise in price causes quantity demanded to fall to 0. A fall in price leads to an infinite quantity demanded (horizontal demand curve).
Cross-price elasticity of demand = $\dfrac{\text{\% change in quantity } \textit{of one good} \text{ demanded}}{\text{\% change in price } \textit{of another good}}$		
Complements	Negative	Quantity demanded of one good falls when the price of another rises.
Substitutes	Positive	Quantity demanded of one good rises when the price of another rises.
Income elasticity of demand = $\dfrac{\text{\% change in quantity demanded}}{\text{\% change in income}}$		
Inferior good	Negative	Quantity demanded falls when income rises.
Normal good, income-inelastic	Positive, less than 1	Quantity demanded rises when income rises, but not as rapidly as income.
Normal good, income-elastic	Greater than 1	Quantity demanded rises when income rises, and more rapidly than income.
Price elasticity of supply = $\dfrac{\text{\% change in quantity supplied}}{\text{\% change in price}}$		
Perfectly inelastic supply	0	Price has no effect on quantity supplied (vertical supply curve).
	Greater than 0, less than ∞	Ordinary upward-sloping supply curve.
Perfectly elastic supply	∞	Any fall in price causes quantity supplied to fall to 0. Any rise in price elicits an infinite quantity supplied (horizontal supply curve).

M o d u l e ⑫ R e v i e w

Solutions appear at the back of the book.

Check Your Understanding

1. After Chelsea's income increased from $12,000 to $18,000 a year, her purchases of CDs increased from 10 to 40 CDs a year. Calculate Chelsea's income elasticity of demand for CDs using the midpoint method.

2. As the price of margarine rises by 20%, a manufacturer of baked goods increases its quantity of butter demanded by 5%. Calculate the cross-price elasticity of demand between butter and margarine. Are butter and margarine substitutes or complements for this manufacturer?

3. Using the midpoint method, calculate the price elasticity of supply for web-design services when the price per hour rises from $100 to $150 and the number of hours supplied increases from 300,000 hours to 500,000. Is supply elastic, inelastic, or unit-elastic?

Multiple-Choice Questions

1. If the cross-price elasticity between two goods is negative, this means that the two goods are
   a. substitutes.
   b. complements.
   c. normal.
   d. inferior.
   e. luxuries.

2. If Kylie buys 200 units of good X when her income is $20,000 and 300 units of good X when her income increases to $25,000, her income elasticity of demand, using the midpoint method, is
   a. 0.06.
   b. 0.5.
   c. 1.65.
   d. 1.8.
   e. 2.00.

3. The income elasticity of demand for a normal good is
   a. zero.
   b. 1.
   c. infinite.
   d. positive.
   e. negative.

4. A perfectly elastic supply curve is
   a. positively sloped.
   b. negatively sloped.
   c. vertical.
   d. horizontal.
   e. U-shaped

5. Which of the following leads to a more inelastic price elasticity of supply?
       I. the use of inputs that are easily obtained
       II. a high degree of substitutability between inputs
       III. a shorter time period in which to supply the good
   a. I only
   b. II only
   c. III only
   d. I and II only
   e. I, II, and III

Critical-Thinking Questions

Assume the price of corn rises by 20% and this causes suppliers to increase the quantity of corn supplied by 40%.
a. Calculate the price elasticity of supply.
b. In this case, is supply elastic or inelastic?
c. Draw a correctly labeled graph of a supply curve illustrating the most extreme case of the category of elasticity you found in part b (either perfectly elastic or perfectly inelastic supply).
d. What would likely be true of the availability of inputs for a firm with the supply curve you drew in part c? Explain.

Module 13
Consumer and Producer Surplus

There is a lively market in second-hand college textbooks. At the end of each term, some students who took a course decide that the money they can make by selling their used books is worth more to them than keeping the books. And some students who are taking the course next term prefer to buy a somewhat battered but less expensive used textbook rather than pay full price for a new one.

Textbook publishers and authors are not happy about these transactions because they cut into sales of new books. But both the students who sell used books and those who buy them clearly benefit from the existence of the market. That is why many college bookstores facilitate their trade, buying used textbooks and selling them alongside the new books.

But can we put a number on what used textbook buyers and sellers gain from these transactions? Can we answer the question *"How much* do the buyers and sellers of textbooks gain from the existence of the used-book market?"

Yes, we can. In this module we will see how to measure benefits, such as those to buyers of used textbooks, from being able to purchase a good—known as *consumer surplus.* And we will see that there is a corresponding measure, *producer surplus,* of the benefits sellers receive from being able to sell a good.

The concepts of consumer surplus and producer surplus are useful for analyzing a wide variety of economic issues. They let us calculate how much benefit producers and consumers receive from the existence of a market. They also allow us to calculate how the welfare of consumers and producers is affected by changes in market prices. Such calculations play a crucial role in evaluating many economic policies.

What information do we need to calculate consumer and producer surplus? Surprisingly, all we need are the demand and supply curves for a good. That is, the supply and demand model isn't just a model of how a competitive market works—it's also a model of how much consumers and producers gain from participating in that market. So our first step will be to learn how consumer and producer surplus can be derived from the demand and supply curves. We will then see how these concepts can be applied to actual economic issues.

Consumer Surplus and the Demand Curve

First-year college students are often surprised by the prices of the textbooks required for their classes. The College Board estimates that in 2006-2007 students at four-year schools spent, on average, $942 for books and supplies. But at the end of the semester, students might again be surprised to find out that they can sell back at least some of the textbooks they used for the semester for a percentage of the purchase price (offsetting some of the cost of textbooks). The ability to purchase used textbooks at the start of the semester and to sell back used textbooks at the end of the semester is beneficial to students on a budget. In fact, the market for used textbooks is a big business in terms of dollars and cents—approximately $1.9 billion in 2004-2005. This market provides a convenient starting point for us to develop the concepts of consumer and producer surplus. We'll use the concepts of consumer and producer surplus to understand exactly how buyers and sellers benefit from a competitive market and how big those benefits are. In addition, these concepts assist in the analysis of what happens when competitive markets don't work well or there is interference in the market.

So let's begin by looking at the market for used textbooks, starting with the buyers. The key point, as we'll see in a minute, is that the demand curve is derived from their tastes or preferences—and that those same preferences also determine how much they gain from the opportunity to buy used books.

Willingness to Pay and the Demand Curve

A used book is not as good as a new book—it will be battered and coffee-stained, may include someone else's highlighting, and may not be completely up to date. How much this bothers you depends on your preferences. Some potential buyers would prefer to buy the used book even if it is only slightly cheaper than a new one, while others would buy the used book only if it is considerably cheaper. Let's define a potential buyer's **willingness to pay** as the maximum price at which he or she would buy a good, in this case a used textbook. An individual won't buy the good if it costs more than this amount but is eager to do so if it costs less. If the price is just equal to an individual's willingness to pay, he or she is indifferent between buying and not buying. For the sake of simplicity, we'll assume that the individual buys the good in this case.

The table in Figure 13.1 on the next page shows five potential buyers of a used book that costs $100 new, listed in order of their willingness to pay. At one extreme is Aleisha, who will buy a second-hand book even if the price is as high as $59. Brad is less willing to have a used book and will buy one only if the price is $45 or less. Claudia is willing to pay only $35 and Darren, only $25. Edwina, who really doesn't like the idea of a used book, will buy one only if it costs no more than $10.

How many of these five students will actually buy a used book? It depends on the price. If the price of a used book is $55, only Aleisha buys one; if the price is $40, Aleisha and Brad both buy used books, and so on. So the information in the table can be used to construct the *demand schedule* for used textbooks.

We can use this demand schedule to derive the market demand curve shown in Figure 13.1. Because we are considering only a small number of consumers, this curve doesn't look like the smooth demand curves we have seen previously, for markets that contained hundreds or thousands of consumers. This demand curve is step-shaped, with alternating horizontal and vertical segments. Each horizontal segment—each step—corresponds to one potential buyer's willingness to pay. However, we'll see shortly that for the analysis of consumer surplus it doesn't matter whether the demand curve is step-shaped, as in this figure, or whether there are many consumers, making the curve smooth.

A consumer's **willingness to pay** for a good is the maximum price at which he or she would buy that good.

figure **13.1** The Demand Curve for Used Textbooks

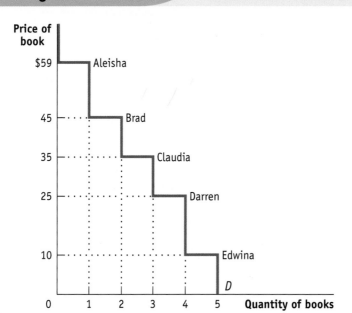

Potential buyers	Willingness to pay
Aleisha	$59
Brad	45
Claudia	35
Darren	25
Edwina	10

With only five potential consumers in this market, the demand curve is step-shaped. Each step represents one consumer, and its height indicates that consumer's willingness to pay—the maximum price at which each will buy a used textbook—as indicated in the table. Aleisha has the highest willingness to pay at $59, Brad has the next highest at $45, and so on down to Edwina with the lowest willingness to pay at $10. At a price of $59, the quantity demanded is one (Aleisha); at a price of $45, the quantity demanded is two (Aleisha and Brad); and so on until you reach a price of $10, at which all five students are willing to purchase a book.

Willingness to Pay and Consumer Surplus

Suppose that the campus bookstore makes used textbooks available at a price of $30. In that case Aleisha, Brad, and Claudia will buy books. Do they gain from their purchases, and if so, how much?

The answer, shown in Table 13.1, is that each student who purchases a book does achieve a net gain but that the amount of the gain differs among students.

Aleisha would have been willing to pay $59, so her net gain is $59 − $30 = $29. Brad would have been willing to pay $45, so his net gain is $45 − $30 = $15. Claudia would

table **13.1**

Consumer Surplus When the Price of a Used Textbook Is $30

Potential buyer	Willingness to pay	Price paid	Individual consumer surplus = Willingness to pay − Price paid
Aleisha	$59	$30	$29
Brad	45	30	15
Claudia	35	30	5
Darren	25	—	—
Edwina	10	—	—
All buyers			Total consumer surplus = $49

have been willing to pay $35, so her net gain is $35 − $30 = $5. Darren and Edwina, however, won't be willing to buy a used book at a price of $30, so they neither gain nor lose.

The net gain that a buyer achieves from the purchase of a good is called that buyer's **individual consumer surplus.** What we learn from this example is that whenever a buyer pays a price less than his or her willingness to pay, the buyer achieves some individual consumer surplus.

The sum of the individual consumer surpluses achieved by all the buyers of a good is known as the **total consumer surplus** achieved in the market. In Table 13.1, the total consumer surplus is the sum of the individual consumer surpluses achieved by Aleisha, Brad, and Claudia: $29 + $15 + $5 = $49.

Economists often use the term **consumer surplus** to refer to both individual and total consumer surplus. We will follow this practice; it will always be clear in context whether we are referring to the consumer surplus achieved by an individual or by all buyers.

Total consumer surplus can be represented graphically. Figure 13.2 reproduces the demand curve from Figure 13.1. Each step in that demand curve is one book wide and represents one consumer. For example, the height of Aleisha's step is $59, her willingness to pay. This step forms the top of a rectangle, with $30—the price she actually pays for a book—forming the bottom. The area of Aleisha's rectangle, ($59 − $30) × 1 = $29, is her consumer surplus from purchasing one book at $30. So the individual consumer surplus Aleisha gains is the *area of the dark blue rectangle* shown in Figure 13.2.

In addition to Aleisha, Brad and Claudia will also each buy a book when the price is $30. Like Aleisha, they benefit from their purchases, though not as much, because they each have a lower willingness to pay. Figure 13.2 also shows the consumer surplus gained by Brad and Claudia; again, this can be measured by the areas of the appropriate rectangles. Darren and Edwina, because they do not buy books at a price of $30, receive no consumer surplus.

The total consumer surplus achieved in this market is just the sum of the individual consumer surpluses received by Aleisha, Brad, and Claudia. So total consumer surplus is equal to the combined area of the three rectangles—the entire shaded area in Figure 13.2. Another way to say this is that total consumer surplus is equal to the area below the demand curve but above the price.

Individual consumer surplus is the net gain to an individual buyer from the purchase of a good. It is equal to the difference between the buyer's willingness to pay and the price paid.

Total consumer surplus is the sum of the individual consumer surpluses of all the buyers of a good in a market.

The term **consumer surplus** is often used to refer to both individual and to total consumer surplus.

figure 13.2

Consumer Surplus in the Used-Textbook Market

At a price of $30, Aleisha, Brad, and Claudia each buy a book but Darren and Edwina do not. Aleisha, Brad, and Claudia get individual consumer surpluses equal to the difference between their willingness to pay and the price, illustrated by the areas of the shaded rectangles. Both Darren and Edwina have a willingness to pay less than $30, so they are unwilling to buy a book in this market; they receive zero consumer surplus. The total consumer surplus is given by the entire shaded area—the sum of the individual consumer surpluses of Aleisha, Brad, and Claudia—equal to $29 + $15 + $5 = $49.

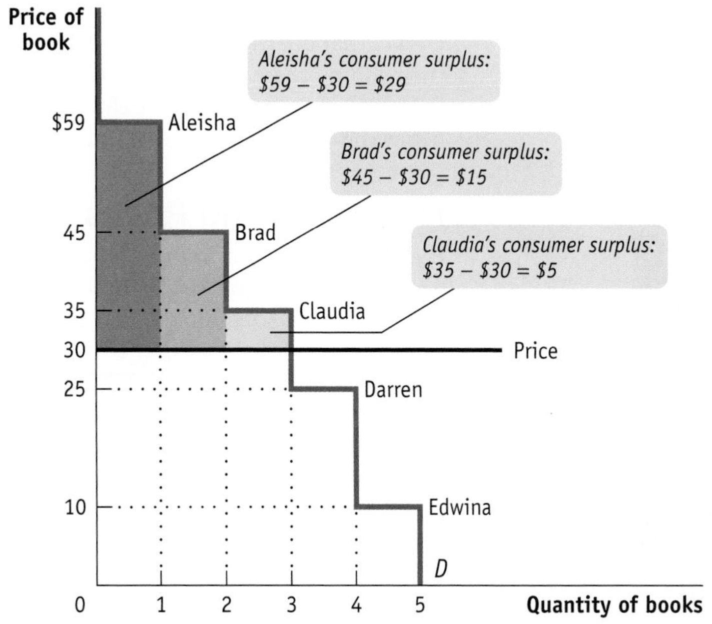

This is worth repeating as a general principle: *The total consumer surplus generated by purchases of a good at a given price is equal to the area below the demand curve but above that price.* The same principle applies regardless of the number of consumers.

When we consider large markets, this graphical representation becomes particularly helpful. Consider, for example, the sales of personal computers to millions of potential buyers. Each potential buyer has a maximum price that he or she is willing to pay. With so many potential buyers, the demand curve will be smooth, like the one shown in Figure 13.3.

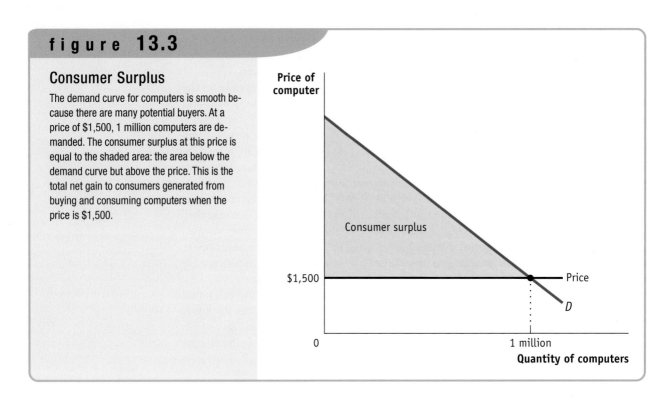

figure 13.3

Consumer Surplus

The demand curve for computers is smooth because there are many potential buyers. At a price of $1,500, 1 million computers are demanded. The consumer surplus at this price is equal to the shaded area: the area below the demand curve but above the price. This is the total net gain to consumers generated from buying and consuming computers when the price is $1,500.

Suppose that at a price of $1,500, a total of 1 million computers are purchased. How much do consumers gain from being able to buy those 1 million computers? We could answer that question by calculating the individual consumer surplus of each buyer and then adding these numbers up to arrive at a total. But it is much easier just to look at Figure 13.3 and use the fact that total consumer surplus is equal to the shaded area below the demand curve but above the price.

How Changing Prices Affect Consumer Surplus

It is often important to know how price *changes* affect consumer surplus. For example, we may want to know the harm to consumers from a frost in Florida that drives up orange prices or consumers' gain from the introduction of fish farming that makes salmon steaks less expensive. The same approach we have used to derive consumer surplus can be used to answer questions about how changes in prices affect consumers.

Let's return to the example of the market for used textbooks. Suppose that the bookstore decided to sell used textbooks for $20 instead of $30. By how much would this fall in price increase consumer surplus?

The answer is illustrated in Figure 13.4. As shown in the figure, there are two parts to the increase in consumer surplus. The first part, shaded dark blue, is the gain of those who would have bought books even at the higher price of $30. Each of the students who would have bought books at $30—Aleisha, Brad, and Claudia—now pays $10 less, and therefore each gains $10 in consumer surplus from the fall in price to $20. So

figure 13.4

Consumer Surplus and a Fall in the Price of Used Textbooks

There are two parts to the increase in consumer surplus generated by a fall in price from $30 to $20. The first is given by the dark blue rectangle: each person who would have bought at the original price of $30—Aleisha, Brad, and Claudia—receives an increase in consumer surplus equal to the total reduction in price, $10. So the area of the dark blue rectangle corresponds to an amount equal to 3 × $10 = $30. The second part is given by the light blue area: the increase in consumer surplus for those who would *not* have bought at the original price of $30 but who buy at the new price of $20—namely, Darren. Darren's willingness to pay is $25, so he now receives consumer surplus of $5. The total increase in consumer surplus is 3 × $10 + $5 = $35, represented by the sum of the shaded areas. Likewise, a rise in price from $20 to $30 would decrease consumer surplus by an amount equal to the sum of the shaded areas.

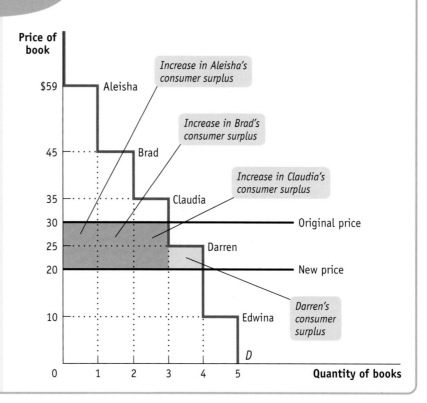

the dark blue area represents the $10 × 3 = $30 increase in consumer surplus to those three buyers. The second part, shaded light blue, is the gain to those who would not have bought a book at $30 but are willing to pay more than $20. In this case that gain goes to Darren, who would not have bought a book at $30 but does buy one at $20. He gains $5—the difference between his willingness to pay of $25 and the new price of $20. So the light blue area represents a further $5 gain in consumer surplus. The total increase in consumer surplus is the sum of the shaded areas, $35. Likewise, a rise in price from $20 to $30 would decrease consumer surplus by an amount equal to the sum of the shaded areas.

Figure 13.4 illustrates that when the price of a good falls, the area under the demand curve but above the price—the total consumer surplus—increases. Figure 13.5 on the next page shows the same result for the case of a smooth demand curve for personal computers. Here we assume that the price of computers falls from $5,000 to $1,500, leading to an increase in the quantity demanded from 200,000 to 1 million units. As in the used-textbook example, we divide the gain in consumer surplus into two parts. The dark blue rectangle in Figure 13.5 corresponds to the dark blue area in Figure 13.4: it is the gain to the 200,000 people who would have bought computers even at the higher price of $5,000. As a result of the price reduction, each receives additional surplus of $3,500. The light blue triangle in Figure 13.5 corresponds to the light blue area in Figure 13.4: it is the gain to people who would not have bought the good at the higher price but are willing to do so at a price of $1,500. For example, the light blue triangle includes the gain to someone who would have been willing to pay $2,000 for a computer and therefore gains $500 in consumer surplus when it is possible to buy a computer for only $1,500. As before, the total gain in consumer surplus is the sum of the shaded areas, the increase in the area under the demand curve but above the price.

What would happen if the price of a good were to rise instead of fall? We would do the same analysis in reverse. Suppose, for example, that for some reason the price of

figure 13.5

A Fall in the Price Increases Consumer Surplus

A fall in the price of a computer from $5,000 to $1,500 leads to an increase in the quantity demanded and an increase in consumer surplus. The change in total consumer surplus is given by the sum of the shaded areas: the total area below the demand curve and between the old and new prices. Here, the dark blue area represents the increase in consumer surplus for the 200,000 consumers who would have bought a computer at the original price of $5,000; they each receive an increase in consumer surplus of $3,500. The light blue area represents the increase in consumer surplus for those willing to buy at a price equal to or greater than $1,500 but less than $5,000. Similarly, a rise in the price of a computer from $1,500 to $5,000 generates a decrease in consumer surplus equal to the sum of the two shaded areas.

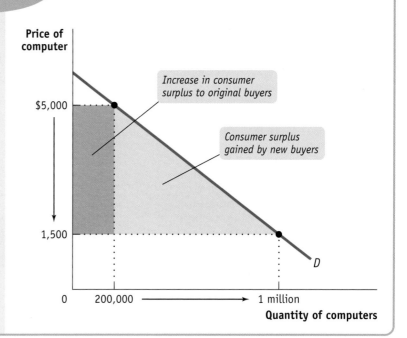

computers rises from $1,500 to $5,000. This would lead to a fall in consumer surplus equal to the sum of the shaded areas in Figure 13.5. This loss consists of two parts. The dark blue rectangle represents the loss to consumers who would still buy a computer, even at a price of $5,000. The light blue triangle represents the loss to consumers who decide not to buy a computer at the higher price.

in real life

A Matter of Life and Death

Each year about 4,000 people in the United States die while waiting for a kidney transplant. In 2009, some 80,000 were on the waiting list. Since the number of those in need of a kidney far exceeds availability, what is the best way to allocate available organs? A market isn't feasible. For understandable reasons, the sale of human body parts is illegal in this country. So the task of establishing a protocol for these situations has fallen to the nonprofit group United Network for Organ Sharing (UNOS).

Under current UNOS guidelines, a donated kidney goes to the person who has been waiting the longest. According to this system, an available kidney would go to a 75-year-old who has been waiting for 2 years instead of to a 25-year-old who has been waiting 6 months, even though the 25-year-old will likely live longer and benefit from the transplanted organ for a longer period of time.

To address this issue, UNOS is devising a new set of guidelines based on a concept it calls "net benefit." According to these new guidelines, kidneys would be allocated on the basis of who will receive the greatest net benefit, where net benefit is measured as the expected increase in lifespan from the transplant. And age is by far the biggest predictor of how long someone will live after a transplant. For example, a typical 25-year-old diabetic will gain an extra 8.7 years of life from a transplant, but a typical 55-year-old diabetic will gain only 3.6 extra years. Under the current system, based on waiting times, transplants lead to about 44,000 extra years of life for recipients; under the new system, that number would jump to 55,000 extra years. The share of kidneys going to those in their 20s would triple; the share going to those 60 and older would be halved.

What does this have to do with consumer surplus? As you may have guessed, the UNOS

concept of "net benefit" is a lot like individual consumer surplus—the individual consumer surplus generated from getting a new kidney. In essence, UNOS has devised a system that allocates donated kidneys according to who gets the greatest individual consumer surplus. In terms of results, then, its proposed "net benefit" system operates a lot like a competitive market.

Producer Surplus and the Supply Curve

Just as some buyers of a good would have been willing to pay more for their purchase than the price they actually pay, some sellers of a good would have been willing to sell it for less than the price they actually receive. We can therefore carry out an analysis of producer surplus and the supply curve that is almost exactly parallel to that of consumer surplus and the demand curve.

Cost and Producer Surplus

Consider a group of students who are potential sellers of used textbooks. Because they have different preferences, the various potential sellers differ in the price at which they are willing to sell their books. The table in Figure 13.6 shows the prices at which several different students would be willing to sell. Andrew is willing to sell the book as long as he can get at least $5; Betty won't sell unless she can get at least $15; Carlos requires $25; Donna requires $35; Engelbert $45.

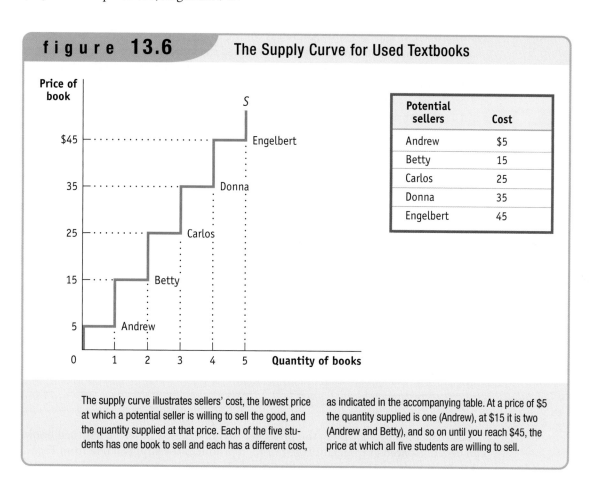

figure 13.6   **The Supply Curve for Used Textbooks**

Potential sellers	Cost
Andrew	$5
Betty	15
Carlos	25
Donna	35
Engelbert	45

The supply curve illustrates sellers' cost, the lowest price at which a potential seller is willing to sell the good, and the quantity supplied at that price. Each of the five students has one book to sell and each has a different cost, as indicated in the accompanying table. At a price of $5 the quantity supplied is one (Andrew), at $15 it is two (Andrew and Betty), and so on until you reach $45, the price at which all five students are willing to sell.

The lowest price at which a potential seller is willing to sell is called the seller's **cost.** So Andrew's cost is $5, Betty's is $15, and so on.

Using the term *cost,* which people normally associate with the monetary cost of producing a good, may sound a little strange when applied to sellers of used textbooks. The students don't have to manufacture the books, so it doesn't cost the student who sells a book anything to make that book available for sale, does it?

Yes, it does. A student who sells a book won't have it later, as part of his or her personal collection. So there is an *opportunity cost* to selling a textbook, even if the owner has completed the course for which it was required. And remember that one of the basic principles of economics is that the true measure of the cost of doing something is

A seller's **cost** is the lowest price at which he or she is willing to sell a good.

Individual producer surplus is the net gain to an individual seller from selling a good. It is equal to the difference between the price received and the seller's cost.

Total producer surplus in a market is the sum of the individual producer surpluses of all the sellers of a good in a market. Economists use the term **producer surplus** to refer both to individual and to total producer surplus.

always its opportunity cost. That is, the real cost of something is what you must give up to get it.

So it is good economics to talk of the minimum price at which someone will sell a good as the "cost" of selling that good, even if he or she doesn't spend any money to make the good available for sale. Of course, in most real-world markets the sellers are also those who produce the good and therefore *do* spend money to make the good available for sale. In this case the cost of making the good available for sale *includes* monetary costs, but it may also include other opportunity costs.

Getting back to the example, suppose that Andrew sells his book for $30. Clearly he has gained from the transaction: he would have been willing to sell for only $5, so he has gained $25. This net gain, the difference between the price he actually gets and his cost—the minimum price at which he would have been willing to sell—is known as his **individual producer surplus.**

Just as we derived the demand curve from the willingness to pay of different consumers, we can derive the supply curve from the cost of different producers. The step-shaped curve in Figure 13.6 shows the supply curve implied by the costs shown in the accompanying table. At a price less than $5, none of the students are willing to sell; at a price between $5 and $15, only Andrew is willing to sell, and so on.

As in the case of consumer surplus, we can add the individual producer surpluses of sellers to calculate the **total producer surplus,** the total net gain to all sellers in the market. Economists use the term **producer surplus** to refer to either total or individual producer surplus. Table 13.2 shows the net gain to each of the students who would sell a used book at a price of $30: $25 for Andrew, $15 for Betty, and $5 for Carlos. The total producer surplus is $25 + $15 + $5 = $45.

table 13.2

Producer Surplus When the Price of a Used Textbook Is $30

Potential seller	Cost	Price received	Individual producer surplus = Price received − Cost
Andrew	$5	$30	$25
Betty	15	30	15
Carlos	25	30	5
Donna	35	—	—
Engelbert	45	—	—
All sellers			Total producer surplus = $45

As with consumer surplus, the producer surplus gained by those who sell books can be represented graphically. Figure 13.7 reproduces the supply curve from Figure 13.6. Each step in that supply curve is one book wide and represents one seller. The height of Andrew's step is $5, his cost. This forms the bottom of a rectangle, with $30, the price he actually receives for his book, forming the top. The area of this rectangle, ($30 − $5) × 1 = $25, is his producer surplus. So the producer surplus Andrew gains from selling his book is the *area of the dark red rectangle* shown in the figure.

Let's assume that the campus bookstore is willing to buy all the used copies of this book that students are willing to sell at a price of $30. Then, in addition to Andrew, Betty and Carlos will also sell their books. They will also benefit from their sales, though not as much as Andrew, because they have higher costs. Andrew, as we have seen, gains $25. Betty gains a smaller amount: since her cost is $15, she gains only $15. Carlos gains even less, only $5.

figure 13.7

Producer Surplus in the Used-Textbook Market

At a price of $30, Andrew, Betty, and Carlos each sells a book but Donna and Engelbert do not. Andrew, Betty, and Carlos get individual producer surpluses equal to the difference between the price and their cost, illustrated here by the shaded rectangles. Donna and Engelbert each has a cost that is greater than the price of $30, so they are unwilling to sell a book and so receive zero producer surplus. The total producer surplus is given by the entire shaded area, the sum of the individual producer surpluses of Andrew, Betty, and Carlos, equal to $25 + $15 + $5 = $45.

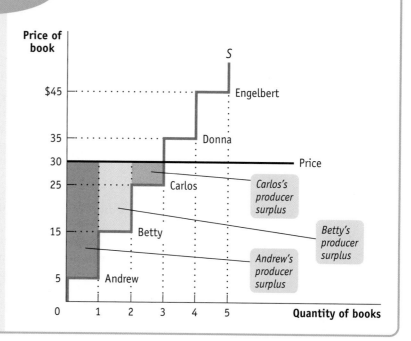

Again, as with consumer surplus, we have a general rule for determining the total producer surplus from sales of a good: *The total producer surplus from sales of a good at a given price is the area above the supply curve but below that price.*

This rule applies both to examples like the one shown in Figure 13.7, where there are a small number of producers and a step-shaped supply curve, and to more realistic examples, where there are many producers and the supply curve is more or less smooth.

Consider, for example, the supply of wheat. Figure 13.8 shows how producer surplus depends on the price per bushel. Suppose that, as shown in

figure 13.8

Producer Surplus

Here is the supply curve for wheat. At a price of $5 per bushel, farmers supply 1 million bushels. The producer surplus at this price is equal to the shaded area: the area above the supply curve but below the price. This is the total gain to producers—farmers in this case—from supplying their product when the price is $5.

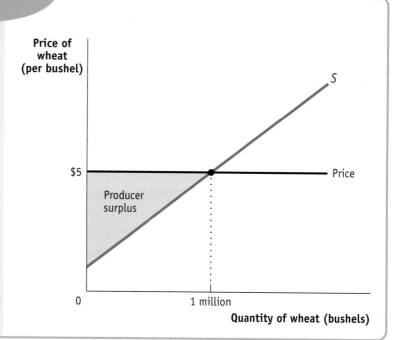

the figure, the price is $5 per bushel and farmers supply 1 million bushels. What is the benefit to the farmers from selling their wheat at a price of $5? Their producer surplus is equal to the shaded area in the figure—the area above the supply curve but below the price of $5 per bushel.

How Changing Prices Affect Producer Surplus

As in the case of consumer surplus, a change in price alters producer surplus. However, although a fall in price increases consumer surplus, it reduces producer surplus. Similarly, a rise in price reduces consumer surplus but increases producer surplus.

To see this, let's first consider a rise in the price of the good. Producers of the good will experience an increase in producer surplus, though not all producers gain the same amount. Some producers would have produced the good even at the original price; they will gain the entire price increase on every unit they produce. Other producers will enter the market because of the higher price; they will gain only the difference between the new price and their cost.

Figure 13.9 is the supply counterpart of Figure 13.5. It shows the effect on producer surplus of a rise in the price of wheat from $5 to $7 per bushel. The increase in producer surplus is the sum of the shaded areas, which consists of two parts. First, there is a dark red rectangle corresponding to the gains to those farmers who would have supplied wheat even at the original $5 price. Second, there is an additional light red triangle that corresponds to the gains to those farmers who would not have supplied wheat at the original price but are drawn into the market by the higher price.

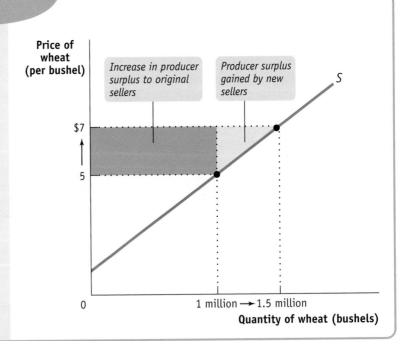

figure 13.9

A Rise in the Price Increases Producer Surplus

A rise in the price of wheat from $5 to $7 leads to an increase in the quantity supplied and an increase in producer surplus. The change in total producer surplus is given by the sum of the shaded areas: the total area above the supply curve but between the old and new prices. The dark red area represents the gain to the farmers who would have supplied 1 million bushels at the original price of $5; they each receive an increase in producer surplus of $2 for each of those bushels. The triangular light red area represents the increase in producer surplus achieved by the farmers who supply the additional 500,000 bushels because of the higher price. Similarly, a fall in the price of wheat generates a reduction in producer surplus equal to the sum of the shaded areas.

If the price were to fall from $7 to $5 per bushel, the story would run in reverse. The sum of the shaded areas would now be the decline in producer surplus, the decrease in the area above the supply curve but below the price. The loss would consist of two parts, the loss to farmers who would still grow wheat at a price of $5 (the dark red rectangle) and the loss to farmers who decide to no longer grow wheat because of the lower price (the light red triangle).

Module 13 Review

Solutions appear at the back of the book.

Check Your Understanding

1. Consider the market for cheese-stuffed jalapeno peppers. There are two consumers, Casey and Josey, and their willingness to pay for each pepper is given in the accompanying table. (Neither is willing to consume more than 4 peppers at any price.) Use the table (i) to construct the demand schedule for peppers for prices of $0.00, $0.10, and so on, up to $0.90, and (ii) to calculate the total consumer surplus when the price of a pepper is $0.40.

Quantity of peppers	Casey's willingness to pay	Josey's willingness to pay
1st pepper	$0.90	$0.80
2nd pepper	0.70	0.60
3rd pepper	0.50	0.40
4th pepper	0.30	0.30

2. Again consider the market for cheese-stuffed jalapeno peppers. There are two producers, Cara and Jamie, and their costs of producing each pepper are given in the accompanying table. (Neither is willing to produce more than 4 peppers at any price.) Use the table (i) to construct the supply schedule for peppers for prices of $0.00, $0.10, and so on, up to $0.90, and (ii) to calculate the total producer surplus when the price of a pepper is $0.70.

Quantity of peppers	Cara's cost	Jamie's cost
1st pepper	$0.10	$0.30
2nd pepper	0.10	0.50
3rd pepper	0.40	0.70
4th pepper	0.60	0.90

Multiple-Choice Questions

1. Refer to the graph below. What is the value of consumer surplus when the market price is $40?

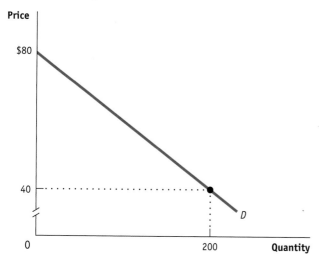

a. $400
b. $800
c. $4,000
d. $8,000
e. $16,000

2. Refer to the graph below. What is the value of producer surplus when the market price is $60?

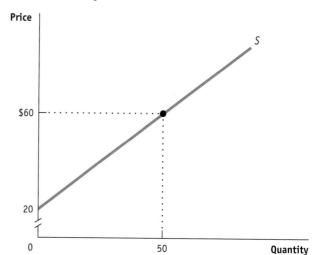

a. $100
b. $150
c. $1,000
d. $1,500
e. $3,000

3. Other things equal, a rise in price will result in which of the following?
   a. Producer surplus will rise; consumer surplus will rise.
   b. Producer surplus will fall; consumer surplus will fall.
   c. Producer surplus will rise; consumer surplus will fall.
   d. Producer surplus will fall; consumer surplus will rise.
   e. Producer surplus will not change; consumer surplus will rise.

4. Consumer surplus is found as the area
   a. above the supply curve and below the price.
   b. below the demand curve and above the price.
   c. above the demand curve and below the price.
   d. below the supply curve and above the price.
   e. below the supply curve and above the demand curve.

5. Allocating kidneys to those with the highest net benefit (where net benefit is measured as the expected increase in lifespan from a transplant) is an attempt to maximize
   a. consumer surplus.
   b. producer surplus.
   c. profit.
   d. equity.
   e. respect for elders.

Critical-Thinking Question

Draw a correctly labeled graph showing a competitive market in equilibrium. On your graph, clearly indicate and label the area of consumer surplus and the area of producer surplus.

Module 14
Efficiency and Deadweight Loss

What you will learn
in this **Module:**

- The meaning and importance of total surplus and how it can be used to illustrate efficiency in markets
- How taxes affect total surplus and can create deadweight loss

Consumer Surplus, Producer Surplus, and Efficiency

Markets are a remarkably effective way to organize economic activity: under the right conditions, they can make society as well off as possible given the available resources. The concepts of consumer and producer surplus can help us deepen our understanding of why this core principle of economics is so.

The Gains from Trade

Let's return to the market for used textbooks, but now consider a much bigger market—say, one at a large state university. There are many potential buyers and sellers, so the market is competitive. Let's line up incoming students who are potential buyers of a book in order of their willingness to pay, so that the entering student with the highest willingness to pay is potential buyer number 1, the student with the next highest willingness to pay is number 2, and so on. Then we can use their willingness to pay to derive a demand curve like the one in Figure 14.1 on the next page. Similarly, we can line up outgoing students, who are potential sellers of the book, in order of their cost, starting with the student with the lowest cost, then the student with the next lowest cost, and so on, to derive a supply curve like the one shown in the same figure.

As we have drawn the curves, the market reaches equilibrium at a price of $30 per book, and 1,000 books are bought and sold at that price. The two shaded triangles show the consumer surplus (blue) and the producer surplus (red) generated by this market. The sum of consumer and producer surplus is known as **total surplus.**

The striking thing about this picture is that both consumers and producers gain—that is, both consumers and producers are better off because there is a market in this good. But this should come as no surprise—it illustrates another core principle of economics: *There are gains from trade*. These gains from trade are the reason everyone is better off participating in a market economy than they would be if each individual tried to be self-sufficient.

Total surplus is the total net gain to consumers and producers from trading in a market. It is the sum of producer and consumer surplus.

figure 14.1

Total Surplus

In the market for used textbooks, the equilibrium price is $30 and the equilibrium quantity is 1,000 books. Consumer surplus is given by the blue area, the area below the demand curve but above the price. Producer surplus is given by the red area, the area above the supply curve but below the price. The sum of the blue and the red areas is total surplus, the total benefit to society from the production and consumption of the good.

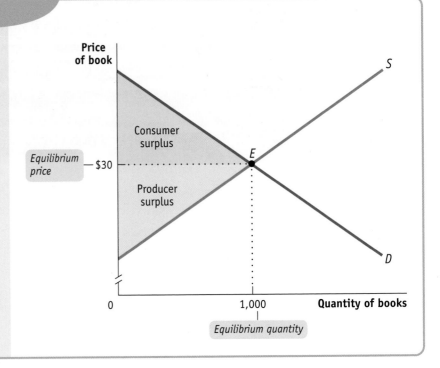

But are we as well off as we could be? This brings us to the question of the efficiency of markets.

The Efficiency of Markets

A market is *efficient* if, once the market has produced its gains from trade, there is no way to make some people better off without making other people worse off. Note that market equilibrium is just *one* way of deciding who consumes a good and who sells a good. To better understand how markets promote efficiency, let's examine some alternatives. Consider the example of kidney transplants discussed earlier in an IRL box. There is not a market for kidneys, and available kidneys currently go to whoever has been on the waiting list the longest. Of course, those who have been waiting the longest aren't necessarily those who would benefit the most from a new kidney.

Similarly, imagine a committee charged with improving on the market equilibrium by deciding who gets and who gives up a used textbook. The committee's ultimate goal would be to bypass the market outcome and come up with another arrangement that would increase total surplus.

Let's consider three approaches the committee could take:

1. It could reallocate consumption among consumers.
2. It could reallocate sales among sellers.
3. It could change the quantity traded.

The Reallocation of Consumption Among Consumers The committee might try to increase total surplus by selling books to different consumers. Figure 14.2 shows why this will result in lower surplus compared to the market equilibrium outcome. Points *A* and *B* show the positions on the demand curve of two potential buyers of used books, Ana and Bob. As we can see from the figure, Ana is willing to pay $35 for a book, but Bob is willing to pay only $25. Since the market equilibrium price is $30, under the market outcome Ana gets a book and Bob does not.

Now suppose the committee reallocates consumption. This would mean taking the book away from Ana and giving it to Bob. Since the book is worth $35 to Ana but only $25 to Bob, this change *reduces total consumer surplus* by $35 − $25 = $10. Moreover, this result

figure 14.2

Reallocating Consumption Lowers Consumer Surplus

Ana (point A) has a willingness to pay of $35. Bob (point B) has a willingness to pay of only $25. At the market equilibrium price of $30, Ana purchases a book but Bob does not. If we rearrange consumption by taking a book from Ana and giving it to Bob, consumer surplus declines by $10 and, as a result, total surplus declines by $10. The market equilibrium generates the highest possible consumer surplus by ensuring that those who consume the good are those who most value it.

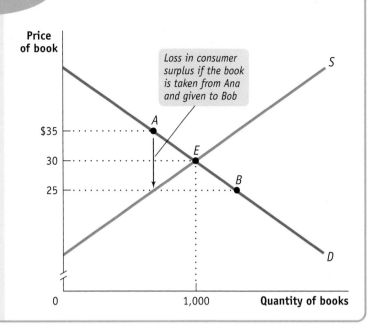

doesn't depend on which two students we pick. Every student who buys a book at the market equilibrium price has a willingness to pay of $30 or more, and every student who doesn't buy a book has a willingness to pay of less than $30. So reallocating the good among consumers always means taking a book away from a student who values it more and giving it to one who values it less. This necessarily reduces total consumer surplus.

The Reallocation of Sales Among Sellers The committee might try to increase total surplus by altering who sells their books, taking sales away from sellers who would have sold their books in the market equilibrium and instead compelling those who would not have sold their books in the market equilibrium to sell them. Figure 14.3 shows why this will result in lower surplus. Here points X and Y show the positions on the supply

figure 14.3

Reallocating Sales Lowers Producer Surplus

Yvonne (point Y) has a cost of $35, $10 more than Xavier (point X), who has a cost of $25. At the market equilibrium price of $30, Xavier sells a book but Yvonne does not. If we rearrange sales by preventing Xavier from selling his book and compelling Yvonne to sell hers, producer surplus declines by $10 and, as a result, total surplus declines by $10. The market equilibrium generates the highest possible producer surplus by assuring that those who sell the good are those who most value the right to sell it.

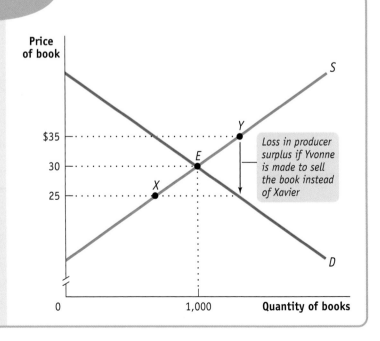

curve of Xavier, who has a cost of $25, and Yvonne, who has a cost of $35. At the equilibrium market price of $30, Xavier would sell his book but Yvonne would not sell hers. If the committee reallocated sales, forcing Xavier to keep his book and Yvonne to sell hers, total producer surplus would be reduced by $35 − $25 = $10. Again, it doesn't matter which two students we choose. Any student who sells a book at the market equilibrium price has a lower cost than any student who keeps a book. So reallocating sales among sellers necessarily increases total cost and reduces total producer surplus.

Changes in the Quantity Traded The committee might try to increase total surplus by compelling students to trade either more books or fewer books than the market equilibrium quantity. Figure 14.4 shows why this will result in lower surplus. It shows all four students: potential buyers Ana and Bob, and potential sellers Xavier and Yvonne. To reduce sales, the committee will have to prevent a transaction that would have occurred in the market equilibrium—that is, prevent Xavier from selling to Ana. Since Ana is willing to pay $35 and Xavier's cost is $25, preventing this transaction reduces total surplus by $35 − $25 = $10. Once again, this result doesn't depend on which two students we pick: any student who would have sold the book in the market equilibrium has a cost of $30 or less, and any student who would have purchased the book in the market equilibrium has a willingness to pay of $30 or more. So preventing any sale that would have occurred in the market equilibrium necessarily reduces total surplus.

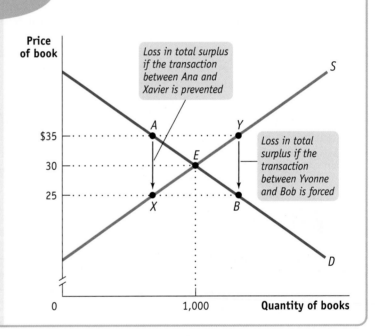

figure 14.4

Changing the Quantity Lowers Total Surplus

If Xavier (point X) were prevented from selling his book to someone like Ana (point A), total surplus would fall by $10, the difference between Ana's willingness to pay ($35) and Xavier's cost ($25). This means that total surplus falls whenever fewer than 1,000 books—the equilibrium quantity—are transacted. Likewise, if Yvonne (point Y) were compelled to sell her book to someone like Bob (point B), total surplus would also fall by $10, the difference between Yvonne's cost ($35) and Bob's willingness to pay ($25). This means that total surplus falls whenever more than 1,000 books are transacted. These two examples show that at market equilibrium, all mutually beneficial transactions—and only mutually beneficial transactions—occur.

Finally, the committee might try to increase sales by forcing Yvonne, who would not have sold her book in the market equilibrium, to sell it to someone like Bob, who would not have bought a book in the market equilibrium. Because Yvonne's cost is $35, but Bob is only willing to pay $25, this transaction reduces total surplus by $10. And once again it doesn't matter which two students we pick—anyone who wouldn't have bought the book has a willingness to pay of less than $30, and anyone who wouldn't have sold has a cost of more than $30.

The key point to remember is that once this market is in equilibrium, there is no way to increase the gains from trade. Any other outcome reduces total surplus. We can summarize our results by stating that an efficient market performs four important functions:

1. It allocates consumption of the good to the potential buyers who most value it, as indicated by the fact that they have the highest willingness to pay.

2. It allocates sales to the potential sellers who most value the right to sell the good, as indicated by the fact that they have the lowest cost.

3. It ensures that every consumer who makes a purchase values the good more than every seller who makes a sale, so that all transactions are mutually beneficial.

4. It ensures that every potential buyer who doesn't make a purchase values the good less than every potential seller who doesn't make a sale, so that no mutually beneficial transactions are missed.

There are three caveats, however. First, although a market may be efficient, it isn't necessarily *fair.* In fact, fairness, or *equity,* is often in conflict with efficiency. We'll discuss this next.

The second caveat is that markets sometimes *fail.* Under some well-defined conditions, markets can fail to deliver efficiency. When this occurs, markets no longer maximize total surplus. We'll take a closer look at market failures in later modules.

Third, even when the market equilibrium maximizes total surplus, this does not mean that it results in the best outcome for every *individual* consumer and producer. Other things equal, each buyer would like to pay a lower price and each seller would like to receive a higher price. So if the government were to intervene in the market—say, by lowering the price below the equilibrium price to make consumers happy or by raising the price above the equilibrium price to make producers happy—the outcome would no longer be efficient. Although some people would be happier, society as a whole would be worse off because total surplus would be lower.

Equity and Efficiency

It's easy to get carried away with the idea that markets are always good and that economic policies that interfere with efficiency are bad. But that would be misguided because there is another factor to consider: society cares about equity, or what's "fair." There is often a trade-off between equity and efficiency: policies that promote equity often come at the cost of decreased efficiency, and policies that promote efficiency often result in decreased equity. So it's important to realize that a society's choice to sacrifice some efficiency for the sake of equity, however it defines equity, may well be a valid one. And it's important to understand that fairness, unlike efficiency, can be very hard to define. Fairness is a concept about which well-intentioned people often disagree.

In fact, the debate about equity and efficiency is at the core of most debates about taxation. Proponents of taxes that redistribute income from the rich to the poor often argue for the fairness of such redistributive taxes. Opponents of taxation often argue that phasing out certain taxes would make the economy more efficient.

Because taxes are ultimately paid out of income, economists classify taxes according to how they vary with the income of individuals. A tax that rises more than in proportion to income, so that high-income taxpayers pay a larger percentage of their income than low-income taxpayers, is a **progressive tax.** A tax that rises less than in proportion to income, so that high-income taxpayers pay a smaller percentage of their income than low-income taxpayers, is a **regressive tax.** A tax that rises in proportion to income, so that all taxpayers pay the same percentage of their income, is a **proportional tax.** The U.S. tax system contains a mixture of progressive and regressive taxes, though it is somewhat progressive overall.

The Effects of Taxes on Total Surplus

To understand the economics of taxes, it's helpful to look at a simple type of tax known as an **excise tax**—a tax charged on each unit of a good or service that is sold. Most tax revenue in the United States comes from other kinds of taxes, but excise taxes

A **progressive tax** rises more than in proportion to income. A **regressive tax** rises less than in proportion to income. A **proportional tax** rises in proportion to income.

An **excise tax** is a tax on sales of a particular good or service.

are common. For example, there are excise taxes on gasoline, cigarettes, and foreign-made trucks, and many local governments impose excise taxes on services such as hotel room rentals. The lessons we'll learn from studying excise taxes apply to other, more complex taxes as well.

The Effect of an Excise Tax on Quantities and Prices

Suppose that the supply and demand for hotel rooms in the city of Potterville are as shown in Figure 14.5. We'll make the simplifying assumption that all hotel rooms are the same. In the absence of taxes, the equilibrium price of a room is $80 per night and the equilibrium quantity of hotel rooms rented is 10,000 per night.

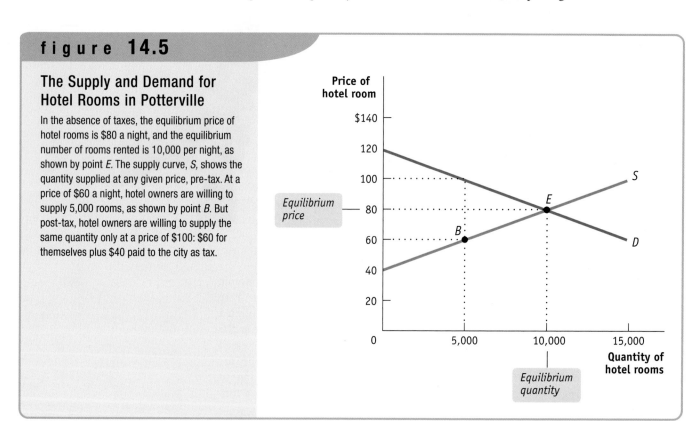

figure 14.5

The Supply and Demand for Hotel Rooms in Potterville

In the absence of taxes, the equilibrium price of hotel rooms is $80 a night, and the equilibrium number of rooms rented is 10,000 per night, as shown by point *E*. The supply curve, *S*, shows the quantity supplied at any given price, pre-tax. At a price of $60 a night, hotel owners are willing to supply 5,000 rooms, as shown by point *B*. But post-tax, hotel owners are willing to supply the same quantity only at a price of $100: $60 for themselves plus $40 paid to the city as tax.

Now suppose that Potterville's government imposes an excise tax of $40 per night on hotel rooms—that is, every time a room is rented for the night, the owner of the hotel must pay the city $40. For example, if a customer pays $80, $40 is collected as a tax, leaving the hotel owner with only $40. As a result, hotel owners are less willing to supply rooms at any given price.

What does this imply about the supply curve for hotel rooms in Potterville? To answer this question, we must compare the incentives of hotel owners *pre-tax* (before the tax is levied) to their incentives *post-tax* (after the tax is levied). From Figure 14.5 we know that pre-tax, hotel owners are willing to supply 5,000 rooms per night at a price of $60 per room. But after the $40 tax per room is levied, they are willing to supply the same amount, 5,000 rooms, only if they receive $100 per room—$60 for themselves plus $40 paid to the city as tax. In other words, in order for hotel owners to be willing to supply the same quantity post-tax as they would have pre-tax, they must receive an additional $40 per room, the amount of the tax. This implies that the post-tax supply curve shifts up by the amount of the tax compared to the pre-tax supply curve. At every quantity supplied, the supply price—the price that producers must receive to produce a given quantity—has increased by $40.

The upward shift of the supply curve caused by the tax is shown in Figure 14.6, where S_1 is the pre-tax supply curve and S_2 is the post-tax supply curve. As you can see, the market equilibrium moves from E, at the equilibrium price of $80 per room and 10,000 rooms rented each night, to A, at a market price of $100 per room and only 5,000 rooms rented each night. A is, of course, on both the demand curve D and the new supply curve S_2. In this case, $100 is the demand price of 5,000 rooms—but in effect hotel owners receive only $60, when you account for the fact that they have to pay the $40 tax. From the point of view of hotel owners, it is as if they were on their original supply curve at point B.

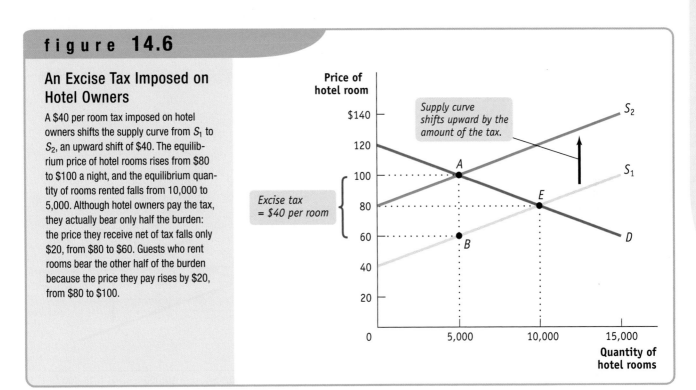

figure 14.6

An Excise Tax Imposed on Hotel Owners

A $40 per room tax imposed on hotel owners shifts the supply curve from S_1 to S_2, an upward shift of $40. The equilibrium price of hotel rooms rises from $80 to $100 a night, and the equilibrium quantity of rooms rented falls from 10,000 to 5,000. Although hotel owners pay the tax, they actually bear only half the burden: the price they receive net of tax falls only $20, from $80 to $60. Guests who rent rooms bear the other half of the burden because the price they pay rises by $20, from $80 to $100.

Let's check this again. How do we know that 5,000 rooms will be supplied at a price of $100? Because the price *net of tax* is $60, and according to the original supply curve, 5,000 rooms will be supplied at a price of $60, as shown by point B in Figure 14.6.

An excise tax *drives a wedge* between the price paid by consumers and the price received by producers. As a result of this wedge, consumers pay more and producers receive less. In our example, consumers—people who rent hotel rooms—end up paying $100 a night, $20 more than the pre-tax price of $80. At the same time, producers—the hotel owners—receive a price net of tax of $60 per room, $20 less than the pre-tax price. In addition, the tax creates missed opportunities: 5,000 potential consumers who would have rented hotel rooms—those willing to pay $80 but not $100 per night—are discouraged from renting rooms. Correspondingly, 5,000 rooms that would have been made available by hotel owners when they receive $80 are not offered when they receive only $60. Like a quota on sales, discussed at the end of the section on supply and demand, this tax leads to inefficiency by distorting incentives and creating missed opportunities for mutually beneficial transactions.

It's important to recognize that as we've described it, Potterville's hotel tax is a tax on the hotel owners, not their guests—it's a tax on the producers, not the consumers. Yet the price received by producers, net of tax, is down by only $20, half the amount of the tax, and the price paid by consumers is up by $20. In effect, half the tax is being paid by consumers.

What would happen if the city levied a tax on consumers instead of producers? That is, suppose that instead of requiring hotel owners to pay $40 a night for each room they rent, the city required hotel *guests* to pay $40 for each night they stayed in a hotel. The answer is shown in Figure 14.7. If a hotel guest must pay a tax of $40 per night, then the price for a room paid by that guest must be reduced by $40 in order for the quantity of hotel rooms demanded post-tax to be the same as that demanded pre-tax. So the demand curve shifts *downward*, from D_1 to D_2, by the amount of the tax. At every quantity demanded, the demand price—the price that consumers must be offered to demand a given quantity—has fallen by $40. This shifts the equilibrium from E to B, where the market price of hotel rooms is $60 and 5,000 hotel rooms are bought and sold. In effect, hotel guests pay $100 when you include the tax. So from the point of view of guests, it is as if they were on their original demand curve at point A.

figure 14.7

An Excise Tax Imposed on Hotel Guests

A $40 per room tax imposed on hotel guests shifts the demand curve from D_1 to D_2, a downward shift of $40. The equilibrium price of hotel rooms falls from $80 to $60 a night, and the quantity of rooms rented falls from 10,000 to 5,000. Although in this case the tax is officially paid by consumers, while in Figure 14.6 the tax was paid by producers, the outcome is the same: after taxes, hotel owners receive $60 per room but guests pay $100. This illustrates a general principle: *The incidence of an excise tax doesn't depend on whether consumers or producers officially pay the tax.*

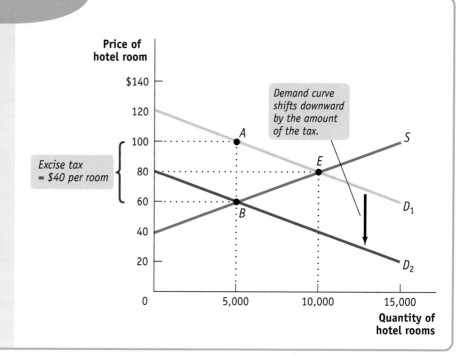

If you compare Figures 14.6 and 14.7, you will notice that the effects of the tax are the same even though different curves are shifted. In each case, consumers pay $100 per unit (including the tax, if it is their responsibility), producers receive $60 per unit (after paying the tax, if it is their responsibility), and 5,000 hotel rooms are bought and sold. *In fact, it doesn't matter who officially pays the tax—the equilibrium outcome is the same.*

This example illustrates a general principle of **tax incidence,** a measure of who really pays a tax: the burden of a tax cannot be determined by looking at who writes the check to the government. In this particular case, a $40 tax on hotel rooms brings about a $20 increase in the price paid by consumers and a $20 decrease in the price received by producers. Regardless of whether the tax is levied on consumers or producers, the incidence of the tax is the same. As we will see next, the burden of a tax depends on the price elasticities of supply and demand.

Price Elasticities and Tax Incidence

We've just learned that the incidence of an excise tax doesn't depend on who officially pays it. In the example shown in Figures 14.5 through 14.7, a tax on hotel rooms falls equally on consumers and producers, no matter on whom the tax is

Tax incidence is the distribution of the tax burden.

levied. But it's important to note that this 50–50 split between consumers and producers is a result of our assumptions in this example. In the real world, the incidence of an excise tax usually falls unevenly between consumers and producers: one group bears more of the burden than the other.

What determines how the burden of an excise tax is allocated between consumers and producers? The answer depends on the shapes of the supply and the demand curves. *More specifically, the incidence of an excise tax depends on the price elasticity of supply and the price elasticity of demand.* We can see this by looking first at a case in which consumers pay most of an excise tax, and then at a case in which producers pay most of the tax.

When an Excise Tax Is Paid Mainly by Consumers Figure 14.8 shows an excise tax that falls mainly on consumers: an excise tax on gasoline, which we set at $1 per gallon. (There really is a federal excise tax on gasoline, though it is actually only about $0.18 per gallon in the United States. In addition, states impose excise taxes between $0.08 and $0.37 per gallon.) According to Figure 14.8, in the absence of the tax, gasoline would sell for $2 per gallon.

figure 14.8

An Excise Tax Paid Mainly by Consumers

The relatively steep demand curve here reflects a low price elasticity of demand for gasoline. The relatively flat supply curve reflects a high price elasticity of supply. The pretax price of a gallon of gasoline is $2.00, and a tax of $1.00 per gallon is imposed. The price paid by consumers rises by $0.95 to $2.95, reflecting the fact that most of the burden of the tax falls on consumers. Only a small portion of the tax is borne by producers: the price they receive falls by only $0.05 to $1.95.

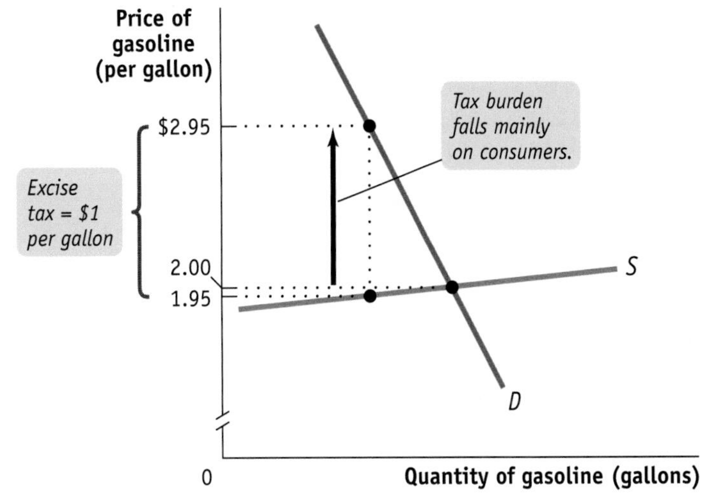

Two key assumptions are reflected in the shapes of the supply and demand curves in Figure 14.8. First, the price elasticity of demand for gasoline is assumed to be very low, so the demand curve is relatively steep. Recall that a low price elasticity of demand means that the quantity demanded changes little in response to a change in price. Second, the price elasticity of supply of gasoline is assumed to be very high, so the supply curve is relatively flat. A high price elasticity of supply means that the quantity supplied changes a lot in response to a change in price.

We have just learned that an excise tax drives a wedge, equal to the size of the tax, between the price paid by consumers and the price received by producers. This wedge drives the price paid by consumers up and the price received by producers down. But as we can see from Figure 14.8, in this case those two effects are very unequal in size. The price received by producers falls only slightly, from $2.00 to $1.95, but the price paid by consumers rises by a lot, from $2.00 to $2.95. This means that consumers bear the greater share of the tax burden.

This example illustrates another general principle of taxation: *When the price elasticity of demand is low and the price elasticity of supply is high, the burden of an excise tax falls mainly on consumers.* Why? A low price elasticity of demand means that consumers have few substitutes and so little alternative to buying higher-priced gasoline. In contrast, a high price elasticity of supply results from the fact that producers have many production substitutes for their gasoline (that is, other uses for the crude oil from which gasoline is refined). This gives producers much greater flexibility in refusing to accept lower prices for their gasoline. And, not surprisingly, the party with the least flexibility—in this case, consumers—gets stuck paying most of the tax. This is a good description of how the burden of the main excise taxes actually collected in the United States today, such as those on cigarettes and alcoholic beverages, is allocated between consumers and producers.

When an Excise Tax Is Paid Mainly by Producers Figure 14.9 shows an example of an excise tax paid mainly by producers, a $5.00 per day tax on downtown parking in a small city. In the absence of the tax, the market equilibrium price of parking is $6.00 per day.

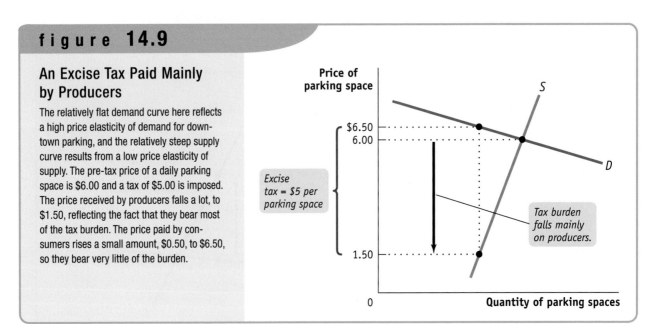

figure 14.9

An Excise Tax Paid Mainly by Producers

The relatively flat demand curve here reflects a high price elasticity of demand for downtown parking, and the relatively steep supply curve results from a low price elasticity of supply. The pre-tax price of a daily parking space is $6.00 and a tax of $5.00 is imposed. The price received by producers falls a lot, to $1.50, reflecting the fact that they bear most of the tax burden. The price paid by consumers rises a small amount, $0.50, to $6.50, so they bear very little of the burden.

We've assumed in this case that the price elasticity of supply is very low because the lots used for parking have very few alternative uses. This makes the supply curve for parking spaces relatively steep. The price elasticity of demand, however, is assumed to be high: consumers can easily switch from the downtown spaces to other parking spaces a few minutes' walk from downtown, spaces that are not subject to the tax. This makes the demand curve relatively flat.

The tax drives a wedge between the price paid by consumers and the price received by producers. In this example, however, the tax causes the price paid by consumers to rise only slightly, from $6.00 to $6.50, but the price received by producers falls a lot, from $6.00 to $1.50. In the end, a consumer bears only $0.50 of the $5 tax burden, with a producer bearing the remaining $4.50.

Again, this example illustrates a general principle: *When the price elasticity of demand is high and the price elasticity of supply is low, the burden of an excise tax falls mainly on producers.* A real-world example is a tax on purchases of existing houses. In many American towns, house prices in desirable locations have risen as well-off outsiders have moved in and purchased homes from the less well-off original occupants, a phenomenon called gentrification. Some of these towns have imposed taxes on house sales intended to extract money from the new arrivals. But this ignores the fact that the price elasticity of demand for houses in a particular town is often high because potential buyers can choose to move to other towns. Furthermore, the price elasticity of supply is often low because most sellers must sell their houses due to job transfers or to provide funds for their retirement. So taxes on home purchases are actually paid mainly by the less well-off sellers—not, as town officials imagine, by wealthy buyers.

The Benefits and Costs of Taxation

When a government is considering whether to impose a tax or how to design a tax system, it has to weigh the benefits of a tax against its costs. We may not think of a tax as something that provides benefits, but governments need money to provide things people want, such as streets, schools, national defense, and health care for those unable to afford it. The benefit of a tax is the revenue it raises for the government to pay for these services. Unfortunately, this benefit comes at a cost—a cost that is normally larger than the amount consumers and producers pay. Let's look first at what determines how much money a tax raises and then at the costs a tax imposes.

istockphoto

The Revenue from an Excise Tax

How much revenue does the government collect from an excise tax? In our hotel tax example, the revenue is equal to the area of the shaded rectangle in Figure 14.10.

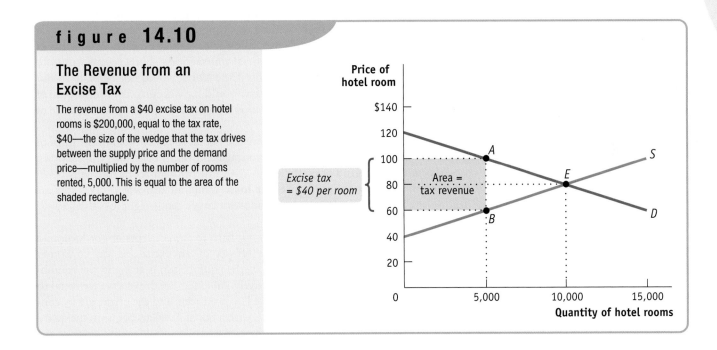

figure 14.10

The Revenue from an Excise Tax

The revenue from a $40 excise tax on hotel rooms is $200,000, equal to the tax rate, $40—the size of the wedge that the tax drives between the supply price and the demand price—multiplied by the number of rooms rented, 5,000. This is equal to the area of the shaded rectangle.

To see why this area represents the revenue collected by a $40 tax on hotel rooms, notice that the *height* of the rectangle is $40, equal to the tax per room. It is also, as we've seen, the size of the wedge that the tax drives between the supply price (the price received by producers) and the demand price (the price paid by consumers). Meanwhile, the *width* of the rectangle is 5,000 rooms, equal to the equilibrium quantity of rooms given the $40 tax. With that information, we can make the following calculations.

The tax revenue collected is:

$$\text{Tax revenue} = \$40 \text{ per room} \times 5{,}000 \text{ rooms} = \$200{,}000$$

The area of the shaded rectangle is:

$$\text{Area} = \text{Height} \times \text{Width} = \$40 \text{ per room} \times 5{,}000 \text{ rooms} = \$200{,}000,$$

or

$$\text{Tax revenue} = \text{Area of shaded rectangle}$$

This is a general principle: *The revenue collected by an excise tax is equal to the area of a rectangle with the height of the tax wedge between the supply price and the demand price and the width of the quantity sold under the tax.*

The Costs of Taxation

What is the cost of a tax? You might be inclined to answer that it is the amount of money taxpayers pay to the government—the tax revenue collected. But suppose the government uses the tax revenue to provide services that taxpayers want. Or suppose that the government simply hands the tax revenue back to taxpayers. Would we say in those cases that the tax didn't actually cost anything?

No—because a tax, like a quota, prevents mutually beneficial transactions from occurring. Consider Figure 14.10 once more. Here, with a $40 tax on hotel rooms, guests pay $100 per room but hotel owners receive only $60 per room. Because of the wedge created by the tax, we know that some transactions didn't occur that would have occurred without the tax. More specifically, we know from the supply and demand curves that there are some potential guests who would be willing to pay up to $90 per night and some hotel owners who would be willing to supply rooms if they received at least $70 per night. If these two sets of people were allowed to trade with each other without the tax, they would engage in mutually beneficial transactions—hotel rooms would be rented. But such deals would be illegal because the $40 tax would not be paid. In our example, 5,000 potential hotel room rentals that would have occurred in the absence of the tax, to the mutual benefit of guests and hotel owners, do not take place because of the tax.

So an excise tax imposes costs over and above the tax revenue collected in the form of inefficiency, which occurs because the tax discourages mutually beneficial transactions. The cost to society of this kind of inefficiency—the value of the forgone mutually beneficial transactions—is called the **deadweight loss.** While all real-world taxes impose some deadweight loss, a badly designed tax imposes a larger deadweight loss than a well-designed one.

To measure the deadweight loss from a tax, we turn to the concepts of producer and consumer surplus. Figure 14.11 shows the effects of an excise tax on consumer and producer surplus. In the absence of the tax, the equilibrium is at E and the equilibrium price and quantity are P_E and Q_E, respectively. An excise tax drives a wedge equal to the amount of the tax between the price received by producers and the price paid by consumers, reducing the quantity sold. In this case, with a tax of T dollars per unit, the quantity sold falls to Q_T. The price paid by consumers rises to P_C, the demand price of the reduced quantity, Q_T, and the price received by producers falls to P_P, the supply price of that quantity. The difference between these prices, $P_C - P_P$, is equal to the excise tax, T.

Using the concepts of producer and consumer surplus, we can show exactly how much surplus producers and consumers lose as a result of the tax. We learned previously that a fall in the price of a good generates a gain in consumer surplus that is equal to the sum of the areas of a rectangle and a triangle. Similarly, a price increase causes a loss to consumers that is represented by the sum of the areas of a rectangle and a triangle. So it's not surprising that in the case of an excise tax, the rise in the price paid by consumers causes a loss equal to the sum of the areas of a rectangle and a triangle: the dark blue rectangle labeled A and the area of the light blue triangle labeled B in Figure 14.11.

The **deadweight loss** (from a tax) is the decrease in total surplus resulting from the tax, minus the tax revenues generated.

figure 14.11

A Tax Reduces Consumer and Producer Surplus

Before the tax, the equilibrium price and quantity are P_E and Q_E, respectively. After an excise tax of T per unit is imposed, the price to consumers rises to P_C and consumer surplus falls by the sum of the dark blue rectangle, labeled A, and the light blue triangle, labeled B. The tax also causes the price to producers to fall to P_P; producer surplus falls by the sum of the dark red rectangle, labeled C, and the light red triangle, labeled F. The government receives revenue from the tax, $Q_T \times T$, which is given by the sum of the areas A and C. Areas B and F represent the losses to consumer and producer surplus that are not collected by the government as revenue; they are the deadweight loss to society of the tax.

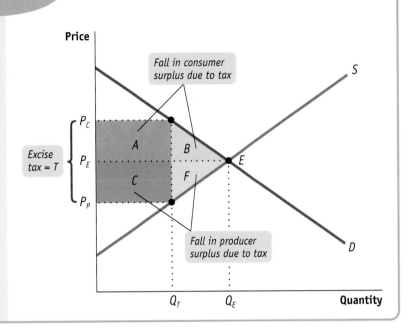

Meanwhile, the fall in the price received by producers leads to a fall in producer surplus. This, too, is equal to the sum of the areas of a rectangle and a triangle. The loss in producer surplus is the sum of the areas of the dark red rectangle labeled C and the light red triangle labeled F in Figure 14.11.

Of course, although consumers and producers are hurt by the tax, the government gains revenue. The revenue the government collects is equal to the tax per unit sold, T, multiplied by the quantity sold, Q_T. This revenue is equal to the area of a rectangle Q_T wide and T high. And we already have that rectangle in the figure: it is the sum of rectangles A and C. So the government gains part of what consumers and producers lose from an excise tax.

But a portion of the loss to producers and consumers from the tax is not offset by a gain to the government—specifically, the two triangles B and F. The deadweight loss caused by the tax is equal to the combined area of these two triangles. It represents the total surplus lost to society because of the tax—that is, the amount of surplus that would have been generated by transactions that now do not take place because of the tax.

Figure 14.12 on the next page is a version of Figure 14.11 that leaves out rectangles A (the surplus shifted from consumers to the government) and C (the surplus shifted from producers to the government) and shows only the deadweight loss, drawn here as a triangle shaded yellow. The base of that triangle is equal to the tax wedge, T; the height of the triangle is equal to the reduction in the quantity transacted due to the tax, $Q_E - Q_T$. Clearly, the larger the tax wedge and the larger the reduction in the quantity transacted, the greater the inefficiency from the tax. But also note an important, contrasting point: if the excise tax somehow *didn't* reduce the quantity bought and sold in this market—if Q_T remained equal to Q_E after the tax was levied—the yellow triangle would disappear and the deadweight loss from the tax would be zero. So if a tax does *not* discourage transactions, it causes no deadweight loss. In this case, the tax simply shifts surplus straight from consumers and producers to the government.

Using a triangle to measure deadweight loss is a technique used in many economic applications. For example, triangles are used to measure the deadweight loss produced by types of taxes other than excise taxes. They are also used to measure the deadweight loss produced by monopoly, another kind of market distortion. And deadweight-loss triangles are often used to evaluate the benefits and costs of public policies besides taxation—such as whether to impose stricter safety standards on a product.

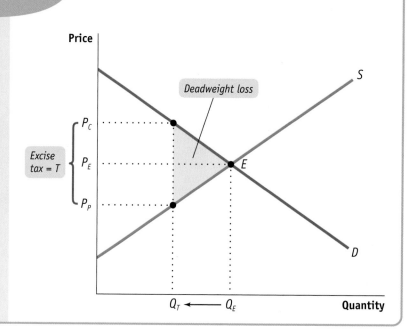

figure 14.12

The Deadweight Loss of a Tax

A tax leads to a deadweight loss because it creates inefficiency: some mutually beneficial transactions never take place because of the tax, namely the transactions $Q_E - Q_T$. The yellow area here represents the value of the deadweight loss: it is the total surplus that would have been gained from the $Q_E - Q_T$ transactions. If the tax had not discouraged transactions—had the number of transactions remained at Q_E—no deadweight loss would have been incurred.

In considering the total amount of inefficiency caused by a tax, we must also take into account something not shown in Figure 14.12: the resources actually used by the government to collect the tax, and by taxpayers to pay it, over and above the amount of the tax. These lost resources are called the **administrative costs** of the tax. The most familiar administrative cost of the U.S. tax system is the time individuals spend filling out their income tax forms or the money they spend on accountants to prepare their tax forms for them. (The latter is considered an inefficiency from the point of view of society because accountants could instead be performing other, non-tax-related services.) Included in the administrative costs that taxpayers incur are resources used to evade the tax, both legally and illegally. The costs of operating the Internal Revenue Service, the arm of the federal government tasked with collecting the federal income tax, are actually quite small in comparison to the administrative costs paid by taxpayers. The total inefficiency caused by a tax is the sum of its deadweight loss and its administrative costs.

Some extreme forms of taxation, such as the *poll tax* instituted by the government of British Prime Minister Margaret Thatcher in 1989, are notably unfair but very efficient. A poll tax is an example of a **lump-sum tax,** a tax that is the same for everyone regardless of any actions people take. The poll tax in Britain was widely perceived as much less fair than the tax structure it replaced, in which local taxes were proportional to property values.

Under the old system, the highest local taxes were paid by the people with the most expensive houses. Because these people tended to be wealthy, they were also best able to bear the burden. But the old system definitely distorted incentives to engage in mutually beneficial transactions and created deadweight loss. People who were considering home improvements knew that such improvements, by making their property more valuable, would increase their tax bills. The result, surely, was that some home improvements that would have taken place without the tax did not take place because of it. In contrast, a lump-sum tax does not distort incentives. Because under a lump-sum tax people have to pay the same amount of tax regardless of their actions, it does not cause them to substitute untaxed goods for a good whose price has been artificially inflated by a tax, as occurs with an excise tax. So lump-sum taxes, although unfair, are better than other taxes at promoting economic efficiency.

The **administrative costs** of a tax are the resources used by government to collect the tax, and by taxpayers to pay (or to evade) it, over and above the amount collected.

A **lump-sum tax** is a tax of a fixed amount paid by all taxpayers.

Module 14 Review

Solutions appear at the back of the book.

Check Your Understanding

1. Using the tables in Check Your Understanding in the preceding module, find the equilibrium price and quantity in the market for cheese-stuffed jalapeno peppers. What is the total surplus in the equilibrium in this market, and who receives it?

2. Consider the market for butter, shown in the accompanying figure. The government imposes an excise tax of $0.30 per pound of butter. What is the price paid by consumers post-tax? What is the price received by producers post-tax? What is the quantity of butter sold? How is the incidence of the tax allocated between consumers and producers? Show this on the figure.

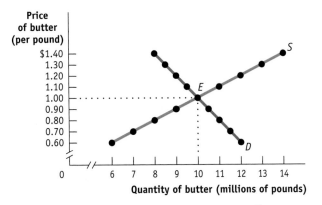

3. The accompanying table shows five consumers' willingness to pay for one can of diet soda each as well as five producers' costs of selling one can of diet soda each. Each consumer buys at most one can of soda; each producer sells at most one can of soda. The government asks your advice about the effects of an excise tax of $0.40 per can of diet soda. Assume that there are no administrative costs from the tax.

	Consumer Willingness to Pay		Producer Cost
Ana	$0.70	Zhang	$0.10
Bernice	0.60	Yves	0.20
Chizuko	0.50	Xavier	0.30
Dagmar	0.40	Walter	0.40
Ella	0.30	Vern	0.50

   a. Without the excise tax, what is the equilibrium price and the equilibrium quantity of soda?

   b. The excise tax raises the price paid by consumers post-tax to $0.60 and lowers the price received by producers post-tax to $0.20. With the excise tax, what is the quantity of soda sold?

   c. Without the excise tax, how much individual consumer surplus does each of the consumers gain? How much individual consumer surplus does each consumer gain with the tax? How much total consumer surplus is lost as a result of the tax?

   d. Without the excise tax, how much individual producer surplus does each of the producers gain? How much individual producer surplus does each producer gain with the tax? How much total producer surplus is lost as a result of the tax?

   e. How much government revenue does the excise tax create?

   f. What is the deadweight loss from the imposition of this excise tax?

Multiple-Choice Questions

1. At market equilibrium in a competitive market, which of the following is necessarily true?

   I. Consumer surplus is maximized.

   II. Producer surplus is maximized.

   III. Total surplus is maximized.

   a. I only
   b. II only
   c. III only
   d. I and II only
   e. I, II, and III

2. When a competitive market is in equilibrium, total surplus can be increased by

   I. reallocating consumption among consumers.

   II. reallocating sales among sellers.

   III. changing the quantity traded.

   a. I only
   b. II only
   c. III only
   d. I, II, and III
   e. None of the above

3. Which of the following is true regarding equity and efficiency in competitive markets?

   a. Competitive markets ensure equity and efficiency.
   b. There is often a trade-off between equity and efficiency.
   c. Competitive markets lead to neither equity nor efficiency.
   d. There is generally agreement about the level of equity and efficiency in a market.
   e. None of the above.

4. An excise tax imposed on sellers in a market will result in which of the following?

    I. an upward shift of the supply curve

    II. a downward shift of the demand curve

    III. deadweight loss

a. I only

b. II only

c. III only

d. I and III only

e. I, II, and III

5. An excise tax will be paid mainly by producers when

a. it is imposed on producers.

b. it is imposed on consumers.

c. the price elasticity of supply is low and the price elasticity of demand is high.

d. the price elasticity of supply is high and the price elasticity of demand is low.

e. the price elasticity of supply is perfectly elastic.

Critical-Thinking Questions

Draw a correctly labeled graph of a competitive market in equilibrium. Use your graph to illustrate the effect of an excise tax imposed on consumers. Indicate each of the following on your graph:

a. the equilibrium price and quantity without the tax, labeled P_E and Q_E

b. the quantity sold in the market post-tax, labeled Q_T

c. the price paid by consumers post-tax, labeled P_C

d. the price received by producers post-tax, labeled P_P

e. the tax revenue generated by the tax, labeled "Tax revenue"

f. The deadweight loss resulting from the tax, labeled "DWL."

© DAJ/Imagestate

What you will learn in this **Module:**

- How consumers make choices about the purchase of goods and services

- Why consumers' general goal is to maximize utility

- Why the principle of diminishing marginal utility applies to the consumption of most goods and services

- How to use marginal analysis to find the optimal consumption bundle

Module 15
Utility Maximization

We have used the demand curve to study consumer responsiveness to changes in prices and discovered its usefulness in predicting how consumers will gain from the availability of goods and services in a market. But where does the demand curve come from? In other words, what lies behind the demand curve? The demand curve represents the tastes, preferences, and resulting choices of individual consumers. Its shape reflects the additional satisfaction, or *utility*, people receive from consuming more and more of a good or service.

Utility: It's All About Getting Satisfaction

When analyzing consumer behavior, we're looking into how people pursue their needs and wants and the subjective feelings that motivate purchases. Yet there is no simple way to measure subjective feelings. How much satisfaction do I get from my third cookie? Is it less or more than the satisfaction you receive from your third cookie? Does it even make sense to ask that question?

Luckily, we don't need to make comparisons between your feelings and mine. The analysis of consumer behavior that follows requires only the assumption that individuals try to maximize some personal measure of the satisfaction gained from consumption. That measure of satisfaction is known as **utility,** a concept we use to understand behavior but don't expect to measure in practice.

Utility is a measure of personal satisfaction.

Utility and Consumption

We can think of consumers as using consumption to "produce" utility, much in the same way that producers use inputs to produce output. As consumers, we do not make explicit calculations of the utility generated by consumption choices, but we must make choices, and we usually base them on at least a rough attempt to achieve greater satisfaction. I can have either soup or salad with my dinner. Which will I enjoy more? I can go to Disney World this year or put the money toward buying a new car. Which will make me happier? These are the types of questions that go into utility maximization.

The concept of utility offers a way to study choices that are made in a more or less rational way.

© Drive Images/Alamy

How do we measure utility? For the sake of simplicity, it is useful to suppose that we can measure utility in hypothetical units called—what else?—**utils.** A *utility function* shows the relationship between a consumer's utility and the combination of goods and services—the *consumption bundle*—he or she consumes.

Figure 15.1 illustrates a utility function. It shows the total utility that Cassie, who likes fried clams, gets from an all-you-can-eat clam dinner. We suppose that her consumption bundle consists of a side of coleslaw, which comes with the meal, plus a number of clams to be determined. The table that accompanies the figure shows how Cassie's total utility depends on the number of clams; the curve in panel (a) of the figure shows that same information graphically.

Cassie's utility function slopes upward over most of the range shown, but it gets flatter as the number of clams consumed increases. And in this example it eventually turns downward. According to the information in the table in Figure 15.1, nine clams is a clam too far. Adding that additional clam actually makes Cassie worse off: it would lower her total utility. If she's rational, of course, Cassie will realize that and not consume the ninth clam.

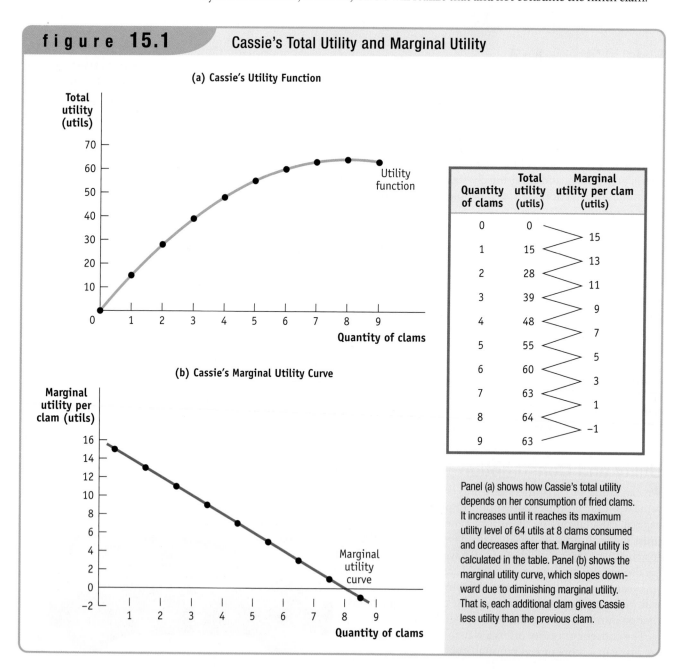

figure 15.1 Cassie's Total Utility and Marginal Utility

(a) Cassie's Utility Function

Utility function

(b) Cassie's Marginal Utility Curve

Marginal utility curve

Quantity of clams	Total utility (utils)	Marginal utility per clam (utils)
0	0	
		15
1	15	
		13
2	28	
		11
3	39	
		9
4	48	
		7
5	55	
		5
6	60	
		3
7	63	
		1
8	64	
		−1
9	63	

Panel (a) shows how Cassie's total utility depends on her consumption of fried clams. It increases until it reaches its maximum utility level of 64 utils at 8 clams consumed and decreases after that. Marginal utility is calculated in the table. Panel (b) shows the marginal utility curve, which slopes downward due to diminishing marginal utility. That is, each additional clam gives Cassie less utility than the previous clam.

So when Cassie chooses how many clams to consume, she will make this decision by considering the *change* in her total utility from consuming one more clam. This illustrates the general point: to maximize *total* utility, consumers must focus on *marginal* utility.

The Principle of Diminishing Marginal Utility

In addition to showing how Cassie's total utility depends on the number of clams she consumes, the table in Figure 15.1 also shows the **marginal utility** generated by consuming each additional clam—that is, the *change* in total utility from consuming one additional clam. The **marginal utility curve** is constructed by plotting points at the midpoint between the numbered quantities since marginal utility is found as consumption levels change. For example, when consumption rises from 1 to 2 clams, marginal utility is 13. Therefore, we place the point corresponding to marginal utility of 13 halfway between 1 and 2 clams.

The marginal utility curve slopes downward because each successive clam adds less to total utility than the previous clam. This is reflected in the table: marginal utility falls from a high of 15 utils for the first clam consumed to −1 for the ninth clam consumed. The fact that the ninth clam has negative marginal utility means that consuming it actually reduces total utility. (Restaurants that offer all-you-can-eat meals depend on the proposition that you can have too much of a good thing.) Not all marginal utility curves eventually become negative. But it is generally accepted that marginal utility curves do slope downward—that consumption of most goods and services is subject to *diminishing marginal utility*.

istockphoto

The basic idea behind the **principle of diminishing marginal utility** is that the additional satisfaction a consumer gets from one more unit of a good or service declines as the amount of that good or service consumed rises. Or, to put it slightly differently, the more of a good or service you consume, the closer you are to being satiated—reaching a point at which an additional unit of the good adds nothing to your satisfaction. For someone who almost never gets to eat a banana, the occasional banana is a marvelous treat (as it was in Eastern Europe before the fall of communism, when bananas were very hard to find). For someone who eats them all the time, a banana is just, well, a banana.

The **marginal utility** of a good or service is the change in total utility generated by consuming one additional unit of that good or service. The **marginal utility curve** shows how marginal utility depends on the quantity of a good or service consumed.

According to the **principle of diminishing marginal utility,** each successive unit of a good or service consumed adds less to total utility than does the previous unit.

Is Marginal Utility Really Diminishing?

Are all goods really subject to diminishing marginal utility? Of course not; there are a number of goods for which, at least over some range, marginal utility is surely *increasing.*

For example, there are goods that require some experience to enjoy. The first time you do it, downhill skiing involves a lot more fear than enjoyment—or so they say: two of the authors have never tried it! It only becomes a pleasurable activity if you do it enough to become reasonably competent. And even some less strenuous forms of consumption take

practice; people who are not accustomed to drinking coffee say it has a bitter taste and can't understand its appeal. (The authors, on the other hand, regard coffee as one of the basic food groups.)

Another example would be goods that only deliver positive utility if you buy enough. The great Victorian economist Alfred Marshall, who more or less invented the supply and demand model, gave the example of wallpaper: buying only enough to do half a room is worse than useless. If you need two rolls of wallpaper to fin-

ish a room, the marginal utility of the second roll is larger than the marginal utility of the first roll.

So why does it make sense to assume diminishing marginal utility? For one thing, most goods don't suffer from these qualifications: nobody needs to learn to like ice cream. Also, although most people don't ski and some people don't drink coffee, those who do ski or drink coffee do enough of it that the marginal utility of one more ski run or one more cup is less than that of the last. So *in the relevant range* of consumption, marginal utility is still diminishing.

The principle of diminishing marginal utility doesn't always apply, but it does apply in the great majority of cases, enough to serve as a foundation for our analysis of consumer behavior.

Budgets and Optimal Consumption

The principle of diminishing marginal utility explains why most people eventually reach a limit, even at an all-you-can-eat buffet where the cost of another clam is measured only in future indigestion. Under ordinary circumstances, however, it costs some additional resources to consume more of a good, and consumers must take that cost into account when making choices.

What do we mean by cost? As always, the fundamental measure of cost is *opportunity cost*. Because the amount of money a consumer can spend is limited, a decision to consume more of one good is also a decision to consume less of some other good.

Budget Constraints and Budget Lines

Consider Sammy, whose appetite is exclusively for clams and potatoes. (There's no accounting for tastes.) He has a weekly income of $20 and since, given his appetite, more of either good is better than less, he spends all of it on clams and potatoes. We will assume that clams cost $4 per pound and potatoes cost $2 per pound. What are his possible choices?

Whatever Sammy chooses, we know that the cost of his consumption bundle cannot exceed the amount of money he has to spend. That is,

(15-1) Expenditure on clams + Expenditure on potatoes ≤ Total income

Consumers always have limited income, which constrains how much they can consume. So the requirement illustrated by Equation 15-1—that a consumer must choose a consumption bundle that costs no more than his or her income—is known as the consumer's **budget constraint.** It's a simple way of saying that a consumer can't spend more than the total amount of income available to him or her. In other words, consumption bundles are affordable when they obey the budget constraint. We call the set of all of Sammy's affordable consumption bundles his **consumption possibilities.** In general, whether or not a particular consumption bundle is included in a consumer's consumption possibilities depends on the consumer's income and the prices of goods and services.

Figure 15.2 shows Sammy's consumption possibilities. The quantity of clams in his consumption bundle is measured on the horizontal axis and the quantity of potatoes on the vertical axis. The downward-sloping line connecting points *A* through *F* shows which consumption bundles are affordable and which are not. Every bundle on or inside this line (the shaded area) is affordable; every bundle outside this line is unaffordable. As an example of one of the points, let's look at point *C*, representing 2 pounds of clams and 6 pounds of potatoes, and check whether it satisfies Sammy's budget constraint. The cost of bundle *C* is 6 pounds of potatoes × $2 per pound + 2 pounds of clams × $4 per pound = $12 + $8 = $20. So bundle *C* does indeed satisfy Sammy's budget constraint: it costs no more than his weekly income of $20. In fact, bundle *C* costs exactly as much as Sammy's income. By doing the arithmetic, you can check that all the other points lying on the downward-sloping line are also bundles at which Sammy spends all of his income.

The downward-sloping line has a special name, the **budget line.** It shows all the consumption bundles available to Sammy when he spends all of his income. It's downward-sloping because when Sammy is spending all of his income, say by consuming at point *A* on the budget line, then in order to consume more clams he must consume fewer potatoes—that is, he must move to a point like *B*. In other words, when

A **budget constraint** limits the cost of a consumer's consumption bundle to no more than the consumer's income.

A consumer's **consumption possibilities** is the set of all consumption bundles that are affordable, given the consumer's income and prevailing prices.

A consumer's **budget line** shows the consumption bundles available to a consumer who spends all of his or her income.

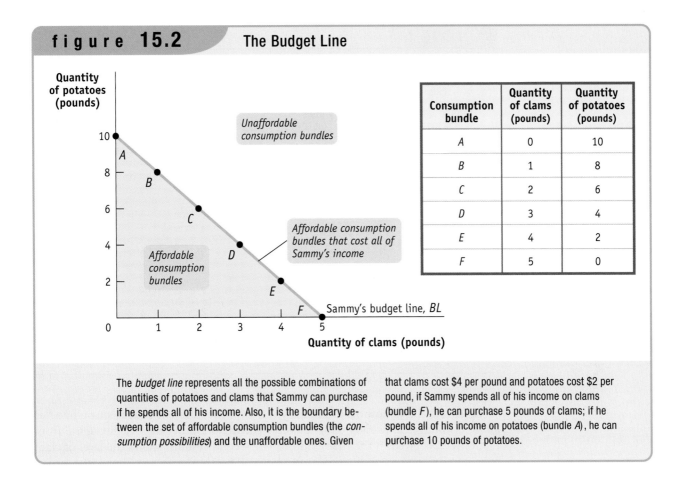

figure **15.2**   The Budget Line

Consumption bundle	Quantity of clams (pounds)	Quantity of potatoes (pounds)
A	0	10
B	1	8
C	2	6
D	3	4
E	4	2
F	5	0

The *budget line* represents all the possible combinations of quantities of potatoes and clams that Sammy can purchase if he spends all of his income. Also, it is the boundary between the set of affordable consumption bundles (the *consumption possibilities*) and the unaffordable ones. Given that clams cost $4 per pound and potatoes cost $2 per pound, if Sammy spends all of his income on clams (bundle *F*), he can purchase 5 pounds of clams; if he spends all of his income on potatoes (bundle *A*), he can purchase 10 pounds of potatoes.

Sammy is on his budget line, the opportunity cost of consuming more clams is consuming fewer potatoes, and vice versa. As Figure 15.2 indicates, any consumption bundle that lies above the budget line is unaffordable.

Do we need to consider the other bundles in Sammy's consumption possibilities, the ones that lie *within* the shaded region in Figure 15.2 bounded by the budget line? The answer is, for all practical situations, no: as long as Sammy doesn't get satiated— that is, as long as his marginal utility from consuming either good is always positive— and he doesn't get any utility from saving income rather than spending it, then he will always choose to consume a bundle that lies on his budget line.

Given that $20 per week budget, next we can consider the culinary dilemma of what point on his budget line Sammy will choose.

The Optimal Consumption Bundle

Because Sammy's budget constrains him to a consumption bundle somewhere along the budget line, a choice to consume a given quantity of clams also determines his potato consumption, and vice versa. We want to find the consumption bundle—represented by a point on the budget line—that maximizes Sammy's total utility. This bundle is Sammy's **optimal consumption bundle.**

Table 15.1 on the next page shows how much utility Sammy gets from different levels of consumption of clams and potatoes, respectively. According to the table, Sammy has a healthy appetite; the more of either good he consumes, the higher his utility. But because he has a limited budget, he must make a trade-off: the more pounds of clams he consumes, the fewer pounds of potatoes, and vice versa. That is, he must choose a point on his budget line.

A consumer's **optimal consumption bundle** is the consumption bundle that maximizes the consumer's total utility given his or her budget constraint.

table **15.1**

Sammy's Utility from Clam and Potato Consumption

Utility from clam consumption		Utility from potato consumption	
Quantity of clams (pounds)	Utility from clams (utils)	Quantity of potatoes (pounds)	Utility from potatoes (utils)
0	0	0	0
1	15	1	11.5
2	25	2	21.4
3	31	3	29.8
4	34	4	36.8
5	36	5	42.5
		6	47.0
		7	50.5
		8	53.2
		9	55.2
		10	56.7

Table 15.2 shows how his total utility varies for the different consumption bundles along his budget line. Each of six possible consumption bundles, *A* through *F* from Figure 15.2, is given in the first column. The second column shows the level of clam consumption corresponding to each choice. The third column shows the utility Sammy gets from consuming those clams. The fourth column shows the quantity of potatoes Sammy can afford *given* the level of clam consumption; this quantity goes down as his clam consumption goes up because he is sliding down the budget line. The fifth column shows the utility he gets from consuming those potatoes. And the final column shows his *total utility*. In this example, Sammy's total utility is the sum of the utility he gets from clams and the utility he gets from potatoes.

Figure 15.3 gives a visual representation of the data shown in Table 15.2. Panel (a) shows Sammy's budget line, to remind us that when he decides to consume more clams he is also deciding to consume fewer potatoes. Panel (b) then shows how his total utility depends on that choice. The horizontal axis in panel (b) has two sets of labels: it shows both the quantity of clams, increasing from left to right, and the quantity of

table **15.2**

Sammy's Budget and Total Utility

Consumption bundle	Quantity of clams (pounds)	Utility from clams (utils)	Quantity of potatoes (pounds)	Utility from potatoes (utils)	Total utility (utils)
A	0	0	10	56.7	56.7
B	1	15	8	53.2	68.2
C	2	25	6	47.0	72.0
D	3	31	4	36.8	67.8
E	4	34	2	21.4	55.4
F	5	36	0	0	36.0

figure 15.3

Optimal Consumption Bundle

Panel (a) shows Sammy's budget line and his six possible consumption bundles. Panel (b) shows how his total utility is affected by his consumption bundle, which must lie on his budget line. The quantity of clams is measured from left to right on the horizontal axis, and the quantity of potatoes is measured from right to left. His total utility is maximized at bundle *C*, where he consumes 2 pounds of clams and 6 pounds of potatoes. This is Sammy's *optimal consumption bundle*.

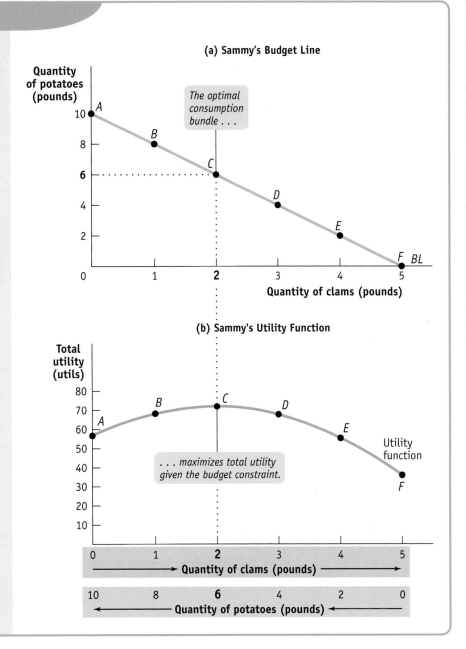

potatoes, increasing from right to left. The reason we can use the same axis to represent consumption of both goods is, of course, that he is constrained by the budget line: the more pounds of clams Sammy consumes, the fewer pounds of potatoes he can afford, and vice versa.

Clearly, the consumption bundle that makes the best of the trade-off between clam consumption and potato consumption, the optimal consumption bundle, is the one that maximizes Sammy's total utility. That is, Sammy's optimal consumption bundle puts him at the top of the total utility curve.

As always, we can find the top of the curve by direct observation. We can see from Figure 15.3 that Sammy's total utility is maximized at point *C*—that his optimal consumption bundle contains 2 pounds of clams and 6 pounds of potatoes. But we know that we usually gain more insight into "how much" problems when we use *marginal analysis*. So in the next section we turn to representing and solving the optimal consumption choice problem with marginal analysis.

Spending the Marginal Dollar

As we've just seen, we can find Sammy's optimal consumption choice by finding the total utility he receives from each consumption bundle on his budget line and then choosing the bundle at which total utility is maximized. But we can use marginal analysis instead, turning Sammy's problem of finding his optimal consumption choice into a "how much" problem. How do we do this? By thinking about choosing an optimal consumption bundle as a problem of *how much to spend on each good*. That is, to find the optimal consumption bundle with marginal analysis we ask the question of whether Sammy can make himself better off by spending a little bit more of his income on clams and less on potatoes, or by doing the opposite—spending a little bit more on potatoes and less on clams. In other words, the marginal decision is a question of how to *spend the marginal dollar*—how to allocate an additional dollar between clams and potatoes in a way that maximizes utility.

Our first step in applying marginal analysis is to ask if Sammy is made better off by spending an additional dollar on either good; and if so, by how much is he better off. To answer this question we must calculate the **marginal utility per dollar** spent on either clams or potatoes—how much additional utility Sammy gets from spending an additional dollar on either good.

Marginal Utility per Dollar

We've already introduced the concept of marginal utility, the additional utility a consumer gets from consuming one more unit of a good or service; now let's see how this concept can be used to derive the related measure of marginal utility per dollar.

Table 15.3 shows how to calculate the marginal utility per dollar spent on clams and potatoes, respectively.

table 15.3

Sammy's Marginal Utility per Dollar

(a) Clams (price of clams = $4 per pound)				(b) Potatoes (price of potatoes = $2 per pound)			
Quantity of clams (pounds)	Utility from clams (utils)	Marginal utility per pound of clams (utils)	Marginal utility per dollar (utils)	Quantity of potatoes (pounds)	Utility from potatoes (utils)	Marginal utility per pound of potatoes (utils)	Marginal utility per dollar (utils)
0	0			0	0		
		15	3.75			11.5	5.75
1	15			1	11.5		
		10	2.50			9.9	4.95
2	25			2	21.4		
		6	1.50			8.4	4.20
3	31			3	29.8		
		3	0.75			7.0	3.50
4	34			4	36.8		
		2	0.50			5.7	2.85
5	36			5	42.5		
						4.5	2.25
				6	47.0		
						3.5	1.75
				7	50.5		
						2.7	1.35
				8	53.2		
						2.0	1.00
				9	55.2		
						1.5	0.75
				10	56.7		

In panel (a) of the table, the first column shows different possible amounts of clam consumption. The second column shows the utility Sammy derives from each amount of clam consumption; the third column then shows the marginal utility, the increase in utility Sammy gets from consuming an additional pound of clams. Panel (b) provides the same information for potatoes. The next step is to derive marginal utility *per dollar* for each good. To do this, we just divide the marginal utility of the good by its price in dollars.

To see why we divide by the price, compare the third and fourth columns of panel (a). Consider what happens if Sammy increases his clam consumption from 2 pounds to 3 pounds. This raises his total utility by 6 utils. But he must spend $4 for that additional pound, so the increase in his utility per additional dollar spent on clams is 6 utils/$4 = 1.5 utils per dollar. Similarly, if he increases his clam consumption from 3 pounds to 4 pounds, his marginal utility is 3 utils but his marginal utility per dollar is 3 utils/$4 = 0.75 utils per dollar. Notice that because of diminishing marginal utility, Sammy's marginal utility per pound of clams falls as the quantity of clams he consumes rises. As a result, his marginal utility per dollar spent on clams also falls as the quantity of clams he consumes rises.

So the last column of panel (a) shows how Sammy's marginal utility per dollar spent on clams depends on the quantity of clams he consumes. Similarly, the last column of panel (b) shows how his marginal utility per dollar spent on potatoes depends on the quantity of potatoes he consumes. Again, marginal utility per dollar spent on each good declines as the quantity of that good consumed rises because of diminishing marginal utility.

We will use the symbols MU_C and MU_P to represent the marginal utility per pound of clams and potatoes, respectively. And we will use the symbols P_C and P_P to represent the price of clams (per pound) and the price of potatoes (per pound). Then the marginal utility per dollar spent on clams is MU_C/P_C and the marginal utility per dollar spent on potatoes is MU_P/P_P. In general, the additional utility generated from an additional dollar spent on a good is equal to:

(15-2) Marginal utility per dollar spent on a good
= Marginal utility of one unit of the good/Price of one unit of the good
= MU_{good}/P_{good}

Next we'll see how this concept helps us determine a consumer's optimal consumption bundle using marginal analysis.

Optimal Consumption

Let's consider Figure 15.4 on the next page. As in Figure 15.3, we can measure both the quantity of clams and the quantity of potatoes on the horizontal axis due to the budget constraint. Along the horizontal axis of Figure 15.4—also as in Figure 15.3—the quantity of clams increases as you move from left to right, and the quantity of potatoes increases as you move from right to left. The curve labeled MU_C/P_C in Figure 15.4 shows Sammy's marginal utility per dollar spent on clams as derived in Table 15.3. Likewise, the curve labeled MU_P/P_P shows his marginal utility per dollar spent on potatoes. Notice that the two curves, MU_C/P_C and MU_P/P_P, cross at the optimal consumption bundle, point C, consisting of 2 pounds of clams and 6 pounds of potatoes. Moreover, Figure 15.4 illustrates an important feature of Sammy's optimal consumption bundle: when Sammy consumes 2 pounds of clams and 6 pounds of potatoes, his marginal utility per dollar spent is the same, 2, for both goods. That is, at the optimal consumption bundle, $MU_C/P_C = MU_P/P_P = 2$.

This isn't an accident. Consider another one of Sammy's possible consumption bundles—say, B in Figure 15.3, at which he consumes 1 pound of clams and 8 pounds of potatoes. The marginal utility per dollar spent on each good is shown by points B_C and B_P in Figure 15.4. At that consumption bundle, Sammy's marginal utility per

figure 15.4

Marginal Utility per Dollar

Sammy's optimal consumption bundle is at point C, where his marginal utility per dollar spent on clams, MU_C/P_C, is equal to his marginal utility per dollar spent on potatoes, MU_P/P_P. This illustrates the optimal consumption rule: *at the optimal consumption bundle, the marginal utility per dollar spent on each good and service is the same.* At any other consumption bundle on Sammy's budget line, such as bundle *B* in Figure 15.3, represented here by points B_C and B_P, consumption is not optimal: Sammy can increase his utility at no additional cost by reallocating his spending.

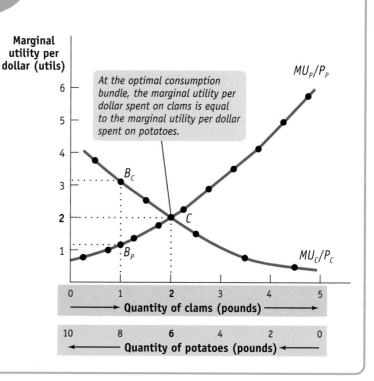

At the optimal consumption bundle, the marginal utility per dollar spent on clams is equal to the marginal utility per dollar spent on potatoes.

dollar spent on clams would be approximately 3, but his marginal utility per dollar spent on potatoes would be only approximately 1. This shows that he has made a mistake: he is consuming too many potatoes and not enough clams.

How do we know this? If Sammy's marginal utility per dollar spent on clams is higher than his marginal utility per dollar spent on potatoes, he has a simple way to make himself better off while staying within his budget: spend $1 less on potatoes and $1 more on clams. By spending an additional dollar on clams, he adds about 3 utils to his total utility; meanwhile, by spending $1 less on potatoes, he subtracts only about 1 util from his total utility. Because his marginal utility per dollar spent is higher for clams than for potatoes, reallocating his spending toward clams and away from potatoes would increase his total utility. On the other hand, if his marginal utility per dollar spent on potatoes is higher, he can increase his utility by spending less on clams and more on potatoes. So if Sammy has in fact chosen his optimal consumption bundle, his marginal utility per dollar spent on clams and potatoes must be equal.

This is a general principle, known as the **optimal consumption rule:** *when a consumer maximizes utility in the face of a budget constraint, the marginal utility per dollar spent on each good or service in the consumption bundle is the same.* That is, for any two goods C and P, the optimal consumption rule says that at the optimal consumption bundle

$$(15\text{-}3) \quad \frac{MU_C}{P_C} = \frac{MU_P}{P_P}$$

It's easiest to understand this rule using examples in which the consumption bundle contains only two goods, but it applies no matter how many goods or services a consumer buys: the marginal utilities per dollar spent for each and every good or service in the optimal consumption bundle are equal.

The main reason for studying consumer behavior is to look behind the market demand curve. At the beginning of this section we explained how the *substitution effect* leads consumers to buy less of a good when its price increases. We used the substitution effect

The **optimal consumption rule** says that in order to maximize utility, a consumer must equate the marginal utility per dollar spent on each good and service in the consumption bundle.

to explain, in general, why the individual demand curve obeys the law of demand. Marginal analysis adds clarity to the utility-maximizing behavior of individuals and explains more precisely how an increase in price leads to less marginal utility per dollar and therefore a decrease in the quantity demanded.

Module 15 Review

Solutions appear at the back of the book.

Check Your Understanding

1. Explain why a rational consumer who has diminishing marginal utility for a good would not consume an additional unit when it generates negative marginal utility, even when that unit is free.

2. In the following two examples, find all the consumption bundles that lie on the consumer's budget line. Illustrate these consumption possibilities in a diagram, and draw the budget line through them.
   a. The consumption bundle consists of movie tickets and buckets of popcorn. The price of each ticket is $10.00, the price of each bucket of popcorn is $5.00, and the consumer's income is $20.00. In your diagram, put movie tickets on the vertical axis and buckets of popcorn on the horizontal axis.
   b. The consumption bundle consists of underwear and socks. The price of each pair of underwear is $4.00, the price of each pair of socks is $2.00, and the consumer's income is $12.00. In your diagram, put pairs of socks on the vertical axis and pairs of underwear on the horizontal axis.

3. In Table 15.3 you can see that the marginal utility per dollar spent on clams and the marginal utility per dollar spent on potatoes are equal when Sammy increases his consumption of clams from 3 pounds to 4 pounds and his consumption of potatoes from 9 pounds to 10 pounds. Explain why this is not Sammy's optimal consumption bundle. Illustrate your answer using a budget line like the one in Figure 15.3.

Multiple-Choice Questions

1. Generally, each successive unit of a good consumed will cause marginal utility to
   a. increase at an increasing rate.
   b. increase at a decreasing rate.
   c. increase at a constant rate.
   d. decrease.
   e. either increase or decrease.

2. Assume there are two goods, good X and good Y. Good X costs $5 and good Y costs $10. If your income is $200, which of the following combinations of good X and good Y is on your budget line?
   a. 0 units of good X and 18 units of good Y
   b. 0 units of good X and 20 units of good Y
   c. 20 units of good X and 0 units of good Y
   d. 10 units of good X and 12 units of good Y
   e. all of the above

3. The optimal consumption rule states that total utility is maximized when all income is spent and
   a. MU/P is equal for all goods.
   b. MU is equal for all goods.
   c. P/MU is equal for all goods.
   d. MU is as high as possible for all goods.
   e. The amount spent on each good is equal.

4. A consumer is spending all of her income and receiving 100 utils from the last unit of good A and 80 utils from the last unit of good B. If the price of good A is $2 and the price of good B is $1, to maximize total utility the consumer should buy
   a. more of good A.
   b. more of good B.
   c. less of good B.
   d. more of both goods.
   e. less of both goods.

5. The optimal consumption bundle is always represented by a point
   a. inside the consumer's budget line.
   b. outside the consumer's budget line.
   c. at the highest point on the consumer's budget line.
   d. on the consumer's budget line.
   e. at the horizontal intercept of the consumer's budget line.

Critical-Thinking Questions

Assume you have an income of $100. The price of good X is $5, and the price of good Y is $20.

a. Draw a correctly labeled budget line with "Quantity of good X" on the horizontal axis and "Quantity of good Y" on the vertical axis. Be sure to correctly label the horizontal and vertical intercepts.

b. With your current consumption bundle, you receive 100 utils from consuming your last unit of good X and 400 utils from consuming your last unit of good Y. Are you maximizing your total utility? Explain.

c. What will happen to the total and marginal utility you receive from consuming good X if you decide to consume another unit of good X? Explain.

Section 3 Review

Summary

Income Effects, Substitution Effects, and Elasticity

1. Changes in the price of a good affect the quantity consumed as a result of the **substitution effect,** and in some cases the **income effect.** Most goods absorb only a small share of a consumer's spending; for these goods, only the substitution effect—buying less of the good that has become relatively more expensive and more of the good that has become relatively cheaper—is significant. The income effect becomes substantial when there is a change in the price of a good that absorbs a large share of a consumer's spending, thereby changing the purchasing power of the consumer's income.

2. Many economic questions depend on the size of consumer or producer responses to changes in prices or other variables. *Elasticity* is a general measure of responsiveness that can be used to answer such questions.

3. The **price elasticity of demand**—the percent change in the quantity demanded divided by the percent change

in the price (dropping the minus sign)—is a measure of the responsiveness of the quantity demanded to changes in the price. In practical calculations, it is usually best to use the **midpoint method,** which calculates percent changes in prices and quantities based on the average of the initial and final values.

Interpreting Price Elasticity of Demand

4. Demand can fall anywhere in the range from **perfectly inelastic,** meaning the quantity demanded is unaffected by the price, to **perfectly elastic,** meaning there is a unique price at which consumers will buy as much or as little as they are offered. When demand is perfectly inelastic, the demand curve is a vertical line; when it is perfectly elastic, the demand curve is a horizontal line.

5. The price elasticity of demand is classified according to whether it is more or less than 1. If it is greater than 1, demand is **elastic;** if it is less than 1, demand is **inelastic;** if it is exactly 1, demand is **unit-elastic.** This classification determines how **total revenue,** the total value

166 section 3 Behind the Demand Curve: Consumer Choice

of sales, changes when the price changes. If demand is elastic, total revenue falls when the price increases and rises when the price decreases. If demand is inelastic, total revenue rises when the price increases and falls when the price decreases.

6. The price elasticity of demand depends on whether there are close substitutes for the good in question, whether the good is a necessity or a luxury, the share of income spent on the good, and the length of time that has elapsed since the price change.

Other Elasticities

7. The **cross-price elasticity of demand** measures the effect of a change in one good's price on the quantity of another good demanded. The cross-price elasticity of demand can be positive, in which case the goods are substitutes, or negative, in which case they are complements.

8. The **income elasticity of demand** is the percent change in the quantity of a good demanded when a consumer's income changes divided by the percent change in income. The income elasticity of demand indicates how intensely the demand for a good responds to changes in income. It can be negative; in that case the good is an inferior good. Goods with positive income elasticities of demand are normal goods. If the income elasticity is greater than 1, a good is **income-elastic;** if it is positive and less than 1, the good is **income-inelastic.**

9. The **price elasticity of supply** is the percent change in the quantity of a good supplied divided by the percent change in the price. If the quantity supplied does not change at all, we have an instance of **perfectly inelastic supply;** the supply curve is a vertical line. If the quantity supplied is zero below some price but infinite above that price, we have an instance of **perfectly elastic supply;** the supply curve is a horizontal line.

10. The price elasticity of supply depends on the availability of resources to expand production and on time. It is higher when inputs are available at relatively low cost and when more time has elapsed since the price change.

Consumer and Producer Surplus

11. The **willingness to pay** of each individual consumer determines the shape of the demand curve. When price is less than or equal to the willingness to pay, the potential consumer purchases the good. The difference between willingness to pay and price is the net gain to the consumer, the **individual consumer surplus.**

12. **Total consumer surplus** in a market, which is the sum of all individual consumer surpluses in a market, is equal to the area below the market demand curve but above the price. A rise in the price of a good reduces consumer surplus; a fall in the price increases consumer surplus. The term **consumer surplus** is often used to refer to both individual and total consumer surplus.

13. The **cost** of each potential producer of a good, the lowest price at which he or she is willing to supply a unit of that good, determines the supply curve. If the price of a good is above a producer's cost, a sale generates a net gain to the producer, known as the **individual producer surplus.**

14. **Total producer surplus** in a market, the sum of the individual producer surpluses in a market, is equal to the area above the market supply curve but below the price. A rise in the price of a good increases producer surplus; a fall in the price reduces producer surplus. The term **producer surplus** is often used to refer to both individual and total producer surplus.

Efficiency and Deadweight Loss

15. **Total surplus,** the total gain to society from the production and consumption of a good, is the sum of consumer and producer surplus.

16. Usually, markets are efficient and achieve the maximum total surplus. Any possible reallocation of consumption or sales, or change in the quantity bought and sold, reduces total surplus. However, society also cares about equity. So government intervention in a market that reduces efficiency but increases equity can be a valid choice by society.

17. A tax that rises more than in proportion to income is a **progressive tax.** A tax that rises less than in proportion to income is a **regressive tax.** A tax that rises in proportion to income is, you guessed it, a **proportional tax.**

18. An **excise tax**—a tax on the purchase or sale of a good—raises the price paid by consumers and reduces the price received by producers, driving a wedge between the two. The **incidence** of the tax—how the burden of the tax is divided between consumers and producers—does not depend on who officially pays the tax.

19. The incidence of an excise tax depends on the price elasticities of supply and demand. If the price elasticity of demand is higher than the price elasticity of supply, the tax falls mainly on producers; if the price elasticity of supply is higher than the price elasticity of demand, the tax falls mainly on consumers.

20. The tax revenue generated by a tax depends on the **tax rate** and on the number of units sold with the tax. Excise taxes cause inefficiency in the form of deadweight loss because they discourage some mutually beneficial transactions. Taxes also impose **administrative costs:** resources used to collect the tax, to pay it (over and above the amount of the tax), and to evade it.

21. An excise tax generates revenue for the government but lowers total surplus. The loss in total surplus exceeds the tax revenue, resulting in a deadweight loss to society. This deadweight loss is represented by a triangle, the area of which equals the value of the transactions discouraged by the tax. The greater the elasticity of demand or supply, or both, the larger the deadweight loss

from a tax. If either demand or supply is perfectly in-elastic, there is no deadweight loss from a tax.

22. A **lump-sum tax** is a tax of a fixed amount paid by all taxpayers. Because a lump-sum tax does not depend on the behavior of taxpayers, it does not discourage mutually beneficial transactions and therefore causes no deadweight loss.

Utility Maximization

23. Consumers maximize a measure of satisfaction called **utility.** We measure utility in hypothetical units called **utils.**

24. A good's or service's **marginal utility** is the additional utility generated by consuming one more unit of the good or service. We usually assume that the **principle of diminishing marginal utility** holds: consumption of another unit of a good or service yields less addi-

tional utility than the previous unit. As a result, the **marginal utility curve** slopes downward.

25. A **budget constraint** limits a consumer's spending to no more than his or her income. It defines the consumer's **consumption possibilities,** the set of all affordable consumption bundles. A consumer who spends all of his or her income will choose a consumption bundle on the **budget line.** An individual chooses the consumption bundle that maximizes total utility, the **optimal consumption bundle.**

26. We use marginal analysis to find the optimal consumption bundle by analyzing how to allocate the marginal dollar. According to the **optimal consumption rule,** with the optimal consumption bundle, the **marginal utility per dollar** spent on each good and service—the marginal utility of a good divided by its price—is the same.

Key Terms

Problems

1. Nile.com, the online bookseller, wants to increase its total revenue. One strategy is to offer a 10% discount on every book it sells. Nile.com knows that its customers can be divided into two distinct groups according to their likely responses to the discount. The accompanying table shows how the two groups respond to the discount.

	Group A (sales per week)	Group B (sales per week)
Volume of sales before the 10% discount	1.55 million	1.50 million
Volume of sales after the 10% discount	1.65 million	1.70 million

   a. Using the midpoint method, calculate the price elasticities of demand for group A and group B.

   b. Explain how the discount will affect total revenue from each group.

   c. Suppose Nile.com knows which group each customer belongs to when he or she logs on and can choose whether or not to offer the 10% discount. If Nile.com wants to increase its total revenue, should discounts be offered to group A or to group B, to neither group, or to both groups?

2. Do you think the price elasticity of demand for Ford sport-utility vehicles (SUVs) will increase, decrease, or remain the same when each of the following events occurs? Explain your answer.

a. Other car manufacturers, such as General Motors, decide to make and sell SUVs.

b. SUVs produced in foreign countries are banned from the American market.

c. Due to ad campaigns, Americans believe that SUVs are much safer than ordinary passenger cars.

d. The time period over which you measure the elasticity lengthens. During that longer time, new models such as four-wheel-drive cargo vans appear.

3. The accompanying table gives part of the supply schedule for personal computers in the United States.

Price per computer	Quantity of computers supplied
$1,100	12,000
900	8,000

a. Using the midpoint method, calculate the price elasticity of supply when the price increases from $900 to $1,100.

b. Suppose firms produce 1,000 more computers at any given price due to improved technology. As price increases from $900 to $1,100, is the price elasticity of supply now greater than, less than, or the same as it was in part a?

c. Suppose a longer time period under consideration means that the quantity supplied at any given price is 20% higher than the figures given in the table. As price increases from $900 to $1,100, is the price elasticity of supply now greater than, less than, or the same as it was in part a?

4. The accompanying table lists the cross-price elasticities of demand for several goods, where the percent quantity change is measured for the first good of the pair, and the percent price change is measured for the second good.

Good	Cross-price elasticities of demand
Air-conditioning units and kilowatts of electricity	−0.34
Coke and Pepsi	+0.63
High-fuel-consuming sport-utility vehicles (SUVs) and gasoline	−0.28
McDonald's burgers and Burger King burgers	+0.82
Butter and margarine	+1.54

a. Explain the sign of each of the cross-price elasticities. What does it imply about the relationship between the two goods in question?

b. Compare the absolute values of the cross-price elasticities and explain their magnitudes. For example, why is the cross-price elasticity of McDonald's burgers and Burger King burgers less than the cross-price elasticity of butter and margarine?

c. Use the information in the table to calculate how a 5% increase in the price of Pepsi affects the quantity of Coke demanded.

d. Use the information in the table to calculate how a 10% decrease in the price of gasoline affects the quantity of SUVs demanded.

5. The accompanying table shows the price and yearly quantity sold of souvenir T-shirts in the town of Crystal Lake according to the average income of the tourists visiting.

Price of T-shirt	Quantity of T-shirts demanded when average tourist income is $20,000	Quantity of T-shirts demanded when average tourist income is $30,000
$4	3,000	5,000
5	2,400	4,200
6	1,600	3,000
7	800	1,800

a. Using the midpoint method, calculate the price elasticity of demand when the price of a T-shirt rises from $5 to $6 and the average tourist income is $20,000. Also calculate it when the average tourist income is $30,000.

b. Using the midpoint method, calculate the income elasticity of demand when the price of a T-shirt is $4 and the average tourist income increases from $20,000 to $30,000. Also calculate it when the price is $7.

6. In each of the following cases, do you think the price elasticity of supply is (i) perfectly elastic; (ii) perfectly inelastic; (iii) elastic, but not perfectly elastic; or (iv) inelastic, but not perfectly inelastic? Explain using a diagram.

a. An increase in demand this summer for luxury cruises leads to a huge jump in the sales price of a cabin on the Queen Mary 2.

b. The price of a kilowatt of electricity is the same during periods of high electricity demand as during periods of low electricity demand.

c. Fewer people want to fly during February than during any other month. The airlines cancel about 10% of their flights as ticket prices fall about 20% during this month.

d. Owners of vacation homes in Maine rent them out during the summer. Due to a soft economy, a 30% decline in the price of a vacation rental leads more than half of homeowners to occupy their vacation homes themselves during the summer.

7. Worldwide, the average coffee grower has increased the amount of acreage under cultivation over the past few years. The result has been that the average coffee plantation produces significantly more coffee than it did 10 to 20 years ago. Unfortunately for the growers, however, this has also been a period in which their total revenues have plunged. In terms of an elasticity, what must be true for these events to have occurred? Illustrate these events with a diagram, indicating the quantity effect and the price effect that gave rise to these events.

8. Determine the amount of consumer surplus generated in each of the following situations.

a. Leon goes to the clothing store to buy a new T-shirt, for which he is willing to pay up to $10. He picks out one he likes with a price tag of exactly $10. When he is paying for it, he learns that the T-shirt has been discounted by 50%.

b. Alberto goes to the CD store hoping to find a used copy of *Nirvana's Greatest Hits* for up to $10. The store has one copy selling for $10, which he purchases.

c. After soccer practice, Stacey is willing to pay $2 for a bottle of mineral water. The 7-Eleven sells mineral water for $2.25 per bottle, so she declines to purchase it.

9. Determine the amount of producer surplus generated in each of the following situations.

a. Gordon lists his old Lionel electric trains on eBay. He sets a minimum acceptable price, known as his *reserve price,* of $75. After five days of bidding, the final high bid is exactly $75. He accepts the bid.

b. So-Hee advertises her car for sale in the used-car section of the student newspaper for $2,000, but she is willing to sell the car for any price higher than $1,500. The best offer she gets is $1,200, which she declines.

c. Sanjay likes his job so much that he would be willing to do it for free. However, his annual salary is $80,000.

10. You are the manager of Fun World, a small amusement park. The accompanying diagram shows the demand curve of a typical customer at Fun World.

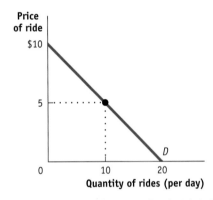

a. Suppose that the price of each ride is $5. At that price, how much consumer surplus does an individual consumer get? (Recall that the area of a right triangle is ½ × the height of the triangle × the base of the triangle.)

b. Suppose that Fun World considers charging an admission fee, even though it maintains the price of each ride at $5. What is the maximum admission fee it could charge? (Assume that all potential customers have enough money to pay the fee.)

c. Suppose that Fun World lowered the price of each ride to zero. How much consumer surplus does an individual consumer get? What is the maximum admission fee Fun World could charge?

11. The accompanying diagram illustrates a taxi driver's individual supply curve. (Assume that each taxi ride is the same distance.)

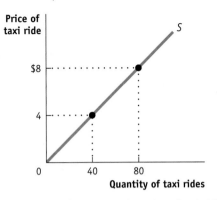

a. Suppose the city sets the price of taxi rides at $4 per ride, and at $4 the taxi driver is able to sell as many taxi rides as he desires. What is this taxi driver's producer surplus? (Recall that the area of a right triangle is ½ × the height of the triangle × the base of the triangle.)

b. Suppose that the city keeps the price of a taxi ride set at $4, but it decides to charge taxi drivers a "licensing fee." What is the maximum licensing fee the city could extract from this taxi driver?

c. Suppose that the city allowed the price of taxi rides to increase to $8 per ride. Again assume that, at this price, the taxi driver sells as many rides as he is willing to offer. How much producer surplus does an individual taxi driver now get? What is the maximum licensing fee the city could charge this taxi driver?

12. Consider the original market for pizza in Collegetown, illustrated in the accompanying table. Collegetown officials decide to impose an excise tax on pizza of $4 per pizza.

Price of pizza	Quantity of pizza demanded	Quantity of pizza supplied
10	0	6
9	1	5
8	2	4
7	3	3
6	4	2
5	5	1
4	6	0
3	7	0
2	8	0
1	9	0

a. What is the quantity of pizza bought and sold after the imposition of the tax? What is the price paid by consumers? What is the price received by producers?

b. Calculate the consumer surplus and the producer surplus after the imposition of the tax. By how much has the imposition of the tax reduced consumer surplus? By how much has it reduced producer surplus?

c. How much tax revenue does Collegetown earn from this tax?

d. Calculate the deadweight loss from this tax.

13. The state needs to raise money, and the governor has a choice of imposing an excise tax of the same amount on one of two previously untaxed goods: either restaurant meals or gasoline. Both the demand for and the supply of restaurant meals are more elastic than the demand for and the supply of gasoline. If the governor wants to minimize the deadweight loss caused by the tax, which good should be taxed? For each good, draw a diagram that illustrates the deadweight loss from taxation.

14. For each of the following situations, decide whether Al has increasing, constant, or diminishing marginal utility.

a. The more economics classes Al takes, the more he enjoys the subject. And the more classes he takes, the easier each one gets, making him enjoy each additional class even more than the one before.

b. Al likes loud music. In fact, according to him, "the louder, the better." Each time he turns the volume up a notch, he adds 5 utils to his total utility.

c. Al enjoys watching reruns of the old sitcom *Friends*. He claims that these episodes are always funny, but he does admit that the more times he sees an episode, the less funny it gets.

d. Al loves toasted marshmallows. The more he eats, however, the fuller he gets and the less he enjoys each additional marshmallow. And there is a point at which he becomes satiated: beyond that point, more marshmallows actually make him feel worse rather than better.

15. Use the concept of marginal utility to explain the following: Newspaper vending machines are designed so that once you have paid for one paper, you could take more than one paper at a time. But soda vending machines, once you have paid for one soda, dispense only one soda at a time.

16. Brenda likes to have bagels and coffee for breakfast. The accompanying table shows Brenda's total utility from various consumption bundles of bagels and coffee.

Consumption bundle		
Quantity of bagels	Quantity of coffee (cups)	Total utility (utils)
0	0	0
0	2	28
0	4	40
1	2	48
1	3	54
2	0	28
2	2	56
3	1	54
3	2	62
4	0	40
4	2	66

Suppose Brenda knows she will consume 2 cups of coffee for sure. However, she can choose to consume different quantities of bagels: she can choose either 0, 1, 2, 3, or 4 bagels.

a. Calculate Brenda's marginal utility from bagels as she goes from consuming 0 bagel to 1 bagel, from 1 bagel to 2 bagels, from 2 bagels to 3 bagels, and from 3 bagels to 4 bagels.

b. Draw Brenda's marginal utility curve of bagels. Does Brenda have increasing, diminishing, or constant marginal utility of bagels?

17. Bernie loves notebooks and Beyoncé CDs. The accompanying table shows the utility Bernie receives from each product.

Quantity of notebooks	Utility from notebooks (utils)	Quantity of CDs	Utility from CDs (utils)
0	0	0	0
2	70	1	80
4	130	2	150
6	180	3	210
8	220	4	260
10	250	5	300

The price of a notebook is $5, the price of a CD is $10, and Bernie has $50 of income to spend.

a. Which consumption bundles of notebooks and CDs can Bernie consume if he spends all his income? Illustrate Bernie's budget line with a diagram, putting notebooks on the horizontal axis and CDs on the vertical axis.

b. Calculate the marginal utility of each notebook and the marginal utility of each CD. Then calculate the marginal utility per dollar spent on notebooks and the marginal utility per dollar spent on CDs.

c. Draw a diagram like Figure 15.4 in which both the marginal utility per dollar spent on notebooks and the marginal utility per dollar spent on CDs are illustrated. Using this diagram and the optimal consumption rule, predict which bundle—from all the bundles on his budget line—Bernie will choose.

18. For each of the following situations, decide whether the bundle Lakshani is considering is optimal or not. If it is not optimal, how could Lakshani improve her overall level of utility? That is, determine which good she should spend more on and which good she should spend less on.

a. Lakshani has $200 to spend on sneakers and sweaters. Sneakers cost $50 per pair, and sweaters cost $20 each. She is thinking about buying 2 pairs of sneakers and 5 sweaters. She tells her friend that the additional utility she would get from the second pair of sneakers is the same as the additional utility she would get from the fifth sweater.

b. Lakshani has $5 to spend on pens and pencils. Each pen costs $0.50 and each pencil costs $0.10. She is thinking about buying 6 pens and 20 pencils. The last pen would add five times as much to her total utility as the last pencil.

c. Lakshani has $50 per season to spend on tickets to football games and tickets to soccer games. Each football ticket costs $10, and each soccer ticket costs $5. She is thinking about buying 3 football tickets and 2 soccer tickets. Her marginal utility from the third football ticket is twice as much as her marginal utility from the second soccer ticket.

Behind the Supply Curve: Profit, Production, and Costs

In the last section we examined the factors that affect consumer choice—the demand side of the supply and demand model. In this section we turn our attention to the factors that affect producer choice and the supply side of the supply and demand model. We'll begin with the concept of profit and examine profit maximization as the goal of a firm. We will then investigate the firm's production function, which shows the relationship between the inputs used for production and the output that is produced. Next we'll consider the costs that influence firms' decisions about supply. The final module in this section introduces the models of market structure used to understand how the supply side of the economy works.

Brand-X Pictures

iStockphoto

Module 16
Defining Profit

Understanding Profit

The primary goal of most firms is to maximize profit. Other goals, such as maximizing market share or protecting the environment, may also figure into a firm's mission. But economic models generally start with the assumption that firms attempt to maximize profit. So we will begin with an explanation of how economists define and calculate profit. In the next module we will look at how firms go about maximizing their profit.

In general, a firm's profit equals its *total revenue*—which is equal to the price of the output times the quantity sold, or $P \times Q$—minus the cost of all the inputs used to produce its output, its *total cost*. That is,

$$\text{Profit} = \text{Total Revenue} - \text{Total Cost}$$

However, there are different types of costs that may be used to calculate different types of profit. To start the discussion of how to calculate profit, we'll look at two different types of costs, *explicit costs* and *implicit costs*.

Explicit versus Implicit Costs

Suppose that, after graduating from high school, you have two options: to go to college or to take a job immediately. You would like to continue your education but are concerned about the cost.

But what exactly is the cost of attending college? Here is where it is important to remember the concept of opportunity cost: the cost of the time spent getting a degree is what you forgo by not taking a job for the years you go to college. The opportunity cost of additional education, like any cost, can be broken into two parts: the *explicit cost* and the *implicit cost*.

An **explicit cost** is a cost that requires an outlay of money. For example, the explicit cost of a year of college includes tuition. An **implicit cost,** though, does not involve an outlay of money; instead, it is measured by the value, in dollar terms, of the benefits that are forgone. For example, the implicit cost of a year spent in college includes the income you would have earned if you had taken a job instead.

A common mistake, both in economic analysis and in real business situations, is to ignore implicit costs and focus exclusively on explicit costs. But often the implicit cost

An **explicit cost** is a cost that involves actually laying out money. An **implicit cost** does not require an outlay of money; it is measured by the value, in dollar terms, of benefits that are forgone.

of an activity is quite substantial—indeed, sometimes it is much larger than the explicit cost.

Table 16.1 gives a breakdown of hypothetical explicit and implicit costs associated with spending a year in college instead of taking a job. The explicit cost consists of tuition, books, supplies, and a computer for doing assignments—all of which require you to spend money. The implicit cost is the salary you would have earned if you had taken a job instead. As you can see, the forgone salary is $35,000 and the explicit cost is $19,500, making the implicit cost more than the explicit cost in this example. So ignoring the implicit cost of an action can lead to a seriously misguided decision.

> The **accounting profit** of a business is the business's total revenue minus the explicit cost and depreciation.

table **16.1**

Opportunity Cost of an Additional Year of School

Explicit cost		Implicit cost	
Tuition	$17,000	Forgone salary	$35,000
Books and supplies	1,000		
Computer	1,500		
Total explicit cost	19,500	Total implicit cost	35,000
Total opportunity cost = Total explicit cost + Total implicit cost = $54,500			

A slightly different way of looking at the implicit cost in this example can deepen our understanding of opportunity cost. The forgone salary is the cost of using your own resources—your time—in going to college rather than working. The use of your *time* for more education, despite the fact that you don't have to spend any money, is still costly to you. This illustrates an important aspect of opportunity cost: in considering the cost of an activity, you should include the cost of using any of your own resources for that activity. You can calculate the cost of using your own resources by determining what they would have earned in their next best alternative use.

Accounting Profit versus Economic Profit

As the example of going to college suggests, taking account of implicit as well as explicit costs can be very important when making decisions. This is true whether the decisions affect individuals, groups, governments, or businesses.

Consider the case of Babette's Cajun Café, a small restaurant in New Orleans. This year Babette brought in $100,000 in revenue. Out of that revenue, she paid her expenses: the cost of food ingredients and other supplies, the cost of wages for her employees, and the rent for her restaurant space. This year her expenses were $60,000. We assume that Babette owns her restaurant equipment—items such as appliances and furnishings. The question is: Is Babette's restaurant profitable?

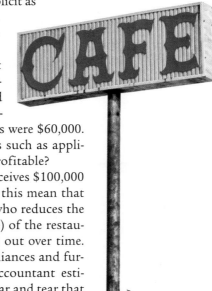

At first it might seem that the answer is obviously yes: she receives $100,000 from her customers and has expenses of only $60,000. Doesn't this mean that she has a profit of $40,000? Not according to her accountant, who reduces the number by $5,000 for the yearly *depreciation* (reduction in value) of the restaurant equipment. Depreciation occurs because equipment wears out over time. As a consequence, every few years Babette must replace her appliances and furnishings. The yearly depreciation amount reflects what an accountant estimates to be the reduction in the value of the machines due to wear and tear that year. This leaves $35,000, which is the business's **accounting profit.** That is,

The **economic profit** of a business is the business's total revenue minus the opportunity cost of its resources. It is usually less than the accounting profit.

The **implicit cost of capital** is the opportunity cost of the capital used by a business—the income the owner could have realized from that capital if it had been used in its next best alternative way.

"I've done the numbers, and I will marry you."

the accounting profit of a business is its total revenue minus its *explicit* cost and depreciation. The accounting profit is the number that Babette has to report on her income tax forms and that she would be obliged to report to anyone thinking of investing in her business.

Accounting profit is a very useful number, but suppose that Babette wants to decide whether to keep her restaurant open or do something else. To make this decision, she will need to calculate her **economic profit**—the total revenue she receives minus her *opportunity* cost, which includes implicit as well as explicit costs. In general, when economists use the simple term *profit,* they are referring to economic profit. (We adopt this simplification in this book.)

Why does Babette's economic profit differ from her accounting profit? Because she may have an implicit cost over and above the explicit cost her accountant has calculated. Businesses can face an implicit cost for two reasons. First, a business's capital—its equipment, buildings, tools, inventory, and financial assets—could have been put to use in some other way. If the business owns its capital, it does not pay any money for its use, but it pays an implicit cost because it does not use the capital in some other way. Second, the owner devotes time and energy to the business that could have been used elsewhere—a particularly important factor in small businesses, whose owners tend to put in many long hours.

If Babette had rented her appliances and furnishings instead of owning them, her rent would have been an explicit cost. But because Babette owns her own equipment, she does not pay rent on them and her accountant deducts an estimate of their depreciation in the profit statement. However, this does not account for the opportunity cost of the equipment—what Babette forgoes by owning it. Suppose that instead of using the equipment in her own restaurant, the best alternative Babette has is to sell the equipment for $50,000 and put the money into a bank account where it would earn yearly interest of $3,000. This $3,000 is an implicit cost of running the business. The **implicit cost of capital** is the opportunity cost of the capital used by a business; it reflects the income that could have been earned if the capital had been used in its next best alternative way. It is just as much a true cost as if Babette had rented her equipment instead of owning it.

Finally, Babette should take into account the opportunity cost of her own time. Suppose that instead of running her own restaurant, she could earn $34,000 as a chef in someone else's restaurant. That $34,000 is also an implicit cost of her business.

Table 16.2, in the column titled Case 1, summarizes the accounting for Babette's Cajun Café, taking both explicit and implicit costs into account. It turns out, unfortunately, that

table **16.2**

Profit at Babette's Cajun Café

	Case 1	Case 2
Revenue	$100,000	$100,000
Explicit cost	−60,000	−60,000
Depreciation	−5,000	−5,000
Accounting profit	**35,000**	**35,000**
Implicit cost of business		
Income Babette could have earned on capital used in the next best way	−3,000	−3,000
Income Babette could have earned as a chef in someone else's restaurant	−34,000	−30,000
Economic profit	**−2,000**	**+2,000**

Farming in the Shadow of Suburbia

Beyond the sprawling suburbs, most of New England is covered by dense forest. But this is not the forest primeval: if you hike through the woods, you encounter many stone walls, relics of the region's agricultural past when stone walls enclosed fields and pastures. In 1880, more than half of New England's land was farmed; by 2009, the amount was down to 10%.

The remaining farms of New England are mainly located close to large metropolitan areas. There farmers get high prices for their produce from city dwellers who are willing to pay a premium for locally grown, extremely fresh fruits and vegetables.

But now even these farms are under economic pressure caused by a rise in the implicit cost of farming close to a metropolitan area. As metropolitan areas have expanded during the last two decades, farmers increasingly ask themselves whether they could do better by selling their land to property developers.

In 2009, the average value of an acre of farmland in the United States as a whole was $2,100; in Rhode Island, the most densely populated of the New England states, the average was $15,300. The Federal Reserve Bank of Boston has noted that "high land prices put intense pressure on the region's farms to generate incomes that are substantial enough to justify keeping the land in agriculture." The important point is that the pressure is intense even if the farmer owns the land because the land is a form of capital used to run the business.

Maintaining the land as a farm instead of selling it to a developer constitutes a large implicit cost of capital. A fact provided by the U.S. Department of Agriculture (USDA) helps us put a dollar figure on the portion of the implicit cost of capital due to development pressure for some Rhode Island farms. In 2004, a USDA program designed to prevent development of Rhode Island farmland by paying owners for the "development rights" to their land paid an average of $4,949 per acre for those rights alone. By 2009, the amount had risen to $15,357.

About two-thirds of New England's farms remaining in business earn very little money. They are maintained as "rural residences" by people with other sources of income—not so much because they are commercially viable, but more out of a personal commitment and the satisfaction these people derive from farm life. Although many businesses have important implicit costs, they can also have important benefits to their owners that go beyond the revenue earned.

although the business makes an accounting profit of $35,000, its economic profit is actually negative. This means that Babette would be better off financially if she closed the restaurant and devoted her time and capital to something else. If, however, some of Babette's cost should fall sufficiently, she could earn a positive economic profit. In that case, she would be better off financially if she continued to operate the restaurant. For instance, consider the column titled Case 2: here we assume that what Babette could earn as a chef employed by someone else has dropped to $30,000 (say, due to a soft labor market). In this case, her economic profit is positive: she is earning more than her explicit and implicit costs and she should keep her restaurant open.

In real life, discrepancies between accounting profit and economic profit are extremely common. As the IRL above explains, this is a message that has found a receptive audience among real-world businesses.

Normal Profit

In the example above, when Babette is earning an economic profit, her total revenue is higher than the sum of her implicit and explicit costs. This means that operating her restaurant makes Babette better off financially than she would be using her resources in any other activity. When Babette earns a negative economic profit (which can also be described as a *loss*), it means that Babette would be better off financially if she devoted her resources to her next best alternative. As this example illustrates, economic profits signal the best use of resources. A positive economic profit indicates that the current use is the best use of resources. A negative economic profit indicates that there is a better alternative use for resources.

An economic profit equal to zero is also known as a **normal profit.** It is an economic profit just high enough to keep a firm engaged in its current activity.

But what about an economic profit *equal to* zero? Most of us would generally think earning zero profit was a bad thing. After all, a firm's goal is to maximize profit—profit is what firms are after! However, an economic profit equal to zero is not bad at all. An economic profit of zero means that the firm could not do any better using its resources in any alternative activity. Another name for an economic profit of zero is a **normal profit.** A firm earning a normal profit is earning just enough to keep it using its resources in its current activity. After all, it can't do any better in any other activity!

Module 16 Review

Solutions appear at the back of the book.

Check Your Understanding

1. Karma and Don run a furniture-refinishing business from their home. Which of the following represent an explicit cost of the business and which represent an implicit cost?
   a. supplies such as paint stripper, varnish, polish, sandpaper, and so on
   b. basement space that has been converted into a workroom
   c. wages paid to a part-time helper
   d. a van that they inherited and use only for transporting furniture
   e. the job at a larger furniture restorer that Karma gave up in order to run the business

2. a. Suppose you are in business earning an accounting profit of $25,000. What is your economic profit if the implicit cost of your capital is $2,000 and the opportunity cost of your time is $23,000? Explain your answer.
   b. What does your answer to part a tell you about the advisability of devoting your time and capital to this business?

Multiple-Choice Questions

1. Which of the following is an example of an *implicit* cost of going out for lunch?
   a. the amount of the tip you leave the waiter
   b. the total bill you charge to your credit card
   c. the cost of gas to drive to the restaurant
   d. the value of the time you spent eating lunch
   e. all of the above

2. Which of the following is an *implicit* cost of attending college?
   a. tuition
   b. books
   c. laptop computer
   d. lab fees
   e. forgone salary

3. Which of the following is the best definition of accounting profit? Accounting profit equals total revenue minus depreciation and total
   a. explicit cost only.
   b. implicit cost only.
   c. explicit cost plus implicit cost.
   d. opportunity cost.
   e. explicit cost plus opportunity cost.

4. Which of the following is considered when calculating economic profit but not accounting profit?
   a. implicit cost
   b. explicit cost
   c. total revenue
   d. marginal cost
   e. All of the above are considered when calculating accounting profit.

5. You sell T-shirts at your school's football games. Each shirt costs $5 to make and sells for $10. Each game lasts two hours and you sell 100 shirts per game. You could always be earning $8 per hour at your other job. Which of the following is correct? Your accounting profit from selling shirts at a game is
   a. $1,000 and your economic profit is $500.
   b. $500 and your economic profit is $1,000.
   c. $500 and your economic profit is $484.
   d. $484 and your economic profit is $500.
   e. $500 and your economic profit is also $500.

Critical-Thinking Questions

Sunny owns and operates Sunny's Sno Cone Stand. Use the data in the table provided to answer the questions below.

Sunny's Sno Cone Stand: January

Price of Sno Cone	$2
Sno Cones sold	2,000
Explicit cost	$400
Depreciation	$100
Implicit cost of capital	$200

a. Calculate Sunny's Sno Cone Stand's total revenue for January.
b. Calculate Sunny's Sno Cone Stand's accounting profit for January.
c. What additional information would Sunny need in order to determine whether or not to continue operating the Sno Cone Stand?
d. Explain how Sunny would determine whether or not to continue operating the business on the basis of these numbers.

Michael Melford/National Geographic/Getty Images

What you will learn in this **Module**:

- The principle of marginal analysis
- How to determine the profit-maximizing level of output using the optimal output rule

Module 17
Profit Maximization

Maximizing Profit

In the previous module we learned about different types of profit, how to calculate profit, and how firms can use profit calculations to make decisions—for instance to determine whether to continue using resources for the same activity or not. In this module we ask the question: what quantity of output would maximize the producer's profit? First we will find the profit-maximizing quantity by calculating the total profit at each quantity for comparison. Then we will use marginal analysis to determine the *optimal output rule,* which turns out to be simple: as our initial discussion of marginal analysis suggested, a producer should produce up until marginal benefit equals marginal cost.

Consider Jennifer and Jason, who run an organic tomato farm. Suppose that the market price of organic tomatoes is $18 per bushel and that Jennifer and Jason can sell as many as they would like at that price. Then we can use the data in Table 17.1 to find their profit-maximizing level of output.

The first column shows the quantity of output in bushels, and the second column shows Jennifer and Jason's total revenue from their output: the market value of their output. Total revenue, *TR*, is equal to the market price multiplied by the quantity of output:

(17-1) $TR = P \times Q$

In this example, total revenue is equal to $18 per bushel times the quantity of output in bushels.

The third column of Table 17.1 shows Jennifer and Jason's total cost, *TC*. The fourth column shows their profit, equal to total revenue minus total cost:

(17-2) $\text{Profit} = TR - TC$

As indicated by the numbers in the table, profit is maximized at an output of five bushels, where profit is equal to $18. But we can gain more insight into the profit-maximizing choice of output by viewing it as a problem of marginal analysis, a task we'll dive into next.

table **17.1**

Profit for Jennifer and Jason's Farm When Market Price Is $18

Quantity of tomatoes Q (bushels)	Total revenue TR	Total cost TC	Profit TR – TC
0	$0	$14	–$14
1	18	30	–12
2	36	36	0
3	54	44	10
4	72	56	16
5	90	72	18
6	108	92	16
7	126	116	10

Using Marginal Analysis to Choose the Profit-Maximizing Quantity of Output

The **principle of marginal analysis** provides a clear message about when to stop doing anything: proceed until *marginal benefit* equals *marginal cost*. To apply this principle, consider the effect on a producer's profit of increasing output by one unit. The marginal benefit of that unit is the additional revenue generated by selling it; this measure has a name—it is called the **marginal revenue** of that output. The general formula for marginal revenue is:

$$(17\text{-}3) \quad \text{Marginal revenue} = \frac{\text{Change in total revenue generated by one additional unit of output}}{1} = \frac{\text{Change in total revenue}}{\text{Change in quantity of output}}$$

or

$$MR = \Delta TR / \Delta Q$$

In this equation, the Greek uppercase delta (the triangular symbol) represents the change in a variable.

The application of the principle of marginal analysis to the producer's decision of how much to produce is called the **optimal output rule,** which states that profit is maximized by producing the quantity at which the marginal revenue of the last unit produced is equal to its marginal cost. As this rule suggests, we will see that Jennifer and Jason maximize their profit by equating marginal revenue and marginal cost.

Note that there may not be any particular quantity at which marginal revenue exactly equals marginal cost. In this case the producer should produce until one more unit would cause marginal benefit to fall below marginal cost. As a common simplification, we can think of marginal cost as rising steadily, rather than jumping from one level at one quantity to a different level at the next quantity. This ensures that marginal cost will equal marginal revenue at some quantity. We employ this simplified approach in what follows.

Consider Table 17.2 on the next page, which provides cost and revenue data for Jennifer and Jason's farm. The second column contains the farm's total cost of output.

According to the **principle of marginal analysis,** every activity should continue until marginal benefit equals marginal cost.

Marginal revenue is the change in total revenue generated by an additional unit of output.

The **optimal output rule** says that profit is maximized by producing the quantity of output at which the marginal revenue of the last unit produced is equal to its marginal cost.

table 17.2

Short-Run Costs for Jennifer and Jason's Farm

Quantity of tomatoes Q (bushels)	Total cost TC	Marginal cost of bushel $MC = \Delta TC/\Delta Q$	Marginal revenue of bushel MR	Net gain of bushel = $MR - MC$
0	$14			
		$16	$18	$2
1	30			
		6	18	12
2	36			
		8	18	10
3	44			
		12	18	6
4	56			
		16	18	2
5	72			
		20	18	−2
6	92			
		24	18	−6
7	116			

The third column shows their marginal cost. Notice that, in this example, marginal cost initially falls as output rises but then begins to increase, so that the marginal cost curve has a "swoosh" shape. (Later it will become clear that this shape has important implications for short-run production decisions.)

The fourth column contains the farm's marginal revenue, which has an important feature: Jennifer and Jason's marginal revenue is assumed to be constant at $18 for every output level. The assumption holds true for a particular type of market—perfectly competitive markets—which we will study in later modules, but for now it is just to make the calculations easier. The fifth and final column shows the calculation of the net gain per bushel of tomatoes, which is equal to marginal revenue minus marginal cost. As you can see, it is positive for the first through fifth bushels; producing each of these bushels raises Jennifer and Jason's profit. For the sixth and seventh bushels, however, net gain is negative: producing them would decrease, not increase, profit. (You can verify this by reexamining Table 17.1.) So five bushels are Jennifer and Jason's profit-maximizing output; it is the level of output at which marginal cost is equal to the market price, $18.

Figure 17.1 shows that Jennifer and Jason's profit-maximizing quantity of output is, indeed, the number of bushels at which the marginal cost of production is equal to marginal revenue (which is equivalent to price in perfectly competitive markets). The figure shows the **marginal cost curve,** MC, drawn from the data in the third column of Table 17.2. We plot the marginal cost of increasing output from one to two bushels halfway between one and two, and so on. The horizontal line at $18 is Jennifer and Jason's **marginal revenue curve.** Note that marginal revenue stays the same regardless of how much Jennifer and Jason sell because we have assumed marginal revenue is constant.

Does this mean that the firm's production decision can be entirely summed up as "produce up to the point where the marginal cost of production is equal to the price"? No, not quite. Before applying the principle of marginal analysis to determine how much to produce, a potential producer must, as a first step, answer an "either-or" question: Should I produce at all? If the answer to that question is yes, the producer then proceeds to the second step—a "how much" decision: maximizing profit by choosing the quantity of output at which marginal cost is equal to price.

The **marginal cost curve** shows how the cost of producing one more unit depends on the quantity that has already been produced.

The **marginal revenue curve** shows how marginal revenue varies as output varies.

figure 17.1

The Firm's Profit-Maximizing Quantity of Output

At the profit-maximizing quantity of output, marginal revenue is equal to marginal cost. It is located at the point where the marginal cost curve crosses the marginal revenue curve, which is a horizontal line at the market price. Here, the profit-maximizing point is at an output of 5 bushels of tomatoes, the output quantity at point *E*.

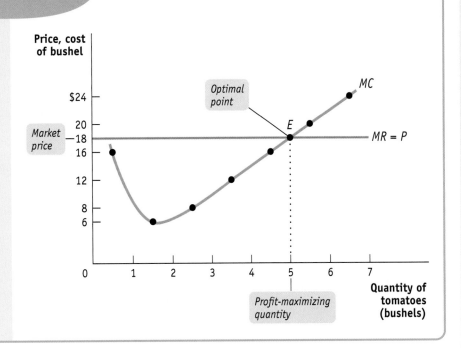

To understand why the first step in the production decision involves an "either–or" question, we need to ask how we determine whether it is profitable or unprofitable to produce at all.

When Is Production Profitable?

Recall that a firm's decision whether or not to stay in a given business depends on its *economic profit*—a measure based on the opportunity cost of resources used in the business. To put it a slightly different way: in the calculation of economic profit, a firm's total cost incorporates the implicit cost—the benefits forgone in the next best use of the firm's resources—as well as the explicit cost in the form of actual cash outlays. In contrast, *accounting profit* is profit calculated using only the explicit costs incurred by the firm. This means that economic profit incorporates the opportunity cost of resources owned by the firm and used in the production of output, while accounting profit does not. As in the example of Babette's Cajun Café, a firm may make positive accounting profit while making zero or even negative economic profit. It's important to understand clearly that a firm's decision to produce or not, to stay in business or to close down permanently, should be based on economic profit, not accounting profit.

So we will assume, as we always do, that the cost numbers given in Tables 17.1 and 17.2 include all costs, implicit as well as explicit, and that the profit numbers in Table 17.1 are economic profit. What determines whether Jennifer and Jason's farm earns a profit or generates a loss? The answer is that whether or not it is profitable depends on the market price of tomatoes—specifically, *whether selling the firm's optimal quantity of output at the market price results in at least a normal profit.*

In the next modules, we look in detail at the two components used to calculate profit; firm revenue (which is determined by the level of production) and firm cost.

Photodisc

Module 17 Review

Solutions appear at the back of the book.

Check Your Understanding

1. Suppose a firm can sell as many units of output as it wants for a price of $15 per unit and faces total costs as indicated in the table below. Use the optimal output rule to determine the profit-maximizing level of output for the firm.

Q	TC
0	$2
1	10
2	20
3	33
4	50
5	71

2. Use the data from Question 1 to graph the firm's MC and MR curves and show the profit-maximizing level of output.

Multiple-Choice Questions

Use the data in the table provided to answer questions 1–3.

Quantity	Total Revenue	Total Cost
Q	TR	TC
0	$0	$14
1	18	30
2	36	36
3	54	44
4	72	56
5	90	72
6	108	92
7	126	116

1. What is the marginal revenue of the third unit of output?
   a. $8
   b. $14
   c. $18
   d. $44
   e. $54

2. What is the marginal cost of the first unit of output?
   a. $0
   b. $14
   c. $16
   d. $18
   e. $30

3. At what level of output is profit maximized?
   a. 0
   b. 1
   c. 3
   d. 5
   e. 7

4. A firm should continue to produce as long as its
   a. total revenue is less than its total costs.
   b. total revenue is greater than its total explicit costs.
   c. accounting profit is greater than its economic profit.
   d. accounting profit is not negative.
   e. economic profit is at least zero.

5. A firm earns a normal profit when its
   a. accounting profit equals 0.
   b. economic profit is positive.
   c. total revenue equals its total costs.
   d. accounting profit equals its economic profit.
   e. economic profit equals its total explicit and implicit costs.

Critical-Thinking Question

Use a graph to illustrate the typical shape of the two curves used to find a firm's profit-maximizing level of output on the basis of the optimal output rule. Assume all units of output can be sold for $5. Indicate the profit-maximizing level of output with a "Q*" on the appropriate axis. (You don't have enough information to provide a specific numerical answer.)

Michael Melford/National Geographic/Getty Images

Module 18
The Production Function

What you will learn in this Module:

- The importance of the firm's production function, the relationship between the quantity of inputs and the quantity of output

- Why production is often subject to diminishing returns to inputs

The Production Function

A *firm* produces goods or services for sale. To do this, it must transform inputs into output. The quantity of output a firm produces depends on the quantity of inputs; this relationship is known as the firm's **production function.** As we'll see, a firm's production function underlies its *cost curves.* As a first step, let's look at the characteristics of a hypothetical production function.

Inputs and Output

To understand the concept of a production function, let's consider a farm that we assume, for the sake of simplicity, produces only one output, wheat, and uses only two inputs, land and labor. This particular farm is owned by a couple named George and Martha. They hire workers to do the actual physical labor on the farm. Moreover, we will assume that all potential workers are of the same quality—they are all equally knowledgeable and capable of performing farmwork.

George and Martha's farm sits on 10 acres of land; no more acres are available to them, and they are currently unable to either increase or decrease the size of their farm by selling, buying, or leasing acreage. Land here is what economists call a **fixed input**—an input whose quantity is fixed for a period of time and cannot be varied. George and Martha are, however, free to decide how many workers to hire. The labor provided by these workers is called a **variable input**—an input whose quantity the firm can vary at any time.

In reality, whether or not the quantity of an input is really fixed depends on the time horizon. In the **long run**—that is, given that a long enough period of time has elapsed—firms can adjust the quantity of any input. So there are no fixed inputs in the long run. In contrast, the **short run** is defined as the time period during which at least one input is fixed. Later, we'll look more carefully at the distinction between the short run and the long run. But for now, we will restrict our attention to the short run and assume that at least one input (land) is fixed.

A **production function** is the relationship between the quantity of inputs a firm uses and the quantity of output it produces.

A **fixed input** is an input whose quantity is fixed for a period of time and cannot be varied.

A **variable input** is an input whose quantity the firm can vary at any time.

The **long run** is the time period in which all inputs can be varied.

The **short run** is the time period in which at least one input is fixed.

George and Martha know that the quantity of wheat they produce depends on the number of workers they hire. Using modern farming techniques, one worker can cultivate the 10-acre farm, albeit not very intensively. When an additional worker is added, the land is divided equally among all the workers: each worker has 5 acres to cultivate when 2 workers are employed, each cultivates $3\frac{1}{3}$ acres when 3 are employed, and so on. So as additional workers are employed, the 10 acres of land are cultivated more intensively and more bushels of wheat are produced. The relationship between the quantity of labor and the quantity of output, for a given amount of the fixed input, constitutes the farm's production function. The production function for George and Martha's farm, where land is the fixed input and labor is the variable input, is shown in the first two columns of the table in Figure 18.1; the diagram there shows the same information graphically. The curve in Figure 18.1 shows how the quantity of output depends on the quantity of the variable input for a given quantity of the fixed input; it is called the farm's **total product curve.** The physical quantity of output, bushels of wheat, is measured on the vertical axis; the quantity of the variable input, labor (that is, the number of workers employed), is measured on the horizontal axis. The total product curve here slopes upward, reflecting the fact that more bushels of wheat are produced as more workers are employed.

Although the total product curve in Figure 18.1 slopes upward along its entire length, the slope isn't constant: as you move up the curve to the right, it flattens out. To understand this changing slope, look at the third column of the table in Figure 18.1, which shows the *change in the quantity of output* generated by adding one more worker. That is, it shows the **marginal product** of labor, or *MPL:* the additional quantity of output from using one more unit of labor (one more worker).

The **total product curve** shows how the quantity of output depends on the quantity of the variable input, for a given quantity of the fixed input.

The **marginal product** of an input is the additional quantity of output produced by using one more unit of that input.

figure 18.1   Production Function and Total Product Curve for George and Martha's Farm

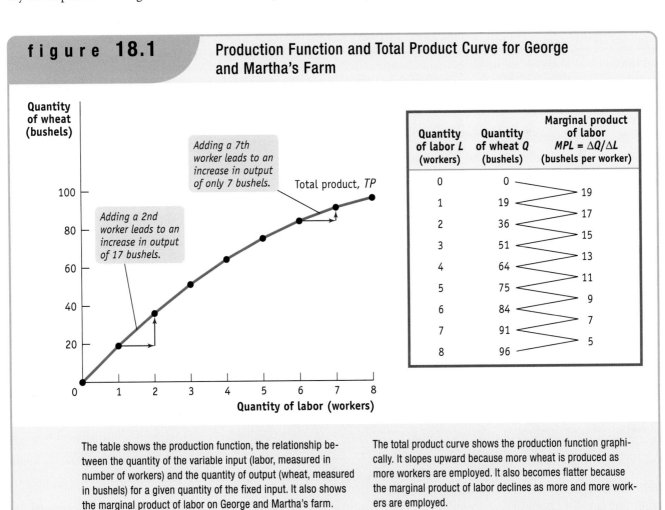

The table shows the production function, the relationship between the quantity of the variable input (labor, measured in number of workers) and the quantity of output (wheat, measured in bushels) for a given quantity of the fixed input. It also shows the marginal product of labor on George and Martha's farm.

The total product curve shows the production function graphically. It slopes upward because more wheat is produced as more workers are employed. It also becomes flatter because the marginal product of labor declines as more and more workers are employed.

In this example, we have data at intervals of 1 worker—that is, we have information on the quantity of output when there are 3 workers, 4 workers, and so on. Sometimes data aren't available in increments of 1 unit—for example, you might have information on the quantity of output only when there are 40 workers and when there are 50 workers. In this case, you can use the following equation to calculate the marginal product of labor:

$$\textbf{(18-1)} \quad \begin{array}{l} \text{Marginal} \\ \text{product} \\ \text{of labor} \end{array} = \begin{array}{l} \text{Change in quantity of} \\ \text{output produced by one} \\ \text{additional unit of labor} \end{array} = \frac{\text{Change in quantity of output}}{\text{Change in quantity of labor}}$$

or

$$MPL = \frac{\Delta Q}{\Delta L}$$

Recall that Δ, the Greek uppercase delta, represents the change in a variable. Now we can explain the significance of the slope of the total product curve: it is equal to the marginal product of labor. The slope of a line is equal to "rise" over "run." This implies that the slope of the total product curve is the change in the quantity of output (the "rise") divided by the change in the quantity of labor (the "run"). And this, as we can see from Equation 18-1, is simply the marginal product of labor. So in Figure 18.1, the fact that the marginal product of the first worker is 19 also means that the slope of the total product curve in going from 0 to 1 worker is 19. Similarly, the slope of the total product curve in going from 1 to 2 workers is the same as the marginal product of the second worker, 17, and so on.

In this example, the marginal product of labor steadily declines as more workers are hired—that is, each successive worker adds less to output than the previous worker. So as employment increases, the total product curve gets flatter.

Figure 18.2 shows how the marginal product of labor depends on the number of workers employed on the farm. The marginal product of labor, *MPL*, is measured on the vertical axis in units of physical output—bushels of wheat—produced per additional worker, and the number of workers employed is measured on the horizontal axis. You can see from the table in Figure 18.1 that if 5 workers are employed instead of 4, output rises from 64 to 75 bushels; in this case the marginal product of labor is

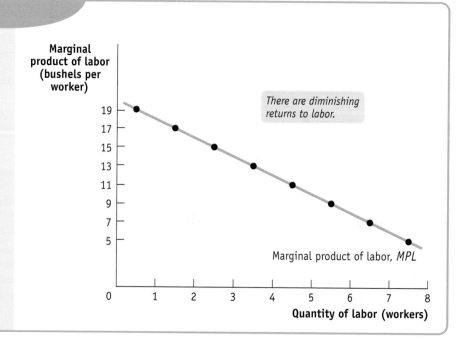

figure 18.2

Marginal Product of Labor Curve for George and Martha's Farm

The marginal product of labor curve plots each worker's marginal product, the increase in the quantity of output generated by each additional worker. The change in the quantity of output is measured on the vertical axis and the number of workers employed on the horizontal axis. The first worker employed generates an increase in output of 19 bushels, the second worker generates an increase of 17 bushels, and so on. The curve slopes downward due to diminishing returns to labor.

11 bushels—the same number found in Figure 18.2. To indicate that 11 bushels is the marginal product when employment rises from 4 to 5, we place the point corresponding to that information halfway between 4 and 5 workers.

In this example the marginal product of labor falls as the number of workers increases. That is, there are *diminishing returns to labor* on George and Martha's farm. In general, there are **diminishing returns to an input** when an increase in the quantity of that input, holding the quantity of all other inputs fixed, reduces that input's marginal product. Due to diminishing returns to labor, the *MPL* curve is negatively sloped.

To grasp why diminishing returns can occur, think about what happens as George and Martha add more and more workers without increasing the number of acres. As the number of workers increases, the land is farmed more intensively and the number of bushels increases. But each additional worker is working with a smaller share of the 10 acres—the fixed input—than the previous worker. As a result, the additional worker cannot produce as much output as the previous worker. So it's not surprising that the marginal product of the additional worker falls.

The crucial point to emphasize about diminishing returns is that, like many propositions in economics, it is an "other things equal" proposition: each successive unit of an input will raise production by less than the last *if the quantity of all other inputs is held fixed.*

What would happen if the levels of other inputs were allowed to change? You can see the answer illustrated in Figure 18.3. Panel (a) shows two total product curves, TP_{10} and TP_{20}. TP_{10} is the farm's total product curve when its total area is 10 acres (the same curve as in Figure 18.1). TP_{20} is the total product curve when the farm's area has increased to 20 acres. Except when 0 workers are employed, TP_{20} lies everywhere above TP_{10} because with more acres available, any given number of workers produces more output. Panel (b) shows the corresponding marginal product of labor curves.

There are **diminishing returns to an input** when an increase in the quantity of that input, holding the levels of all other inputs fixed, leads to a decline in the marginal product of that input.

With diminishing marginal returns to labor, as more and more workers are added to a fixed amount of land, each worker adds less to total output than the previous worker.

---

figure 18.3   Total Product, Marginal Product, and the Fixed Input

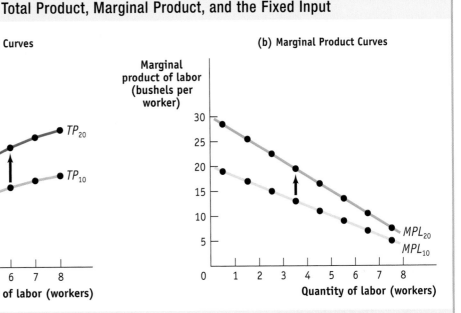

This figure shows how the quantity of output—illustrated by the total product curve—and marginal product depend on the level of the fixed input. Panel (a) shows two total product curves for George and Martha's farm, TP_{10} when their farm is 10 acres and TP_{20} when it is 20 acres. With more land, each worker can produce more wheat. So an increase in the fixed input shifts the total product curve up from TP_{10} to TP_{20}. This also implies that the marginal product of each worker is higher when the farm is 20 acres than when it is 10 acres. As a result, an increase in acreage also shifts the marginal product of labor curve up from MPL_{10} to MPL_{20}. Panel (b) shows the marginal product of labor curves. Note that both marginal product of labor curves still slope downward due to diminishing returns to labor.

Was Malthus Right?

In 1798, Thomas Malthus, an English pastor, authored the book *An Essay on the Principle of Population,* which introduced the principle of diminishing returns to an input. Malthus's writings were influential in his own time and continue to provoke heated argument to this day.

Malthus argued that as a country's population grew but its land area remained fixed, it would become increasingly difficult to grow enough food. Though more intensive cultivation of the land could increase yields, as the marginal product of labor declined, each successive farmer would add less to the total than the last.

From this argument, Malthus drew a powerful conclusion—that misery was the normal condition of humankind. In a country with a small population and abundant land (a description of the United States at the time), he argued, families would be large and the population would grow rapidly. Ultimately, the pressure of population on the land would reduce the condition of most people to a level at which starvation and disease held the population in check. (Arguments like this led the historian Thomas Carlyle to dub economics the "dismal science.")

Happily, over the long term, Malthus's predictions have turned out to be wrong. World population has increased from about 1 billion when Malthus wrote to more than 6.8 billion in 2010, but in most of the world people eat better now than ever before. So was Malthus completely wrong? And do his incorrect predictions refute the idea of diminishing returns? No, on both counts.

First, the Malthusian story is a pretty accurate description of 57 of the last 59 centuries: peasants in eighteenth-century France probably did not live much better than Egyptian peasants in the age of the pyramids. Yet diminishing returns does not mean that using more labor to grow food on a given amount of land will lead to a decline in the marginal product of labor—*if*

there is also a radical improvement in farming technology. Fortunately, since the eighteenth century, technological progress has been so rapid that it has alleviated much of the limits imposed by diminishing returns. Diminishing returns implies that the marginal product declines when *all* other things—including technology—remain the same. So the happy fact that Malthus's predictions were wrong does not invalidate the concept of diminishing returns.

Typically, however, technological progress relaxes the limits imposed by diminishing returns only over the very long term. This was demonstrated in 2008 when bad weather, an ethanol-driven increase in the demand for corn, and a brisk rise in world income led to soaring world grain prices. As farmers scrambled to plant more acreage, they ran up against limits in the availability of inputs like land and fertilizer. Hopefully, we can prove Malthus wrong again before long.

MPL_{10} is the marginal product of labor curve given 10 acres to cultivate (the same curve as in Figure 18.2), and MPL_{20} is the marginal product of labor curve given 20 acres. Both curves slope downward because, in each case, the amount of land is fixed, albeit at different levels. But MPL_{20} lies everywhere above MPL_{10}, reflecting the fact that the marginal product of the same worker is higher when he or she has more of the fixed input to work with.

Figure 18.3 demonstrates a general result: the position of the total product curve depends on the quantities of other inputs. If you change the quantities of the other inputs, both the total product curve and the marginal product curve of the remaining input will shift. The importance of the "other things equal" assumption in discussing diminishing returns is illustrated in the IRL above.

Module (18) Review

Solutions appear at the back of the book.

Check Your Understanding

1. Bernie's ice-making company produces ice cubes using a 10-ton machine and electricity (along with water, which we will ignore as an input for simplicity). The quantity of output, measured in pounds of ice, is given in the accompanying table.

   a. What is the fixed input? What is the variable input?

   b. Construct a table showing the marginal product of the variable input. Does it show diminishing returns?

   c. Suppose a 50% increase in the size of the fixed input increases output by 100% for any given amount of the variable input. What is the fixed input now? Construct a table showing the quantity of output and the marginal product in this case.

Quantity of electricity (kilowatts)	Quantity of ice (pounds)
0	0
1	1,000
2	1,800
3	2,400
4	2,800

Multiple-Choice Questions

1. A production function shows the relationship between inputs and
   a. fixed costs.
   b. variable costs.
   c. total revenue.
   d. output.
   e. profit.

2. Which of the following defines the short run?
   a. less than a year
   b. when all inputs are fixed
   c. when no inputs are variable
   d. when only one input is variable
   e. when at least one input is fixed

3. The slope of the total product curve is also known as
   a. marginal product.
   b. marginal cost.
   c. average product.
   d. average revenue.
   e. profit.

4. Diminishing returns to an input ensures that as a firm continues to produce, the total product curve will have what kind of slope?
   a. negative decreasing
   b. positive decreasing
   c. negative increasing
   d. positive increasing
   e. positive constant

5. Historically, the limits imposed by diminishing returns have been alleviated by
   a. investment in capital.
   b. increases in the population.
   c. discovery of more land.
   d. Thomas Malthus.
   e. economic models.

Critical-Thinking Question

Use the data in the table below to graph the production function and the marginal product of labor. Do the data illustrate diminishing returns to labor? Explain.

Quantity of labor L	Quantity of output Q
0	0
1	19
2	36
3	51
4	64
5	75
6	84
7	91
8	96

© Terrance Klassen/AgeFotostock

What you will learn in this Module:

- The various types of cost a firm faces, including fixed cost, variable cost, and total cost

- How a firm's costs generate marginal cost curves and average cost curves

Module 19
Firm Costs

From the Production Function to Cost Curves

Now that we have learned about the firm's production function, we can use that knowledge to develop its cost curves. To see how a firm's production function is related to its cost curves, let's turn once again to George and Martha's farm. Once George and Martha know their production function, they know the relationship between inputs of labor and land and output of wheat. But if they want to maximize their profits, they need to translate this knowledge into information about the relationship between the quantity of output and cost. Let's see how they can do this.

To translate information about a firm's production function into information about its cost, we need to know how much the firm must pay for its inputs. We will assume that George and Martha face either an explicit or an implicit cost of $400 for the use of the land. As we learned previously, it is irrelevant whether George and Martha must rent the land for $400 from someone else or whether they own the land themselves and forgo earning $400 from renting it to someone else. Either way, they pay an opportunity cost of $400 by using the land to grow wheat. Moreover, since the land is a fixed input for which George and Martha pay $400 whether they grow one bushel of wheat or one hundred, its cost is a **fixed cost,** denoted by *FC*—a cost that does not depend on the quantity of output produced. In business, a fixed cost is often referred to as an "overhead cost."

We also assume that George and Martha must pay each worker $200. Using their production function, George and Martha know that the number of workers they must hire depends on the amount of wheat they intend to produce. So the cost of labor, which is equal to the number of workers multiplied by $200, is a **variable cost,** denoted by *VC*—a cost that depends on the quantity of output produced. Adding the fixed cost and the variable cost of a given quantity of output gives the **total cost,** or *TC*, of that quantity of output. We can express the relationship among fixed cost, variable cost, and total cost as an equation:

(19-1)   Total cost = Fixed cost + Variable cost

or

$$TC = FC + VC$$

A **fixed cost** is a cost that does not depend on the quantity of output produced. It is the cost of the fixed input.

A **variable cost** is a cost that depends on the quantity of output produced. It is the cost of the variable input.

The **total cost** of producing a given quantity of output is the sum of the fixed cost and the variable cost of producing that quantity of output.

The table in Figure 19.1 shows how total cost is calculated for George and Martha's farm. The second column shows the number of workers employed, L. The third column shows the corresponding level of output, Q, taken from the table in Figure 18.1. The fourth column shows the variable cost, VC, equal to the number of workers multiplied by $200. The fifth column shows the fixed cost, FC, which is $400 regardless of the quantity of wheat produced. The sixth column shows the total cost of output, TC, which is the variable cost plus the fixed cost.

The first column labels each row of the table with a letter, from A to I. These labels will be helpful in understanding our next step: drawing the **total cost curve,** a curve that shows how total cost depends on the quantity of output.

George and Martha's total cost curve is shown in the diagram in Figure 19.1, where the horizontal axis measures the quantity of output in bushels of wheat and the vertical axis measures total cost in dollars. Each point on the curve corresponds to one row of the table in Figure 19.1. For example, point A shows the situation when 0 workers are employed: output is 0, and total cost is equal to fixed cost, $400. Similarly, point B shows the situation when 1 worker is employed: output is 19 bushels, and total cost is $600, equal to the sum of $400 in fixed cost and $200 in variable cost.

Like the total product curve, the total cost curve slopes upward: due to the increasing variable cost, the more output produced, the higher the farm's total cost.

> The **total cost curve** shows how total cost depends on the quantity of output.

figure 19.1

Total Cost Curve for George and Martha's Farm

The table shows the variable cost, fixed cost, and total cost for various output quantities on George and Martha's 10-acre farm. The total cost curve shows how total cost (measured on the vertical axis) depends on the quantity of output (measured on the horizontal axis). The labeled points on the curve correspond to the rows of the table. The total cost curve slopes upward because the number of workers employed, and hence total cost, increases as the quantity of output increases. The curve gets steeper as output increases due to diminishing returns to labor.

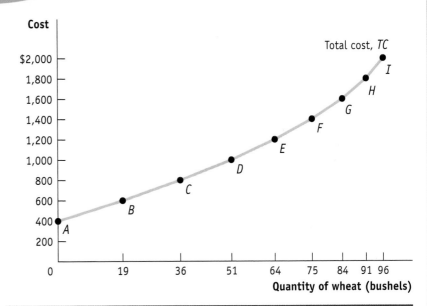

Point on graph	Quantity of labor L (workers)	Quantity of wheat Q (bushels)	Variable cost VC	Fixed cost FC	Total cost $TC = FC + VC$
A	0	0	$0	$400	$400
B	1	19	200	400	600
C	2	36	400	400	800
D	3	51	600	400	1,000
E	4	64	800	400	1,200
F	5	75	1,000	400	1,400
G	6	84	1,200	400	1,600
H	7	91	1,400	400	1,800
I	8	96	1,600	400	2,000

But unlike the total product curve, which gets flatter as employment rises, the total cost curve gets *steeper*. That is, the slope of the total cost curve is greater as the amount of output produced increases. As we will soon see, the steepening of the total cost curve is also due to diminishing returns to the variable input. Before we can see why, we must first look at the relationships among several useful measures of cost.

Two Key Concepts: Marginal Cost and Average Cost

We've just learned how to derive a firm's total cost curve from its production function. Our next step is to take a deeper look at total cost by deriving two extremely useful measures: *marginal cost* and *average cost*. As we'll see, these two measures of the cost of production have a somewhat surprising relationship to each other. Moreover, they will prove to be vitally important in later modules, where we will use them to analyze the firm's output decision and the market supply curve.

Marginal Cost

Marginal cost is the added cost of doing something one more time. In the context of production, marginal cost is the change in total cost generated by producing one more unit of output. We've already seen that marginal product is easiest to calculate if data on output are available in increments of one unit of input. Similarly, marginal cost is easiest to calculate if data on total cost are available in increments of one unit of output because the increase in total cost for each unit is clear. When the data come in less convenient increments, it's still possible to calculate marginal cost over each interval. But for the sake of simplicity, let's work with an example in which the data come in convenient one-unit increments.

Selena's Gourmet Salsas produces bottled salsa; Table 19.1 shows how its costs per day depend on the number of cases of salsa it produces per day. The firm has a fixed

table **19.1**

Costs at Selena's Gourmet Salsas

Quantity of salsa Q (cases)	Fixed cost FC	Variable cost VC	Total cost TC = FC + VC	Marginal cost of case MC = ΔTC/ΔQ
0	$108	$0	$108	
				$12
1	108	12	120	
				36
2	108	48	156	
				60
3	108	108	216	
				84
4	108	192	300	
				108
5	108	300	408	
				132
6	108	432	540	
				156
7	108	588	696	
				180
8	108	768	876	
				204
9	108	972	1,080	
				228
10	108	1,200	1,308	

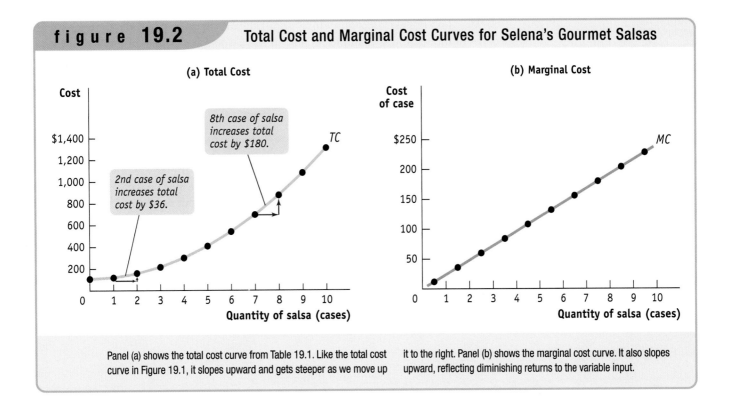

figure 19.2   Total Cost and Marginal Cost Curves for Selena's Gourmet Salsas

(a) Total Cost

8th case of salsa increases total cost by $180.

2nd case of salsa increases total cost by $36.

(b) Marginal Cost

Panel (a) shows the total cost curve from Table 19.1. Like the total cost curve in Figure 19.1, it slopes upward and gets steeper as we move up it to the right. Panel (b) shows the marginal cost curve. It also slopes upward, reflecting diminishing returns to the variable input.

cost of $108 per day, shown in the second column, which is the daily rental cost of its food-preparation equipment. The third column shows the variable cost, and the fourth column shows the total cost. Panel (a) of Figure 19.2 plots the total cost curve. Like the total cost curve for George and Martha's farm in Figure 19.1, this curve slopes upward, getting steeper as quantity increases.

The significance of the slope of the total cost curve is shown by the fifth column of Table 19.1, which indicates marginal cost—the additional cost of each additional unit. The general formula for marginal cost is:

(19-2)   Marginal cost = $\dfrac{\text{Change in total cost generated by one additional unit of output}}{} = \dfrac{\text{Change in total cost}}{\text{Change in quantity of output}}$

or

$$MC = \frac{\Delta TC}{\Delta Q}$$

As in the case of marginal product, marginal cost is equal to "rise" (the increase in total cost) divided by "run" (the increase in the quantity of output). So just as marginal product is equal to the slope of the total product curve, marginal cost is equal to the slope of the total cost curve.

Now we can understand why the total cost curve gets steeper as it increases from left to right: as you can see in Table 19.1, marginal cost at Selena's Gourmet Salsas rises as output increases. And because marginal cost equals the slope of the total cost curve, a higher marginal cost means a steeper slope. Panel (b) of Figure 19.2 shows the marginal cost curve corresponding to the data in Table 19.1. Notice that, as in Figure 17.1, we plot the marginal cost for increasing output from 0 to 1 case of salsa halfway between 0 and 1, the marginal cost for increasing output from 1 to 2 cases of salsa halfway between 1 and 2, and so on.

iStockphoto

Why does the marginal cost curve slope upward? Because there are diminishing returns to inputs in this example. As output increases, the marginal product of the variable input declines. This implies that more and more of the variable input must be used to produce each additional unit of output as the amount of output already produced rises. And since each unit of the variable input must be paid for, the additional cost per additional unit of output also rises.

Recall that the flattening of the total product curve is also due to diminishing returns: if the quantities of other inputs are fixed, the marginal product of an input falls as more of that input is used. The flattening of the total product curve as output increases and the steepening of the total cost curve as output increases are just flip-sides of the same phenomenon. That is, as output increases, the marginal cost of output also increases because the marginal product of the variable input decreases. Our next step is to introduce another measure of cost: *average cost.*

Average Cost

In addition to total cost and marginal cost, it's useful to calculate **average total cost,** often simply called **average cost.** The average total cost is total cost divided by the quantity of output produced; that is, it is equal to total cost per unit of output. If we let *ATC* denote average total cost, the equation looks like this:

$$(19\text{-}3) \quad ATC = \frac{\text{Total cost}}{\text{Quantity of output}} = \frac{TC}{Q}$$

Average total cost is important because it tells the producer how much the *average* or *typical* unit of output costs to produce. Marginal cost, meanwhile, tells the producer how much *one more* unit of output costs to produce. Although they may look very similar, these two measures of cost typically differ. And confusion between them is a major source of error in economics, both in the classroom and in real life. Table 19.2 uses data from Selena's Gourmet Salsas to calculate average total cost. For example, the total cost of producing 4 cases of salsa is $300, consisting of $108 in fixed cost and $192 in variable cost (from Table 19.1). So the average total cost of producing 4 cases of salsa is

table **19.2**

Average Costs for Selena's Gourmet Salsas

Quantity of salsa Q (cases)	Total cost TC	Average total cost of case $ATC = TC/Q$	Average fixed cost of case $AFC = FC/Q$	Average variable cost of case $AVC = VC/Q$
1	$120	$120.00	$108.00	$12.00
2	156	78.00	54.00	24.00
3	216	72.00	36.00	36.00
4	300	75.00	27.00	48.00
5	408	81.60	21.60	60.00
6	540	90.00	18.00	72.00
7	696	99.43	15.43	84.00
8	876	109.50	13.50	96.00
9	1,080	120.00	12.00	108.00
10	1,308	130.80	10.80	120.00

$300/4 = $75. You can see from Table 19.2 that as the quantity of output increases, average total cost first falls, then rises.

Figure 19.3 plots that data to yield the *average total cost curve,* which shows how average total cost depends on output. As before, cost in dollars is measured on the vertical axis and quantity of output is measured on the horizontal axis. The average total cost curve has a distinctive U shape that corresponds to how average total cost first falls and then rises as output increases. Economists believe that such **U-shaped average total cost curves** are the norm for firms in many industries.

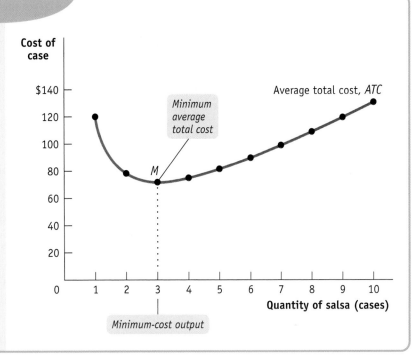

figure 19.3

Average Total Cost Curve for Selena's Gourmet Salsas

The average total cost curve at Selena's Gourmet Salsas is U-shaped. At low levels of output, average total cost falls because the "spreading effect" of falling average fixed cost dominates the "diminishing returns effect" of rising average variable cost. At higher levels of output, the opposite is true and average total cost rises. At point *M,* corresponding to an output of three cases of salsa per day, average total cost is at its minimum level, the minimum average total cost.

To help our understanding of why the average total cost curve is U-shaped, Table 19.2 breaks average total cost into its two underlying components, *average fixed cost* and *average variable cost.* **Average fixed cost,** or *AFC,* is fixed cost divided by the quantity of output, also known as the fixed cost per unit of output. For example, if Selena's Gourmet Salsas produces 4 cases of salsa, average fixed cost is $108/4 = $27 per case. **Average variable cost,** or *AVC,* is variable cost divided by the quantity of output, also known as variable cost per unit of output. At an output of 4 cases, average variable cost is $192/4 = $48 per case. Writing these in the form of equations:

(19-4) $AFC = \dfrac{\text{Fixed cost}}{\text{Quantity of output}} = \dfrac{FC}{Q}$

$AVC = \dfrac{\text{Variable cost}}{\text{Quantity of output}} = \dfrac{VC}{Q}$

Average total cost is the sum of average fixed cost and average variable cost; it has a U shape because these components move in opposite directions as output rises.

Average fixed cost falls as more output is produced because the numerator (the fixed cost) is a fixed number but the denominator (the quantity of output) increases as more is produced. Another way to think about this relationship is that, as more output is produced, the fixed cost is spread over more units of output; the end result is that the

A **U-shaped average total cost curve** falls at low levels of output and then rises at higher levels.

Average fixed cost is the fixed cost per unit of output.

Average variable cost is the variable cost per unit of output.

fixed cost *per unit of output*—the average fixed cost—falls. You can see this effect in the fourth column of Table 19.2: average fixed cost drops continuously as output increases. Average variable cost, however, rises as output increases. As we've seen, this reflects diminishing returns to the variable input: each additional unit of output adds more to variable cost than the previous unit because increasing amounts of the variable input are required to make another unit.

So increasing output has two opposing effects on average total cost—the "spreading effect" and the "diminishing returns effect":

- *The spreading effect.* The larger the output, the greater the quantity of output over which fixed cost is spread, leading to lower average fixed cost.

- *The diminishing returns effect.* The larger the output, the greater the amount of variable input required to produce additional units, leading to higher average variable cost.

At low levels of output, the spreading effect is very powerful because even small increases in output cause large reductions in average fixed cost. So at low levels of output, the spreading effect dominates the diminishing returns effect and causes the average total cost curve to slope downward. But when output is large, average fixed cost is already quite small, so increasing output further has only a very small spreading effect. Diminishing returns, however, usually grow increasingly important as output rises. As a result, when output is large, the diminishing returns effect dominates the spreading effect, causing the average total cost curve to slope upward. At the bottom of the U-shaped average total cost curve, point *M* in Figure 19.3, the two effects exactly balance each other. At this point average total cost is at its minimum level, the minimum average total cost.

Figure 19.4 brings together in a single picture the four other cost curves that we have derived from the total cost curve for Selena's Gourmet Salsas: the marginal cost curve (*MC*), the average total cost curve (*ATC*), the average variable cost curve (*AVC*), and the average fixed cost curve (*AFC*). All are based on the information in Tables 19.1 and 19.2. As before, cost is measured on the vertical axis and the quantity of output is measured on the horizontal axis.

figure 19.4

Marginal Cost and Average Cost Curves for Selena's Gourmet Salsas

Here we have the family of cost curves for Selena's Gourmet Salsas: the marginal cost curve (*MC*), the average total cost curve (*ATC*), the average variable cost curve (*AVC*), and the average fixed cost curve (*AFC*). Note that the average total cost curve is U-shaped and the marginal cost curve crosses the average total cost curve at the bottom of the U, point *M*, corresponding to the minimum average total cost from Table 19.2 and Figure 19.3.

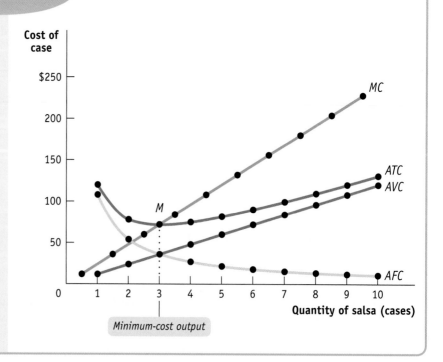

Let's take a moment to note some features of the various cost curves. First of all, marginal cost slopes upward—the result of diminishing returns that make an additional unit of output more costly to produce than the one before. Average variable cost also slopes upward—again, due to diminishing returns—but is flatter than the marginal cost curve. This is because the higher cost of an additional unit of output is averaged across all units, not just the additional unit, in the average variable cost measure. Meanwhile, average fixed cost slopes downward because of the spreading effect.

Finally, notice that the marginal cost curve intersects the average total cost curve from below, crossing it at its lowest point, point M in Figure 19.4. This last feature is our next subject of study.

Minimum Average Total Cost

For a U-shaped average total cost curve, average total cost is at its minimum level at the bottom of the U. Economists call the quantity of output that corresponds to the minimum average total cost the **minimum-cost output.** In the case of Selena's Gourmet Salsas, the minimum-cost output is three cases of salsa per day.

In Figure 19.4, the bottom of the U is at the level of output at which the marginal cost curve crosses the average total cost curve from below. Is this an accident? No—it reflects general principles that are always true about a firm's marginal cost and average total cost curves:

- At the minimum-cost output, average total cost *is equal to* marginal cost.

- At output less than the minimum-cost output, marginal cost *is less than* average total cost and average total cost is falling.

- And at output greater than the minimum-cost output, marginal cost *is greater than* average total cost and average total cost is rising.

To understand these principles, think about how your grade in one course—say, a 3.0 in physics—affects your overall grade point average. If your GPA before receiving that grade was more than 3.0, the new grade lowers your average.

Similarly, if marginal cost—the cost of producing one more unit—is less than average total cost, producing that extra unit lowers average total cost. This is shown in Figure 19.5 by the movement from A_1 to A_2. In this case, the marginal cost of producing

The **minimum-cost output** is the quantity of output at which average total cost is lowest—it corresponds to the bottom of the U-shaped average total cost curve.

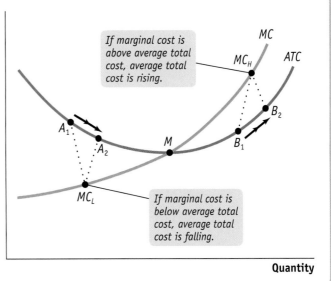

figure 19.5

The Relationship Between the Average Total Cost and the Marginal Cost Curves

To see why the marginal cost curve (*MC*) must cut through the average total cost curve (*ATC*) at the minimum average total cost (point *M*), corresponding to the minimum-cost output, we look at what happens if marginal cost is different from average total cost. If marginal cost is *less* than average total cost, an increase in output must reduce average total cost, as in the movement from A_1 to A_2. If marginal cost is *greater* than average total cost, an increase in output must increase average total cost, as in the movement from B_1 to B_2.

an additional unit of output is low, as indicated by the point MC_L on the marginal cost curve. When the cost of producing the next unit of output is less than average total cost, increasing production reduces average total cost. So any quantity of output at which marginal cost is less than average total cost must be on the downward-sloping segment of the U.

But if your grade in physics is more than the average of your previous grades, this new grade raises your GPA. Similarly, if marginal cost is greater than average total cost, producing that extra unit raises average total cost. This is illustrated by the movement from B_1 to B_2 in Figure 19.5, where the marginal cost, MC_H, is higher than average total cost. So any quantity of output at which marginal cost is greater than average total cost must be on the upward-sloping segment of the U.

Finally, if a new grade is exactly equal to your previous GPA, the additional grade neither raises nor lowers that average—it stays the same. This corresponds to point M in Figure 19.5: when marginal cost equals average total cost, we must be at the bottom of the U because only at that point is average total cost neither falling nor rising.

Does the Marginal Cost Curve Always Slope Upward?

Up to this point, we have emphasized the importance of diminishing returns, which lead to a marginal product curve that always slopes downward and a marginal cost curve that always slopes upward. In practice, however, economists believe that marginal cost curves often slope *downward* as a firm increases its production from zero up to some low level, sloping upward only at higher levels of production: marginal cost curves look like the curve labeled MC in Figure 19.6.

This initial downward slope occurs because a firm often finds that, when it starts with only a very small number of workers, employing more workers and expanding output allows its workers to specialize in various tasks. This, in turn, lowers the firm's marginal cost as it expands output. For example, one individual producing salsa would have to perform all the tasks involved: selecting and preparing the ingredients, mixing the salsa, bottling and labeling it, packing it into cases, and so on. As more workers are employed, they can divide the tasks, with each worker specializing in one or a few aspects of salsa-making. This specialization leads to *increasing returns* to the hiring of additional workers and results in a marginal cost curve that initially slopes downward.

figure 19.6

More Realistic Cost Curves

A realistic marginal cost curve has a "swoosh" shape. Starting from a very low output level, marginal cost often falls as the firm increases output. That's because hiring additional workers allows greater specialization of their tasks and leads to increasing returns. Once specialization is achieved, however, diminishing returns to additional workers set in and marginal cost rises. The corresponding average variable cost curve is now U-shaped, like the average total cost curve.

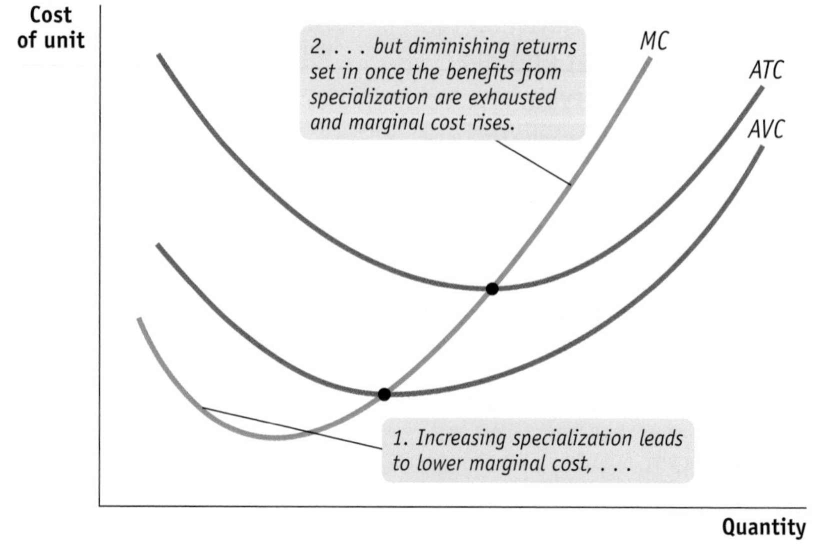

2. . . . but diminishing returns set in once the benefits from specialization are exhausted and marginal cost rises.

1. Increasing specialization leads to lower marginal cost, . . .

But once there are enough workers to have completely exhausted the benefits of further specialization, diminishing returns to labor set in and the marginal cost curve changes direction and slopes upward. So typical marginal cost curves actually have the "swoosh" shape shown by *MC* in Figure 19.6. For the same reason, average variable cost curves typically look like *AVC* in Figure 19.6: they are U-shaped rather than strictly upward sloping.

However, as Figure 19.6 also shows, the key features we saw from the example of Selena's Gourmet Salsas remain true: the average total cost curve is U-shaped, and the marginal cost curve passes through the point of minimum average total cost.

Module 19 Review

Solutions appear at the back of the book.

Check Your Understanding

1. Alicia's Apple Pies is a roadside business. Alicia must pay $9.00 in rent each day. In addition, it costs her $1.00 to produce the first pie of the day, and each subsequent pie costs 50% more to produce than the one before. For example, the second pie costs $1.00 × 1.5 = $1.50 to produce, and so on.
   a. Calculate Alicia's marginal cost, variable cost, average fixed cost, average variable cost, and average total cost as her daily pie output rises from 0 to 6. (*Hint:* The variable cost of two pies is just the marginal cost of the first pie, plus the marginal cost of the second, and so on.)

   b. Indicate the range of pies for which the spreading effect dominates and the range for which the diminishing returns effect dominates.
   c. What is Alicia's minimum-cost output? Explain why making one more pie lowers Alicia's average total cost when output is lower than the minimum-cost output. Similarly, explain why making one more pie raises Alicia's average total cost when output is greater than the minimum-cost output.

Multiple-Choice Questions

1. When a firm is producing zero output, total cost equals
   a. zero.
   b. variable cost.
   c. fixed cost.
   d. average total cost.
   e. marginal cost.

2. Which of the following statements is true?
   I. Marginal cost is the change in total cost generated by one additional unit of output.
   II. Marginal cost is the change in variable cost generated by one additional unit of output.
   III. The marginal cost curve must cross the minimum of the average total cost curve.
   a. I only
   b. II only
   c. III only
   d. I and II only
   e. I, II, and III

3. Which of the following is correct?
   a. AVC is the change in total cost generated by one additional unit of output.
   b. MC = TC/Q
   c. The average cost curve crosses at the minimum of the marginal cost curve.

   d. The AFC curve slopes upward.
   e. AVC = ATC − AFC

4. The slope of the total cost curve equals
   a. variable cost.
   b. average variable cost.
   c. average total cost.
   d. average fixed cost.
   e. marginal cost.

5.

Q	VC	TC
0	$0	$40
1	20	60
2	50	90
3	90	130
4	140	180
5	200	240

On the basis of the data in the table above, what is the marginal cost of the third unit of output?
   a. 40
   b. 50
   c. 60
   d. 90
   e. 130

Critical-Thinking Question

Draw a correctly labeled graph showing a firm with an upward sloping *MC* curve and typically shaped *ATC, AVC,* and *AFC* curves.

© Modern Landscapes/Alamy

Module 20
Long-Run Costs and Economies of Scale

What you will learn
in this **Module:**

- Why a firm's costs may differ between the short run and the long run

- How a firm can enjoy economies of scale

Up to this point, we have treated fixed cost as completely outside the control of a firm because we have focused on the short run. But all inputs are variable in the long run: this means that in the long run, even "fixed cost" may change. *In the long run, in other words, a firm's fixed cost becomes a variable it can choose.* For example, given time, Selena's Gourmet Salsas can acquire additional food-preparation equipment or dispose of some of its existing equipment. In this module, we will examine how a firm's costs behave in the short run and in the long run. We will also see that the firm will choose its fixed cost in the long run based on the level of output it expects to produce.

Short-Run versus Long-Run Costs

Let's begin by supposing that Selena's Gourmet Salsas is considering whether to acquire additional food-preparation equipment. Acquiring additional machinery will affect its total cost in two ways. First, the firm will have to either rent or buy the additional equipment; either way, that will mean a higher fixed cost in the short run. Second, if the workers have more equipment, they will be more productive: fewer workers will be needed to produce any given output, so variable cost for any given output level will be reduced.

The table in Figure 20.1 on the next page shows how acquiring an additional machine affects costs. In our original example, we assumed that Selena's Gourmet Salsas had a fixed cost of $108. The left half of the table shows variable cost as well as total cost and average total cost assuming a fixed cost of $108. The average total cost curve for this level of fixed cost is given by ATC_1 in Figure 20.1. Let's compare that to a situation in which the firm buys additional food-preparation equipment, doubling its fixed cost to $216 but reducing its variable cost at any given level of output. The right half of the table shows the firm's variable cost, total cost, and average total cost with this higher level of fixed cost. The average total cost curve corresponding to $216 in fixed cost is given by ATC_2 in Figure 20.1.

figure **20.1**

Choosing the Level of Fixed Cost for Selena's Gourmet Salsas

There is a trade-off between higher fixed cost and lower variable cost for any given output level, and vice versa. ATC_1 is the average total cost curve corresponding to a fixed cost of $108; it leads to lower fixed cost and higher variable cost. ATC_2 is the average total cost curve corresponding to a higher fixed cost of $216 but lower variable cost. At low output levels, at 4 or fewer cases of salsa per day, ATC_1 lies below ATC_2: average total cost is lower with only $108 in fixed cost. But as output goes up, average total cost is lower with the higher amount of fixed cost, $216: at more than 4 cases of salsa per day, ATC_2 lies below ATC_1.

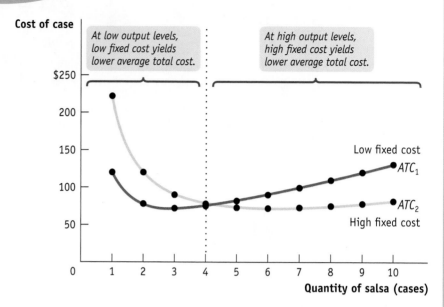

	Low fixed cost (FC = $108)			High fixed cost (FC = $216)		
Quantity of salsa (cases)	High variable cost	Total cost	Average total cost of case ATC_1	Low variable cost	Total cost	Average total cost of case ATC_2
1	$12	$120	$120.00	$6	$222	$222.00
2	48	156	78.00	24	240	120.00
3	108	216	72.00	54	270	90.00
4	192	300	75.00	96	312	78.00
5	300	408	81.60	150	366	73.20
6	432	540	90.00	216	432	72.00
7	588	696	99.43	294	510	72.86
8	768	876	109.50	384	600	75.00
9	972	1,080	120.00	486	702	78.00
10	1,200	1,308	130.80	600	816	81.60

From the figure you can see that when output is small, 4 cases of salsa per day or fewer, average total cost is smaller when Selena forgoes the additional equipment and maintains the lower fixed cost of $108: ATC_1 lies below ATC_2. For example, at 3 cases per day, average total cost is $72 without the additional machinery and $90 with the additional machinery. But as output increases beyond 4 cases per day, the firm's average total cost is lower if it acquires the additional equipment, raising its fixed cost to $216. For example, at 9 cases of salsa per day, average total cost is $120 when fixed cost is $108 but only $78 when fixed cost is $216.

Why does average total cost change like this when fixed cost increases? When output is low, the increase in fixed cost from the additional equipment outweighs the reduction in variable cost from higher worker productivity—that is, there are too few units of output over which to spread the additional fixed cost. So if Selena plans to produce 4 or fewer cases per day, she would be better off choosing the lower level of fixed cost, $108, to achieve a lower average total cost of production. When planned output is high, however, she should acquire the additional machinery.

In general, for each output level there is some choice of fixed cost that minimizes the firm's average total cost for that output level. So when the firm has a desired output level that it expects to maintain over time, it should choose the optimal fixed cost for that level—that is, the level of fixed cost that minimizes its average total cost.

Now that we are studying a situation in which fixed cost can change, we need to take *time* into account when discussing average total cost. All of the average total cost curves we have considered until now are defined for a given level of fixed cost—that is, they are defined for the short run, the period of time over which fixed cost doesn't vary. To reinforce that distinction, for the rest of this module we will refer to these average total cost curves as "short-run average total cost curves."

For most firms, it is realistic to assume that there are many possible choices of fixed cost, not just two. The implication: for such a firm, many possible short-run average total cost curves will exist, each corresponding to a different choice of fixed cost and so giving rise to what is called a firm's "family" of short-run average total cost curves.

At any given time, a firm will find itself on one of its short-run cost curves, the one corresponding to its current level of fixed cost; a change in output will cause it to move along that curve. If the firm expects that change in output level to be long-standing, then it is likely that the firm's current level of fixed cost is no longer optimal. Given sufficient time, it will want to adjust its fixed cost to a new level that minimizes average total cost for its new output level. For example, if Selena had been producing 2 cases of salsa per day with a fixed cost of $108 but found herself increasing her output to 8 cases per day for the foreseeable future, then in the long run she should purchase more equipment and increase her fixed cost to a level that minimizes average total cost at the 8-cases-per-day output level.

Suppose we do a thought experiment and calculate the lowest possible average total cost that can be achieved for each output level if the firm were to choose its fixed cost for each output level. Economists have given this thought experiment a name: the *long-run average total cost curve*. Specifically, the **long-run average total cost curve,** or *LRATC,* is the relationship between output and average total cost when fixed cost has been chosen to minimize average total cost *for each level of output*. If there are many possible choices of fixed cost, the long-run average total cost curve will have the familiar, smooth U shape, as shown by *LRATC* in Figure 20.2.

The **long-run average total cost curve** shows the relationship between output and average total cost when fixed cost has been chosen to minimize average total cost for each level of output.

figure 20.2

Short-Run and Long-Run Average Total Cost Curves

Short-run and long-run average total cost curves differ because a firm can choose its fixed cost in the long run. If Selena has chosen the level of fixed cost that minimizes short-run average total cost at an output of 6 cases, and actually produces 6 cases, then she will be at point *C* on *LRATC* and *ATC*₆. But if she produces only 3 cases, she will move to point *B*. If she expects to produce only 3 cases for a long time, in the long run she will reduce her fixed cost and move to point *A* on *ATC*₃. Likewise, if she produces 9 cases (putting her at point *Y*) and expects to continue this for a long time, she will increase her fixed cost in the long run and move to point *X*.

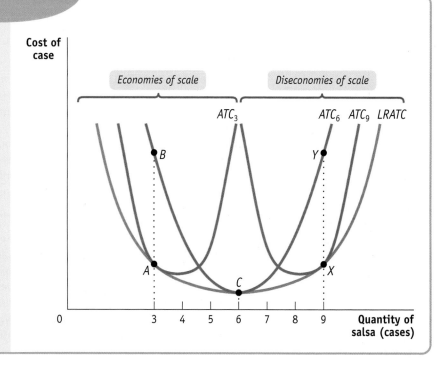

We can now draw the distinction between the short run and the long run more fully. In the long run, when a producer has had time to choose the fixed cost appropriate for its desired level of output, that producer will be at some point on the long-run average total cost curve. But if the output level is altered, the firm will no longer be on its long-run average total cost curve and will instead be moving along its current short-run average total cost curve. It will not be on its long-run average total cost curve again until it readjusts its fixed cost for its new output level.

Figure 20.2 illustrates this point. The curve ATC_3 shows short-run average total cost if Selena has chosen the level of fixed cost that minimizes average total cost at an output of 3 cases of salsa per day. This is confirmed by the fact that at 3 cases per day, ATC_3 touches $LRATC$, the long-run average total cost curve. Similarly, ATC_6 shows short-run average total cost if Selena has chosen the level of fixed cost that minimizes average total cost if her output is 6 cases per day. It touches $LRATC$ at 6 cases per day. And ATC_9 shows short-run average total cost if Selena has chosen the level of fixed cost that minimizes average total cost if her output is 9 cases per day. It touches $LRATC$ at 9 cases per day.

Suppose that Selena initially chose to be on ATC_6. If she actually produces 6 cases of salsa per day, her firm will be at point C on both its short-run and long-run average total cost curves. Suppose, however, that Selena ends up producing only 3 cases of salsa per day. In the short run, her average total cost is indicated by point B on ATC_6; it is no longer on $LRATC$. If Selena had known that she would be producing only 3 cases per day, she would have been better off choosing a lower level of fixed cost, the one corresponding to ATC_3, thereby achieving a lower average total cost. Then her firm would have found itself at point A on the long-run average total cost curve, which lies below point B.

Suppose, conversely, that Selena ends up producing 9 cases per day even though she initially chose to be on ATC_6. In the short run her average total cost is indicated by point Y on ATC_6. But she would be better off purchasing more equipment and incurring a higher fixed cost in order to reduce her variable cost and move to ATC_9. This would allow her to reach point X on the long-run average total cost curve, which lies below Y. The distinction between short-run and long-run average total costs is extremely important in making sense of how real firms operate over time. A company that has to increase output suddenly to meet a surge in demand will typically find that in the short run its average total cost rises sharply because it is hard to get extra production out of existing facilities. But given time to build new factories or add machinery, short-run average total cost falls.

Returns to Scale

What determines the shape of the long-run average total cost curve? It is the influence of *scale,* the size of a firm's operations, on its long-run average total cost of production. Firms that experience *scale effects* in production find that their long-run average total cost changes substantially depending on the quantity of output they produce. There are **economies of scale** when long-run average total cost declines as output increases. As you can see in Figure 20.2, Selena's Gourmet Salsas experiences economies of scale over output levels ranging from 0 up to 6 cases of salsa per day—the output levels over which the long-run average total cost curve is declining. Economies of scale can result from **increasing returns to scale,** which exist when output increases more than in proportion to an increase in all inputs. For example, if Selena could double all of her inputs and make more than twice as much salsa, she would be experiencing increasing returns to scale. With twice the inputs (and costs) and more than twice the salsa, she would be enjoying decreasing long-run average total costs, and thus economies of scale. Increasing returns to scale therefore imply economies of scale, although economies of scale exist whenever long-run average total cost is falling, whether or not all inputs are increasing by the same proportion.

In contrast, there are **diseconomies of scale** when long-run average total cost increases as output increases. For Selena's Gourmet Salsas, decreasing returns to scale occur at output levels greater than 6 cases, the output levels over which its long-run

There are **economies of scale** when long-run average total cost declines as output increases.

There are **increasing returns to scale** when output increases more than in proportion to an increase in all inputs. For example, with increasing returns to scale, doubling all inputs would cause output to more than double.

There are **diseconomies of scale** when long-run average total cost increases as output increases.

average total cost curve is rising. Diseconomies of scale can result from **decreasing returns to scale,** which exist when output increases less than in proportion to an increase in all inputs—doubling the inputs results in less than double the output. When output increases directly in proportion to an increase in all inputs—doubling the inputs results in double the output—the firm is experiencing **constant returns to scale.**

What explains these scale effects in production? The answer ultimately lies in the firm's technology of production. Economies of scale often arise from the increased *specialization* that larger output levels allow—a larger scale of operation means that individual workers can limit themselves to more specialized tasks, becoming more skilled and efficient at doing them. Another source of economies of scale is a very large initial setup cost; in some industries—such as auto manufacturing, electricity generating, and petroleum refining—it is necessary to pay a high fixed cost in the form of plant and equipment before producing any output. A third source of economies of scale, found in certain high-tech industries such as software development, is *network externalities,* a topic covered in a later module. As we'll see when we study monopoly, increasing returns have very important implications for how firms and industries behave and interact.

Diseconomies of scale—the opposite scenario—typically arise in large firms due to problems of coordination and communication: as a firm grows in size, it becomes ever more difficult and therefore costly to communicate and to organize activities. Although economies of scale induce firms to grow larger, diseconomies of scale tend to limit their size.

There are **decreasing returns to scale** when output increases less than in proportion to an increase in all inputs.

There are **constant returns to scale** when output increases directly in proportion to an increase in all inputs.

A **sunk cost** is a cost that has already been incurred and is nonrecoverable. A sunk cost should be ignored in a decision about future actions.

Sunk Costs

To complete our discussion of costs, we need to include the concept of sunk costs. When making decisions, knowing what to ignore is important. Although we have devoted much attention to costs that are important to take into account when making a decision, some costs should be ignored when doing so. This section presents the kind of costs that people should ignore when making decisions—what economists call *sunk costs*—and explains why they should be ignored.

To gain some intuition, consider the following scenario. You own a car that is a few years old, and you have just replaced the brake pads at a cost of $250. But then you find out that the entire brake system is defective and also must be replaced. This will cost you an additional $1,500. Alternatively, you could sell the car and buy another of comparable quality, but with no brake defects, by spending an additional $1,600. What should you do: fix your old car, or sell it and buy another?

Some might say that you should take the latter option. After all, this line of reasoning goes, if you repair your car, you will end up having spent $1,750: $1,500 for the brake system and $250 for the brake pads. If you were instead to sell your old car and buy another, you would spend only $1,600.

But this reasoning, although it sounds plausible, is wrong. It ignores the fact that you have *already* spent $250 on brake pads, and that $250 is *nonrecoverable*. That is, having already been spent, the $250 cannot be recouped. Therefore, it should be ignored and should have no effect on your decision whether to repair your car and keep it or not. From a rational viewpoint, the real cost at this time of repairing and keeping your car is $1,500, not $1,750. So the correct decision is to repair your car and keep it rather than spend $1,600 on a new car.

In this example, the $250 that has already been spent and cannot be recovered is what economists call a **sunk cost.** Sunk costs should be ignored in making decisions because they have no influence on future costs and benefits. It's like the old saying, "There's no use crying over spilled milk": once something can't be recovered, it is irrelevant in making decisions about what to do in the future. This applies equally to individuals, firms, and governments—regardless of how much has been spent on a project in the past, if the future costs exceed the future benefits, the project should not continue.

It is often psychologically hard to ignore sunk costs. And if, in fact, you haven't yet incurred the costs, then you should take them into consideration. That is, if you had known

© Greatstock Photographic Library / Alamy

There's No Business Like Snow Business

Anyone who has lived both in a snowy city, like Chicago, and in a city that only occasionally experiences significant snowfall, like Washington, D.C., is aware of the differences in total cost that arise from making different choices about fixed cost.

In Washington, even a minor snowfall—say, an inch or two overnight—is enough to create chaos during the next morning's commute. The same snowfall in Chicago has hardly any effect at all. The reason is not that Washingtonians are wimps and Chicagoans are made of sterner stuff; it is that Washington, where it rarely snows, has only a fraction as many snowplows

and other snow-clearing equipment as cities where heavy snow is a fact of life.

In this sense Washington and Chicago are like two producers who expect to produce different levels of output, where the "output" is snow removal. Washington, which rarely has significant snow, has chosen a low level of fixed cost in the form of snow-clearing equipment. This makes sense under normal circumstances but leaves the city unprepared when major snow does fall. Chicago, which knows that it will face lots of snow, chooses to accept the higher fixed cost that leaves it in a position to respond effectively.

A lesson in returns to scale: cities with higher average annual snowfall maintain larger snowplow fleets.

at the beginning that it would cost $1,750 to repair your car, then the right choice *at that time* would have been to buy a new car for $1,600. But once you have already paid the $250 for brake pads, you should no longer include it in your decision making about your next actions. It may be hard to "let bygones be bygones," but it is the right way to make a decision.

Summing Up Costs: The Short and Long of It

If a firm is to make the best decisions about how much to produce, it has to understand how its costs relate to the quantity of output it chooses to produce. Table 20.1 provides a quick summary of the concepts and measures of cost you have learned about.

table 20.1

Concepts and Measures of Cost

	Measurement	Definition	Mathematical term
Short run	Fixed cost	Cost that does not depend on the quantity of output produced	FC
	Average fixed cost	Fixed cost per unit of output	$AFC = FC/Q$
Short run and long run	Variable cost	Cost that depends on the quantity of output produced	VC
	Average variable cost	Variable cost per unit of output	$AVC = VC/Q$
	Total cost	The sum of fixed cost (short run) and variable cost	$TC = FC$ (short run) $+ VC$
	Average total cost (average cost)	Total cost per unit of output	$ATC = TC/Q$
	Marginal cost	The change in total cost generated by producing one more unit of output	$MC = \Delta TC/\Delta Q$
Long run	Long-run average total cost	Average total cost when fixed cost has been chosen to minimize average total cost for each level of output	$LRATC$

Module 20 Review

Solutions appear at the back of the book.

Check Your Understanding

1. The accompanying table shows three possible combinations of fixed cost and average variable cost. Average variable cost is constant in this example. (It does not vary with the quantity of output produced.)

Choice	Fixed cost	Average variable cost
1	$8,000	$1.00
2	12,000	0.75
3	24,000	0.25

   a. For each of the three choices, calculate the average total cost of producing 12,000, 22,000, and 30,000 units. For each of these quantities, which choice results in the lowest average total cost?

   b. Suppose that the firm, which has historically produced 12,000 units, experiences a sharp, permanent increase in demand that leads it to produce 22,000 units. Explain how its average total cost will change in the short run and in the long run.

   c. Explain what the firm should do instead if it believes the change in demand is temporary.

2. In each of the following cases, explain whether the firm is likely to experience economies of scale or diseconomies of scale and why.

   a. an interior design firm in which design projects are based on the expertise of the firm's owner

   b. a diamond-mining company

Multiple-Choice Questions

1. In the long run,
   a. all inputs are variable.
   b. all inputs are fixed.
   c. some inputs are variable and others are fixed.
   d. a firm will go out of business.
   e. firms increase in size.

2. Which of the following is always considered the long run?
   a. 1 month
   b. 1 year
   c. 5 years
   d. 10 years
   e. none of the above

3. Which of the following statements is generally correct?
   I. The long-run average total cost curve is U-shaped.
   II. The short-run average total cost curve is U-shaped.
   III. Firms tend to experience economies of scale at low levels of production and diseconomies of scale at high levels of production.
   a. I only
   b. II only
   c. III only
   d. I and II only
   e. I, II, and III

4. When making decisions, which of the following costs should be ignored?
   a. average costs
   b. total costs
   c. marginal costs
   d. sunk costs
   e. None—no costs should be ignored.

5. Economies of scale will allow which of the following types of cities to lower their average total cost of clearing snow by investing in larger snow plow fleets? Cities with
   a. more people.
   b. more existing snow plows.
   c. less snowfall.
   d. larger budgets.
   e. more snowfall.

Critical-Thinking Question

Draw a correctly labeled graph showing a short-run average total cost curve and the corresponding long-run average total cost curve. On your graph, identify the areas of economies and diseconomies of scale.

© Chris A Crumley/Alamy

Module 21
Introduction to Market Structure

You may have noticed that this section is titled "Behind the Supply Curve," but we have yet to mention any supply curve. The reason is that to discuss the supply curve in a market, we need to identify the type of market we are looking at. In this module we will learn about the basic characteristics of the four major types of markets in the economy.

Types of Market Structure

The real world holds a mind-boggling array of different markets. Patterns of firm behavior vary as widely as the markets themselves: in some markets firms are extremely competitive; in others, they seem somehow to coordinate their actions to limit competition; and some markets are monopolies in which there is no competition at all. In order to develop principles and make predictions about markets and firm behavior, economists have developed four primary models of market structure: *perfect competition, monopoly, oligopoly,* and *monopolistic competition.*

This system of market structure is based on two dimensions:

- the number of firms in the market (one, few, or many)
- whether the goods offered are identical or *differentiated*

Differentiated goods are goods that are different but considered at least somewhat substitutable by consumers (think Coke versus Pepsi).

Figure 21.1 on the next page provides a simple visual summary of the types of market structure classified according to the two dimensions. In *perfect competition* many firms each sell an identical product. In *monopoly,* a single firm sells a single, undifferentiated product. In *oligopoly,* a few firms—more than one but not a large number—sell products that may be either identical or differentiated. And in *monopolistic competition,* many firms each sell a differentiated product (think of producers of economics textbooks).

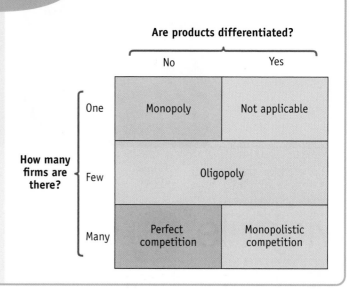

figure 21.1

Types of Market Structure

The behavior of any given firm and the market it occupies are analyzed using one of four models of market structure—monopoly, oligopoly, perfect competition, or monopolistic competition. This system for categorizing market structure is based on two dimensions: (1) whether products are differentiated or identical and (2) the number of firms in the industry—one, a few, or many.

Are products differentiated?

		No	Yes
How many firms are there?	One	Monopoly	Not applicable
	Few	Oligopoly	
	Many	Perfect competition	Monopolistic competition

Perfect Competition

Suppose that Yves and Zoe are neighboring farmers, both of whom grow organic tomatoes. Both sell their output to the same grocery store chains that carry organic foods; so, in a real sense, Yves and Zoe compete with each other.

Does this mean that Yves should try to stop Zoe from growing tomatoes or that Yves and Zoe should form an agreement to grow fewer? Almost certainly not: there are hundreds or thousands of organic tomato farmers (let's not forget Jennifer and Jason!), and Yves and Zoe are competing with all those other growers as well as with each other. Because so many farmers sell organic tomatoes, if any one of them produced more or fewer, there would be no measurable effect on market prices.

When people talk about business competition, they often imagine a situation in which two or three rival firms are struggling for advantage. But economists know that when a business focuses on a few main competitors, it's actually a sign that competition is fairly limited. As the example of organic tomatoes suggests, when the number of competitors is large, it doesn't even make sense to identify rivals and engage in aggressive competition because each firm is too small within the scope of the market to make a significant difference.

We can put it another way: Yves and Zoe are *price-takers*. A firm is a **price-taker** when its actions cannot affect the market price of the good or service it sells. As a result, a price-taking firm takes the market price as given. When there is enough competition—when competition is what economists call "perfect"—then every firm is a price-taker. There is a similar definition for consumers: a **price-taking consumer** is a consumer who cannot influence the market price of the good or service by his or her actions. That is, the market price is unaffected by how much or how little of the good the consumer buys.

Defining Perfect Competition

In a **perfectly competitive market,** all market participants, both consumers and producers, are price-takers. That is, neither consumption decisions by individual consumers nor production decisions by individual producers affect the market price of the good.

The supply and demand model is a model of a perfectly competitive market. It depends fundamentally on the assumption that no individual buyer or seller of a good,

A **price-taking firm** is a firm whose actions have no effect on the market price of the good or service it sells.

A **price-taking consumer** is a consumer whose actions have no effect on the market price of the good or service he or she buys.

A **perfectly competitive market** is a market in which all market participants are price-takers.

such as coffee beans or organic tomatoes, believes that it is possible to individually affect the price at which he or she can buy or sell the good. For a firm, being a price-taker means that the demand curve is a horizontal line at the market price. If the firm charged more than the market price, buyers would go to any of the many alternative sellers of the same product. And it is unnecessary to charge a lower price because, as an insignificantly small part of the perfectly competitive market, the firm can sell all that it wants at the market price.

As a general rule, consumers are indeed price-takers. Instances in which consumers are able to affect the prices they pay are rare. It is, however, quite common for producers to have a significant ability to affect the prices they receive, a phenomenon we'll address later. So the model of perfect competition is appropriate for some but not all markets. An industry in which firms are price-takers is called a **perfectly competitive industry.** Clearly, some industries aren't perfectly competitive; in later modules we'll focus on industries that don't fit the perfectly competitive model.

Under what circumstances will all firms be price-takers? As we'll discover next, there are two necessary conditions for a perfectly competitive industry and a third condition is often present as well.

> A **perfectly competitive industry** is an industry in which firms are price-takers.
>
> A firm's **market share** is the fraction of the total industry output accounted for by that firm's output.
>
> A good is a **standardized product,** also known as a **commodity,** when consumers regard the products of different firms as the same good.

Two Necessary Conditions for Perfect Competition

The markets for major grains, such as wheat and corn, are perfectly competitive: individual wheat and corn farmers, as well as individual buyers of wheat and corn, take market prices as given. In contrast, the markets for some of the food items made from these grains—in particular, breakfast cereals—are by no means perfectly competitive. There is intense competition among cereal brands, but not *perfect* competition. To understand the difference between the market for wheat and the market for shredded wheat cereal is to understand the two necessary conditions for perfect competition.

First, for an industry to be perfectly competitive, it must contain many firms, none of whom have a large **market share.** A firm's market share is the fraction of the total industry output accounted for by that firm's output. The distribution of market share constitutes a major difference between the grain industry and the breakfast cereal industry. There are thousands of wheat farmers, none of whom account for more than a tiny fraction of total wheat sales. The breakfast cereal industry, however, is dominated by four firms: Kellogg's, General Mills, Post, and Quaker Foods. Kellogg's alone accounts for about one-third of all cereal sales. Kellogg's executives know that if they try to sell more corn flakes, they are likely to drive down the market price of corn flakes. That is, they know that their actions influence market prices—due to their tremendous size, changes in their production will significantly affect the overall quantity supplied. It makes sense to assume that firms are price-takers only when they are numerous and relatively small.

Second, an industry can be perfectly competitive only if consumers regard the products of all firms as equivalent. This clearly isn't true in the breakfast cereal market: consumers don't consider Cap'n Crunch to be a good substitute for Wheaties. As a result, the maker of Wheaties has some ability to increase its price without fear that it will lose all its customers to the maker of Cap'n Crunch. Contrast this with the case of a **standardized product,** sometimes known as a **commodity,** which is a product that consumers regard as the same good even when it comes from different firms. Because wheat is a standardized product, consumers regard the output of one wheat producer as a perfect substitute for that of another producer. Consequently, one farmer cannot increase the price for his or her wheat without losing all sales to other wheat farmers. So the second necessary condition for a perfectly competitive industry is that the industry output is a standardized product. (See the IRL that follows.)

Scott Bauer/ARS/USDA

What's a Standardized Product?

A perfectly competitive industry must produce a standardized product. But is it enough for the products of different firms actually to be the same? No: people must also *think* that they are the same. And producers often go to great lengths to convince consumers that they have a distinctive, or *differentiated*, product, even when they don't.

Consider, for example, champagne—not the super-expensive premium champagnes, but the more ordinary stuff. Most people cannot tell the difference between champagne actually produced in the Champagne region of France, where the product originated, and similar products from Spain or California. But the French government has sought and obtained legal protection for the winemakers of Champagne, ensuring that around the world only bubbly wine from that region can be called champagne. If it's from someplace else, all the seller can do is say that it was produced using the *méthode Champenoise*. This creates a differentiation in the minds of consumers and lets the champagne producers of Champagne charge higher prices.

Similarly, Korean producers of *kimchi,* the spicy fermented cabbage that is the Korean national side dish, are doing their best to convince consumers that the same product packaged by Japanese firms is just not the real thing. The purpose is, of course, to ensure higher prices for Korean *kimchi.*

So is an industry perfectly competitive if it sells products that are indistinguishable except in name but that consumers, for whatever reason, don't think are standardized? No. When it comes to defining the nature of competition, the consumer is always right.

An industry has **free entry and exit** when new firms can easily enter into the industry and existing firms can easily leave the industry.

Free Entry and Exit

All perfectly competitive industries have many firms with small market shares, producing a standardized product. Most perfectly competitive industries are also characterized by one more feature: it is easy for new firms to enter the industry or for firms that are currently in the industry to leave. That is, no obstacles in the form of government regulations or limited access to key resources prevent new firms from entering the market. And no additional costs are associated with shutting down a company and leaving the industry. Economists refer to the arrival of new firms into an industry as *entry;* they refer to the departure of firms from an industry as *exit.* When there are no obstacles to entry into or exit from an industry, we say that the industry has **free entry and exit.**

Free entry and exit is not strictly necessary for perfect competition. However, it ensures that the number of firms in an industry can adjust to changing market conditions. And, in particular, it ensures that firms in an industry cannot act to keep other firms out.

To sum up, then, perfect competition depends on two necessary conditions. First, the industry must contain many firms, each having a small market share. Second, the industry must produce a standardized product. In addition, perfectly competitive industries are normally characterized by free entry and exit.

Monopoly

The De Beers monopoly of South Africa was created in the 1880s by Cecil Rhodes, a British businessman. By 1880, mines in South Africa already dominated the world's supply of diamonds. There were, however, many mining companies, all competing with each other. During the 1880s Rhodes bought the great majority of those mines and consolidated them into a single company, De Beers. By 1889, De Beers controlled almost all of the world's diamond production.

De Beers, in other words, became a *monopolist.* But what does it mean to be a monopolist? And what do monopolists do?

Defining Monopoly

As we mentioned earlier, the supply and demand model of a market is not universally valid. Instead, it's a model of perfect competition, which is only one of several types of market structure. A market will be perfectly competitive only if there are many firms, all of which produce the same good. Monopoly is the most extreme departure from perfect competition.

A **monopolist** is a firm that is the only producer of a good that has no close substitutes. An industry controlled by a monopolist is known as a **monopoly.**

In practice, true monopolies are hard to find in the modern American economy, partly because of legal obstacles. A contemporary entrepreneur who tried to consolidate all the firms in an industry the way Rhodes did would soon find himself in court, accused of breaking *antitrust* laws, which are intended to prevent monopolies from emerging. Monopolies do, however, play an important role in some sectors of the economy.

Why Do Monopolies Exist?

A monopolist making profits will not go unnoticed by others. (Recall that this is "economic profit," revenue over and above the opportunity costs of the firm's resources.) But won't other firms crash the party, grab a piece of the action, and drive down prices and profits in the long run? If possible, yes, they will. For a profitable monopoly to persist, something must keep others from going into the same business; that "something" is known as a **barrier to entry.** There are four principal types of barriers to entry: control of a scarce resource or input, economies of scale, technological superiority, and government-created barriers.

Control of a Scarce Resource or Input A monopolist that controls a resource or input crucial to an industry can prevent other firms from entering its market. Cecil Rhodes made De Beers into a monopolist by establishing control over the mines that produced the great bulk of the world's diamonds.

Economies of Scale Many Americans have natural gas piped into their homes for cooking and heating. Invariably, the local gas company is a monopolist. But why don't rival companies compete to provide gas?

In the early nineteenth century, when the gas industry was just starting up, companies did compete for local customers. But this competition didn't last long; soon local gas companies became monopolists in almost every town because of the large fixed cost of providing a town with gas lines. The cost of laying gas lines didn't depend on how much gas a company sold, so a firm with a larger volume of sales had a cost advantage: because it was able to spread the fixed cost over a larger volume, it had a lower average total cost than smaller firms.

The natural gas industry is one in which average total cost falls as output increases, resulting in economies of scale and encouraging firms to grow larger. In an industry characterized by economies of scale, larger firms are more profitable and drive out smaller ones. For the same reason, established firms have a cost advantage over any potential entrant—a potent barrier to entry. So economies of scale can both give rise to and sustain a monopoly.

A monopoly created and sustained by economies of scale is called a **natural monopoly.** The defining characteristic of a natural monopoly is that it possesses economies of scale over the range of output that is relevant for the industry. The source of this condition is large fixed costs: when large fixed costs are required to operate, a given quantity of output is produced at lower average total cost by one large firm than by two or more smaller firms.

The most visible natural monopolies in the modern economy are local utilities—water, gas, electricity, local land-line phone service, and, in most locations, cable television. As we'll see later, natural monopolies pose a special challenge to public policy.

A **monopolist** is the only producer of a good that has no close substitutes. An industry controlled by a monopolist is known as a **monopoly.**

To earn economic profits, a monopolist must be protected by a **barrier to entry**—something that prevents other firms from entering the industry.

A **natural monopoly** exists when economies of scale provide a large cost advantage to a single firm that produces all of an industry's output.

Technological Superiority A firm that maintains a consistent technological advantage over potential competitors can establish itself as a monopolist. For example, from the 1970s through the 1990s, the chip manufacturer Intel was able to maintain a consistent advantage over potential competitors in both the design and production of microprocessors, the chips that run computers. But technological superiority is typically not a barrier to entry over the longer term: over time competitors will invest in upgrading their technology to match that of the technology leader. In fact, in the last few years Intel found its technological superiority eroded by a competitor, Advanced Micro Devices (also known as AMD), which now produces chips approximately as fast and as powerful as Intel chips.

We should note, however, that in certain high-tech industries, technological superiority is not a guarantee of success against competitors. Some high-tech industries are characterized by *network externalities,* a condition that arises when the value of a good to a consumer rises as the number of other people who also use the good rises. In these industries, the firm possessing the largest network—the largest number of consumers currently using its product—has an advantage over its competitors in attracting new customers, an advantage that may allow it to become a monopolist. Microsoft is often cited as an example of a company with a technologically inferior product—its computer operating system—that grew into a monopolist through the phenomenon of network externalities.

Government-Created Barriers In 1998 the pharmaceutical company Merck introduced Propecia, a drug effective against baldness. Despite the fact that Propecia was very profitable and other drug companies had the know-how to produce it, no other firms challenged Merck's monopoly. That's because the U.S. government had given Merck the sole legal right to produce the drug in the United States. Propecia is an example of a monopoly protected by government-created barriers.

The most important legally created monopolies today arise from *patents* and *copyrights.* A **patent** gives an inventor the sole right to make, use, or sell that invention for a period that in most countries lasts between 16 and 20 years. Patents are given to the creators of new products, such as drugs or mechanical devices. Similarly, a **copyright** gives the creator of a literary or artistic work the sole right to profit from that work, usually for a period equal to the creator's lifetime plus 70 years.

The justification for patents and copyrights is a matter of incentives. If inventors were not protected by patents, they would gain little reward from their efforts: as soon as a valuable invention was made public, others would copy it and sell products based on it. And if inventors could not expect to profit from their inventions, then there would be no incentive to incur the costs of invention in the first place. Likewise for the creators of literary or artistic works. So the law allows a monopoly to exist temporarily by granting property rights that encourage invention and creation. Patents and copyrights are temporary because the law strikes a compromise. The higher price for the good that holds while the legal protection is in effect compensates inventors for the cost of invention; conversely, the lower price that results once the legal protection lapses benefits consumers.

Because the lifetime of the temporary monopoly cannot be tailored to specific cases, this system is imperfect and leads to some missed opportunities. In some cases there can be significant welfare issues. For example, the violation of American drug patents by pharmaceutical companies in poor countries has been a major source of controversy, pitting the needs of poor patients who cannot afford to pay retail drug prices against the interests of drug manufacturers who have incurred high research costs to discover these drugs. To solve this problem, some American drug companies and poor countries have negotiated deals in which the patents are honored but the American companies sell their drugs at deeply discounted prices. (This is an example of *price discrimination,* which we'll learn more about later.)

A **patent** gives an inventor a temporary monopoly in the use or sale of an invention.

A **copyright** gives the creator of a literary or artistic work the sole right to profit from that work.

Oligopoly

An industry with only a few firms is known as an **oligopoly;** a producer in such an industry is known as an **oligopolist.**

Oligopolists compete with each other for sales. But oligopolists aren't like producers in a perfectly competitive industry, who take the market as given. Oligopolists know their decisions about how much to produce will affect the market price. That is, like monopolists, oligopolists have some *market power*. Economists refer to a situation in which firms compete but also possess market power—which enables them to affect market prices—as **imperfect competition.** There are two important forms of imperfect competition: oligopoly and *monopolistic competition.* Of these, oligopoly is probably the more important in practice.

Many familiar goods and services are supplied by only a few competing sellers, which means the industries in question are oligopolies. For example, most air routes are served by only two or three airlines: in recent years, regularly scheduled shuttle service between New York and either Boston or Washington, D.C., has been provided only by Delta and US Airways. Three firms—Chiquita, Dole, and Del Monte, which own huge banana plantations in Central America—control 65% of world banana exports. Most cola beverages are sold by Coca-Cola and Pepsi. This list could go on for many pages.

It's important to realize that an oligopoly isn't necessarily made up of large firms. What matters isn't size per se; the question is how many competitors there are. When a small town has only two grocery stores, grocery service there is just as much an oligopoly as air shuttle service between New York and Washington.

Why are oligopolies so prevalent? Essentially, an oligopoly is the result of the same factors that sometimes produce a monopoly, but in somewhat weaker form. Probably the most important source of oligopolies is the existence of economies of scale, which give bigger firms a cost advantage over smaller ones. When these effects are very strong, as we have seen, they lead to a monopoly; when they are not that strong, they lead to an industry with a small number of firms. For example, larger grocery stores typically have lower costs than smaller stores. But the advantages of large scale taper off once grocery stores are reasonably large, which is why two or three stores often survive in small towns.

Photodisc

Is It an Oligopoly or Not?

In practice, it is not always easy to determine an industry's market structure just by looking at the number of sellers. Many oligopolistic industries contain a number of small "niche" firms, which don't really compete with the major players. For example, the U.S. airline industry includes a number of regional airlines such as New Mexico Airlines, which flies propeller planes between Albuquerque and Carlsbad, New Mexico; if you count these carriers, the U.S. airline industry contains nearly one hundred firms, which doesn't sound like competition among a small group. But there are only a handful of national competitors like American and United, and on many routes, as we've seen, there are only two or three competitors.

To get a better picture of market structure, economists often use two measures of market power: **concentration ratios** and the **Herfindahl–Hirschman Index.** Concentration ratios measure the percentage of industry sales accounted for by the "X" largest firms, where "X" can equal any number of firms. For example, the four-firm concentration ratio is the percentage of sales accounted for by the four largest firms and the eight-firm concentration ratio is the percentage of industry sales accounted for by the eight largest firms. Let's say that the largest four firms account for 25%, 20%, 15%, and 10% of industry sales; then the four-firm concentration ratios would equal 70 (25+20+15+10). And if the next largest four firms in that industry account for 9%, 8%, 6%, and 2% of sales, the eight-firm concentration ratio would equal 95 (70 +9+8+6+2). The

An **oligopoly** is an industry with only a small number of firms. A producer in such an industry is known as an **oligopolist.**

When no one firm has a monopoly, but producers nonetheless realize that they can affect market prices, an industry is characterized by **imperfect competition.**

Concentration ratios measure the percentage of industry sales accounted for by the "X" largest firms, for example the four-firm concentration ratio or the eight-firm concentration ratio.

Herfindahl–Hirschman Index, or HHI, is the square of each firm's share of market sales summed over the industry. It gives a picture of the industry market structure.

Courtesy of Henry M. Trotter

four- and eight-firm concentration ratios are the most commonly used. A higher concentration ratio signals a market is more concentrated and thus is more likely to be an oligopoly.

Another measure of market concentration is the Herfindahl-Hirschman index, or HHI. The HHI for an industry is the square of each firm's share of market sales summed over the firms in the industry. Unlike concentration ratios, the HHI takes into account the distribution of market sales among the top firms by squaring each firm's market share, thereby giving more weight to larger firms. For example, if an industry contains only 3 firms and their market shares are 60%, 25%, and 15%, then the HHI for the industry is:

$$HHI = 60^2 + 25^2 + 15^2 = 4,450$$

By squaring each market share, the HHI calculation produces numbers that are much larger when a larger share of an industry output is dominated by fewer firms. This is confirmed by the data in Table 21.1. Here, the indices for industries dominated by a small number of firms, like the personal computer operating systems industry or the wide-body aircraft industry, are many times larger than the index for the retail grocery industry, which has numerous firms of approximately equal size.

table **21.1**

The HHI for Some Oligopolistic Industries

Industry	HHI	Largest firms
PC operating systems	9,182	Microsoft, Linux
Wide-body aircraft	5,098	Boeing, Airbus
Diamond mining	2,338	De Beers, Alrosa, Rio Tinto
Automobiles	1,432	GM, Ford, Chrysler, Toyota, Honda, Nissan, VW
Movie distributors	1,096	Buena Vista, Sony Pictures, 20th Century Fox, Warner Bros., Universal, Paramount, Lionsgate
Internet service providers	750	SBC, Comcast, AOL, Verizon, Road Runner, Earthlink, Charter, Qwest
Retail grocers	321	Walmart, Kroger, Sears, Target, Costco, Walgreens, Ahold, Albertsons

Sources: Canadian Government; Diamond Facts 2006; www.w3counter.com; Planet retail; Autodata; Reuters; ISP Planet; Swivel. Data cover 2006–2007.

Monopolistic Competition

Leo manages the Wonderful Wok stand in the food court of a big shopping mall. He offers the only Chinese food there, but there are more than a dozen alternatives, from Bodacious Burgers to Pizza Paradise. When deciding what to charge for a meal, Leo knows that he must take those alternatives into account: even people who normally prefer stir-fry won't order a $15 lunch from Leo when they can get a burger, fries, and drink for $4.

But Leo also knows that he won't lose all his business even if his lunches cost a bit more than the alternatives. Chinese food isn't the same thing as burgers or pizza. Some people will really be in the mood for Chinese that day, and they will buy from Leo even if they could have dined more cheaply on burgers. Of course, the reverse is also true: even if Chinese is a bit cheaper, some people will choose burgers instead. In other words, Leo does have some market power: he has *some* ability to set his own price.

So how would you describe Leo's situation? He definitely isn't a price-taker, so he isn't in a situation of perfect competition. But you wouldn't exactly call him a monopolist, either. Although he's the only seller of Chinese food in that food court, he does face competition from other food vendors.

Yet it would also be wrong to call him an oligopolist. Oligopoly, remember, involves competition among a small number of interdependent firms in an industry protected by some—albeit limited—barriers to entry and whose profits are highly interdependent. Because their profits are highly interdependent, oligopolists have an incentive to collude, tacitly or explicitly. But in Leo's case there are *lots* of vendors in the shopping mall, too many to make tacit collusion feasible.

Defining Monopolistic Competition

Monopolistic competition is a market structure in which there are many competing firms in an industry, each firm sells a differentiated product, and there is free entry into and exit from the industry in the long run.

Economists describe Leo's situation as one of **monopolistic competition.** Monopolistic competition is particularly common in service industries such as the restaurant and gas station industries, but it also exists in some manufacturing industries. It involves three conditions:

- a large number of competing firms,
- differentiated products, and
- free entry into and exit from the industry in the long run.

In a monopolistically competitive industry, each producer has some ability to set the price of her differentiated product. But exactly how high she can set it is limited by the competition she faces from other existing and potential firms that produce close, but not identical, products.

Large Numbers In a monopolistically competitive industry there are many firms. Such an industry does not look either like a monopoly, where the firm faces no competition, or like an oligopoly, where each firm has only a few rivals. Instead, each seller has many competitors. For example, there are many vendors in a big food court, many gas stations along a major highway, and many hotels at a popular beach resort.

Differentiated Products In a monopolistically competitive industry, each firm has a product that consumers view as somewhat distinct from the products of competing firms. Such product differentiation can come in the form of different styles or types, different locations, or different levels of quality. At the same time, though, consumers see these competing products as close substitutes. If Leo's food court contained 15 vendors selling exactly the same kind and quality of food, there would be perfect competition: any seller who tried to charge a higher price would have no customers. But suppose that Wonderful Wok is the only Chinese food vendor, Bodacious Burgers is the only hamburger stand, and so on. The result of this differentiation is that each vendor has some ability to set his or her own price: each firm has some—albeit limited—market power.

Free Entry and Exit in the Long Run In monopolistically competitive industries, new firms, with their own distinct products, can enter the industry freely in the long run. For example, other food vendors would open outlets in the food court if they thought it would be profitable to do so. In addition, firms will exit the industry if they find they are not covering their costs in the long run.

Monopolistic competition, then, differs from the three market structures we have examined so far. It's not the same as perfect competition: firms have some power to set prices. It's not pure monopoly: firms face some competition. And it's not the same as oligopoly: there are many firms and free entry, which eliminates the potential for collusion that is so important in oligopoly. As we'll see in a later section, competition among the sellers of differentiated products is the key to understanding how monopolistic competition works.

Now that we have introduced the idea of market structure and presented the four principal models of market structure, we can proceed in the next two sections to use the cost curves we have developed to build each of the four market structure models. These models will allow us to explain and predict firm behavior (e.g., price and quantity determination) and analyze individual markets.

Solutions appear at the back of the book.

Check Your Understanding

1. In each of the following situations, what type of market structure do you think the industry represents?
   a. There are three producers of aluminum in the world, a good sold in many places.
   b. There are thousands of farms that produce indistinguishable soybeans to thousands of buyers.
   c. Many designers sell high-fashion clothes. Each designer has a distinctive style and a somewhat loyal clientele.
   d. A small town in the middle of Alaska has one bicycle shop.

Multiple-Choice Questions

1. Which of the following is true for a perfectly competitive industry?
   I. There are many firms, each with a large market share.
   II. The firms in the industry produce a standardized product.
   III. There are barriers to entry and exit.
   a. I only
   b. II only
   c. III only
   d. I and II only
   e. I, II, and III

2. Which of the following is true for a monopoly?
   I. There is only one firm.
   II. The firm produces a product with many close substitutes.
   III. The industry has free entry and exit.
   a. I only
   b. II only
   c. III only
   d. I and II only
   e. I, II, and III

3. Which of the following is true for an oligopoly?
   I. There are a few firms, each with a large market share.
   II. The firms in the industry are interdependent.
   III. The industry experiences diseconomies of scale.
   a. I only
   b. II only
   c. III only
   d. I and II only
   e. I, II, and III

4. Which of the following is true for a monopolistically competitive industry?
   I. There are many firms, each with a small market share.
   II. The firms in the industry produce a standardized product.
   III. Firms are price-takers.
   a. I only
   b. II only
   c. III only
   d. I and II only
   e. I, II, and III

5. Which of the following is an example of differentiated products?
   a. Coke and Pepsi
   b. automobiles and bicycles
   c. trucks and gasoline
   d. stocks and bonds
   e. gold and silver

Critical-Thinking Question

a. Draw a correctly labeled graph of a perfectly competitive firm's demand curve if the market price is $10.
b. What does the firm's marginal revenue equal any time it sells one more unit of its output?

Section **4** Review

Summary

Defining Profit

1. The cost of using a resource for a particular activity is the opportunity cost of that resource. Some opportunity costs are **explicit costs;** they involve a direct payment of cash. Other opportunity costs, however, are **implicit costs;** they involve no outlay of money but represent the inflows of cash that are forgone. Both explicit and implicit costs should be taken into account when making decisions. Firms use capital and their owners' time, so firms should base decisions on **economic profit,** which takes into account implicit costs such as the opportunity cost of the owners' time and the **implicit cost of capital. Accounting profit,** which firms calculate for the purposes of taxes and public reporting, is often considerably larger than economic profit because it includes only explicit costs and depreciation, not implicit costs. Finally, **normal profit** is a term used to describe an economic profit equal to zero—a profit just high enough to justify the use of resources in an activity.

Profit Maximization

2. A producer chooses output according to the **optimal output rule:** produce the quantity at which marginal revenue equals marginal cost. The **marginal revenue** for each unit of output is shown by the **marginal revenue curve.** More generally, the **principle of marginal analysis** suggests that every activity should continue until marginal benefit equals marginal cost.

The Production Function

3. The relationship between inputs and output is represented by a firm's **production function.** In the **short run,** the quantity of a **fixed input** cannot be varied but the quantity of a **variable input,** by definition, can. In the **long run,** the quantities of all inputs can be varied. For a given amount of the fixed input, the **total product curve** shows how the quantity of output changes as the quantity of the variable input changes. The **marginal product** of an input is the increase in output that results from using one more unit of that input.

4. There are **diminishing returns to an input** when its marginal product declines as more of the input is used, holding the quantity of all other inputs fixed.

Firm Costs

5. **Total cost,** represented by the **total cost curve,** is equal to the sum of **fixed cost,** which does not depend on output, and **variable cost,** which does depend on output. Due to diminishing returns, marginal cost, the increase in total cost generated by producing one more unit of output, normally increases as output increases.

6. **Average total cost** (also known as **average cost**) is the total cost divided by the quantity of output. Economists believe that **U-shaped average total cost curves** are typical because average total cost consists of two parts: **average fixed cost,** which falls when output increases (the spreading effect), and **average variable cost,** which rises with output (the diminishing returns effect).

7. When average total cost is U-shaped, the bottom of the U is the level of output at which average total cost is minimized, the point of **minimum-cost output.** This is also the point at which the **marginal cost curve** crosses the average total cost curve from below. Due to gains from specialization, the marginal cost curve may slope downward initially before sloping upward, giving it a "swoosh" shape.

Long-Run Costs and Economies of Scale

8. In the long run, a firm can change its fixed input and its level of fixed cost. By accepting higher fixed cost, a firm can lower its variable cost for any given output level, and vice versa. The **long-run average total cost curve** shows the relationship between output and average total cost when fixed cost has been chosen to minimize average total cost at each level of output. A firm moves along its short-run average total cost curve as it changes the quantity of output, and it returns to a point on both its short-run and long-run average total cost curves once it has adjusted fixed cost to its new output level.

9. As output increases, there are **economies of scale** if long-run average total cost decreases and **diseconomies of scale** if long-run average total cost increases. As all inputs are increased by the same proportion, there are **increasing returns to scale** if output increases by a larger proportion than the inputs; **decreasing returns to scale** if output increases by a smaller proportion; and **constant returns to scale** if output increases by the same proportion.

10. **Sunk costs** are expenditures that have already been made and cannot be recovered. Sunk costs should be ignored in making decisions about future actions because what is important is a comparison of future costs and future benefits.

Introduction to Market Structure

11. There are four main types of market structure based on the number of firms in the industry and product differentiation: perfect competition, monopoly, oligopoly, and monopolistic competition.

12. A **monopolist** is a producer who is the sole supplier of a good without close substitutes. An industry controlled by a monopolist is a **monopoly.**

13. To persist, a monopoly must be protected by a **barrier to entry.** This can take the form of control of a natural resource or input, increasing returns to scale that give rise to a **natural monopoly,** technological superiority, or government rules that prevent entry by other firms, such as **patents** or **copyrights.**

14. In a **perfectly competitive market** all firms are **price-taking firms** and all consumers are **price-taking consumers**—no one's actions can influence the market price. Consumers are normally price-takers, but firms often are not. In a **perfectly competitive industry,** every firm in the industry is a price-taker.

15. There are two necessary conditions for a perfectly competitive industry: there are many firms, none of which has a large **market share,** and the industry produces a **standardized product** or **commodity**—goods that consumers regard as equivalent. A third condition is often satisfied as well: **free entry and exit** into and from the industry.

16. Many industries are **oligopolies:** there are only a few sellers. Oligopolies exist for more or less the same reasons that monopolies exist, but in weaker form. They are characterized by **imperfect competition:** firms compete but possess some market power.

17. Monopolistic competition is a market structure in which there are many competing firms, each producing a differentiated product, and there is free entry and exit in the long run. Product differentiation takes three main forms: by style or type, by location, and by quality. The extent of imperfect competition can be measured by the **concentration ratio,** or the **Herfindahl-Hirschman Index.**

Key Terms

Problems

1. Hiro owns and operates a small business that provides economic consulting services. During the year he spends $55,000 on traveling to clients and other expenses, and the computer that he owns depreciates by $2,000. If he didn't use the computer, he could sell it and earn yearly interest of $100 on the money created through this sale. Hiro's total revenue for the year is $100,000. Instead of working as a consultant for the year, he could teach economics at a small local college and make a salary of $50,000.

  a. What is Hiro's accounting profit?

  b. What is Hiro's economic profit?

  c. Should Hiro continue working as a consultant, or should he teach economics instead?

2. Jackie owns and operates a Web-design business. Her computing equipment depreciates by $5,000 per year. She runs the business out of a room in her home. If she didn't use the room as her business office, she could rent it out for $2,000 per year. Jackie knows that if she didn't run her own business, she could return to her previous job at a large software company that would pay her a salary of $60,000 per year. Jackie has no other expenses.

  a. How much total revenue does Jackie need to make in order to break even in the eyes of her accountant? That is, how much total revenue would give Jackie an accounting profit of just zero?

  b. How much total revenue does Jackie need to make in order for her to want to remain self-employed? That is, how much total revenue would give Jackie an economic profit of just zero?

3. You own and operate a bike store. Each year, you receive revenue of $200,000 from your bike sales, and it costs you $100,000 to obtain the bikes. In addition, you pay $20,000 for electricity, taxes, and other expenses per year. Instead of running the bike store, you could become an accountant and receive a yearly salary of $40,000. A large clothing retail chain wants to expand and offers to rent the store from you for $50,000 per year. How do you explain to your friends that despite making a profit, it is too costly for you to continue running your store?

4. Suppose you have just paid a nonrefundable fee of $1,000 for your meal plan for this academic term. This allows you to eat dinner in the cafeteria every evening.

  a. You are offered a part-time job in a restaurant where you can eat for free each evening. Your parents say that you should eat dinner in the cafeteria anyway, since you have already paid for those meals. Are your parents right? Explain why or why not.

  b. You are offered a part-time job in a different restaurant where, rather than being able to eat for free, you receive only a large discount on your meals. Each meal there will cost you $2; if you eat there each evening this semester, it will add up to $200. Your roommate says that you should eat in the restaurant since it costs less than the $1,000 that you paid for the meal plan. Is your roommate right? Explain why or why not.

5. You have bought a $10 ticket in advance for the college soccer game, a ticket that cannot be resold. You know that going to the soccer game will give you a benefit equal to $20. After you have bought the ticket, you hear that there will be a professional baseball post-season game at the same time. Tickets to the baseball game cost $20, and you know that going to the baseball game will give you a benefit equal to $35. You tell your friends the following: "If I had known about the baseball game before buying the ticket to the soccer game, I would have gone to the baseball game instead. But now that I already have the ticket to the soccer game, it's better for me to just go to the soccer game." Are you making the correct decision? Justify your answer by calculating the benefits and costs of your decision.

6. You are the manager of a gym, and you have to decide how many customers to admit each hour. Assume that each customer stays exactly one hour. Customers are costly to admit because they inflict wear and tear on the exercise equipment. Moreover, each additional customer generates more wear and tear than the customer before. As a result, the gym faces increasing marginal cost. The accompanying table shows the marginal cost associated with each number of customers per hour.

Quantity of customers per hour	Marginal cost of customer
0	
	$14.00
1	
	14.50
2	
	15.00
3	
	15.50
4	
	16.00
5	
	16.50
6	
	17.00
7	

  a. Suppose that each customer pays $15.25 for a one-hour workout. Use the principle of marginal analysis to find the optimal number of customers that you should admit per hour.

  b. You increase the price of a one-hour workout to $16.25. What is the optimal number of customers per hour that you should admit now?

7. Georgia and Lauren are economics students who go to a karate class together. Both have to choose how many classes to go to per week. Each class costs $20. The accompanying table shows Georgia's and Lauren's estimates of the marginal benefit that each of them gets from each class per week.

Quantity of Classes	Lauren's marginal benefit of each class	Georgia's marginal benefit of each class
0		
	$23	$28
1		
	19	22
2		
	14	15
3		
	8	7
4		

a. Use marginal analysis to find Lauren's optimal number of karate classes per week. Explain your answer.

b. Use marginal analysis to find Georgia's optimal number of karate classes per week. Explain your answer.

8. Changes in the prices of key commodities can have a significant impact on a company's bottom line. According to a September 27, 2007, article in the *Wall Street Journal,* "Now, with oil, gas and electricity prices soaring, companies are beginning to realize that saving energy can translate into dramatically lower costs." Another *Wall Street Journal* article, dated September 9, 2007, states, "Higher grain prices are taking an increasing financial toll." Energy is an input into virtually all types of production; corn is an input into the production of beef, chicken, high-fructose corn syrup, and ethanol (the gasoline substitute fuel).

a. Explain how the cost of energy can be both a fixed cost and a variable cost for a company.

b. Suppose energy is a fixed cost and energy prices rise. What happens to the company's average total cost curve? What happens to its marginal cost curve? Illustrate your answer with a diagram.

c. Explain why the cost of corn is a variable cost but not a fixed cost for an ethanol producer.

d. When the cost of corn goes up, what happens to the average total cost curve of an ethanol producer? What happens to its marginal cost curve? Illustrate your answer with a diagram.

9. Marty's Frozen Yogurt is a small shop that sells cups of frozen yogurt in a university town. Marty owns three frozen-yogurt machines. His other inputs are refrigerators, frozen-yogurt mix, cups, sprinkle toppings, and, of course, workers. He estimates that his daily production function when he varies the number of workers employed (and at the same time, of course, yogurt mix, cups, and so on) is as shown in the accompanying table.

Quantity of labor (workers)	Quantity of frozen yogurt (cups)
0	0
1	110
2	200
3	270
4	300
5	320
6	330

a. What are the fixed inputs and variable inputs in the production of cups of frozen yogurt?

b. Draw the total product curve. Put the quantity of labor on the horizontal axis and the quantity of frozen yogurt on the vertical axis.

c. What is the marginal product of the first worker? The second worker? The third worker? Why does marginal product decline as the number of workers increases?

10. The production function for Marty's Frozen Yogurt is given in Problem 9. Marty pays each of his workers $80 per day. The cost of his other variable inputs is $0.50 per cup of yogurt. His fixed cost is $100 per day.

a. What is Marty's variable cost and total cost when he produces 110 cups of yogurt? 200 cups? Calculate variable and total cost for every level of output given in Problem 9.

b. Draw Marty's variable cost curve. On the same diagram, draw his total cost curve.

c. What is the marginal cost per cup for the first 110 cups of yogurt? For the next 90 cups? Calculate the marginal cost for all remaining levels of output.

11. The production function for Marty's Frozen Yogurt is given in Problem 9. The costs are given in Problem 10.

a. For each of the given levels of output, calculate the average fixed cost (*AFC*), average variable cost (*AVC*), and average total cost (*ATC*) per cup of frozen yogurt.

b. On one diagram, draw the *AFC, AVC,* and *ATC* curves.

c. What principle explains why the *AFC* declines as output increases? What principle explains why the *AVC* increases as output increases? Explain your answers.

d. How many cups of frozen yogurt are produced when average total cost is minimized?

12. The accompanying table shows a car manufacturer's total cost of producing cars.

Quantity of cars	TC
0	$500,000
1	540,000
2	560,000
3	570,000
4	590,000
5	620,000
6	660,000
7	720,000
8	800,000
9	920,000
10	1,100,000

a. What is this manufacturer's fixed cost?

b. For each level of output, calculate the variable cost (*VC*). For each level of output except zero, calculate the average variable cost (*AVC*), average total cost (*ATC*), and average fixed cost (*AFC*). What is the minimum-cost output?

c. For each level of output, calculate this manufacturer's marginal cost (*MC*).

d. On one diagram, draw the manufacturer's *AVC, ATC,* and *MC* curves.

13. Labor costs represent a large percentage of total costs for many firms. According to a September 1, 2007, *Wall Street Journal* article, U.S. labor costs were up 0.9% during the preceding three months and 0.8% over the three months preceding those.

a. When labor costs increase, what happens to average total cost and marginal cost? Consider a case in which labor costs are only variable costs and a case in which they are both variable and fixed costs.

An increase in labor productivity means each worker can produce more output. Recent data on productivity show that labor productivity in the U.S. nonfarm business sector grew 2% for each of the years 2005, 2006, and 2007. Annual growth in labor productivity averaged 1.5% from the mid-1970s to mid-1990s, 2.6% in the past decade, and 4% for a couple of years in the early 2000s.

b. When productivity growth is positive, what happens to the total product curve and the marginal product of labor curve? Illustrate your answer with a diagram.

c. When productivity growth is positive, what happens to the marginal cost curve and the average total cost curve? Illustrate your answer with a diagram.

d. If labor costs are rising over time on average, why would a company want to adopt equipment and methods that increase labor productivity?

14. Magnificent Blooms is a florist specializing in floral arrangements for weddings, graduations, and other events. The firm has a fixed cost associated with space and equipment of $100 per day. Each worker is paid $50 per day. The daily production function for Magnificent Blooms is shown in the accompanying table.

Quantity of labor (workers)	Quantity of floral arrangements
0	0
1	5
2	9
3	12
4	14
5	15

a. Calculate the marginal product of each worker. What principle explains why the marginal product per worker declines as the number of workers employed increases?

b. Calculate the marginal cost of each level of output. What principle explains why the marginal cost per floral arrangement increases as the number of arrangements increases?

15. You have the information shown in the accompanying table about a firm's costs. Complete the missing data.

Quantity	TC	MC	ATC	AVC
0	$20		—	—
		$20		
1	?		?	?
		10		
2	?		?	?
		16		
3	?		?	?
		20		
4	?		?	?
		24		
5	?		?	?

16. Evaluate each of the following statements. If a statement is true, explain why; if it is false, identify the mistake and try to correct it.

    a. A decreasing marginal product tells us that marginal cost must be rising.

    b. An increase in fixed cost increases the minimum-cost output.

    c. An increase in fixed cost increases marginal cost.

    d. When marginal cost is above average total cost, average total cost must be falling.

17. Mark and Jeff operate a small company that produces souvenir footballs. Their fixed cost is $2,000 per month. They can hire workers for $1,000 per worker per month. Their monthly production function for footballs is as given in the accompanying table.

Quantity of labor (workers)	Quantity of footballs
0	0
1	300
2	800
3	1,200
4	1,400
5	1,500

a. For each quantity of labor, calculate average variable cost (AVC), average fixed cost (AFC), average total cost (ATC), and marginal cost (MC).

b. On one diagram, draw the AVC, ATC, and MC curves.

c. At what level of output is Mark and Jeff's average total cost minimized?

18. You produce widgets. Currently you produce 4 widgets at a total cost of $40.

    a. What is your average total cost?

    b. Suppose you could produce one more (the fifth) widget at a marginal cost of $5. If you do produce that fifth widget, what will your average total cost be? Has your average total cost increased or decreased? Why?

    c. Suppose instead that you could produce one more (the fifth) widget at a marginal cost of $20. If you do produce that fifth widget, what will your average total cost be? Has your average total cost increased or decreased? Why?

Market Structures: Perfect Competition and Monopoly

The preceding section explained how factors including the number of firms in the industry, the type of product sold, and the existence of barriers to entry determine the market power of firms. We learned about the four basic market structures—perfect competition, monopoly, oligopoly, and monopolistic competition. We can think about these structures as falling along a spectrum from perfect competition at one end to monopoly at the other, with monopolistic competition and oligopoly lying in between. To shed more light on the market structure spectrum, consider two very different markets introduced in previous sections: the market for organic tomatoes and the market for diamonds.

In the United States, a growing interest in healthy living has steadily increased the demand for products such as organically grown fruits and vegetables. Over the past decade, the markets for these products have been healthy as well, with an average growth rate of 20% per year. It costs a bit more to grow crops without chemical fertilizers and pesticides, but consumers are willing to pay higher prices for the benefits of fruits and vegetables grown the natural way. The farmers in each area who pioneered organic farming techniques had little competition and many prospered thanks to these higher prices.

But with profits as a lure for expanded production, the high prices were unlikely to persist. Over time, farmers already producing organically would increase their capacity, and conventional farmers

Bjorn Andren/Nordic Photos/Getty Images

would enter the organic food fray, increasing supply and driving down price. With a large and growing number of buyers and sellers, undifferentiated products, and few barriers to entry, the organic food market increasingly resembles a *perfectly competitive* market.

In contrast, the market for diamonds is dominated by one supplier, De Beers. For generations, diamonds have been valued not just for their attractive appearance, but also for their rarity. But geologists will tell you that diamonds aren't all that rare. In fact, they are fairly common and only seem rare compared to other gem-quality stones. This is because De Beers *makes* them rare: the company controls most of the world's diamond mines and limits the quantity supplied to the market. This makes De Beers resemble a *monopolist,* the sole (or almost sole) producer of a good. Because De Beers controls so much of the world's diamond supply, other firms have considerable difficulty trying to enter the diamond market and increase the quantity of the gems available.

In this section we will study how markets like those for organic tomatoes and diamonds differ, and how these markets respond to market conditions. We will see how firms positioned at opposite ends of the spectrum of market power—from perfect competition to monopoly—make key decisions about output and prices. Then, in the next section, we will complete our exploration of market structure with a closer look at oligopoly and monopolistic competition.

© UpperCut Images/Alamy

Module 22
Introduction to Perfect Competition

Recall the example of the market for organic tomatoes from our earlier discussions. Jennifer and Jason run an organic tomato farm. But many other organic tomato farmers, such as Yves and Zoe, sell their output to the same grocery store chains. Since organic tomatoes are a standardized product, consumers don't care which farmer produces the organic tomatoes they buy. And because so many farmers sell organic tomatoes, no individual farmer has a large market share, which means that no individual farmer can have a measurable effect on market prices. These farmers are price-taking producers and their customers are price-taking consumers. The market for organic tomatoes meets the two necessary conditions for perfect competition: there are many producers each with a small market share, and the firms produce a standardized product. In this module, we build the model of perfect competition and use it to look at a representative firm in the market.

Production and Profits

Jennifer and Jason's tomato farm will maximize its profit by producing bushels of tomatoes up to the point at which marginal revenue equals marginal cost. We know this from the producer's *optimal output rule*: profit is maximized by producing the quantity at which the marginal revenue of the last unit produced is equal to its marginal cost. Always remember, $MR = MC$ at the optimal quantity of output. This will be true for any profit-maximizing firm in any market structure.

We can review how to apply the optimal output rule with the help of Table 22.1, which provides various short-run cost measures for Jennifer and Jason's farm. The second column contains the farm's variable cost, and the third column shows its total cost of output based on the assumption that the farm incurs a fixed cost of $14. The fourth column shows their marginal cost. Notice that, in this example, the marginal cost initially falls as output rises but then begins to increase, so that the marginal cost curve has the familiar "swoosh" shape.

The fifth column contains the farm's marginal revenue, which has an important feature: Jennifer and Jason's marginal revenue is constant at $18 for every output level.

table 22.1

Short-Run Costs for Jennifer and Jason's Farm

Quantity of tomatoes Q (bushels)	Variable cost VC	Total cost TC	Marginal cost of bushel $MC = \Delta TC/\Delta Q$	Marginal revenue of bushel MR	Net gain of bushel = MR − MC
0	$0	$14			
			$16	$18	$2
1	16	30			
			6	18	12
2	22	36			
			8	18	10
3	30	44			
			12	18	6
4	42	56			
			16	18	2
5	58	72			
			20	18	−2
6	78	92			
			24	18	−6
7	102	116			

The sixth and final column shows the calculation of the net gain per bushel of tomatoes, which is equal to marginal revenue minus marginal cost—or, equivalently in this case, market price minus marginal cost. As you can see, it is positive for the 1st through 5th bushels; producing each of these bushels raises Jennifer and Jason's profit. For the 6th bushel, however, net gain is negative: producing it would decrease, not increase, profit. So 5 bushels are Jennifer and Jason's profit-maximizing output; it is the level of output at which marginal cost rises from a level below market price to a level above market price, passing through the market price of $18 along the way.

This example illustrates an application of the optimal output rule to the particular case of a price-taking firm—the **price-taking firm's optimal output rule:** *price equals marginal cost at the price-taking firm's optimal quantity of output.* That is, a price-taking firm's profit is maximized by producing the quantity of output at which the market price is equal to the marginal cost of the last unit produced. Why? Because *in the case of a price-taking firm, marginal revenue is equal to the market price.* A price-taking firm cannot influence the market price by its actions. It always takes the market price as given because it cannot lower the market price by selling more or raise the market price by selling less. So, for a price-taking firm, the additional revenue generated by producing one more unit is always the market price. We will need to keep this fact in mind in future modules, in which we will learn that in the three other market structures, firms are *not* price takers. Therefore, marginal revenue is *not* equal to the market price.

Figure 22.1 on the next page shows Jennifer and Jason's profit-maximizing quantity of output. The figure shows the marginal cost curve, *MC,* drawn from the data in the fourth column of Table 22.1. We plot the marginal cost of increasing output from 1 to 2 bushels halfway between 1 and 2, and likewise for each incremental change. The horizontal line at $18 is Jennifer and Jason's marginal revenue curve. Remember that whenever a firm is a price-taker, its marginal revenue curve is a horizontal line at the market price: it can sell as much as it likes at the market price. Regardless of whether it sells more or less, the market price is unaffected. In effect, the individual firm faces a horizontal, perfectly elastic demand curve for its output—an individual demand curve that is equivalent to its marginal revenue curve. In fact, the horizontal line with the height of the market price represents the perfectly competitive

The **price-taking firm's optimal output rule** says that a price-taking firm's profit is maximized by producing the quantity of output at which the market price is equal to the marginal cost of the last unit produced.

figure 22.1

The Price-Taking Firm's Profit-Maximizing Quantity of Output

At the profit-maximizing quantity of output, the market price is equal to marginal cost. It is located at the point where the marginal cost curve crosses the marginal revenue curve, which is a horizontal line at the market price and represents the firm's demand curve. Here, the profit-maximizing point is at an output of 5 bushels of tomatoes, the output quantity at point *E*.

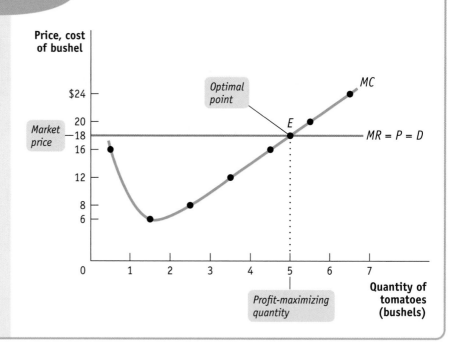

firm's demand, marginal revenue, and *average revenue*—the average amount of revenue taken in per unit—because price equals average revenue whenever every unit is sold for the same price. The marginal cost curve crosses the marginal revenue curve at point *E*. Sure enough, the quantity of output at *E* is 5 bushels.

Does this mean that the price-taking firm's production decision can be entirely summed up as "produce up to the point where the marginal cost of production is equal to the price"? No, not quite. Before applying the principle of marginal analysis to determine how much to produce, a potential producer must as a first step answer an "either–or" question: should it produce at all? If the answer to that question is yes, it then proceeds to the second step—a "how much" decision: maximizing profit by choosing the quantity of output at which marginal cost is equal to price.

To understand why the first step in the production decision involves an "either–or" question, we need to ask how we determine whether it is profitable or unprofitable to produce at all. In the next module we'll see that unprofitable firms shut down in the long run, but tolerate losses in the short run up to a certain point.

When Is Production Profitable?

Remember that firms make their production decisions with the goal of maximizing *economic profit*—a measure based on the opportunity cost of resources used by the firm. In the calculation of economic profit, a firm's total cost incorporates the implicit cost—the benefits forgone in the next best use of the firm's resources—as well as the explicit cost in the form of actual cash outlays. In contrast, *accounting profit* is profit calculated using only the explicit costs incurred by the firm. This means that economic profit incorporates all of the opportunity cost of resources owned by the firm and used in the production of output, while accounting profit does not. A firm may make positive accounting profit while making zero or even negative economic profit. It's important to understand that a firm's decisions of how much to produce, and whether or not to stay in business, should be based on economic profit, not accounting profit.

So we will assume, as usual, that the cost numbers given in Table 22.1 include all costs, implicit as well as explicit. What determines whether Jennifer

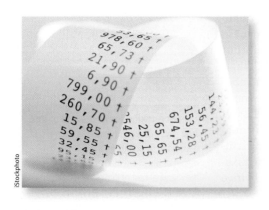

table **22.2**

Short-Run Average Costs for Jennifer and Jason's Farm

Quantity of tomatoes Q (bushels)	Variable cost VC	Total cost TC	Short-run average variable cost of bushel AVC = VC/Q	Short-run average total cost of bushel ATC = TC/Q
1	$16.00	$30.00	$16.00	$30.00
2	22.00	36.00	11.00	18.00
3	30.00	44.00	10.00	14.67
4	42.00	56.00	10.50	14.00
5	58.00	72.00	11.60	14.40
6	78.00	92.00	13.00	15.33
7	102.00	116.00	14.57	16.57

and Jason's farm earns a profit or generates a loss? This depends on the market price of tomatoes—specifically, *whether the market price is more or less than the farm's minimum average total cost.*

In Table 22.2 we calculate short-run average variable cost and short-run average total cost for Jennifer and Jason's farm. These are short-run values because we take fixed cost as given. (We'll turn to the effects of changing fixed cost shortly.) The short-run average total cost curve, *ATC,* is shown in Figure 22.2, along with the marginal cost curve, *MC,* from Figure 22.1. As you can see, average total cost is minimized at point *C,* corresponding to an output of 4 bushels—the *minimum-cost output*—and an average total cost of $14 per bushel.

figure **22.2**

Costs and Production in the Short Run

This figure shows the marginal cost curve, *MC,* and the short-run average total cost curve, *ATC.* When the market price is $14, output will be 4 bushels of tomatoes (the minimum-cost output), represented by point *C.* The price of $14 is equal to the firm's minimum average total cost, so at this price the firm breaks even.

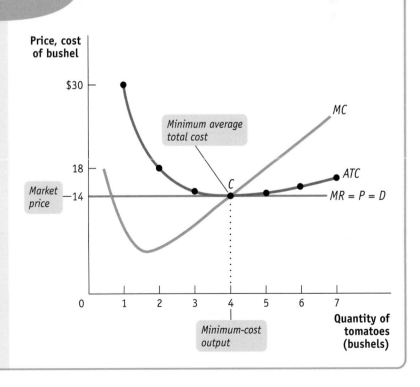

To see how these curves can be used to decide whether production is profitable or unprofitable, recall that profit is equal to total revenue minus total cost, $TR - TC$. This means:

- If the firm produces a quantity at which $TR > TC$, the firm is profitable.
- If the firm produces a quantity at which $TR = TC$, the firm breaks even.
- If the firm produces a quantity at which $TR < TC$, the firm incurs a loss.

We can also express this idea in terms of revenue and cost per unit of output. If we divide profit by the number of units of output, Q, we obtain the following expression for profit per unit of output:

(22-1) $\text{Profit}/Q = TR/Q - TC/Q$

TR/Q is average revenue, which is the market price. TC/Q is average total cost. So a firm is profitable if the market price for its product is more than the average total cost of the quantity the firm produces; a firm experiences losses if the market price is less than the average total cost of the quantity the firm produces. This means:

- If the firm produces a quantity at which $P > ATC$, the firm is profitable.
- If the firm produces a quantity at which $P = ATC$, the firm breaks even.
- If the firm produces a quantity at which $P < ATC$, the firm incurs a loss.

In summary, in the short run a firm will maximize profit by producing the quantity of output at which $MC = MR$. A perfectly competitive firm is a price-taker, so it can sell as many units of output as it would like at the market price. This means that for a perfectly competitive firm it is always true that $MR = P$. The firm is profitable, or breaks even, as long as the market price is greater than, or equal to, average total cost. In the next module, we develop the perfect competition model using graphs to analyze the firm's level of profit.

Module ㉒ Review

Solutions appear at the back of the book.

Check Your Understanding

1. Refer to the graph provided.

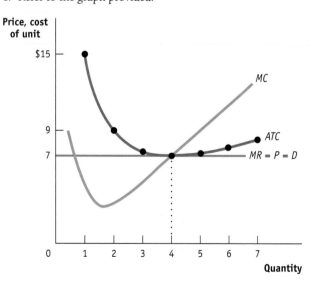

   a. At what level of output does the firm maximize profit? Explain how you know.
   b. At the profit-maximizing quantity of output, is the firm profitable, does it just break even, or does it earn a loss? Explain.

2. If a firm has a total cost of $500 at a quantity of 50 units, and it is at that quantity that average total cost is minimized for the firm, what is the lowest price that would allow the firm to break even (that is, earn a normal profit)? Explain.

Multiple-Choice Questions

1. A perfectly competitive firm will maximize profit at the quantity at which the firm's marginal revenue equals
   a. price.
   b. average revenue.
   c. total cost.
   d. marginal cost.
   e. demand.

2. Which of the following is correct for a perfectly competitive firm?
   I. The marginal revenue curve is the demand curve.
   II. The firm maximizes profit when price equals marginal cost.
   III. The market demand curve is horizontal.
   a. I only
   b. II only
   c. III only
   d. I and II only
   e. I, II, and III

3. A firm is profitable if
   a. $TR < TC.$
   b. $AR < ATC.$
   c. $MC < ATC.$
   d. $ATC < P.$
   e. $ATC > MC.$

4. If a firm has a total cost of $200, its profit-maximizing level of output is 10 units, and it is breaking even (that is, earning a normal profit), what is the market price?
   a. $200
   b. $100
   c. $20
   d. $10
   e. $2

5. What is the firm's profit if the price of its product is $5 and it produces 500 units of output at a total cost of $1,000?
   a. $5,000
   b. $2,500
   c. $1,500
   d. −$1,500
   e. −$2,500

Critical-Thinking Questions

Refer to the table provided. Price is equal to $14.
a. Calculate the firm's marginal cost at each quantity.
b. Determine the firm's profit-maximizing level of output.
c. Calculate the firm's profit at the profit-maximizing level of output.

Short-Run Costs for Jennifer and Jason's Farm

Quantity of tomatoes Q (bushels)	Variable cost VC	Total cost TC
0	$0	$14
1	16	30
2	22	36
3	30	44
4	42	56
5	58	72
6	78	92
7	102	116

What you will learn in this Module:

- How to evaluate a perfectly competitive firm's situation using a graph
- How to determine a perfect competitor's profit or loss
- How a firm decides whether to produce or shut down in the short run

Module 23
Graphing Perfect Competition

We have just learned that for a perfectly competitive firm, a comparison of the market price to the firm's average total cost determines whether the firm is earning a profit, taking a loss, or breaking even with a normal profit of zero. Now we can evaluate the profitability of perfectly competitive firms in a variety of situations.

Interpreting Perfect Competition Graphs

Figure 23.1 illustrates how the market price determines whether a firm is profitable. It also shows how profits are depicted graphically. Each panel shows the marginal cost curve, *MC*, and the short-run average total cost curve, *ATC*. Average total cost is minimized at point *C*. Panel (a) shows the case in which the market price of tomatoes is $18 per bushel. Panel (b) shows the case in which the market price of tomatoes is lower, $10 per bushel.

In panel (a), we see that at a price of $18 per bushel the profit-maximizing quantity of output is 5 bushels, indicated by point *E*, where the marginal cost curve, *MC*, intersects the marginal revenue curve, *MR*—which for a price-taking firm is a horizontal line at the market price. At that quantity of output, average total cost is $14.40 per bushel, indicated by point *Z*. Since the price per bushel exceeds the average total cost per bushel, Jennifer and Jason's farm is profitable.

Jennifer and Jason's total profit when the market price is $18 is represented by the area of the shaded rectangle in panel (a). To see why, notice that total profit can be expressed in terms of profit per unit:

(23-1) $\text{Profit} = TR - TC = (TR/Q - TC/Q) \times Q$

or, equivalently, because *P* is equal to *TR/Q* and *ATC* is equal to *TC/Q*,

$$\text{Profit} = (P - ATC) \times Q$$

figure 23.1

Profitability and the Market Price

In panel (a) the market price is $18. The farm is profitable because price exceeds minimum average total cost, the break-even price, $14. The farm's optimal output choice is indicated by point *E*, corresponding to an output of 5 bushels. The average total cost of producing 5 bushels is indicated by point *Z* on the *ATC* curve, corresponding to an amount of $14.40. The vertical distance between *E* and *Z* corresponds to the farm's per-unit profit, $18.00 − $14.40 = $3.60. Total profit is given by the area of the shaded rectangle, 5 × $3.60 = $18.00. In panel (b) the market price is $10; the farm is unprofitable because the price falls below the minimum average total cost, $14. The farm's optimal output choice when producing is indicated by point *A*, corresponding to an output of 3 bushels. The farm's per-unit loss, $14.67 − $10.00 = $4.67, is represented by the vertical distance between *A* and *Y*. The farm's total loss is represented by the shaded rectangle, 3 × $4.67 = $14.00 (adjusted for rounding error).

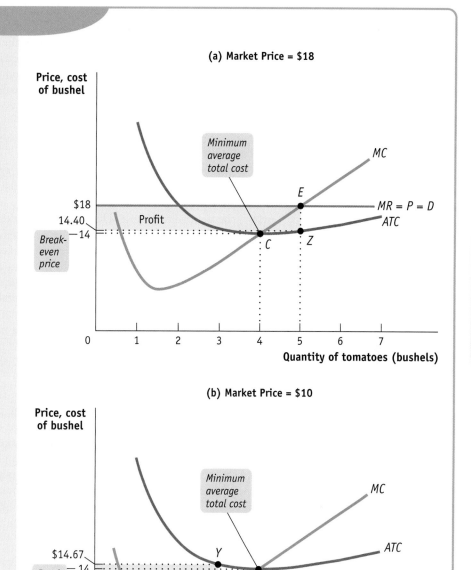

The height of the shaded rectangle in panel (a) corresponds to the vertical distance between points *E* and *Z*. It is equal to $P − ATC = $18.00 − $14.40 = $3.60 per bushel. The shaded rectangle has a width equal to the output: $Q = 5$ bushels. So the area of that rectangle is equal to Jennifer and Jason's profit: 5 bushels × $3.60 profit per bushel = $18.

What about the situation illustrated in panel (b)? Here the market price of tomatoes is $10 per bushel. Producing until price equals marginal cost leads to a profit-maximizing output of 3 bushels, indicated by point *A*. At this output, Jennifer and Jason have an average total cost of $14.67 per bushel, indicated by point *Y*. At their profit-maximizing output quantity—3 bushels—average total cost exceeds the market price. This means that Jennifer and Jason's farm generates a loss, not a profit.

How much do they lose by producing when the market price is $10? On each bushel they lose $ATC - P = \$14.67 - \$10.00 = \$4.67$, an amount corresponding to the vertical distance between points A and Y. And they produce 3 bushels, which corresponds to the width of the shaded rectangle. So the total value of the losses is $\$4.67 \times 3 = \$14.00$ (adjusted for rounding error), an amount that corresponds to the area of the shaded rectangle in panel (b).

But how does a producer know, in general, whether or not its business will be profitable? It turns out that the crucial test lies in a comparison of the market price to the firm's *minimum average total cost*. On Jennifer and Jason's farm, average total cost reaches its minimum, $14, at an output of 4 bushels, indicated by point C. Whenever the market price exceeds the minimum average total cost, there are output levels for which the average total cost is less than the market price. In other words, the producer can find a level of output at which the firm makes a profit. So Jennifer and Jason's farm will be profitable whenever the market price exceeds $14. And they will achieve the highest possible profit by producing the quantity at which marginal cost equals price.

Conversely, if the market price is less than the minimum average total cost, there is no output level at which price exceeds average total cost. As a result, the firm will be unprofitable at any quantity of output. As we saw, at a price of $10—an amount less than the minimum average total cost—Jennifer and Jason did indeed lose money. By producing the quantity at which marginal cost equaled price, Jennifer and Jason did the best they could, but the best they could do was a loss of $14. Any other quantity would have increased the size of their loss.

The minimum average total cost of a price-taking firm is called its **break-even price,** the price at which it earns zero economic profit (which we now know as a *normal profit*). A firm will earn positive profit when the market price is above the break-even price, and it will suffer losses when the market price is below the break-even price. Jennifer and Jason's break-even price of $14 is the price at point C in Figure 23.1.

So the rule for determining whether a firm is profitable depends on a comparison of the market price of the good to the firm's break-even price—its minimum average total cost:

- Whenever the market price exceeds the minimum average total cost, the producer is profitable.

- Whenever the market price equals the minimum average total cost, the producer breaks even.

- Whenever the market price is less than the minimum average total cost, the producer is unprofitable.

The Short-Run Production Decision

You might be tempted to say that if a firm is unprofitable because the market price is below its minimum average total cost, it shouldn't produce any output. In the short run, however, this conclusion isn't right. In the short run, sometimes the firm should produce even if price falls below minimum average total cost. The reason is that total cost includes *fixed cost*—cost that does not depend on the amount of output produced and can be altered only in the long run. In the short run, fixed cost must still be paid, regardless of whether or not a firm produces. For example, if Jennifer and Jason have rented a tractor for the year, they have to pay the rent on the tractor regardless of whether they produce any tomatoes. *Since it cannot be changed in the short run, their fixed cost is irrelevant to their decision about whether to produce or shut down in the short run.* Although fixed cost should play no role in the decision about whether to produce in the short run, another type of cost—variable cost—does matter. Part of the variable cost for Jennifer and Jason is the wage cost of

iStockphoto

workers who must be hired to help with planting and harvesting. Variable cost can be eliminated by *not* producing, which makes it a critical consideration when determining whether or not to produce in the short run.

Let's turn to Figure 23.2: it shows both the short-run average total cost curve, *ATC*, and the short-run average variable cost curve, *AVC*, drawn from the information in Table 22.1. Recall that the difference between the two curves—the vertical distance between them—represents average fixed cost, the fixed cost per unit of output, *FC/Q*. Because the marginal cost curve has a "swoosh" shape—falling at first before rising—the short-run average variable cost curve is U-shaped: the initial fall in marginal cost causes average variable cost to fall as well, and then the rise in marginal cost eventually pulls average variable cost up again. The short-run average variable cost curve reaches its minimum value of $10 at point *A*, at an output of 3 bushels.

figure 23.2

The Short-Run Individual Supply Curve

When the market price equals or exceeds Jennifer and Jason's *shut-down price* of $10, the minimum average variable cost indicated by point *A*, they will produce the output quantity at which marginal cost is equal to price. So at any price equal to or above the minimum average *variable* cost, the short-run individual supply curve is the firm's marginal cost curve; this corresponds to the upward-sloping segment of the individual supply curve. When market price falls below minimum average variable cost, the firm ceases operation in the short run. This corresponds to the vertical segment of the individual supply curve along the vertical axis.

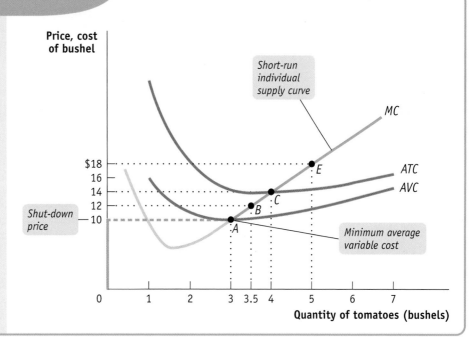

The Shut-Down Price

We are now prepared to analyze the optimal production decision in the short run. We have two cases to consider:

- When the market price is below the minimum average *variable* cost
- When the market price is greater than or equal to the minimum average *variable* cost

When the market price is below the minimum average variable cost, the price the firm receives per unit is not covering its variable cost per unit. A firm in this situation should cease production immediately. Why? Because there is no level of output at which the firm's total revenue covers its variable cost—the cost it can avoid by not operating. In this case the firm maximizes its profit by not producing at all—by, in effect, minimizing its loss. It will still incur a fixed cost in the short run, but it will no longer incur any variable cost. This means that the minimum average variable cost determines the **shut-down price,** the price at which the firm ceases production in the short run.

When price is greater than minimum average variable cost, however, the firm should produce in the short run. In this case, the firm maximizes profit—or minimizes loss—by choosing the output level at which its marginal cost is equal to the market price. For example, if the market price of tomatoes is $18 per bushel, Jennifer and Jason should

A firm will cease production in the short run if the market price falls below the **shut-down price,** which is equal to minimum average variable cost.

produce at point *E* in Figure 23.2, corresponding to an output of 5 bushels. Note that point *C* in Figure 23.2 corresponds to the farm's break-even price of $14 per bushel. Since *E* lies above *C*, Jennifer and Jason's farm will be profitable; they will generate a per-bushel profit of $18.00 − $14.40 = $3.60 when the market price is $18.

But what if the market price lies between the shut-down price and the break-even price—that is, between the minimum average *variable* cost and the minimum average *total* cost? In the case of Jennifer and Jason's farm, this corresponds to prices anywhere between $10 and $14—say, a market price of $12. At $12, Jennifer and Jason's farm is not profitable; since the market price is below the minimum average total cost, the farm is losing (on average) the difference between price and average total cost on every unit produced. Yet even though the market price isn't covering Jennifer and Jason's average total cost, it is covering their average variable cost and some—but not all—of the average fixed cost. If a firm in this situation shuts down, it will incur no variable cost but it will incur the *full* fixed cost. As a result, shutting down will generate an even greater loss than continuing to operate.

This means that whenever price falls between minimum average total cost and minimum average variable cost, the firm is better off producing some output in the short run. The reason is that by producing, it can cover its variable cost and at least some of its fixed cost, even though it is incurring a loss. In this case, the firm maximizes profit—that is, minimizes loss—by choosing the quantity of output at which its marginal cost is equal to the market price. So if Jennifer and Jason face a market price of $12 per bushel, their profit-maximizing output is given by point *B* in Figure 23.2, corresponding to an output of 3.5 bushels.

It's worth noting that the decision to produce when the firm is covering its variable cost but not all of its fixed cost is similar to the decision to ignore a *sunk cost,* a concept we studied previously. You may recall that a sunk cost is a cost that has already been incurred and cannot be recouped; and because it cannot be changed, it should have no effect on any current decision. In the short-run production decision, fixed cost is, in effect, like a sunk cost—it has been spent, and it can't be recovered in the short run. This comparison also illustrates why variable cost does indeed matter in the short run: it can be avoided by not producing.

And what happens if the market price is exactly equal to the shut-down price, the minimum average variable cost? In this instance, the firm is indifferent between producing 3 units or 0 units. As we'll see shortly, this is an important point when looking at the behavior of an industry as a whole. For the sake of clarity, we'll assume that the firm, although indifferent, does indeed produce output when price is equal to the shut-down price.

Putting everything together, we can now draw the **short-run individual supply curve** of Jennifer and Jason's farm, the red line in Figure 23.2; it shows how the profit-maximizing quantity of output in the short run depends on the price. As you can see, the curve is in two segments. The upward-sloping red segment starting at point *A* shows the short-run profit-maximizing output when market price is equal to or above

the shut-down price of $10 per bushel. As long as the market price is equal to or above the shut-down price, Jennifer and Jason will produce the quantity of output at which marginal cost is equal to the market price. So at market prices equal to or above the shut-down price, the firm's short-run supply curve corresponds to its marginal cost curve. But at any market price below the minimum average variable cost, in this case, $10 per bushel—the firm shuts down and output drops to zero in the short run. This corresponds to the vertical segment of the curve that lies on top of the vertical axis.

Do firms sometimes shut down temporarily without going out of business? Yes. In fact, in some industries temporary shut-downs are routine. The most common examples are industries in which demand is highly seasonal, like outdoor amusement parks in climates with cold winters. Such parks would have to offer very low prices to entice customers during the colder months—prices so low that the owners would not cover their variable cost (principally wages and electricity). The wiser choice economically is to shut down until warm weather brings enough customers who are willing to pay a higher price.

Changing Fixed Cost

Although fixed cost cannot be altered in the short run, in the long run firms can acquire or get rid of machines, buildings, and so on. In the long run the level of fixed cost is a matter of choice, and a firm will choose the level of fixed cost that minimizes the average total cost for its desired output level. Now we will focus on an even bigger question facing a firm when choosing its fixed cost: whether to incur *any* fixed cost at all by continuing to operate.

In the long run, a firm can always eliminate fixed cost by selling off its plant and equipment. If it does so, of course, it can't produce any output—it has exited the industry. In contrast, a new firm can take on some fixed cost by acquiring machines and other resources, which puts it in a position to produce—it can enter the industry. In most perfectly competitive industries the set of firms, although fixed in the short run, changes in the long run as some firms enter or exit the industry.

Consider Jennifer and Jason's farm once again. In order to simplify our analysis, we will sidestep the issue of choosing among several possible levels of fixed cost. Instead, we will assume that if they operate at all, Jennifer and Jason have only one possible choice of fixed cost: $14. Alternatively, they can choose a fixed cost of zero if they exit the industry. It is changes in fixed cost that cause short-run average total cost curves to differ from long-run total cost curves, so with this assumption, Jennifer and Jason's short-run and long-run average total cost curves are one and the same.

Suppose that the market price of organic tomatoes is consistently less than the break-even price of $14 over an extended period of time. In that case, Jennifer and Jason never fully cover their total cost: their business runs at a persistent loss. In the long run, then, they can do better by closing their business and leaving the industry. In other words, *in the long run* firms will exit an industry if the market price is consistently less than their break-even price—their minimum average total cost.

Conversely, suppose that the price of organic tomatoes is consistently above the break-even price, $14, for an extended period of time. Because their farm is profitable, Jennifer and Jason will remain in the industry and continue producing. But things won't stop there. The organic tomato industry meets the criterion of *free entry*: there are many potential organic tomato producers because the necessary inputs are easy to obtain. And the cost curves of those potential producers are likely to be similar to those of Jennifer and Jason, since the technology used by other producers is likely to be very similar to that used by Jennifer and Jason. If the price is high enough to generate profits for existing producers, it will also attract some of these potential producers into the industry. So *in the long run* a price in excess of $14 should lead to entry: new producers will come into the organic tomato industry.

As we will see shortly, exit and entry lead to an important distinction between the *short-run industry supply curve* and the *long-run industry supply curve*.

Summing Up: The Perfectly Competitive Firm's Profitability and Production Conditions

In this module we've studied what's behind the supply curve for a perfectly competitive, price-taking firm. A perfectly competitive firm maximizes profit, or minimizes loss, by producing the quantity that equates price and marginal cost. The exception is if price is below minimum average variable cost in the short run, or below minimum average total cost in the long run, in which case the firm is better off shutting down.

table **23.1**

Summary of the Perfectly Competitive Firm's Profitability and Production Conditions

Profitability condition (minimum *ATC* = break-even price)	Result
P > minimum *ATC*	Firm profitable. Entry into industry in the long run.
P = minimum *ATC*	Firm breaks even. No entry into or exit from industry in the long run.
P < minimum *ATC*	Firm unprofitable. Exit from industry in the long run.

Production condition (minimum *AVC* = shut-down price)	Result
P > minimum *AVC*	Firm produces in the short run. If *P* < minimum *ATC*, firm covers variable cost and some but not all of fixed cost. If *P* > minimum *ATC*, firm covers all variable cost and fixed cost.
P = minimum *AVC*	Firm indifferent between producing in the short run or not. Just covers variable cost.
P < minimum *AVC*	Firm shuts down in the short run. Does not cover variable cost.

Table 23.1 summarizes the perfectly competitive firm's profitability and production conditions. It also relates them to entry into and exit from the industry in the long run. Now that we understand how a perfectly competitive *firm* makes its decisions, we can go on to look at the supply curve for a perfectly competitive *market* and the long-run equilibrium in perfect competition.

in real life

Prices Are Up . . . but So Are Costs

In 2005 Congress passed the Energy Policy Act, mandating that by the year 2012, 7.5 billion gallons of alternative fuel—mostly corn-based ethanol—be added to the American fuel supply with the goal of reducing gasoline consumption. The unsurprising result of this mandate: the demand for corn skyrocketed, along with its price. In spring 2007, the price of corn was 50% higher than it had been a year earlier.

This development caught the eye of American farmers like Ronnie Gerik of Aquilla, Texas, who, in response to surging corn prices, reduced the size of his cotton crop and increased his corn acreage by 40%. He was not alone; within a year, the amount of U.S. acreage planted in corn increased by 15%.

Although this sounds like a sure way to make a profit, Gerik was actually taking a big gamble: even though the price of corn increased, so did the cost of the raw materials needed to grow it—by 20%. Consider the cost of just two inputs:

fertilizer and fuel. Corn requires more fertilizer than other crops and, with more farmers planting corn, the increased demand for fertilizer led to a price increase. Corn also has to be transported farther away from the farm than cotton; at the same time that Gerik began shifting to greater corn production, diesel fuel became very expensive. Moreover, corn is much more sensitive to the amount of rainfall than a crop like cotton. So farmers who plant corn in drought-prone places like Texas are increasing their risk of loss. Gerik had to incorporate into his calculations his best guess of what a dry spell would cost him.

Despite all of this, what Gerik did made complete economic sense. By planting more corn, he was moving up his individual short-run supply curve for corn production. And because his individual supply curve is his marginal cost curve, his costs also went up because he had to use more inputs—inputs that had become more expensive to obtain.

Courtesy of Ronnie Gerik.

Although Gerik was taking a big gamble when he cut the size of his cotton crop to plant more corn, his decision made good economic sense.

So the moral of this story is that farmers will increase their corn acreage until the marginal cost of producing corn is approximately equal to the market price of corn—which shouldn't come as a surprise because corn production satisfies all the requirements of a perfectly competitive industry.

Module 23 Review

Solutions appear at the back of the book.

Check Your Understanding

1. Draw a short-run diagram showing a U-shaped average total cost curve, a U-shaped average variable cost curve, and a "swoosh"-shaped marginal cost curve. On it, indicate the range of prices for which the following actions are optimal. Explain your answers.
   a. The firm shuts down immediately.
   b. The firm operates in the short run despite sustaining a loss.
   c. The firm operates while making a profit.

2. The state of Maine has a very active lobster industry, which harvests lobsters during the summer months. During the rest of the year, lobsters can be obtained by restaurants from producers in other parts of the world, but at a much higher price. Maine is also full of "lobster shacks," roadside restaurants serving lobster dishes that are open only during the summer. Supposing that the market demand for lobster dishes remains the same throughout the year, explain why it is optimal for lobster shacks to operate only during the summer.

Multiple-Choice Questions

For questions 1–3, refer to the graph provided.

Market Price = $20

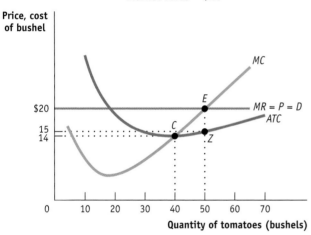

1. The firm's total revenue is equal to
   a. $14.
   b. $20.
   c. $560.
   d. $750.
   e. $1,000.

2. The firm's total cost is equal to
   a. $14.
   b. $15.
   c. $560.
   d. $750.
   e. $1,000.

3. The firm is earning a
   a. profit equal to $5.
   b. profit equal to $250.
   c. loss equal to $15.
   d. loss equal to $750.
   e. loss equal to $250.

4. A firm should continue to produce in the short run as long as price is at least equal to
   a. *MR*.
   b. *MC*.
   c. minimum *ATC*.
   d. minimum *AVC*.
   e. *AFC*.

5. At prices that motivate the firm to produce at all, the short-run supply curve for a perfect competitor corresponds to which curve?
   a. the *ATC* curve
   b. the *AVC* curve
   c. the *MC* curve
   d. the *AFC* curve
   e. the *MR* curve

Critical-Thinking Questions

Refer to the graph provided.

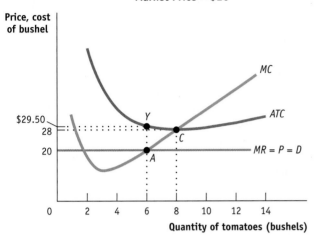

Market Price = $20

a. Assuming it is appropriate for the firm to produce in the short run, what is the firm's profit-maximizing level of output?

b. Calculate the firm's total revenue.

c. Calculate the firm's total cost.

d. Calculate the firm's profit or loss.

e. If *AVC* were $22 at the profit-maximizing level of output, would the firm produce in the short run? Explain why or why not.

Getty Images

Module 24
Long-Run Outcomes in Perfect Competition

Up to this point we have been discussing the perfectly competitive firm's short-run situation—whether to produce or not, and if so, whether the firm earns a positive profit, breaks even with a normal profit, or takes a loss. In this module, we look at the long-run situation in a perfectly competitive market. We will see that perfect competition leads to some interesting and desirable market outcomes. Later, we will contrast these outcomes with the outcomes in monopolistic and imperfectly competitive markets.

The Industry Supply Curve

Why will an increase in the demand for organic tomatoes lead to a large price increase at first but a much smaller increase in the long run? The answer lies in the behavior of the **industry supply curve**—the relationship between the price and the total output of an industry as a whole. The industry supply curve is what we referred to in earlier modules as the supply curve or the market supply curve. But here we take some extra care to distinguish between the *individual supply curve* of a single firm and the supply curve of the industry as a whole.

As you might guess from the previous module, the industry supply curve must be analyzed in somewhat different ways for the short run and the long run. Let's start with the short run.

The Short-Run Industry Supply Curve

Recall that in the short run the number of firms in an industry is fixed—there is no entry or exit. And you may also remember that the industry supply curve is the horizontal sum of the individual supply curves of all firms—you find it by summing the total output across all suppliers at every given price. We will do that exercise here under the assumption that all the firms are alike—an assumption that makes the derivation particularly simple. So let's assume that there are 100 organic tomato farms, each with the same costs as Jennifer and Jason's farm. Each of these 100 farms will have an individual short-run supply curve like the one in Figure 23.2 from the previous module, which is reprinted on the next page for your convenience.

The **industry supply curve** shows the relationship between the price of a good and the total output of the industry as a whole.

figure **23.2**

The Short-Run Individual Supply Curve

When the market price equals or exceeds Jennifer and Jason's *shut-down price* of $10, the minimum average variable cost indicated by point *A*, they will produce the output quantity at which marginal cost is equal to price. So at any price equal to or above the minimum average *variable* cost, the short-run individual supply curve is the firm's marginal cost curve; this corresponds to the upward-sloping segment of the individual supply curve. When market price falls below minimum average variable cost, the firm ceases operation in the short run. This corresponds to the vertical segment of the individual supply curve along the vertical axis.

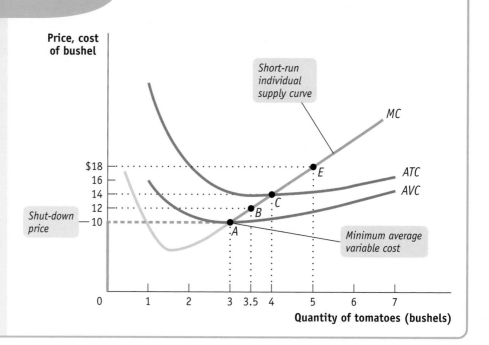

The **short-run industry supply curve** shows how the quantity supplied by an industry depends on the market price, given a fixed number of firms.

At a price below $10, no farms will produce. At a price of more than $10, each farm will produce the quantity of output at which its marginal cost is equal to the market price. As you can see from Figure 23.2, this will lead each farm to produce 4 bushels if the price is $14 per bushel, 5 bushels if the price is $18, and so on. So if there are 100 organic tomato farms and the price of organic tomatoes is $18 per bushel, the industry as a whole will produce 500 bushels, corresponding to 100 farms × 5 bushels per farm. The result is the **short-run industry supply curve,** shown as *S* in Figure 24.1. This curve shows the quantity that producers will supply at each price, *taking the number of farms as given.*

figure **24.1**

The Short-Run Market Equilibrium

The short-run industry supply curve, *S*, is the industry supply curve taking the number of producers—here, 100—as given. It is generated by adding together the individual supply curves of the 100 producers. Below the shut-down price of $10, no producer wants to produce in the short run. Above $10, the short-run industry supply curve slopes upward, as each producer increases output as price increases. It intersects the demand curve, *D*, at point E_{MKT}, the point of short-run market equilibrium, corresponding to a market price of $18 and a quantity of 500 bushels.

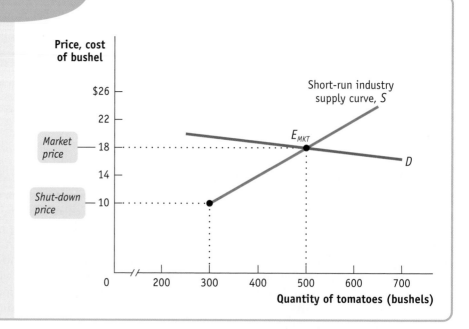

The market demand curve, labeled D in Figure 24.1, crosses the short-run industry supply curve at E_{MKT}, corresponding to a price of $18 and a quantity of 500 bushels. Point E_{MKT} is a **short-run market equilibrium:** the quantity supplied equals the quantity demanded, taking the number of farms as given. But the long run may look quite different because in the long run farms may enter or exit the industry.

The Long-Run Industry Supply Curve

Suppose that in addition to the 100 farms currently in the organic tomato business, there are many other potential organic tomato farms. Suppose also that each of these potential farms would have the same cost curves as existing farms, like the one owned by Jennifer and Jason, upon entering the industry.

When will additional farms enter the industry? Whenever existing farms are making a profit—that is, whenever the market price is above the break-even price of $14 per bushel, the minimum average total cost of production. For example, at a price of $18 per bushel, new farms will enter the industry.

What will happen as additional farms enter the industry? Clearly, the quantity supplied at any given price will increase. The short-run industry supply curve will shift to the right. This will, in turn, alter the market equilibrium and result in a lower market price. Existing farms will respond to the lower market price by reducing their output, but the total industry output will increase because of the larger number of farms in the industry.

Figure 24.2 illustrates the effects of this chain of events on an existing farm and on the market; panel (a) shows how the market responds to entry, and panel (b) shows

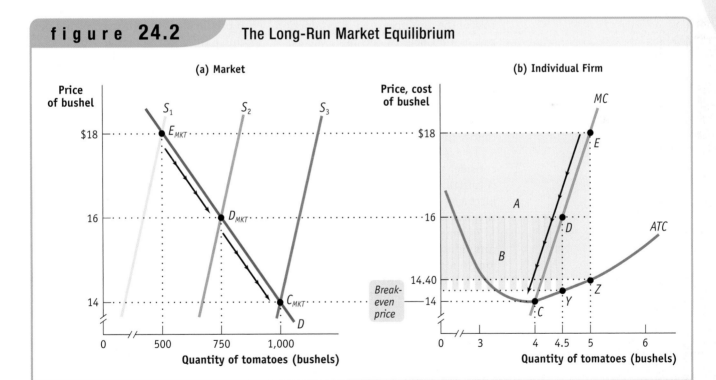

figure 24.2   **The Long-Run Market Equilibrium**

Point E_{MKT} of panel (a) shows the initial short-run market equilibrium. Each of the 100 existing producers makes an economic profit, illustrated in panel (b) by the green rectangle labeled A, the profit of an existing firm. Profits induce entry by additional producers, shifting the short-run industry supply curve outward from S_1 to S_2 in panel (a), resulting in a new short-run equilibrium at point D_{MKT}, at a lower market price of $16 and higher industry output. Existing firms re-duce output and profit falls to the area given by the striped rectangle labeled B in panel (b). Entry continues to shift out the short-run industry supply curve, as price falls and industry output increases yet again. Entry ceases at point C_{MKT} on supply curve S_3 in panel (a). Here market price is equal to the break-even price; existing producers make zero economic profits and there is no incentive for entry or exit. Therefore C_{MKT} is also a long-run market equilibrium.

how an individual existing farm responds to entry. (Note that these two graphs have been rescaled in comparison to Figures 23.2 and 24.1 to better illustrate how profit changes in response to price.) In panel (a), S_1 is the initial short-run industry supply curve, based on the existence of 100 producers. The initial short-run market equilibrium is at E_{MKT}, with an equilibrium market price of $18 and a quantity of 500 bushels. At this price existing farms are profitable, which is reflected in panel (b): an existing farm makes a total profit represented by the green shaded rectangle labeled A when the market price is $18.

These profits will induce new producers to enter the industry, shifting the short-run industry supply curve to the right. For example, the short-run industry supply curve when the number of farms has increased to 167 is S_2. Corresponding to this supply curve is a new short-run market equilibrium labeled D_{MKT}, with a market price of $16 and a quantity of 750 bushels. At $16, each farm produces 4.5 bushels, so that industry output is $167 \times 4.5 = 750$ bushels (rounded). From panel (b) you can see the effect of the entry of 67 new farms on an existing farm: the fall in price causes it to reduce its output, and its profit falls to the area represented by the striped rectangle labeled B.

Although diminished, the profit of existing farms at D_{MKT} means that entry will continue and the number of farms will continue to rise. If the number of farms rises to 250, the short-run industry supply curve shifts out again to S_3, and the market equilibrium is at C_{MKT}, with a quantity supplied and demanded of 1,000 bushels and a market price of $14 per bushel.

Like E_{MKT} and D_{MKT}, C_{MKT} is a short-run equilibrium. But it is also something more. Because the price of $14 is each farm's break-even price, an existing producer makes zero economic profit—neither a profit nor a loss, earning only the opportunity cost of the resources used in production—when producing its profit-maximizing output of 4 bushels. At this price there is no incentive either for potential producers to enter or for existing producers to exit the industry. So C_{MKT} corresponds to a **long-run market equilibrium**—a situation in which the quantity supplied equals the quantity demanded, given that sufficient time has elapsed for producers to either enter or exit the industry. In a long-run market equilibrium, all existing and potential producers have fully adjusted to their optimal long-run choices; as a result, no producer has an incentive to either enter or exit the industry.

To explore further the difference between short-run and long-run equilibrium, consider the effect of an increase in demand on an industry with free entry that is initially in long-run equilibrium. Panel (b) in Figure 24.3 shows the market adjustment; panels (a) and (c) show how an existing individual firm behaves during the process.

In panel (b) of Figure 24.3, D_1 is the initial demand curve and S_1 is the initial short-run industry supply curve. Their intersection at point X_{MKT} is both a short-run and a long-run market equilibrium because the equilibrium price of $14 leads to zero economic profit—and therefore neither entry nor exit. It corresponds to point X in panel (a), where an individual existing firm is operating at the minimum of its average total cost curve.

Now suppose that the demand curve shifts out for some reason to D_2. As shown in panel (b), in the short run, industry output moves along the short-run industry supply curve, S_1, to the new short-run market equilibrium at Y_{MKT}, the intersection of S_1 and D_2. The market price rises to $18 per bushel, and industry output increases from Q_X to Q_Y. This corresponds to an existing firm's movement from X to Y in panel (a) as the firm increases its output in response to the rise in the market price.

But we know that Y_{MKT} is not a long-run equilibrium because $18 is higher than minimum average total cost, so existing firms are making economic profits. This will lead additional firms to enter the industry. Over time entry will cause the short-run industry supply curve to shift to the right. In the long run, the short-run industry supply curve will have shifted out to S_2, and the equilibrium will be at Z_{MKT}—with the price

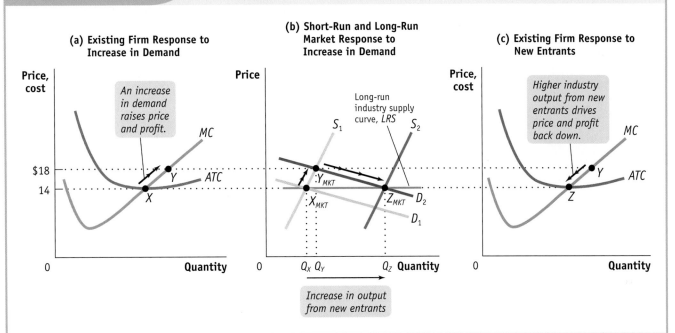

(a) Existing Firm Response to Increase in Demand

(b) Short-Run and Long-Run Market Response to Increase in Demand

(c) Existing Firm Response to New Entrants

Increase in output from new entrants

Panel (b) shows how an industry adjusts in the short and long run to an increase in demand; panels (a) and (c) show the corresponding adjustments by an existing firm. Initially the market is at point X_{MKT} in panel (b), a short-run and long-run equilibrium at a price of $14 and industry output of Q_X. An existing firm makes zero economic profit, operating at point X in panel (a) at minimum average total cost. Demand increases as D_1 shifts rightward to D_2, in panel (b), raising the market price to $18. Existing firms increase their output, and industry output moves along the short-run industry supply curve S_1 to a short-run equilibrium at Y_{MKT}. Correspondingly, the existing firm in panel (a) moves from point X to point Y. But at a price of $18 existing firms are profitable. As shown in panel (b), in the long run

new entrants arrive and the short-run industry supply curve shifts rightward, from S_1 to S_2. There is a new equilibrium at point Z_{MKT}, at a lower price of $14 and higher industry output of Q_Z. An existing firm responds by moving from Y to Z in panel (c), returning to its initial output level and zero economic profit. Production by new entrants accounts for the total increase in industry output, $Q_Z - Q_X$. Like X_{MKT}, Z_{MKT} is also a short-run and long-run equilibrium: with existing firms earning zero economic profit, there is no incentive for any firms to enter or exit the industry. The horizontal line passing through X_{MKT} and Z_{MKT}, LRS, is the *long-run industry supply curve*: at the break-even price of $14, producers will produce any amount that consumers demand in the long run.

falling back to $14 per bushel and industry output increasing yet again, from Q_Y to Q_Z. Like X_{MKT} before the increase in demand, Z_{MKT} is both a short-run and a long-run market equilibrium.

The effect of entry on an existing firm is illustrated in panel (c), in the movement from Y to Z along the firm's individual supply curve. The firm reduces its output in response to the fall in the market price, ultimately arriving back at its original output quantity, corresponding to the minimum of its average total cost curve. In fact, every firm that is now in the industry—the initial set of firms and the new entrants—will operate at the minimum of its average total cost curve, at point Z. This means that the entire increase in industry output, from Q_X to Q_Z, comes from production by new entrants.

The line LRS that passes through X_{MKT} and Z_{MKT} in panel (b) is the **long-run industry supply curve.** It shows how the quantity supplied by an industry responds to the price, given that firms have had time to enter or exit the industry.

In this particular case, the long-run industry supply curve is horizontal at $14. In other words, in this industry supply is *perfectly elastic* in the long run: given time to enter or exit, firms will supply any quantity that consumers demand at a price of $14.

The **long-run industry supply curve** shows how the quantity supplied responds to the price once producers have had time to enter or exit the industry.

Perfectly elastic long-run supply is actually a good assumption for many industries. In this case we speak of there being *constant costs across the industry*: each firm, regardless of whether it is an incumbent or a new entrant, faces the same cost structure (that is, they each have the same cost curve). Industries that satisfy this condition are industries in which there is a perfectly elastic supply of inputs—industries like agriculture or bakeries. In other industries, however, even the long-run industry supply curve slopes upward. The usual reason for this is that producers must use some input that is in limited supply (that is, their supply is at least somewhat inelastic). As the industry expands, the price of that input is driven up. Consequently, the cost structure for firms becomes higher than it was when the industry was smaller. An example is beach front resort hotels, which must compete for a limited quantity of prime beachfront property. Industries that behave like this are said to have *increasing costs across the industry*. Finally, it is possible for the long-run industry supply curve to slope downward, a condition that occurs when the cost structure for firms becomes lower as the industry expands. This is the case in industries such as the electric car industry, in which increased output allows for economies of scale in the production of lithium batteries and other specialized inputs, and thus lower input prices. A downward-sloping industry supply curve indicates *decreasing costs across the industry*.

Regardless of whether the long-run industry supply curve is horizontal, upward sloping, or downward sloping, the long-run price elasticity of supply is *higher* than the short-run price elasticity whenever there is free entry and exit. As shown in Figure 24.4, the long-run industry supply curve is always flatter than the short-run industry supply curve. The reason is entry and exit: a high price caused by an increase in demand attracts entry by new firms, resulting in a rise in industry output and an eventual fall in price; a low price caused by a decrease in demand induces existing firms to exit, leading to a fall in industry output and an eventual increase in price.

The distinction between the short-run industry supply curve and the long-run industry supply curve is very important in practice. We often see a sequence of events like that shown in Figure 24.3: an increase in demand initially leads to a large price

figure 24.4

Comparing the Short-Run and Long-Run Industry Supply Curves

The long-run industry supply curve may slope upward, but it is always flatter—more elastic—than the short-run industry supply curve. This is because of entry and exit: a higher price attracts new entrants in the long run, resulting in a rise in industry output and a fall in price; a lower price induces existing producers to exit in the long run, generating a fall in industry output and a rise in price.

Price

Short-run industry supply curve, *S*

Long-run industry supply curve, *LRS*

The long-run industry supply curve is always flatter—more elastic—than the short-run industry supply curve.

Quantity

increase, but prices return to their initial level once new firms have entered the industry. Or we see the sequence in reverse: a fall in demand reduces prices in the short run, but they return to their initial level as producers exit the industry.

The Cost of Production and Efficiency in Long-Run Equilibrium

Our analysis leads us to three conclusions about the cost of production and efficiency in the long-run equilibrium of a perfectly competitive industry. These results will be important in our upcoming discussion of how monopoly gives rise to inefficiency.

First, in a perfectly competitive industry in equilibrium, the value of marginal cost is the same for all firms. That's because all firms produce the quantity of output at which marginal cost equals the market price, and as price-takers they all face the same market price.

Second, in a perfectly competitive industry with free entry and exit, each firm will have zero economic profit in the long-run equilibrium. Each firm produces the quantity of output that minimizes its average total cost—corresponding to point Z in panel (c) of Figure 24.3. So the total cost of producing the industry's output is minimized in a perfectly competitive industry.

The third and final conclusion is that the long-run market equilibrium of a perfectly competitive industry is efficient: no mutually beneficial transactions go unexploited. To understand this, recall a fundamental requirement for efficiency: all consumers who are willing to pay an amount greater than or equal to the sellers' cost actually get the good. We also learned that when a market is efficient (except under certain, well-defined conditions), the market price matches all consumers willing to pay at least the market price with all sellers who have a cost of production that is less than or equal to the market price.

So in the long-run equilibrium of a perfectly competitive industry, production is efficient: costs are minimized and no resources are wasted. In addition, the allocation of goods to consumers is efficient: every consumer willing to pay the cost of producing the good gets it. Indeed, no mutually beneficial transaction is left unexploited. Moreover, this condition tends to persist over time as the environment changes: the force of competition makes producers responsive to changes in consumers' desires and to changes in technology.

in real life

A Crushing Reversal

For some reason, starting in the mid-1990s, Americans began drinking a lot more wine. Part of this increase in demand may have reflected a booming economy, but the surge in wine consumption continued even after the economy stumbled in 2001. By 2006, Americans were consuming 59% more wine than they did in 1993—a total of 2.4 gallons of wine per year per U.S. resident.

At first, the increase in wine demand led to sharply higher prices; between 1993 and 2000, the price of red wine grapes rose approximately 50%, and California grape growers earned high profits. Then, as the discussions of long-run supply foretell, there was a rapid expansion of the industry, both because existing grape growers expanded their capacity and because new growers entered the industry. Between 1994 and 2002, production of red wine grapes almost doubled. The result was predictable: the price of grapes fell as the supply curve shifted out. As demand growth slowed in 2002, prices plunged by 17%. The effect was to end the California wine industry's expansion. In fact, some grape

producers began to exit the industry. By 2004, U.S. grape production had fallen by 20% compared to 2002.

Check Your Understanding

1. Which of the following events will induce firms to enter an industry? Which will induce firms to exit? When will entry or exit cease? Explain your answer.
   a. A technological advance lowers the fixed cost of production of every firm in the industry.
   b. The wages paid to workers in the industry go up for an extended period of time.
   c. A permanent change in consumer tastes increases demand for the good.
   d. The price of a key input rises due to a long-term shortage of that input.

2. Assume that the egg industry is perfectly competitive and is in long-run equilibrium with a perfectly elastic long-run industry supply curve. Health concerns about cholesterol then lead to a decrease in demand. Construct a figure similar to Figure 24.3, showing the short-run behavior of the industry and how long-run equilibrium is reestablished.

Multiple-Choice Questions

1. In the long run, a perfectly competitive firm will earn
   a. a negative market return.
   b. a positive profit.
   c. a loss.
   d. a normal profit.
   e. excess profit.

2. With perfect competition, efficiency is generally attained in
   a. the short run but not the long run.
   b. the long run but not the short run.
   c. both the short run and the long run.
   d. neither the short run nor the long run.
   e. specific firms only.

3. Compared to the short-run industry supply curve, the long-run industry supply curve will be more
   a. elastic.
   b. inelastic.
   c. steeply sloped.
   d. profitable.
   e. accurate.

4. Which of the following is generally true for perfect competition?
      I. There is free entry and exit.
      II. Long-run market equilibrium is efficient.
      III. Firms maximize profits at the output level where $P = MC$.
   a. I only
   b. II only
   c. III only
   d. I and II only
   e. I, II, and III

5. Which of the following will happen in response if perfectly competitive firms are earning positive economic profit?
   a. Firms will exit the industry.
   b. The short-run industry supply curve will shift right.
   c. The short-run industry supply curve will shift left.
   d. Firm output will increase.
   e. Market price will increase.

Critical-Thinking Question

Draw correctly labeled side-by-side graphs to show the long-run adjustment that would take place if perfectly competitive firms were earning a profit.

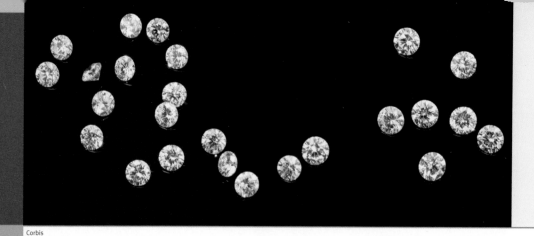

Corbis

Module 25
Introduction
to Monopoly

In this module we turn to monopoly, the market structure at the opposite end of the spectrum from perfect competition. A monopolist's profit-maximizing decision is subtly different from that of a price-taking producer, but it has large implications for the output produced and the welfare created. We will see the crucial role that market demand plays in leading a monopolist to behave differently from a firm in a perfectly competitive industry.

The Monopolist's Demand Curve and Marginal Revenue

Recall the firm's optimal output rule: a profit-maximizing firm produces the quantity of output at which the marginal cost of producing the last unit of output equals marginal revenue—the change in total revenue generated by the last unit of output. That is, $MR = MC$ at the profit-maximizing quantity of output. Although the optimal output rule holds for *all* firms, decisions about price and the quantity of output differ between monopolies and perfectly competitive industries due to differences in the demand curves faced by monopolists and perfectly competitive firms.

We have learned that even though the *market* demand curve always slopes downward, each of the firms that make up a perfectly competitive industry faces a horizontal, *perfectly elastic* demand curve, like D_C in panel (a) of Figure 25.1. Any attempt by an individual firm in a perfectly competitive industry to charge more than the going market price will cause the firm to lose all its sales. It can, however, sell as much as it likes at the market price. We saw that the marginal revenue of a perfectly competitive firm is simply the market price. As a result, the price-taking firm's optimal output rule is to produce the output level at which the marginal cost of the last unit produced is equal to the market price.

A monopolist, in contrast, is the sole supplier of its good. So its demand curve is simply the market demand curve, which slopes downward, like D_M in panel (b) of

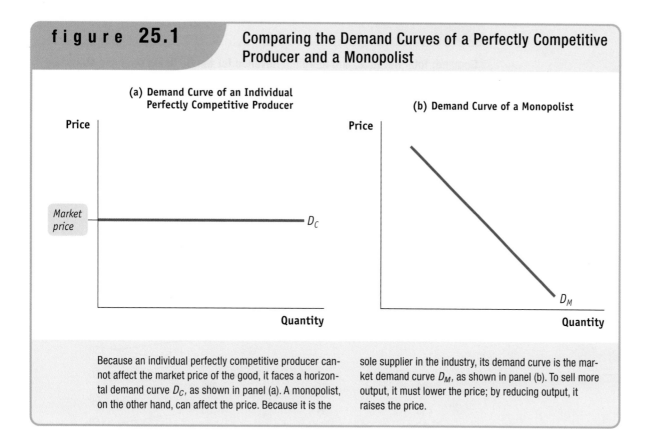

figure 25.1   Comparing the Demand Curves of a Perfectly Competitive Producer and a Monopolist

(a) Demand Curve of an Individual Perfectly Competitive Producer

Price

Market price — D_C

Quantity

(b) Demand Curve of a Monopolist

Price

D_M

Quantity

Because an individual perfectly competitive producer cannot affect the market price of the good, it faces a horizontal demand curve D_C, as shown in panel (a). A monopolist, on the other hand, can affect the price. Because it is the sole supplier in the industry, its demand curve is the market demand curve D_M, as shown in panel (b). To sell more output, it must lower the price; by reducing output, it raises the price.

Figure 25.1. This downward slope creates a "wedge" between the price of the good and the marginal revenue of the good. Table 25.1 on the next page shows how this wedge develops. The first two columns of Table 25.1 show a hypothetical demand schedule for De Beers diamonds. For the sake of simplicity, we assume that all diamonds are exactly alike. And to make the arithmetic easy, we suppose that the number of diamonds sold is far smaller than is actually the case. For instance, at a price of $500 per diamond, we assume that only 10 diamonds are sold. The demand curve implied by this schedule is shown in panel (a) of Figure 25.2 on page 611.

The third column of Table 25.1 shows De Beers's total revenue from selling each quantity of diamonds—the price per diamond multiplied by the number of diamonds sold. The last column shows marginal revenue, the change in total revenue from producing and selling another diamond.

Clearly, after the 1st diamond, the marginal revenue a monopolist receives from selling one more unit is less than the price at which that unit is sold. For example, if De Beers sells 10 diamonds, the price at which the 10th diamond is sold is $500. But the marginal revenue—the change in total revenue in going from 9 to 10 diamonds—is only $50.

Why is the marginal revenue from that 10th diamond less than the price? Because an increase in production by a monopolist has two opposing effects on revenue:

- *A quantity effect.* One more unit is sold, increasing total revenue by the price at which the unit is sold (in this case, +$500).

- *A price effect.* In order to sell that last unit, the monopolist must cut the market price on *all* units sold. This decreases total revenue (in this case, by $9 \times -\$50 = -\$450$).

The quantity effect and the price effect are illustrated by the two shaded areas in panel (a) of Figure 25.2. Increasing diamond sales from 9 to 10 means moving down the demand curve from *A* to *B*, reducing the price per diamond from $550 to $500. The green-shaded area represents the quantity effect: De Beers sells the 10th diamond at a price of $500. This is offset, however, by the price effect, represented by the orange-shaded area. In order to

table **25.1**

Demand, Total Revenue, and Marginal Revenue for the De Beers Diamond Monopoly

Price of diamond P	Quantity of diamonds demanded Q	Total revenue $TR = P \times Q$	Marginal revenue $MR = \Delta TR/\Delta Q$
$1,000	0	$0	
			$950
950	1	950	
			850
900	2	1,800	
			750
850	3	2,550	
			650
800	4	3,200	
			550
750	5	3,750	
			450
700	6	4,200	
			350
650	7	4,550	
			250
600	8	4,800	
			150
550	9	4,950	
			50
500	10	5,000	
			−50
450	11	4,950	
			−150
400	12	4,800	
			−250
350	13	4,550	
			−350
300	14	4,200	
			−450
250	15	3,750	
			−550
200	16	3,200	
			−650
150	17	2,550	
			−750
100	18	1,800	
			−850
50	19	950	
			−950
0	20	0	

sell that 10th diamond, De Beers must reduce the price on all its diamonds from $550 to $500. So it loses $9 \times \$50 = \$450$ in revenue, the orange-shaded area. So, as point C indicates, the total effect on revenue of selling one more diamond—the marginal revenue—derived from an increase in diamond sales from 9 to 10 is only $50.

Point C lies on the monopolist's marginal revenue curve, labeled MR in panel (a) of Figure 25.2 and taken from the last column of Table 25.1. The crucial point about the monopolist's marginal revenue curve is that it is always *below* the demand curve. That's because of the price effect, which means that a monopolist's marginal revenue from selling an additional unit is always less than the price the monopolist receives for that unit. It is the price effect that creates the wedge between the monopolist's marginal revenue curve and the demand curve: in order to sell an additional diamond, De Beers must cut the market price on all units sold.

In fact, this wedge exists for any firm that possesses market power, such as an oligopolist, except in the case of price discrimination as explained in a later module. Having market

figure 25.2

A Monopolist's Demand, Total Revenue, and Marginal Revenue Curves

Panel (a) shows the monopolist's demand and marginal revenue curves for diamonds from Table 25.1. The marginal revenue curve lies below the demand curve. To see why, consider point *A* on the demand curve, where 9 diamonds are sold at $550 each, generating total revenue of $4,950. To sell a 10th diamond, the price on all 10 diamonds must be cut to $500, as shown by point *B*. As a result, total revenue increases by the green area (the quantity effect: +$500) but decreases by the orange area (the price effect: −$450). So the marginal revenue from the 10th diamond is $50 (the difference between the green and orange areas), which is much lower than its price, $500. Panel (b) shows the monopolist's total revenue curve for diamonds. As output goes from 0 to 10 diamonds, total revenue increases. It reaches its maximum at 10 diamonds—the level at which marginal revenue is equal to 0—and declines thereafter. The quantity effect dominates the price effect when total revenue is rising; the price effect dominates the quantity effect when total revenue is falling.

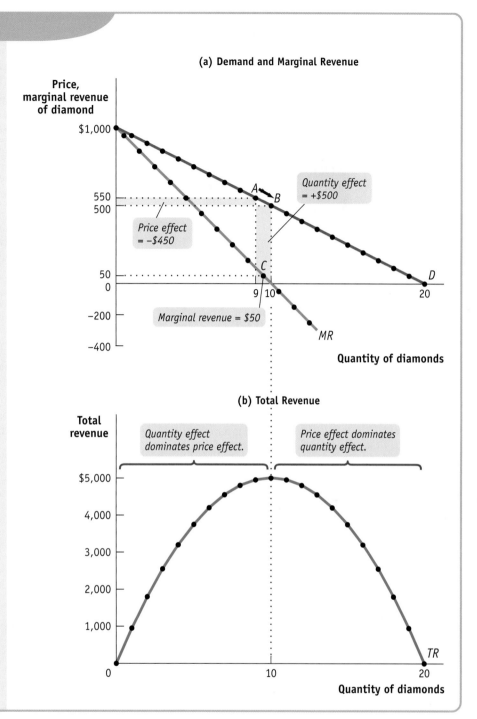

(a) Demand and Marginal Revenue

Price, marginal revenue of diamond

Quantity effect = +$500

Price effect = −$450

Marginal revenue = $50

MR

Quantity of diamonds

(b) Total Revenue

Total revenue

Quantity effect dominates price effect.

Price effect dominates quantity effect.

TR

Quantity of diamonds

power means that the firm faces a downward-sloping demand curve. As a result, there will always be a price effect from an increase in output for a firm with market power that charges every customer the same price. So for such a firm, the marginal revenue curve always lies below the demand curve.

Take a moment to compare the monopolist's marginal revenue curve with the marginal revenue curve for a perfectly competitive firm, which has no market power. For such a firm there is no price effect from an increase in output: its marginal revenue curve is simply its horizontal demand curve. So for a perfectly competitive firm, market price and marginal revenue are always equal.

Corbis

To emphasize how the quantity and price effects offset each other for a firm with market power, De Beers's total revenue curve is shown in panel (b) of Figure 25.2. Notice that it is hill-shaped: as output rises from 0 to 10 diamonds, total revenue increases. This reflects the fact that *at low levels of output, the quantity effect is stronger than the price effect:* as the monopolist sells more, it has to lower the price on only very few units, so the price effect is small. As output rises beyond 10 diamonds, total revenue actually falls. This reflects the fact that *at high levels of output, the price effect is stronger than the quantity effect:* as the monopolist sells more, it now has to lower the price on many units of output, making the price effect very large. Correspondingly, the marginal revenue curve lies below zero at output levels above 10 diamonds. For example, an increase in diamond production from 11 to 12 yields only $400 for the 12th diamond, simultaneously reducing the revenue from diamonds 1 through 11 by $550. As a result, the marginal revenue of the 12th diamond is −$150.

The Monopolist's Profit-Maximizing Output and Price

To complete the story of how a monopolist maximizes profit, we now bring in the monopolist's marginal cost. Let's assume that there is no fixed cost of production; we'll also assume that the marginal cost of producing an additional diamond is constant at $200, no matter how many diamonds De Beers produces. Then marginal cost will always equal average total cost, and the marginal cost curve (and the average total cost curve) is a horizontal line at $200, as shown in Figure 25.3.

figure 25.3

The Monopolist's Profit-Maximizing Output and Price

This figure shows the demand, marginal revenue, and marginal cost curves. Marginal cost per diamond is constant at $200, so the marginal cost curve is horizontal at $200. According to the optimal output rule, the profit-maximizing quantity of output for the monopolist is at $MR = MC$, shown by point A, where the marginal cost and marginal revenue curves cross at an output of 8 diamonds. The price De Beers can charge per diamond is found by going to the point on the demand curve directly above point A, which is point B here—a price of $600 per diamond. It makes a profit of $400 × 8 = $3,200. A perfectly competitive industry produces the output level at which $P = MC$, given by point C, where the demand curve and marginal cost curves cross. So a competitive industry produces 16 diamonds, sells at a price of $200, and makes zero profit.

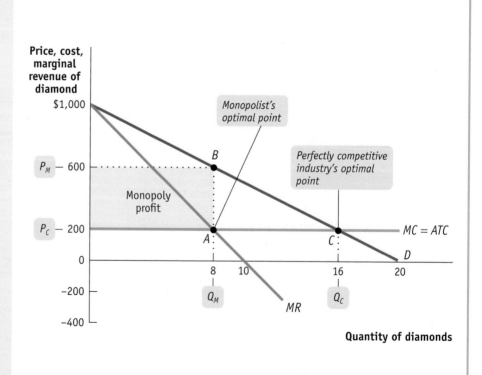

To maximize profit, the monopolist compares marginal cost with marginal revenue. If marginal revenue exceeds marginal cost, De Beers increases profit by producing more; if marginal revenue is less than marginal cost, De Beers increases profit by producing less. So the monopolist maximizes its profit by using the optimal output rule:

(25-1) $MR = MC$ at the monopolist's profit-maximizing quantity of output

The monopolist's optimal point is shown in Figure 25.3. At *A,* the marginal cost curve, *MC,* crosses the marginal revenue curve, *MR.* The corresponding output level, 8 diamonds, is the monopolist's profit-maximizing quantity of output, Q_M. The price at which consumers demand 8 diamonds is $600, so the monopolist's price, P_M, is $600—corresponding to point *B.* The average total cost of producing each diamond is $200, so the monopolist earns a profit of $600 − $200 = $400 per diamond, and total profit is 8 × $400 = $3,200, as indicated by the shaded area.

Monopoly versus Perfect Competition

When Cecil Rhodes consolidated many independent diamond producers into De Beers, he converted a perfectly competitive industry into a monopoly. We can now use our analysis to see the effects of such a consolidation.

Let's look again at Figure 25.3 and ask how this same market would work if, instead of being a monopoly, the industry were perfectly competitive. We will continue to assume that there is no fixed cost and that marginal cost is constant, so average total cost and marginal cost are equal.

If the diamond industry consists of many perfectly competitive firms, each of those producers takes the market price as given. That is, each producer acts as if its marginal revenue is equal to the market price. So each firm within the industry uses the price-taking firm's optimal output rule:

(25-2) $P = MC$ at the perfectly competitive firm's profit-maximizing quantity of output.

In Figure 25.3, this would correspond to producing at *C,* where the price per diamond, P_C, is $200, equal to the marginal cost of production. So the profit-maximizing output of an industry under perfect competition, Q_C, is 16 diamonds.

But does the perfectly competitive industry earn any profit at *C?* No: the price of $200 is equal to the average total cost per diamond. So there is no economic profit for this industry when it produces at the perfectly competitive output level.

We've already seen that once the industry is consolidated into a monopoly, the result is very different. The monopolist's marginal revenue is influenced by the price effect, so that marginal revenue is less than the price. That is,

(25-3) $P > MR = MC$ at the monopolist's profit-maximizing quantity of output

As we've already seen, the monopolist produces less than the competitive industry—8 diamonds rather than 16. The price under monopoly is $600, compared with only $200 under perfect competition. The monopolist earns a positive profit, but the competitive industry does not.

So, we can see that compared with a competitive industry, a monopolist does the following:

- produces a smaller quantity: $Q_M < Q_C$
- charges a higher price: $P_M > P_C$
- earns a profit

Monopoly Behavior and the Price Elasticity of Demand

A monopolist faces marginal revenue that is lower than the market price. But how much lower? The answer depends on the *price elasticity of demand.*

Remember that the price elasticity of demand determines how total revenue from sales changes when the price changes. If the price elasticity is greater than 1 (demand is elastic), a fall in the price increases total revenue because the rise in the quantity demanded outweighs the lower price of each unit sold. If the price elasticity is less than 1 (demand is inelastic), a lower price reduces total revenue.

When a monopolist increases output by one unit, it must reduce the market price in order to sell that unit. If the price elasticity of demand is less than 1, this will actually reduce revenue—that is, marginal revenue will be negative. The monopolist can increase revenue by producing more only if the price elasticity of demand is greater than 1; the higher the elasticity, the closer the additional revenue is to the initial market price.

What this tells us is that the difference between monopoly behavior and perfectly competitive behavior depends on the price elasticity of demand. A monopolist that faces highly elastic demand will behave almost like a firm in a perfectly competitive industry.

For example, Amtrak has a monopoly on intercity passenger service in the Northeast Corridor, but it has very little ability to raise prices: potential train travelers will switch to cars and

KAREN BLEIER/AFP/Getty Images

planes. In contrast, a monopolist that faces less elastic demand—like most cable TV companies—will behave very differently from a perfect competitor: it will charge much higher prices and restrict output more.

Monopoly: The General Picture

Figure 25.3 involved specific numbers and assumed that marginal cost was constant, there was no fixed cost, and therefore, that the average total cost curve was a horizontal line. Figure 25.4 shows a more general picture of monopoly in action: D is the market demand curve; MR, the marginal revenue curve; MC, the marginal cost curve; and ATC, the average total cost curve. Here we return to the usual assumption that the marginal cost curve has a "swoosh" shape and the average total cost curve is U-shaped.

figure 25.4

The Monopolist's Profit

In this case, the marginal cost curve has a "swoosh" shape and the average total cost curve is U-shaped. The monopolist maximizes profit by producing the level of output at which $MR = MC$, given by point A, generating quantity Q_M. It finds its monopoly price, P_M, from the point on the demand curve directly above point A, point B here. The average total cost of Q_M is shown by point C. Profit is given by the area of the shaded rectangle.

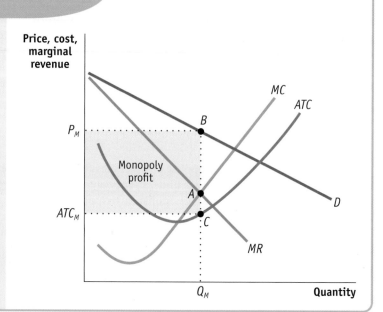

Applying the optimal output rule, we see that the profit-maximizing level of output, identified as the quantity at which marginal revenue and marginal cost intersect (see point A), is Q_M. The monopolist charges the highest price possible for this quantity, P_M, found at the height of the demand curve at Q_M (see point B). At the profit-maximizing level of output, the monopolist's average total cost is ATC_M (see point C).

Recalling how we calculated profit in Equation 23-1, profit is equal to the difference between total revenue and total cost. So we have

(25-4) $\text{Profit} = TR - TC$
$$= (P_M \times Q_M) - (ATC_M \times Q_M)$$
$$= (P_M - ATC_M) \times Q_M.$$

Profit is equal to the area of the shaded rectangle in Figure 25.4, with a height of $P_M - ATC_M$ and a width of Q_M.

We learned that a perfectly competitive industry can have profits *in the short run but not in the long run*. In the short run, price can exceed average total cost, allowing a perfectly competitive firm to make a profit. But we also know that this cannot persist. In the long run, any profit in a perfectly competitive industry will be competed away as new firms enter the market. In contrast, while a monopoly can earn a profit or a loss in the short run, barriers to entry make it possible for a monopolist to make positive profits in the long run.

The STRUGGLING U.S. Postal Service takes a LESSON from the POWER COMPANIES...

WHOOPS! STAMP SHORTAGE! NOW THEY'RE TWO BUCKS EACH

Reprinted with special permission of King Feature Syndicate.

Module 25 Review

Solutions appear at the back of the book.

Check Your Understanding

1. Use the accompanying total revenue schedule of Emerald, Inc., a monopoly producer of 10-carat emeralds, to calculate the items listed in parts a–d. Then answer part e.

Quantity of emeralds demanded	Total revenue
1	$100
2	186
3	252
4	280
5	250

    a. the demand schedule (Hint: the average revenue at each quantity indicates the price at which that quantity would be demanded.)

    b. the marginal revenue schedule

    c. the quantity effect component of marginal revenue at each output level

    d. the price effect component of marginal revenue at each output level

    e. What additional information is needed to determine Emerald, Inc.'s profit-maximizing output?

2. Replicate Figure 25.3 and use your graph to show what happens to the following when the marginal cost of diamond production rises from $200 to $400. Use the information in Table 25.1 to identify specific numbers for prices and quantities on your graph.

    a. the marginal cost curve

    b. the profit-maximizing price and quantity

    c. the profit of the monopolist

    d. the quantity that would be produced if the diamond industry were perfectly competitive, and the associated profit

Multiple-Choice Questions

Refer to the graph provided for questions 1–4.

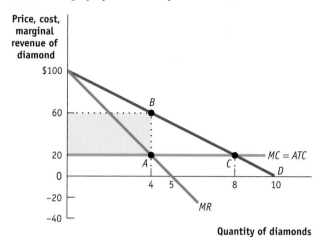

1. The monopolist's profit-maximizing output is
   a. 0.
   b. 4.
   c. 5.
   d. 8.
   e. 10.

2. The monopolist's total revenue equals
   a. $80.
   b. $160.
   c. $240.

   d. $300.
   e. $480.

3. The monopolist's total cost equals
   a. $20.
   b. $80.
   c. $160.
   d. $240.
   e. $480.

4. The monopolist is earning a profit equal to
   a. $0.
   b. $40.
   c. $80.
   d. $160.
   e. $240.

5. How does a monopoly differ from a perfectly competitive industry with the same costs?
   - I. It produces a smaller quantity.
   - II. It charges a higher price.
   - III. It earns normal profits in the long run.
   a. I only
   b. II only
   c. III only
   d. I and II only
   e. I, II, and III

Critical-Thinking Question

a. Draw a graph showing a monopoly earning a normal profit in the short run.

b. Can a monopoly earn a normal profit in the long run? Explain.

Module 26
Monopoly and Public Policy

What you will learn in this Module:

- The effects of the difference between perfect competition and monopoly on society's welfare

- How policy-makers address the problems posed by monopoly

It's good to be a monopolist, but it's not so good to be a monopolist's customer. A monopolist, by reducing output and raising prices, benefits at the expense of consumers. But buyers and sellers always have conflicting interests. Is the conflict of interest under monopoly any different from what it is under perfect competition?

The answer is yes, because monopoly is a source of inefficiency: the losses to consumers from monopoly behavior are larger than the gains to the monopolist. Because monopoly leads to net losses for the economy, governments often try either to prevent the emergence of monopolies or to limit their effects. In this module, we will see why monopoly leads to inefficiency and examine the policies governments adopt in an attempt to prevent this inefficiency.

Welfare Effects of Monopoly

By holding output below the level at which marginal cost is equal to the market price, a monopolist increases its profit but hurts consumers. To assess whether this is a net benefit or loss to society, we must compare the monopolist's gain in profit to the consumers' loss. And what we learn is that the consumers' loss is larger than the monopolist's gain. Monopoly causes a net loss for society.

To see why, let's return to the case in which the marginal cost curve is horizontal, as shown in the two panels of Figure 26.1 on the next page. Here the marginal cost curve is MC, the demand curve is D, and, in panel (b), the marginal revenue curve is MR.

Panel (a) shows what happens if this industry is perfectly competitive. Equilibrium output is Q_C; the price of the good, P_C, is equal to marginal cost, and marginal cost is also equal to average total cost because there is no fixed cost and marginal cost is constant. Each firm is earning exactly its average total cost per unit of output, so there is no producer surplus in this equilibrium. The consumer surplus generated by the market is equal to the area of the blue-shaded triangle CS_C shown in panel (a). Since there is no producer surplus when the industry is perfectly competitive, CS_C also represents the total surplus.

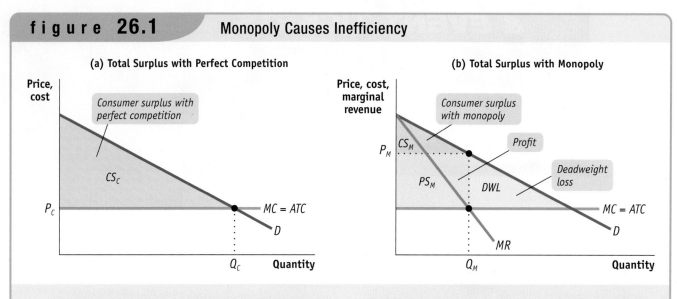

(a) Total Surplus with Perfect Competition

(b) Total Surplus with Monopoly

Panel (a) depicts a perfectly competitive industry: output is Q_C, and market price, P_C, is equal to *MC*. Since price is exactly equal to each producer's average total cost of production per unit, there is no producer surplus. So total surplus is equal to consumer surplus, the entire shaded area. Panel (b) depicts the industry under monopoly: the mo-

nopolist decreases output to Q_M and charges P_M. Consumer surplus (blue area) has shrunk: a portion of it has been captured as profit (green area), and a portion of it has been lost to deadweight loss (yellow area), the value of mutually beneficial transactions that do not occur because of monopoly behavior. As a result, total surplus falls.

Panel (b) shows the results for the same market, but this time assuming that the industry is a monopoly. The monopolist produces the level of output, Q_M, at which marginal cost is equal to marginal revenue, and it charges the price, P_M. The industry now earns profit—which is also the producer surplus in this case—equal to the area of the green rectangle, PS_M. Note that this profit is part of what was consumer surplus in the perfectly competitive market, and consumer surplus with the monopoly shrinks to the area of the blue triangle, CS_M.

By comparing panels (a) and (b), we see that in addition to the redistribution of surplus from consumers to the monopolist, another important change has occurred: the sum of profit and consumer surplus—total surplus—is *smaller* under monopoly than under perfect competition. That is, the sum of CS_M and PS_M in panel (b) is less than the area CS_C in panel (a). Previously, we analyzed how taxes could cause *deadweight loss* for society. Here we show that a monopoly creates deadweight loss equal to the area of the yellow triangle, *DWL*. So monopoly produces a net loss for society.

This net loss arises because some mutually beneficial transactions do not occur. There are people for whom an additional unit of the good is worth more than the marginal cost of producing it but who don't consume it because they are not willing to pay the monopoly price, P_M. Indeed, by driving a wedge between price and marginal cost, a monopoly acts much like a tax on consumers and produces the same kind of inefficiency.

So monopoly power detracts from the welfare of society as a whole and is a source of market failure. Is there anything government policy can do about it?

Preventing Monopoly Power

Policy toward monopolies depends crucially on whether or not the industry in question is a natural monopoly, one in which increasing returns to scale ensure that a bigger producer has lower average total cost. If the industry is *not* a natural monopoly, the best policy is to prevent a monopoly from arising or break it up if it already exists.

Government policy used to prevent or eliminate monopolies is known as *antitrust policy,* which we will discuss in a later module. For now, let's focus on the more difficult problem of dealing with a natural monopoly.

Dealing with a Natural Monopoly

Breaking up a monopoly that isn't natural is clearly a good idea: the gains to consumers outweigh the loss to the producer. But it's not so clear whether a natural monopoly, one in which large producers have lower average total costs than small producers, should be broken up, because this would raise average total cost. For example, a town government that tried to prevent a single company from dominating local gas supply—which, as we've discussed, is almost surely a natural monopoly—would raise the cost of providing gas to its residents.

Yet even in the case of a natural monopoly, a profit-maximizing monopolist acts in a way that causes inefficiency—it charges consumers a price that is higher than marginal cost and, by doing so, prevents some potentially beneficial transactions. Also, it can seem unfair that a firm that has managed to establish a monopoly position earns a large profit at the expense of consumers.

What can public policy do about this? There are two common answers.

Public Ownership

In many countries, the preferred answer to the problem of natural monopoly has been **public ownership.** Instead of allowing a private monopolist to control an industry, the government establishes a public agency to provide the good and protect consumers' interests.

The advantage of public ownership, in principle, is that a publicly owned natural monopoly can set prices based on the criterion of efficiency rather than profit maximization. In a perfectly competitive industry, profit-maximizing behavior *is* efficient because producers set price equal to marginal cost; that is why there is no economic argument for public ownership of, say, wheat farms.

Experience suggests, however, that public ownership as a solution to the problem of natural monopoly often works badly in practice. One reason is that publicly owned firms are often less eager than private companies to keep costs down or offer high-quality products. Another is that publicly owned companies all too often end up serving political interests—providing contracts or jobs to people with the right connections.

Regulation

In the United States, the more common answer has been to leave the industry in private hands but subject it to regulation. In particular, most local utilities, like electricity, telephone service, natural gas, and so on, are covered by **price regulation** that limits the prices they can charge.

Figure 26.2 on the next page shows an example of price regulation of a natural monopoly—a highly simplified version of a local gas company. The company faces a demand curve, *D,* with an associated marginal revenue curve, *MR.* For simplicity, we assume that the firm's total cost consists of two parts: a fixed cost and a variable cost that is the same for every unit. So marginal cost is constant in this case, and the marginal cost curve (which here is also the average variable cost curve) is the horizontal line *MC.* The average total cost curve is the downward-sloping curve *ATC;* it slopes downward because the higher the output, the lower the average fixed cost (the fixed cost per unit of output). Because average total cost slopes downward over the range of output relevant for market demand, this is a natural monopoly.

In **public ownership** of a monopoly, the good is supplied by the government or by a firm owned by the government.

Price regulation limits the price that a monopolist is allowed to charge.

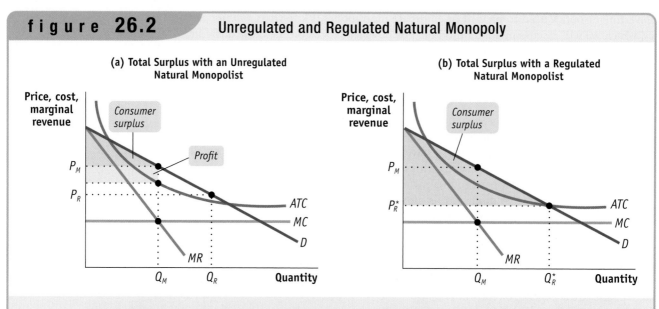

figure 26.2 Unregulated and Regulated Natural Monopoly

(a) Total Surplus with an Unregulated Natural Monopolist

Price, cost, marginal revenue

Consumer surplus

Profit

P_M

P_R

ATC

MC

D

MR

Q_M Q_R Quantity

(b) Total Surplus with a Regulated Natural Monopolist

Price, cost, marginal revenue

Consumer surplus

P_M

P_R^*

ATC

MC

D

MR

Q_M Q_R^* Quantity

This figure shows the case of a natural monopolist. In panel (a), if the monopolist is allowed to charge P_M, it makes a profit, shown by the green area; consumer surplus is shown by the blue area. If it is regulated and must charge the lower price, P_R, output increases from Q_M to Q_R and consumer surplus increases. Panel (b)

shows what happens when the monopolist must charge a price equal to average total cost, the price P_R^*. Output expands to Q_R^*, and consumer surplus is now the entire blue area. The monopolist makes zero profit. This is the greatest total surplus possible without the monopoly incurring losses.

Panel (a) illustrates a case of natural monopoly without regulation. The unregulated natural monopolist chooses the monopoly output Q_M and charges the price P_M. Since the monopolist receives a price greater than average total cost, she or he earns a profit, represented by the green-shaded rectangle in panel (a). Consumer surplus is given by the blue-shaded triangle.

Now suppose that regulators impose a price ceiling on local gas deliveries—one that falls below the monopoly price P_M but above average total cost, say, at P_R in panel (a). At that price the quantity demanded is Q_R.

Does the company have an incentive to produce that quantity? Yes. If the price the monopolist can charge is fixed at P_R by regulators, the firm can sell any quantity between zero and Q_R for the same price, P_R. Because it doesn't have to lower its price to sell more (up to Q_R), there is no price effect to bring marginal revenue below price, so the regulated price becomes the marginal revenue for the monopoly just like the market price is the marginal revenue for a perfectly competitive firm. With marginal revenue being above marginal cost and price exceeding average cost, the firm expands output to meet the quantity demanded, Q_R. This policy has appeal because at the regulated price, the monopolist produces more at a lower price.

Of course, the monopolist will not be willing to produce at all in the long run if the regulated price means producing at a loss. That is, the price ceiling has to be set high enough to allow the firm to cover its average total cost. Panel (b) shows a situation in which regulators have pushed the price down as far as possible, at the level where the average total cost curve crosses the demand curve. At any lower price the firm loses money. The price here, P_R^*, is the best regulated price: the monopolist is just willing to operate and produces Q_R^*, the quantity demanded at that price. Consumers and society gain as a result.

The welfare effects of this regulation can be seen by comparing the shaded areas in the two panels of Figure 26.2. Consumer surplus is increased by the regulation, with the gains coming from two sources. First, profits are eliminated and added instead to consumer surplus. Second, the larger output and lower price leads to an overall welfare gain—an increase in total surplus. In fact, panel (b) illustrates the largest total surplus possible.

Must Monopoly Be Controlled?

Sometimes the cure is worse than the disease. Some economists have argued that the best solution, even in the case of a natural monopoly, may be to live with it. The case for doing nothing is that attempts to control monopoly will, one way or another, do more harm than good.

The following IRL describes the case of cable television, a natural monopoly that has been alternately regulated and deregulated as politicians change their minds about the appropriate policy.

in real life

Cable Dilemmas

Most price regulation in the United States goes back a long way: electricity, local phone service, water, and gas have been regulated in most places for generations. But cable television is a relatively new industry. Until the late 1970s, only rural areas too remote to support local broadcast stations were served by cable. After 1972, new technology and looser rules made it profitable to offer cable service to major metropolitan areas; new networks like HBO and CNN emerged to take advantage of the possibilities.

Until recently, local cable TV was a natural monopoly: running cable through a town entails large fixed costs that don't depend on how many people actually subscribe. Having more than one cable company would involve a lot of wasteful duplication. But if the local cable company is a monopoly, should its prices be regulated?

At first, most local governments thought so, and cable TV was subject to price regulation. In 1984, however, Congress passed a law prohibiting most local governments from regulating cable prices. (The law was the result both of

widespread skepticism about whether price regulation was actually a good idea and of intensive lobbying by the cable companies.)

After the law went into effect, however, cable television rates increased sharply. The resulting consumer backlash led to a new law, in 1992, which once again allowed local governments to set limits on cable prices.

Was the second round of regulation a success? As measured by the prices of "basic" cable service, it was: after rising rapidly during the period of deregulation, the cost of basic service leveled off.

However, price regulation in cable applies only to "basic" service. Cable operators can try to evade the restrictions by charging more for premium channels like HBO or by offering fewer channels in the "basic" package. So some skeptics have questioned whether current regulation has actually been effective.

Yet technological change has begun providing relief to consumers in some areas. Although cable TV is a natural monopoly, there is now another means of delivering video programs to

FiOS TV It rivals reality.   verizon

Stringer/Getty Images

homes: over a high-speed fiber-optic Internet connection. In some locations, fiber-optic Internet providers have begun competing aggressively with traditional cable TV companies. Studies have shown that when a second provider enters a market, prices can drop significantly, as much as 30%. In fact, the United States is currently behind on this front: today 60% of households in Hong Kong watch TV programs delivered over the Internet. What will these changes mean for the cable TV monopolies? Stay tuned.

Module 26 Review

Solutions appear at the back of the book.

Check Your Understanding

1. What policy should the government adopt in the following cases? Explain.
   a. Internet service in Anytown, OH, is provided by cable. Customers feel they are being overcharged, but the cable company claims it must charge prices that let it recover the costs of laying cable.

   b. The only two airlines that currently fly to Alaska need government approval to merge. Other airlines wish to fly to Alaska but need government-allocated landing slots to do so.

2. True or false? Explain your answer.
   a. Society's welfare is lower under monopoly because some consumer surplus is transformed into profit for the monopolist.
   b. A monopolist causes inefficiency because there are consumers who are willing to pay a price greater than or equal to marginal cost but less than the monopoly price.

3. Suppose a monopolist mistakenly believes that her or his marginal revenue is always equal to the market price. Assuming constant marginal cost and no fixed cost, draw a diagram comparing the level of profit, consumer surplus, total surplus, and deadweight loss for this misguided monopolist compared to a smart monopolist. Explain your findings.

Multiple-Choice Questions

1. Which of the following statements is true of a monopoly as compared to a perfectly competitive market with the same costs?

   I. Consumer surplus is smaller.
   II. Profit is smaller.
   III. Deadweight loss is smaller.

   a. I only
   b. II only
   c. III only
   d. I and II only
   e. I, II, and III

2. Which of the following is true of a natural monopoly?
   a. It experiences diseconomies of scale.
   b. *ATC* is lower if there is a single firm in the market.
   c. It occurs in a market that relies on natural resources for its production.
   d. There are decreasing returns to scale in the industry.
   e. The government must provide the good or service to achieve efficiency.

3. Which of the following government actions is the most common for a natural monopoly in the United States?
   a. prevent its formation
   b. break it up using antitrust laws

   c. use price regulation
   d. public ownership
   e. elimination of the market

4. Which of the following markets is an example of a regulated natural monopoly?
   a. local cable TV
   b. gasoline
   c. cell phone service
   d. organic tomatoes
   e. diamonds

5. Which of the following is most likely to be higher for a regulated natural monopoly than for an unregulated natural monopoly?
   a. product variety
   b. quantity
   c. price
   d. profit
   e. deadweight loss

Critical-Thinking Questions

Draw a correctly labeled graph of a natural monopoly. Use your graph to identify each of the following:

a. consumer surplus if the market were somehow able to operate as a perfectly competitive market
b. consumer surplus with the monopoly
c. monopoly profit
d. deadweight loss with the monopoly

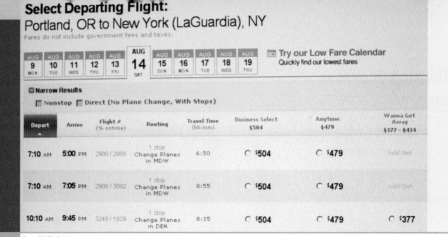

Select Departing Flight:
Portland, OR to New York (LaGuardia), NY
Fares do not include government fees and taxes.

Dena Digilio Betz

Module 27
Price Discrimination

Up to this point, we have considered only the case of a monopolist who charges all consumers the same price. However, monopolists want to maximize their profits and often they do so by charging different prices for the same product. In this module we look at how monopolists increase their profits by engaging in *price discrimination*.

Price Discrimination Defined

A monopolist who charges everyone the same price is known as a **single-price monopolist.** As the term suggests, not all monopolists do this. In fact, many monopolists find that they can increase their profits by selling the same good to different customers for different prices: they practice **price discrimination.**

An example of price discrimination that travelers encounter regularly involves airline tickets. Although there are a number of airlines, most routes in the United States are serviced by only one or two carriers, which, as a result, have market power and can influence prices. So any regular airline passenger quickly becomes aware that the simple question "How much will it cost me to fly there?" rarely has a simple answer. If you are willing to buy a nonrefundable ticket a month in advance and stay over a Saturday night, the round trip may cost only $150—or less if you are a senior citizen or a student. But if you have to go on a business trip tomorrow, which happens to be Tuesday, and want to come back on Wednesday, the same round trip might cost $550. Yet the business traveler and the visiting grandparent receive the same product.

You might object that airlines are not usually monopolies—that in most flight markets the airline industry is an oligopoly. In fact, price discrimination takes place under oligopoly and monopolistic competition as well as monopoly. But it doesn't happen under perfect competition. And once we've seen why monopolists sometimes price-discriminate, we'll be in a good position to understand why it happens in other cases, too.

A **single-price monopolist** charges all consumers the same price.

Sellers engage in **price discrimination** when they charge different prices to different consumers for the same good.

The Logic of Price Discrimination

To get a preliminary view of why price discrimination might be more profitable than charging all consumers the same price, imagine that Air Sunshine offers the only nonstop flights between Bismarck, North Dakota, and Ft. Lauderdale, Florida. Assume that there are no capacity problems—the airline can fly as many planes as the number of passengers warrants. Also assume that there is no fixed cost. The marginal cost to the airline of providing a seat is $125 however many passengers it carries.

Further assume that the airline knows there are two kinds of potential passengers. First, there are business travelers, 2,000 of whom want to travel between the destinations each week. Second, there are high school students, 2,000 of whom also want to travel each week.

Will potential passengers take the flight? It depends on the price. The business travelers, it turns out, really need to fly; they will take the plane as long as the price is no more than $550. Since they are flying purely for business, we assume that cutting the price below $550 will not lead to any increase in business travel. The students, however, have less money and more time; if the price goes above $150, they will take the bus. The implied demand curve is shown in Figure 27.1.

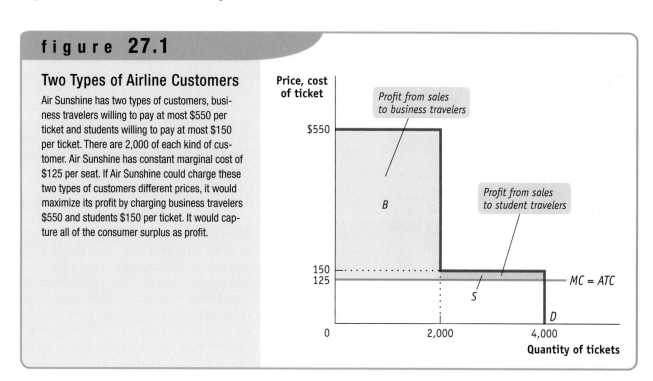

figure 27.1

Two Types of Airline Customers

Air Sunshine has two types of customers, business travelers willing to pay at most $550 per ticket and students willing to pay at most $150 per ticket. There are 2,000 of each kind of customer. Air Sunshine has constant marginal cost of $125 per seat. If Air Sunshine could charge these two types of customers different prices, it would maximize its profit by charging business travelers $550 and students $150 per ticket. It would capture all of the consumer surplus as profit.

So what should the airline do? If it has to charge everyone the same price, its options are limited. It could charge $550; that way it would get as much as possible out of the business travelers but lose the student market. Or it could charge only $150; that way it would get both types of travelers but would make significantly less money from sales to business travelers.

We can quickly calculate the profits from each of these alternatives. If the airline charged $550, it would sell 2,000 tickets to the business travelers, earning a total revenue of 2,000 × $550 = $1.1 million and incurring costs of 2,000 × $125 = $250,000; so its profit would be $850,000, illustrated by the shaded area B in Figure 27.1. If the airline charged only $150, it would sell 4,000 tickets, receiving revenue of 4,000 × $150 = $600,000 and incurring costs of 4,000 × $125 = $500,000; so its profit would be $100,000. If the airline must charge everyone the same price, charging the higher price and forgoing sales to students is clearly more profitable.

What the airline would really like to do, however, is charge the business travelers the full $550 but offer $150 tickets to the students. That's a lot less than the price paid by business travelers, but it's still above marginal cost; so if the airline could sell those extra 2,000 tickets to students, it would make an additional $50,000 in profit. That is, it would make a profit equal to the areas B plus S in Figure 27.1.

It would be more realistic to suppose that there is some "give" in the demand of each group: at a price below $550, there would be some increase in business travel; and at a price above $150, some students would still purchase tickets. But this, it turns out, does not do away with the argument for price discrimination. The important point is that the two groups of consumers differ in their *sensitivity to price*—that a high price has a larger effect in discouraging purchases by students than by business travelers. As long as different groups of customers respond differently to the price, a monopolist will find that it can capture more consumer surplus and increase its profit by charging them different prices.

Price Discrimination and Elasticity

A more realistic description of the demand that airlines face would not specify particular prices at which different types of travelers would choose to fly. Instead, it would distinguish between the groups on the basis of their sensitivity to the price—their price elasticity of demand.

Suppose that a company sells its product to two easily identifiable groups of people—business travelers and students. It just so happens that business travelers are very insensitive to the price: there is a certain amount of the product they just have to have whatever the price, but they cannot be persuaded to buy much more than that no mat-

On many airline routes, the fare you pay depends on the type of traveler you are.

ter how cheap it is. Students, though, are more flexible: offer a good enough price and they will buy quite a lot, but raise the price too high and they will switch to something else. Which approach is best for the company in this case?

The answer is the one already suggested by our simplified example: the company should charge business travelers, with their low price elasticity of demand, a higher price than it charges students, with their high price elasticity of demand.

The actual situation of the airlines is very much like this hypothetical example. Business travelers typically place a high priority on being in the right place at the right time and are not very sensitive to the price. But leisure travelers are fairly sensitive to the price: faced with a high price, they might take the bus, drive to another airport to get a lower fare, or skip the trip altogether.

So why doesn't an airline simply announce different prices for business and leisure customers? First, this would probably be illegal. (U.S. law places some limits on the ability of companies to practice blatant price discrimination.) Second, even if it were legal, it would be a hard policy to enforce: business travelers might be willing to wear casual clothing and claim they were visiting family in Ft. Lauderdale in order to save $400.

So what the airlines do—quite successfully—is impose rules that indirectly have the effect of charging business and leisure travelers different fares. Business travelers usually travel during the week and want to be home on the weekend, so the round-trip fare is much higher if you don't stay over a Saturday night. The requirement of a weekend stay for a cheap ticket effectively separates business travelers from leisure travelers. Similarly, business travelers often visit several cities in succession rather than make a simple round trip; so round-trip fares are much lower than twice the one-way fare. Many business trips are scheduled on short notice, so fares are much lower if you book far in advance. Fares are also lower if you travel standby, taking your chances on whether you actually get a seat—business travelers have to make it to that meeting; people visiting their relatives don't. And because customers must show their ID at check-in, airlines make sure there are no resales of tickets between the two groups that would undermine their ability to price-discriminate—students can't buy cheap tickets and resell them to business travelers. Look at the rules that govern ticket pricing, and you will see an ingenious implementation of profit-maximizing price discrimination.

Perfect Price Discrimination

Let's return to the example of business travelers and students traveling between Bismarck and Ft. Lauderdale, illustrated in Figure 27.1, and ask what would happen if the airline could distinguish between the two groups of customers in order to charge each a different price.

Clearly, the airline would charge each group its *willingness to pay*—that is, the maximum that each group is willing to pay. For business travelers, the willingness to pay is $550; for students, it is $150. As we have assumed, the marginal cost is $125 and does not depend on output, making the marginal cost curve a horizontal line. And as we noted earlier, we can easily determine the airline's profit: it is the sum of the areas of rectangle *B* and rectangle *S*.

In this case, the consumers do not get any consumer surplus! The entire surplus is captured by the monopolist in the form of profit. When a monopolist is able to capture the entire surplus in this way, we say that the monopolist achieves **perfect price discrimination.**

In general, the greater the number of different prices charged, the closer the monopolist is to perfect price discrimination. Figure 27.2 on the next page shows a monopolist facing a downward-sloping demand curve, a monopolist who we assume is able to charge different prices to different groups of consumers, with the consumers who are willing to pay the most being charged the most. In panel (a) the monopolist charges two different prices; in panel (b) the monopolist charges three different prices. Two things are apparent:

- The greater the number of prices the monopolist charges, the lower the lowest price—that is, some consumers will pay prices that approach marginal cost.
- The greater the number of prices the monopolist charges, the more money extracted from consumers.

With a very large number of different prices, the picture would look like panel (c), a case of perfect price discrimination. Here, every consumer pays the most he or she is willing to pay, and the entire consumer surplus is extracted as profit.

Both our airline example and the example in Figure 27.2 can be used to make another point: a monopolist who can engage in perfect price discrimination doesn't cause any inefficiency! The reason is that the source of inefficiency is eliminated: all potential consumers who are willing to purchase the good at a price equal to or above marginal cost are able to do so. The perfectly price-discriminating monopolist manages to "scoop up" all consumers by offering some of them lower prices than others.

Perfect price discrimination is almost never possible in practice. At a fundamental level, the inability to achieve perfect price discrimination is a problem of prices as economic signals. When prices work as economic signals, they convey the information needed to ensure that all mutually beneficial transactions will indeed occur: the market price signals the seller's cost, and a consumer signals willingness to pay by purchasing the good whenever that willingness to pay is at least as high as the market price. The problem in reality, however, is that prices are often not perfect signals: a consumer's true willingness to pay can be disguised, as by a business traveler who claims to be a student when buying a ticket in order to obtain a lower fare. When such disguises work, a monopolist cannot achieve perfect price discrimination. However, monopolists do try to move in the direction of perfect price discrimination through a variety of pricing strategies. Common techniques for price discrimination include the following:

- *Advance purchase restrictions.* Prices are lower for those who purchase well in advance (or in some cases for those who purchase at the last minute). This separates those who are likely to shop for better prices from those who won't.
- *Volume discounts.* Often the price is lower if you buy a large quantity. For a consumer who plans to consume a lot of a good, the cost of the last unit—the marginal cost to the consumer—is considerably less than the average price. This separates those who plan to buy a lot, and so are likely to be more sensitive to price, from those who don't.

Perfect price discrimination takes place when a monopolist charges each consumer his or her willingness to pay—the maximum that the consumer is willing to pay.

figure **27.2**   Price Discrimination

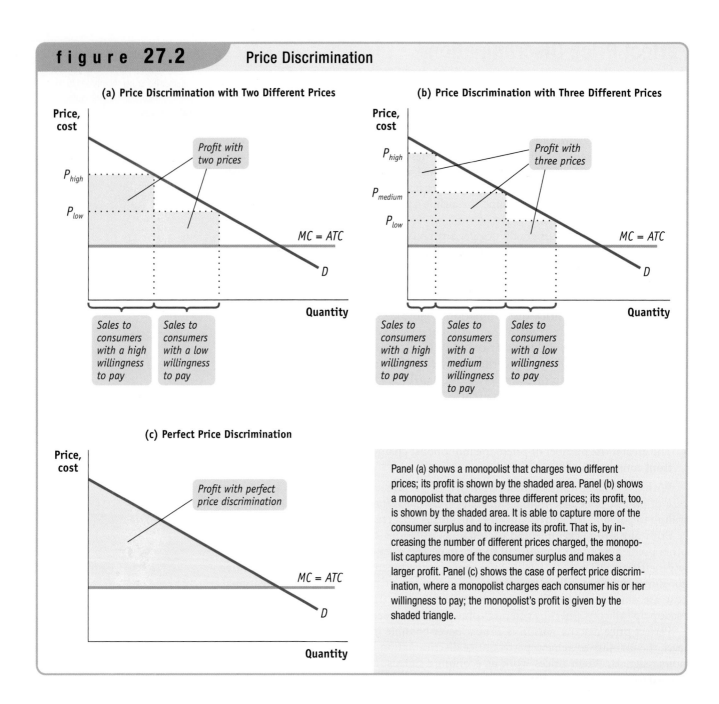

(a) Price Discrimination with Two Different Prices

Price, cost

P_{high}

P_{low}

Profit with two prices

MC = ATC

D

Quantity

Sales to consumers with a high willingness to pay

Sales to consumers with a low willingness to pay

(b) Price Discrimination with Three Different Prices

Price, cost

P_{high}

P_{medium}

P_{low}

Profit with three prices

MC = ATC

D

Quantity

Sales to consumers with a high willingness to pay

Sales to consumers with a medium willingness to pay

Sales to consumers with a low willingness to pay

(c) Perfect Price Discrimination

Price, cost

Profit with perfect price discrimination

MC = ATC

D

Quantity

Panel (a) shows a monopolist that charges two different prices; its profit is shown by the shaded area. Panel (b) shows a monopolist that charges three different prices; its profit, too, is shown by the shaded area. It is able to capture more of the consumer surplus and to increase its profit. That is, by increasing the number of different prices charged, the monopolist captures more of the consumer surplus and makes a larger profit. Panel (c) shows the case of perfect price discrimination, where a monopolist charges each consumer his or her willingness to pay; the monopolist's profit is given by the shaded triangle.

■ *Two-part tariffs.* In a discount club like Costco or Sam's Club (which are not monopolists but monopolistic competitors), you pay an annual fee (the first part of the tariff) in addition to the price of the item(s) you purchase (the second part of the tariff). So the full price of the first item you buy is in effect much higher than that of subsequent items, making the two-part tariff behave like a volume discount.

Our discussion also helps explain why government policies on monopoly typically focus on preventing deadweight loss, not preventing price discrimination—unless it causes serious issues of equity. Compared to a single-price monopolist, price discrimination—even when it is not perfect—can increase the efficiency of the market. When a single, medium-level price is replaced by a high price and a low price, some consumers who were formerly priced out of the market will be able to purchase the good. The price discrimination increases efficiency because more of the units for which the willingness to pay (as indicated by the height of the demand curve) exceeds the marginal cost are produced and sold. Consider a drug that is disproportionately prescribed to senior citizens, who are often on fixed incomes and so are very sensitive to price. A policy that allows a drug company to charge senior citizens a low price and everyone else a high price will serve more consumers and create more total surplus than a situation in which everyone is charged the same price. But price discrimination that creates serious concerns about equity is likely to be prohibited—for example, an ambulance service that charges patients based on the severity of their emergency.

Module 27 Review

Solutions appear at the back of the book.

Check Your Understanding

1. True or false? Explain your answer.
   a. A single-price monopolist sells to some customers that would not find the product affordable if purchasing from a price-discriminating monopolist.
   b. A price-discriminating monopolist creates more inefficiency than a single-price monopolist because it captures more of the consumer surplus.
   c. Under price discrimination, a customer with highly elastic demand will pay a lower price than a customer with inelastic demand.

2. Which of the following are cases of price discrimination and which are not? In the cases of price discrimination, identify the consumers with high price elasticity of demand and those with low price elasticity of demand.
   a. Damaged merchandise is marked down.
   b. Restaurants have senior citizen discounts.
   c. Food manufacturers place discount coupons for their merchandise in newspapers.
   d. Airline tickets cost more during the summer peak flying season.

Multiple-Choice Questions

1. Which of the following characteristics is necessary in order for a firm to price-discriminate?
   a. free entry and exit
   b. differentiated product
   c. many sellers
   d. some control over price
   e. horizontal demand curve

2. Price discrimination
   a. is the opposite of volume discounts.
   b. is a practice limited to movie theaters and the airline industry.
   c. can lead to increased efficiency in the market.
   d. rarely occurs in the real world.
   e. helps to increase the profits of perfect competitors.

3. With perfect price discrimination, consumer surplus
   a. is maximized.
   b. equals zero.
   c. is increased.
   d. cannot be determined.
   e. is the area below the demand curve above MC.

4. Which of the following is a technique used by price discriminating monopolists?
   I. advance purchase restrictions
   II. two-part tariffs
   III. volume discounts
   a. I only
   b. II only
   c. III only
   d. I and II only
   e. I, II, and III

5. A price discriminating monopolist will charge a higher price to consumers with
   a. a more inelastic demand.
   b. a less inelastic demand.
   c. higher income.
   d. lower willingness to pay.
   e. less experience in the market.

Critical-Thinking Question

Draw a correctly labeled graph showing a monopoly practicing perfect price discrimination. On your graph, identify the monopoly's profit. What does consumer surplus equal in this case? Explain.

Summary

Introduction to Perfect Competition

1. A producer chooses output according to the **price-taking firm's optimal output rule:** produce the quantity at which price equals marginal cost. However, a firm that produces the optimal quantity may not be profitable.

Graphing Perfect Competition

2. A firm is profitable if total revenue exceeds total cost or, equivalently, if the market price exceeds its **break-even price**—minimum average total cost. If market price exceeds the break-even price, the firm is profitable. If market price is less than minimum average total cost, the firm is unprofitable. If market price is equal to minimum average total cost, the firm breaks even. When profitable, the firm's per-unit profit is $P - ATC$; when unprofitable, its per-unit loss is $ATC - P$.

3. Fixed cost is irrelevant to the firm's optimal short-run production decision. The short-run production decision depends on the firm's **shut-down price**—its minimum average variable cost—and the market price. When the market price is equal to or exceeds the shut-down price, the firm produces the output quantity at which marginal cost equals the market price. When the market

price falls below the shut-down price, the firm ceases production in the short run. This generates the firm's **short-run individual supply curve.**

4. Fixed cost matters over time. If the market price is below minimum average total cost for an extended period of time, firms will exit the industry in the long run. If market price is above minimum average total cost, existing firms are profitable and new firms will enter the industry in the long run.

Long-Run Outcomes in Perfect Competition

5. The **industry supply curve** depends on the time period (short run or long run). When the number of firms is fixed, the **short-run industry supply curve** applies. The **short-run market equilibrium** occurs where the short-run industry supply curve and the demand curve intersect.

6. With sufficient time for entry into and exit from an industry, the **long-run industry supply curve** applies. The **long-run market equilibrium** occurs at the intersection of the long-run industry supply curve and the demand curve. At this point, no producer has an incentive to enter or exit. The long-run industry supply curve is often horizontal. It may slope upward if there is

limited supply of an input, resulting in increasing costs across the industry. It may even slope downward, as in the case of decreasing costs across the industry. But the long-run industry supply curve is always more elastic than the short-run industry supply curve.

7. In the long-run market equilibrium of a competitive industry, profit maximization leads each firm to produce at the same marginal cost, which is equal to the market price. Free entry and exit means that each firm earns zero economic profit—producing the output corresponding to its minimum average total cost. So the total cost of production of an industry's output is minimized. The outcome is efficient because every consumer with willingness to pay greater than or equal to marginal cost gets the good.

Introduction to Monopoly

8. The key difference between a monopoly and a perfectly competitive industry is that a single, perfectly competitive firm faces a horizontal demand curve but a monopolist faces a downward-sloping demand curve. This gives the monopolist market power, the ability to raise the market price by reducing output.

9. The marginal revenue of a monopolist is composed of a quantity effect (the price received from the additional unit) and a price effect (the reduction in the price at which all units are sold). Because of the price effect, a monopolist's marginal revenue is always less than the market price, and the marginal revenue curve lies below the demand curve.

10. At the monopolist's profit-maximizing output level, marginal cost equals marginal revenue, which is less than market price. At the perfectly competitive firm's profit-maximizing output level, marginal cost equals the market price. So in comparison to perfectly competitive industries, monopolies produce less, charge higher prices, and can earn profits in both the short run and the long run.

Monopoly and Public Policy

11. A monopoly creates deadweight losses by charging a price above marginal cost: the loss in consumer surplus exceeds the monopolist's profit. This makes monopolies a source of market failure and governments often make policies to prevent or end them.

12. Natural monopolies also cause deadweight losses. To limit these losses, governments sometimes impose **public ownership** and at other times impose **price regulation.** A price ceiling on a monopolist, as opposed to a perfectly competitive industry, need not cause shortages and can increase total surplus.

Price Discrimination

13. Not all monopolists are **single-price monopolists.** Monopolists, as well as oligopolists and monopolistic competitors, often engage in **price discrimination** to make higher profits, using various techniques to differentiate consumers based on their sensitivity to price and charging those with less elastic demand higher prices. A monopolist that achieves **perfect price discrimination** charges each consumer a price equal to his or her willingness to pay and captures the total surplus in the market. Although perfect price discrimination creates no inefficiency, it is practically impossible to implement.

Key Terms

Price-taking firm's optimal output rule, p. 229
Break-even price, p. 236
Shut-down price, p. 237
Short-run individual supply curve, p. 238
Industry supply curve, p. 243

Short-run industry supply curve, p. 244
Short-run market equilibrium, p. 245
Long-run market equilibrium, p. 246
Long-run industry supply curve, p. 247
Public ownership, p. 263

Price regulation, p. 263
Single-price monopolist, p. 268
Price discrimination, p. 268
Perfect price discrimination, p. 271

Problems

1. For each of the following, is the industry perfectly competitive? Referring to market share, standardization of the product, and/or free entry and exit, explain your answers.

   a. aspirin

   b. Alicia Keys concerts

   c. SUVs

2. Kate's Katering provides catered meals, and the catered meals industry is perfectly competitive. Kate's machinery costs $100 per day and is the only fixed input. Her variable cost consists of the wages paid to the cooks and the food ingredients. The variable cost per day associated with each level of output is given in the accompanying table.

Quantity of meals	VC
0	$0
10	200
20	300
30	480
40	700
50	1,000

   a. Calculate the total cost, the average variable cost, the average total cost, and the marginal cost for each quantity of output.

   b. What is the break-even price? What is the shut-down price?

   c. Suppose that the price at which Kate can sell catered meals is $21 per meal. In the short run, will Kate earn a profit? In the short run, should she produce or shut down?

   d. Suppose that the price at which Kate can sell catered meals is $17 per meal. In the short run, will Kate earn a profit? In the short run, should she produce or shut down?

   e. Suppose that the price at which Kate can sell catered meals is $13 per meal. In the short run, will Kate earn a profit? In the short run, should she produce or shut down?

3. Bob produces DVD movies for sale, which requires a building and a machine that copies the original movie onto a DVD. Bob rents a building for $30,000 per month and rents a machine for $20,000 a month. Those are his fixed costs. His variable costs per month are given in the accompanying table.

Quantity of DVDs	VC
0	$0
1,000	5,000
2,000	8,000
3,000	9,000
4,000	14,000
5,000	20,000
6,000	33,000
7,000	49,000
8,000	72,000
9,000	99,000
10,000	150,000

   a. Calculate Bob's average variable cost, average total cost, and marginal cost for each quantity of output.

   b. There is free entry into the industry, and anyone who enters will face the same costs as Bob. Suppose that currently the price of a DVD is $25. What will Bob's profit be? Is this a long-run equilibrium? If not, what will the price of DVD movies be in the long run?

4. Consider Bob's DVD company described in Problem 3. Assume that DVD production is a perfectly competitive industry. For each of the following questions, explain your answers.

   a. What is Bob's break-even price? What is his shut-down price?

   b. Suppose the price of a DVD is $2. What should Bob do in the short run?

   c. Suppose the price of a DVD is $7. What is the profit-maximizing quantity of DVDs that Bob should produce? What will his total profit be? Will he produce or shut down in the short run? Will he stay in the industry or exit in the long run?

   d. Suppose instead that the price of DVDs is $20. Now what is the profit-maximizing quantity of DVDs that Bob should produce? What will his total profit be now? Will he produce or shut down in the short run? Will he stay in the industry or exit in the long run?

5. Consider again Bob's DVD company described in Problem 3.

   a. Draw Bob's marginal cost curve.

   b. Over what range of prices will Bob produce no DVDs in the short run?

   c. Draw Bob's individual supply curve.

6. **a.** A profit-maximizing business incurs an economic loss of $10,000 per year. Its fixed cost is $15,000 per year. Should it produce or shut down in the short run? Should it stay in the industry or exit in the long run?

   b. Suppose instead that this business has a fixed cost of $6,000 per year. Should it produce or shut down in the short run? Should it stay in the industry or exit in the long run?

7. The first sushi restaurant opens in town. Initially, people are very cautious about eating tiny portions of raw fish, as this is a town where large portions of grilled meat have always been popular. Soon, however, an influential health report warns consumers against grilled meat and suggests that they increase their consumption of fish, especially raw fish. The sushi restaurant becomes very popular and its profit increases.

   a. What will happen to the short-run profit of the sushi restaurant? What will happen to the number of sushi restaurants in town in the long run? Will the first sushi restaurant be able to sustain its short-run profit over the long run? Explain your answers.

   b. Local steakhouses suffer from the popularity of sushi and start incurring losses. What will happen to the number of steakhouses in town in the long run? Explain your answer.

8. A perfectly competitive firm has the following short-run total costs:

Quantity	TC
0	$5
1	10
2	13
3	18
4	25
5	34
6	45

Market demand for the firm's product is given by the following market demand schedule:

Price	Quantity demanded
$12	300
10	500
8	800
6	1,200
4	1,800

a. Calculate this firm's marginal cost and, for all output levels except zero, the firm's average variable cost and average total cost.

b. There are 100 firms in this industry that all have costs identical to those of this firm. Draw the short-run industry supply curve. In the same diagram, draw the market demand curve.

c. What is the market price, and how much profit will each firm make?

9. A new vaccine against a deadly disease has just been discovered. Presently, 55 people die from the disease each year. The new vaccine will save lives, but it is not completely safe. Some recipients of the shots will die from adverse reactions. The projected effects of the inoculation are given in the accompanying table:

Percent of population inoculated	Total deaths due to disease	Total deaths due to inoculation	Marginal benefit of inoculation	Marginal cost of inoculation	"Profit" of inoculation
0	55	0	—	—	—
10	45	0	—	—	—
20	36	1	—	—	—
30	28	3	—	—	—
40	21	6	—	—	—
50	15	10	—	—	—
60	10	15	—	—	—
70	6	20	—	—	—
80	3	25	—	—	—
90	1	30	—	—	—
100	0	35	—	—	—

a. What are the interpretations of "marginal benefit" and "marginal cost" here? Calculate marginal benefit and marginal cost per each 10% increase in the rate of inoculation. Write your answers in the table.

b. What proportion of the population should optimally be inoculated?

c. What is the interpretation of "profit" here? Calculate the profit for all levels of inoculation.

10. The production of agricultural products like wheat is one of the few examples of a perfectly competitive industry. In this question, we analyze results from a study released by the U.S. Department of Agriculture about wheat production in the United States in 1998 and make some comparisons to wheat production in 2010.

    a. The average variable cost per acre planted with wheat was $107 per acre. Assuming a yield of 50 bushels per acre, calculate the average variable cost per bushel of wheat.

b. The average price of wheat received by a farmer in 1998 was $2.65 per bushel. Do you think the average farm would have exited the industry in the short run? Explain.

c. With a yield of 50 bushels of wheat per acre, the average total cost per farm was $3.80 per bushel. The harvested acreage for rye (a type of wheat) in the United States fell from 418,000 acres in 1998 to 250,000 in 2010. Using the information on prices and costs here and in parts a and b, explain why this might have happened.

d. Using the above information, do you think the prices of wheat were higher or lower prior to 1998? Why?

11. Skyscraper City has a subway system for which a one-way fare is $1.50. There is pressure on the mayor to reduce the fare by one-third, to $1.00. The mayor is dismayed, thinking that this will mean Skyscraper City is losing one-third of its revenue from sales of subway tickets. The mayor's economic adviser reminds her that she is focusing only on the price effect and ignoring the quantity effect. Explain why the mayor's estimate of a one-third loss of revenue is likely to be an overestimate. Illustrate with a diagram.

12. Consider an industry with the demand curve (*D*) and marginal cost curve (*MC*) shown in the accompanying diagram. There is no fixed cost. If the industry is a single-price monopoly, the monopolist's marginal revenue curve would be *MR*. Answer the following questions by naming the appropriate points or areas.

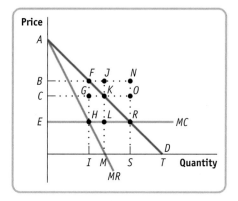

a. If the industry is perfectly competitive, what will be the total quantity produced? At what price?

b. Which area reflects consumer surplus under perfect competition?

c. If the industry is a single-price monopoly, what quantity will the monopolist produce? Which price will it charge?

d. Which area reflects the single-price monopolist's profit?

e. Which area reflects consumer surplus under single-price monopoly?

f. Which area reflects the deadweight loss to society from single-price monopoly?

g. If the monopolist can price-discriminate perfectly, what quantity will the perfectly price-discriminating monopolist produce?

13. Bob, Bill, Ben, and Brad Baxter have just made a documentary movie about their basketball team. They are thinking about making the movie available for download on the Internet, and they can act as a single-price monopolist if they choose to. Each time the movie is downloaded, their Internet service provider charges them a fee of $4. The Baxter brothers are arguing about which price to charge customers per download. The accompanying table shows the demand schedule for their film.

Price of download	Quantity of downloads demanded
$10	0
8	1
6	3
4	6
2	10
0	15

a. Calculate the total revenue and the marginal revenue per download.

b. Bob is proud of the film and wants as many people as possible to download it. Which price would he choose? How many downloads would be sold?

c. Bill wants as much total revenue as possible. Which price would he choose? How many downloads would be sold?

d. Ben wants to maximize profit. Which price would he choose? How many downloads would be sold?

e. Brad wants to charge the efficient price. Which price would he choose? How many downloads would be sold?

14. Suppose that De Beers is a single-price monopolist in the market for diamonds. De Beers has five potential customers: Raquel, Jackie, Joan, Mia, and Sophia. Each of these customers will buy at most one diamond—and only if the price is just equal to, or lower than, her willingness to pay. Raquel's willingness to pay is $400; Jackie's, $300; Joan's, $200; Mia's, $100; and Sophia's, $0. De Beers's marginal cost per diamond is $100. This leads to the demand schedule for diamonds shown in the accompanying table.

Price of diamond	Quantity of diamonds demanded
$500	0
400	1
300	2
200	3
100	4
0	5

a. Calculate De Beers's total revenue and its marginal revenue. From your calculation, draw the demand curve and the marginal revenue curve.

b. Explain why De Beers faces a downward-sloping demand curve.

c. Explain why the marginal revenue from an additional diamond sale is less than the price of the diamond.

d. Suppose De Beers currently charges $200 for its diamonds. If it lowers the price to $100, how large is the price effect? How large is the quantity effect?

e. Add the marginal cost curve to your diagram from part a, and determine which quantity maximizes the company's profit and which price De Beers will charge.

15. Use the demand schedule for diamonds given in Problem 14. The marginal cost of producing diamonds is constant at $100. There is no fixed cost.

a. If De Beers charges the monopoly price, how large is the individual consumer surplus that each buyer experiences? Calculate total consumer surplus by summing the individual consumer surpluses. How large is producer surplus?

Suppose that upstart Russian and Asian producers enter the market and the market becomes perfectly competitive.

b. What is the perfectly competitive price? What quantity will be sold in this perfectly competitive market?

c. At the competitive price and quantity, how large is the consumer surplus that each buyer experiences? How large is total consumer surplus? How large is producer surplus?

d. Compare your answer to part c to your answer to part a. How large is the deadweight loss associated with monopoly in this case?

16. Use the demand schedule for diamonds given in Problem 14. De Beers is a monopolist, but it can now price-discriminate perfectly among all five of its potential customers. De Beers's marginal cost is constant at $100. There is no fixed cost.

a. If De Beers can price-discriminate perfectly, to which customers will it sell diamonds and at what prices?

b. How large is each individual consumer surplus? How large is total consumer surplus? Calculate producer surplus by summing the producer surplus generated by each sale.

17. Download Records decides to release an album by the group Mary and the Little Lamb. It produces the album with no fixed cost, but the total cost of downloading an album to a CD and paying Mary her royalty is $6 per album. Download Records can act as a single-price monopolist. Its marketing division finds that the demand schedule for the album is as shown in the accompanying table.

Price of album	Quantity of albums demanded
$22	0
20	1,000
18	2,000
16	3,000
14	4,000
12	5,000
10	6,000
8	7,000

a. Calculate the total revenue and the marginal revenue per album.

b. The marginal cost of producing each album is constant at $6. To maximize profit, what level of output should Download Records choose, and which price should it charge for each album?

c. Mary renegotiates her contract and now needs to be paid a higher royalty per album. So the marginal cost rises to be constant at $14. To maximize profit, what level of output should Download Records now choose, and which price should it charge for each album?

18. The accompanying diagram illustrates your local electricity company's natural monopoly. The diagram shows the demand curve for kilowatt-hours (kWh) of electricity, the company's marginal revenue (MR) curve, its marginal cost (MC) curve, and its average total cost (ATC) curve. The government wants to regulate the monopolist by imposing a price ceiling.

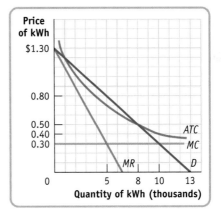

a. If the government does not regulate this monopolist, which price will it charge? Illustrate the inefficiency this creates by shading the deadweight loss from monopoly.

b. If the government imposes a price ceiling equal to the marginal cost, $0.30, will the monopolist make a profit or lose money? Shade the area of profit (or loss) for the monopolist. If the government does impose this price ceiling, do you think the firm will continue to produce in the long run?

c. If the government imposes a price ceiling of $0.50, will the monopolist make a profit, lose money, or break even?

19. The movie theater in Collegetown serves two kinds of customers: students and professors. There are 900 students and 100 professors in Collegetown. Each student's willingness to pay for a movie ticket is $5. Each professor's willingness to pay for a movie ticket is $10. Each will buy at most one ticket. The movie theater's marginal cost per ticket is constant at $3, and there is no fixed cost.

a. Suppose the movie theater cannot price-discriminate and needs to charge both students and professors the same price per ticket. If the movie theater charges $5, who will buy tickets and what will the movie theater's profit be? How large is consumer surplus?

b. If the movie theater charges $10, who will buy movie tickets and what will the movie theater's profit be? How large is consumer surplus?

c. Now suppose that, if it chooses to, the movie theater can price-discriminate between students and professors by requiring students to show their student ID. If the movie theater charges students $5 and professors $10, how much profit will the movie theater make? How large is consumer surplus?

20. A monopolist knows that in order to expand the quantity of output it produces from 8 to 9 units, it must lower the price of its output from $2 to $1. Calculate the quantity effect and the price effect. Use these results to calculate the monopolist's marginal revenue of producing the 9th unit. The marginal cost of producing the 9th unit is positive. Is it a good idea for the monopolist to produce the 9th unit?

section 6

Market Structures: Imperfect Competition

The agricultural products company Archer Daniels Midland (also known as ADM) has often described itself as "supermarket to the world." In 1993, executives from ADM and its Japanese competitor Ajinomoto met to discuss the market for lysine, an additive used in animal feed. In this and subsequent meetings, the two companies joined with several other producers to set targets for the price of lysine, behavior known as *price-fixing*. Each company agreed to limit its production to achieve the price targets, with the goal of raising industry profits. But what the companies were doing was illegal, and the FBI had bugged the meeting room with a camera hidden in a lamp. Over the past few years, there have been numerous investigations and some convictions for price-fixing in a variety of industries, from insurance to college education to computer chips. Despite its illegality, some firms continue to attempt to fix the price of their products.

In the fast food market, it is the legal practice of *product differentiation* that occupies the minds of marketing executives. Fast-food producers go to great lengths to convince

you they have something special to offer beyond the ordinary burger: it's flame broiled or 100% beef or super-thick or lathered with special sauce. Or maybe they offer chicken or fish or roast beef. And the differentiation dance goes on in the pizza industry as well. Pizza Hut offers cheese in the crust. Papa John's claims "better ingredients." Dominoes has a "new recipe," and if you don't want thin crust, the alternative isn't "regular," it's "hand tossed"! The slogans and logos for fast-food restaurants often seem to differ more than the food itself.

To understand why ADM engaged in illegal price-fixing and why fast-food joints go to great lengths to differentiate their patties and pizzas, we need to understand the two market structures in between perfect competition and monopoly in the spectrum of market power—oligopoly and monopolistic competition. The models of these two market structures are at the same time more complicated and more realistic than those we studied in the previous section. Indeed, they describe the behavior of most of the firms in the real world.

What you will learn
in this **Module:**

- Why oligopolists have an
  incentive to act in ways that
  reduce their combined profit
- Why oligopolies can benefit
  from collusion

Module 28
Introduction to
Oligopoly

Earlier we learned that an oligopoly is an industry with only a few sellers. But what number constitutes a "few"? There is no universal answer, and it is not always easy to determine an industry's market structure just by looking at the number of sellers. Economists use various measures to gain a better picture of market structure, including *concentration ratios* and the *Herfindahl-Hirschman Index,* as explained in Module 21.

In addition to having a small number of sellers in the industry, an oligopoly is characterized by **interdependence,** a relationship in which the outcome (profit) of each firm depends on the actions of the other firms in the market. This is not true for monopolies because, by definition, they have no other firms to consider. On the other hand, competitive markets contain so many firms that no one firm has a significant effect on the outcome of the others. However, in an oligopoly, an industry with few sellers, the outcome for each seller depends on the behavior of the others. Interdependence makes studying a market much more interesting because firms must observe and predict the behavior of other firms. But it is also more complicated. To understand the strategies of oligopolists, we must do more than find the point where the *MC* and *MR* curves intersect!

Understanding Oligopoly

How much will a firm produce? Up to this point, we have always answered: the quantity that maximizes its profit. When a firm is a perfect competitor or a monopolist, we can assume that the firm will use its cost curves to determine its profit-maximizing output. When it comes to oligopoly, however, we run into some difficulties.

A Duopoly Example

Let's begin looking at the puzzle of oligopoly with the simplest version, an industry in which there are only two firms—a **duopoly**—and each is known as a **duopolist.**

Firms are **interdependent** when the outcome (profit) of each firm depends on the actions of the other firms in the market.

An oligopoly consisting of only two firms is a **duopoly.** Each firm is known as a **duopolist.**

Imagine that there are only two producers of lysine (the animal feed additive mentioned in the section opener). To make things even simpler, suppose that once a company has incurred the fixed cost needed to produce lysine, the marginal cost of producing another pound is zero. So the companies are concerned only with the revenue they receive from sales.

Table 28.1 shows a hypothetical demand schedule for lysine and the total revenue of the industry at each price–quantity combination.

Sellers engage in **collusion** when they cooperate to raise their joint profits. A **cartel** is a group of producers that agree to restrict output in order to increase prices and their joint profits.

table **28.1**

Demand Schedule for Lysine

Price of lysine (per pound)	Quantity of lysine demanded (millions of pounds)	Total revenue (millions)
$12	0	$0
11	10	110
10	20	200
9	30	270
8	40	320
7	50	350
6	60	360
5	70	350
4	80	320
3	90	270
2	100	200
1	110	110
0	120	0

If this were a perfectly competitive industry, each firm would have an incentive to produce more as long as the market price was above marginal cost. Since the marginal cost is assumed to be zero, this would mean that at equilibrium, lysine would be provided for free. Firms would produce until price equals zero, yielding a total output of 120 million pounds and zero revenue for both firms.

However, with only two firms in the industry, it would seem foolish to allow price and revenue to plummet to zero. Each would realize that with more production comes a lower market price. So each firm would, like a monopolist, see that profits would be higher if it and its rival limited their production.

So how much will the two firms produce?

One possibility is that the two companies will engage in **collusion**— they will cooperate to raise their joint profits. The strongest form of collusion is a **cartel,** a group of producers with an agreement to work together to limit output and increase price, and therefore profit. The world's most famous cartel is the Organization of Petroleum Exporting Countries (OPEC).

As its name indicates, OPEC is actually a cartel made up of governments rather than firms. There's a reason for this: cartels among firms are illegal in the United States and many other jurisdictions. But let's ignore the law for a moment. Suppose the firms producing lysine were to form a cartel and that this cartel decided to act

AP Photo/Hans Punz

OPEC representatives discuss the cartel's policies of cooperation.

as if it were a monopolist, maximizing total industry profits. It's obvious from Table 28.1 that in order to maximize the combined profits of the firms, this cartel should set total industry output at 60 million pounds of lysine, which would sell at a price of $6 per pound, leading to revenue of $360 million, the maximum possible. Then the only question would be how much of that 60 million pounds each firm gets to produce. A "fair" solution might be for each firm to produce 30 million pounds and receive revenues of $180 million.

But even if the two firms agreed on such a deal, they might have a problem: each of the firms would have an incentive to break its word and produce more than the agreed-upon quantity.

Collusion and Competition

Suppose that the presidents of the two lysine producers were to agree that each would produce 30 million pounds of lysine over the next year. Both would understand that this plan maximizes their combined profits. And both would have an incentive to cheat.

To see why, consider what would happen if one firm honored its agreement, producing only 30 million pounds, but the other ignored its promise and produced 40 million pounds. This increase in total output would drive the price down from $6 to $5 per pound, the price at which 70 million pounds are demanded. The industry's total revenue would fall from $360 million ($6 × 60 million pounds) to $350 million ($5 × 70 million pounds). However, the cheating firm's revenue would *rise*, from $180 million to $200 million. Since we are assuming a marginal cost of zero, this would mean a $20 million increase in profits.

But both firms' presidents might make exactly the same calculation. And if *both* firms were to produce 40 million pounds of lysine, the price would drop to $4 per pound. So each firm's profits would fall, from $180 million to $160 million.

The incentive to cheat motivates the firms to produce more than the quantity that maximizes their joint profits rather than limiting output as a true monopolist would. We know that a profit-maximizing monopolist sets marginal cost (which in this case is zero) equal to marginal revenue. But what is marginal revenue? Recall that producing an additional unit of a good has two effects:

1. A positive *quantity* effect: one more unit is sold, increasing total revenue by the price at which that unit is sold.

2. A negative *price* effect: in order to sell one more unit, the monopolist must cut the market price on *all* units sold.

The negative price effect is the reason marginal revenue for a monopolist is less than the market price. But when considering the effect of increasing production, a firm is concerned only with the price effect on its *own* units of output, not on those of its fellow oligopolists. In the lysine example, both duopolists suffer a negative price effect if one firm decides to produce extra lysine and so drives down the price. But each firm cares only about the portion of the negative price effect that falls on the lysine it produces.

This tells us that an individual firm in an oligopolistic industry faces a smaller price effect from an additional unit of output than a monopolist; therefore, the marginal revenue that such a firm calculates is higher. So it will seem to be profitable for any one firm in an oligopoly to increase production, even if that increase reduces the profits of the industry as a whole. But if everyone thinks that way, the result is that everyone earns a lower profit!

Until now, we have been able to analyze producer behavior by asking what a producer should do to maximize profits. But even if the duopolists are both trying to maximize profits, what does this predict about their behavior? Will they engage in collusion, reaching and holding to an agreement that maximizes their combined profits? Or will they engage in **noncooperative behavior,** with each firm acting in its own self-interest, even though this has the effect of driving down everyone's profits? Both strategies can be carried out with a goal of profit maximization. Which will actually describe their behavior?

When firms ignore the effects of their actions on each other's profits, they engage in **noncooperative behavior.**

Now you see why oligopoly presents a puzzle: there are only a small number of players, making collusion a real possibility. If there were dozens or hundreds of firms, it would be safe to assume they would behave noncooperatively. Yet, when there are only a handful of firms in an industry, it's hard to determine whether collusion will actually occur.

Since collusion is ultimately more profitable than noncooperative behavior, firms have an incentive to collude if they can. One way to do so is to formalize it—sign an agreement (maybe even make a legal contract) or establish some financial incentives for the companies to set their prices high. But in the United States and many other nations, firms can't do that—at least not legally. A contract among firms to keep prices high would be unenforceable, and it could be a one-way ticket to jail. The same goes for an informal agreement. In fact, executives from rival firms rarely meet without lawyers present, who make sure that the conversation does not stray into inappropriate territory. Even hinting at how nice it would be if prices were higher can bring an unwelcome interview with the Justice Department or the Federal Trade Commission. For example, in 2003 the Justice Department launched a price-fixing case against Monsanto and other large producers of genetically modified seed. The Justice Department was alerted by a series of meetings held between Monsanto and Pioneer Hi-Bred International, two companies that account for 60% of the U.S. market in maize and soybean seed. These companies, parties to a licensing agreement involving genetically modified seed, claimed that no illegal discussions of price-fixing occurred in those meetings. But the fact that the two firms discussed prices as part of the licensing agreement was enough to trigger action by the Justice Department.

Bryan Smith/Zuma Press

Competing with Prices versus Competing with Quantities

Sometimes, as we've seen, oligopolistic firms just ignore the rules. But more often they develop strategies for making the best of the situation depending on what they know, or assume, about the other firms' behavior. The uncertainties of oligopoly behavior make it harder to model than the behavior of monopolists or perfectly competitive firms, but models do exist. One such model is an example of *price competition* developed by French economist Joseph Bertrand. According to the *Bertrand model,* oligopolists repeatedly undercut each others' prices—charging a bit less than the others to steal their customers—until price reaches the level of marginal cost, as under perfect competition. Another French economist, Augustin Cournot, focused instead on *quantity competition,* which had oligopolists choosing quantities and charging as much as possible for those quantities, rather than choosing prices and selling as much as possible at those prices. According to the *Cournot model,* each oligopolist treats the output of its competitors as fixed, and restricts output to that quantity that will maximize profit given the fixed output of others. The firms' restriction of output in the Cournot model results in lower overall output levels, and higher prices, than under perfect competition, and each firm earns a positive economic profit.

Consider American Airlines and British Airways, which we will assume are duopolists with exclusive rights to fly the Chicago–London route. When the economy is strong and lots of people want to fly between Chicago and London, American Airlines and British Airways might assume the number of passengers the other can carry is constrained, for example by the number of landing slots or terminal gates available. In this environment they are likely to behave according to the Cournot model and price above marginal cost—say, charging $800 per round trip. But when the business climate is poor, the two airlines are likely to find that they have lots of empty seats at a fare of $800 and that capacity constraints are no longer an issue. What will they do?

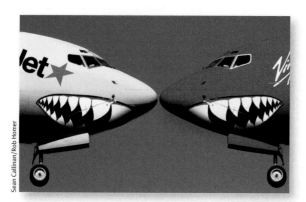

In the absence of collusion, price competition among oligopolists can be intense, as with the airfare war between Jetstar and Virgin Blue that has led to $300 fares to Bali.

Recent history tells us they will engage in a price war by slashing ticket prices. If American Airlines were to try to maintain a price of $800, it would soon find itself undercut by British Airways, which would charge $750 and steal its customers. In turn, American Airlines would undercut British Airways by charging $700—and so on. As long as each firm finds that it can capture the customers by cutting price, each will continue cutting until price is equal to marginal cost. (Going any lower would cause them to incur an avoidable loss.) This is the outcome Bertrand predicted.

Oligopolists would, understandably, prefer to avoid Bertrand behavior because it earns them zero profits. Lacking an environment that imposes constraints on their output capacity, firms try other means of avoiding direct price competition—such as producing products that are not perfect substitutes but are instead differentiated. We'll examine this strategy in more detail in a later module. For now, we note that producing differentiated products allows oligopolists to cultivate a loyal set of customers and to charge prices higher than marginal cost.

Collusion is another approach to dodging the profit-suppressing effects of competition. In the next module, we'll see why informal collusion often works but sometimes fails.

The Great Vitamin Conspiracy

It was a bitter pill to swallow. In the late 1990s, some of the world's largest drug companies (mainly European and Japanese) agreed to pay billions of dollars in damages to customers after being convicted of a huge conspiracy to rig the world vitamin market.

The conspiracy began in 1989 when the Swiss company Roche and the German company BASF began secret talks about raising prices for vitamins. Soon a French company, Rhone-Poulenc, joined in, followed by several Japanese companies and other companies around the world. The members of the group, which referred to itself as "Vitamins, Inc.," met regularly—sometimes at hotels, sometimes at the private homes of executives—to set prices and divide up markets for "bulk" vitamins (like vitamin A, vitamin C, and so on). These bulk vitamins are sold mainly to other companies, such as animal feed makers, food producers, and so on, which include them in their products. Indeed, it was the animal feed companies that grew suspicious about the prices they were being charged, which led to a series of investigations. The case eventually broke open when Rhone-Poulenc made a deal with U.S. officials to provide evidence of the conspiracy. The French company was concerned that rumors about price-fixing would lead U.S. officials to block its planned merger with another company.

How could it have happened?

The main answer probably lies in different national traditions about how to treat oligopolists. The United States has a long tradition of taking tough legal action against price-fixing. European governments, however, have historically been much less stringent. Indeed, in the past some European governments have actually encouraged major companies to form cartels. But European antitrust law has changed recently to become more like U.S. antitrust law. Despite this change, however, the cultural tradition of forming cartels as normal business practice lingers within the boardrooms of some European companies.

Module 28 Review

Solutions appear at the back of the book.

Check Your Understanding

1. Explain whether each of the following characteristics will increase or decrease the likelihood that a firm will collude with other firms in an oligopoly to restrict output.
   a. The firm's initial market share is small. (Hint: Think about the price effect.)

   b. The firm has a cost advantage over its rivals.
   c. The firm's customers face additional costs when they switch from one firm's product to another firm's product.
   d. The firm and its rivals are currently operating at maximum production capacity, which cannot be altered in the short run.

Multiple-Choice Questions

1. When firms cooperate to raise their joint profits, they are necessarily
   a. colluding.
   b. in a cartel.
   c. a monopoly.
   d. in a duopoly.
   e. in a competitive industry.

2. Use the information in the table below on market shares in the search engine industry and measures of market power (defined in the module "Introduction to Market Structure") to determine which of the following statements are correct.

Search Engine	Market share
Google	44%
Yahoo	29
MSN	13
AOL	6
Ask	5
Other	3

   I. The 4-firm concentration ratio is 92.
   II. The Herfindahl-Hirschman index is 3,016.
   III. The industry is likely to be an oligopoly.
   a. I only
   b. II only
   c. III only
   d. I and II only
   e. I, II, and III

3. An agreement among several producers to restrict output and increase profit is necessary for
   a. cooperation.
   b. collusion.
   c. monopolization.
   d. a cartel.
   e. competition.

4. Oligopolists engage in which of the following types of behavior?
   I. quantity competition
   II. price competition
   III. cooperative behavior
   a. I only
   b. II only
   c. III only
   d. I and II only
   e. I, II, and III

5. Which of the following will make it easier for firms in an industry to maintain positive economic profit?
   a. a ban on cartels
   b. a small number of firms in the industry
   c. a lack of product differentiation
   d. low start-up costs for new firms
   e. the assumption by firms that other firms have variable output levels

Critical-Thinking Questions

a. What are the two major reasons we don't see cartels among oligopolistic industries in the United States?
b. Explain the difference between behavior under the Cournot model and behavior under the Bertrand model.

Frances M. Roberts

What you will learn in this **Module:**

- How our understanding of oligopoly can be enhanced by using game theory

- The concept of the prisoners' dilemma

- How repeated interactions among oligopolists can result in collusion in the absence of any formal agreement

Module 29
Game Theory

Games Oligopolists Play

In our duopoly example and in real life, each oligopolistic firm realizes both that its profit depends on what its competitor does and that its competitor's profit depends on what it does. That is, the two firms are in a situation of interdependence, whereby each firm's decision significantly affects the profit of the other firm (or firms, in the case of more than two).

In effect, the two firms are playing a "game" in which the profit of each player depends not only on its own actions but on those of the other player (or players). In order to understand more fully how oligopolists behave, economists, along with mathematicians, developed the area of study of such games, known as **game theory.** It has many applications, not just to economics but also to military strategy, politics, and other social sciences.

Let's see how game theory helps us understand oligopoly.

The Prisoners' Dilemma

Game theory deals with any situation in which the reward to any one player—the **payoff**—depends not only on his or her own actions but also on those of other players in the game. In the case of oligopolistic firms, the payoff is simply the firm's profit.

When there are only two players, as in a lysine duopoly, the interdependence between the players can be represented with a **payoff matrix** like that shown in Figure 29.1. Each row corresponds to an action by one player; each column corresponds to an action by the other. For simplicity, let's assume that each firm can pick only one of two alternatives: produce 30 million pounds of lysine or produce 40 million pounds.

The matrix contains four boxes, each divided by a diagonal line. Each box shows the payoff to the two firms that results from a pair of choices; the number below the diagonal shows Firm 1's profits, the number above the diagonal shows Firm 2's profits.

These payoffs show what we concluded from our earlier analysis: the combined profit of the two firms is maximized if they each produce 30 million pounds. Either firm can, however, increase its own profits by producing 40 million pounds if the other produces only 30 million pounds. But if both produce the larger quantity, both will have lower profits than if they had both held their output down.

The study of behavior in situations of interdependence is known as **game theory.**

The reward received by a player in a game, such as the profit earned by an oligopolist, is that player's **payoff.**

A **payoff matrix** shows how the payoff to each of the participants in a two-player game depends on the actions of both. Such a matrix helps us analyze situations of interdependence.

figure 29.1

A Payoff Matrix

Two firms must decide how much lysine to produce. The profits of the two firms are *interdependent*: each firm's profit depends not only on its own decision but also on the other's decision. Each row represents an action by Firm 1, each column one by Firm 2. Both firms will be better off if they both choose the lower output; but it is in each firm's individual interest to choose the higher output.

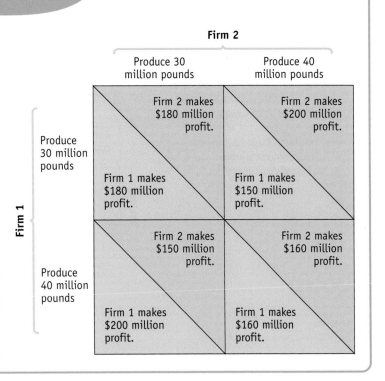

Firm 2

	Produce 30 million pounds	Produce 40 million pounds
Firm 1 — Produce 30 million pounds	Firm 2 makes $180 million profit. / Firm 1 makes $180 million profit.	Firm 2 makes $200 million profit. / Firm 1 makes $150 million profit.
Produce 40 million pounds	Firm 2 makes $150 million profit. / Firm 1 makes $200 million profit.	Firm 2 makes $160 million profit. / Firm 1 makes $160 million profit.

The particular situation shown here is a version of a famous—and seemingly paradoxical—case of interdependence that appears in many contexts. Known as the **prisoners' dilemma,** it is a type of game in which the payoff matrix implies the following:

- Each player has an incentive, regardless of what the other player does, to cheat—to take an action that benefits it at the other's expense.

- When both players cheat, both are worse off than they would have been if neither had cheated.

The original illustration of the prisoners' dilemma occurred in a fictional story about two accomplices in crime—let's call them Thelma and Louise—who have been caught by the police. The police have enough evidence to put them behind bars for 5 years. They also know that the pair have committed a more serious crime, one that carries a 20-year sentence; unfortunately, they don't have enough evidence to convict the women on that charge. To do so, they would need each of the prisoners to implicate the other in the second crime.

So the police put the miscreants in separate cells and say the following to each: "Here's the deal: if neither of you confesses, you know that we'll send you to jail for 5 years. If you confess and implicate your partner, and she doesn't do the same, we reduce your sentence from 5 years to 2. But if your partner confesses and you don't, you'll get the maximum 20 years. And if both of you confess, we'll give you both 15 years."

Figure 29.2 on the next page shows the payoffs that face the prisoners, depending on the decision of each to remain silent or to confess. (Usually the payoff matrix reflects the players' payoffs, and higher payoffs are better than lower payoffs. This case is an exception: a higher number of years in prison is bad, not good!) Let's assume that the prisoners have no way to communicate and that they have not sworn an oath not to harm each other or anything of that sort. So each acts in her own self-interest. What will they do?

The **prisoners' dilemma** is a game based on two premises: (1) Each player has an incentive to choose an action that benefits itself at the other player's expense; and (2) When both players act in this way, both are worse off than if they had acted cooperatively.

The Kobal Collection

The critically acclaimed 1991 movie *Thelma and Louise* was innovative in depicting two female characters running from the law.

figure 29.2

The Prisoners' Dilemma

Each of two prisoners, held in separate cells, is offered a deal by the police—a light sentence if she confesses and implicates her accomplice but her accomplice does not do the same, a heavy sentence if she does not confess but her accomplice does, and so on. It is in the joint interest of both prisoners not to confess; it is in each one's individual interest to confess.

Louise

	Don't confess	Confess
Don't confess	Louise gets 5-year sentence. / Thelma gets 5-year sentence.	Louise gets 2-year sentence. / Thelma gets 20-year sentence.
Confess	Louise gets 20-year sentence. / Thelma gets 2-year sentence.	Louise gets 15-year sentence. / Thelma gets 15-year sentence.

Thelma

An action is a **dominant strategy** when it is a player's best action regardless of the action taken by the other player.

A **Nash equilibrium,** also known as a **noncooperative equilibrium,** is the result when each player in a game chooses the action that maximizes his or her payoff, given the actions of other players.

Mathematician and Nobel Laureate John Forbes Nash proposed one of the key ideas in game theory.

The answer is clear: both will confess. Look at it first from Thelma's point of view: she is better off confessing, regardless of what Louise does. If Louise doesn't confess, Thelma's confession reduces her own sentence from 5 years to 2. If Louise *does* confess, Thelma's confession reduces her sentence from 20 to 15 years. Either way, it's clearly in Thelma's interest to confess. And because she faces the same incentives, it's clearly in Louise's interest to confess, too. To confess in this situation is a type of action that economists call a *dominant strategy.* An action is a **dominant strategy** when it is the player's best action regardless of the action taken by the other player. It's important to note that not all games have a dominant strategy—it depends on the structure of payoffs in the game. But in the case of Thelma and Louise, it is clearly in the interest of the police to structure the payoffs so that confessing is a dominant strategy for each person. As long as the two prisoners have no way to make an enforceable agreement that neither will confess (something they can't do if they can't communicate, and the police certainly won't allow them to do so because the police want to compel each one to confess), the dominant strategy exists as the best alternative.

So if each prisoner acts rationally in her own interest, both will confess. Yet if neither of them had confessed, both would have received a much lighter sentence! In a prisoners' dilemma, each player has a clear incentive to act in a way that hurts the other player—but when both make that choice, it leaves both of them worse off.

When Thelma and Louise both confess, they reach an *equilibrium* of the game. We have used the concept of equilibrium many times in this book; it is an outcome in which no individual or firm has any incentive to change his or her action. In game theory, this kind of equilibrium, in which each player takes the action that is best for her, given the actions taken by other players, is known as a **Nash equilibrium,** after the mathematician and Nobel Laureate John Nash. (Nash's life was chronicled in the best-selling biography *A Beautiful Mind,* which was made into a movie.) Because the players in a Nash equilibrium do not take into account the effect of their actions on others, this is also known as a **noncooperative equilibrium.**

In the prisoners' dilemma, the Nash equilibrium happens to be an equilibrium of two dominant strategies—a *dominant strategy equilibrium*—but Nash equilibria can exist when there is no dominant strategy at all. For example, suppose that after serving time in jail, Thelma and Louise are disheartened by the mutual distrust that led them to confess, and each wants nothing more than to avoid seeing the other. On a Saturday night, they might each have to choose between going to the nightclub and going to the movie theater. Neither has a dominant strategy because the best strategy for each depends on what the other is doing. However, Thelma going to the nightclub and Louise going to the movie theater is a Nash equilibrium because each player takes the action that is best given the action of the other. Thelma going to the movie theater and Louise going to the nightclub is also a Nash equilibrium, because again, neither wants to change her behavior given what the other is doing.

Now look back at Figure 29.1: the two firms face a prisoners' dilemma just like Thelma and Louise did after the crimes. Each firm is better off producing the higher output, regardless of what the other firm does. Yet if both produce 40 million pounds, both are worse off than if they had followed their agreement and produced only 30 million pounds. In both cases, then, the pursuit of individual self-interest—the effort to maximize profits or to minimize jail time—has the perverse effect of hurting both players.

Prisoners' dilemmas appear in many situations. The upcoming IRL describes an example from the days of the Cold War. Clearly, the players in any prisoners' dilemma would be better off if they had some way of enforcing cooperative behavior: if Thelma and Louise had both sworn to a code of silence, or if the two firms had signed an enforceable agreement not to produce more than 30 million pounds of lysine.

But we know that in the United States an agreement setting the output levels of two oligopolists isn't just unenforceable, it's illegal. So it seems that a noncooperative equilibrium is the only possible outcome. Or is it?

Overcoming the Prisoners' Dilemma: Repeated Interaction and Tacit Collusion

Thelma and Louise are playing what is known as a *one-shot* game—they play the game with each other only once. They get to choose once and for all whether to confess or deny, and that's it. However, most of the games that oligopolists play aren't one-shot games; instead, the players expect to play the game repeatedly with the same rivals. An oligopolist usually expects to be in business for many years, and knows that a decision today about whether to cheat is likely to affect the decisions of other firms in the future. So a smart oligopolist doesn't just decide what to do based on the effect on profit in the short run. Instead, it engages in **strategic behavior,** taking into account the effects of its action on the future actions of other players. And under some conditions oligopolists that behave strategically can manage to behave as if they had a formal agreement to collude.

Suppose that our two firms expect to be in the lysine business for many years and therefore expect to play the game of cheat versus collude shown in Figure 29.1 many times. Would they really betray each other time and again?

Probably not. Suppose that each firm considers two strategies. In one strategy it always cheats, producing 40 million pounds of lysine each year, regardless of what the other firm does. In the other strategy, it starts with good behavior, producing only 30 million pounds in the first year, and watches to see what its rival does. If the other firm also keeps its production down, each firm will stay cooperative, producing 30 million pounds again for the next year. But if one firm produces 40 million pounds, the other firm will take the gloves off and also produce 40 million pounds next year. This latter strategy—start by behaving cooperatively, but thereafter do whatever the other player did in the previous period—is generally known as **tit for tat.**

Playing "tit for tat" is a form of strategic behavior because it is intended to influence the future actions of other players. The "tit for tat" strategy offers a reward to

A firm engages in **strategic behavior** when it attempts to influence the future behavior of other firms.

A strategy of **tit for tat** involves playing cooperatively at first, then doing whatever the other player did in the previous period.

the other player for cooperative behavior—if you behave cooperatively, so will I. It also provides a punishment for cheating—if you cheat, don't expect me to be nice in the future.

The payoff to each firm of each of these strategies would depend on which strategy the other chooses. Consider the four possibilities, shown in Figure 29.3:

1. If one firm plays "tit for tat" and so does the other, both firms will make a profit of $180 million each year.

2. If one firm plays "always cheat" but the other plays "tit for tat," one makes a profit of $200 million the first year but only $160 million per year thereafter.

3. If one firm plays "tit for tat" but the other plays "always cheat," one makes a profit of only $150 million in the first year but $160 million per year thereafter.

4. If one firm plays "always cheat" and the other does the same, both firms will make a profit of $160 million each year.

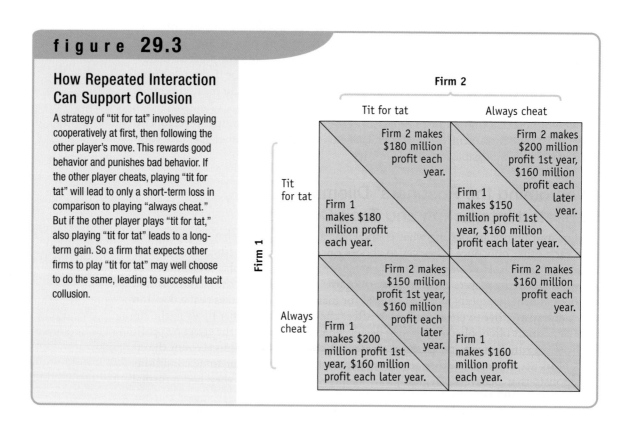

figure 29.3

How Repeated Interaction Can Support Collusion

A strategy of "tit for tat" involves playing cooperatively at first, then following the other player's move. This rewards good behavior and punishes bad behavior. If the other player cheats, playing "tit for tat" will lead to only a short-term loss in comparison to playing "always cheat." But if the other player plays "tit for tat," also playing "tit for tat" leads to a long-term gain. So a firm that expects other firms to play "tit for tat" may well choose to do the same, leading to successful tacit collusion.

Which strategy is better? In the first year, one firm does better playing "always cheat," whatever its rival's strategy: it assures itself that it will get either $200 million or $160 million. (Which of the two payoffs it actually receives depends on whether the other plays "tit for tat" or "always cheat.") This is better than what it would get in the first year if it played "tit for tat": either $180 million or $150 million. But by the second year, a strategy of "always cheat" gains the firm only $160 million per year for the second and all subsequent years, regardless of the other firm's actions. Over time, the total amount gained by playing "always cheat" is less than the amount gained by playing "tit for tat": for the second and all subsequent years, it would never get any less than $160 million and would get as much as $180 million if the other firm played "tit for tat" as well. Which strategy, "always cheat" or "tit for tat," is more profitable depends on two things: how many years each firm expects to play the game and what strategy its rival follows.

If the firm expects the lysine business to end in the near future, it is in effect playing a one-shot game. So it might as well cheat and grab what it can. Even if the firm expects to remain in the lysine business for many years (therefore to find itself repeatedly playing this game) and, for some reason, expects the other firm will always cheat, it should also always cheat. That is, the firm should follow the old rule, "Do unto others before they do unto you."

But if the firm expects to be in the business for a long time and thinks the other firm is likely to play "tit for tat," it will make more profits over the long run by playing "tit for tat," too. It could have made some extra short-term profit by cheating at the beginning, but this would provoke the other firm into cheating, too, and would, in the end, mean less profit.

The lesson of this story is that when oligopolists expect to compete with each other over an extended period of time, each individual firm will often conclude that it is in its own best interest to be helpful to the other firms in the industry. So it will restrict its output in a way that raises the profit of the other firms, expecting them to return the favor. Despite the fact that firms have no way of making an enforceable agreement to limit output and raise prices (and are in legal jeopardy if they even discuss prices), they manage to act "as if" they had such an agreement. When this type of unspoken agreement comes about, we say that the firms are engaging in **tacit collusion.**

When firms limit production and raise prices in a way that raises each other's profits, even though they have not made any formal agreement, they are engaged in **tacit collusion.**

in real life

Prisoners of the Arms Race

Between World War II and the late 1980s, the United States and the Soviet Union were locked in a seemingly endless struggle that never broke out into open war. During this Cold War, both countries spent huge sums on arms, sums that were a significant drain on the U.S. economy and eventually proved a crippling burden for the Soviet Union, whose underlying economic base was much weaker. Yet neither country was ever able to achieve a decisive military advantage.

As many people pointed out, both nations would have been better off if they had both spent less on arms. Yet the arms race continued for 40 years.

Why? As political scientists were quick to notice, one way to explain the arms race was to suppose that the two countries were locked in a classic prisoners' dilemma. Each government would have liked to achieve decisive mil-

itary superiority, and each feared military inferiority. But both would have preferred a stalemate with low military spending to one with high spending. However, each government rationally chose to engage in high spending. If its rival did not spend heavily, this would lead to military superiority; not spending heavily would lead to inferiority if the other government continued its arms buildup. So the countries were trapped.

The answer to this trap could have been an agreement not to spend as much; indeed, the two sides tried repeatedly to negotiate limits on some kinds of weapons. But these agreements weren't very effective. In the end the issue was resolved as heavy military spending hastened the collapse of the Soviet Union in 1991.

Unfortunately, the logic of an arms race has not disappeared. A nuclear arms race has devel-

TASS/Soufoto

oped between Pakistan and India, neighboring countries with a history of mutual antagonism. In 1998 the two countries confirmed the unrelenting logic of the prisoners' dilemma: both publicly tested their nuclear weapons in a tit-for-tat sequence, each seeking to prove to the other that it could inflict just as much damage as its rival.

Check Your Understanding

1. Suppose world leaders Nikita and Margaret are engaged in an arms race and face the decision of whether to build a missile. Answer the following questions using the information in the payoff matrix below, which shows how each set of actions will affect the utility of the players (the numbers represent utils gained or lost).

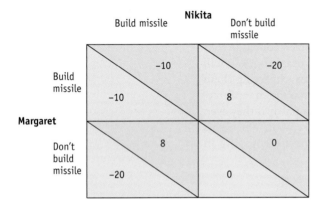

a. Identify any Nash equilibria that exist in this game, and explain why they do or do not exist.

b. Which set of actions maximizes the total payoff for Nikita and Margaret?

c. Why is it unlikely that they will choose the payoff-maximizing set of actions without some communication?

2. For each of the following characteristics of an industry, explain whether the characteristic makes it more likely that oligopolists will play noncooperatively rather than engaging in tacit collusion.

a. Each oligopolist expects several new firms to enter the market in the future.

b. It is very difficult for a firm to detect whether another firm has raised output.

c. The firms have coexisted while maintaining high prices for a long time.

Multiple-Choice Questions

1. Each player has an incentive to choose an action that, when both players choose it, makes them both worse off. This situation describes
   a. a dominant strategy.
   b. the prisoners' dilemma.
   c. interdependence.
   d. Nash equilibrium.
   e. tit for tat.

2. Which of the following types of oligopoly behavior is/are illegal?
       I. tacit collusion
       II. cartel formation
       III. tit for tat
   a. I only
   b. II only
   c. III only
   d. I and II only
   e. I, II, and III

3. A situation in which each player in a game chooses the action that maximizes his or her payoff, given the actions of the other players, ignoring the effects of his or her action on the payoffs received by others, is known as a:
   a. dominant strategy.
   b. cooperative equilibrium.
   c. Nash equilibrium.
   d. strategic situation.
   e. prisoners' dilemma.

4. In the context of the Thelma and Louise story in the module, suppose that Louise discovers Thelma's action (confess or don't confess) before choosing her own action.

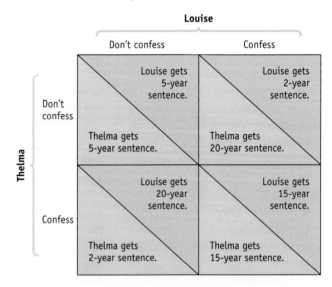

Based on the payoff matrix provided, Louise will
a. confess whether or not Thelma confessed.
b. not confess only if Thelma confessed.
c. not confess only if Thelma didn't confess.
d. not confess regardless of whether or not Thelma confessed.
e. confess only if Thelma did not confess.

5. Which of the following is true on the basis of the payoff matrix provided in Question 4?
   a. Louise has no dominant strategy, but Thelma does.
   b. Thelma has no dominant strategy, but Louise does.
   c. Both Thelma and Louise have a dominant strategy.
   d. Neither Thelma nor Louise has a dominant strategy.
   e. Louise has a dominant strategy only if Thelma confesses.

Critical-Thinking Question

Draw a clearly labeled payoff matrix illustrating the following situation. There are two firms, "Firm A" and "Firm B." Each firm must decide whether to charge a high price or a low price. If one firm charges a high price and the other a low price, the firm charging the high price will earn low profits while the firm charging the low price will earn high profits. If both firms charge a high price, both earn high profits and if both firms charge low prices, both earn low profits.

© Richard Levine/Alamy

What you will learn in this **Module**:

- The legal constraints of antitrust policy

- The factors that limit tacit collusion

- The cause and effect of price wars, product differentiation, price leadership, and nonprice competition

- The importance of oligopoly in the real world

Module 30
Oligopoly in Practice

Previously, we described the cartel known as "Vitamins, Inc.," which effectively sustained collusion for many years. The conspiratorial dealings of the vitamin makers were not, fortunately, the norm. But how do oligopolies usually work in practice? The answer depends both on the legal framework that limits what firms can do and on the underlying ability of firms in a given industry to cooperate without formal agreements. In this module we will explore a variety of oligopoly behaviors and how antitrust laws limit oligopolists' attempts to maximize their profits.

The Legal Framework

To understand oligopoly pricing in practice, we must be familiar with the legal constraints under which oligopolistic firms operate. In the United States, oligopoly first became an issue during the second half of the nineteenth century, when the growth of railroads—themselves an oligopolistic industry—created a national market for many goods. Large firms producing oil, steel, and many other products soon emerged. The industrialists quickly realized that profits would be higher if they could limit price competition. So many industries formed cartels—that is, they signed formal agreements to limit production and raise prices. Until 1890, when the first federal legislation against such cartels was passed, this was perfectly legal.

However, although these cartels were legal, their agreements weren't legally *enforceable*—members of a cartel couldn't ask the courts to force a firm that was violating its agreement to reduce its production. And firms often did violate their agreements, for the reason already suggested by our duopoly example in the previous module: there is always a temptation for each firm in a cartel to produce more than it is supposed to.

In 1881 clever lawyers at John D. Rockefeller's Standard Oil Company came up with a solution—the so-called *trust*. In a trust, shareholders of all the major companies in an industry placed their shares in the hands of a board of trustees who controlled the companies. This, in effect, merged the companies into a single firm that could then engage in monopoly pricing. In this way, the Standard Oil Trust established what was essentially a monopoly of the oil industry, and it was soon followed by trusts in sugar, whiskey, lead, cottonseed oil, and linseed oil.

Eventually, there was a public backlash, driven partly by concern about the economic effects of the trust movement and partly by fear that the owners of the trusts were simply becoming too powerful. The result was the Sherman Antitrust Act of 1890, which was intended both to prevent the creation of more monopolies and to break up existing ones. At first this law went largely unenforced. But over the decades that followed, the federal government became increasingly committed to making it difficult for oligopolistic industries either to become monopolies or to behave like them. Such efforts are known to this day as **antitrust policy.**

One of the most striking early actions of antitrust policy was the breakup of Standard Oil in 1911. Its components formed the nuclei of many of today's large oil companies—Standard Oil of New Jersey became Exxon, Standard Oil of New York became Mobil, and so on. In the 1980s a long-running case led to the breakup of Bell Telephone, which once had a monopoly on both local and long-distance phone service in the United States. As we mentioned earlier, the Justice Department reviews proposed mergers between companies in the same industry and will bar mergers that it believes will reduce competition.

Among advanced countries, the United States is unique in its long tradition of antitrust policy. Until recently, other advanced countries did not have policies against price-fixing, and some even supported the creation of cartels, believing that it would help their own firms compete against foreign rivals. But the situation has changed radically over the past 20 years, as the European Union (EU)—an international body with the duty of enforcing antitrust policy for its member countries—has converged toward U.S. practices. Today, EU and U.S. regulators often target the same firms because price-fixing has "gone global" as international trade has expanded. During the early 1990s, the United States instituted an amnesty program in which a price-fixer receives a much-reduced penalty if it provides information on its co-conspirators. (Remember that the Great Vitamin Conspiracy was busted when a French company, Rhone-Poulenc, revealed the cartel in order to get favorable treatment from U.S. regulators.) In addition, Congress substantially increased maximum fines levied upon conviction. These two new policies clearly made informing on cartel partners a dominant strategy, and it has paid off: in recent years, executives from Belgium, Britain, Canada, France, Germany, Italy, Mexico, the Netherlands, South Korea, and Switzerland, as well as from the United States, have been convicted in U.S. courts of cartel crimes. As one lawyer commented, "You get a race to the courthouse" as each conspirator seeks to be the first to come clean.

Life has gotten much tougher over the past few years if you want to operate a cartel. So what's an oligopolist to do?

Tacit Collusion and Price Wars

If real life were as simple as our lysine story, it probably wouldn't be necessary for the company presidents to meet or do anything that could land them in jail. Both firms would realize that it was in their mutual interest to restrict output to 30 million pounds each and that any short-term gains to either firm from producing more would be much less than the later losses as the other firm retaliated. So even without any explicit agreement, the firms would probably have achieved the tacit collusion needed to maximize their combined profits.

Real industries are nowhere near that simple; nonetheless, in most oligopolistic industries, most of the time, the sellers do appear to succeed in keeping prices above their noncooperative level. Tacit collusion, in other words, is the normal state of oligopoly.

Although tacit collusion is common, it rarely allows an industry to push prices all the way up to their monopoly level; collusion is usually far from perfect. A variety of factors make it hard for an industry to coordinate on high prices.

Large Numbers

Suppose that there were three instead of two firms in the lysine industry and that each was currently producing only 20 million pounds. In that case any one firm that decided to produce an extra 10 million pounds would gain more in short-term profits—and lose less once another firm responded in kind—than in our original example because it has fewer units on which to feel the price effect. The general point is that the

Antitrust policy involves efforts by the government to prevent oligopolistic industries from becoming or behaving like monopolies.

In 1911, Standard Oil was broken up into 34 separate companies, 3 of which later became Chevron, Conoco, and Exxon.

more firms there are in an oligopoly, the less is the incentive of any one firm to behave cooperatively, taking into account the impact of its actions on the profits of the other firms. Large numbers of firms in an industry also make the monitoring of price and output levels more difficult, and typically indicate low barriers to entry.

Complex Products and Pricing Schemes

In our simplified lysine example the two firms produce only one product. In reality, however, oligopolists often sell thousands or even tens of thousands of different products. A Walmart Supercenter sells over 100,000 items! Under these circumstances, as when there are a large number of firms, keeping track of what other firms are producing and what prices they are charging is difficult. This makes it hard to determine whether a firm is cheating on the tacit agreement.

Differences in Interests

In the lysine example, a tacit agreement for the firms to split the market equally is a natural outcome, probably acceptable to both firms. In other situations, however, firms often differ both in their perceptions about what is fair and in their real interests.

For example, suppose that one firm in a duopoly was a long-established producer and the other a more recent entrant into the industry. The long-established firm might feel that it deserved to continue producing more than the newer firm, but the newer firm might feel that it was entitled to 50% of the business.

Alternatively, suppose that the newer firm's marginal costs were lower than the long-established firm's. Even if they could agree on market shares, they would then disagree about the profit-maximizing level of output.

Bargaining Power of Buyers

Often oligopolists sell not to individual consumers but to large buyers—other industrial enterprises, nationwide chains of stores, and so on. These large buyers are in a position to bargain for lower prices from the oligopolists: they can ask for a discount from an oligopolist, and warn that they will go to a competitor if they don't get it. An important reason large retailers like Target are able to offer lower prices to customers than small retailers is precisely their ability to use their size to extract lower prices from their suppliers.

These difficulties in enforcing tacit collusion have sometimes led companies to defy the law and create illegal cartels. We've already examined the cases of the lysine industry and the bulk vitamin industry. An older, classic example was the U.S. electrical equipment conspiracy of the 1950s, which led to the indictment of and jail sentences for some executives. The industry was one in which tacit collusion was especially difficult because of all the reasons just mentioned. There were many firms—40 companies were indicted. They produced a very complex array of products, often more or less custom-built for particular clients. They differed greatly in size, from giants like General Electric to family firms with only a few dozen employees. And the customers in many cases were large buyers like electrical utilities, which would normally try to force suppliers to compete for their business. Tacit collusion just didn't seem practical—so executives met secretly and illegally to decide who would bid what price for which contract.

The IRL describes yet another price-fixing conspiracy: the one between the very posh auction houses Sotheby's and Christie's.

Because tacit collusion is often hard to achieve, most oligopolies charge prices that are well below what the same industry would charge if it were controlled by a monopolist—or what they would charge if they were able to collude explicitly. In addition, sometimes tacit collusion breaks down and aggressive price competition amounts to a **price war**. A price war sometimes precipitates a collapse of prices to their noncooperative level, or even lower, as sellers try to put each other out of business or at least punish what they regard as cheating.

A **price war** occurs when tacit collusion breaks down and aggressive price competition causes prices to collapse.

The Art of Conspiracy

If you want to sell a valuable work of art, there are really only two places to go: Christie's, the London-based auction house, or Sotheby's, its New York counterpart and competitor. Both are classy operations—literally: many of the employees of Christie's come from Britain's aristocracy, and many of Sotheby's come from blue-blooded American families that might as well have titles. They're not the sort of people you would expect to be seeking plea bargains from prosecutors.

But on October 6, 2000, Diana D. Brooks, the very upper-class former president of Sotheby's, pleaded guilty to a conspiracy. With her counterpart at Christie's, she had engaged in the illegal practice of price-fixing—agreeing on the fees they would charge people who sold artwork through either house. As part of her guilty plea, and in an effort to avoid going to jail, she agreed to help in the investigation of her boss, the former chairman of Sotheby's.

Why would such upper-crust types engage in illegal practices? For the same reasons that respectable electrical equipment industry executives did. By definition, no two works of art are alike; it wasn't easy for the two houses to collude tacitly because it was too hard to determine what commissions they were charging on any given transaction. To increase profits, then, the companies felt that they needed to reach a detailed agreement. They did, and they got caught.

AFP/Getty Images

Product Differentiation and Price Leadership

In many oligopolies, firms produce products that consumers regard as similar but not identical. A $10 difference in the price won't make many customers switch from a Ford to a Chrysler, or vice versa. Sometimes the differences between products are real, like differences between Froot Loops and Wheaties; sometimes, they exist mainly in the minds of consumers, like differences between brands of vodka (which is *supposed* to be tasteless). Either way, the effect is to reduce the intensity of competition among the firms: consumers will not all rush to buy whichever product is cheapest.

As you might imagine, oligopolists welcome the extra market power that comes when consumers think that their product is different from that of competitors. So in many oligopolistic industries, firms make considerable efforts to create the perception that their product is different—that is, they engage in **product differentiation.**

A firm that tries to differentiate its product may do so by altering what it actually produces, adding "extras," or choosing a different design. It may also use advertising and marketing campaigns to create a differentiation in the minds of consumers, even though its product is more or less identical to the products of rivals.

A classic case of how products may be perceived as different even when they are really pretty much the same is over-the-counter medication. For many years there were only three widely sold pain relievers—aspirin, ibuprofen, and acetaminophen. Yet each of these generic pain relievers were marketed under a number of brand names. And each brand used a marketing campaign implying some special superiority.

Whatever the nature of product differentiation, oligopolists producing differentiated products often reach a tacit understanding not to compete on price. For example, during the years when the great majority of cars sold in the United States were produced by the Big Three auto companies (General Motors, Ford, and Chrysler), there was an unwritten rule that none of the three companies would try to gain market share by making its cars noticeably cheaper than those of the other two.

But then who would decide on the overall price of cars? The answer was normally General Motors: as the biggest of the three, it would announce its prices for the year

Product differentiation is an attempt by a firm to convince buyers that its product is different from the products of other firms in the industry.

first; and the other companies would adopt similar prices. This pattern of behavior, in which one company tacitly sets prices for the industry as a whole, is known as **price leadership.**

Interestingly, firms that have a tacit agreement not to compete on price often engage in vigorous **nonprice competition**—adding new features to their products, spending large sums on ads that proclaim the inferiority of their rivals' offerings, and so on.

Perhaps the best way to understand the mix of cooperation and competition in such industries is with a political analogy. During the long Cold War between the United States and the Soviet Union, the two countries engaged in intense rivalry for global influence. They not only provided financial and military aid to their allies; they sometimes supported forces trying to overthrow governments allied with their rival (as the Soviet Union did in Vietnam in the 1960s and early 1970s, and as the United States did in Afghanistan from 1979 until the collapse of the Soviet Union in 1991). They even sent their own soldiers to support allied governments against rebels (as the United States did in Vietnam and the Soviet Union did in Afghanistan). But they did not get into direct military confrontations with each other; open warfare between the two superpowers was regarded by both as too dangerous—and tacitly avoided.

Price wars aren't as serious as shooting wars, but the principle is the same.

How Important Is Oligopoly?

We have seen that, across industries, oligopoly is far more common than either perfect competition or monopoly. When we try to analyze oligopoly, the economist's usual way of thinking—asking how self-interested individuals would behave, then analyzing their interaction—does not work as well as we might hope because we do not know whether rival firms will engage in noncooperative behavior or manage to engage in some kind of collusion. Given the prevalence of oligopoly, then, is the analysis we developed in earlier modules, which was based on perfect competition, still useful?

The conclusion of the great majority of economists is yes. For one thing, important parts of the economy are fairly well described by perfect competition. And even though many industries are oligopolistic, in many cases the limits to collusion keep prices relatively close to marginal costs—in other words, the industry behaves "almost" as if it were perfectly competitive.

Cars line up for gasoline in 1973 after the U.S. government imposed price controls.

It is also true that predictions from supply and demand analysis are often valid for oligopolies. For example, we saw that price controls will produce shortages. Strictly speaking, this conclusion is certain only for perfectly competitive industries. But in the 1970s, when the U.S. government imposed price controls on the definitely oligopolistic oil industry, the result was indeed to produce shortages and lines at the gas pumps.

So how important is it to take account of oligopoly? Most economists adopt a pragmatic approach. As we have seen here, the analysis of oligopoly is far more difficult and messy than that of perfect competition; so in situations where they do not expect the complications associated with oligopoly to be crucial, economists prefer to adopt the working assumption of perfectly competitive markets. They always keep in mind the possibility that oligopoly might be important; they recognize that there are important issues, from antitrust policies to price wars, that make trying to understand oligopolistic behavior crucial.

Module **30** Review

Solutions appear at the back of the book.

Check Your Understanding

1. For each of the following industry practices, explain whether the practice supports the conclusion that there is tacit collusion in this industry.
   a. For many years the price in the industry has changed infrequently, and all the firms in the industry charge the same price. The largest firm publishes a catalog containing a "suggested" retail price. Changes in price coincide with changes in the catalog.
   b. There has been considerable variation in the market shares of the firms in the industry over time.
   c. Firms in the industry build into their products unnecessary features that make it hard for consumers to switch from one company's products to another's.
   d. Firms meet yearly to discuss their annual sales forecasts.
   e. Firms tend to adjust their prices upward at the same times.

Multiple-Choice Questions

1. Having which of the following makes it easier for oligopolies to coordinate on raising prices?
   a. a large number of firms
   b. differentiated products
   c. buyers with bargaining power
   d. identical perceptions of fairness
   e. complex pricing schemes

2. Which of the following led to the passage of the first antitrust laws?
   I. growth of the railroad industry
   II. the emergence of the Standard Oil Company
   III. increased competition in agricultural industries
   a. I only
   b. II only
   c. III only
   d. I and II only
   e. I, II, and III

3. When was the first federal legislation against cartels passed?
   a. 1776
   b. 1800
   c. 1890
   d. 1900
   e. 1980

4. Which of the following industries has been prosecuted for creating an illegal cartel?
   a. the lysine industry
   b. the art auction house industry
   c. the U.S. electrical equipment industry
   d. the bulk vitamin industry
   e. all of the above

5. Oligopolists engage in tacit collusion in order to
   a. raise prices.
   b. increase output.
   c. share profits.
   d. increase market share.
   e. all of the above.

Critical-Thinking Question

List four factors that make it difficult for firms to form a cartel.
Explain each.

AP Photo/Kiichiro Sato

Module 31
Introduction to Monopolistic Competition

What you will learn in this **Module:**

• How prices and profits are determined in monopolistic competition, both in the short run and in the long run

• How monopolistic competition can lead to inefficiency and excess capacity

Understanding Monopolistic Competition

Suppose an industry is monopolistically competitive: it consists of many producers, all competing for the same consumers but offering differentiated products. How does such an industry behave?

As the term *monopolistic competition* suggests, this market structure combines some features typical of monopoly with others typical of perfect competition. Because each firm is offering a distinct product, it is in a way like a monopolist: it faces a downward-sloping demand curve and has some market power—the ability within limits to determine the price of its product. However, unlike a pure monopolist, a monopolistically competitive firm does face competition: the amount of its product it can sell depends on the prices and products offered by other firms in the industry.

The same, of course, is true of an oligopoly. In a monopolistically competitive industry, however, there are *many* producers, as opposed to the small number that defines an oligopoly. This means that the "puzzle" of oligopoly—whether firms will collude or behave noncooperatively—does not arise in the case of monopolistically competitive industries. True, if all the gas stations or all the restaurants in a town could agree—explicitly or tacitly—to raise prices, it would be in their mutual interest to do so. But such collusion is virtually impossible when the number of firms is large and, by implication, there are no barriers to entry. So in situations of monopolistic competition, we can safely assume that firms behave noncooperatively and ignore the potential for collusion.

Monopolistic Competition in the Short Run

We introduced the distinction between short-run and long-run equilibrium when we studied perfect competition. The short-run equilibrium of an industry takes the number of firms as given. The long-run equilibrium, by contrast, is reached only after enough time has elapsed for firms to enter or exit the industry. To analyze monopolistic competition, we focus first on the short run and then on how an industry moves from the short run to the long run.

Panels (a) and (b) of Figure 31.1 show two possible situations that a typical firm in a monopolistically competitive industry might face in the short run. In each case, the firm looks like any monopolist: it faces a downward-sloping demand curve, which implies a downward-sloping marginal revenue curve.

We assume that every firm has an upward-sloping marginal cost curve but that it also faces some fixed costs, so that its average total cost curve is U-shaped. This assumption doesn't matter in the short run; but, as we'll see shortly, it is crucial to understanding the long-run equilibrium.

In each case the firm, in order to maximize profit, sets marginal revenue equal to marginal cost. So how do these two figures differ? In panel (a) the firm is profitable; in panel (b) it is unprofitable. (Recall that we are referring always to economic profit and not accounting profit—that is, a profit given that all factors of production are earning their opportunity costs.)

In panel (a) the firm faces the demand curve D_P and the marginal revenue curve MR_P. It produces the profit-maximizing output Q_P, the quantity at which marginal revenue is equal to marginal cost, and sells it at the price P_P. This price is above the average total cost at this output, ATC_P. The firm's profit is indicated by the area of the shaded rectangle.

In panel (b) the firm faces the demand curve D_U and the marginal revenue curve MR_U. It chooses the quantity Q_U at which marginal revenue is equal to marginal cost.

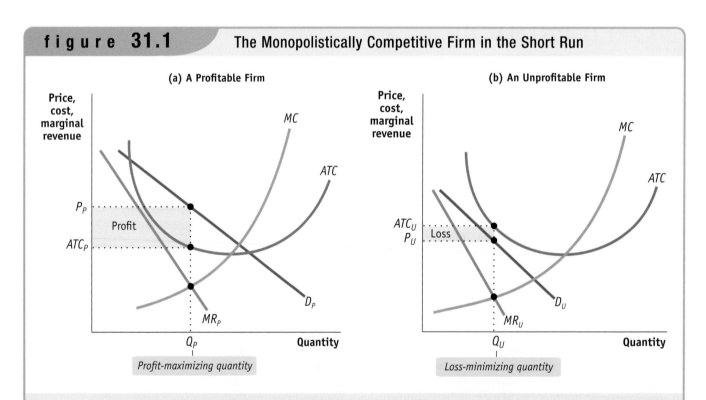

figure 31.1   The Monopolistically Competitive Firm in the Short Run

The firm in panel (a) can be profitable for some output quantities: the quantities for which its average total cost curve, *ATC*, lies below its demand curve, D_P. The profit-maximizing output quantity is Q_P, the output at which marginal revenue, MR_P, is equal to marginal cost, *MC*. The firm charges price P_P and earns a profit, represented by the area of the green shaded rectangle. The firm in panel (b), however, can never be profitable because its average total cost curve lies above its demand curve, D_U, for every output quantity. The best that it can do if it produces at all is to produce quantity Q_U and charge price P_U. This generates a loss, indicated by the area of the yellow shaded rectangle. Any other output quantity results in a greater loss.

However, in this case the price P_U is *below* the average total cost ATC_U; so at this quantity the firm loses money. Its loss is equal to the area of the shaded rectangle. Since Q_U is the profit-maximizing quantity—which means, in this case, the loss-minimizing quantity—there is no way for a firm in this situation to make a profit. We can confirm this by noting that at any quantity of output, the average total cost curve in panel (b) lies above the demand curve D_U. Because $ATC > P$ at all quantities of output, this firm always suffers a loss.

As this comparison suggests, the key to whether a firm with market power is profitable or unprofitable in the short run lies in the relationship between its demand curve and its average total cost curve. In panel (a) the demand curve D_P crosses the average total cost curve, meaning that some of the demand curve lies above the average total cost curve. So there are some price–quantity combinations available at which price is higher than average total cost, indicating that the firm can choose a quantity at which it makes positive profit.

In panel (b), by contrast, the demand curve D_U does not cross the average total cost curve—it always lies below it. So the price corresponding to each quantity demanded is always less than the average total cost of producing that quantity. There is no quantity at which the firm can avoid losing money.

These figures, showing firms facing downward-sloping demand curves and their associated marginal revenue curves, look just like ordinary monopoly graphs. The "competition" aspect of monopolistic competition comes into play, however, when we move from the short run to the long run.

Monopolistic Competition in the Long Run

Obviously, an industry in which existing firms are losing money, like the one in panel (b) of Figure 31.1, is not in long-run equilibrium. When existing firms are losing money, some firms will *exit* the industry. The industry will not be in long-run equilibrium until the persistent losses have been eliminated by the exit of some firms.

It may be less obvious that an industry in which existing firms are earning profits, like the one in panel (a) of Figure 31.1, is also not in long-run equilibrium. Given there is *free entry* into the industry, persistent profits earned by the existing firms will lead to the entry of additional producers. The industry will not be in long-run equilibrium until the persistent profits have been eliminated by the entry of new producers.

How will entry or exit by other firms affect the profit of a typical existing firm? Because the differentiated products offered by firms in a monopolistically competitive industry are available to the same set of customers, entry or exit by other firms will affect the demand curve facing every existing producer. If new gas stations open along a highway, each of the existing gas stations will no longer be able to sell as much gas as before at any given price. So, as illustrated in panel (a) of Figure 31.2 on the next page, entry of additional producers into a monopolistically competitive industry will lead to a *leftward* shift of the demand curve and the marginal revenue curve facing a typical existing producer.

In the long-run, profit lures new firms to enter an industry.

Conversely, suppose that some of the gas stations along the highway close. Then each of the remaining stations will be able to sell more gasoline at any given price. So as illustrated in panel (b), exit of firms from an industry leads to a *rightward* shift of the demand curve and marginal revenue curve facing a typical remaining producer.

The industry will be in long-run equilibrium when there is neither entry nor exit. This will occur only when every firm earns zero profit. So in the long run, a monopolistically competitive industry will end up in **zero-profit equilibrium,** in which firms just manage to cover their costs at their profit-maximizing output quantities.

We have seen that a firm facing a downward-sloping demand curve will earn positive profit if any part of that demand curve lies above its average total cost curve; it

In the long run, a monopolistically competitive industry ends up in **zero-profit equilibrium:** each firm makes zero profit at its profit-maximizing quantity.

figure **31.2**

Entry and Exit Shift Existing Firms' Demand Curves and Marginal Revenue Curves

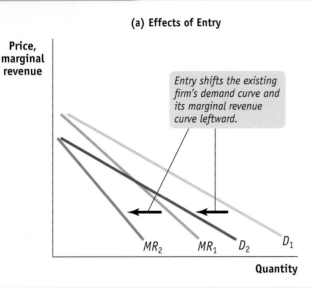

(a) Effects of Entry

Price, marginal revenue

Entry shifts the existing firm's demand curve and its marginal revenue curve leftward.

MR_2 MR_1 D_2 D_1

Quantity

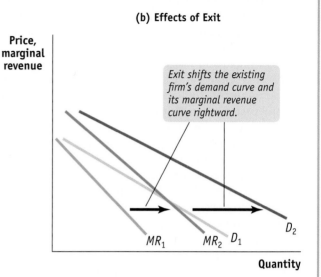

(b) Effects of Exit

Price, marginal revenue

Exit shifts the existing firm's demand curve and its marginal revenue curve rightward.

MR_1 MR_2 D_1 D_2

Quantity

Entry will occur in the long run when existing firms are profitable. In panel (a), entry causes each existing firm's demand curve and marginal revenue curve to shift to the left. The firm receives a lower price for every unit it sells, and its profit falls. Entry will cease when firms make zero profit. Exit will occur in the long run when existing firms are unprofitable. In panel (b), exit from the industry shifts each remaining firm's demand curve and marginal revenue curve to the right. The firm receives a higher price for every unit it sells, and profit rises. Exit will cease when the remaining firms make zero profit.

will incur a loss if its entire demand curve lies below its average total cost curve. So in zero-profit equilibrium, the firm must be in a borderline position between these two cases; its demand curve must just touch its average total cost curve. That is, the demand curve must be just *tangent* to the average total cost curve at the firm's profit-maximizing output quantity—the output quantity at which marginal revenue equals marginal cost.

If this is not the case, the firm operating at its profit-maximizing quantity will find itself making either a profit or loss, as illustrated in the panels of Figure 31.1. But we also know that free entry and exit means that this cannot be a long-run equilibrium. Why? In the case of a profit, new firms will enter the industry, shifting the demand curve of every existing firm leftward until all profit is eliminated. In the case of a loss, some existing firms exit and so shift the demand curve of every remaining firm to the right until all losses are eliminated. All entry and exit ceases only when every existing firm makes zero profit at its profit-maximizing quantity of output.

Figure 31.3 shows a typical monopolistically competitive firm in such a zero-profit equilibrium. The firm produces Q_{MC}, the output at which $MR_{MC} = MC$, and charges price P_{MC}. At this price and quantity, represented by point Z, the demand curve is just tangent to its average total cost curve. The firm earns zero profit because price, P_{MC}, is equal to average total cost, ATC_{MC}.

The normal long-run condition of a monopolistically competitive industry, then, is that each producer is in the situation shown in Figure 31.3. Each producer acts like a monopolist, facing a downward-sloping demand curve and setting marginal cost equal to marginal revenue so as to maximize profit. But this is just enough to achieve zero economic profit. The producers in the industry are like monopolists without monopoly profit.

figure 31.3

The Long-Run Zero-Profit Equilibrium

If existing firms are profitable, entry will occur and shift each existing firm's demand curve leftward. If existing firms are unprofitable, each remaining firm's demand curve shifts rightward as some firms exit the industry. Entry and exit will cease when every existing firm makes zero profit at its profit-maximizing quantity. So, in long-run zero-profit equilibrium, the demand curve of each firm is tangent to its average total cost curve at its profit-maximizing quantity: at the profit-maximizing quantity, Q_{MC}, price, P_{MC}, equals average total cost, ATC_{MC}. A monopolistically competitive firm is like a monopolist without monopoly profits.

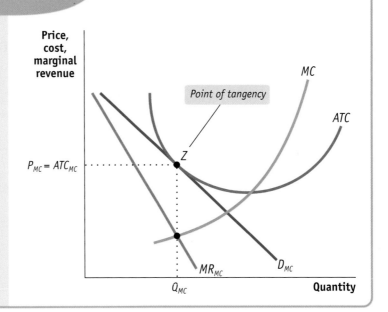

in real life

Hits and Flops

On the face of it, the movie business seems to meet the criteria for monopolistic competition. Movies compete for the same consumers; each movie is different from the others; new companies can and do enter the business. But where's the zero-profit equilibrium? After all, some movies are enormously profitable.

The key is to realize that for every successful blockbuster, there are several flops—and that the movie studios don't know in advance which will be which. (One observer of Hollywood summed up his conclusions as follows: "Nobody knows anything.") And by the time it becomes clear that a movie will be a flop, it's too late to cancel it.

The difference between movie-making and the type of monopolistic competition we model in this section is that the fixed costs of making a movie are also *sunk costs*—once they've been incurred, they can't be recovered.

Yet there is still, in a way, a zero-profit equilibrium. If movies on average were highly profitable, more studios would enter the industry and more movies would be made. If movies on average lost money, fewer movies would be made. In fact, as you might expect, the movie industry on average earns just about enough to cover the cost of production—that is, it earns roughly zero economic profit.

This kind of situation—in which firms earn zero profit on average but have a mixture of highly profitable hits and money-losing

flops—can be found in other industries characterized by high up-front sunk costs. A notable example is the pharmaceutical industry, in which many research projects lead nowhere but a few lead to highly profitable drugs.

Monopolistic Competition versus Perfect Competition

In a way, long-run equilibrium in a monopolistically competitive industry looks a lot like long-run equilibrium in a perfectly competitive industry. In both cases, there are many firms; in both cases, profits have been competed away; in both cases, the price received by every firm is equal to the average total cost of production.

However, the two versions of long-run equilibrium are different—in ways that are economically significant.

Price, Marginal Cost, and Average Total Cost

Figure 31.4 compares the long-run equilibrium of a typical firm in a perfectly competitive industry with that of a typical firm in a monopolistically competitive industry. Panel (a) shows a perfectly competitive firm facing a market price equal to its minimum average total cost; panel (b) reproduces Figure 31.3. Comparing the panels, we see two important differences.

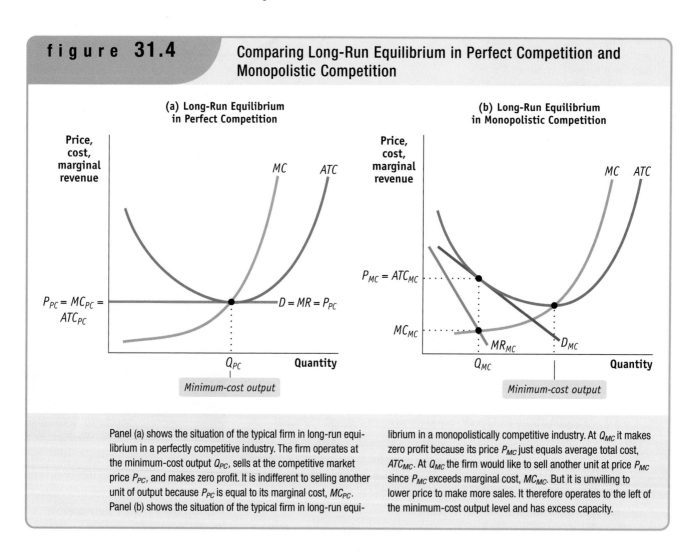

| figure 31.4 | Comparing Long-Run Equilibrium in Perfect Competition and Monopolistic Competition |

(a) Long-Run Equilibrium in Perfect Competition

(b) Long-Run Equilibrium in Monopolistic Competition

Panel (a) shows the situation of the typical firm in long-run equilibrium in a perfectly competitive industry. The firm operates at the minimum-cost output Q_{PC}, sells at the competitive market price P_{PC}, and makes zero profit. It is indifferent to selling another unit of output because P_{PC} is equal to its marginal cost, MC_{PC}. Panel (b) shows the situation of the typical firm in long-run equi-

librium in a monopolistically competitive industry. At Q_{MC} it makes zero profit because its price P_{MC} just equals average total cost, ATC_{MC}. At Q_{MC} the firm would like to sell another unit at price P_{MC} since P_{MC} exceeds marginal cost, MC_{MC}. But it is unwilling to lower price to make more sales. It therefore operates to the left of the minimum-cost output level and has excess capacity.

First, in the case of the perfectly competitive firm shown in panel (a), the price, P_{PC}, received by the firm at the profit-maximizing quantity, Q_{PC}, is equal to the firm's marginal cost of production, MC_{PC}, at that quantity of output. By contrast, at the profit-maximizing quantity chosen by the monopolistically competitive firm in panel (b), Q_{MC}, the price, P_{MC}, is *higher* than the marginal cost of production, MC_{MC}.

This difference translates into a difference in the attitude of firms toward consumers. A wheat farmer, who can sell as much wheat as he likes at the going market price, would not get particularly excited if you offered to buy some more wheat at the market price. Since he has no desire to produce more at that price and can sell the wheat to someone else, you are not doing him a favor.

But if you decide to fill up your tank at Jamil's gas station rather than at Katy's, you are doing Jamil a favor. He is not willing to cut his price to get more customers—he's already made the best of that trade-off. But if he gets a few more customers than he expected at the posted price, that's good news: an additional sale at the *posted* price increases his revenue more than it increases his cost because the posted price exceeds marginal cost.

The fact that monopolistic competitors, unlike perfect competitors, want to sell more at the going price is crucial to understanding why they engage in activities like advertising that help increase sales.

The other difference between monopolistic competition and perfect competition that is visible in Figure 31.4 involves the position of each firm on its average total cost curve. In panel (a), the perfectly competitive firm produces at point Q_{PC}, at the bottom of the U-shaped *ATC* curve. That is, each firm produces the quantity at which average total cost is minimized—the *minimum-cost output*. As a consequence, the total cost of industry output is also minimized.

Firms in a monopolistically competitive industry have **excess capacity:** they produce less than the output at which average total cost is minimized.

Under monopolistic competition, in panel (b), the firm produces at Q_{MC}, on the *downward-sloping* part of the U-shaped *ATC* curve: it produces less than the quantity that would minimize average total cost. This failure to produce enough to minimize average total cost is sometimes described as the **excess capacity** issue. The typical vendor in a food court or a gas station along a road is not big enough to take maximum advantage of available cost savings. So the total cost of industry output is not minimized in the case of a monopolistically competitive industry.

Some people have argued that, because every monopolistic competitor has excess capacity, monopolistically competitive industries are inefficient. But the issue of efficiency under monopolistic competition turns out to be a subtle one that does not have a clear answer.

Is Monopolistic Competition Inefficient?

A monopolistic competitor, like a monopolist, charges a price that is above marginal cost. As a result, some people who are willing to pay at least as much for an egg roll at Wonderful Wok as it costs to produce it are deterred from doing so. In monopolistic competition, some mutually beneficial transactions go unexploited.

Furthermore, it is often argued that monopolistic competition is subject to a further kind of inefficiency: that the excess capacity of every monopolistic competitor implies *wasteful duplication* because monopolistically competitive industries offer too many varieties. According to this argument, it would be better if there were only two or three vendors in the food court, not six or seven. If there were fewer vendors, they would each have lower average total costs and so could offer food more cheaply.

Is this argument against monopolistic competition right—that it lowers total surplus by causing inefficiency? Not necessarily. It's true that if there were fewer gas stations along a highway, each gas station would sell more gasoline and so would have a lower cost per gallon. But there is a drawback: motorists would be inconvenienced because gas stations would be farther apart. The point is that the diversity of products offered in a monopolistically competitive industry is beneficial to consumers. So the higher price consumers pay because of excess capacity is offset to some extent by the value they receive from greater diversity.

There is, in other words, a trade-off: more producers mean higher average total costs but also greater product diversity. Does a monopolistically competitive industry arrive at the socially optimal point in this trade-off? Probably not—but it is hard to say whether there are too many firms or too few! Most economists now believe that duplication of effort and excess capacity in monopolistically competitive industries are not large problems in practice.

Module 31 Review

Solutions appear at the back of the book.

Check Your Understanding

1. Suppose a monopolistically competitive industry composed of firms with U-shaped average total cost curves is in long-run equilibrium. For each of the following changes, explain how the industry is affected in the short run and how it adjusts to a new long-run equilibrium.
   a. a technological change that increases fixed cost for every firm in the industry
   b. a technological change that decreases marginal cost for every firm in the industry

2. Why is it impossible for firms in a monopolistically competitive industry to join together to form a monopoly that is capable of maintaining positive economic profit in the long run?

3. Indicate whether the following statements are true or false, and explain your answers.
   a. Like a firm in a perfectly competitive industry, a firm in a monopolistically competitive industry is willing to sell a good at any price that equals or exceeds marginal cost.
   b. Suppose there is a monopolistically competitive industry in long-run equilibrium that possesses excess capacity. All the firms in the industry would be better off if they merged into a single firm and produced a single product, but whether consumers would be made better off by this is ambiguous.
   c. Fads and fashions are more likely to arise in industries characterized by monopolistic competition or oligopoly than in those characterized by perfect competition or monopoly.

Multiple-Choice Questions

1. Which of the following is a characteristic of monopolistic competition?
   a. a standardized product
   b. many sellers
   c. barriers to entry
   d. positive long-run profits
   e. a perfectly elastic demand curve

2. Which of the following results is possible for a monopolistic competitor in the short run?
   I. positive economic profit
   II. normal profit
   III. loss
   a. I only
   b. II only
   c. III only
   d. I and II only
   e. I, II, and III

3. Which of the following results is possible for a monopolistic competitor in the long run?
   I. positive economic profit
   II. normal profit
   III. loss
   a. I only
   b. II only
   c. III only
   d. I and II only
   e. I, II, and III

4. Which of the following best describes a monopolistic competitor's demand curve?
   a. upward sloping
   b. downward sloping
   c. U-shaped
   d. horizontal
   e. vertical

5. The long-run outcome in a monopolistically competitive industry results in
   a. inefficiency because firms earn positive economic profits.
   b. efficiency due to excess capacity.
   c. inefficiency due to product diversity.
   d. efficiency because price exceeds marginal cost.
   e. a trade-off between higher average total cost and more product diversity.

Critical-Thinking Question

Draw a correctly labeled graph for a monopolistically competitive firm in long-run equilibrium. Label the distance on the quantity axis that represents excess capacity.

Alamy

Module 32
Product Differentiation and Advertising

In a previous module we saw that product differentiation often plays an important role in oligopolistic industries. In such industries, product differentiation reduces the intensity of competition between firms when tacit collusion cannot be achieved. Product differentiation plays an even more crucial role in monopolistically competitive industries. Because tacit collusion is virtually impossible when there are many producers, product differentiation is the only way monopolistically competitive firms can acquire some market power. In this module, we look at how oligopolists and monopolistic competitors differentiate their products in order to maximize profits.

How Firms Differentiate Their Products

How do firms in the same industry—such as fast-food vendors, gas stations, or chocolate makers—differentiate their products? Sometimes the difference is mainly in the minds of consumers rather than in the products themselves. We'll discuss the role of advertising and the importance of brand names in achieving this kind of product differentiation later. But, in general, firms differentiate their products by—surprise!—actually making them different.

The key to product differentiation is that consumers have different preferences and are willing to pay somewhat more to satisfy those preferences. Each producer can carve out a market niche by producing something that caters to the particular preferences of some group of consumers better than the products of other firms. There are three important forms of product differentiation: differentiation by style or type, differentiation by location, and differentiation by quality.

Differentiation by Style or Type

The sellers in Leo's food court offer different types of fast food: hamburgers, pizza, Chinese food, Mexican food, and so on. Each consumer arrives at the food court with some preference for one or another of these offerings. This preference may depend on the consumer's mood, her diet, or what she has already eaten that day. These preferences will not make consumers indifferent to price: if Wonderful Wok were to charge $15 for an egg roll, everybody would go to Bodacious Burgers or Pizza Paradise instead. But some people will choose a more expensive meal if that type of food is closer to their preference. So the products of the different vendors are substitutes, but they aren't *perfect* substitutes—they are *imperfect substitutes*.

Vendors in a food court aren't the only sellers who differentiate their offerings by type. Clothing stores concentrate on women's or men's clothes, on business attire or sportswear, on trendy or classic styles, and so on. Auto manufacturers offer sedans, minivans, sport-utility vehicles, and sports cars, each type aimed at drivers with different needs and tastes.

Books offer yet another example of differentiation by type and style. Mysteries are differentiated from romances; among mysteries, we can differentiate among hard-boiled detective stories, whodunits, and police procedurals. And no two writers of hard-boiled detective stories are exactly alike: Raymond Chandler and Sue Grafton each have their devoted fans.

In fact, product differentiation is characteristic of most consumer goods. As long as people differ in their tastes, producers find it possible and profitable to offer variety.

Differentiation by Location

Gas stations along a road offer differentiated products. True, the gas may be exactly the same. But the location of the stations is different, and location matters to consumers: it's more convenient to stop for gas near your home, near your workplace, or near wherever you are when the gas gauge gets low.

In fact, many monopolistically competitive industries supply goods differentiated by location. This is especially true in service industries, from dry cleaners to hairdressers, where customers often choose the seller who is closest rather than cheapest.

Differentiation by Quality

Do you have a craving for chocolate? How much are you willing to spend on it? You see, there's chocolate and then there's chocolate: although ordinary chocolate may not be very expensive, gourmet chocolate can cost several dollars per bite.

With chocolate, as with many goods, there is a range of possible qualities. You can get a usable bicycle for less than $100; you can get a much fancier bicycle for 10 times as much. It all depends on how much the additional quality matters to you and how much you will miss the other things you could have purchased with that money.

Because consumers vary in what they are willing to pay for higher quality, producers can differentiate their products by quality—some offering lower-quality, inexpensive products and others offering higher-quality products at a higher price.

istockphoto

Product differentiation, then, can take several forms. Whatever form it takes, however, there are two important features of industries with differentiated products: *competition among sellers* and *value in diversity*.

Competition among sellers means that even though sellers of differentiated products are not offering identical goods, they are to some extent competing for a limited market. If more businesses enter the market, each will find that it sells a lower quantity at any given price. For example, if a new gas station opens along a road, each of the existing gas stations will sell a bit less.

Value in diversity refers to the gain to consumers from the proliferation of differentiated products. A food court with eight vendors makes consumers happier than one with only six vendors, even if the prices are the same, because some customers will get a meal that is closer to what they had in mind. A road on which there is a gas station every two miles is more convenient for motorists than a road where gas stations are five miles apart. When a product is available in many different qualities, fewer people are forced to pay for more quality than they need or to settle for lower quality than they

Any Color, So Long as It's Black

The early history of the auto industry offers a classic illustration of the power of product differentiation.

The modern automobile industry was created by Henry Ford, who first introduced assembly-line production. This technique made it possible for him to offer the famous Model T at a far lower price than anyone else was charging for a car; by 1920, Ford dominated the automobile business.

Ford's strategy was to offer just one style of car, which maximized his economies of scale in production but made no concessions to differences in consumers' tastes. He supposedly declared that customers could get the Model T in "any color, so long as it's black."

This strategy was challenged by Alfred P. Sloan, who had merged a number of smaller automobile companies into General Motors. Sloan's strategy was to offer a range of car types, differentiated by quality and price. Chevrolets were basic cars that directly challenged the Model T, Buicks were bigger and more expensive, and so on up to Cadillacs. And you could get each model in several different colors.

By the 1930s the verdict was clear: customers preferred a range of styles, and General Motors, not Ford, became the dominant auto manufacturer for the rest of the twentieth century.

want. There are, in other words, benefits to consumers from a greater diversity of available products.

As we'll see next, competition among the sellers of differentiated products is the key to understanding how monopolistic competition works.

Controversies About Product Differentiation

Up to this point, we have assumed that products are differentiated in a way that corresponds to some real desire of consumers. There is real convenience in having a gas station in your neighborhood; Chinese food and Mexican food are really different from each other.

In the real world, however, some instances of product differentiation can seem puzzling if you think about them. What is the real difference between Crest and Colgate toothpaste? Between Energizer and Duracell batteries? Or a Marriott and a Hilton hotel room? Most people would be hard-pressed to answer any of these questions. Yet the producers of these goods make considerable efforts to convince consumers that their products are different from and better than those of their competitors.

No discussion of product differentiation is complete without spending at least a bit of time on the two related issues—and puzzles—of *advertising* and *brand names*.

The Role of Advertising

Wheat farmers don't advertise their wares on TV, but car dealers do. That's not because farmers are shy and car dealers are outgoing; it's because advertising is worthwhile only in industries in which firms have at least some market power. The purpose of advertisements is to persuade people to buy more of a seller's product at the going price. A perfectly competitive firm, which can sell as much as it likes at the going market price, has no incentive to spend money persuading consumers to buy more. Only a firm that has some market power, and which therefore charges a price that is above marginal cost, can gain from advertising. (Industries that are more or less perfectly competitive, like the milk industry, do advertise—but these ads are sponsored by an association on behalf of the industry as a whole, not on behalf of a particular farm.)

Given that advertising "works," it's not hard to see why firms with market power would spend money on it. But the big question about advertising is, *why* does it work? A related question is whether advertising is, from society's point of view, a waste of resources.

Not all advertising poses a puzzle. Much of it is straightforward: it's a way for sellers to inform potential buyers about what they have to offer (or, occasionally, for buyers to inform potential sellers about what they want). Nor is there much controversy about the economic usefulness of ads that provide information: the real estate ad that declares "sunny, charming, 2 bedrooms, 1 bath, a/c" tells you things you need to know (even if a few euphemisms are involved—"charming," of course, means "small").

But what information is being conveyed when a TV actress proclaims the virtues of one or another toothpaste or a sports hero declares that some company's batteries are better than those inside that pink mechanical rabbit? Surely nobody believes that the sports star is an expert on batteries—or that he chose the company that he personally believes makes the best batteries, as opposed to the company that offered to pay him the most. Yet companies believe, with good reason, that money spent on such promotions increases their sales—and that they would be in big trouble if they stopped advertising but their competitors continued to do so.

Why are consumers influenced by ads that do not really provide any information about the product? One answer is that consumers are not as rational as economists typically assume. Perhaps consumers' judgments, or even their tastes, can be influenced by things that economists think ought to be irrelevant, such as which company has hired the most charismatic celebrity to endorse its product. And there is surely some truth to this. Consumer rationality is a useful working assumption; it is not an absolute truth.

However, another answer is that consumer response to advertising is not entirely irrational because ads can serve as indirect "signals" in a world where consumers don't have good information about products. Suppose, to take a common example, that you need to avail yourself of some local service that you don't use regularly—body work on your car, say, or furniture moving. You turn to the Yellow Pages, where you see a number of small listings and several large display ads. You know that those display ads are large because the firms paid extra for them; still, it may be quite rational to call one of the firms with a big display ad. After all, the big ad probably means that it's a relatively large, successful company—otherwise, the company wouldn't have found it worth spending the money for the larger ad.

The same principle may partly explain why ads feature celebrities. You don't really believe that the supermodel prefers that watch; but the fact that the watch manufacturer is willing and able to pay her fee tells you that it is a major company that is likely to stand behind its product. According to this reasoning, an expensive advertisement serves to establish the quality of a firm's products in the eyes of consumers.

The possibility that it is rational for consumers to respond to advertising also has some bearing on the question of whether advertising is a waste of resources. If ads work by manipulating only the weak-minded, the $149 billion U.S. businesses spent on advertising in 2007 would have been an economic waste—except to the extent that ads sometimes provide entertainment. To the extent that advertising conveys important information, however, it is an economically productive activity after all.

Brand Names

You've been driving all day, and you decide that it's time to find a place to sleep. On your right, you see a sign for the Bates Motel; on your left, you see a sign for a Motel 6, or a Best Western, or some other national chain. Which one do you choose?

© Jonathan Larsen/Diadem Images/Alamy

A **brand name** is a name owned by a particular firm that distinguishes its products from those of other firms.

Unless they were familiar with the area, most people would head for the chain. In fact, most motels in the United States are members of major chains; the same is true of most fast-food restaurants and many, if not most, stores in shopping malls.

Motel chains and fast-food restaurants are only one aspect of a broader phenomenon: the role of **brand names,** names owned by particular companies that differentiate their products in the minds of consumers. In many cases, a company's brand name is the most important asset it possesses: clearly, McDonald's is worth far more than the sum of the deep-fat fryers and hamburger grills the company owns.

In fact, companies often go to considerable lengths to defend their brand names, suing anyone else who uses them without permission. You may talk about blowing your nose on a kleenex or xeroxing a term paper, but unless the product in question comes from Kleenex or Xerox, legally the seller must describe it as a facial tissue or a photocopier.

As with advertising, with which they are closely linked, the social usefulness of brand names is a source of dispute. Does the preference of consumers for known brands reflect consumer irrationality? Or do brand names convey real information? That is, do brand names create unnecessary market power, or do they serve a real purpose?

As in the case of advertising, the answer is probably some of both. On the one hand, brand names often do create unjustified market power. Consumers often pay more for brand-name goods in the supermarket even though consumer experts assure us that the cheaper store brands are equally good. Similarly, many common medicines, like aspirin, are cheaper—with no loss of quality—in their generic form.

On the other hand, for many products the brand name does convey information. A traveler arriving in a strange town can be sure of what awaits in a Holiday Inn or a McDonald's; a tired and hungry traveler may find this preferable to trying an independent hotel or restaurant that might be better—but might be worse.

In addition, brand names offer some assurance that the seller is engaged in repeated interaction with its customers and so has a reputation to protect. If a traveler eats a bad meal at a restaurant in a tourist trap and vows never to eat there again, the restaurant owner may not care, since the chance is small that the traveler will be in the same area again in the future. But if that traveler eats a bad meal at McDonald's and vows never to eat at a McDonald's again, that matters to the company. This gives McDonald's an incentive to provide consistent quality, thereby assuring travelers that quality controls are in place.

Module 32 Review

Solutions appear at the back of the book.

Check Your Understanding

1. For each of the following types of advertising, explain whether it is likely to be useful or wasteful from the standpoint of consumers.
   a. advertisements explaining the benefits of aspirin
   b. advertisements for Bayer aspirin
   c. advertisements that state how long a plumber or an electrician has been in business

2. Some industry analysts have stated that a successful brand name is like a barrier to entry. Explain why this might be true.

Multiple-Choice Questions

1. Which of the following is a form of product differentiation?
       I. style or type
       II. location
       III. quality
   a. I only
   b. II only
   c. III only
   d. I and II only
   e. I, II, and III

2. In which of the following market structures will individual firms advertise?
       I. perfect competition
       II. oligopoly
       III. monopolistic competition
   a. I only
   b. II only
   c. III only
   d. II and III only
   e. I, II, and III

3. Advertising is an attempt to affect which of the following?
   a. consumer tastes and preferences
   b. consumer income
   c. the price of complements
   d. the price of substitutes
   e. input prices

4. Brand names generally serve to
   a. waste resources.
   b. decrease firm profits.
   c. confuse consumers.
   d. decrease information.
   e. signal quality.

5. Which of the following is true of advertising expenditures in monopolistic competition? Monopolistic competitors
   a. will not advertise.
   b. use only informational advertising.
   c. waste resources on advertising.
   d. attempt to create popular brand names.
   e. earn long-run profits through advertising.

Critical-Thinking Question

When is product differentiation socially efficient? Explain. When is it not socially efficient? Explain.

Section 6 Review

Summary

Introduction to Oligopoly

1. Many industries are oligopolies, characterized by a small number of sellers. The smallest type of oligopoly, a **duopoly,** has only two sellers. Oligopolies exist for more or less the same reasons that monopolies exist, but in weaker form. They are characterized by imperfect competition: firms compete but possess market power.

2. Predicting the behavior of oligopolists poses something of a puzzle. The firms in an oligopoly could maximize their combined profits by acting as a **cartel,** setting output levels for each firm as if they were a sin-

gle monopolist; to the extent that firms manage to do this, they engage in **collusion.** But each individual firm has an incentive to produce more than the agreed upon quantity of output—to engage in **noncooperative behavior.** Informal collusion is likely to be easier to achieve in industries in which firms face capacity constraints.

Game Theory

3. The situation of **interdependence,** in which each firm's profit depends noticeably on what other firms do, is the subject of **game theory.** In the case of a game

with two players, the **payoff** of each player depends on both its own actions and on the actions of the other; this interdependence can be shown in a **payoff matrix.** Depending on the structure of payoffs in the payoff matrix, a player may have a **dominant strategy**—an action that is always the best regardless of the other player's actions.

4. Some **duopolists** face a particular type of game known as a **prisoners' dilemma;** if each acts independently on its own interest, the resulting **Nash equilibrium** or **noncooperative equilibrium** will be bad for both. However, firms that expect to play a game repeatedly tend to engage in **strategic behavior,** trying to influence each other's future actions. A particular strategy that seems to work well in such situations is **tit for tat,** which often leads to **tacit collusion.**

Oligopoly in Practice

5. In order to limit the ability of oligopolists to collude and act like monopolists, most governments pursue **antitrust policy** designed to make collusion more difficult. In practice, however, tacit collusion is widespread.

6. A variety of factors make tacit collusion difficult: a large numbers of firms, complex products and pricing, differences in interests, and buyers with bargaining power. When tacit collusion breaks down, there can be a **price war.** Oligopolists try to avoid price wars in various ways, such as through **product differentiation** and through **price leadership,** in which one firm sets prices for the industry. Another approach is **nonprice competition,** such as advertising.

Introduction to Monopolistic Competition

7. Monopolistic competition is a market structure in which there are many competing producers, each producing a differentiated product, and there is free entry and exit in the long run.

8. Short-run profits will attract the entry of new firms in the long run. This reduces the quantity each existing producer sells at any given price and shifts its demand curve to the left. Short-run losses will induce exit by some firms in the long run. This shifts the demand curve of each remaining firm to the right.

9. In the long run, a monopolistically competitive industry is in **zero-profit equilibrium:** at its profit-maximizing quantity, the demand curve for each existing firm is tangent to its average total cost curve. There are zero profits in the industry and no entry or exit.

10. In long-run equilibrium, firms in a monopolistically competitive industry sell at a price greater than marginal cost. They also have **excess capacity** because they produce less than the minimum-cost output; as a result, they have higher costs than firms in a perfectly competitive industry. Whether or not monopolistic competition is inefficient is ambiguous because consumers value the product diversity that it creates.

Product Competition and Advertising

11. Product differentiation takes three main forms: style or type, location, and quality. Firms will engage in advertising to increase demand for their products and enhance their market power. Advertising and **brand names** that provide useful information to consumers are valuable to society. Advertisements can be wasteful from a societal standpoint when their only purpose is to create market power.

Key Terms

Interdependence, p. 282
Duopoly, p. 282
Duopolist, p. 282
Collusion, p. 283
Cartel, p. 639
Noncooperative behavior, p. 284
Game theory, p. 288
Payoff, p. 288

Payoff matrix, p. 288
Prisoners' dilemma, p. 289
Dominant strategy, p. 290
Nash equilibrium, p. 290
Noncooperative equilibrium, p. 291
Strategic behavior, p. 291
Tit for tat, p. 647
Tacit collusion, p. 293

Antitrust policy, p. 297
Price war, p. 298
Product differentiation, p. 299
Price leadership, p. 300
Nonprice competition, p. 300
Zero-profit equilibrium, p. 305
Excess capacity, p. 309
Brand name, p. 316

Problems

1. The accompanying table presents market share data for the U.S. breakfast cereal market in 2006.

Company	Market Share
Kellogg	30%
General Mills	26
PepsiCo (Quaker Oats)	14
Kraft	13
Private Label	11
Other	6

Source: Advertising Age

a. Use the data provided to calculate the Herfindahl–Hirschman Index (HHI) for the market.

b. Based on this HHI, what type of market structure is the U.S. breakfast cereal market?

2. The accompanying table shows the demand schedule for vitamin D. Suppose that the marginal cost of producing vitamin D is zero.

Price of vitamin D (per ton)	Quantity of vitamin D demanded (tons)
$8	0
7	10
6	20
5	30
4	40
3	50
2	60
1	70

a. Assume that BASF is the only producer of vitamin D and acts as a monopolist. It currently produces 40 tons of vitamin D at $4 per ton. If BASF were to produce 10 more tons, what would be the price effect for BASF? What would be the quantity effect? Would BASF have an incentive to produce those 10 additional tons?

b. Now assume that Roche enters the market by also producing vitamin D and the market is now a duopoly. BASF and Roche agree to produce 40 tons of vitamin D in total, 20 tons each. BASF cannot be punished for deviating from the agreement with Roche. If BASF, on its own, were to deviate from that agreement and produce 10 more tons, what would be the price effect for BASF? What would be the quantity effect for BASF? Would BASF have an incentive to produce those 10 additional tons?

3. The market for olive oil in New York City is controlled by two families, the Sopranos and the Contraltos. Both families will ruthlessly eliminate any other family that attempts to enter the New York City olive oil market. The marginal cost of producing olive oil is constant and equal to $40 per gallon. There is no fixed cost. The accompanying table gives the market demand schedule for olive oil.

Price of olive oil (per gallon)	Quantity of olive oil demanded (gallons)
$100	1,000
90	1,500
80	2,000
70	2,500
60	3,000
50	3,500
40	4,000
30	4,500
20	5,000
10	5,500

a. Suppose the Sopranos and the Contraltos form a cartel. For each of the quantities given in the table, calculate the total revenue for their cartel and the marginal revenue for each additional gallon. How many gallons of olive oil would the cartel sell in total and at what price? The two families share the market equally (each produces half of the total output of the cartel). How much profit does each family make?

b. Uncle Junior, the head of the Soprano family, breaks the agreement and sells 500 more gallons of olive oil than under the cartel agreement. Assuming the Contraltos maintain the agreement, how does this affect the price for olive oil and the profits earned by each family?

c. Anthony Contralto, the head of the Contralto family, decides to punish Uncle Junior by increasing his sales by 500 gallons as well. How much profit does each family earn now?

4. In France, the market for bottled water is controlled by two large firms, Perrier and Evian. Each firm has a fixed cost of €1 million and a constant marginal cost of €2 per liter of bottled water (€1 = 1 euro). The following table gives the market demand schedule for bottled water in France.

Price of bottled water (per liter)	Quantity of bottled water demanded (millions of liters)
€10	0
9	1
8	2
7	3
6	4
5	5
4	6
3	7
2	8
1	9

a. Suppose the two firms form a cartel and act as a monopolist. Calculate marginal revenue for the cartel. What will the monopoly price and output be? Assuming the firms divided the output evenly, how much will each produce and what will each firm's profits be?

b. Now suppose Perrier decides to increase production by 1 million liters. Evian doesn't change its production. What will the new market price and output be? What is Perrier's profit? What is Evian's profit?

c. What if Perrier increases production by 3 million liters? Evian doesn't change its production. What would its output and profits be relative to those in part b?

d. What do your results tell you about the likelihood of cheating on such agreements?

5. To preserve the North Atlantic fish stocks, it is decided that only two fishing fleets, one from the United States and the other from the European Union (EU), can fish in those waters. The accompanying table shows the market demand schedule per week for fish from these waters. The only costs are fixed costs, so fishing fleets maximize profit by maximizing revenue.

Price of fish (per pound)	Quantity of fish demanded (pounds)
$17	1,800
16	2,000
15	2,100
14	2,200
12	2,300

a. If both fishing fleets collude, what is the revenue-maximizing output for the North Atlantic fishery? What price will a pound of fish sell for?

b. If both fishing fleets collude and share the output equally, what is the revenue to the EU fleet? To the U.S. fleet?

c. Suppose the EU fleet cheats by expanding its own catch by 100 pounds per week. The U.S. fleet doesn't change its catch. What is the revenue to the U.S. fleet? To the EU fleet?

d. In retaliation for the cheating by the EU fleet, the U.S. fleet also expands its catch by 100 pounds per week. What is the revenue to the U.S. fleet? To the EU fleet?

6. Suppose that the fisheries agreement in Problem 5 breaks down, so that the fleets behave noncooperatively. Assume that the United States and the EU each can send out either one or two fleets. The more fleets in the area, the more fish they catch in total but the lower the catch of each fleet. The accompany-

ing matrix shows the profit (in dollars) per week earned by the two sides.

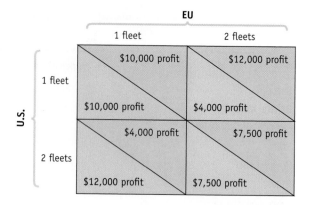

a. What is the noncooperative Nash equilibrium? Will each side choose to send out one or two fleets?

b. Suppose that the fish stocks are being depleted. Each region considers the future and comes to a "tit-for-tat" agreement whereby each side will send only one fleet out as long as the other does the same. If either of them breaks the agreement and sends out a second fleet, the other will also send out two and will continue to do so until its competitor sends out only one fleet. If both play this "tit-for-tat" strategy, how much profit will each make every week?

7. Untied and Air "R" Us are the only two airlines operating flights between Collegeville and Bigtown. That is, they operate in a duopoly. Each airline can charge either a high price or a low price for a ticket. The accompanying matrix shows their payoffs, in profits per seat (in dollars), for any choice that the two airlines can make.

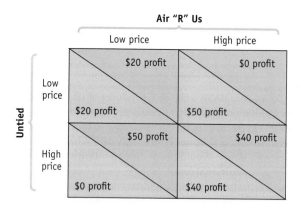

a. Suppose the two airlines play a one-shot game—that is, they interact only once and never again. What will be the Nash equilibrium in this one-shot game?

b. Now suppose the two airlines play this game twice. And suppose each airline can play one of two strategies: it can play either "always charge the low price" or "tit for tat"—that is, start off charging the high price in the first period, and then in the second period do whatever the other airline did in the previous period. Write down the payoffs to Untied from the following four possibilities:

   i. Untied plays "always charge the low price" when Air "R" Us also plays "always charge the low price."

   ii. Untied plays "always charge the low price" when Air "R" Us plays "tit for tat."

   iii. Untied plays "tit for tat" when Air "R" Us plays "always charge the low price."

   iv. Untied plays "tit for tat" when Air "R" Us also plays "tit for tat."

8. Suppose that Coke and Pepsi are the only two producers of cola drinks, making them duopolists. Both companies have zero marginal cost and a fixed cost of $100,000.

a. Assume first that consumers regard Coke and Pepsi as perfect substitutes. Currently both are sold for $0.20 per can, and at that price each company sells 4 million cans per day.

   i. How large is Pepsi's profit?

   ii. If Pepsi were to raise its price to $0.30 cents per can, and Coke did not respond, what would happen to Pepsi's profit?

b. Now suppose that each company advertises to differentiate its product from the other company's. As a result of advertising, Pepsi realizes that if it raises or lowers its price, it will sell less or more of its product, as shown by the demand schedule in the accompanying table.

Price of Pepsi (per can)	Quantity of Pepsi demanded (millions of cans)
$0.10	5
0.20	4
0.30	3
0.40	2
0.50	1

If Pepsi now were to raise its price to $0.30 per can, what would happen to its profit?

c. Comparing your answer to part a(i) and to part b, what is the maximum amount Pepsi would be willing to spend on advertising?

9. Philip Morris and R.J. Reynolds spend huge sums of money each year to advertise their tobacco products in an attempt to steal customers from each other. Suppose each year Philip Morris and R.J. Reynolds have to decide whether or not they want to spend money on advertising. If neither firm advertises, each will earn a profit of $2 million. If they both advertise, each will earn a profit of $1.5 million. If one firm advertises and the other does not, the firm that advertises will earn a profit of $2.8 million and the other firm will earn $1 million.

a. Use a payoff matrix to depict this problem.

b. Suppose Philip Morris and R.J. Reynolds can write an enforceable contract about what they will do. What is the cooperative solution to this game?

c. What is the Nash equilibrium without an enforceable contract? Explain why this is the likely outcome.

10. Use the three conditions for monopolistic competition discussed in this section to decide which of the following firms are likely to be operating as monopolistic competitors. If they are not monopolistically competitive firms, are they monopolists, oligopolists, or perfectly competitive firms?

a. a local band that plays for weddings, parties, and so on

b. Minute Maid, a producer of individual-serving juice boxes

c. your local dry cleaner

d. a farmer who produces soybeans

11. You are thinking of setting up a coffee shop. The market structure for coffee shops is monopolistic competition. There are three Starbucks shops, and two other coffee shops very much like Starbucks, in your town already. In order for you to have some degree of market power, you may want to differentiate your coffee shop. Thinking about the three different ways in which products can be differentiated, explain how you would decide whether you should copy Starbucks or whether you should sell coffee in a completely different way.

12. The restaurant business in town is a monopolistically competitive industry in long-run equilibrium. One restaurant owner asks for your advice. She tells you that, each night, not all tables in her restaurant are full. She also tells you that if she lowered the prices on her menu, she would attract more customers and that doing so would lower her average total cost. Should she lower her prices? Draw a diagram showing the demand curve, marginal revenue curve, marginal cost curve, and average total cost curve for this restaurant to explain your advice. Show in your diagram what would happen to the restaurant owner's profit if she were to lower the price so that she sells the minimum-cost output.

13. The market structure of the local gas station industry is monopolistic competition. Suppose that currently each gas station incurs a loss. Draw a diagram for a typical gas station to show this short-run situation. Then, in a separate diagram, show what will happen to the typical gas station in the long run. Explain your reasoning.

14. The local hairdresser industry has the market structure of monopolistic competition. Your hairdresser boasts that he is making a profit and that if he continues to do so, he will be able to retire in five years. Use a diagram to illustrate your hairdresser's current situation. Do you expect this to last? In a separate diagram, draw what you expect to happen in the long run. Explain your reasoning.

15. Magnificent Blooms is a florist in a monopolistically competitive industry. It is a successful operation, producing the quantity that minimizes its average total cost and making a profit. The owner also says that at its current level of output, its marginal cost is above marginal revenue. Illustrate the current situation of Magnificent Blooms in a diagram. Answer the following questions by illustrating with a diagram.

    a. In the short run, could Magnificent Blooms increase its profit?

    b. In the long run, could Magnificent Blooms increase its profit?

16. "In both the short run and in the long run, the typical firm in monopolistic competition and a monopolist each make a profit." Do you agree with this statement? Explain your reasoning.

17. The market for clothes has the structure of monopolistic competition. What impact will fewer firms in this industry have on you as a consumer? Address the following issues:

    a. variety of clothes

    b. differences in quality of service

    c. price

18. For each of the following situations, decide whether advertising is directly informative about the product or simply an indirect signal of its quality. Explain your reasoning.

    a. Golf champion Tiger Woods drives a Buick in a TV commercial and claims that he prefers it to any other car.

    b. A newspaper ad states, "For sale: 1999 Honda Civic, 160,000 miles, new transmission."

    c. McDonald's spends millions of dollars on an advertising campaign that proclaims: "I'm lovin' it."

    d. Subway advertises one of its sandwiches by claiming that it contains 6 grams of fat and fewer than 300 calories.

19. In each of the following cases, explain how the advertisement functions as a signal to a potential buyer. Explain what information the buyer lacks that is being supplied by the advertisement and how the information supplied by the advertisement is likely to affect the buyer's willingness to buy the good.

    a. "Looking for work. Excellent references from previous employers available."

    b. "Electronic equipment for sale. All merchandise carries a one-year, no-questions-asked warranty."

    c. "Car for sale by original owner. All repair and maintenance records available."

20. The accompanying table shows the Herfindahl–Hirschman Index (HHI) for the restaurant, cereal, movie, and laundry detergent industries as well as the advertising expenditures of the top 10 firms in each industry in 2006. Use the information in the table to answer the following questions.

Industry	HHI	Advertising expenditures (millions)
Restaurants	179	$1,784
Cereal	2,098	732
Movie studios	918	3,324
Laundry detergent	2,068	132

    a. Which market structure—oligopoly or monopolistic competition—best characterizes each of the industries?

    b. Based on your answer to part a, which type of market structure has higher advertising expenditures? Use the characteristics of each market structure to explain why this relationship might exist.

section 7

Factor Markets

Does higher education pay? Yes, it does: In the modern economy, employers are willing to pay a premium for workers with more education. And the size of that premium has increased a lot over the last few decades. Back in 1973 workers with advanced degrees, such as law degrees or MBAs, earned only 76% more than those who had only graduated from high school. By 2009, the premium for an advanced degree had risen to over 112%.

Who decided that the wages of workers with advanced degrees would rise so much compared with those of high school grads? The answer, of course, is that nobody decided it. Wage rates are prices, the prices of different kinds of labor; and they are decided, like other prices, by supply and demand.

Still, there is a qualitative difference between the wage rate of high school grads and the price of used textbooks: the wage rate isn't the price of a *good;* it's the price of a *factor of production.* And although markets for factors of production are in many ways similar to those for goods, there are also some important differences.

In this section, we examine *factor markets,* the markets in which the factors of production such as labor, land, and capital are traded. Factor markets, like goods markets, play a crucial role in the economy: they allocate productive resources to firms and help ensure that those resources are used efficiently.

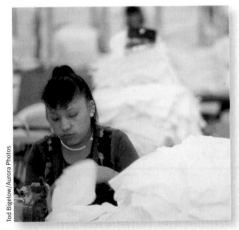

Tod Bigelow/Aurora Photos

Jon Feingersch/Corbis

If you've ever had doubts about attending college, consider this: factory workers with only high school degrees will make much less than college grads. The present discounted value of the difference in lifetime earnings is as much as $300,000.

323

What you will learn in this **Module:**

- How factors of production—resources like land, labor, and capital—are traded in factor markets

- How factor markets determine the factor distribution of income

- How the demand for a factor of production is determined

Module 33
Introduction and Factor Demand

The Economy's Factors of Production

You may recall that we have already defined a factor of production in the context of the circular-flow diagram; it is any resource that is used by firms to produce goods and services, items that are consumed by households. The markets in which factors of production are bought and sold are called *factor markets*, and the prices in factor markets are known as *factor prices*.

What are these factors of production, and why do factor prices matter?

The Factors of Production

Economists divide factors of production into four principal classes. The first is *labor*, the work done by human beings. The second is *land*, which encompasses resources provided by nature. The third is capital, which can be divided into two categories: **physical capital**—often referred to simply as "capital"—consists of manufactured resources such as equipment, buildings, tools, and machines. In the modern economy, **human capital,** the improvement in labor created by education and knowledge, and embodied in the workforce, is at least equally significant. Technological progress has boosted the importance of human capital and made technical sophistication essential to many jobs, thus helping to create the premium for workers with advanced degrees. The final factor of production, *entrepreneurship,* is a unique resource that is not purchased in an easily identifiable factor market like the other three. It refers to risk-taking activities that bring together resources for innovative production.

Why Factor Prices Matter: The Allocation of Resources

The factor prices determined in factor markets play a vital role in the important process of allocating resources among firms.

Consider the example of Mississippi and Louisiana in the aftermath of Hurricane Katrina, the costliest hurricane ever to hit the U.S. mainland. The states had an urgent

Physical capital—often referred to simply as "capital"—consists of manufactured productive resources such as equipment, buildings, tools, and machines.

Human capital is the improvement in labor created by education and knowledge that is embodied in the workforce.

need for workers in the building trades—everything from excavation to roofing—to repair or replace damaged structures. What ensured that those needed workers actually came? The factor market: the high demand for workers drove up wages. During 2005, the average U.S. wage grew at a rate of around 6%. But in areas heavily affected by Katrina, the average wage during the fall of 2005 grew by 30% more than the national rate, and some areas saw twice that rate of increase. Over time, these higher wages led large numbers of workers with the right skills to move temporarily to these states to do the work.

In other words, the market for a factor of production—construction workers—allocated that factor of production to where it was needed.

In this sense factor markets are similar to goods markets, which allocate goods among consumers. But there are two features that make factor markets special. Unlike in a goods market, demand in a factor market is what we call **derived demand.** That is, demand for the factor is derived from demand for the firm's output. The second feature is that factor markets are where most of us get the largest shares of our income (government transfers being the next largest source of income in the economy).

In the months after Hurricane Katrina, home repair signs like these were abundant throughout New Orleans.

Factor Incomes and the Distribution of Income

Most American families get most of their income in the form of wages and salaries—that is, they get their income by selling labor. Some people, however, get most of their income from physical capital: when you own stock in a company, what you really own is a share of that company's physical capital. Some people get much of their income from rents earned on land they own. And successful entrepreneurs earn income in the form of profits.

Obviously, then, the prices of factors of production have a major impact on how the economic "pie" is sliced among different groups. For example, a higher wage rate, other things equal, means that a larger proportion of the total income in the economy goes to people who derive their income from labor and less goes to those who derive their income from capital, land, or entrepreneurship. Economists refer to how the economic pie is sliced as the "distribution of income." Specifically, factor prices determine the **factor distribution of income**—how the total income of the economy is divided among labor, land, capital, and entrepreneurship.

The factor distribution of income in the United States has been quite stable over the past few decades. In other times and places, however, large changes have taken place in the factor distribution. One notable example: during the Industrial Revolution, the share of total income earned by landowners fell sharply, while the share earned by capital owners rose.

The Factor Distribution of Income in the United States

When we talk about the factor distribution of income, what are we talking about in practice?

In the United States, as in all advanced economies, payments to labor account for most of the economy's total income. Figure 33.1 on the next page shows the factor distribution of income in the United States in 2009: in that year, 70.9% of total income in the economy took the form of "compensation of employees"—a number that includes

The demand for a factor is a **derived demand.** It results from (that is, it is derived from) the demand for the output being produced.

The **factor distribution of income** is the division of total income among land, labor, capital, and entrepreneurship.

figure **33.1**

Factor Distribution of Income in the United States in 2009

In 2009, compensation of employees accounted for most income earned in the United States—70.9% of the total. Most of the remainder—consisting of earnings paid in the form of interest, corporate profits, and rent—went to owners of physical capital. Finally, proprietors' income—9.2% of the total—went to individual owners of businesses as compensation for their labor, entrepreneurship, and capital expended in their businesses.

Source: Bureau of Economic Analysis.

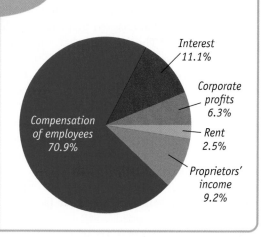

Interest 11.1%

Corporate profits 6.3%

Rent 2.5%

Proprietors' income 9.2%

Compensation of employees 70.9%

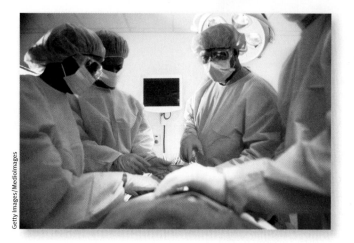

both wages and benefits such as health insurance. This number has been quite stable over the long run; 37 years earlier, in 1972, compensation of employees was very similar, at 72.2% of total income.

Much of what we call compensation of employees is really a return on human capital. A surgeon isn't just supplying the services of a pair of ordinary hands (at least the patient hopes not!): that individual is also supplying the result of many years and hundreds of thousands of dollars invested in training and experience. We can't directly measure what fraction of wages is really a payment for education and training, but many economists believe that labor resources created through additional human capital has become *the* most important factor of production in modern economies.

Marginal Productivity and Factor Demand

All economic decisions are about comparing costs and benefits—and usually about comparing marginal costs and marginal benefits. This goes both for a consumer, deciding whether to buy more goods or services, and for a firm, deciding whether to hire an additional worker.

Although there are some important exceptions, most factor markets in the modern American economy are perfectly competitive. This means that most buyers and sellers of factors are price-takers because they are too small relative to the market to do anything but accept the market price. And in a competitive labor market, it's clear how to define the marginal cost an employer pays for a worker: it is simply the worker's wage rate. But what is the marginal benefit of that worker? To answer that question, we return to the production function, which relates inputs to output. For now we assume that all firms are price-takers in their output markets—that is, they operate in a perfectly competitive industry.

Value of the Marginal Product

Figure 33.2 shows the production function for wheat on George and Martha's farm, as introduced in the module "The Production Function." Panel (a) uses the total product curve to show how total wheat production depends on the number of workers employed on the farm; panel (b) shows how the *marginal product of labor,* the increase in output from employing one more worker, depends on the number of workers employed. Table 33.1

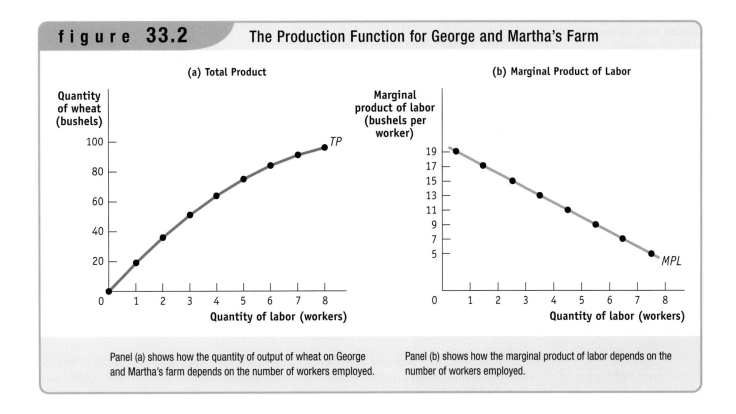

(a) Total Product

(b) Marginal Product of Labor

Panel (a) shows how the quantity of output of wheat on George and Martha's farm depends on the number of workers employed.

Panel (b) shows how the marginal product of labor depends on the number of workers employed.

shows the numbers behind the figure. Note: sometimes the marginal product (*MP*) is called the *marginal physical product* or *MPP*. These two terms are the same; the extra "P" just emphasizes that the term refers to the quantity of physical output being produced, not the monetary value of that output.

If workers are paid $200 each and wheat sells for $20 per bushel, how many workers should George and Martha employ to maximize profit?

table **33.1**

Employment and Output for George and Martha's Farm

Quantity of labor *L* (workers)	Quantity of wheat *Q* (bushels)	Marginal product of labor $MPL = \frac{\Delta Q}{\Delta L}$ (bushels per worker)
0	0	
		19
1	19	
		17
2	36	
		15
3	51	
		13
4	64	
		11
5	75	
		9
6	84	
		7
7	91	
		5
8	96	

Earlier we showed how to answer this question in several steps. First, we used information from the production function to derive the firm's total cost and its marginal cost. Then we used the *price-taking firm's optimal output rule:* a price-taking firm's profit is maximized by producing the quantity of output at which the marginal cost is equal to the market price. Having determined the optimal quantity of output, we went back to the production function to find the optimal number of workers—which was simply the number of workers needed to produce the optimal quantity of output.

As you might have guessed, marginal analysis provides a more direct way to find the number of workers that maximizes a firm's profit. This alternative approach is just a different way of looking at the same thing. But it gives us more insight into the demand for factors as opposed to the supply of goods.

To see how this alternative approach works, suppose that George and Martha are deciding whether to employ another worker. The increase in *cost* from employing another worker is the wage rate, W. The *benefit* to George and Martha from employing another worker is the value of the extra output that worker can produce. What is this value? It is the marginal product of labor, MPL, multiplied by the price per unit of output, P. This amount—the extra value of output generated by employing one more unit of labor—is known as the **value of the marginal product** of labor, or $VMPL$:

(33-1)   Value of the marginal product of labor $= VMPL = P \times MPL$

So should George and Martha hire another worker? Yes, if the value of the extra output is more than the cost of the additional worker—that is, if $VMPL > W$. Otherwise, they should not.

The hiring decision is made using marginal analysis, by comparing the marginal benefit from hiring another worker ($VMPL$) with the marginal cost (W). And as with any decision that is made on the margin, the optimal choice is made by equating marginal benefit with marginal cost (or if they're never equal, by continuing to hire until the marginal cost of one more unit would exceed the marginal benefit). That is, to maximize profit, George and Martha will employ workers up to the point at which, for the last worker employed,

(33-2) $VMPL = W$.

This rule isn't limited to labor; it applies to any factor of production. The value of the marginal product of any factor is its marginal product times the price of the good it produces. And as a general rule, profit-maximizing, price-taking firms will keep adding more units of each factor of production until the value of the marginal product of the last unit employed is equal to the factor's price.

This rule is consistent with our previous analysis. We saw that a profit-maximizing firm chooses the level of output at which the price of the good it produces equals the marginal cost of producing that good. It turns out that if the level of output is chosen so that price equals marginal cost, then it is also true that with the amount of labor required to produce that output level, the value of the marginal product of labor will equal the wage rate.

Now let's look more closely at why choosing the level of employment to equate $VMPL$ and W works, and at how it helps us understand factor demand.

Value of the Marginal Product and Factor Demand

Table 33.2 shows the value of the marginal product of labor on George and Martha's farm when the price of wheat is $20 per bushel. In Figure 33.3, the horizontal axis shows the number of workers employed; the vertical axis measures the value of the marginal product of labor *and* the wage rate. The curve shown is the **value of the marginal product curve** of labor. This curve, like the marginal product of labor curve, slopes downward because of diminishing returns to labor in production. That is, the value of the

table 33.2

Value of the Marginal Product of Labor for George and Martha's Farm

Quantity of labor *L* (workers)	Marginal product of labor *MPL* (bushels per worker)	Value of the marginal product of labor $VMPL = P \times MPL$
0		
	19	$380
1		
	17	340
2		
	15	300
3		
	13	260
4		
	11	220
5		
	9	180
6		
	7	140
7		
	5	100
8		

marginal product of each worker is less than that of the preceding worker because the marginal product of each worker is less than that of the preceding worker.

We have just seen that to maximize profit, George and Martha hire workers until the wage rate is equal to the value of the marginal product of the last worker employed. Let's use the example to see how this principle really works.

figure 33.3

The Value of the Marginal Product Curve

This curve shows how the value of the marginal product of labor depends on the number of workers employed. It slopes downward because of diminishing returns to labor in production. To maximize profit, George and Martha choose the level of employment at which the value of the marginal product of labor is equal to the market wage rate. For example, at a wage rate of $200 the profit-maximizing level of employment is 5 workers, shown by point *A*. The value of the marginal product curve of a factor is the producer's individual demand curve for that factor.

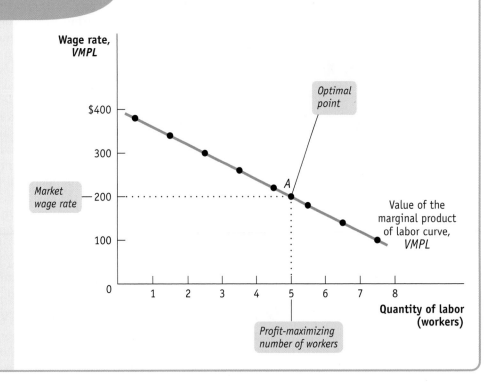

Assume that George and Martha currently employ 3 workers and that these workers must be paid the market wage rate of $200. Should they employ an additional worker?

Looking at Table 33.2, we see that if George and Martha currently employ 3 workers, the value of the marginal product of an additional worker is $260. So if they employ an additional worker, they will increase the value of their production by $260 but increase their cost by only $200, yielding an increased profit of $60. In fact, a firm can always increase profit by employing one more unit of a factor of production as long as the value of the marginal product produced by that unit exceeds the factor price.

Alternatively, suppose that George and Martha employ 8 workers. By reducing the number of workers to 7, they can save $200 in wages. In addition, the value of the marginal product of the 8th worker is only $100. So, by reducing employment by one worker, they can increase profit by $200 − $100 = $100. In other words, a firm can always increase profit by employing one less unit of a factor of production as long as the value of the marginal product produced by that unit is less than the factor price.

Using this method, we can see from Table 33.2 that the profit-maximizing employment level is 5 workers, given a wage rate of $200. The value of the marginal product of the 5th worker is $220, so adding the 5th worker results in $20 of additional profit. But George and Martha should not hire more than 5 workers: the value of the marginal product of the 6th worker is only $180, $20 less than the cost of that worker. So, to maximize profit, George and Martha should employ workers up to but not beyond the point at which the value of the marginal product of the last worker employed is equal to the wage rate.

Look again at the value of the marginal product curve in Figure 33.3. To determine the profit-maximizing level of employment, we set the value of the marginal product of labor equal to the price of labor—a wage rate of $200 per worker. This means that the

Firms keep hiring more workers until the value of the marginal product of labor equals the wage rate.

profit-maximizing level of employment is at point *A,* corresponding to an employment level of 5 workers. If the wage rate were higher, we would simply move up the curve and decrease the number of workers employed: if the wage rate were lower than $200, we would move down the curve and increase the number of workers employed.

In this example, George and Martha have a small farm in which the potential employment level varies from 0 to 8 workers, and they hire workers up to the point at which the value of the marginal product of another worker would fall below the wage rate. For a larger farm with many employees, the value of the marginal product of labor falls only slightly when an additional worker is employed. As a result, there will be some worker whose value of the marginal product almost exactly equals the wage rate. (In keeping with the George and Martha example, this means that some worker generates a value of the marginal product of approximately $200.) In this case, the firm maximizes profit by choosing a level of employment at which the value of the marginal product of the last worker hired *equals* (to a very good approximation) the wage rate.

In the interest of simplicity, we will assume from now on that firms use this rule to determine the profit-maximizing level of employment. *This means that the value of the marginal product of labor curve is the individual firm's labor demand curve.* And in general, a firm's value of the marginal product curve for any factor of production is that firm's individual demand curve for that factor of production.

Shifts of the Factor Demand Curve

As in the case of ordinary demand curves, it is important to distinguish between movements along the factor demand curve and shifts of the factor demand curve. What causes factor demand curves to shift? There are three main causes:

- Changes in the prices of goods
- Changes in the supply of other factors
- Changes in technology

Changes in the Prices of Goods Remember that factor demand is derived demand: if the price of the good that is produced with a factor changes, so will the value of the marginal product of the factor. That is, in the case of labor demand, if P changes, $VMPL$ = $P \times MPL$ will change at any given level of employment.

Figure 33.4 illustrates the effects of changes in the price of wheat, assuming that $200 is the current wage rate. Panel (a) shows the effect of an *increase* in the price of wheat. This shifts the value of the marginal product of labor curve upward because $VMPL$ rises at any given level of employment. If the wage rate remains unchanged at $200, the optimal point moves from point A to point B: the profit-maximizing level of employment rises.

Panel (b) shows the effect of a *decrease* in the price of wheat. This shifts the value of the marginal product of labor curve downward. If the wage rate remains unchanged at $200, the optimal point moves from point A to point C: the profit-maximizing level of employment falls.

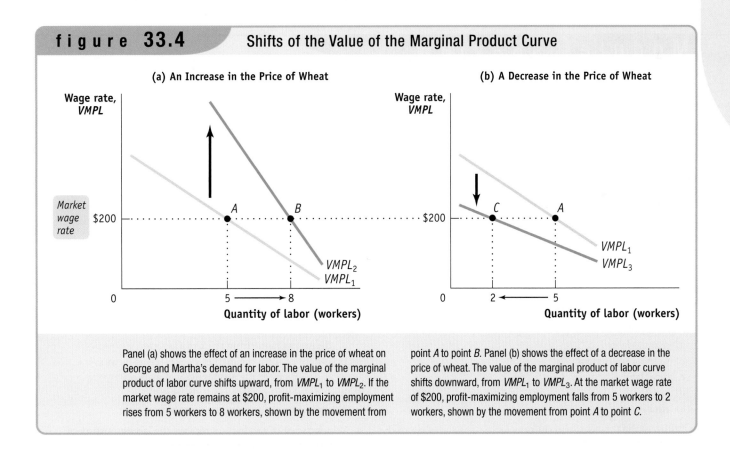

figure 33.4   Shifts of the Value of the Marginal Product Curve

Panel (a) shows the effect of an increase in the price of wheat on George and Martha's demand for labor. The value of the marginal product of labor curve shifts upward, from $VMPL_1$ to $VMPL_2$. If the market wage rate remains at $200, profit-maximizing employment rises from 5 workers to 8 workers, shown by the movement from point A to point B. Panel (b) shows the effect of a decrease in the price of wheat. The value of the marginal product of labor curve shifts downward, from $VMPL_1$ to $VMPL_3$. At the market wage rate of $200, profit-maximizing employment falls from 5 workers to 2 workers, shown by the movement from point A to point C.

Changes in the Supply of Other Factors Suppose that George and Martha acquire more land to cultivate—say, by clearing a woodland on their property. Each worker now produces more wheat because each one has more land to work with. As a result, the marginal product of labor on the farm rises at any given level of employment. This has the same effect as an increase in the price of wheat, which is illustrated in panel (a) of Figure 33.4: the value of the marginal product of labor curve shifts upward, and at any given wage rate the profit-maximizing level of employment rises. Similarly, suppose

George and Martha cultivate less land. This leads to a fall in the marginal product of labor at any given employment level. Each worker produces less wheat because each has less land to work with. As a result, the value of the marginal product of labor curve shifts downward—as in panel (b) of Figure 33.4—and the profit-maximizing level of employment falls.

Changes in Technology In general, the effect of technological progress on the demand for any given factor can go either way: improved technology can either increase or decrease the demand for a given factor of production.

How can technological progress decrease factor demand? Consider horses, which were once an important factor of production. The development of substitutes for horse power, such as automobiles and tractors, greatly reduced the demand for horses.

The usual effect of technological progress, however, is to increase the demand for a given factor, often because it raises the marginal product of the factor. In particular, although there have been persistent fears that machinery would reduce the demand for labor, over the long run the U.S. economy has seen both large wage increases and large increases in employment, suggesting that technological progress has greatly increased labor demand.

Module 33 Review

Solutions appear at the back of the book.

Check Your Understanding

1. Suppose that the government places price controls on the market for college professors, imposing a wage that is lower than the market wage. Describe the effect of this policy on the production of college degrees. What sectors of the economy do you think would be adversely affected by this policy? What sectors of the economy might benefit?

2. a. Suppose service industries, such as retailing and banking, experience an increase in demand. These industries use relatively more labor than nonservice industries. Does the demand curve for labor shift to the right, shift to the left, or remain unchanged?

   b. Suppose diminishing fish populations off the coast of Maine lead to policies restricting the use of the most productive types of nets in that area. The result is a decrease in the number of fish caught per day by commercial fishers in Maine. The price of fish is unaffected. Does the demand curve for fishers in Maine shift to the right, shift to the left, or remain unchanged?

Multiple-Choice Questions

1. Which of the following is an example of *physical* capital?
   a. manual labor
   b. welding equipment
   c. farm land
   d. lumber
   e. education

2. Which of the following can shift the factor demand curve to the right?
      I. an increase in the price of the good being produced
      II. an increase in the factor's marginal productivity
      III. a technological advance
   a. I only
   b. II only
   c. III only
   d. I and II only
   e. I, II, and III

3. Factor market demand is called a *derived* demand because it
   a. derives its name from the Latin *factorus*.
   b. is derived from the market wage received by workers.
   c. is derived from the productivity of workers.
   d. is derived from the product market.
   e. derives its shape from the price of the factor.

4. Which factor of production receives the largest portion of income in the United States?
   a. land
   b. labor
   c. physical capital
   d. entrepreneurship
   e. interest

5. The individual firm's demand curve for labor is
    a. the *VMPL* curve.
    b. upward sloping.
    c. horizontal at the level of the product price.
    d. vertical.
    e. equal to the *MPL* curve.

Critical-Thinking Questions

Draw a separate, correctly labeled graph illustrating the effect of each of the following changes on the demand for labor. Adopt the usual *ceteris paribus* assumption that all else remains unchanged in each case.

a. The price of the product being produced decreases.
b. Worker productivity increases.
c. Firms invest in more capital to be used by workers.

What you will learn in this **Module:**

- How to determine supply and demand in the markets for land and capital
- How to find equilibrium in the land and capital markets
- How the demand for factors leads to the marginal productivity theory of income distribution

Module 34
The Markets for Land and Capital

In Figure 33.1 we saw the factor distribution of income and found that approximately 70% of total income in the economy took the form of compensation for employees. Because labor is such an important resource, it is often used as the example in discussions of factor markets. But land and capital are critical resources as well, and their markets have unique characteristics worthy of examination. In this module we look more closely at the markets for land and capital before moving on to discuss the labor market further in the next module.

Land and Capital

In the previous module we used a labor market example to explain why a firm's individual demand curve for a factor is its value of the marginal product curve. Now we look at the distinguishing characteristics of demand and supply in land and capital markets, and how the equilibrium price and quantity of these factors are determined.

Demand in the Markets for Land and Capital

If we maintain the assumption that the markets for goods and services are perfectly competitive, the result that we derived for demand in the labor market also applies to other factors of production. Suppose, for example, that a farmer is considering whether to rent an additional acre of land for the next year. He or she will compare the cost of renting that acre with the value of the additional output generated by employing an additional acre—the value of the marginal product of an acre of land. To maximize profit, the farmer will rent more land up until the value of the marginal product of an acre of land is equal to the rental rate per acre. The same is true for capital: the decision of whether to rent an additional piece of equipment comes down to a comparison of the additional cost of the equipment with the value of the additional output it generates.

What if the farmer already owns the land or the firm already owns the equipment? As discussed in the module "Defining Profit" in the context of Babette's Cajun Café, even if you own land or capital, there is an implicit cost—the opportunity cost—of using it for a given activity because it could be used for something else, such as renting it out to other firms at the market rental rate. So a profit-maximizing firm employs additional units of land and capital until the cost of the last unit employed, explicit or implicit, is equal to the value of the marginal product of that unit. We call the explicit cost of renting a unit of land or capital for a set period of time its **rental rate.**

The **rental rate** of either land or capital is the cost, explicit or implicit, of using a unit of that asset for a given period of time.

As with labor, due to diminishing returns, the value of the marginal product curve and therefore the individual firm's demand curves for land and capital slope downward.

Supply in the Markets for Land and Capital

Figure 34.1 illustrates the markets for land and capital. The red curve in panel (a) is the supply curve for land. As we have drawn it, the supply curve for land is relatively steep and therefore relatively inelastic. This reflects the fact that finding new supplies of land for production is typically difficult and expensive—for example, creating new farmland through expensive irrigation.

The red curve in panel (b) is the supply curve for capital. In contrast to the supply curve for land, the supply curve for capital is relatively flat and therefore relatively elastic. That's because the supply of capital is relatively responsive to price: capital is typically paid for with the savings of investors, and the amount of savings that investors make available is relatively responsive to the rental rate for capital.

As in the case of supply curves for goods and services, the supply curve for a factor of production will shift as the factor becomes more or less available. For example, the supply of farmland could decrease as a result of a drought or the supply of capital could increase as a result of a government policy to promote investment. Because of diminishing returns, when the supply of land or capital changes, its marginal product will change.

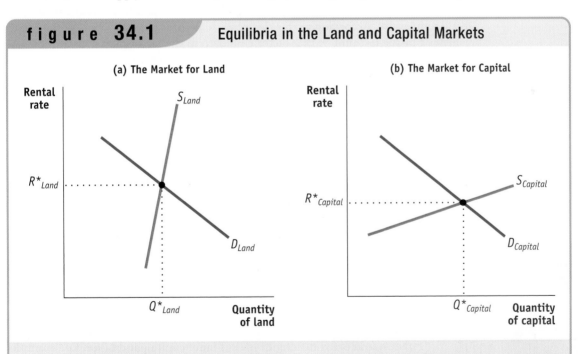

figure 34.1   Equilibria in the Land and Capital Markets

Panel (a) illustrates equilibrium in the market for land; panel (b) illustrates equilibrium in the market for capital. The supply curve for land is relatively steep, reflecting the high cost of increasing the quantity of productive land. The supply curve for capital, in contrast, is relatively flat, due to the relatively high responsiveness of savings to changes in the rental rate for capital. The equilibrium rental rates for land and capital, as well as the equilibrium quantities transacted, are given by the intersections of the demand and supply curves. In a competitive land market, each unit of land will be paid the equilibrium value of the marginal product of land, R^*_{Land}. Likewise, in a competitive capital market, each unit of capital will be paid the equilibrium value of the marginal product of capital, $R^*_{Capital}$.

When the supply of land or capital decreases, the marginal product and rental rate increase. For example, if the number of available delivery trucks decreased, the additional benefit from the last truck used would be higher than before—it would serve more critical delivery needs—and firms would pay more for it. Likewise, when the supply of land or capital increases, the marginal product and rental rate decrease.

Equilibrium in Land and Capital Markets

The equilibrium rental rate and quantity in the land and capital markets are found at the intersection of the supply and demand curves in Figure 34.1. Panel (a) shows the equilibrium in the market for land. Summing all of the firm demand curves for land gives us the market demand curve for land. The equilibrium rental rate for land is R^*_{Land}, and the equilibrium quantity of land employed in production is Q^*_{Land}. In a competitive land market, each unit of land will be paid the equilibrium value of the marginal product of land.

Panel (b) shows the equilibrium in the market for capital. The equilibrium rental rate for capital is $R^*_{Capital}$, and the equilibrium quantity of capital employed in production is $Q^*_{Capital}$. In a competitive capital market, each unit of capital will be paid the equilibrium value of the marginal product of capital.

Now that we know how equilibrium rental rates and quantities are determined in land and capital markets, we can learn how these markets influence the factor distribution of income. To do this, we look more closely at marginal productivity in factor markets.

Marginal Productivity Theory

The **marginal productivity theory of income distribution** sums up what we have learned about payments to factors when goods markets and factor markets are perfectly competitive. According to this theory, each factor is paid the value of the output generated by the last unit of that factor employed in the factor market as a whole—its equilibrium value of the marginal product. To understand why the marginal productivity theory of income distribution is important, look back at Figure 33.1, which shows the factor distribution of income in the United States, and ask yourself this question: who or what determined that labor would get 70.9% of total U.S. income? Why not 90% or 50%?

The answer, according to this theory, is that the division of income among the economy's factors of production isn't arbitrary: in the economy-wide factor market, the price paid for each factor is equal to the increase in the value of output generated by the last unit of that factor employed in the market. If a unit of labor is paid more than a unit of capital, it is because at the equilibrium quantity of each factor, the value of the marginal product of labor exceeds the value of the marginal product of capital.

So far we have treated factor markets as if every unit of each factor were identical. That is, as if all land were identical, all labor were identical, and all capital were identical. But in reality factors differ considerably with respect to productivity. For instance, land resources differ in their ability to produce crops and workers have different skills and abilities. Rather than thinking of one land market for all land resources in an economy, and similarly one capital market and one labor market, we can instead think of different markets for different types of land, capital, and labor. For example, the market for computer programmers is different from the market for pastry chefs.

When we consider that there are separate factor markets for different types of factors, the marginal productivity theory of income distribution still holds. That is, when the labor market for computer programmers is in equilibrium, the wage rate earned by all computer programmers is equal to the market's equilibrium value of the marginal product—the value of the marginal product of the last computer programmer hired in that market. The

Help Wanted!

Hamill Manufacturing of Pennsylvania makes precision components for military helicopters and nuclear submarines. Their highly skilled senior machinists are well paid compared to other workers in manufacturing, earning nearly $70,000 in 2006, excluding benefits. Like most skilled machinists in the United States, Hamill's machinists are very productive: according to the National Mechanists Association, in 2006 each skilled American machinist generated approximately $120,000 in yearly revenue.

But there is a $50,000 difference between the salary paid to Hamill machinists and the revenue they generate. Does this mean that the marginal productivity theory of income distribution doesn't hold? Doesn't the theory imply that machinists should be paid $120,000, the average revenue that each one generates? The answer is no, for two reasons. First, the $120,000 figure is averaged over *all machinists currently employed.* The theory says that machinists will be paid the value

of the marginal product of the *last machinist hired,* and due to diminishing returns to labor, that value will be lower than the average over all machinists currently employed. Second, a worker's equilibrium wage rate includes other costs, such as employee benefits, that have to be added to the $70,000 salary. The marginal productivity theory of income distribution says that workers are paid a wage rate, *including all benefits,* equal to the value of the marginal product. At Hamill, the machinists have job security and good benefits, which add to their salary. Including these benefits, machinists' total compensation will be equal to the value of the marginal product of the last machinist employed.

In Hamill's case, there is yet another factor that explains the $50,000 gap: there are not enough machinists at the current wage rate. Although the company increased the number of employees from 85 in 2004 to 110 in 2006, they would like to hire more. Why doesn't Hamill

Source: Courtesy U.S. Air Force

raise its wages in order to attract more skilled machinists? The problem is that the work they do is so specialized that it is hard to hire from the outside, even when the company raises wages as an inducement. To address this problem, Hamill is now spending a significant amount of money training each new hire. In the end, it does appear that the marginal productivity theory of income distribution holds.

---

marginal productivity theory can explain the distribution of income among different types of land, labor, and capital as well as the distribution of income among the factors of production. At the end of this section we look more closely at the distribution of income between different types of labor and the extent to which the marginal productivity theory of income distribution explains differences in workers' wages.

Module 34 Review

Solutions appear at the back of the book.

Check Your Understanding

1. Explain how each of the following events would affect the equilibrium rental rate and the equilibrium quantity in the land market.
   a. Developers improve the process of filling in coastal waters with rocks and soil to form large new areas of land.
   b. New fertilizers improve the productivity of each acre of farmland.

2. Explain the following statement: "When firms in different industries all compete for the same land, the value of the marginal product of the last unit of land rented will be equal across all firms, regardless of whether they are in different industries."

Multiple-Choice Questions

1. The implicit cost of capital that you own is
   a. the rental rate.
   b. greater than the rental rate.
   c. the original purchase price of the capital.
   d. greater than the original purchase price of the capital.
   e. zero because you already own it.

2. Which of the following is true in relation to a very steep supply curve for land?

   I. It is relatively elastic.
   II. The quantity of land is very responsive to price changes.
   III. Finding new supplies of land is relatively expensive and difficult.

   a. I only
   b. II only
   c. III only
   d. I and II only
   e. I, II, and III

3. The explicit cost of land you don't own is equal to the
   a. rental rate.
   b. interest rate.
   c. profit received from using that land.
   d. market wage rate.
   e. marginal product of land.

4. A firm will continue to employ more land until its value of the marginal product of land is
   a. zero.
   b. maximized.
   c. equal to the rental rate.
   d. equal to the wage rate.
   e. equal to the value of the marginal product of labor and capital.

5. According to the marginal productivity theory of income distribution,
   a. each unit of a factor will be paid the value of its marginal product.
   b. as more of a factor is used, its marginal productivity increases.
   c. factors that receive higher payments are less productive.
   d. capital should receive the highest portion of factor income.
   e. each factor is paid the equilibrium value of its marginal product.

Critical-Thinking Question

Draw a correctly labeled graph showing how the market rental rate and quantity of land are determined in the land market. On your graph, be sure to include each of the following: the supply and demand curves for land, the equilibrium rental rate, the equilibrium quantity of land employed, and correct labels on the axes.

© LOOK Die Bildagentur der Fotografen GmbH/Alamy

What you will learn in this **Module:**

- The way in which a worker's decision about time preference gives rise to labor supply

- How to find equilibrium in the labor market

Module 35
The Market for Labor

At the beginning of this section we looked at the determinants of labor demand and how the wage rate influences the quantity of labor demanded by firms. Now we complete our development of the labor market model by adding the supply of labor and exploring the determination of equilibrium wage and quantity in the labor market.

The Supply of Labor

There are only 24 hours in a day, so to supply labor is to give up leisure, which presents a dilemma of sorts. For this and other reasons, as we'll see, the labor market looks different from markets for goods and services.

Work versus Leisure

In the labor market, the roles of firms and households are the reverse of what they are in markets for goods and services. A good such as wheat is supplied by firms and demanded by households; labor, though, is demanded by firms and supplied by households. How do people decide how much labor to supply?

As a practical matter, most people have limited control over their work hours: sometimes a worker has little choice but to take a job for a set number of hours per week. However, there is often flexibility to choose among different careers and employment situations that involve varying numbers of work hours. There is a range of part-time and full-time jobs; some are strictly 9:00 A.M. to 5:00 P.M., others have much longer or shorter work hours. Some people work two jobs; others don't work at all. And self-employed people have many work-hour options. To simplify our study of labor supply, we will imagine an individual who can choose to work as many or as few hours as he or she likes.

Why wouldn't such an individual work as many hours as possible? Because workers are human beings, too, and have other uses for their time. An hour spent on the job is an hour not spent on other, presumably more pleasant, activities. So the decision about how much labor to supply involves making a decision about **time allocation**—how many hours to spend on different activities.

By working, people earn income that they can use to buy goods. The more hours an individual works, the more goods he or she can afford to buy. But this increased purchasing

Decisions about labor supply result from decisions about **time allocation:** how many hours to spend on different activities.

339

power comes at the expense of a reduction in **leisure,** the time spent not working. (Leisure doesn't necessarily mean time goofing off. It could mean time spent with one's family, pursuing hobbies, exercising, and so on.) And though purchased goods yield utility, so does leisure. Indeed, we can think of leisure itself as a normal good, which most people would like to consume more of as their incomes increase.

How does a rational individual decide how much leisure to consume? By making a marginal comparison, of course. In analyzing consumer choice, we asked how a utility-maximizing consumer uses a marginal *dollar.* In analyzing labor supply, we ask how an individual uses a marginal *hour.*

Consider Clive, an individual who likes both leisure and the goods money can buy. Suppose that his wage rate is $10 per hour. In deciding how many hours he wants to work, he must compare the marginal utility of an additional hour of leisure with the additional utility he gets from $10 worth of goods. If $10 worth of goods adds more to his total utility than an additional hour of leisure, he can increase his total utility by giving up an hour of leisure in order to work an additional hour. If an extra hour of leisure adds more to his total utility than $10 worth of goods, he can increase his total utility by working one fewer hour in order to gain an hour of leisure.

At Clive's optimal level of labor supply, then, the marginal utility he receives from one hour of leisure is equal to the marginal utility he receives from the goods that his hourly wage can purchase. This is very similar to the *optimal consumption rule* we encountered previously, except that it is a rule about time rather than money.

Our next step is to ask how Clive's decision about time allocation is affected when his wage rate changes.

Wages and Labor Supply

Suppose that Clive's wage rate doubles, from $10 to $20 per hour. How will he change his time allocation?

You could argue that Clive will work longer hours because his incentive to work has increased: by giving up an hour of leisure, he can now gain twice as much money as before. But you could equally well argue that he will work less because he doesn't need to work as many hours to generate the income required to pay for the goods he wants.

As these opposing arguments suggest, the quantity of labor Clive supplies can either rise or fall when his wage rate rises. To understand why, let's recall the distinction between *substitution effects* and *income effects.* We have seen that a price change affects consumer choice in two ways: by changing the opportunity cost of a good in terms of other goods (the substitution effect) and by making the consumer richer or poorer (the income effect).

Now think about how a rise in Clive's wage rate affects his demand for leisure. The opportunity cost of leisure—the amount of money he gives up by taking an hour off instead of working—rises. That substitution effect gives him an incentive, other things equal, to consume less leisure and work longer hours. Conversely, a higher wage rate makes Clive richer—and this income effect leads him, other things equal, to want to consume *more* leisure and supply less labor because leisure is a normal good.

So in the case of labor supply, the substitution effect and the income effect work in opposite directions. If the substitution effect is so powerful that it dominates the income effect, an increase in Clive's wage rate leads him to supply *more* hours of labor. If the income effect is so powerful that it dominates the substitution effect, an increase in the wage rate leads him to supply *fewer* hours of labor.

We see, then, that the **individual labor supply curve**—the relationship between the wage rate and the number of hours of labor supplied by an individual worker—does not necessarily slope upward. If the income effect dominates, a higher wage rate will reduce the quantity of labor supplied.

Leisure is time available for purposes other than earning money to buy marketed goods.

The **individual labor supply curve** shows how the quantity of labor supplied by an individual depends on that individual's wage rate.

Figure 35.1 illustrates the two possibilities for labor supply. If the substitution effect dominates the income effect, the individual labor supply curve slopes upward; panel (a) shows an increase in the wage rate from $10 to $20 per hour leading to a *rise* in the number of hours worked from 40 to 50. However, if the income effect dominates, the quantity of labor supplied goes down when the wage rate increases. Panel (b) shows the same rise in the wage rate leading to a *fall* in the number of hours worked from 40 to 30.

Economists refer to an individual labor supply curve that contains both upward-sloping and downward-sloping segments as a "backward-bending labor supply curve." At lower wage rates, the substitution effect dominates the income effect. At higher wage rates, the income effect eventually dominates the substitution effect.

figure 35.1   The Individual Labor Supply Curve

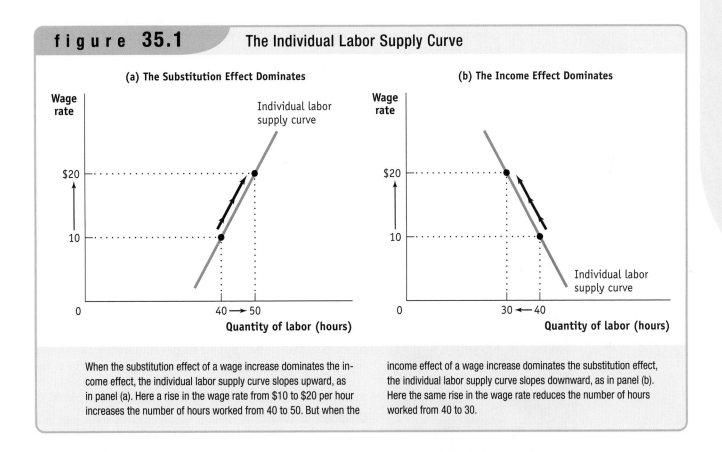

When the substitution effect of a wage increase dominates the income effect, the individual labor supply curve slopes upward, as in panel (a). Here a rise in the wage rate from $10 to $20 per hour increases the number of hours worked from 40 to 50. But when the

income effect of a wage increase dominates the substitution effect, the individual labor supply curve slopes downward, as in panel (b). Here the same rise in the wage rate reduces the number of hours worked from 40 to 30.

Is a backward-bending labor supply curve a real possibility? Yes: many labor economists believe that income effects on the supply of labor may be somewhat stronger than substitution effects at high wage rates. The most compelling piece of evidence for this belief comes from Americans' increasing consumption of leisure over the past century. At the end of the nineteenth century, wages adjusted for inflation were only about one-eighth what they are today; the typical work week was 70 hours, and very few workers retired at age 65. Today the typical work week is less than 40 hours, and most people retire at age 65 or earlier. So it seems that Americans have chosen to take advantage of higher wages in part by consuming more leisure.

Shifts of the Labor Supply Curve

Now that we have examined how income and substitution effects shape the individual labor supply curve, we can turn to the market labor supply curve. In any labor market, the market supply curve is the horizontal sum of the individual labor supply curves of all workers in that market. A change in any factor *other than the wage* that alters workers' willingness to supply labor causes a shift of the labor supply curve. A variety of factors can lead to such shifts, including changes in preferences and social norms, changes in population, changes in opportunities, and changes in wealth.

Changes in Preferences and Social Norms Changes in preferences and social norms can lead workers to increase or decrease their willingness to work at any given wage. A striking example of this phenomenon is the large increase in the number of employed women—particularly married, employed women—that has occurred in the United States since the 1960s. Until that time, women who could afford to largely avoided working outside the home. Changes in preferences and norms in post–World War II America (helped along by the invention of labor-saving home appliances such as washing machines, the trend for more people to live in cities, and higher female education levels) have induced large numbers of American women to join the workforce—a phenomenon often observed in other countries that experience similar social and technological changes.

Changes in Population Changes in the population size generally lead to shifts of the labor supply curve. A larger population tends to shift the labor supply curve rightward as more workers are available at any given wage; a smaller population tends to shift the labor supply curve leftward due to fewer available workers. Currently the size of the U.S. labor force grows by approximately 1% per year, a result of immigration from other countries and, in comparison to other developed countries, a relatively high birth rate. As a result, the labor supply curve in the United States is shifting to the right.

Changes in Opportunities At one time, teaching was the only occupation considered suitable for well-educated women. However, as opportunities in other professions opened up to women starting in the 1960s, many women left teaching and chose other careers.

Women now choose among myriad careers.

This generated a leftward shift of the supply curve for teachers, reflecting a fall in the willingness to work at any given wage and forcing school districts to pay more to maintain an adequate teaching staff. These events illustrate a general result: when superior alternatives arise for workers in another labor market, the supply curve in the original labor market shifts leftward as workers move to the new opportunities. Similarly, when opportunities diminish in one labor market—say, layoffs in the manufacturing industry due to increased foreign competition—the supply in alternative labor markets increases as workers move to these other markets.

Changes in Wealth A person whose wealth increases will buy more normal goods, including leisure. So when a class of workers experiences a general increase in wealth—say, due to a stock market boom—the income effect from the wealth increase will shift the labor supply curve associated with those workers leftward as workers consume more leisure and work less. Note that *the income effect caused by a change in wealth shifts the labor supply curve,* but *the income effect from a wage rate increase—*as we discussed in the case of the individual labor supply curve—*is a movement along the labor supply curve.* The following IRL illustrates how such a change in the wealth levels of many families during the late 1990s led to a shift of the market labor supply curve associated with their employable children.

Equilibrium in the Labor Market

Now that we have discussed the labor supply curve, we can use the supply and demand curves for labor to determine the equilibrium wage and level of employment in the labor market.

The Decline of the Summer Job

Come summertime, resort towns along the New Jersey shore find themselves facing a recurring annual problem: a serious shortage of lifeguards. Traditionally, lifeguard positions, together with many other seasonal jobs, have been filled mainly by high school and college students. But in recent years a growing number of young Americans have chosen not to take summer jobs. In 1979, 71% of Americans between the ages of 16 and 19 were in the summer workforce. Twenty years later that number had fallen to 63%; and by 2009, it was 33%. Data show that young men in particular have become much less willing to take summer jobs.

One explanation for the decline in the summer labor supply is that more students feel they should devote their summers to additional study. But an important factor in the decline is increasing household affluence. As a result, many teenagers no longer feel pressured to contribute to household finances by taking a summer job; that is, the income effect leads to a reduced labor supply. Another factor points to the substitution effect: increased competition from immigrants, who are now doing the jobs typically done by teenagers (mowing lawns, delivering pizzas), has led to a decline in wages. So many teenagers forgo summer work and consume leisure instead.

Figure 35.2 illustrates the labor market as a whole. The *market labor demand curve*, like the market demand curve for a good, is the horizontal sum of all the individual labor demand curves of all the firms that hire labor. And recall that a price-taking firm's labor demand curve is the same as its value of the marginal product of labor curve. As discussed above, the labor supply curve is upward sloping.

The equilibrium wage rate is the wage rate at which the quantity of labor supplied is equal to the quantity of labor demanded. In Figure 35.2, this leads to an equilibrium wage rate of W^* and the corresponding equilibrium employment level of L^*. (The equilibrium wage rate is also known as the market wage rate.)

But this labor market assumes we have perfect competition in both the product market and the factor market. What if either the product or factor market is not perfectly competitive?

figure 35.2

Equilibrium in the Labor Market

The market labor demand curve is the horizontal sum of the individual labor demand curves of all producers. Here the equilibrium wage rate is W^*, the equilibrium employment level is L^*, and every producer hires labor up to the point at which $VMPL = W^*$. So labor is paid its equilibrium value of the marginal product, that is, the value of the marginal product of the last worker hired in the labor market as a whole.

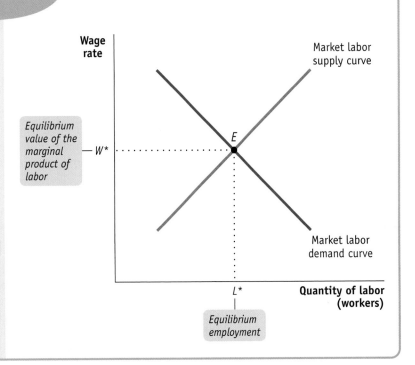

When the Product Market Is Not Perfectly Competitive

When the product market is perfectly competitive, the wage rate is equal to the value of the marginal product of labor at equilibrium. In other market structures this is not the case. For example, in a monopoly, the demand curve for the product faced by the monopolist slopes downward. This means that to sell an additional unit of output, the monopolist must lower the price. As a result, the additional revenue received from selling one more unit for a monopolist is not simply the price like it was for a perfect competitor. It is less than the price by the amount of the *price effect* explained previously—the decreased revenue on units that could have been sold at a higher price if the price hadn't been lowered to sell another unit. How does this affect hiring? To determine its demand for workers, the monopolist must multiply the marginal product of labor by the *marginal revenue* received from selling the additional output. This is called the **marginal revenue product of labor** or **MRPL**.

$$\text{(35-1)} \quad MRPL = MPL \times MR$$

Table 35.1 shows the calculation of a firm's marginal revenue product of labor.

table 35.1

Marginal Revenue Product of Labor with Imperfect Competition in the Product Market

Quantity of Labor (L)	Quantity of Output (Q)	Marginal Product of labor (MPL)	Product Price (P)	Total Revenue (TR) = P×Q	Marginal Revenue (MR) = ΔTR/ΔQ	Marginal Revenue Product of labor (MRPL) = MPL×MR
0	0			$0.00		
		10			$10.00	$100.00
1	10		$10.00	100.00		
		9			9.58	86.20
2	19		9.80	186.20		
		8			9.13	73.00
3	27		9.60	259.20		
		7			8.63	60.40
4	34		9.40	319.60		
		6			8.07	48.40
5	40		9.20	368.00		

For a perfectly competitive firm, marginal revenue equals price, so *VMPL* and *MRPL* are equivalent. The two concepts measure the same thing: the value to the firm of hiring an additional worker. The term *MRPL* is a more general term that applies to firms in both perfect competition and imperfect competition. The general rule is that *a profit-maximizing firm in an imperfectly competitive product market employs each factor of production up to the point at which the marginal revenue product of the last unit of the factor employed is equal to that factor's cost.*

In the case of a firm operating in an imperfectly competitive product market, the demand curve for a factor is the marginal revenue product curve, as shown in Figure 35.3.

When the Labor Market Is Not Perfectly Competitive

There are also important differences when considering an imperfectly competitive *labor* market rather than a perfectly competitive labor market. One major difference is the *marginal factor cost*. The marginal factor cost is the additional cost of hiring one more unit of a factor of production. For example, the **marginal factor cost of labor** (**MFCL**) is the additional cost of hiring one more unit of labor. With perfect competition in the labor market, each firm is so small that it can hire as much labor as it wants at the market wage. The firm's hiring decision does not affect the market. This means

The demand curve for labor for a firm operating in an imperfectly competitive product market is the marginal revenue product of labor curve. The **marginal revenue product of labor (MRPL)** is equal to the marginal product of labor times the marginal revenue received from selling the additional output. The marginal revenue product of land and the marginal revenue product of capital are equivalent concepts.

The **marginal factor cost of labor (MFCL)** is the additional cost of hiring an additional worker. The marginal factor cost of land and the marginal factor cost of capital are equivalent concepts.

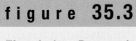

figure 35.3

Firm Labor Demand with Imperfect Competition

A firm's labor demand curve is the marginal revenue product of labor curve, which differs from the value of the marginal product of labor curve when there is imperfect competition in the product market (as with a monopoly, for example). With perfect competition, the marginal revenue product of labor ($MPL \times MR$) and the value of the marginal product of labor ($MPL \times P$) are the same because $MR = P$.

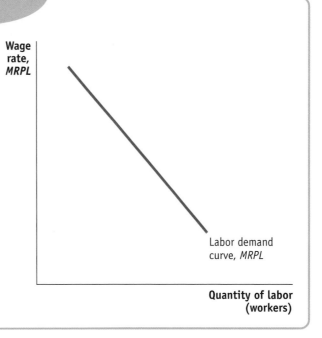

that with perfect competition in the labor market, the additional cost of hiring another worker (the *MFCL*) is always equal to the market wage, and the labor supply curve faced by an individual firm is horizontal, as shown in Figure 35.4.

The labor supply curve faced by a firm is very different in a labor market characterized by imperfect competition: it is upward sloping and the marginal factor cost is above the market wage. Unlike a perfect competitor that is small and cannot affect the market, a firm in an imperfectly competitive labor market is large enough to affect the market wage. For example, a labor market in which there is only one firm hiring labor is called a **monopsony**. A **monopsonist** is the single buyer of a factor. Perhaps you've

A **monopsonist** is a single buyer in a factor market. A market in which there is a monopsonist is a **monopsony**.

figure 35.4

Firm Labor Supply in a Perfectly Competitive Labor Market

In a perfectly competitive labor market, the labor supply curve faced by an individual firm is horizontal at the market equilibrium wage because the firm is so small relative to the market that it can hire all the labor that it wants at the market wage. For this reason, the labor supply curve for a firm in a perfectly competitive labor market is equivalent to the marginal factor cost of labor curve.

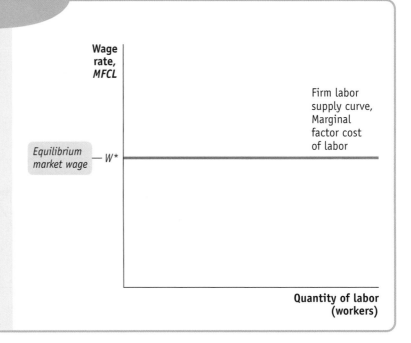

seen a small town where one firm, such as a meatpacking company or a lumber mill, hires most of the labor—that's an example of a monopsony. Since the firm already hires most of the available labor in the town, if it wants to hire more workers it has to offer higher wages to attract them. The higher wages go to all workers, not just the workers hired last. Therefore, the additional cost of hiring an additional worker (*MFCL*) is *higher* than the wage: it is the wage plus the raises paid to all workers. The calculation of *MFCL* is shown in Table 35.2.

table **35.2**

Marginal Factor Cost of Labor with Imperfect Competition in the Labor Market

Quantity of Labor (*L*)	Wage (*W*)	Total Labor Cost (= *L* × *W*)	Marginal Factor Cost of Labor (*MFCL*)
0	$0	$0	
			$6
1	6	6	
			8
2	7	14	
			10
3	8	24	
			12
4	9	36	
			14
5	10	50	

The fact that a firm in an imperfectly competitive labor market must raise the wage to hire more workers means that the *MFCL* curve is *above* the labor supply curve, as shown in Figure 35.5. The explanation for this is similar to the explanation for why the monopolist's marginal revenue curve is below the demand curve. To sell one more, the monopolist has to lower the price, so the additional revenue is the price minus the losses on the units that would otherwise sell at the higher price.

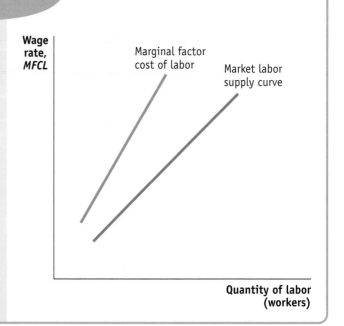

figure 35.5

Supply of Labor and Marginal Factor Cost in an Imperfectly Competitive Market

The marginal factor cost of labor curve is above the market labor supply curve because, to hire more workers in an imperfectly competitive labor market (such as a monopsony), the firm must raise the wage and pay everyone more. This makes the additional cost of hiring another worker higher than the wage rate.

Here, to hire an additional worker, the monopolist has to raise the wage, so the marginal factor cost is the wage plus the wage increase for those workers who could otherwise be hired at the lower wage.

Equilibrium in the Imperfectly Competitive Labor Market

In a perfectly competitive labor market, firms hire labor until the value of the marginal product of labor equals the market wage. With imperfect competition in a factor market, a firm will hire additional workers until the marginal revenue product of labor equals the marginal factor cost of labor. Note that the marginal revenue product of labor for a perfectly competitive firm is the same as the value of the marginal product of labor and that the marginal factor cost of labor for a perfectly competitive firm is the market wage. The terms *marginal revenue product* and *marginal factor cost* are generally applicable to the analysis of any market structure. The terms we used previously, *value of the marginal product* and *wage,* refer to the specific cases of perfect competition in the product market and labor market respectively. Thus, we can generalize and say that every firm hires workers up to the point at which the marginal revenue product of labor equals the marginal factor cost of labor:

(35-2) Hire workers until $MRPL = MFCL$

Equilibrium in the labor market with imperfect competition is shown in Figure 35.6. Once an imperfectly competitive firm has determined the optimal number of workers to hire, L^*, it finds the wage necessary to hire that number of workers by starting at the point on the labor supply curve above the optimal number of workers, and looking straight to the left to see the wage level at that point, W^*.

Let's put the information we just learned together, again referring to Figure 35.6: The labor demand curve is the marginal revenue product curve. In an imperfectly competitive labor market, the firm must offer a higher wage to hire more workers, so

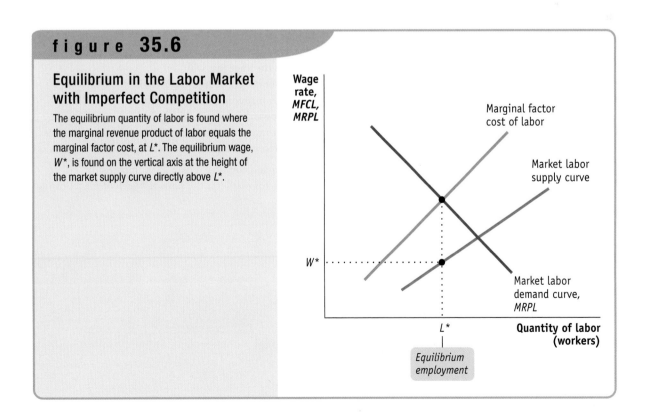

figure 35.6

Equilibrium in the Labor Market with Imperfect Competition

The equilibrium quantity of labor is found where the marginal revenue product of labor equals the marginal factor cost, at L^*. The equilibrium wage, W^*, is found on the vertical axis at the height of the market supply curve directly above L^*.

Wage rate, MFCL, MRPL

Marginal factor cost of labor

Market labor supply curve

W^*

Market labor demand curve, MRPL

L^*

Quantity of labor (workers)

Equilibrium employment

the marginal factor cost curve is above the labor supply curve. The equilibrium quantity of labor is found where the marginal revenue product equals the marginal factor cost, as represented by L^* on the graph. The firm will pay the wage required to hire L^* workers, which is found on the supply curve above L^*. The labor supply curve shows that the quantity of labor supplied is equal to L^* at a wage of W^*. The equilibrium wage in the market is thus W^*. Note that, unlike the wage in a perfectly competitive labor market, the wage in the imperfectly competitive labor market is less than the marginal factor cost of labor.

We have learned how firms determine the optimal amount of land, labor, or capital to hire in factor markets. But often there are different combinations of factors that a firm can use to produce the same level of output. In the next module, we look at how a firm chooses between alternative input combinations for producing a given level of output.

Module 35 Review

Solutions appear at the back of the book.

Check Your Understanding

1. Formerly, Clive was free to work as many or as few hours per week as he wanted. But a new law limits the maximum number of hours he can work per week to 35. Explain under what circumstances, if any, he is made
   a. worse off.
   b. equally well off.
   c. better off.

2. Explain in terms of the income and substitution effects how a fall in Clive's wage rate can induce him to work more hours than before.

Multiple-Choice Questions

1. Which of the following is necessarily true if you work more when your wage rate increases?
   a. The income effect is large.
   b. The substitution effect is small.
   c. The income effect dominates the substitution effect.
   d. The substitution effect dominates the income effect.
   e. The income effect equals the substitution effect.

2. Which of the following will cause you to work more as your wage rate decreases?
   - I. the income effect
   - II. the substitution effect
   - III. a desire for leisure
   a. I only
   b. II only
   c. III only
   d. I and II only
   e. I, II, and III

3. Which of the following will shift the supply curve for labor to the right?
   a. a decrease in the labor force participation rate of women
   b. a decrease in population
   c. an increase in wealth

d. a decrease in the opportunity cost of leisure
   e. an increase in labor market opportunities for women

4. An increase in the wage rate will
   a. shift the labor supply curve to the right.
   b. shift the labor supply curve to the left.
   c. cause an upward movement along the labor supply curve.
   d. cause a downward movement along the labor supply curve.
   e. have no effect on the quantity of labor supplied.

5. The factor demand curve for a firm in an imperfectly competitive factor market is the same as which of the following curves?
   a. *VMP*
   b. *MPP*
   c. *MFC*
   d. *MRP*
   e. *MP*

Critical-Thinking Questions

a. Draw a correctly labeled graph showing a perfectly competitive labor market in equilibrium. On your graph, be sure to label the labor demand curve, the labor supply curve, marginal revenue product of labor, the equilibrium wage (W^*), and the equilibrium quantity of labor (L^*).

b. On your graph, illustrate how a decrease in the price of the product made by the firm would affect the equilibrium wage and quantity of labor. Label the resulting wage rate W_2 and the resulting quantity of labor L_2.

Module 36
The Cost-Minimizing Input Combination

In the past three modules we discussed the markets for factors of production—land, capital, and labor—and how firms determine the optimal quantity of each factor to hire. But firms don't determine how much of each input to hire separately. Production requires multiple inputs, and firms must decide what *combination* of inputs to use to produce their output. In this module, we will look at how firms decide the optimal combination of factors for producing the desired level of output.

Alternative Input Combinations

In many instances a firm can choose among a number of alternative combinations of inputs that will produce a given level of output. For example, on George and Martha's wheat farm, the decision might involve labor and capital. To produce their optimal quantity of wheat, they could choose to have a relatively *capital-intensive* operation by investing in several tractors and other mechanized farm equipment and hiring relatively little labor. Alternatively, they could have a more *labor-intensive* operation by hiring a lot of workers to do much of the planting and harvesting by hand. The same amount of wheat can be produced using many different combinations of capital and labor. George and Martha must determine which combination of inputs will maximize their profits.

To begin our study of the optimal combination of inputs, we'll look at the relationship between the inputs used for production. Depending on the situation, inputs can be either substitutes or complements.

Substitutes and Complements in Factor Markets

Early in this book we discussed substitutes and complements in the context of the supply and demand model. Two goods are *substitutes* if a rise in the price of one good makes consumers more willing to buy the other good. For example, an increase in the price of oranges will cause some buyers to switch from purchasing oranges to purchasing tangerines. When buyers tend to consume two goods together, the goods are known as *complements*. For example, cereal and milk are considered complements because many people consume them together. If the price of cereal increases, people will buy less cereal and therefore need less milk. The decision about how much of a good to buy is influenced by the prices of related goods.

The concepts of substitutes and complements also apply to a firm's purchase of inputs. And just as the price of related goods affects consumers' purchasing decisions, the price of other inputs can affect a firm's decision about how much of an input it will use. In some situations, capital and labor are substitutes. For example, George and Martha can produce the same amount of wheat by substituting more tractors for fewer farm workers. Likewise, ATM machines can substitute for bank tellers.

Capital and labor can also be complements when more of one increases the marginal product of the other. For example, a farm worker is more productive when George and Martha buy a tractor, and each tractor requires a worker to drive it. Office workers are more productive when they can use faster computers, and doctors are more productive with modern X-ray machines. In these cases the quantity and quality of capital available affect the marginal product of labor, and thus the demand for labor. Given the relationship between inputs, how does a firm determine which of the possible combinations to use?

Determining the Optimal Input Mix

If several alternative input combinations can be used to produce the optimal level of output, a profit-maximizing firm will select the input combination with the lowest cost. This process is known as cost minimization.

Cost Minimization

How does a firm determine the combination of inputs that maximizes profits? Let's consider this question using an example.

Imagine you manage a grocery store chain and you need to decide the right combination of self-checkout stations and cashiers at a new store. Table 36.1 shows the alternative combinations of capital (self-checkout stations) and labor (cashiers) you can hire to check out customers shopping at the store. If the store puts in 20 self-checkout stations, you will need to hire 1 cashier to monitor every 5 stations for a total of 4 cashiers. However, trained cashiers are faster than customers at scanning goods, so the store could check out the same number of customers using 10 cashiers and only 10 self-checkout stations.

If you can check out the same number of customers using either of these combinations of capital and labor, how do you decide which combination of inputs to use? By finding the input combination that costs the least—the cost-minimizing input combination.

table **36.1**

Cashiers and Self-Checkout Stations

	Capital (self-checkout stations)	Labor (cashiers)
	Rental rate = $1,000/month	Wage rate = $1,600/month
a.	20	4
b.	10	10

Assume that the cost to rent, operate, and maintain a self-checkout station for a month is $1,000 and hiring a cashier costs $1,600 per month. The cost of each input combination from Table 36.1 is shown below.

a. cost of capital $20 \times \$1,000 = \$20,000$
   cost of labor $4 \times \$1,600 = \underline{\$\ \ 6,400}$
   TOTAL $\$26,400$

b. cost of capital $10 \times \$1,000 = \$10,000$
   cost of labor $10 \times \$1,600 = \underline{\$16,000}$
   TOTAL $\$26,000$

Clearly, your firm would choose the lower cost combination, combination b, and hire 10 cashiers and put in 10 self-checkout stations.

When firms must choose between alternative combinations of inputs, they evaluate the cost of each combination and select the one that minimizes the cost of production. This can be done by calculating the total cost of each alternative combination of inputs, as shown in this example. However, because the number of possible combinations can be very large, it is more practical to use marginal analysis to find the cost-minimizing level of output–which brings us to the cost-minimization rule.

The Cost-Minimization Rule

We already know that the additional output that results from hiring an additional unit of an input is the marginal product (*MP*) of that input. Firms want to receive the highest possible marginal product from each dollar spent on inputs. To do this, firms adjust their hiring of inputs until the marginal product per dollar is equal for all inputs. This is the **cost-minimization rule.** When the inputs are labor and capital, this amounts to equating the marginal product of labor (*MPL*) per dollar spent on wages to the marginal product of capital (*MPK*) per dollar spent to rent capital:

(36-1) $MPL/\text{Wage} = MPK/\text{Rental rate}$

To understand why cost minimization occurs when the marginal product per dollar is equal for all inputs, let's start by looking at two counterexamples. Consider a situation in which the marginal product of labor per dollar is greater than the marginal product of capital per dollar. This situation is described by Equation 36-2:

(36-2) $MPL/\text{Wage} > MPK/\text{Rental rate}$

Suppose the marginal product of labor is 20 units and the marginal product of capital is 100 units. If the wage is $10 and the rental rate for capital is $100, then the marginal product per dollar will be 20/$10 = 2 units of output per dollar for labor and 100/$100 = 1 units of output per dollar for capital. The firm is receiving 2 additional units of output for each dollar spent on labor and only 1 additional unit of output for each dollar spent on capital. In this case, the firm gets more additional output for its money by hiring labor, so it should hire more labor and less capital. Because of diminishing returns, as the firm hires more labor, the marginal product of labor falls and as it hires less capital, the marginal product of capital rises. The firm will continue to substitute labor for capital until the falling marginal product of labor per dollar meets the rising marginal product of capital per dollar and the two are equivalent. That is, the firm will adjust its hiring of capital and labor until the marginal product per dollar spent on each input is equal, as in Equation 36-1.

Next, consider a situation in which the marginal product of capital per dollar is greater than the marginal product of labor per dollar. This situation is described by Equation 36-3:

(36-3) $MPL/\text{Wage} < MPK/\text{Rental rate}$

Self-checkout lines have reduced the need for many stores to hire extra cashiers.

A firm determines the cost-minimizing combination of inputs using the **cost-minimization rule:** hire factors so that the marginal product per dollar spent on each factor is the same.

Let's continue with the assumption that the marginal product of labor for the last unit of labor hired is 20 units and the marginal product of capital for the last unit of capital hired is 100 units. If the wage is $10 and the rental rate for capital is $25, then the marginal product per dollar will be 20/$10 = 2 units of output per dollar for labor and 100/$25 = 4 units of output per dollar for capital. The firm is receiving 4 additional units of output for each dollar spent on capital and only 2 additional units of output for each dollar spent on labor. In this case, the firm gets more additional output for its money by hiring capital, so it should hire more capital and less labor. Because of diminishing returns, as the firm hires more capital, the marginal product of capital falls, and as it hires less labor, the marginal product of labor rises. The firm will continue to hire more capital and less labor until the falling marginal product of capital per dollar meets the rising marginal product of labor per dollar to satisfy the cost-minimization rule. That is, the firm will adjust its hiring of capital and labor until the marginal product per dollar spent on each input is equal.

The cost-minimization rule is analogous to the optimal consumption rule (introduced in the module "Utility Maximization"): consumers maximize their utility by choosing the combination of goods so that the marginal utility per dollar is equal for all goods.

So far in this section we have learned how factor markets determine the equilibrium price and quantity in the markets for land, labor, and capital and how firms determine the combination of inputs they will hire. But how well do these models of factor markets explain the distribution of factor incomes in our economy? Earlier we considered how the marginal productivity theory of income distribution explains the factor distribution of income. In the final module in this section we look at the distribution of income in *labor* markets and consider to what extent the marginal productivity theory of income distribution explains wage differences.

Module 36 Review

Solutions appear at the back of the book.

Check Your Understanding

1. A firm produces its output using only capital and labor. Labor costs $100 per worker per day and capital costs $200 per unit per day. If the marginal product of the last worker employed is 500 and the marginal product of the last unit of capital employed is 1,000, is the firm employing the cost-minimizing combination of inputs? Explain.

Multiple-Choice Questions

1. An automobile factory employs either assembly line workers or robotic arms to produce automobile engines. In this case, labor and capital are considered
   a. independent.
   b. complements.
   c. substitutes.
   d. supplements.
   e. human capital.

2. If an increase in the amount of capital employed by a firm leads to an increase in the marginal product of labor, labor and capital are considered
   a. independent.
   b. complements.
   c. substitutes.
   d. supplements.
   e. human capital.

3. If the marginal product of labor per dollar is greater than the marginal product of capital per dollar, which of the following is true? The firm should
   a. not change its employment of capital and labor.
   b. hire more capital.
   c. hire more labor.
   d. hire less labor.
   e. hire more capital and labor.

4. The cost-minimization rule states that costs are minimized when
   a. *MP* per dollar is equal for all factors.
   b. ($MP \times P$) is equal for all factors.
   c. each factor's *MP* is the same.
   d. *MRP* is maximized.
   e. *MFC* is minimized.

5. A firm currently produces its desired level of output. Its marginal product of labor is 400, its marginal product of capital is 1,000, the wage rate is $20 and the rental rate of capital is $100. In that case, the firm should

a. employ more capital and more labor.
b. employ less labor and less capital.
c. employ less labor and more capital.
d. employ less capital and more labor.
e. not change its allocation of capital and labor.

Critical-Thinking Questions

Refer to the table below. Assume that the wage is $10 per day and the price of pencils is $1.

Quantity of labor (workers)	Quantity of pencils produced
0	0
1	40
2	90
3	120
4	140
5	150
6	160
7	166

a. What is the *MPL* of the 4th worker?
b. What is the *MPL* per dollar of the 5th worker?
c. How many workers would the firm hire if it hired every worker for whom the marginal product per dollar is greater than or equal to 1 pencil per dollar?
d. If the marginal product per dollar spent on labor is 1 pencil per dollar, the marginal product of the last unit of capital hired is 100 pencils per dollar, and the rental rate is $50 per day, is the firm minimizing its cost? Explain.

What you will learn
in this **Module:**

- Labor market applications of
  the marginal productivity
  theory of income distribution

- Sources of wage disparities
  and the role of discrimination

Module 37
Theories of Income Distribution

In the module "The Markets for Land and Capital," we introduced the factor distribution of income and explained how the *marginal productivity theory of income distribution* helps to explain how income is divided among factors of production in an economy. We also considered how the markets for factors of production are broken down. There are different markets for different types of factors. For example, there are different labor markets for different types of labor, such as for computer programmers, pastry chefs, and economists. In this module, we look at the marginal productivity theory of income distribution and the extent to which it explains wage disparities between workers.

The Marginal Productivity Theory of Income Distribution

According to the marginal productivity theory of income distribution, the division of income among the economy's factors of production is determined by each factor's marginal productivity at the market equilibrium. If we consider an economy-wide factor market, the price paid for *all* factors in the economy is equal to the increase in the value of output generated by the last unit of the factor employed in the market. But what about the distribution of income among different labor markets and workers? Does the marginal productivity theory of income distribution help to explain why some workers earn more than others?

Marginal Productivity and Wage Inequality

A large part of the observed inequality in wages can be explained by considerations that are consistent with the marginal productivity theory of income distribution. In particular, there are three well-understood sources of wage differences across occupations and individuals.

The first is the existence of **compensating differentials:** across different types of jobs, wages are often higher or lower depending on how attractive or unattractive the

Compensating differentials are wage differences across jobs that reflect the fact that some jobs are less pleasant or more dangerous than others.

The **equilibrium value of the marginal product** of a factor is the additional value produced by the last unit of that factor employed in the factor market as a whole.

job is. Workers in unpleasant or dangerous jobs receive a higher wage than workers in jobs that require the same skill, training, and effort but lack the unpleasant or dangerous qualities. For example, truckers who haul hazardous chemicals are paid more than truckers who haul bread. For any *particular* job, the marginal productivity theory of income distribution generally holds true. For example, hazardous-load truckers are paid a wage equal to the **equilibrium value of the marginal product** of the last person employed in the market for hazardous-load truckers.

A second reason for wage inequality that is clearly consistent with marginal productivity theory is differences in talent. People differ in their abilities: a high-ability person, by producing a better product that commands a higher price compared to a lower-ability person, generates a higher value of the marginal product. And these differences in the value of the marginal product translate into differences in earning potential. We all know that this is true in sports: practice is important, but 99.99% (at least) of the population just doesn't have what it takes to control a soccer ball like Lionel Messi or hit a tennis ball like Serena Williams. The same is true, though less obvious, in other fields of endeavor.

A third, very important reason for wage differences is differences in the quantity of *human capital*. Recall that human capital—education and training—is at least as important in the modern economy as physical capital in the form of buildings and machines. Different people "embody" quite different quantities of human capital, and a person with more human capital typically generates a higher value of the marginal product by producing more or better products. So differences in human capital account for substantial differences in wages. People with high levels of human capital, such as surgeons or engineers, generally receive high wages.

The most direct way to see the effect of human capital on wages is to look at the relationship between education levels and earnings. Figure 37.1 shows earnings differentials by gender, ethnicity, and three education levels for people 25 years or older in 2009. As you can see, regardless of gender or ethnicity, higher education is associated with higher median earnings. For example, in 2009 white females with 9 to 12 years of

figure 37.1

Earnings Differentials by Education, Gender, and Ethnicity, 2009

It is clear that, regardless of gender or ethnicity, education pays: those with a high school diploma earn more than those without one, and those with a college degree earn substantially more than those with only a high school diploma. Other patterns are evident as well: for any given education level, white males earn more than every other group, and males earn more than females for any given ethnic group.

Source: Bureau of Labor Statistics.

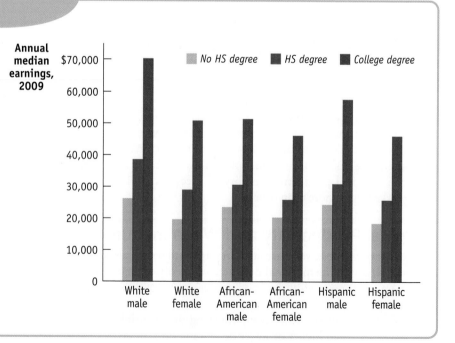

schooling but without a high school diploma had median earnings 30% less than those with a high school diploma and 60% less than those with a college degree—and similar patterns exist for the other five groups. Additional data show that surgeons—an occupation that requires steady hands and many years of formal training—earned an average of $219,770 in 2009.

Because even now men typically have had more years of education than women and whites more years than non-whites, differences in education level are part of the explanation for earnings differences.

It's also important to realize that formal education is not the only source of human capital; on-the-job training and experience are also very important. This point was highlighted by a 2003 National Science Foundation report on earnings differences between male and female scientists and engineers. The study was motivated by concerns over the male–female earnings gap: the median salary for women in science and engineering is about 24% less than the median salary for men. The study found that women in these occupations are, on average, younger than men and have considerably less experience than their male counterparts. This difference in age and experience, according to the study, explained most of the earnings differential. Differences in job tenure and experience can partly explain one notable aspect of Figure 37.1: that, across all ethnicities, women's median earnings are less than men's median earnings for any given education level.

But it's also important to emphasize that earnings differences arising from differences in human capital are not necessarily "fair." A society in which non-white children typically receive a poor education because they live in underfunded school districts, and then go on to earn low wages because they are poorly educated, may have labor markets that are well described by marginal productivity theory (and earnings consistent with the earnings differentials across ethnic groups shown in Figure 37.1). Yet many people would still consider the resulting distribution of income unfair.

Still, many observers think that actual wage differentials cannot be entirely explained by compensating differentials, differences in talent, and differences in human capital. They believe that market power, *efficiency wages,* and discrimination also play an important role. We will examine these forces next.

> **Unions** are organizations of workers that try to raise wages and improve working conditions for their members by bargaining collectively.

Market Power

The marginal productivity theory of income distribution is based on the assumption that factor markets are perfectly competitive. In such markets we can expect workers to be paid the equilibrium value of their marginal product, regardless of who they are. But how valid is this assumption?

We studied markets that are *not* perfectly competitive in previous modules; now let's touch briefly on the ways in which labor markets may deviate from the competitive assumption.

One undoubted source of differences in wages between otherwise similar workers is **unions**—organizations that try to raise wages and improve working conditions for their members. Labor unions, when successful, replace one-on-one wage deals between workers and employers with "collective bargaining," in which the employer negotiates wages with union representatives. Without question, this leads to higher wages for those workers who are represented by unions. In 2009, the median weekly earnings of union members in the United States were $908, compared with $710 for workers not represented by unions—about a 22% difference.

Just as workers can sometimes organize to demand higher wages than they would otherwise receive, employers can sometimes organize to pay *lower* wages than would result from competition. For example, health care workers—doctors, nurses, and so on—sometimes argue that health maintenance organizations (HMOs) are engaged in a collective effort to hold down their wages.

Union members rally to demand higher wages.

Collective action, either by workers or by employers, is less common in the United States than it used to be. Several decades ago, around 30% of U.S. workers were union members. Today, however, union membership in the United States is relatively limited: less than 7.2% of the employees of private businesses are represented by unions. And although there are fields like health care in which a few large firms account for a sizable share of employment in certain geographical areas, the sheer size of the U.S. labor market and the ease with which most workers can move in search of higher-paying jobs probably mean that concerted efforts to hold wages below the unrestrained market equilibrium level rarely occur and even more rarely succeed.

Efficiency Wages

A second source of wage inequality is the phenomenon of *efficiency wages*—a type of incentive scheme used by employers to motivate workers to work hard and to reduce worker turnover. Suppose a worker performs a job that is extremely important but that the employer can observe how well the job is being performed only at infrequent intervals. This would be true, for example, for childcare providers. Then it often makes sense for the employer to pay more than the worker could earn in an alternative job—that is, more than the equilibrium wage. Why? Because earning a premium makes losing this job and having to take the alternative job quite costly for the worker. So a worker who happens to be observed performing poorly and is therefore fired is now worse off for having to accept a lower-paying job. The threat of losing a job that pays a premium motivates the worker to perform well and avoid being fired. Likewise, paying a premium also reduces worker turnover—the frequency with which an employee leaves a job voluntarily. Despite the fact that it may take no more effort and skill to be a childcare provider than to be an office worker, efficiency wages show why it often makes economic sense for a parent to pay a caregiver more than the equilibrium wage of an office worker.

The **efficiency-wage model** explains why we may observe wages offered above their equilibrium level. Like the price floors we studied in the module "Supply and Demand: Price Controls"—and, in particular, much like the minimum wage—this phenomenon leads to a surplus of labor in labor markets that are characterized by the efficiency-wage model. This surplus of labor translates into unemployment—some workers are actively searching for a high-paying efficiency-wage job but are unable to get one, and other more fortunate but no more deserving workers are able to find work. As a result, two workers with exactly the same profile—the same skills and job history—may earn different wages: the worker who is lucky enough to get an efficiency-wage job earns more than the worker who gets a standard job (or who remains unemployed while searching for a higher-paying job). Efficiency wages are a response to a type of market failure that arises from the fact that some employees don't always perform as well as they should and are able to hide that fact. As a result, employers use above-equilibrium wages to motivate their employees, leading to an inefficient outcome.

Discrimination

It is an ugly fact that throughout history there has been discrimination against workers who are considered to be of the wrong race, ethnicity, gender, or other characteristics. How does this fit into our economic models?

The main insight economic analysis offers is that discrimination is *not* a natural consequence of market competition. On the contrary, market forces tend to work against discrimination. To see why, consider the incentives that would exist if social convention dictated that women be paid, say, 30% less than men with equivalent qualifications and experience. A company whose management was itself unbiased would then be able to reduce its costs by hiring women rather than men—and such companies would have an advantage over other companies that hired men despite their higher cost. The result would be to create an excess demand for female workers, which would tend to drive up their wages.

According to the **efficiency-wage model,** some employers pay an above-equilibrium wage as an incentive for better performance and loyalty.

But if market competition works against discrimination, how is it that so much discrimination has taken place? The answer is twofold. First, when labor markets don't work well, employers may have the ability to discriminate without hurting their profits. For example, market interferences (such as unions or minimum-wage laws) or market failures (such as efficiency wages) can lead to wages that are above their equilibrium levels. In these cases, there are more job applicants than there are jobs, leaving employers free to discriminate among applicants. In research published in the *American Economic Review*, two economists, Marianne Bertrand and Sendhil Mullainathan, documented discrimination in hiring by sending fictitious résumés to prospective employers on a random basis. Applicants with "white-sounding" names such as Emily Walsh were 50% more likely to be contacted than applicants with "African-American-sounding" names such as Lakisha Washington. Also, applicants with white-sounding names and good credentials were much more likely to be contacted than those without such credentials. By contrast, potential employers seemed to ignore the credentials of applicants with African-American-sounding names.

Second, discrimination has sometimes been institutionalized in government policy. This institutionalization has made it easier to maintain discrimination against market pressure. For example, at one time in the United States, African-Americans were barred from attending "whites-only" public schools and universities in many parts of the country and forced to attend inferior schools. Although market competition tends to work against *current* discrimination, it is not a remedy for past discrimination, which typically has had an impact on the education and experience of its victims and thereby reduces their income. The following IRL illustrates the way in which government policy enforced discrimination in the world's most famous racist regime, that of the former government of South Africa.

Wage Disparities in Practice

Wage rates in the United States cover a very wide range. In 2009, hundreds of thousands of workers received the legal federal minimum of $7.25 per hour. At the other extreme, the chief executives of several companies were paid more than $100 million for

in real life

The Economics of Apartheid

The Republic of South Africa is the richest nation in Africa, but it also has a harsh political history. Until the peaceful transition to majority rule in 1994, the country was controlled by its white minority, Afrikaners, the descendants of European (mainly Dutch) immigrants. This minority imposed an economic system known as apartheid, which overwhelmingly favored white interests over those of native Africans and other groups considered "non-white," such as Asians.

The origins of apartheid go back to the early years of the twentieth century, when large numbers of white farmers began moving into South Africa's growing cities. There they discovered, to their horror, that they did not automatically earn higher wages than other races. But they had the

right to vote—and non-whites did not. And so the South African government instituted "job-reservation" laws designed to ensure that only whites got jobs that paid well. The government also set about creating jobs for whites in government-owned industries. As Allister Sparks notes in *The Mind of South Africa* (1990), in its efforts to provide high-paying jobs for whites, the country "eventually acquired the largest amount of nationalized industry of any country outside the Communist bloc."

In other words, racial discrimination was possible because it was backed by the power of the government, which prevented markets from following their natural course. A postscript: in 1994, in one of the political miracles of modern times, the white regime

ceded power and South Africa became a full-fledged democracy. Apartheid was abolished. Unfortunately, large racial differences in earnings remain. The main reason is that apartheid created huge disparities in human capital, which will persist for many years to come.

the year, which works out to $20,000 per hour even if they worked 100-hour weeks. Leaving out these extremes, there is still a huge range of wage rates. Are people really that different in their marginal productivities?

A particular source of concern is the existence of systematic wage differences across gender and ethnicity. Figure 37.2 compares annual median earnings in 2009 of workers 25 years or older classified by gender and ethnicity. As a group, white males had the highest earnings. Women (averaging across all ethnicities) earned only about 76% as much; African-American workers (male and female combined) only 69% as much; and Hispanic workers only 64% as much.

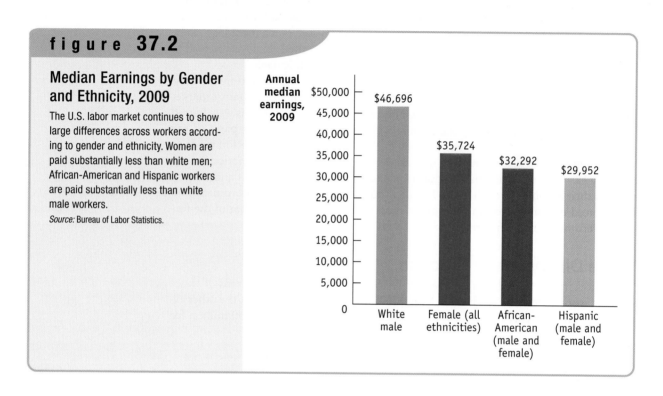

figure 37.2

Median Earnings by Gender and Ethnicity, 2009

The U.S. labor market continues to show large differences across workers according to gender and ethnicity. Women are paid substantially less than white men; African-American and Hispanic workers are paid substantially less than white male workers.

Source: Bureau of Labor Statistics.

We are a nation founded on the belief that all men are created equal—and if the Constitution were rewritten today, we would say that *all people* are created equal. So why do they receive such unequal pay? In part, the pay differences may be due to differences in marginal productivity, but we also must allow for the possible effects of other influences.

Is the Marginal Productivity Theory of Income Distribution Really True?

Although the marginal productivity theory of income distribution is a well-established part of economic theory, closely linked to the analysis of markets in general, it is a source of some controversy. There are two main objections to it.

First, in the real world we see large disparities in income between workers who, in the eyes of some observers, should receive the same payment. Perhaps the most conspicuous examples in the United States are the large differences in the average wages between women and men and among various racial and ethnic groups. Do these wage differences really reflect differences in marginal productivity, or is something else going on?

Second, many people wrongly believe that the marginal productivity theory of income distribution gives a *moral* justification for the distribution of income, implying that the existing distribution is fair and appropriate. This misconception sometimes leads other people, who believe that the current distribution of income is unfair, to reject marginal productivity theory.

So Does Marginal Productivity Theory Work?

The main conclusion you should draw from this discussion is that the marginal productivity theory of income distribution is not a perfect description of how factor incomes are determined but that it works pretty well. The deviations are important. But, by and large, in a modern economy with well-functioning labor markets, factors of production are paid the equilibrium value of the marginal product—the value of the marginal product of the last unit employed in the market as a whole.

It's important to emphasize, once again, that this does not mean that the factor distribution of income is morally justified.

Module 37 Review

Solutions appear at the back of the book.

Check Your Understanding

1. Assess each of the following statements. Do you think they are true, false, or ambiguous? Explain.
   a. The marginal productivity theory of income distribution is inconsistent with the presence of income disparities associated with gender, race, or ethnicity.
   b. Companies that engage in workplace discrimination but whose competitors do not are likely to earn less profit as a result of their actions.
   c. Workers who are paid less because they have less experience are not the victims of discrimination.

Multiple-Choice Questions

1. Which group of U.S. workers had the highest median earnings in 2009?
   a. white males
   b. females (all ethnicities)
   c. African-Americans (males and female)
   d. Hispanics
   e. African-American males

2. Which of the following sources of wage differences is/are consistent with the marginal productivity theory of income distribution?
   - I. talent
   - II. discrimination
   - III. efficiency wages
   a. I only
   b. II only
   c. III only
   d. I and II only
   e. I, II, and III

3. Compensating differentials mean that which of the following leads to higher wages for some jobs?
   a. danger
   b. discrimination
   c. marginal productivity
   d. market power
   e. a surplus of labor

4. Which of the following is a result in the efficiency-wage model?
   a. compensating differentials
   b. surpluses of labor
   c. shortages of labor
   d. discrimination
   e. increased productivity

5. Which of the following statements regarding the marginal productivity theory of income distribution is correct?
   a. Each worker should earn a wage based on his or her marginal productivity.
   b. The wage rate should equal the rental rate.
   c. Workers with higher marginal products always receive a higher wage than workers with lower marginal products.
   d. The factor distribution of income is morally justified.
   e. With well-functioning labor markets, each factor is paid the equilibrium value of the marginal product of that factor.

Critical-Thinking Question

List three different economic concepts that explain wage differences when the marginal productivity theory of income distribution does not. Explain each.

Section 7 Review

Summary

Introduction and Factor Demand

1. Just as there are markets for goods and services, there are markets for factors of production, including labor, land, and both **physical capital** and **human capital.** These markets determine the **factor distribution of income.**

2. A profit-maximizing, price-taking firm will keep employing more units of a factor until the factor's price is equal to the **value of the marginal product**—the marginal product of the factor multiplied by the price of the output it produces. The **value of the marginal product curve** is therefore the price-taking firm's demand curve for a factor. Factor demand is often referred to as a **derived demand** because it is derived from the demand for the producer's output.

3. The market demand curve for labor is the horizontal sum of the individual demand curves of firms in that market. It shifts for three main reasons: changes in output price, changes in the supply of other factors, and technological changes.

The Markets for Land and Capital

4. When a competitive labor market is in equilibrium, the market wage is equal to the **equilibrium value of the marginal product** of labor, the additional value produced by the last worker hired in the labor market as a whole. The same principle applies to other factors of production: the **rental rate** of land or capital is equal to the equilibrium value of the marginal product. This insight leads to the **marginal productivity theory of income distribution,** according to which each factor is paid the value of the marginal product of the last unit of that factor employed in the factor market as a whole.

The Market for Labor

5. Labor supply is the result of decisions about **time allocation,** with each worker facing a trade-off between

leisure and work. An increase in the hourly wage rate tends to increase work hours via the substitution effect but decrease work hours via the income effect. If the net result is that a worker increases the quantity of labor supplied in response to a higher wage, the **individual labor supply curve** slopes upward. If the net result is that a worker decreases work hours, the individual labor supply curve—unlike supply curves for goods and services—slopes downward.

6. The market labor supply curve is the horizontal sum of the individual labor supply curves of all workers in that market. It shifts for four main reasons: changes in preferences and social norms, changes in population, changes in opportunities, and changes in wealth.

7. When a firm is not a price-taker in a factor market, the firm will consider the **marginal revenue product** and the **marginal factor cost** when determining how much of a factor to hire. These concepts are equivalent to the value of the marginal product and the wage (or the price of the factor) in a perfectly competitive market.

8. A **monopsonist** is the single buyer of a factor. A market in which there is a monopsonist is a **monopsony.**

The Cost-Minimizing Input Combination

9. Firms will determine the optimal input combination using the **cost-minimization rule:** When a firm uses the cost-minimizing combination of inputs, the marginal product of labor divided by the wage rate is equal to the marginal product of capital divided by the rental rate.

Theories of Income Distribution

10. Large disparities in wages raise questions about the validity of the marginal productivity theory of income distribution. Many disparities can be explained by **compensating differentials** and by differences in

talent, job experience, and human capital across workers. Market interference in the forms of **unions** and collective action by employers also creates wage disparities. The **efficiency-wage model,** which arises from a type of market failure, shows how wage disparities can result from employers' attempts to increase

worker performance. Free markets tend to diminish discrimination, but discrimination remains a real source of wage disparity. Discrimination is typically maintained either through problems in labor markets or (historically) through institutionalization in government policies.

Key Terms

Physical capital, p. 324
Human capital, p. 324
Derived demand, p. 325
Factor distribution of income, p. 325
Value of the marginal product, p. 328
Value of the marginal product curve, p. 328
Rental rate, p. 335

Marginal productivity theory of income distribution, p. 336
Time allocation, p. 339
Leisure, p. 340
Individual labor supply curve, p. 340
Marginal revenue product of labor, p. 344
Marginal factor cost of labor, p. 344

Monopsonist, p. 345
Monopsony, p. 345
Cost-minimization rule, p. 352
Compensating differentials, p. 355
Equilibrium value of the marginal product, p. 356
Unions, p. 357
Efficiency-wage model, p. 358

Problems

1. In 2007, national income in the United States was $11,186.9 billion. In the same year, 137 million workers were employed, at an average wage of $57,526 per worker per year.

   a. How much compensation of employees was paid in the United States in 2007?

   b. Analyze the factor distribution of income. What percentage of national income was received in the form of compensation to employees in 2007?

   c. Suppose that a huge wave of corporate downsizing leads many terminated employees to open their own businesses. What is the effect on the factor distribution of income?

   d. Suppose the supply of labor rises due to an increase in the retirement age. What happens to the percentage of national income received in the form of compensation of employees?

2. Marty's Frozen Yogurt has the production function per day shown in the accompanying table. The equilibrium wage rate for a worker is $80 per day. Each cup of frozen yogurt sells for $2.

Quantity of labor (workers)	Quantity of frozen yogurt (cups)
0	0
1	110
2	200
3	270
4	300
5	320
6	330

   a. Calculate the marginal product of labor for each worker and the value of the marginal product of labor per worker.

   b. How many workers should Marty employ?

3. Patty's Pizza Parlor has the production function per hour shown in the accompanying table. The hourly wage rate for each worker is $10. Each pizza sells for $2.

Quantity of labor (workers)	Quantity of pizza
0	0
1	9
2	15
3	19
4	22
5	24

   a. Calculate the marginal product of labor for each worker and the value of the marginal product of labor per worker.

   b. Draw the value of the marginal product of labor curve. Use your diagram to determine how many workers Patty should employ.

   c. Now the price of pizza increases to $4. Calculate the value of the marginal product of labor per worker, and draw the new value of the marginal product of labor curve in your diagram. Use your diagram to determine how many workers Patty should employ now.

4. The production function for Patty's Pizza Parlor is given in the table in Problem 3. The price of pizza is $2, but the hourly wage rate rises from $10 to $15. Use a diagram to determine how Patty's demand for workers responds as a result of this wage rate increase.

5. Patty's Pizza Parlor initially had the production function given in the table in Problem 3. A worker's hourly wage rate was $10, and pizza sold for $2. Now Patty buys a new high-tech pizza oven that allows her workers to become twice as productive as before. That is, the first worker now produces 18 pizzas per hour instead of 9, and so on.

a. Calculate the new marginal product of labor and the new value of the marginal product of labor.

b. Use a diagram to determine how Patty's hiring decision responds to this increase in the productivity of her workforce.

6. Jameel runs a driver education school. The more driving instructors he hires, the more driving lessons he can sell. But because he owns a limited number of training automobiles, each additional driving instructor adds less to Jameel's output of driving lessons. The accompanying table shows Jameel's production function per day. Each driving lesson can be sold at $35 per hour.

Quantity of labor (driving instructors)	Quantity of driving lessons (hours)
0	0
1	8
2	15
3	21
4	26
5	30
6	33

Determine Jameel's labor demand schedule (his demand schedule for driving instructors) for each of the following daily wage rates for driving instructors: $160, $180, $200, $220, $240, and $260.

7. Dale and Dana work at a self-service gas station and convenience store. Dale opens up every day, and Dana arrives later to help stock the store. They are both paid the current market wage of $9.50 per hour. But Dale feels he should be paid much more because the revenue generated from the gas pumps he turns on every morning is much higher than the revenue generated by the items that Dana stocks. Assess this argument.

8. A *New York Times* article published in September 2007 observed that the wage of farmworkers in Mexico is $11 an hour but the wage of immigrant Mexican farmworkers in California is $9 an hour.

a. Assume that the output sells for the same price in the two countries. Does this imply that the marginal product of labor of farmworkers is higher in Mexico or in California? Explain your answer, and illustrate with a diagram that shows the demand and supply curves for labor in the respective markets. In your diagram, assume that the quantity supplied of labor for any given wage rate is the same for Mexican farmworkers as it is for immigrant Mexican farmworkers in California.

b. Now suppose that farmwork in Mexico is more arduous and more dangerous than farmwork in California. As a result, the quantity supplied of labor for any given wage rate is not the same for Mexican farmworkers as it is for immigrant Mexican farmworkers in California. How does this change your answer to part a? What concept best accounts for the difference between wage rates between Mexican farmworkers and immigrant Mexican farmworkers in California?

c. Illustrate your answer to part b with a diagram. In this diagram, assume that the quantity of labor demanded for any given wage rate is the same for Mexican employers as it is for Californian employers.

9. Kendra is the owner of Wholesome Farms, a commercial dairy. Kendra employs labor, land, and capital. In her operations, Kendra can substitute between the amount of labor she employs and the amount of capital she employs. That is, to produce the same quantity of output she can use more labor and less land; similarly, to produce the same quantity of output she can use less labor and more land. However, if she uses more land, she must use more of both labor and capital; if she uses less land, she can use less of both labor and capital. Let w^* represent the annual cost of labor in the market, let r_L^* represent the annual cost of a unit of land in the market, and let r_K^* represent the annual cost of a unit of capital in the market.

a. Suppose that Kendra can maximize her profits by employing less labor and more capital than she is currently using but the same amount of land. What three conditions must now hold for Kendra's operations (involving her value of the marginal product of labor, land and capital) for this to be true?

b. Kendra believes that she can increase her profits by renting and using more land. What three conditions must hold (involving her value of the marginal product of labor, land, and capital) for this to be true?

10. Research consistently finds that despite nondiscrimination policies, African-American workers on average receive lower wages than white workers do. What are the possible reasons for this? Are these reasons consistent with marginal productivity theory?

11. Greta is an enthusiastic amateur gardener and spends a lot of her free time working in her yard. She also has demanding and well-paid employment as a freelance advertising consultant. Because the advertising business is going through a difficult time, the hourly consulting fee Greta can charge falls. Greta decides to spend more time gardening and less time consulting. Explain her decision in terms of income and substitution effects.

12. Wendy works at a fast-food restaurant. When her wage rate was $5 per hour, she worked 30 hours per week. When her wage rate rose to $6 per hour, she decided to work 40 hours. But when her wage rate rose further to $7, she decided to work only 35 hours.

a. Draw Wendy's individual labor supply curve.

b. Is Wendy's behavior irrational, or can you find a rational explanation? Explain your answer.

13. You are the governor's economic policy adviser. The governor wants to put in place policies that encourage employed people to work more hours at their jobs and that encourage unemployed people to find and take jobs. Assess each of the following policies in terms of reaching that goal. Explain your reasoning in terms of income and substitution effects, and indicate when the impact of the policy may be ambiguous.

a. The state income tax rate is lowered, which has the effect of increasing workers' after-tax wage rate.

b. The state income tax rate is increased, which has the effect of decreasing workers' after-tax wage rate.

c. The state property tax rate is increased, which reduces workers' after-tax income.

14. A study by economists at the Federal Reserve Bank of Boston found that between 1965 and 2003 the average American's leisure time increased by between 4 and 8 hours a week. The study claims that this increase is primarily driven by a rise in wage rates.

   a. Use the income and substitution effects to describe the labor supply for the average American. Which effect dominates?

   b. The study also finds an increase in female labor force participation—more women are choosing to hold jobs rather than exclusively perform household tasks. For the average woman who has newly entered the labor force, which effect dominates?

   c. Draw typical individual labor supply curves that illustrate your answers to part a and part b above.

Market Failure and the Role of Government

For many people in the northeastern United States, there is no better way to relax than to fish in one of the region's thousands of lakes. But in the 1960s, avid fishermen noticed something alarming: lakes that had formerly teemed with fish were now almost empty. What had happened?

The answer was acid rain, caused mainly by coal-burning power plants. When coal is burned, it releases sulfur dioxide and nitric oxide into the atmosphere; these gases react with water, producing sulfuric acid and nitric acid. The result in the Northeast, downwind from the nation's industrial heartland, was rain sometimes as acidic as lemon juice. Acid rain didn't just kill fish; it also damaged trees and crops, and in time even began to dissolve limestone buildings.

You'll be glad to hear that the acid rain problem today is much less serious than it was in the 1960s. Power plants have reduced their emissions by switching to low-sulfur coal and installing scrubbers in their smokestacks. But they didn't do this out of the goodness of their hearts; they did it in response to government policy. Without such government intervention, power companies would have had no incentive to take the environmental effects of their actions into account.

The Gulf of Mexico oil spill of 2010 is among the reminders that environmental problems persist. Neglected pollution is one of several reasons why markets sometimes fail to deliver efficient quantities of goods and services. We've already seen that inefficiency can arise from market power, which allows monopolists and colluding oligopolists to charge prices above marginal cost, thereby preventing mutually beneficial transactions from occurring. In this section we will consider other reasons for market failure. First we will see that inefficiency can arise from *externalities*, which create a conflict between the best interests of an individual or a firm and the best interests of society as a whole. Then we will focus on how the characteristics of goods often determine whether markets can deliver them efficiently. Finally, we look at the role of government in addressing market failures. The investigation of sources of inefficiency will deepen our understanding of the types of policy that can make society better off.

AP/Wide World Photos

For many polluters, acid rain is someone else's problem.

iStockphoto

Module 38
Introduction to Externalities

The Economics of Pollution

Pollution is a bad thing. Yet most pollution is a side effect of activities that provide us with good things: our air is polluted by power plants generating the electricity that lights our cities, and our rivers are sullied by fertilizer runoff from farms that grow our food. Why shouldn't we accept a certain amount of pollution as the cost of a good life?

Actually, we do. Even highly committed environmentalists don't think that we can or should completely eliminate pollution—even an environmentally conscious society would accept *some* pollution as the cost of producing useful goods and services. What environmentalists argue is that unless there is a strong and effective environmental policy, our society will generate *too much* pollution—too much of a bad thing. And the great majority of economists agree.

To see why, we need a framework that lets us think about how much pollution a society *should* have. We'll then be able to see why a market economy, left to itself, will produce more pollution than it should. We'll start by adopting a framework to study the problem under the simplifying assumption that the amount of pollution emitted by a polluter is directly observable and controllable.

Costs and Benefits of Pollution

How much pollution should society allow? We learned previously that "how much" decisions always involve comparing the marginal benefit from an additional unit of something with the marginal cost of that additional unit. The same is true of pollution.

The **marginal social cost of pollution** is the additional cost imposed on society as a whole by an additional unit of pollution. For example, acid rain harms fisheries, crops, and forests; and each additional ton of sulfur dioxide released into the atmosphere increases the harm.

The **marginal social benefit of pollution** is the additional benefit to society from an additional unit of pollution. This concept may seem counterintuitive—what's good

The **marginal social cost of pollution** is the additional cost imposed on society as a whole by an additional unit of pollution.

The **marginal social benefit of pollution** is the additional gain to society as a whole from an additional unit of pollution.

about pollution? However, pollution avoidance requires the use of money and inputs that could otherwise be used for other purposes. For example, to reduce the quantity of sulfur dioxide they emit, power companies must either buy expensive low-sulfur coal or install special scrubbers to remove sulfur from their emissions. The more sulfur dioxide they are allowed to emit, the lower are these avoidance costs. If we calculated how much money the power industry would save if it were allowed to emit an additional ton of sulfur dioxide, that savings would be the marginal benefit to society of emitting that ton of sulfur dioxide.

Using hypothetical numbers, Figure 38.1 shows how we can determine the **socially optimal quantity of pollution**—the quantity of pollution that makes society as well off as possible, taking all costs and benefits into account. The upward-sloping marginal social cost curve, labeled *MSC,* shows how the marginal cost to society of an additional ton of pollution emissions varies with the quantity of emissions. (An upward slope is likely because nature can often safely handle low levels of pollution but is increasingly harmed as pollution reaches high levels.) The marginal social benefit curve, labeled *MSB,* is downward sloping because it is progressively harder, and therefore more expensive, to achieve a further reduction in pollution as the total amount of pollution falls—increasingly more expensive technology must be used. As a result, as pollution falls, the cost savings to a polluter of being allowed to emit one more ton rises.

> The **socially optimal quantity of pollution** is the quantity of pollution that society would choose if all the costs and benefits of pollution were fully accounted for.

---

figure 38.1

The Socially Optimal Quantity of Pollution

Pollution yields both costs and benefits. Here the curve *MSC* shows how the marginal cost to society as a whole from emitting one more ton of pollution emissions depends on the quantity of emissions. The curve *MSB* shows how the marginal benefit to society as a whole of emitting an additional ton of pollution emissions depends on the quantity of pollution emissions. The socially optimal quantity of pollution is Q_{OPT}; at that quantity, the marginal social benefit of pollution is equal to the marginal social cost, corresponding to $200.

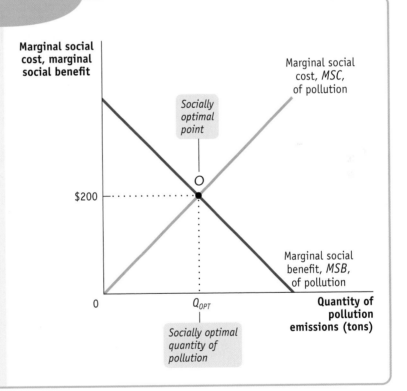

The socially optimal quantity of pollution in this example isn't zero. It's Q_{OPT}, the quantity corresponding to point *O*, where the marginal social benefit curve crosses the marginal social cost curve. At Q_{OPT}, the marginal social benefit from an additional ton of emissions and its marginal social cost are equalized at $200.

But will a market economy, left to itself, arrive at the socially optimal quantity of pollution? No, it won't.

An **external cost** is an uncompensated cost that an individual or firm imposes on others.

Pollution: An External Cost

Pollution yields both benefits and costs to society. But in a market economy without government intervention, those who benefit from pollution—like the owners of power companies—decide how much pollution occurs. They have no incentive to take into account the costs of pollution that they impose on others.

To see why, remember the nature of the benefits and costs from pollution. For polluters, the benefits take the form of monetary savings: by emitting an extra ton of sulfur dioxide, any given polluter saves the cost of buying expensive, low-sulfur coal or installing pollution-control equipment. So the benefits of pollution accrue directly to the polluters.

The costs of pollution, though, fall on people who have no say in the decision about how much pollution takes place: for example, people who fish in northeastern lakes do not control the decisions of power plants.

Figure 38.2 shows the result of this asymmetry between who reaps the benefits and who pays the costs. In a market economy without government intervention to protect the environment, only the benefits of pollution are taken into account in choosing the quantity of pollution. So the quantity of emissions won't be the socially optimal quantity Q_{OPT}; it will be Q_{MKT}, the quantity at which the marginal social benefit of an additional ton of pollution is zero, but the marginal social cost of that additional ton is much larger—$400. The quantity of pollution in a market economy without government intervention will be higher than its socially optimal quantity.

The reason is that in the absence of government intervention, those who derive the benefit from pollution—the owners of polluting firms—don't have to compensate those who bear the cost. So the marginal cost of pollution to any given polluter is zero (the assumption being that the polluter isn't also the pollution victim): polluters have no incentive to limit the amount of emissions. For example, before the Clean Air Act of 1970, midwestern power plants used the cheapest type of coal available, despite the fact that cheap coal generated more pollution, and they did nothing to scrub their emissions.

The environmental cost of pollution is perhaps the best-known and most important example of an **external cost**—an uncompensated cost that an individual or firm

figure 38.2

Why a Market Economy Produces Too Much Pollution

In the absence of government intervention, the quantity of pollution will be Q_{MKT}, the quantity at which the marginal social benefit of pollution equals the price polluters pay for each unit of pollution they emit: $0. This is an inefficiently high quantity of pollution because the marginal social cost, $400, greatly exceeds the marginal social benefit, $0.

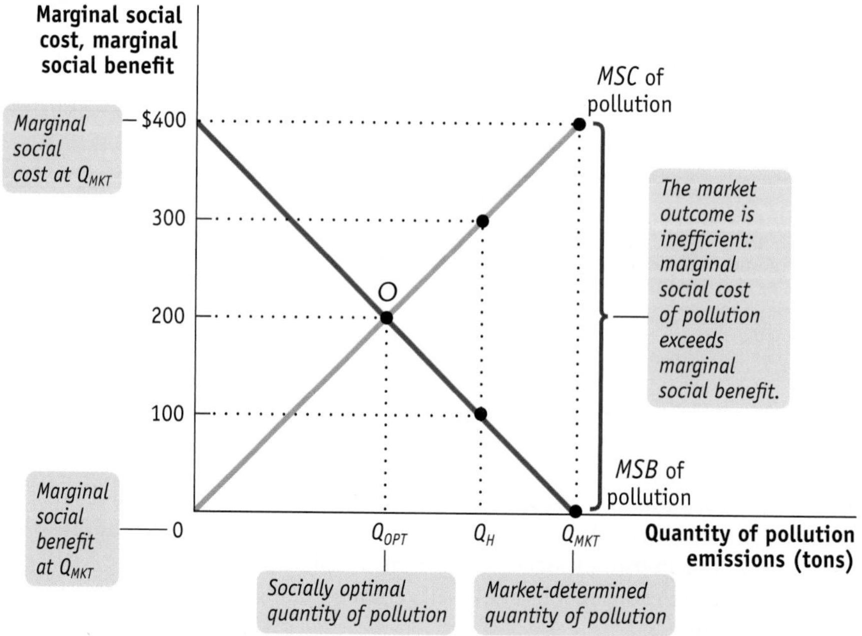

imposes on others. There are many other examples of external costs besides pollution. Another important, and certainly familiar, external cost is traffic congestion—an individual who chooses to drive during rush hour increases congestion and so increases the travel time of other drivers.

We'll see in the next module that there are also important examples of **external benefits,** benefits that individuals or firms confer on others without receiving compensation. External costs and external benefits are jointly known as **externalities.** External costs are called **negative externalities** and external benefits are called **positive externalities.**

As we've already suggested, externalities can lead to individual decisions that are not optimal for society as a whole. Let's take a closer look at why, focusing on the case of pollution.

Traffic congestion is a negative externality.

Talking and Driving

Why is that woman in the car in front of us driving so erratically? Is she drunk? No, she's talking on her cell phone.

Traffic safety experts take the risks posed by driving while talking very seriously. Using hands-free, voice-activated phones doesn't seem to help much because the main danger is distraction. As one traffic safety consultant put it, "It's not where your eyes are; it's where your head is." And we're not talking about a trivial problem. One estimate suggests that people who talk on their cell phones while driving may be responsible for 600 or more traffic deaths each year.

The National Safety Council urges people not to use phones while driving. But a growing number of people say that voluntary standards aren't enough; they want the use of cell phones while driving made illegal, as it already is in eight states and the District of Columbia, as well as in Japan, Israel, and many other countries.

Why not leave the decision up to the driver? Because the risk posed by driving while talking isn't just a risk to the driver; it's also a safety risk to others—especially people in other cars. Even if you decide that the benefit to you of taking that call is worth the cost, you

aren't taking into account the cost to other people. Driving while talking, in other words, generates a serious—sometimes fatal—negative externality.

The Inefficiency of Excess Pollution

We have just shown that in the absence of government action, the quantity of pollution will be *inefficient:* polluters will pollute up to the point at which the marginal social benefit of pollution is zero, as shown by quantity Q_{MKT} in Figure 38.2. Recall that an outcome is inefficient if some people could be made better off without making others worse off. We have already seen why the equilibrium quantity in a perfectly competitive market with no externalities is the efficient quantity of the good, the quantity that maximizes total surplus. Here, we can use a variation of that analysis to show how the presence of a negative externality upsets that result.

Because the marginal social benefit of pollution is zero at Q_{MKT}, reducing the quantity of pollution by one ton would subtract very little from the total social benefit from pollution. In other words, the benefit to polluters from that last unit of pollution is very low—virtually zero. Meanwhile, the marginal social cost imposed on the rest of society of that last ton of pollution at Q_{MKT} is quite high—$400. In other words, by reducing

An **external benefit** is a benefit that an individual or firm confers on others without receiving compensation.

External costs and benefits are known as **externalities.**

External costs are **negative externalities,** and external benefits are **positive externalities.**

the quantity of pollution at Q_{MKT} by one ton, the total social cost of pollution falls by $400, but total social benefit falls by virtually zero. So total surplus rises by approximately $400 if the quantity of pollution at Q_{MKT} is reduced by one ton.

If the quantity of pollution is reduced further, there will be more gains in total surplus, though they will be smaller. For example, if the quantity of pollution is Q_H in Figure 38.2, the marginal social benefit of a ton of pollution is $100, but the marginal social cost is still much higher at $300. This means that reducing the quantity of pollution by one ton leads to a net gain in total surplus of approximately $300 − $100 = $200. Thus Q_H is still an inefficiently high quantity of pollution. Only if the quantity of pollution is reduced to Q_{OPT}, where the marginal social cost and the marginal social benefit of an additional ton of pollution are both $200, is the outcome efficient.

Private Solutions to Externalities

Can the private sector solve the problem of externalities without government intervention? Bear in mind that when an outcome is inefficient, there is potentially a deal that makes people better off. Why don't individuals find a way to make that deal?

In an influential 1960 article, economist and Nobel laureate Ronald Coase pointed out that in an ideal world the private sector could indeed deal with all externalities. According to the **Coase theorem,** even in the presence of externalities, an economy can reach an efficient solution, provided that the legal rights of the parties are clearly defined and the costs of making a deal are sufficiently low. In some cases it takes a lot of time, or even money, to bring the relevant parties together, negotiate a deal, and carry out the terms of the deal. The costs of making a deal are known as **transaction costs.**

To get a sense of Coase's argument, imagine two neighbors, Mick and Christina, who both like to barbecue in their backyards on summer afternoons. Mick likes to play golden oldies on his boombox while barbecuing, but this annoys Christina, who can't stand that kind of music.

Who prevails? You might think it depends on the legal rights involved in the case: if the law says that Mick has the right to play whatever music he wants, Christina just has to suffer; if the law says that Mick needs Christina's consent to play music in his backyard, Mick has to live without his favorite music while barbecuing.

But as Coase pointed out, the outcome need not be determined by legal rights, because Christina and Mick can make a private deal as long as the legal rights are clearly defined. Even if Mick has the right to play his music, Christina could pay him not to. Even if Mick can't play the music without an OK from Christina, he can offer to pay her to give that OK. These payments allow them to reach an efficient solution, regardless of who has the legal upper hand. If the benefit of the music to Mick exceeds its cost to Christina, the music will go on; if the benefit to Mick is less than the cost to Christina, there will be silence.

The implication of Coase's analysis is that externalities need not lead to inefficiency because individuals have an incentive to make mutually beneficial deals—deals that lead them to take externalities into account when making decisions. When individuals *do* take externalities into account when making decisions, economists say that they **internalize the externalities.** If externalities are fully internalized, as when Mick must forgo a payment from Christina *equal to the external cost he imposes on her* in order to play music, the outcome is efficient even without government intervention.

Why can't individuals always internalize externalities? Our barbecue example implicitly assumes the transaction costs are low enough for Mick and Christina to be able to make a deal. In many situations involving externalities, however, transaction costs prevent individuals from making efficient deals. Examples of transaction costs include the following:

- *The costs of communication among the interested parties.* Such costs may be very high if many people are involved.

- *The costs of making legally binding agreements.* Such costs may be high if expensive legal services are required.

Thank You for Not Smoking

New Yorkers call them the "shiver-and-puff people"—the smokers who stand outside their workplaces, even in the depths of winter, to take a cigarette break. Over the past couple of decades, rules against smoking in spaces shared by others have become ever stricter. This is partly a matter of personal dislike—nonsmokers really don't like to smell other people's cigarette smoke—but it also reflects concerns over the health risks of second-hand smoke. As the Surgeon General's warning on many packs says, "Smoking causes lung cancer, heart disease, emphysema, and may complicate pregnancy." And there's no question that being in the same room as someone who smokes exposes you to at least some health risk.

Second-hand smoke, then, is clearly an example of a negative externality. But how important is it? Putting a dollar-and-cents value on it—that is, measuring the marginal social cost of cigarette smoke—requires researchers to not only estimate the health effects but also put a value on these effects. Despite the difficulty, economists have tried. A paper published in 1993 in the *Journal of Economic Perspectives* surveyed the research on the external costs of both cigarette smoking and alcohol consumption.

According to this paper, conclusions regarding the health costs of cigarettes depend on whether the costs imposed on members of smokers' families, including unborn children, are counted along with the costs borne by

smokers. If not, the external costs of second-hand smoke have been estimated at about $0.19 per pack smoked. (Using this method of calculation, $0.19 corresponds to the *average* social cost of smoking per pack at the current level of smoking in society.) A 2005 study raised this estimate to $0.52 per pack smoked. If the effects on smokers' families are included, the number rises considerably—family members who live with smokers are exposed to a lot more smoke. (They are also exposed to the risk of fire, which alone is estimated at $0.09 per pack.) If you include the effects of smoking by pregnant women on their unborn children's future health, the cost is immense—$4.80 per pack, which is more than twice the wholesale price charged by cigarette manufacturers.

- *Costly delays involved in bargaining.* Even if there is a potentially beneficial deal, both sides may hold out in an effort to extract more favorable terms, leading to increased effort and forgone utility.

In some cases, transaction costs are low enough to allow individuals to resolve externality problems. For example, while filming *A League of Their Own* on location in a neighborhood ballpark, director Penny Marshall paid a man $100 to stop using his noisy chainsaw nearby. But in many other cases, transaction costs are too high to make it possible to deal with externalities through private action. For example, tens of millions of people are adversely affected by acid rain. It would be prohibitively expensive to try to make a deal among all those people and all those power companies.

When transaction costs prevent the private sector from dealing with externalities, it is time to look for government solutions—the subject of the next module.

Module 38 Review

Solutions appear at the back of the book.

Check Your Understanding

1. Wastewater runoff from large poultry farms adversely affects residents in neighboring homes. Explain the following:
   a. why this is considered an externality problem
   b. the efficiency of the outcome with neither government intervention nor a private deal
   c. how the socially optimal outcome is determined and how it compares with the no-intervention, no-deal outcome

2. According to Yasmin, any student who borrows a book from the university library and fails to return it on time imposes a negative externality on other students. She claims that rather than charging a modest fine for late returns, the library should charge a huge fine, so that borrowers will never return a book late. Is Yasmin's economic reasoning correct?

Multiple-Choice Questions

1. The socially optimal level of pollution is
   a. less than that created by the market, but not zero.
   b. more than that created by the market.
   c. whatever the market creates.
   d. determined by firms.
   e. zero.

2. Which of the following is a source of negative externalities?
   a. loud conversations in a library
   b. smokestack scrubbers
   c. a beautiful view
   d. national defense
   e. a decision to purchase dressy but uncomfortable shoes.

3. Inefficiencies created by externalities can be dealt with through
   a. government actions only.
   b. private actions only.
   c. market outcomes only.
   d. either private or government actions.
   e. neither private nor government actions.

4. The Coase theorem asserts that, under the right circumstances, inefficiencies created by externalities can be dealt with through
   a. lawsuits.
   b. private bargaining.
   c. vigilante actions.
   d. government policies.
   e. mediation.

5. Which of the following makes it more likely that private solutions to externality problems will succeed?
   a. high transaction costs
   b. high prices for legal services
   c. delays in the bargaining process
   d. a small number of affected parties
   e. loosely defined legal rights

Critical-Thinking Questions

a. Define the marginal social cost of pollution.
b. Define the marginal social benefit of pollution, and explain why polluting more can provide benefits to a firm even when it could produce the same quantity of output without polluting as much.
c. Define the socially optimal level of pollution.

iStockphoto

What you will learn in this **Module:**

* How external benefits and costs cause inefficiency in the markets for goods

* Why some government policies to deal with externalities, such as emissions taxes, tradable emissions permits, and Pigouvian subsidies, are efficient, although others, including environmental standards, are not

Module **39**
Externalities and Public Policy

Policies Toward Pollution

Before 1970 there were no rules governing the amount of sulfur dioxide that power plants in the United States could emit—which is why acid rain got to be such a problem. In 1970, the Clean Air Act set rules about sulfur dioxide emissions; thereafter, the acidity of rainfall declined significantly. Economists argued, however, that a more flexible system of rules that exploited the effectiveness of markets could achieve lower pollution levels at a lower cost. In 1990 this theory was put into effect with a modified version of the Clean Air Act. And guess what? The economists were right!

In this module we'll look at the policies governments use to deal with pollution and at how economic analysis has been used to improve those policies.

Environmental Standards

Because the economy, and life itself, depend on a viable environment, external costs that threaten the environment—air pollution, water pollution, habitat destruction, and so on, are worthy of attention. Protection of the environment has become a major focus of government in every advanced nation. In the United States, the Environmental Protection Agency is the principal enforcer of environmental policies at the national level and is supported by the actions of state and local governments.

How does a country protect its environment? At present the main policy tools are **environmental standards,** rules that protect the environment by specifying actions by producers and consumers. A familiar example is the law that requires almost all vehicles to have catalytic converters, which reduce the emission of chemicals that can cause smog and lead to health problems. Other rules require communities to treat their sewage, factories to limit their pollution emissions, and homes to be painted with lead-free paint, among many other examples.

Environmental standards came into widespread use in the 1960s and 1970s with considerable success. Since the United States passed the Clean Air Act in 1970, for example, the emission of air pollutants has fallen by more than a third, even though the

Environmental standards are rules that protect the environment by specifying limits or actions for producers and consumers.

Environmental standards are helping to erase the Los Angeles smog.

population has grown by a third and the size of the economy has more than doubled. Even in Los Angeles, still famous for its smog, the air has improved dramatically: in 1988 ozone levels in the surrounding South Coast Air Basin exceeded federal standards on 178 days; in 2008, on only 28 days.

Despite these successes, economists believe that when regulators can control a polluter's emissions directly, there are more efficient ways than environmental standards to deal with pollution. By using methods grounded in economic analysis, society can achieve a cleaner environment at lower cost. Most current environmental standards are inflexible and don't allow reductions in pollution to be achieved at the lowest possible cost. For example, two power plants—plant A and plant B—might be ordered to reduce pollution by the same percentage, even if their costs of achieving that objective are very different.

How does economic theory suggest that pollution should be controlled? We'll examine two approaches: taxes and tradable permits. As we'll see, either approach can achieve the efficient outcome at the minimum feasible cost.

Emissions Taxes

One way to deal with pollution directly is to charge polluters an **emissions tax.** Emissions taxes are taxes that depend on the amount of pollution a firm produces. For example, power plants might be charged $200 for every ton of sulfur dioxide they emit.

Consider the socially optimal quantity of pollution, Q_{OPT}, shown in Figure 39.1. At that quantity of pollution, the marginal social benefit and the marginal social cost of an additional ton of emissions are equal at $200. But in the absence of government intervention, power companies have no incentive to limit pollution to the socially optimal quantity Q_{OPT}; instead, they will push pollution up to the quantity Q_{MKT}, at which the marginal social benefit is zero.

An **emissions tax** is a tax that depends on the amount of pollution a firm produces.

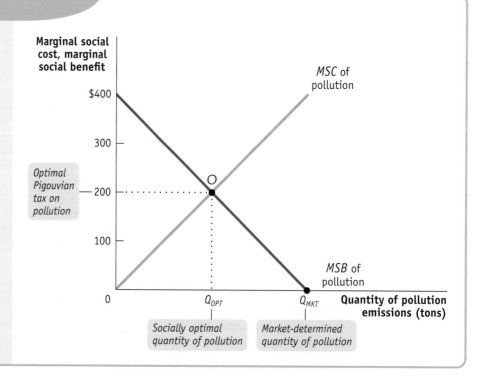

figure 39.1

In Pursuit of the Efficient Quantity of Pollution

The market determined quantity of pollution, Q_{MKT}, is too high because polluters don't pay the marginal social cost, and thus pollute beyond the socially optimal quantity, Q_{OPT}, at which marginal social cost equals marginal social benefit. A Pigouvian tax of $200—the value of the marginal social cost of pollution when it equals the marginal social benefit of pollution—gives polluters the incentive to emit only the socially optimal quantity of pollution. Another solution is to provide permits for only the socially optimal quantity of pollution.

It's now easy to see how an emissions tax can solve the problem. If power companies are required to pay a tax of $200 per ton of emissions, they face a marginal cost of $200 per ton and have an incentive to reduce emissions to Q_{OPT}, the socially optimal quantity. This illustrates a general result: an emissions tax equal to the marginal social cost at the socially optimal quantity of pollution induces polluters to internalize the externality—to take into account the true cost to society of their actions.

Why is an emissions tax an efficient way (that is, a cost-minimizing way) to reduce pollution but environmental standards generally are not? Because an emissions tax ensures that the marginal benefit of pollution is equal for all sources of pollution, but an environmental standard does not. Figure 39.2 shows a hypothetical industry consisting of only two plants, plant A and plant B. We'll assume that plant A uses newer technology than plant B and so has a lower cost of reducing pollution. Reflecting this difference in costs, plant A's marginal benefit of pollution curve, MB_A, lies below plant B's marginal benefit of pollution curve, MB_B. Because it is more costly for plant B to reduce its pollution at any output quantity, an additional ton of pollution is worth more to plant B than to plant A.

In the absence of government action, polluters will pollute until the marginal social benefit of an additional unit of emissions is equal to zero. Recall that the marginal

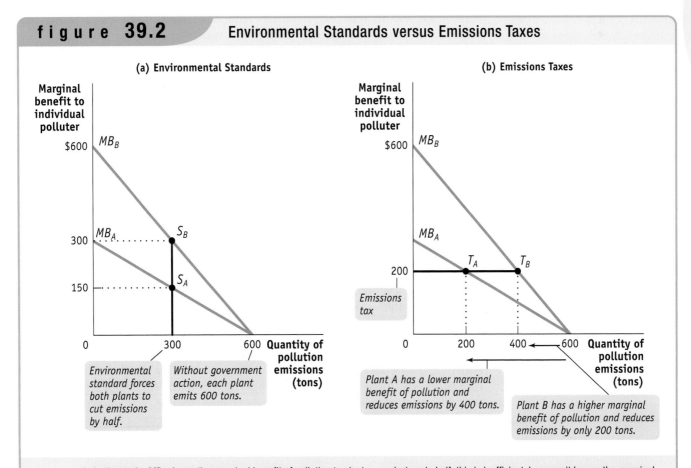

figure 39.2   Environmental Standards versus Emissions Taxes

In both panels, MB_A shows the marginal benefit of pollution to plant A and MB_B shows the marginal benefit of pollution to plant B. In the absence of government intervention, each plant would emit 600 tons. However, the cost of reducing emissions is lower for plant A, as shown by the fact that MB_A lies below MB_B. Panel (a) shows the result of an environmental standard that requires both plants to cut emissions in half; this is inefficient, because it leaves the marginal benefit of pollution higher for plant B than for plant A. Panel (b) shows that an emissions tax achieves the same quantity of overall pollution efficiently: faced with an emissions tax of $200 per ton, both plants reduce pollution to the point where its marginal benefit is $200.

social benefit of pollution is the cost savings, at the margin, to polluters of an additional unit of pollution. As a result, without government intervention each plant will pollute until its own marginal benefit of pollution is equal to zero. This corresponds to an emissions quantity of 600 tons each for plants A and B—the quantity of pollution at which MB_A and MB_B are each equal to zero. So although plant A and plant B value a ton of emissions differently, without government action they will each choose to emit the same amount of pollution.

Now suppose that the government decides that overall pollution from this industry should be cut in half, from 1,200 tons to 600 tons. Panel (a) of Figure 39.2 shows how this might be achieved with an environmental standard that requires each plant to cut its emissions in half, from 600 to 300 tons. The standard has the desired effect of reducing overall emissions from 1,200 to 600 tons but accomplishes it in an inefficient way. As you can see from panel (a), the environmental standard leads plant A to produce at point S_A, where its marginal benefit of pollution is $150, but plant B produces at point S_B, where its marginal benefit of pollution is twice as high, $300.

This difference in marginal benefits between the two plants tells us that the same quantity of pollution can be achieved at lower total cost by allowing plant B to pollute more than 300 tons but inducing plant A to pollute less. In fact, the efficient way to reduce pollution is to ensure that at the industry-wide outcome, the marginal benefit of pollution is the same for all plants. When each plant values a unit of pollution equally, there is no way to rearrange pollution reduction among the various plants that achieves the optimal quantity of pollution at a lower total cost.

We can see from panel (b) how an emissions tax achieves exactly that result. Suppose both plant A and plant B pay an emissions tax of $200 per ton so that the marginal cost of an additional ton of emissions to each plant is now $200 rather than zero. As a result, plant A produces at T_A and plant B produces at T_B. So plant A reduces its pollution more than it would under an inflexible environmental standard, cutting its emissions from 600 to 200 tons; meanwhile, plant B reduces its pollution less, going from 600 to 400 tons. In the end, total pollution—600 tons—is the same as under the environmental standard, but total surplus is higher. That's because the reduction in pollution has been achieved efficiently, allocating most of the reduction to plant A, the plant that can reduce emissions at lower cost.

The term *emissions tax* may convey the misleading impression that taxes are a solution to only one kind of external cost, pollution. In fact, taxes can be used to discourage any activity that generates negative externalities, such as driving during rush hour or operating a noisy bar in a residential area. In general, taxes designed to reduce external costs are known as **Pigouvian taxes,** after the economist A.C. Pigou, who emphasized their usefulness in a classic 1920 book, *The Economics of Welfare.* Look again at Figure 39.1. In our example, the optimal Pigouvian tax is $200; as you can see from Figure 39.1, this corresponds to the marginal social cost of pollution at the optimal output quantity, Q_{OPT}.

Are there any problems with emissions taxes? The main concern is that in practice government officials usually aren't sure at what level the tax should be set. If they set the tax too low, there will be too little improvement in the environment; if they set it too high, emissions will be reduced by more than is efficient. This uncertainty cannot be eliminated, but the nature of the risks can be changed by using an alternative strategy, issuing tradable emissions permits.

Tradable Emissions Permits

Tradable emissions permits are licenses to emit limited quantities of pollutants that can be bought and sold by polluters. They are usually issued to polluting firms according to some formula reflecting their history. For example, each power plant might be issued permits equal to 50% of its emissions before the system went into

Taxes designed to reduce external costs are known as **Pigouvian taxes.**

Tradable emissions permits are licenses to emit limited quantities of pollutants that can be bought and sold by polluters.

effect. The more important point, however, is that these permits are *tradable.* Firms with differing costs of reducing pollution can now engage in mutually beneficial transactions: those that find it easier to reduce pollution will sell some of their permits to those that find it more difficult. In other words, firms will use transactions in permits to reallocate pollution reduction among themselves, so that in the end those with the lowest cost will reduce their pollution the most and those with the highest cost will reduce their pollution the least. Assume that the government issues 300 permits each to plant A and plant B, where one permit allows the emission of one ton of pollution. Under a system of tradable emissions permits, commonly known as a *cap-and-trade program,* plant A will find it profitable to sell 100 of its 300 government-issued permits to plant B. The effect of a cap-and-trade program is to create a market in rights to pollute.

Just like emissions taxes, tradable permits provide polluters with an incentive to take the marginal social cost of pollution into account. To see why, suppose that the market price of a permit to emit one ton of sulfur dioxide is $200. Then every plant has an incentive to limit its emissions of sulfur dioxide to the point where its marginal benefit of emitting another ton of pollution is $200. This is obvious for plants that buy rights to pollute: if a plant must pay $200 for the right to emit an additional ton of sulfur dioxide, it faces the same incentives as a plant facing an emissions tax of $200 per ton. But it's equally true for plants that have more permits than they plan to use: by *not* emitting a ton of sulfur dioxide, a plant frees up a permit that it can sell for $200, so the opportunity cost of a ton of emissions to the plant's owner is $200.

In short, tradable emissions permits have the same cost-minimizing advantage as emissions taxes over environmental standards: either system ensures that those who can reduce pollution most cheaply are the ones who do so. The socially optimal quantity of pollution shown in Figure 39.1 could be efficiently achieved either way: by imposing an emissions tax of $200 per ton of pollution or by issuing tradable permits to emit Q_{OPT} tons of pollution. If regulators choose to issue Q_{OPT} permits, where one permit allows the release of one ton of emissions, then the equilibrium market price of a permit among polluters will indeed be $200. Why? You can see from Figure 39.1 that at Q_{OPT}, only polluters with a marginal benefit of pollution of $200 or more will buy a permit. And the last polluter who buys—who has a marginal benefit of exactly $200— sets the market price.

It's important to realize that emissions taxes and tradable permits do more than induce polluting industries to reduce their output. Unlike rigid environmental standards, emissions taxes and tradable permits provide incentives to create and use technology that emits less pollution—new technology that lowers the socially optimal level of pollution. The main effect of the permit system for sulfur dioxide has been to change *how* electricity is produced rather than to reduce the nation's electricity output. For example, power companies have shifted to the use of alternative fuels such as low-sulfur coal and natural gas; they have also installed scrubbers that take much of the sulfur dioxide out of a power plant's emissions.

The main problem with tradable emissions permits is the flip-side of the problem with emissions taxes: because it is difficult to determine the optimal quantity of pollution, governments can find themselves either issuing too many permits (that is, they don't reduce pollution enough) or issuing too few (that is, they reduce pollution too much).

After first relying on environmental standards, the U.S. government has turned to a system of tradable permits to control acid rain. Current proposals would extend the system to other major sources of pollution. And in 2005 the European Union created an emissions-trading scheme with the purpose of controlling emissions of carbon dioxide, a greenhouse gas. The European Union scheme is part of a larger global market for the trading of greenhouse gas permits. The IRL that follows describes these two systems in greater detail.

Cap and Trade

The tradable emissions permit systems for both acid rain in the United States and greenhouse gases in the European Union are examples of *cap and trade programs:* the government sets a *cap* (a total amount of pollution that can be emitted), issues tradable emissions permits, and enforces a yearly rule that a polluter must hold a number of permits equal to the amount of pollution emitted. The goal is to set the cap low enough to generate environmental benefits and, at the same time, to give polluters flexibility in meeting environmental standards and motivate them to adopt new technologies that will lower the cost of reducing pollution.

In 1994 the United States began a cap and trade system for the sulfur dioxide emissions that cause acid rain by issuing permits to power plants based on their historical consumption of

coal. The cap of 8.95 million tons set for 2010 was about half the level of sulfur dioxide emissions in 1980. Economists who have analyzed the sulfur dioxide cap and trade system point to another reason for its success: it would have been a lot more expensive—80% more to be exact—to reduce emissions by this much using a non-market-based regulatory policy.

The European Union cap and trade scheme is the world's only mandatory trading scheme for greenhouse gases and covers all 27 member nations of the European Union. Available data indicate that within the system, 3,093 metric tons of emissions were transacted in 2008 and 6,326 metric tons in 2009, an astonishing increase of 105%. Although it is still too early to evaluate the system's performance, at the time of this writing the U.S. Senate was impressed

enough with the preliminary results to consider proposing an American cap and trade system for greenhouse gases.

Despite all this good news, however, cap and trade systems are not silver bullets for the world's pollution problems. Although they are appropriate for pollution that's geographically dispersed, like sulfur dioxide and greenhouse gases, they don't work for pollution that's localized, like mercury or lead contamination. In addition, the amount of overall reduction in pollution depends on the level of the cap. Under industry pressure, regulators run the risk of issuing too many permits, effectively eliminating the cap. Finally, there must be vigilant monitoring of compliance if the system is to work. Without oversight of how much a polluter is actually emitting, there is no way to know for sure that the rules are being followed.

Production, Consumption, and Externalities

Nobody imposes external costs like pollution out of malice. Pollution, traffic congestion, and other negative externalities are side effects of activities, like electricity generation, manufacturing, or driving, that are otherwise desirable. We've just learned how government regulators can move the market to the socially optimal quantity when the side effects can be directly controlled. But as we cautioned earlier, in some cases it's not possible to directly control the side effects, only the activities that cause them can be influenced. As we'll see shortly, government policies in these situations must instead be geared to changing the levels of production and consumption that create externalities, which in turn changes the levels of the externalities themselves.

This approach, although slightly more complicated, has several advantages. First, for activities that generate external *costs,* it gives us a clear understanding of how the desirable activity is affected by policies designed to manage its side effects. Second, it helps us think about a question that is different but related to the problem of external costs: what should be done when an activity generates external *benefits.* It's important to realize that not all externalities are negative. There are, in fact, many positive externalities that we encounter every day; for example, a neighbor's bird-feeder has the side effect of maintaining the local wild bird population for everyone's enjoyment. And a beautiful flower garden in front of a neighbor's house can be enjoyed by many passersby.

Using the approach of targeting the activity behind the externalities, we'll now turn our attention to the topic of positive externalities.

Private versus Social Benefits

Earlier, we pointed out that getting a flu shot has benefits to people beyond the person getting the shot. Under some conditions, getting a flu vaccination reduces the expected number of *other* people who get the flu by as much as 1.5. This prompted one economist to suggest a new T-shirt slogan, one particularly suited for the winter months: "Kiss Me, I'm Vaccinated!" When you get vaccinated against the flu, it's likely that you're conferring a substantial benefit on those around you—a benefit for others that you are not compensated for. In other words, getting a flu shot generates a positive externality.

The government can directly control the external costs of pollution because it can measure emissions. In contrast, it can't observe the reduction in flu cases caused by you getting a flu shot, so it can't directly control the external benefits—say, by rewarding you based on how many fewer people caught the flu because of your actions. So if the government wants to influence the level of external benefits from flu vaccinations, it must target the original activity—getting a flu shot.

Your flu shot provides positive externalities to those whom you would otherwise make sick.

From the point of view of society as a whole, a flu shot carries both costs (the price you pay for the shot, which compensates the vaccine maker and your health care provider for the inputs and factors of production necessary to grow the vaccine and deliver it to your bloodstream) and benefits. Those benefits are the private benefit that accrues to you from not getting the flu yourself, but they also include the external benefits that accrue to others from a lower likelihood of catching the flu. However, you have no incentive to take into account the beneficial side effects that are generated by your actions. As a result, in the absence of government intervention, too few people will choose to be vaccinated.

Panel (a) of Figure 39.3 illustrates this point. The market demand curve for flu shots is represented by the curve *D*; the market, or industry, supply curve is given by the curve *S*. In the absence of government intervention, market equilibrium will be at point E_{MKT}, with Q_{MKT} flu shots being bought and sold at the market price of P_{MKT}.

figure 39.3   Positive Externalities and Consumption

(a) Positive Externality

Price, marginal social benefit of flu shot

Marginal external benefit

S

P_{MSB}
P_{OPT}
P_{MKT}

O

E_{MKT}

MSB of flu shots

D

Q_{MKT} Q_{OPT} Quantity of flu shots

(b) Optimal Pigouvian Subsidy

Price of flu shot

Price to producers after subsidy

Optimal Pigouvian subsidy

Price to consumers after subsidy

S

O

E_{MKT}

D

Q_{MKT} Q_{OPT} Quantity of flu shots

Consumption of flu shots generates external benefits, so the marginal social benefit curve, *MSB*, of flu shots, corresponds to the demand curve, *D*, shifted upward by the marginal external benefit. Panel (a) shows that without government action, the market produces Q_{MKT}. It is lower than the socially optimal quantity of consumption, Q_{OPT}, the quantity at which *MSB* crosses the

supply curve, *S*. At Q_{MKT}, the marginal social benefit of another flu shot, P_{MSB}, is greater than the marginal private benefit to consumers of another flu shot, P_{MKT}. Panel (b) shows how an optimal Pigouvian subsidy to consumers, equal to the marginal external benefit, moves consumption to Q_{OPT} by lowering the price paid by consumers.

The **marginal private benefit** of a good is the marginal benefit that accrues to consumers of a good, not including any external benefits.

The **marginal social benefit of a good** is the marginal private benefit plus the marginal external benefit.

The **marginal external benefit** of a good is the addition to external benefits created by one more unit of the good.

A **Pigouvian subsidy** is a payment designed to encourage purchases and activities that yield external benefits.

A **technology spillover** is an external benefit that results when knowledge spreads among individuals and firms.

At that point, the marginal cost to society of another flu shot is equal to the marginal benefit *gained by the individual consumer who purchases that flu shot,* measured by the market price.

So far we have studied goods in the absence of external benefits, so the marginal benefit to the consumer has been no different from the marginal benefit to society. When a good like flu shots creates positive externalities, there is a difference between the marginal benefit to the consumer, which we'll distinguish by calling it the **marginal private benefit,** and the marginal benefit to society, called the **marginal social benefit of a good** (or similarly, of a service or activity). The difference between the marginal private benefit (MPB) and the marginal social benefit (MSB) is the **marginal external benefit** (MEB) that indicates the increase in external benefits to society from an additional unit of the good:

(39-1) $MSB = MPB + MEB$

The demand curve represents the marginal benefit that accrues to *consumers of the good:* the marginal private benefit. It does not incorporate the benefits to society as a whole from consuming the good—in this case, the reduction in the number of flu cases. As you can see from panel (a) of Figure 39.3, the marginal social benefit curve, *MSB,* corresponds to the demand curve, *D, shifted upward* by the amount of the marginal external benefit.

With the marginal social benefit curve and the supply curve, we can find the socially optimal quantity of a good or activity that generates external benefits: it is the quantity Q_{OPT}, the quantity that corresponds to point O at which *MSB* and *S* cross. Because the external benefit is not accounted for in market decisions, Q_{OPT} is greater than Q_{MKT}; it's the quantity at which the marginal cost of a good (measured by *S*) is equal to the marginal social benefit (measured by *MSB*).

So left to its own, a market will bring about too little production and consumption of a good or activity that generates external benefits. Correspondingly, without government action, the price to consumers of such a good or activity is too high: at the market output level Q_{MKT}, the unregulated market price is P_{MKT} and the marginal benefit to consumers of an additional flu shot is lower than P_{MSB}, the true marginal benefit to society of an additional flu shot.

How can the economy be induced to produce Q_{OPT}, the socially optimal level of flu shots shown in Figure 39.3? The answer is by a **Pigouvian subsidy:** a payment designed to encourage activities that yield external benefits. The optimal Pigouvian subsidy, shown in panel (b) of Figure 39.3, is equal to the marginal external benefit of consuming another unit of flu shots. In this example, a Pigouvian subsidy works by lowering the price of consuming the good: consumers pay a price for a flu shot that is equal to the market price *minus* the subsidy. In 2001, Japan began a program of subsidizing 71% of the cost of flu shots for the elderly in large cities. A 2005 study found that the subsidy significantly reduced the incidence of pneumonia, and influenza-caused mortality, at a net benefit to Japanese society of $1.08 billion dollars.

The most important single source of external benefits in the modern economy is the creation of knowledge. In high-tech industries such as the semiconductor, software design, and bioengineering industries, innovations by one firm are quickly emulated by rival firms and put to use in the development of further advancements in related industries. This spreading of cutting-edge information among high-tech firms is known as **technology spillover.** Such spillovers often take place through face-to-face contact. For example, bars and restaurants in California's Silicon Valley are famed for their technical chitchat. Workers know that the best way to keep up with the latest technological innovations is to hang around in the right places, have a drink, and gossip. Such informal contact helps to spread useful knowledge, which may also explain why so many high-tech firms are clustered close to one another.

Private versus Social Costs

Now let's turn briefly to consider a case in which production of a good creates external costs—namely, the livestock industry. Whatever it is—cows, pigs, chicken, sheep, or salmon—livestock farming produces prodigious amounts of what is euphemistically known as "muck." But that's not all: scientists estimate that the amount of methane gas produced by livestock currently rivals the amount caused by the burning of fossil fuels in the creation of greenhouse gases. From the point of view of society as a whole, then, the cost of livestock farming includes both direct production costs (payments for factors of production and inputs) and the external environmental costs imposed as a by-product of farming.

The social cost of livestock production is felt beyond the farm.

When a good like pork involves negative externalities, there is a difference between the marginal cost to the *firm,* which we distinguish as the **marginal private cost,** and the marginal cost to *society,* the **marginal social cost of a good** (or likewise of a service or activity). The difference between the marginal private cost (*MPC*) and the marginal social cost (*MSC*) is the **marginal external cost** (*MEC*)—the increase in external costs to society from an additional unit of the good:

(39-2) $MSC = MPC + MEC$

Panel (a) in Figure 39.4 shows the marginal social cost curve, *MSC,* of livestock; it corresponds to the industry supply curve, *S, shifted upward* by the amount of the marginal external cost. (Recall that in a competitive industry, the industry supply curve is the horizontal sum of the individual firms' supply curves, which are the same as their

The **marginal private cost** of a good is the marginal cost of producing that good, not including any external costs.

The **marginal social cost of a good** is equal to the marginal private cost of production plus its marginal external cost.

The **marginal external cost** of a good is the increase in external costs created by one more unit of the good.

figure 39.4   Negative Externalities and Production

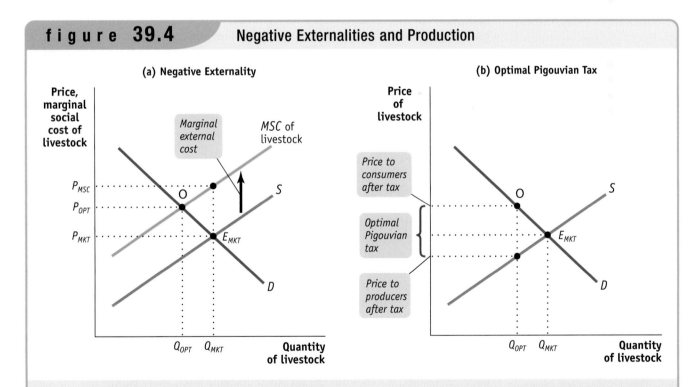

Livestock production generates external costs, so the marginal social cost curve, *MSC,* of livestock, corresponds to the supply curve, *S,* shifted upward by the marginal external cost. Panel (a) shows that without government action, the market produces the quantity Q_{MKT}. It is greater than the socially optimal quantity of livestock production, Q_{OPT}, the quantity at which *MSC* crosses

the demand curve, *D.* At Q_{MKT}, the market price, P_{MKT}, is less than P_{MSC}, the true marginal cost to society of livestock production. Panel (b) shows how an optimal Pigouvian tax on livestock production, equal to its marginal external cost, moves the production to Q_{OPT}, resulting in lower output and a higher price to consumers.

marginal cost curves.) In the absence of government intervention, the market equilibrium will be at point E_{MKT}, yielding an equilibrium quantity of Q_{MKT} and an equilibrium price of P_{MKT}.

The ever-important socially optimal quantity of a good is the quantity at which *marginal social benefit equals marginal social cost*. In the livestock example, this criterion is met at point O, where the MSC and D curves cross. Why can we substitute the demand curve for marginal social benefit in this case? Because although the demand curve represents the marginal benefit to consumers—the marginal private benefit—there are no external benefits to separate the marginal private benefit from the marginal social benefit. That means that when $MSC = D$ and there are no external benefits, it is also true that $MSC = MPB = MSB$.

Unfortunately, the market equilibrium quantity Q_{MKT} is greater than Q_{OPT}, the socially optimal quantity of livestock. So left to its own, the market produces too much of a good that generates an external cost in production, and the price to consumers of such a good is too low: P_{MKT} is less than P_{MSC}, the true marginal cost to society of another unit of livestock. As panel (b) of Figure 39.4 shows, an optimal Pigouvian tax on livestock production, equal to the marginal external cost, moves the market to the socially optimal level of production, Q_{OPT}.

In the flu shot example, we explained that the socially optimal quantity was found where the MSB and S curves crossed. That point met the $MSB = MSC$ criterion for the socially optimal quantity as well because in the absence of external costs, marginal social cost equals marginal private cost, which is indicated by the supply curve. That is, when $MSB = S$ and there are no external costs, it is also true that $MSB = MPC = MSC$.

At this point, you might ask whether a regulator would choose a method of control that targets pollution directly, such as a cap and trade program, or control the production of the associated good with a Pigouvian tax. Generally, it is a good idea to target the pollution directly whenever feasible. The main reason is that this method creates incentives for the invention and adoption of production methods that create less pollution. For example, the AgCert company has found a way to capture greenhouse gases emitted from animal waste for use as tradable emissions reductions in a cap and trade program.

Network Externalities

There is one type of externality that has no inherently favorable or adverse effect on society at large, but it does affect other users of the associated good or service. Suppose you were the only user of Twitter in the world. What would it be worth to you? The answer, of course, is nothing. Twitter derives its value only from the fact that other people also use Twitter and you can send or receive tweets. In general, the more people who use Twitter, the more valuable it is to you.

A **network externality** exists when the value to an individual of a good or service depends on how many other people use the same good or service. Sometimes referred to as the "fax machine effect," the phenomenon of network externalities is so named because the classic examples involve networks of telephones, computers, and transportation systems. When it comes to sharing digital information, it helps to have more users of the same software, hardware, and online networking services. In other contexts, it's better to have more users of the same stock exchanges, gauges of railroad line, and sizes of electrical plugs, among many examples. Congestion creates a form of negative network externality: it can make things worse for you when more people use the same highway, elevator, or swimming pool.

A good is subject to a **network externality** when the value of the good to an individual is greater when more other people also use the good.

Module ⏺39 Review

Solutions appear at the back of the book.

Check Your Understanding

1. Some opponents of tradable emissions permits object to them on the grounds that polluters that sell their permits benefit monetarily from their involvement in polluting the environment. Assess this argument.

2. For each of the following cases, explain whether an external cost or an external benefit is created and identify an appropriate policy response.
   a. Trees planted in urban areas improve air quality and lower summer temperatures.
   b. Water-saving toilets reduce the need to pump water from rivers and aquifers. The cost of a gallon of water to homeowners is virtually zero.
   c. Old computer monitors contain toxic materials that pollute the environment when improperly disposed of.

Multiple-Choice Questions

1. Which of the following policy tools is inefficient even when correctly administered?
   a. environmental standards
   b. emissions taxes
   c. tradable emissions permits
   d. Pigouvian taxes
   e. cap and trade programs

2. An efficient Pigouvian subsidy for a good is set equal to the good's
   a. external cost.
   b. marginal social benefit.
   c. marginal external cost.
   d. marginal external benefit.
   e. price at which $MSC = MSB$.

3. Which of the following is true in the case of a positive externality?
   a. $MSC > MSB$
   b. $MPB > MSC$
   c. $MSB > MPB$
   d. $MPB > MSB$
   e. $MSC > MPC$

4. One example of a source of external benefits is
   a. technology spillover.
   b. traffic congestion.
   c. pollution.
   d. subsidies for polluters.
   e. taxes on environmental conservation.

5. Marginal social benefit equals marginal private benefit plus
   a. marginal external benefit.
   b. marginal private cost.
   c. total external benefit.
   d. total external cost.
   e. marginal social cost.

Critical-Thinking Question

The use of plastic water bottles creates external costs as the result of plastic production, bottle transportation, litter, and waste disposal. Draw a correctly labeled graph showing how the market will determine the quantity of water bottles purchased. On the same graph, show the marginal external cost, the socially optimal quantity of water bottles, and the size of a Pigouvian tax that could be used to achieve the socially optimal quantity of water bottles.

© imac/Alamy

Module 40
Public Goods

In this module, we take a somewhat different approach to the question of why markets sometimes fail. Here we focus on how the characteristics of goods often determine whether markets can deliver them efficiently. When goods have the "wrong" characteristics, the resulting market failures resemble those associated with externalities or market power. This alternative way of looking at sources of inefficiency deepens our understanding of why markets sometimes don't work well and how government can take actions that improve the welfare of society.

Private Goods—And Others

What's the difference between installing a new bathroom in a house and building a municipal sewage system? What's the difference between growing wheat and fishing in the open ocean?

These aren't trick questions. In each case there is a basic difference in the characteristics of the goods involved. Bathroom appliances and wheat have the characteristics necessary to allow markets to work efficiently. Public sewage systems and fish in the sea do not.

Let's look at these crucial characteristics and why they matter.

Characteristics of Goods

Goods like bathroom fixtures and wheat have two characteristics that are essential if a good is to be provided in efficient quantities by a market economy.

- They are **excludable:** suppliers of the good can prevent people who don't pay from consuming it.
- They are **rival in consumption:** the same unit of the good cannot be consumed by more than one person at the same time.

When a good is both excludable and rival in consumption, it is called a **private good.** Wheat is an example of a private good. It is *excludable:* the farmer can sell a bushel to one consumer without having to provide wheat to everyone in the county. And it is *rival in consumption:* if I eat bread baked with a farmer's wheat, that wheat cannot be consumed by someone else.

But not all goods possess these two characteristics. Some goods are **nonexcludable**—the supplier cannot prevent consumption of the good by people who do not pay for it.

What you will learn
in this Module:

- How public goods are characterized and why markets fail to supply efficient quantities of public goods
- What common resources are and why they are overused
- What artificially scarce goods are and why they are underconsumed
- How government intervention in the production and consumption of these types of goods can make society better off
- Why finding the right level of government intervention is often difficult

A good is **excludable** if the supplier of that good can prevent people who do not pay from consuming it.

A good is **rival in consumption** if the same unit of the good cannot be consumed by more than one person at the same time.

A good that is both excludable and rival in consumption is a **private good.**

When a good is **nonexcludable,** the supplier cannot prevent consumption by people who do not pay for it.

A good is **nonrival in consumption** if more than one person can consume the same unit of the good at the same time.

Fire protection is one example: a fire department that puts out fires before they spread protects the whole city, not just people who have made contributions to the Firemen's Benevolent Association. An improved environment is another: pollution can't be ended for some users of a river while leaving the river foul for others.

Nor are all goods rival in consumption. Goods are **nonrival in consumption** if more than one person can consume the same unit of the good at the same time. TV programs are nonrival in consumption: your decision to watch a show does not prevent other people from watching the same show.

Because goods can be either excludable or nonexcludable, and either rival or nonrival in consumption, there are four types of goods, illustrated by the matrix in Figure 40.1:

- *Private goods,* which are excludable and rival in consumption, like wheat
- *Public goods,* which are nonexcludable and nonrival in consumption, like a public sewer system
- *Common resources,* which are nonexcludable but rival in consumption, like clean water in a river
- *Artificially scarce goods,* which are excludable but nonrival in consumption, like pay-per-view movies on cable TV

figure 40.1

Four Types of Goods

There are four types of goods. The type of a good depends on (1) whether or not it is excludable—whether a producer can prevent someone from consuming it; and (2) whether or not it is rival in consumption—whether it is impossible for the same unit of a good to be consumed by more than one person at the same time.

	Rival in consumption	Nonrival in consumption
Excludable	**Private goods** • Wheat • Bathroom fixtures	**Artificially scarce goods** • Pay-per-view movies • Computer software
Non-excludable	**Common resources** • Clean water • Biodiversity	**Public goods** • Public sanitation • National defense

There are, of course, many other characteristics that distinguish between types of goods—necessities versus luxuries, normal versus inferior, and so on. Why focus on whether goods are excludable and rival in consumption?

Why Markets Can Supply Only Private Goods Efficiently

As we learned in earlier modules, markets are typically the best means for a society to deliver goods and services to its members; that is, markets are efficient except in the case of market power, externalities, or other instances of market failure. One source of market failure is rooted in the nature of the good itself: markets cannot supply goods and services efficiently unless they are private goods—excludable and rival in consumption.

To see why excludability is crucial, suppose that a farmer had only two choices: either produce no wheat or provide a bushel of wheat to every resident of the county who wants it, whether or not that resident pays for it. It seems unlikely that anyone would grow wheat under those conditions.

Yet the operator of a public sewage system consisting of pipes that anyone can dump sewage into faces pretty much the same problem as our hypothetical farmer.

A sewage system makes the whole city cleaner and healthier—but that benefit accrues to all the city's residents, whether or not they pay the system operator. The general point is that if a good is nonexcludable, rational consumers won't be willing to pay for it—they will take a "free ride" on anyone who *does* pay. So there is a **free-rider problem.** Examples of the free-rider problem are familiar from daily life. One example you may have encountered happens when students are required to do a group project. There is often a tendency of some group members to shirk their responsibilities, relying on others in the group to get the work done. The shirkers *free-ride* on someone else's effort.

When the benefits from a group project are nonexcludable, there is a temptation to free-ride on the efforts of others.

Because of the free-rider problem, the forces of self-interest alone do not lead to an efficient level of production for a nonexcludable good. Even though consumers would benefit from increased production of the good, no one individual is willing to pay for more, and so no producer is willing to supply it. The result is that nonexcludable goods suffer from *inefficiently low production* in a market economy. In fact, in the face of the free-rider problem, self-interest may not ensure that any amount of the good—let alone the efficient quantity—is produced.

Goods that are excludable and nonrival in consumption, like pay-per-view movies, suffer from a different kind of inefficiency. As long as a good is excludable, it is possible to earn a profit by making it available only to those who pay. Therefore, producers are willing to supply an excludable good. But the marginal cost of letting an additional viewer watch a pay-per-view movie is zero because it is nonrival in consumption. So the efficient price to the consumer is also zero—or, to put it another way, individuals should watch TV movies up to the point where their marginal benefit is zero. But if the cable company actually charges viewers $4, viewers will consume the good only up to the point where their marginal benefit is $4. When consumers must pay a price greater than zero for a good that is nonrival in consumption, the price they pay is higher than the marginal cost of allowing them to consume that good, which is zero. So in a market economy goods that are nonrival in consumption suffer from *inefficiently low consumption*.

Now we can see why private goods are the only goods that will be produced and consumed in efficient quantities in a competitive market. (That is, a private good will be produced and consumed in efficient quantities in a market free of market power, externalities, and other sources of market failure.) Because private goods are excludable, producers can charge for them and so have an incentive to produce them. And because they are also rival in consumption, it is efficient for consumers to pay a positive price— a price equal to the marginal cost of production. If one or both of these characteristics are lacking, a market economy will lack the incentives to bring about efficient quantities of the good.

Yet there are crucial goods that don't meet these criteria—and in these cases, the government can offer assistance.

Public Goods

A **public good** is the exact opposite of a private good: it is both nonexcludable and nonrival in consumption. A public sewage system is an example of a public good: you can't keep a river clean without making it clean for everyone who lives near its banks, and my protection from sewage contamination does not prevent my neighbor from being protected as well.

Here are some other examples of public goods:

- *Disease prevention*. When a disease is stamped out, no one can be excluded from the benefit, and one person's health doesn't prevent others from being healthy.

Goods that are nonexcludable suffer from the **free-rider problem:** individuals have no incentive to pay for their own consumption and instead will take a "free ride" on anyone who does pay.

A **public good** is both nonexcludable and nonrival in consumption.

- *National defense.* A strong military protects all citizens.
- *Scientific research.* In many cases new findings provide widespread benefits that are not excludable or rival.

Because these goods are nonexcludable, they suffer from the free-rider problem, so private firms would produce inefficiently low quantities of them. And because they are nonrival in consumption, it would be inefficient to charge people for consuming them. As a result, society must find nonmarket methods for providing these goods.

Providing Public Goods

Public goods are provided in a variety of ways. The government doesn't always get involved—in many cases a non-governmental solution has been found for the free-rider problem. But these solutions are usually imperfect in some way.

Some public goods are supplied through voluntary contributions. For example, private donations help support public radio and a considerable amount of scientific research. But private donations are insufficient to finance large programs of great importance, such as the Centers for Disease Control and national defense.

Some public goods are supplied by self-interested individuals or firms because those who produce them are able to make money in an indirect way. The classic example is broadcast television, which in the United States is supported entirely by advertising. The downside of such indirect funding is that it skews the nature and quantity of the public goods that are supplied, while imposing additional costs on consumers. TV stations show the programs that yield the most advertising revenue (that is, programs best suited for selling antacids, hair-loss remedies, antihistamines, and the like to the segment of the population that buys them), which are not necessarily the programs people most want to see. And viewers must endure many commercials.

Some potentially public goods are deliberately made excludable and therefore subject to charge, like pay-per-view movies. In the United Kingdom, where most television programming is paid for by a yearly license fee assessed on every television owner (£145.50, or about $229 in 2010), television viewing is made artificially excludable by the use of "television detection vans": vans that roam neighborhoods in an attempt to detect televisions in non-licensed households and fine them. However, as noted earlier, when suppliers charge a price greater than zero for a nonrival good, consumers will consume an inefficiently low quantity of that good.

In small communities, a high level of social encouragement or pressure can be brought to bear on people to contribute money or time to provide the efficient level of a public good. Volunteer fire departments, which depend both on the volunteered services of the firefighters themselves and on contributions from local residents, are a good example. But as communities grow larger and more anonymous, social pressure is increasingly difficult to apply, compelling larger towns and cities to tax residents and depend on salaried firefighters for fire protection services.

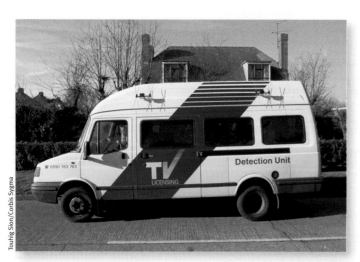

On the prowl: a British TV detection van at work.

As this last example suggests, when other solutions fail, it is up to the government to provide public goods. Indeed, the most important public goods—national defense, the legal system, disease control, fire protection in large cities, and so on—are provided by government and paid for by taxes. Economic theory tells us that the provision of public goods is one of the crucial roles of government.

How Much of a Public Good Should Be Provided?

In some cases, the provision of a public good is an "either-or" decision: a city can either have a sewage system—or not. But in most cases, governments must decide not only whether to provide a public good but also *how much* of that public good to provide. For example, street cleaning is a public good—but how often should the streets be cleaned? Once a month? Twice a month? Every other day?

Imagine a city with only two residents, Ted and Alice. Assume that the public good in question is street cleaning and that Ted and Alice truthfully tell the government how much they value a unit of the public good, one unit being one street cleaning per month. Specifically, each of them tells the government his or her *willingness to pay* for another unit of the public good supplied—an amount that corresponds to that individual's *marginal private benefit* from another unit of the public good.

Using this information along with information on the cost of providing the good, the government can use marginal analysis to find the efficient level of providing the public good: the level at which the *marginal social benefit* of the public good is equal to the marginal social cost of producing it. Recall that the marginal social benefit of a good is the benefit that accrues to society as a whole from the consumption of one additional unit of the good.

But what is the marginal social benefit of another unit of a public good—a unit that generates utility for *all* consumers, not just one consumer, because it is nonexcludable and nonrival in consumption? This question leads us to an important principle: *In the special case of a public good, the marginal social benefit of a unit of the good is equal to the sum of the marginal private benefits enjoyed by all consumers of that unit.* Or to consider it from a slightly different angle, if a consumer could be compelled to pay for a unit before consuming it (the good is made excludable), then the marginal social benefit of a unit is equal to the *sum* of each consumer's willingness to pay for that unit. Using this principle, the marginal social benefit of an additional street cleaning per month is equal to Ted's marginal private benefit from that additional cleaning *plus* Alice's marginal private benefit.

Why? Because a public good is nonrival in consumption—Ted's benefit from a cleaner street does not diminish Alice's benefit from that same clean street, and vice versa. Because Ted and Alice can simultaneously "consume" the same unit of street cleaning, the marginal social benefit is the *sum* of their marginal private benefits. And the efficient quantity of a public good is the quantity at which the marginal social benefit is equal to the marginal social cost of providing it.

Figure 40.2 on the next page illustrates the efficient provision of a public good, showing three marginal benefit curves. Panel (a) shows Ted's marginal private benefit curve from street cleaning, MPB_T: he would be willing to pay $25 for the city to clean its streets once a month, an additional $18 to have it done a second time, and so on. Panel (b) shows Alice's marginal private benefit curve from street cleaning, MPB_A. Panel (c) shows the marginal social benefit curve from street cleaning, MSB: it is the vertical sum of MPB_T and MPB_A.

To maximize society's welfare, the government should increase the quantity of street cleanings until the marginal social benefit of an additional cleaning would fall below the marginal social cost. Suppose that the marginal social cost is $6 per cleaning. Then the city should clean its streets 5 times per month, because the marginal social benefit of each of the first 5 cleanings is more than $6, but going from 5 to 6 cleanings would yield a marginal social benefit of only $2, which is less than the marginal social cost.

One fundamental rationale for the existence of government is that it provides a way for citizens to tax themselves in order to provide public goods—particularly a vital public good like national defense. Responsible governments try to estimate both the social benefits and the social costs of providing a public good, a process known as *cost-benefit analysis.*

figure 40.2

A Public Good

(a) Ted's Marginal Private Benefit Curve

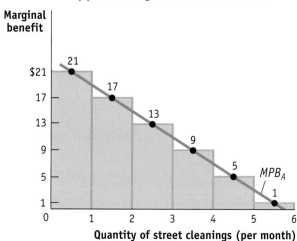

(b) Alice's Marginal Private Benefit Curve

(c) The Marginal Social Benefit Curve

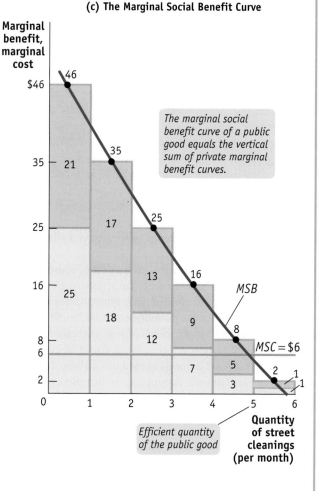

The marginal social benefit curve of a public good equals the vertical sum of private marginal benefit curves.

Panel (a) shows Ted's marginal private benefit curve, MPB_T, and panel (b) shows Alice's marginal private benefit curve, MPB_A. Panel (c) shows the marginal social benefit of the public good, equal to the *sum* of the marginal private benefits to all consumers (in this case, Ted and Alice). The marginal social benefit curve, *MSB*, is the vertical sum of the marginal private benefit curves MPB_T and MPB_A. At a constant marginal social cost of $6, there should be 5 street cleanings per month, because the marginal social benefit of going from 4 to 5 cleanings is $8 ($3 for Ted plus $5 for Alice), but the marginal social benefit of going from 5 to 6 cleanings is only $2.

Of course, if society really consisted of only two individuals, they would probably manage to strike a deal to provide the good. But imagine a city with a million residents, each of whose marginal private benefit from a good is only a tiny fraction of the marginal social benefit. It would be impossible for people to reach a voluntary agreement to pay for the efficient level of a good like street cleaning—the potential for free-riding would make it too difficult to make and enforce an agreement among so many people. But they could and would vote to tax themselves to pay for a city-wide sanitation department.

Voting as a Public Good

It's a sad fact that many Americans who are eligible to vote don't bother to. As a result, their interests tend to be ignored by politicians. But what's even sadder is that this self-defeating behavior may be completely rational.

As the economist Mancur Olson pointed out in a famous book titled *The Logic of Collective Action,* voting is a public good, one that suffers from severe free-rider problems.

Imagine that you are one of a million people who would stand to gain the equivalent of $100 each if some plan is passed in a statewide referendum—say, a plan to improve public schools. And suppose that the opportunity cost of the time it would take you to vote is $10. Will you be sure to go to the polls and vote for the referendum? If you are rational, the answer is

no! The reason is that it is very unlikely that your vote will decide the issue, either way. If the measure passes, you benefit, even if you didn't bother to vote—the benefits are nonexcludable. If the measure doesn't pass, your vote would not have changed the outcome. Either way, by not voting—by free-riding on those who do vote—you save $10.

Of course, many people do vote out of a sense of civic duty. But because political action is a public good, in general people devote too little effort to defending their own interests.

The result, Olson pointed out, is that when a large group of people share a common political interest, they are likely to exert too little effort promoting their cause and so will be ig-

nored. Conversely, small, well-organized interest groups that act on issues narrowly targeted in their favor tend to have disproportionate power.

Is this a reason to distrust democracy? Winston Churchill said it best: "Democracy is the worst form of government, except for all the other forms that have been tried."

Common Resources

A **common resource** is a good that is nonexcludable but is rival in consumption. An example is the stock of fish in a fishing area, like the fisheries off the coast of New England. Traditionally, anyone who had a boat could go out to sea and catch fish—fish in the sea were a nonexcludable good. Yet the total number of fish is limited: the fish that one person catches are no longer available to be caught by someone else. So fish in the sea are rival in consumption.

Other examples of common resources include clean air, water, and the diversity of animal and plant species on the planet (biodiversity). In each of these cases the fact that the good is rival in consumption, and yet nonexcludable, poses a serious problem.

The Problem of Overuse

Because common resources are nonexcludable, individuals cannot be charged for their use. But the resources are rival in consumption, so an individual who uses a unit depletes the resource by making that unit unavailable to others. As a result, a common resource is subject to **overuse:** an individual will continue to use it until his or her marginal private benefit is equal to his or her marginal private cost, ignoring the cost that this action inflicts on society as a whole.

Fish are a classic example of a common resource. Particularly in heavily fished waters, my fishing imposes a cost on others by reducing the fish population and making it harder for others to catch fish. But I have no personal incentive to take this cost into account, since I cannot be charged for fishing. As a result, from society's point of view, I catch too many fish. Traffic congestion is another example of overuse of a common resource. A major highway during rush hour can accommodate only a certain number of vehicles per hour. If I decide to drive to work alone rather than carpool or work at home, I cause many other people to have a longer commute; but I have no incentive to take these consequences into account.

A **common resource** is nonexcludable and rival in consumption: you can't stop me from consuming the good, and more consumption by me means less of the good available for you.

Overuse is the depletion of a common resource that occurs when individuals ignore the fact that their use depletes the amount of the resource remaining for others.

In the case of a common resource, as in the earlier examples involving marginal external costs, the *marginal social cost* of my use of that resource is higher than my *marginal private cost,* the cost to me of using an additional unit of the good. Figure 40.3 illustrates this point. It shows the demand curve for fish, which measures the marginal private benefit of fish (as well as the marginal social benefit because there are no external benefits from catching and consuming fish). The figure also shows the supply curve for fish, which measures the marginal private cost of production of the fishing industry. We know that the industry supply curve is the horizontal sum of each individual fisherman's supply curve—equivalent to his or her marginal private cost curve. The fishing industry supplies the quantity Q_{MKT} at which its marginal private cost equals the price. But the efficient quantity is Q_{OPT}, the quantity of fish that equates the marginal social benefit (as reflected by the demand curve) to the marginal social cost, not to the fishing industry's marginal private cost of production. Thus, the market outcome results in overuse of the common resource.

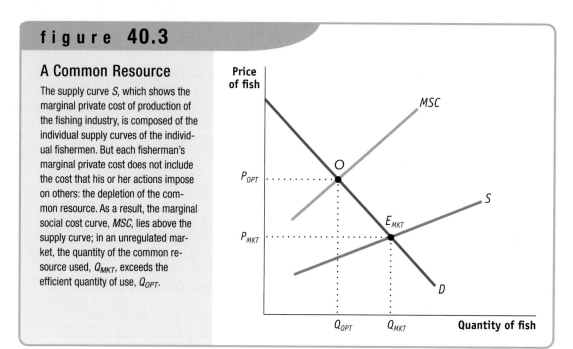

figure 40.3

A Common Resource

The supply curve *S,* which shows the marginal private cost of production of the fishing industry, is composed of the individual supply curves of the individual fishermen. But each fisherman's marginal private cost does not include the cost that his or her actions impose on others: the depletion of the common resource. As a result, the marginal social cost curve, *MSC,* lies above the supply curve; in an unregulated market, the quantity of the common resource used, Q_{MKT}, exceeds the efficient quantity of use, Q_{OPT}.

As we noted, there is a close parallel between the problem of managing a common resource and the problem posed by negative externalities. In the case of an activity that generates a negative externality, the marginal social cost of production is greater than the marginal private cost of production, the difference being the marginal external cost imposed on society. Here, the loss to society arising from a fisher's depletion of the common resource plays the same role as the external cost when there is a negative externality. In fact, many negative externalities (such as pollution) can be thought of as involving common resources (such as clean air).

The Efficient Use and Maintenance of a Common Resource

Because common resources pose problems similar to those created by negative externalities, the solutions are also similar. To ensure efficient use of a common resource, society must find a way to get individual users of the resource to take into account the costs they impose on others. This is the same principle as that of getting individuals to internalize a negative externality that arises from their actions.

There are three principal ways to induce people who use common resources to internalize the costs they impose on others:

■ Tax or otherwise regulate the use of the common resource

■ Create a system of tradable licenses for the right to use the common resource

■ Make the common resource excludable and assign property rights to some individuals

The first two solutions overlap with the approaches to private goods with negative externalities. Just as governments use Pigouvian excise taxes to temper the consumption of alcohol, they use alternative forms of Pigouvian taxes to reduce the use of common resources. For example, in some countries there are "congestion charges" on those who drive during rush hour, in effect charging them for the use of highway space, a common resource. Likewise, visitors to national parks in the United States must pay an entry fee that is essentially a Pigouvian tax.

A second way to correct the problem of overuse is to create a system of tradable licenses for the use of the common resource, much like the systems designed to address negative externalities. The policy maker issues the number of licenses that corresponds to the efficient level of use of the good. Making the licenses tradable ensures that the right to use the good is allocated efficiently—that is, those who end up using the good (those willing to pay the most for a license) are those who gain the most from its use.

If it weren't for fees and restrictions, some common resources would be overrun.

But when it comes to common resources, often the most natural solution is simply to assign property rights. At a fundamental level, common resources are subject to overuse because *nobody owns them*. The essence of ownership of a good—the *property right* over the good—is that you can limit who can and cannot use the good as well as how much of it can be used. When a good is nonexcludable, in a very real sense no one owns it because a property right cannot be enforced—and consequently no one has an incentive to use it efficiently. So one way to correct the problem of overuse is to make the good excludable and assign property rights over it to someone. The good now has an owner who has an incentive to protect the value of the good—to use it efficiently rather than overuse it. This solution is applicable when currently nonexcludable goods can be made excludable, as with the privatization of parks and even roads, but it cannot be applied to resources that are inherently nonexcludable, including the air and flowing water.

Artificially Scarce Goods

An **artificially scarce good** is a good that is excludable but nonrival in consumption. As we've already seen, pay-per-view movies are a familiar example. The marginal cost to society of allowing an individual to watch a movie is zero because one person's viewing doesn't interfere with other people's viewing. Yet cable companies prevent an individual from seeing a movie if he or she hasn't paid. Goods like computer software and audio files, which are valued for the information they embody (and are sometimes called "information goods"), are also artificially scarce.

Markets will supply artificially scarce goods because their excludability allows firms to charge people for them. However, since the efficient price is equal to the marginal cost of zero and the actual price is something higher than that, the good is "artificially scarce" and consumption is inefficiently low. The problem is that, unless the producer can somehow earn revenue from producing and selling the good, none will be produced, which is likely to be worse than a positive but inefficiently low quantity.

Artificially scarce good is a good that is excludable but nonrival in consumption.

We have seen that, in the cases of public goods, common resources, and artificially scarce goods, a market economy will not provide adequate incentives for efficient levels of production and consumption. Fortunately for the sake of market efficiency, most goods are private goods. Food, clothing, shelter, and most other desirable things in life are excludable and rival in consumption, so the types of market failure discussed in this module are important exceptions rather than the norm.

Module 40 Review

Solutions appear at the back of the book.

Check Your Understanding

1. For each of the following goods, indicate whether it is excludable, whether it is rival in consumption, and what kind of good it is.
   a. a public space such as a park
   b. a cheese burrito
   c. information from a website that is password-protected
   d. publicly announced information about the path of an incoming hurricane

2. Which of the goods in Question 1 will be provided by a private producer without government intervention? Which will not be? Explain your answer.

Multiple-Choice Questions

1. Which of the following types of goods are always nonrival in consumption?
   a. public goods
   b. private goods
   c. common resources
   d. inferior goods
   e. goods provided by the government

2. The free-rider problem occurs in the case of
   a. private goods.
   b. common resources.
   c. artificially scarce goods.
   d. motorcycles.
   e. all of the above.

3. Public goods are sometimes provided through which of the following means?
       I. voluntary contributions
      II. individual self-interest
     III. the government
   a. I only
   b. II only
   c. III only
   d. I and III only
   e. I, II, and III

4. Market provision of a public good will lead to
   a. the efficient quantity.
   b. the efficient price.
   c. inefficiently high production of the good.
   d. inefficiently low production of the good.
   e. none of the good being provided.

5. The overuse of a common resource can be reduced by which of the following?
   a. a Pigouvian tax
   b. government regulations
   c. tradable licenses
   d. the assignment of property rights
   e. all of the above

Critical-Thinking Questions

a. Identify and explain the two characteristics shared by every public good.
b. Suppose a new resident moves to a community that purchases a public good for the benefit of every member of the community. What is the additional cost of providing the public good to the new community member? Explain.

AP Photo/The Record, Mike McMahon

What you will learn in this **Module:**

- The three major antitrust laws and how they are used to promote competition

- How government regulation is used to prevent inefficiency in the case of natural monopoly

- The pros and cons of using marginal cost pricing and average cost pricing to regulate prices in natural monopolies

Module 41
Public Policy to Promote Competition

Promoting Competition

We have seen that, in general, equilibrium in a competitive market with no externalities is efficient. On the other hand, imperfectly competitive markets—for example, those with a monopoly or an oligopoly—generally create inefficient outcomes. Concern about the higher prices, lower quantities, and lower quality of goods that can result from imperfect competition has led to public policies to promote competition. These policies include antitrust laws and direct government regulation.

As we discussed in the module "Monopoly and Public Policy," public policy toward monopoly depends crucially on whether or not the industry in question is a natural monopoly. The most common approach to a natural monopoly is for the government to allow one firm to exist but to regulate that firm to increase the quantity and lower the price relative to the monopoly outcome.

In this module, we first focus on ways to promote competition in cases that don't involve natural monopolies. If the industry is *not* a natural monopoly, the best policy is to prevent monopoly from arising or break it up if it already exists. These policies are carried out through antitrust laws. Later in this module we will turn to the more difficult problem of dealing with natural monopoly.

Antitrust Policy

As we discussed in the module "Oligopoly in Practice," imperfect competition first became an issue in the United States during the second half of the nineteenth century when industrialists formed trusts to facilitate monopoly pricing. By having shareholders place their shares in the hands of a board of trustees, major companies in effect merged into a single firm. That is, they created monopolies.

Eventually, there was a public backlash, driven partly by concern about the economic effects of the trust movement, partly by fear that the owners of the trusts were simply becoming too powerful. The result was the Sherman Antitrust Act of 1890, which was intended both to prevent the creation of more monopolies and to break up existing ones. Following the Sherman Act, government passed several other acts intended to clarify antitrust policy.

The Sherman Antitrust Act of 1890

When Microsoft Corporation bundled its Internet Explorer web browser software with its Windows operating system, the makers of competing Netscape Navigator cried foul. Netscape advocates claimed the immediate availability of Internet Explorer to Windows users would create unfair competition. The plaintiffs sought protection under the cornerstone of U.S. antitrust policy (known in many other countries as "competition policy"), the Sherman Antitrust Act. This Act was the first of three major federal antitrust laws in the United States, followed by the Clayton Antitrust Act and the Federal Trade Commission Act, both passed in 1914. The Department of Justice, which has an Antitrust Division charged with enforcing antitrust laws, describes the goals of antitrust laws as protecting competition, ensuring lower prices, and promoting the development of new and better products. It emphasizes that firms in competitive markets attract consumers by cutting prices and increasing the quality of products or services. Competition and profit opportunities also stimulate businesses to find new and more efficient production methods.

The Sherman Antitrust Act of 1890 has two important provisions, each of which outlaws a particular type of activity. The first provision makes it illegal to create a contract, combination, or conspiracy that unreasonably restrains interstate trade. The second provision outlaws the monopolization of any part of interstate commerce. In addition, under the law, the Department of Justice is empowered to bring civil claims and criminal prosecutions when the law is violated. Indeed, it was the Department of Justice that filed suit against Microsoft in the web browser case. The initial court ruling, by the way, was that Microsoft should be broken up into one company that sold Windows and another that sold other software components. After that ruling was overturned on appeal, a final settlement kept Microsoft intact, but prohibited various forms of predatory behavior and practices that could create barriers to entry.

As the ambiguities of the Microsoft case suggest, the law provides little detail regarding what constitutes "restraining trade." And the law does not make it illegal to *be* a monopoly but to "monopolize," that is, to take illegal actions to become a monopoly. If you are the only firm in an industry because no other firm chooses to enter the market, you are not in violation of the Sherman Act.

The two provisions of the Sherman Act give very broad, general descriptions of the activities it makes illegal. The act does not provide details regarding specific actions or activities that it prohibits. The vague nature of the Sherman Act led to the subsequent passage of two additional major antitrust laws.

The Clayton Antitrust Act of 1914

The Clayton Antitrust Act of 1914 was intended to clarify the Sherman Act, which did not identify specific firm behaviors that were illegal. The Clayton Act outlaws four specific firm behaviors; price discrimination, anticompetitive practices (exclusive dealing and tying arrangements), anticompetitive mergers and acquisitions, and interlocking directorates (two corporate boards of directors that share at least one director in common).

You are already familiar with the topic of price discrimination from our discussion of market structures. The Clayton Act makes it illegal to charge different prices to different customers for the same product. Obviously, there are exceptions to this rule that allow the price discrimination we see in practice, for example, at movie theaters where children pay a different price from adults.

By prohibiting exclusive dealing, the Clayton Act makes it illegal for a firm to refuse to do business with you just because you also do business with its competitors. If a firm had the dominant product in a given market, exclusive dealing could allow it to gain monopoly power in other markets. For example, a company that sells an extremely popular felt-tip marker—the only one of its kind—could set a condition that customers who want to purchase the marker must purchase all of their office supplies from the company. This would allow the marker company to expand its existing market power into the market for other office supplies.

The Clayton Act outlaws tying arrangements because, otherwise, a firm could expand its monopoly power for a dominant product by "tying" the purchase of one product to the purchase of a dominant product in another market. Tying arrangements occur when a firm stipulates that it will sell you a specific product, say a printer, only if you buy something else, such as printer paper, at the same time. In this case, tying the printer and paper together expands the firm's printer market power into the market for paper. In this way, as with exclusive dealing, tying arrangements can lessen competition by allowing a firm to expand its market power from one market into another.

Mergers and acquisitions happen fairly often in the U.S. economy; most are not illegal despite the Clayton Act stipulations. The Justice Department regularly reviews proposed mergers between companies in the same industry and, under the Clayton Act, bars any that they determine would significantly reduce competition. To evaluate proposed mergers, they often use the measures we discussed in the oligopoly modules: *concentration ratios* and the *Herfindahl-Hirschman Index*. But the Justice Department is not the only agency responsible for enforcing antitrust laws. Another of our major antitrust laws created and empowers the Federal Trade Commission to enforce antitrust laws.

The Federal Trade Commission promotes fair practices, free entry by firms, and the virtues of competitive markets.

The Federal Trade Commission Act of 1914

Passed in 1914, the Federal Trade Commission Act prohibits unfair methods of competition in interstate commerce and created the Federal Trade Commission (FTC) to enforce the Act. The FTC Act outlaws unfair competition, including "unfair or deceptive acts." The FTC Act also outlaws some of the same practices included in the Sherman and Clayton Acts. In addition, it specifically outlaws price fixing (including the setting of minimum resale prices), output restrictions, and actions that prevent the entry of new firms. The FTC's goal is to promote lower prices, higher output, and free entry—all characteristics of competitive markets (as opposed to monopolies and oligopolies).

Dealing with Natural Monopoly

Antitrust laws are designed to promote competition by preventing business behaviors that concentrate market power. But what if a market is a natural monopoly? As you will recall, a natural monopoly occurs when economies of scale make it efficient to have only one firm in a market. Now we turn from promoting competition to establishing a monopoly, but seeking a public policy to prevent the relatively high prices and low quantities that result when there is only one firm.

Breaking up a monopoly that isn't natural is clearly a good idea: the gains to consumers outweigh the loss to the firm. But what about the situation in which a large firm has a lower average total cost than many small firms—the case of natural monopoly we discussed in the module "Introduction to Market Structure"? The goal in these circumstances is to retain the advantage of lower average total cost that results from a single producer and still curb the inefficiency associated with a monopoly. In the module "Monopoly and Public Policy," we presented two ways to do this—public ownership and price regulation.

While there are a few examples of public ownership in the United States, such as Amtrak, a provider of passenger rail service, the more common answer has been to leave the industry in private hands but subject it to regulation.

Price Regulation Most local utilities are natural monopolies with regulated prices. By having only one firm produce in the market, society benefits from increased efficiency. That is, the average cost of production is lower due to economies of scale. But without price regulation, these firms would be tempted to restrict output and raise price. How, then, do regulators determine an appropriate price?

Since the purpose of regulation is to achieve efficiency in the market, a logical place to set price is at the level at which the marginal cost curve intersects the demand curve. This is called **marginal cost pricing.** (Because we are no longer discussing situations with externalities, we will refer to a single marginal cost that is both marginal social cost and marginal private cost.) We have seen that it is efficient for a competitive firm to set price equal to marginal cost. So should regulators require marginal cost pricing?

Figure 41.1 illustrates this situation. In the case of a natural monopoly, the firm is operating on the downward-sloping portion of its average total cost curve (it is experiencing economies of scale). When average total cost is falling, it must be that marginal cost is below average total cost, pulling it down. If the firm had to set price equal to marginal cost and sell Q_1 units (the quantity demanded when price equals marginal cost), price would be below average total cost and the firm would incur a loss: for each unit sold, the firm would lose the difference between average total cost and price. The firm would not continue to operate at a loss in the long run unless it received a subsidy equal to the amount of the loss. Government could require the efficient price and subsidize the firm, resulting in an overall increase in efficiency for society. But firm subsidies funded from tax revenues are often politically unpopular. What other options do regulators have?

figure 41.1

Price Setting for a Regulated Monopoly

This figure shows the marginal cost curve, *MC*, and the average total cost curve, *ATC*. When price is set equal to marginal cost (where the *MC* curve crosses the demand curve), the firm incurs a loss. When price is set equal to average total cost (where *ATC* crosses the demand curve) the firm breaks even, but price and quantity are not at the efficient level.

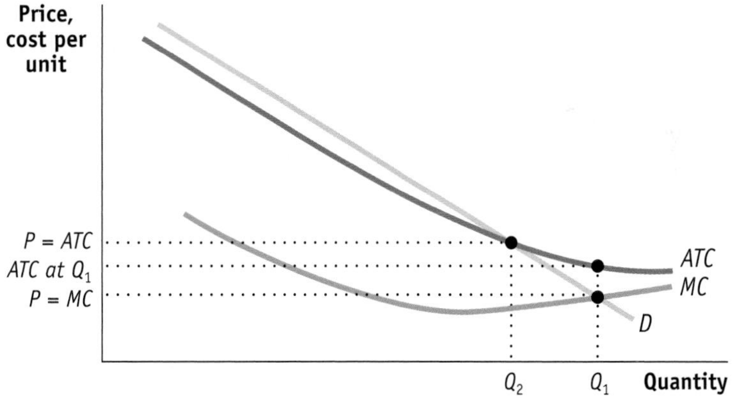

If regulators want to set the price so that the firm does not require a subsidy, they can set the price at which the demand curve intersects the average total cost curve and the firm breaks even. This is called **average cost pricing.** As Figure 41.1 illustrates, average cost pricing results in output level Q_2. The result, a lower quantity at a higher price than with marginal cost pricing, seems to fly in the face of what antitrust regulation is all about. But remember that there are always trade-offs, and it may be best to avoid subsidizing a loss even if it results in less than the efficient quantity.

Allowing a natural monopoly to exist permits the firm to produce at a lower average total cost than if multiple firms produced in the same market. And price regulation seeks to prevent the inefficiency that results when an unregulated monopoly limits output and raises price. This all looks terrific: consumers are better off, monopoly

Marginal cost pricing occurs when regulators set a monopoly's price equal to its marginal cost to achieve efficiency.

Average cost pricing occurs when regulators set a monopoly's price equal to its average cost to prevent the firm from incurring a loss.

profits are avoided, and overall welfare increases. Unfortunately, things are rarely that easy in practice. The main problem is that regulators don't always have the information required to set the price exactly at the level at which the demand curve crosses the average total cost curve. Sometimes they set it too low, creating shortages; at other times they set it too high, increasing inefficiency. Also, regulated monopolies, like publicly owned firms, tend to exaggerate their costs to regulators and to provide inferior quality to consumers.

in real life

The Regulated Price of Power

Power doesn't come cheap, and we're not just talking about the nearly $2 billion spent on congressional races in 2010. By 2017, Georgia Power plans to add two 1,100-megawatt nuclear reactors to its Vogtle Electric Generating Plant in eastern Georgia at an estimated cost of $14 billion. In Kentucky, Louisville Gas and Electric will spend $1.2 billion to add a 750-megawatt coal-fired generating unit. With high start-up costs like these, power plants are natural monopolies. If many plants competed for customers in the same region, none would sell enough energy to warrant the cost of each plant. Here we see the spreading effect from the module "Firm Costs" in action—having just one plant allows the production level to be relatively high and the average fixed cost to be tolerably low.

On October 6, 2010, U.S. Interior Secretary Ken Salazar and representatives from Cape Wind Associates signed the lease for a wind farm off the coast of Massachusetts. The $2.5 billion project will generate 468 megawatts of electricity. With lower output and higher start-up costs than the coal-fired power plant, the spreading effect is smaller, making the average fixed cost and the average total cost relatively high. If regulators set prices for this natural monopoly in accordance with average total cost, we would expect coal-fired plants to be held to a lower price per kilowatt-hour (kWh) than the relatively expensive wind power plants. Indeed, Cape Wind plans to charge 19 cents per kWh, more than twice the 8 cents per kWh allowed for electricity from coal-fired plants in Kentucky and Massachusetts.

Why the interest in generating energy from wind when energy from coal is cheaper for the consumer? The dynamics of supply and demand provide one reason: as supplies of coal decrease and energy demand increases, the equilibrium price for coal energy will rise, helping investments in wind energy to pay off. Another reason relates to the external costs discussed in the module "Externalities and Public Policies": wind turbines create no emissions. The U.S. Department of Energy reports that if 20 percent of the nation's energy needs were satisfied with wind, carbon dioxide emissions would fall by 825 million metric tons annually. Like coal-fired power plants, wind farms do create some negative externalities. The potential for noise and obstructed views elicit cries of "not in my back yard (or even five miles off my coast)!" As with lunches, there's no such thing as a free kWh, which highlights the importance of cost-benefit analysis.

Module 41 Review

Solutions appear at the back of the book.

Check Your Understanding

1. Would each of the following business practices be legal under antitrust law? Explain.
   a. You have a patent for a superior fax machine and therefore are the only person able to sell that type of fax machine. In order to buy your fax machine, you require the purchaser to buy a service contract from you (even though other firms provide excellent service for your machine).
   b. You have invented a new type of correction fluid that does an amazing job covering up mistakes made on paper forms.

   In order to buy your correction fluid, you require purchasers to buy all of their office supplies from you.
   c. You own a car dealership and plan to buy the dealership across the street and merge the two companies. There are several other car dealerships in town.
   d. You and your only other competitor in the state have an agreement that, any time a new firm tries to enter the market, you will drop your prices for long enough to run the new entrant out of business before returning to your previous prices.

2. The IRL in this module discusses the possibility that regulators set prices for wind energy on the basis of average total cost. Explain why policymakers who don't want to pay subsidies would choose average cost pricing over marginal cost pricing in the market for wind energy.

Multiple-Choice Questions

1. The Sherman Antitrust Act of 1890 sought to do which of the following?
   a. break up existing monopolies
   b. prevent the creation of new monopolies
   c. stop monopoly behavior engaged in by trusts
   d. respond to the increasing power of trusts in the economy
   e. all of the above

2. A natural monopoly exists when, over the relevant range, increasing the output level results in a lower
   a. total cost.
   b. average total cost.
   c. average variable cost.
   d. average fixed cost.
   e. marginal cost.

3. Which of the following is the most common policy approach to a natural monopoly?
   a. public ownership
   b. price regulation
   c. quantity regulation
   d. quality regulation
   e. a breakup of the monopoly into smaller firms

For questions 4 and 5, refer to the graph provided.

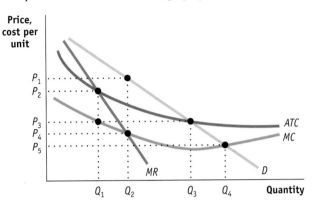

4. Without government intervention, a monopolist will produce _____ and charge _____.
   a. Q_3, P_3
   b. Q_2, P_4
   c. Q_2, P_1
   d. Q_1, P_3
   e. Q_1, P_2

5. The lowest regulated price the government could expect this monopolist to maintain in the long run is
   a. P_1.
   b. P_2.
   c. P_3.
   d. P_4.
   e. P_5.

Critical-Thinking Question

List and describe three different public policy approaches to monopoly.

Module 42

Income Inequality and Income Distribution

What you will learn in this Module:

- What defines poverty, what causes poverty, and the consequences of poverty
- How income inequality in America has changed over time
- How programs like Social Security affect poverty and income inequality

For at least the past 70 years, every U.S. president has promised to do his best to reduce poverty. In 1964 President Lyndon Johnson went so far as to declare a "war on poverty," creating a number of new programs to aid the poor. Antipoverty programs account for a significant part of the U.S. *welfare state*—the system whereby the government takes responsibility for the welfare of its citizens—although social insurance programs are an even larger part. In this module, we look at the problem of poverty and the issue of income distribution, and learn how public policy can affect them.

The Problem of Poverty

What, exactly, do we mean by poverty? Any definition is somewhat arbitrary. Since 1965, however, the U.S. government has maintained an official definition of the **poverty threshold,** a minimum annual income that is considered adequate to purchase the necessities of life. Families whose incomes fall below the poverty threshold are considered poor.

The official poverty threshold depends on the size and composition of a family. In 2009 the poverty threshold for an adult living alone was $10,956; for a household consisting of two adults and two children, it was $21,756.

Trends in Poverty

Contrary to popular misconceptions, although the official poverty threshold is adjusted each year to reflect changes in the cost of living, it has *not* been adjusted upward over time to reflect the long-term rise in the standard of living of the average American family. As a result, as the economy grows and becomes more prosperous, and average incomes rise, you might expect the percentage of the population living below the poverty threshold to steadily decline.

Somewhat surprisingly, however, this hasn't happened. Figure 42.1 on the next page shows the U.S. **poverty rate**—the percentage of the population living below the poverty

The **poverty threshold** is the annual income below which a family is officially considered poor.

The **poverty rate** is the percentage of the population with incomes below the poverty threshold.

figure 42.1

Trends in the U.S Poverty Rate, 1959–2009

The poverty rate fell sharply from the 1960s to the early 1970s but has not shown a clear trend since then.

Source: U.S. Census Bureau

U.S. poverty rate

25%

20

15

10

1959 1970 1980 1990 2000 2009

Year

threshold—from 1959 to 2009. As you can see, the poverty rate fell steeply during the 1960s and early 1970s. Since then, however, it has fluctuated up and down, with no clear trend. In fact, in 2009 the poverty rate was higher than it had been in 1973.

Who Are the Poor?

Many Americans probably hold a stereotyped image of poverty: an African-American or Hispanic family with no husband present and the female head of the household unemployed at least part of the time. This picture isn't completely off-base: poverty is disproportionately high among African-Americans and Hispanics as well as among female-headed households. But a majority of the poor don't fit the stereotype.

In 2009, about 43.5 million Americans were in poverty—14.3% of the population, or about one in seven persons. About one-quarter of the poor were African-American and a roughly equal number, Hispanic. Within these two groups, poverty rates were well above the national average: 25.9% of African-Americans and 25.3% of Hispanics. But there was also widespread poverty among non-Hispanic whites, who had a poverty rate of 9.4%.

There is also a correlation between family makeup and poverty. Female-headed families with no husband present had a very high poverty rate: 32.5%. Married couples were much less likely to be poor, with a poverty rate of only 5.8%; still, about 39% of poor families were married couples.

iStockphoto

What really stands out from the data, however, is the association between poverty and lack of adequate employment. Adults who work full time are very unlikely to be poor: only 3.6% of full-time workers were poor in 2008. Adults who worked part time or not at all during the year made up 87.3% of the poor in 2008. Many industries, particularly in the retail and service sectors, now rely primarily on part-time workers. Part-time work typically lacks benefits such as health plans, paid vacation days, and retirement benefits, and it also usually pays a lower hourly wage than comparable full-time work. As a result, many of the poor are members of what analysts call the *working poor:* workers whose income falls at or below the poverty threshold.

What Causes Poverty?

Poverty is often blamed on lack of education, and educational attainment clearly has a strong positive effect on income level—those with more education earn, on average, higher incomes than those with less education. For example, in 1979 the average hourly wage of men with a college degree was 36% higher than that of men with only a high school diploma; by 2009 the "college premium" had increased to 81%. Lack of proficiency in English is also a barrier to higher income. For example, Mexican-born male workers in the United States—two-thirds of whom have not graduated from high school and many of whom have poor English skills—earn less than half of what native-born men earn. And it's important not to overlook the role of racial and gender discrimination; although less pervasive today than 50 years ago, discrimination still erects formidable barriers to advancement for many Americans. Non-whites earn less and are less likely to be employed than whites with comparable levels of education. Studies find that African-American males suffer persistent discrimination by employers in favor of whites, African-American women, and Hispanic immigrants. Women earn lower incomes than men with similar qualifications.

In addition, one important source of poverty that should not be overlooked is bad luck. Many families find themselves impoverished when a wage-earner loses a job or a family member falls seriously ill.

Consequences of Poverty

The consequences of poverty are often severe, particularly for children. Currently, more than 17.4% of children in the United States live in poverty. Poverty is often associated with a lack of access to health care, which can lead to further health problems that erode the ability to attend school and work later in life. Affordable housing is also frequently a problem, leading poor families to move often and disrupting school and work schedules. Recent medical studies have shown that children raised in severe poverty tend to suffer from lifelong learning disabilities. As a result, American children growing up in or near poverty don't have an equal chance at the starting line: they tend to be at a disadvantage throughout their lives. For example, even talented children who come from poor families are unlikely to finish college.

Table 42.1 shows the results of a long-term survey conducted by the U.S. Department of Education, which tracked a group of students who were in eighth grade in 1988. That year, the students took a mathematics test that the study used as an indicator of their innate ability; the study also scored students by the socioeconomic status of their families, a measure that took into account their parents' income and employment. As you can see, the results were disturbing: only 29% of students who were in the highest-scoring 25% on the test but whose parents were of low status finished college. By contrast, the equally talented children of high-status parents had a 74% chance of finishing college—and children of high-status parents had a 30% chance of finishing college even if they had low test scores. What this tells us is that

table 42.1

Percent of Eighth-Graders Finishing College, 1988

	Mathematics test score in bottom quartile	Mathematics test score in top quartile
Parents in bottom quartile	3%	29%
Parents in top quartile	30	74

Source: National Center for Education Statistics, *The Condition of Education 2003*, p. 47.

The Impeccable Economic Logic of Early Childhood Intervention Programs

One of the most vexing problems facing any society is how to break what researchers call the "cycle of poverty": children who grow up with disadvantaged socioeconomic backgrounds are far more likely to remain trapped in poverty as adults, even after we account for differences in ability. They are more likely to be unemployed or underemployed, to engage in crime, and to suffer chronic health problems.

Early childhood intervention has offered some hope of breaking the cycle. A 2006 study by the RAND Corporation found that high-quality early-childhood programs that focus on education and health care lead to significant social, intellectual, and financial advantages for kids who would otherwise be at risk of dropping out of high school and of engaging in criminal behavior. Children in programs like Head Start were less likely to engage in such destructive behaviors and more likely to end up with a job and to earn a high salary later in life. Another study by researchers at the University of Pittsburgh in 2003 looked at early-childhood intervention programs from a dollars-and-cents perspective, finding from $4 to $7 in benefits for every $1 spent on early-childhood intervention programs. The study also pointed to one program whose participants, by age 20, were 26% more likely to have finished high school, 35% less likely to have been charged in juvenile court, and 40% less likely to have repeated a grade compared to individuals of similar socioeconomic background who did not attend preschool. The observed external benefits to society of these programs are so large that the Brookings Institution predicts that providing high-quality preschool education to every American child would result in an increase in GDP, the total value of a country's domestic output, by almost 2%, representing over 3 million more jobs.

poverty is, to an important degree, self-perpetuating: the children of the poor start at such a disadvantage relative to other Americans that it's very hard for them to achieve a better life.

Economic Inequality

The United States is a rich country. In 2008, the average U.S. household had an income of more than $68,000, far exceeding the poverty threshold. How is it possible, then, that so many Americans still live in poverty? The answer is that income is unequally distributed, with many households earning much less than the average and others earning much more.

Table 42.2 shows the distribution of pre-tax income among U.S. families in 2008—income before federal income taxes are paid—as estimated by the Census Bureau. Households are grouped into *quintiles*, each containing 20% or one-fifth of the popula-

table **42.2**

U.S. Income Distribution in 2008

Income group	Income range	Average income	Percent of total income
Bottom quintile	Less than $20,712	$11,656	3.4%
Second quintile	$20,712 to $39,000	29,517	8.6
Third quintile	$39,000 to $62,725	50,132	14.7
Fourth quintile	$62,725 to $100,240	79,760	23.3
Top quintile	More than $100,240	171,057	50.0
Top 5%	More than $180,000	294,709	21.5
Mean Income = $68,424		**Median Income = $50,303**	

Source: U.S. Census Bureau.

tion. The first, or bottom, quintile contains households whose income put them below the 20th percentile in income, the second quintile contains households whose income put them between the 20th and 40th percentiles, and so on. The Census Bureau also provides data on the 5% of families with the highest incomes.

For each group, Table 42.2 shows three numbers. The second column shows the range of incomes that define the group. For example, in 2008, the bottom quintile consisted of households with annual incomes of less than $20,712; the next quintile of households with incomes between $20,712 and $39,000; and so on. The third column shows the average income in each group, ranging from $11,656 for the bottom fifth to $294,709 for the top 5 percent. The fourth column shows the percentage of total U.S. income received by each group.

At the bottom of Table 42.2 are two useful numbers for thinking about the incomes of American households. **Mean household income,** also called average household income, is the total income of all U.S. households divided by the number of households. **Median household income** is the income of a household in the exact middle of the income distribution—the level of income at which half of all households have lower income and half have higher income. It's very important to realize that these two numbers do not measure the same thing. Economists often illustrate the difference by asking people first to imagine a room containing several dozen more or less ordinary wage-earners and then to think about what happens to the mean and median incomes of the people in the room if a billionaire Wall Street tycoon walks in. The mean income soars, because the tycoon's income pulls up the average, but median income hardly rises at all. This example helps explain why economists generally regard median income as a better guide to the economic status of typical American families than mean income: mean income is strongly affected by the incomes of a relatively small number of very-high-income Americans, who are not representative of the population as a whole; median income is not.

What we learn from Table 42.2 is that income in the United States is quite unequally distributed. The average income of the poorest fifth of families is less than a quarter of the average income of families in the middle, and the richest fifth have an average income more than three times that of families in the middle. The incomes of the richest fifth of the population are, on average, about 15 times as high as those of the poorest fifth. In fact, the distribution of income in America has become more unequal since 1980, rising to a level that has made it a significant political issue. The IRL on the next page discusses long-term trends in U.S. income inequality, which declined in the 1930s and 1940s, was stable for more than 30 years after World War II, but began rising again in the late 1970s.

It's often convenient to have a single number that summarizes a country's level of income inequality. The **Gini coefficient,** the most widely used measure of inequality, is based on how disparately income is distributed across the quintiles. A country with a perfectly equal distribution of income—that is, one in which the bottom 20% of the population received 20% of the income, the bottom 40% of the population received 40% of the income, and so on—would have a Gini coefficient of 0. At the other extreme, the highest possible value for the Gini coefficient is 1—the level it would attain if all of a country's income went to just one person.

One way to get a sense of what Gini coefficients mean in practice is to look at international comparisons. Upcoming Figure 42.2 shows the most recent estimates of the Gini coefficient for many of the world's countries. Aside from a few countries in Africa, the highest levels of income inequality are found in Latin America; countries with a high degree of inequality, such as Brazil, have Gini coefficients close to 0.6. The most equal distributions of income are in Europe, especially in Scandinavia; countries with very equal income distributions, such as Sweden, have Gini coefficients around 0.25. Compared to other wealthy countries, the United States, with a Gini coefficient of 0.468 in 2009, has unusually high inequality, though it isn't as unequal as in Latin America.

How serious an issue is income inequality? In a direct sense, high income inequality means that some people don't share in a nation's overall prosperity. As we've seen, rising inequality explains how it's possible that the U.S. poverty rate has failed to fall for the

Mean household income is the average income across all households.

Median household income is the income of the household lying in the middle of the income distribution.

The **Gini coefficient** is a number that summarizes a country's level of income inequality based on how unequally income is distributed across the quintiles.

Long-Term Trends in Income Inequality in the United States

Does inequality tend to rise, fall, or stay the same over time? The answer is yes—all three. Over the course of the past century, the United States has gone through periods characterized by all three trends: an era of falling inequality during the 1930s and 1940s, an era of stable inequality for about 35 years after World War II, and an era of rising inequality over the past generation.

Detailed U.S. data on income by quintiles, as shown in Table 42.2, are only available starting in 1947. Panel (a) of the figure below shows the annual rate of growth of income, adjusted for inflation, for each quintile over two periods: from 1947 to 1980, and from 1980 to 2008. In the first period, income within each group grew at about the same rate—that is, there wasn't much change in the inequality of income, just growing incomes across the board. After 1980, however, incomes grew much more quickly at the top than in the middle, and more quickly in the middle than at the bottom. So inequality has increased substantially since 1980. Overall, inflation-adjusted income for the top quintile rose 48% between 1980 and 2008, but it rose only 8.7% for the bottom quintile.

Although detailed data on income distribution aren't available before 1947, economists have instead used other information including income tax data to estimate the share of income going to

the top 10% of the population all the way back to 1917. Panel (b) of the figure shows this measure from 1917 to 2008. These data, like the more detailed data available since 1947, show that American inequality was more or less stable between 1947 and the late 1970s but has risen substantially since. The longer-term data also show, however, that the relatively equal distribution of 1947 was something new. In the late nineteenth century, often referred to as the Gilded Age, American income was very unequally distributed; this high level of inequality persisted into the 1930s. But inequality declined sharply between the late 1930s and the end of World War II. In a famous paper, Claudia Goldin and Robert Margo, two economic historians, dubbed this narrowing of income inequality "the Great Compression."

The Great Compression roughly coincided with World War II, a period during which the U.S. government imposed special controls on wages and prices. Evidence indicates that these controls were applied in ways that reduced inequality—for example, it was much easier for employers to get approval to increase the wages of their lowest-paid employees than to increase executive salaries. What remains puzzling is that the equality imposed by wartime controls lasted for decades after those controls were lifted in 1946.

Since the 1970s, as we've already seen, inequality has increased substantially. In fact, pretax income appears to be as unequally distributed

in America today as it was in the 1920s, prompting many commentators to describe the current state of the nation as a new Gilded Age—albeit one in which the effects of inequality are moderated by taxes and the existence of the welfare state. There is intense debate among economists about the causes of this widening inequality. The most popular explanation is rapid technological change, which has increased the demand for highly skilled or talented workers more rapidly than the demand for other workers, leading to a rise in the wage gap between the highly skilled and other workers. Growing international trade may also have contributed by allowing the United States to import labor-intensive products from low-wage countries rather than making them domestically, reducing the demand for less skilled American workers and depressing their wages. Rising immigration may be yet another source. On average, immigrants have lower education levels than native-born workers and increase the supply of low-skilled labor while depressing low-skilled wages.

All of these explanations, however, fail to account for one key feature: much of the rise in inequality doesn't reflect a rising gap between highly educated workers and those with less education, but rather growing differences among highly educated workers themselves. For example, schoolteachers and top business executives have similarly high levels

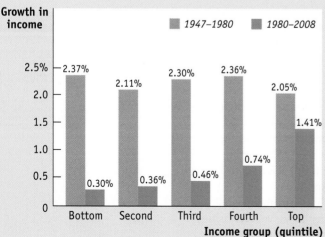

(a) Rates of Income Growth Since 1947

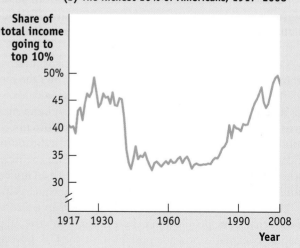

(b) The Richest 10% of Americans, 1917–2008

of education, but executive paychecks have risen dramatically and teachers' salaries have not. For some reason, the economy now pays a few "superstars"—a group that includes literal superstars in the entertainment world but also such groups as Wall Street traders and top corporate executives—much higher incomes than it did a generation ago. It's still not entirely clear what caused the change.

past 35 years even though the country as a whole has become considerably richer. Also, extreme inequality, as found in Latin America, is often associated with political instability, because of tension between a wealthy minority and the rest of the population.

It's important to realize, however, that the data shown in Table 42.2 overstate the true degree of inequality in America, for several reasons. One is that the data represent a snapshot for a single year, whereas the incomes of many individual families fluctuate over time. That is, many of those near the bottom in any given year are having an unusually bad year and many of those at the top are having an unusually good one. Over time, their incomes will revert to a more normal level. So a table showing average incomes within quintiles over a longer period, such as a decade, would not show as much inequality. Furthermore, a family's income tends to vary over its life cycle: most people earn considerably less in their early working years than they will later in life, and then experience a considerable drop in income when they retire. Consequently, the numbers in Table 42.2, which combine young workers, mature workers, and retirees, show more inequality than would a table that compares families of similar ages.

Despite these qualifications, there is a considerable amount of genuine inequality in the United States. Moreover, the fact that families' incomes fluctuate from year to year

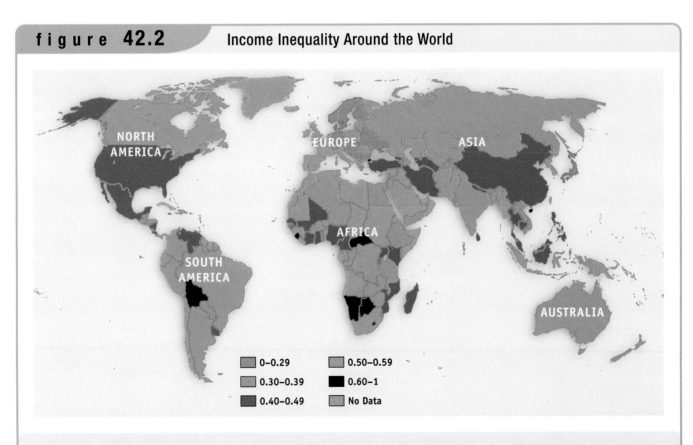

figure 42.2   Income Inequality Around the World

Legend:
- 0–0.29
- 0.30–0.39
- 0.40–0.49
- 0.50–0.59
- 0.60–1
- No Data

The highest levels of income inequality are found in Africa and Latin America. The most equal distributions of income are in Europe, especially in Scandinavia. Compared to other wealthy countries, the United States, with a Gini coefficient of 0.468 in 2009, has unusually high inequality.

Source: World Bank, *Human Development Report 2007–2008*

isn't entirely good news. Measures of inequality in a given year *do* overstate true inequality. But those year-to-year fluctuations are part of a problem that worries even affluent families—economic insecurity.

Economic Insecurity

The rationale for the welfare state rests in part on the benefits of reducing economic insecurity, which afflicts even relatively well-off families. One source of economic insecurity is the risk of a sudden loss of income, as occurs when a family member loses a job and either spends an extended period without work or is forced to take a new job that pays considerably less. In a given year, according to recent estimates, about one in six American families will see their income cut in half. Related estimates show that the percentage of people who find themselves below the poverty threshold for at least one year over the course of a decade is several times higher than the percentage of people below the poverty threshold in any given year.

Even if a family doesn't face a loss in income, it can face a surge in expenses. The most common reason for such surges is a medical problem that requires expensive treatment, such as heart disease or cancer. Many Americans have health insurance that covers a large share of their expenses in such cases, but a substantial number either do not have health insurance or rely on insurance provided by the government.

U.S. Antipoverty Programs

U.S. antipoverty programs include three huge programs—Social Security, Medicare, and Medicaid—several other fairly big programs, including Temporary Assistance for Needy Families, food stamps, the Earned Income Tax Credit, and a number of smaller programs. Table 42.3 shows one useful way to categorize these programs, along with the amount spent on each listed program in 2009.

First, the table distinguishes between programs that are **means-tested** and those that are not. In means-tested programs, benefits are available only to families or individuals whose income and/or wealth falls below some minimum. Basically, means-tested programs are poverty programs designed to help only those with low incomes. By contrast, non-means-tested programs provide their benefits to everyone, although, as we'll see, they tend in practice to reduce income inequality by increasing the incomes of the poor by a larger proportion than the incomes of the rich.

Second, the table distinguishes between programs that provide monetary transfers that beneficiaries can spend as they choose and those that provide **in-kind benefits,** which are given in the form of goods or services rather than money. As the numbers suggest, in-kind benefits are dominated by Medicare and Medicaid, which pay for health care.

table 42.3

Major U.S. Welfare State Programs, 2009

	Monetary transfers	In-kind
Means-tested	Temporary Assistance for Needy Families: $20.1 billion	Food stamps: $54.6 billion
	Supplemental Security Income: $42.4 billion	Medicaid: $369.3 billion
	Earned Income Tax Credit: $66.6 billion	
Not means-tested	Social Security: $664 billion	Medicare: $500.3 billion
	Unemployment insurance: $129.4 billion	

A **means-tested** program is available only to individuals or families whose incomes fall below a certain level.

An **in-kind benefit** is a benefit given in the form of goods or services.

Means-Tested Programs

When people use the term *welfare,* they're often referring to monetary aid to poor families. The main source of such monetary aid in the United States is Temporary Assistance for Needy Families, or TANF. This program does not aid everyone who is poor; it is available only to poor families with children and only for a limited period of time.

TANF was introduced in the 1990s to replace a highly controversial program known as Aid to Families with Dependent Children, or AFDC. The older program was widely accused of creating perverse incentives for the poor, including encouraging family breakup. Partly as a result of the change in programs, the benefits of modern "welfare" are considerably less generous than those available a generation ago, once the data are adjusted for inflation. Also, TANF contains time limits, so welfare recipients—even single parents—must eventually seek work. As you can see from Table 42.3, TANF is a relatively small part of the modern U.S. welfare state.

Other means-tested programs, though more expensive, are less controversial. The Supplemental Security Income program aids disabled Americans who are unable to work and have no other source of income. The Supplemental Nutrition Assistance Program (formerly known as the Food Stamp Program) helps low-income families and individuals to buy food staples.

Finally, economists use the term **negative income tax** for a program that supplements the earnings of low-income workers. For example, in the United States, the Earned Income Tax Credit (EITC) provides additional income to millions of workers. It has become more generous as traditional welfare has become less generous. As an incentive to work, only workers who earn income are eligible for the EITC. And as an incentive to work more, over a certain range of incomes, the more a worker earns, the higher the amount of EITC received. That is, the EITC acts as a negative income tax for low-wage workers. In 2009, married couples with two children earning less than $12,570 per year received EITC payments equal to 40% of their earnings. Payments were slightly lower for single-parent families or workers without children. At higher incomes, the EITC is phased out, disappearing at an income of $40,295 in 2009.

Social Security and Unemployment Insurance

Social Security, the largest program in the U.S. welfare state, is a non-means-tested program that guarantees retirement income to qualifying older Americans. It also provides benefits to workers who become disabled and "survivor benefits" to family members of workers who die. Social Security is supported by a dedicated tax on wages: the Social Security portion of the payroll tax pays for Social Security benefits. The benefits workers receive on retirement depend on their taxable earnings during their working years: the more you earn up to the maximum amount subject to Social Security taxes ($106,800 in 2010), the more you receive in retirement. Benefits are not, however, strictly proportional to earnings. Instead, they're determined by a formula that gives high earners more than low earners, but with a sliding scale that makes the program relatively more generous for low earners.

Because most senior citizens don't receive pensions from their former employers, and most don't own enough assets to live off the income from their assets, Social Security benefits are an enormously important source of income for them. Fully 60% of Americans 65 and older rely on Social Security for more than half their income, and 20% have no income at all except for Social Security.

Unemployment insurance, although a much smaller amount of government transfers than Social Security, is another key social insurance program. It provides workers who lose their jobs with about 35% of their previous salary until they find a new job or until 26 weeks have passed. (This period is sometimes extended when the economy is in a slump.) Unemployment insurance is financed by a tax on employers.

A **negative income tax** is a program that supplements the income of low-income workers.

AP Photo/Rich Pedroncelli

The Supplemental Nutrition Assistance Program helps those with low-incomes put food on the table. Purchases are made using an electronic benefits transfer card that works like a debit card but can be used only to purchase food.

The Effects of Programs on Poverty and Inequality

Because the people who receive government transfers tend to be different from those who are taxed to pay for those transfers, the U.S. welfare state has the effect of redistributing income from some people to others. Each year the Census Bureau estimates the effect of this redistribution in a report titled "The Effects of Government Taxes and Transfers on Income and Poverty." The report calculates only the *direct* effects of taxes and transfers, without taking into account changes in behavior that the taxes and transfers might cause. For example, the report doesn't try to estimate how many older Americans who are now retired would still be working if they weren't receiving Social Security checks. As a result, the estimates are only a partial indicator of the true effects of the welfare state. Nonetheless, the results are striking.

Table 42.4 shows how taxes and government transfers affected the poverty threshold for the population as a whole and for different age groups in 2008. It shows two numbers for each group: the percentage of the group that *would have had* incomes below the poverty threshold if the government neither collected taxes nor made transfers, and the percentage that actually fell below the poverty threshold once taxes and transfers were taken into account. (For technical reasons, the second number is somewhat lower than the standard measure of the poverty rate.) Overall, the combined effect of taxes and transfers is to cut the U.S. poverty rate nearly in half. The elderly derived the greatest benefits from redistribution, which reduced their potential poverty rate of 47.4% to an actual poverty rate of 9.7%.

table **42.4**

Effects of Taxes and Transfers on the Poverty Rate, 2008

Group (by age)	Poverty rate without taxes and transfers	Poverty rate with taxes and transfers
All	21.4%	12.1%
Under 18	22.0	15.9
18 to 64	15.9	11.1
65 and over	47.4	9.7

Source: Census.gov, ASEC: Table 2. Percent of Persons in Poverty, by Definition of Income and Selected Characteristics: 2008

Table 42.5 shows the effects of taxes and transfers on the share of aggregate income going to each quintile of the income distribution in 2005. Like Table 42.4, it shows both what the distribution of income *would have been* if there were no taxes or government transfers and the actual distribution of income taking into account both

table **42.5**

Effects of Taxes and Transfers on the Income Distribution, 2005

Quintiles	Share of aggregate income without taxes and transfers	Share of aggregate income with taxes and transfers
Bottom quintile	1.5%	4.4%
Second quintile	7.3	9.9
Third quintile	14.0	15.3
Fourth quintile	23.4	23.1
Top quintile	53.8	47.3

Source: U.S. Census Bureau.

taxes and transfers. The effect of government programs was to increase the share of income going to the poorest 60% of the population, especially the share going to the poorest 20%, while reducing the share of income going to the richest 20%.

The Debate Over Income Redistribution

The goals of income redistribution seem laudable: to help the poor, protect everyone from financial risk, and ensure that people can afford essential health care. But good intentions don't always make for good policy. There is an intense debate about how large the antipoverty programs should be, a debate that partly reflects differences in philosophy but also reflects concern about the possibly counterproductive effects of antipoverty programs. Disputes about the role of government in income redistribution are also one of the defining issues of modern politics.

Problems with Income Redistribution

There are two different lines of argument against antipoverty programs. One is based on philosophical concerns about the proper role of government. Some political theorists believe that redistributing income is not a legitimate role of government—that government's role should be limited to maintaining the rule of law, providing public goods, and managing externalities.

The more conventional argument against income redistribution involves the trade-off between efficiency and equity. A government with extensive antipoverty programs requires more revenue, and thus higher marginal tax rates, than one that limits itself mainly to the provision of public goods such as national defense. Table 42.6 shows "social expenditure," a measure that roughly corresponds to welfare state spending, as a percentage of GDP in the United States, Britain, and France; it also compares this with an estimate of the marginal tax rate faced by an average wage-earner, including payroll taxes paid by employers and state and local taxes. As you can see, France's large welfare state goes along with a high marginal rate of taxation. Some, but not all, economists believe that this high rate of taxation is a major reason the French work substantially fewer hours per year than Americans.

table 42.6

Social Expenditure and Marginal Tax Rates

	Social expenditure in 2005 (% of GDP)	Marginal tax rate in 2008
US	16.3%	34.4%
UK	22.1	38.8
France	29.5	52.0

Sources: OECD Social Expenditure Database; OECD Taxing Wages Database.

The trade-off between antipoverty programs and high marginal tax rates seems to suggest that we should try to hold down the cost of these programs. One way to do this is to means-test benefits: make them available only to those who need them. But means-testing, it turns out, creates a different kind of trade-off between equity and efficiency. Consider the following example: Suppose there is some means-tested benefit, worth $2,000 per year that is available only to families with incomes of less than $20,000 per year. Now suppose that a family currently has an income of $19,500 but that one family member is deciding whether to take a new job that will raise the family's income to $20,500. Well, taking that job will actually make the family worse off because it will gain $1,000 in earnings but lose the $2,000 government benefit.

This situation, in which earning more actually leaves a family worse off through lost benefits, is known as a *notch*. It is a well-known problem with programs that aid the poor and behaves much like a high marginal tax rate on income. Most welfare state programs are designed to avoid creating a notch. This is typically done by setting a sliding scale for benefits such that they fall off gradually as the recipient's income rises. As long as benefits are reduced by less than a dollar for every additional dollar earned, there is an incentive to work more if possible. Current programs are not always successful in providing incentives for work. The combined effects of the major means-tested programs shown in Table 42.3, plus additional means-tested programs such as housing aid that are offered by some state and local governments, can be to create very high effective marginal tax rates. For example, one 2005 study found that a family consisting of two adults and two children that raised its annual income from $20,000—just above the poverty threshold in 2005—to $35,000 would find almost all of its increase in after-tax income offset by the loss of benefits such as food stamps, the Earned Income Tax Credit, and Medicaid.

The Politics of Income Redistribution

In 1791, in the early phase of the French Revolution, France had a sort of congress, the National Assembly, in which representatives were seated according to social class: nobles, who pretty much liked the way things were, sat on the right; commoners, who wanted big changes, sat on the left. Ever since, it has been common in political discourse to talk about politicians as being on the "right" (more conservative) or on the "left" (more liberal).

But what do modern politicians on the left and right disagree about? In the modern United States, they mainly disagree about the appropriate size of antipoverty programs.

You might think that saying that political debate is really about just one thing—how big should government's involvement in income redistribution be—is a huge oversimplification. But political scientists have found that once you carefully rank members of Congress from right to left, a congressperson's position in that ranking does a very good job of predicting his or her votes on proposed legislation. Modern politics isn't completely one-dimensional—but it comes pretty close.

The same studies that show a strong left–right spectrum in U.S. politics also show strong polarization between the major parties on this spectrum. Thirty years ago there was a substantial overlap between the parties: some Democrats were to the right of some Republicans, or, if you prefer, some Republicans were to the left of some Democrats. Today, however, the rightmost Democrats appear to be to the left of the leftmost Republicans. There's nothing necessarily wrong with this. Although it's common to decry "partisanship," it's hard to see why members of different political parties shouldn't have different views about policy.

Can economic analysis help resolve this political conflict? Only up to a point.

Some of the political controversy over the welfare state involves differences in opinion about the trade-offs we have just discussed: if you believe that the disincentive effects of generous benefits and high taxes are very large, you're likely to look less favorably on welfare state programs than if you believe they're fairly small. Economic analysis, by improving our knowledge of the facts, can help resolve some of these differences.

To an important extent, however, differences of opinion on income redistribution reflect differences in values and philosophy. And those are differences economics can't resolve.

Module 42 Review

Solutions appear at the back of the book.

Check Your Understanding

1. Recall that the poverty threshold is not adjusted to reflect changes in the standard of living. As a result, is the poverty threshold a relative or an absolute measure of poverty? That is, does it define poverty according to how poor someone is relative to others or according to some fixed measure that doesn't change over time? Explain.

Multiple-Choice Questions

1. Which of the following is true of the U.S. poverty rate?
   a. It fell in the 1960s.
   b. There has been a clear upward trend since 1973.
   c. It was lower in 2009 than in 1973.
   d. It has remained unchanged since the mid 1970s.
   e. It has been steadily decreasing since 1959.

2. In 2009, approximately what percentage of the U.S. population lived in poverty?
   a. 2%
   b. 12%
   c. 20%
   d. 26%
   e. 32%

3. Average household income in the United States in 2008 was approximately
   a. $12,000.
   b. $22,000.
   c. $33,000.
   d. $48,201.
   e. $68,000.

4. Programs designed to help only those with low incomes are called
   a. welfare programs.
   b. in-kind programs.
   c. means-tested programs.
   d. income maintenance programs.
   e. social programs.

5. If a country has a perfectly equal distribution of income, its Gini coefficient equals
   a. 0.
   b. 1.
   c. 10.
   d. 50.
   e. 100.

Critical-Thinking Question

In your opinion, what is the strongest argument for and against government programs to redistribute income? To what extent can economics be used to resolve the debate?

Section 8 Review

Summary

Introduction to Externalities

1. When pollution can be directly observed and controlled, government policies should be geared directly to producing the **socially optimal quantity of pollution,** the quantity at which the **marginal social cost of pollution** is equal to the **marginal social benefit of pollution.** In the absence of government intervention, a market produces too much pollution because polluters take only their benefit from polluting into account, not the costs imposed on others.

2. The cost to society of pollution from a power plant is an example of an **external cost;** the benefit to neighbors of beautiful flowers planted in your yard is an example of an **external benefit.** External costs and benefits are jointly known as **externalities,** with external costs called **negative externalities** and external benefits called **positive externalities.**

3. According to the **Coase theorem,** when externalities exist, bargaining will cause individuals to **internalize the externalities,** making government intervention unnecessary, as long as property rights are clearly defined and **transaction costs**—the costs of making a deal—are sufficiently low. However, in many cases transaction costs are too high to permit such deals.

Externalities and Public Policy

4. Governments often deal with pollution by imposing **environmental standards,** an approach, economists argue, that is usually inefficient. Two efficient (cost-minimizing) methods for reducing pollution are **emissions taxes,** a form of **Pigouvian tax,** and **tradable emissions permits.** The optimal Pigouvian tax on pollution is equal to its marginal social cost at the socially optimal quantity of pollution. These methods also provide incentives for the creation and adoption of production technologies that cause less pollution.

5. When a good yields external benefits, such as **technology spillovers,** the **marginal social benefit of the good** is equal to the **marginal private benefit** accruing to consumers plus its **marginal external benefit.** Without government intervention, the market produces too little of the good. An optimal **Pigouvian subsidy** to producers, equal to the marginal external benefit, moves the market to the socially optimal quantity of production. This yields higher output and a higher price to producers.

6. When there are external costs from production, the **marginal social cost of a good** exceeds its **marginal private cost** to producers, the difference being the **marginal external cost.** Without government action, the market produces too much of the good. The optimal Pigouvian tax on production of the good is equal to its marginal external cost, yielding lower output and a higher price to consumers. A system of tradable production permits for the right to produce the good can also achieve efficiency at minimum cost.

7. Communications, transportation, and high-technology goods are frequently subject to **network externalities,** which arise when the value of the good to an individual is greater when more people use the good.

Public Goods

8. Goods may be classified according to whether or not they are **excludable,** meaning that people can be prevented from consuming them, and whether or not they are **rival in consumption,** meaning that one person's consumption of them affects another person's consumption of them.

9. Free markets can deliver efficient levels of production and consumption for **private goods,** which are both excludable and rival in consumption. When goods are nonexcludable, nonrival in consumption, or both, free markets cannot achieve efficient outcomes.

10. When goods are **nonexcludable,** there is a **free-rider problem:** consumers will not pay for the good, leading to inefficiently low production. When goods are **nonrival in consumption,** any positive price leads to inefficiently low consumption.

11. A **public good** is nonexcludable and nonrival in consumption. In most cases a public good must be supplied by the government. The marginal social benefit of a public good is equal to the sum of the marginal private benefits to each consumer. The efficient quantity of a public good is the quantity at which marginal social benefit equals the marginal social cost of providing the good. As with a positive externality, the marginal social benefit is greater than any one individual's marginal private benefit, so no individual is willing to provide the efficient quantity.

12. One rationale for the presence of government is that it allows citizens to tax themselves in order to provide public goods. Governments use cost-benefit analysis to determine the efficient provision of a public good. Such analysis is difficult, however, because individuals have an incentive to overstate the good's value to them.

13. A **common resource** is rival in consumption but nonexcludable. It is subject to **overuse,** because an individual does not take into account the fact that his or her use depletes the amount available for others. This is similar to the problem with a negative externality: the marginal social cost of an individual's use of a common resource is always higher than his or her marginal private cost. Pigouvian taxes, the creation of a system of tradable licenses, and the assignment of property rights are possible solutions.

14. **Artificially scarce goods** are excludable but nonrival in consumption. Because no marginal cost arises from allowing another individual to consume the good, the efficient price is zero. A positive price compensates the producer for the cost of production but leads to inefficiently low consumption.

Public Policy to Promote Competition

15. Antitrust laws and regulation are used to promote competition. When the industry in question is a natural monopoly, price regulation is used.

16. The Sherman Act, the Clayton Act, and the Federal Trade Commission Act were the first major antitrust laws.

17. **Marginal cost pricing** and **average cost pricing** are examples of price regulation used in the case of natural monopoly to allow efficiencies from large scale production without allowing the deadweight loss that results from unregulated monopoly.

Income Inequality and Income Distribution

18. Despite the fact that the **poverty threshold** is adjusted according to the cost of living but not according to the standard of living, and that the average income in the United States has risen substantially over the last 30 years, the **poverty rate,** the percentage of the population with an income below the poverty threshold, is no lower than it was 30 years ago. There are various causes

of poverty: lack of education, the legacy of discrimination, and bad luck. The consequences of poverty are particularly harmful for children.

19. **Median household income,** the income of a family at the center of the income distribution, is a better indicator of the income of the typical household than **mean household income** because it is not distorted by the inclusion of a small number of very wealthy households. The **Gini coefficient,** a number that summarizes a country's level of income inequality based on how unequally income is distributed across quintiles, is used to compare income inequality across countries.

20. **Means-tested** programs target aid to people whose income falls below a certain level. The major **in-kind benefits** programs are Medicare and Medicaid, which pay for medical care. Due to concerns about the effects on incentives to work and on family cohesion, aid to poor families has become significantly less generous even as the **negative income tax** has become more generous. Social Security, the largest U.S. welfare program, has significantly reduced poverty among the elderly. Unemployment insurance is another key social insurance program.

Key Terms

Marginal social cost of pollution, p. 368
Marginal social benefit of pollution, p. 368
Socially optimal quantity of pollution, p. 369
External cost, p. 370
External benefit, p. 371
Externalities, p. 371
Negative externalities, p. 371
Positive externalities, p. 371
Coase theorem, p. 372
Transaction costs, p. 372
Internalize the externalities, p. 372
Environmental standards, p. 375
Emissions taxes, p. 376
Pigouvian taxes, p. 378
Tradable emissions permits, p. 378

Marginal private benefit, p. 382
Marginal social benefit of a good, p. 382
Marginal external benefit, p. 382
Pigouvian subsidy, p. 382
Technology spillover, p. 382
Marginal private cost, p. 383
Marginal social cost of a good, p. 383
Marginal external cost, p. 383
Network externality, p. 384
Excludable, p. 387
Rival in consumption, p. 387
Private good, p. 387
Nonexcludable, p. 387
Nonrival in consumption, p. 388
Free-rider problem, p. 389

Public good, p. 389
Common resource, p. 393
Overuse, p. 393
Artificially scarce good, p. 395
Marginal cost pricing, p. 401
Average cost pricing, p. 401
Poverty threshold, p. 405
Poverty rate, p. 405
Mean household income, p. 409
Median household income, p. 409
Gini coefficient, p. 409
Means-tested, p. 412
In-kind benefits, p. 412
Negative income tax, p. 413

Problems

1. What type of externality (positive or negative) is present in each of the following examples? Is the marginal social benefit of the activity greater than or equal to the marginal benefit to the individual? Is the marginal social cost of the activity greater than or equal to the marginal cost to the individual? Without intervention, will there be too little or too much (relative to what would be socially optimal) of this activity?

   a. Mr. Chau plants lots of colorful flowers in his front yard.

   b. Your next-door neighbor likes to build bonfires in his backyard, and sparks often drift onto your house.

   c. Maija, who lives next to an apple orchard, decides to keep bees to produce honey.

   d. Justine buys a large SUV that consumes a lot of gasoline.

2. The loud music coming from the sorority next to your dorm is a negative externality that can be directly quantified. The accompanying table shows the marginal social benefit and the marginal social cost per decibel (dB, a measure of volume) of music.

Volume of music (dB)	Marginal social benefit of dB	Marginal social cost of dB
90		
	$36	$0
91		
	30	2
92		
	24	4
93		
	18	6
94		
	12	8
95		
	6	10
96		
	0	12
97		

a. Draw the marginal social benefit curve and the marginal social cost curve. Use your diagram to determine the socially optimal volume of music.

b. Only the members of the sorority benefit from the music and they bear none of the cost. Which volume of music will they choose?

c. The college imposes a Pigouvian tax of $3 per decibel of music played. From your diagram, determine the volume of music the sorority will now choose.

3. Many dairy farmers in California are adopting a new technology that allows them to produce their own electricity from methane gas captured from animal wastes. (One cow can produce up to 2 kilowatts a day.) This practice reduces the amount of methane gas released into the atmosphere. In addition to reducing their own utility bills, the farmers are allowed to sell any electricity they produce at favorable rates.

a. Explain how the ability to earn money from capturing and transforming methane gas behaves like a Pigouvian tax on methane gas pollution and can lead dairy farmers to emit the efficient amount of methane gas pollution.

b. Suppose some dairy farmers have lower costs of transforming methane into electricity than others. Explain how this system leads to an efficient allocation of emissions reduction among farmers.

4. The accompanying table shows the total revenue and the total cost that accrue to steel producers from producing steel. Producing a ton of steel imposes a marginal external cost of $60 per ton.

Quantity of steel (tons)	Total revenue	Total cost to producers
1	$115	$ 10
2	210	30
3	285	60
4	340	100
5	375	150

a. Calculate the marginal revenue per ton of steel and the marginal cost per ton of steel to steel producers. Then calculate the marginal social cost per ton of steel.

b. What is the market equilibrium quantity of steel production?

c. What is the socially optimal quantity of steel production?

d. What is the optimal Pigouvian tax to remedy the problem created by the negative externality?

5. Voluntary environmental programs were extremely popular in the United States, Europe, and Japan in the 1990s. Part of their popularity stems from the fact that these programs do not require legislative authority, which is often hard to obtain. The 33/50 program started by the Environmental Protection Agency (EPA) is an example of such a program. With this program, the EPA attempted to reduce industrial emissions of 17 toxic chemicals by providing information on relatively inexpensive methods of pollution control. Companies were asked to voluntarily commit to reducing emissions from their 1988 levels by 33% by 1992 and by 50% by 1995. The program actually met its second target by 1994.

a. As in Figure 39.2 draw marginal benefit curves for pollution generated by two plants, A and B, in 1988. Assume that without government intervention, each plant emits the same amount of pollution, but that at all levels of pollution less than this amount, plant A's marginal benefit of polluting is less than that of plant B. Label the vertical axis "Marginal benefit to individual polluter" and the horizontal axis "Quantity of pollution emissions." Mark the quantity of pollution each plant produces without government action.

b. Do you expect the total quantity of pollution before the program was put in place to have been less than or more than the optimal quantity of pollution? Why?

c. Suppose the plants whose marginal benefit curves you depicted in part a were participants in the 33/50 program. In a replica of your graph from part a, mark targeted levels of pollution in 1995 for the two plants. Compare the amounts by which the two plants reduced emissions. Was this solution necessarily efficient?

d. What kind of environmental policy does the 33/50 program most closely resemble? What is the main shortcoming of such a policy? Compare it to two other types of environmental policy discussed.

6. Smoking produces a negative externality because it imposes a health risk on others who inhale second-hand smoke. Cigarette smoking also causes productivity losses to the economy due to the shorter expected life span of a smoker. The U.S. Centers for Disease Control (CDC) has estimated the average social cost of smoking a single pack of cigarettes for different states by taking these negative externalities into account. The accompanying table provides the price of cigarettes and the estimated average social cost of smoking in five states.

State	Cigarette retail price with taxes (per pack)	CDC estimate of smoking cost in 2006 (per pack)
California	$4.40	$15.10
New York	5.82	21.91
Florida	3.80	10.14
Texas	4.76	9.94
Ohio	4.60	9.19

a. At the current level of consumption, what is the optimal retail price of a pack of cigarettes in the different states? Is the current price below or above this optimal price? Does this suggest that the current level of consumption is too high or too low? Explain your answer.

b. In order to deal with negative externalities, state governments currently impose excise taxes on cigarettes. Are current taxes set at the optimal level? Justify your answer.

c. What is the correct size of an additional Pigouvian tax on cigarette sales in the different states if the CDC's estimate for smoking cost does not change with an increase in the retail price of cigarettes?

7. Education is an example of an activity that generates a positive externality: acquiring more education benefits the individual student and having a more highly educated workforce is good for the economy as a whole. The accompanying table illustrates the marginal benefit to Sian per year of education and the marginal cost per year of education. Each year of education has a marginal external benefit to society equal to $8,000. Assume that the marginal social cost is the same as the marginal cost paid by an individual student.

Quantity of education (years)	Sian's marginal benefit per year	Sian's marginal cost per year
9		
	$20,000	$15,000
10		
	19,000	16,000
11		
	18,000	17,000
12		
	17,000	18,000
13		
	16,000	19,000
14		
	15,000	20,000
15		
	14,000	21,000
16		
	13,000	22,000
17		

a. Find Sian's market equilibrium number of years of education.

b. Calculate the marginal social benefit schedule. What is the socially optimal number of years of education?

c. You are in charge of education funding. Would you use a Pigouvian tax or a Pigouvian subsidy to induce Sian to choose the socially optimal amount of education? How high would you set this tax or subsidy per year of education?

8. Planting a tree improves the environment: trees transform greenhouse gases into oxygen, improve water retention in the soil, and improve soil quality. Assume that the value of this environmental improvement to society is $10 for the expected lifetime of the tree. The following table contains a hypothetical demand schedule for trees to be planted.

Price of tree	Quantity of trees demanded (thousands)
$30	0
25	6
20	12
15	18
10	24
5	30
0	36

a. Assume that the marginal cost of producing a tree for planting is constant at $20. Draw a diagram that shows the market equilibrium quantity and price for trees to be planted.

b. What type of externality is generated by planting a tree? Draw a diagram that shows the optimal number of trees planted. How does this differ from the market outcome?

c. On your diagram from part b, indicate the optimal Pigouvian tax/subsidy (as the case may be). Explain how this moves the market to the optimal outcome.

9. The government is involved in providing many goods and services. For each of the goods or services listed, determine whether it is rival or nonrival in consumption and whether it is excludable or nonexcludable. What type of good is it? Without government involvement, would the quantity provided be efficient, inefficiently low, or inefficiently high?

a. street signs

b. Amtrak rail service

c. regulations limiting pollution

d. an interstate highway without tolls

e. a lighthouse on the coast

10. An economist gives the following advice to a museum director: "You should introduce 'peak pricing': at times when the museum has few visitors, you should admit visitors for free. And at times when the museum has many visitors, you should charge a higher admission fee."

a. When the museum is quiet, is it rival or nonrival in consumption? Is it excludable or nonexcludable? What type of good is the museum at those times? What would be the efficient price to charge visitors during that time, and why?

b. When the museum is busy, is it rival or nonrival in consumption? Is it excludable or nonexcludable? What type of good is the museum at those times? What would be the efficient price to charge visitors during that time, and why?

11. In many planned communities, various aspects of community living are subject to regulation by a homeowners' association. These rules can regulate house architecture; require snow removal from sidewalks; exclude outdoor equipment, such as backyard swimming pools; require appropriate conduct in shared spaces such as the community clubhouse; and so on. Suppose there has been some conflict in one such community because some homeowners feel that some of the regulations mentioned above are overly intrusive. You have been called in to mediate. Using what you have learned about public goods and common resources, how would you decide what types of regulations are warranted and what types are not?

12. A residential community has 100 residents who are concerned about security. The accompanying table gives the total cost of hiring a 24-hour security service as well as each individual resident's total benefit.

Quantity of security guards	Total cost	Total individual benefit to each resident
0	$ 0	$ 0
1	150	10
2	300	16
3	450	18
4	600	19

  a. Explain why the security service is a public good for the residents of the community.

  b. Calculate the marginal cost, the individual marginal benefit for each resident, and the marginal social benefit.

  c. If an individual resident were to decide about hiring and paying for security guards on his or her own, how many guards would that resident hire?

  d. If the residents act together, how many security guards will they hire?

13. The accompanying table shows Tanisha's and Ari's individual marginal benefit of different numbers of street cleanings per month. Suppose that the marginal cost of street cleanings is constant at $9 each.

Quantity of street cleanings per month	Tanisha's individual marginal benefit	Ari's individual marginal benefit
0		
	$10	$8
1		
	6	4
2		
	2	1
3		

  a. If Tanisha had to pay for street cleaning on her own, how many street cleanings would there be?

  b. Calculate the marginal social benefit of street cleaning. What is the optimal number of street cleanings?

  c. Consider the optimal number of street cleanings. The last street cleaning of that number costs $9. Is Tanisha willing to pay for that last cleaning on her own? Is Ari willing to pay for that last cleaning on his own?

14. Anyone with a radio receiver can listen to public radio, which is funded largely by donations.

  a. Is public radio excludable or nonexcludable? Is it rival in consumption or nonrival? What type of good is it?

  b. Should the government support public radio? Explain your reasoning.

  c. In order to finance itself, public radio decides to transmit only to satellite radios, for which users have to pay a fee. What type of good is public radio then? Will the quantity of radio listening be efficient? Why or why not?

15. Your economics teacher assigns a group project for the course. Describe the free-rider problem that can lead to a suboptimal outcome for your group. To combat this problem, the instructor asks you to evaluate the contribution of your peers in a confidential report. Will this evaluation have the desired effects?

16. The accompanying table shows six consumers' willingness to pay (his or her individual marginal benefit) for one MP3 file copy of a Dr. Dre album. The marginal cost of making the file accessible to one additional consumer is constant, at zero.

Consumer	Individual marginal benefit
Adriana	$ 2
Bhagesh	15
Chizuko	1
Denzel	10
Emma	5
Frank	4

  a. What would be the efficient price to charge for a download of the file?

  b. All six consumers are able to download the file for free from a file-sharing service, Pantster. Which consumers will download the file? What will be the total consumer surplus to those consumers?

  c. Pantster is shut down for copyright law infringement. In order to download the file, consumers now have to pay $4.99 at a commercial music site. Which consumers will download the file? What will be the total consumer surplus to those consumers? How much producer surplus accrues to the commercial music site? What is the total surplus? What is the deadweight loss from the new pricing policy?

17. Software has historically been an artificially scarce good—it is nonrival because the cost of replication is negligible once the investment to write the code is made, but software companies make it excludable by charging for user licenses. Recently, however, open-source software has emerged, most of which is free to download and can be modified and maintained by anyone.

  a. Discuss the free-rider problem that might exist in the development of open-source software. What effect might this have on quality? Why does this problem not exist for proprietary software, such as the products of a company like Microsoft or Adobe?

b. Some argue that open-source software serves an unsatisfied market demand that proprietary software ignores. Draw a typical diagram that illustrates how proprietary software may be underproduced. Put the price and marginal cost of software on the vertical axis and the quantity of software on the horizontal axis. Draw a typical demand curve and a marginal cost curve (MC) that is always equal to zero. Assume that the software company charges a positive price, P, for the software. Label the equilibrium point and the efficient point.

18. In developing a vaccine for the H1N1 virus, a pharmaceutical company incurs a very high fixed cost. The marginal cost of delivering the vaccine to patients, however, is negligible (consider it to be equal to zero). The pharmaceutical company holds the exclusive patent to the vaccine. You are a regulator who must decide what price the pharmaceutical company is allowed to charge.

   a. Draw a diagram that shows the price for the vaccine that would arise if the company is unregulated, and label it P_M. What is the efficient price for the vaccine? Show the deadweight loss that arises from the price P_M.

   b. On another diagram, show the lowest price that the regulator can enforce that would still induce the pharmaceutical company to develop the vaccine. Label it P^*. Show the deadweight loss that arises from this price. How does it compare to the deadweight loss that arises from the price P_M?

   c. Suppose you have accurate information about the pharmaceutical company's fixed cost. How could you use price regulation of the pharmaceutical company, combined with a subsidy to the company, to have the efficient quantity of the vaccine provided at the lowest cost to the government?

19. According to a report from the U.S. Census Bureau, "the average [lifetime] earnings of a full-time, year-round worker with a high school education are about $1.2 million compared with $2.1 million for a college graduate." This indicates that there is a considerable benefit to a graduate from investing in his or her own education. Tuition at most state universities covers only about two-thirds to three-quarters of the cost, so the state applies a Pigouvian subsidy to college education. If a Pigouvian subsidy is appropriate, is the externality created by a college education a positive or a negative externality? What does this imply about the differences between the costs and benefits to students compared to social costs and benefits? What are some reasons for the differences?

20. Fishing for sablefish has been so intensive that sablefish were threatened with extinction. After several years of banning such fishing, the government is now proposing to introduce tradable vouchers, each of which entitles its holder to a catch of a certain size. Explain how fishing generates a negative externality and how the voucher scheme may overcome the inefficiency created by this externality.

21. The two dry-cleaning companies in Collegetown, College Cleaners and Big Green Cleaners, are a major source of air pollution. Together they currently produce 350 units of air pollution, which the town wants to reduce to 200 units. The accompanying table shows the current pollution level produced by each company and each company's marginal cost of reducing its pollution. The marginal cost is constant.

Companies	Initial pollution level (units)	Marginal cost of reducing pollution (per unit)
College Cleaners	230	$5
Big Green Cleaners	120	2

   a. Suppose that Collegetown passes an environmental standards law that limits each company to 100 units of pollution. What would be the total cost to the two companies of each reducing its pollution emissions to 100 units?

   Suppose instead that Collegetown issues 100 pollution vouchers to each company, each entitling the company to one unit of pollution, and that these vouchers can be traded.

   b. How much is each pollution voucher worth to College Cleaners? to Big Green Cleaners? (That is, how much would each company, at most, be willing to pay for one more voucher?)

   c. Who will sell vouchers and who will buy them? How many vouchers will be traded?

   d. What is the total cost to the two companies of the pollution controls under this voucher system?

22. Ronald owns a cattle farm at the source of a long river. His cattle's waste flows into the river and down many miles to where Carla lives. Carla gets her drinking water from the river. By allowing his cattle's waste to flow into the river, Ronald imposes a negative externality on Carla. In each of the two following cases, do you think that through negotiation, Ronald and Carla can find an efficient solution? What might this solution look like?

   a. There are no telephones, and for Carla to talk to Ronald, she has to travel for two days on a rocky road.

   b. Carla and Ronald both have e-mail access, making it costless for them to communicate.

23. **a.** EAuction and EMarketplace are two competing Internet auction sites, where buyers and sellers transact goods. Each auction site earns money by charging sellers for listing their goods. EAuction has decided to eliminate fees for the first transaction for sellers that are new to their site. Explain why this is likely to be a good strategy for EAuction in its competition with EMarketplace.

   b. EMarketplace complained to the Justice Department that EAuction's practice of eliminating fees for new sellers was anticompetitive and would lead to monopolization of the Internet auction industry. Is EMarketplace correct? How should the Justice Department respond?

c. EAuction stopped its practice of eliminating fees for new sellers. But since it provided much better technical service than its rival, EMarketplace, buyers and sellers came to prefer EAuction. Eventually, EMarketplace closed down, leaving EAuction as a monopolist. Should the Justice Department intervene to break EAuction into two companies? Explain.

d. EAuction is now a monopolist in the Internet auction industry. It also owns a site that handles payments over the Internet, called PayForIt. It is competing with another Internet payment site, called PayBuddy. EAuction has now stipulated that any transaction on its auction site must use PayForIt, rather than PayBuddy, for the payment. Should the Justice Department intervene? Explain.

Appendix

The modules in this Appendix present optional material. The economics of information, indifference curves, and international trade are an important part of contemporary economic theory, and you will be sure to see these topics in future courses.

iStockphoto

What you will learn in this **Module:**

- The special problems posed by private information—situations in which some people know things that other people do not (also known as *asymmetric information*)

- How information asymmetries can lead to the problem of adverse selection (otherwise known as the *lemons problem*)

- How firms deal with the need for information, using screening and signaling

- How information asymmetries can lead to the problem of moral hazard

Module 43
The Economics
of Information

Private Information: What You Don't Know Can Hurt You

Markets do very well at dealing with situations in which nobody knows what is going to happen. However, markets have much more trouble with situations in which *some people know things that other people don't know*—situations of **private information** (also known as "asymmetric information"). As we will see, private information can distort economic decisions and sometimes prevent mutually beneficial economic transactions from taking place.

Why is some information private? The most important reason is that people generally know more about themselves than other people do. For example, you know whether or not you are a careful driver; but unless you have already been in several accidents, your auto insurance company does not. You are more likely to have a better estimate than your health insurance company of whether or not you will need an expensive medical procedure. And if you are selling me your used car, you are more likely to be aware of any problems with it than I am.

But why should such differences in who knows what be a problem? It turns out that there are two distinct sources of trouble: *adverse selection,* which arises from having private information about the way things are, and *moral hazard,* which arises from having private information about what people do.

Adverse Selection: The Economics of Lemons

Suppose that someone offers to sell you an almost brand-new car—purchased just three months ago, with only 2,000 miles on the odometer and no dents or scratches. Will you be willing to pay almost the same for it as for a car direct from the dealer?

Probably not, for one main reason: you cannot help but wonder why this car is being sold. Is it because the owner has discovered that something is wrong with it—that it is a "lemon"? Having driven the car for a while, the owner knows more about it than you do—and people are more likely to sell cars that give them trouble.

Private information is information that some people have that others do not.

You might think that the fact that sellers of used cars know more about them than buyers do represents an advantage to the sellers. But potential buyers know that potential sellers are likely to offer them lemons—they just don't know exactly which car is a lemon. Because potential buyers of a used car know that potential sellers are more likely to sell lemons than good cars, buyers will offer a lower price than they would if they had a guarantee of the car's quality. Worse yet, this poor opinion of used cars tends to be self-reinforcing, precisely because it depresses the prices that buyers offer. Used cars sell at a discount because buyers expect a disproportionate share of those cars to be lemons. Even a used car that is not a lemon would sell only at a large discount because buyers don't know whether it's a lemon or not. But potential sellers who have good cars are unwilling to sell them at a deep discount, except under exceptional circumstances. So good used cars are rarely offered for sale, and used cars that are offered for sale have a strong tendency to be lemons. (This is why people who have a compelling reason to sell a car, such as moving overseas, make a point of revealing that information to potential buyers—as if to say "This car is not a lemon!")

The end result, then, is not only that used cars sell for low prices but also that there are a large number of used cars with hidden problems. Equally important, many potentially beneficial transactions—sales of good cars by people who would like to get rid of them to people who would like to buy them—end up being frustrated by the inability of potential sellers to convince potential buyers that their cars are actually worth the higher price demanded. So some mutually beneficial trades between those who want to sell used cars and those who want to buy them go unexploited.

Although economists sometimes refer to situations like this as the "lemons problem" (the issue was introduced in a famous 1970 paper by economist and Nobel laureate George Akerlof entitled "The Market for Lemons"), the more formal name of the problem is **adverse selection.** The reason for the name is obvious: because the potential sellers know more about the quality of what they are selling than the potential buyers, they have an incentive to select the worst things to sell.

Adverse selection does not apply only to used cars. It is a problem for many parts of the economy—notably for insurance companies, and most notably for health insurance companies. Suppose that a health insurance company were to offer a standard policy to everyone with the same premium. The premium would reflect the *average* risk of incurring a medical expense. But that would make the policy look very expensive to healthy people, who know that they are less likely than the average person to incur medical expenses. So healthy people would be less likely than less healthy people to buy the policy, leaving the health insurance company with exactly the customers it doesn't want: people with a higher-than-average risk of needing medical care, who would find the premium to be a good deal. In order to cover its expected losses from this sicker customer pool, the health insurance company is compelled to raise premiums, driving away more of the remaining healthier customers, and so on. Because the insurance company can't determine who is healthy and who is not, it must charge everyone the same premium, thereby discouraging healthy people from purchasing policies and encouraging unhealthy people to buy policies.

Adverse selection can lead to a phenomenon called an *adverse selection death spiral* as the market for health insurance collapses: insurance companies refuse to offer policies because there is no premium at which the company can cover its losses. Because of the severe adverse selection problems, governments in many advanced countries assume the role of providing health insurance to their citizens. The U.S. government, through its various health insurance programs including Medicare, Medicaid, and the Children's Health Insurance Program, now disburses more than half the total payments for medical care in the United States.

In general, people or firms faced with the problem of adverse selection follow one of several well-established strategies for dealing with it. One strategy is **screening:** using observable information to make inferences about private information. If you apply to purchase health insurance, you'll find that the insurance company will demand documentation of your health status in an attempt to "screen out" sicker applicants, whom

Adverse selection occurs when one person knows more about the way things are than other people do. Adverse selection exists, for example, when sellers offer items of particularly low (hidden) quality for sale, and when the people with the greatest need for insurance are those most likely to purchase it.

Adverse selection can be reduced through **screening:** using observable information about people to make inferences about their private information.

Adverse selection can be diminished by people **signaling** their private information through actions that credibly reveal what they know.

A long-term **reputation** allows an individual to assure others that he or she isn't concealing adverse private information.

they will refuse to insure or will insure only at very high premiums. Auto insurance also provides a very good example. An insurance company may not know whether you are a careful driver, but it has statistical data on the accident rates of people who resemble your profile—and it uses those data in setting premiums. A 19-year-old male who drives a sports car and has already had a fender-bender is likely to pay a very high premium. A 40-year-old female who drives a minivan and has never had an accident is likely to pay much less. In some cases, this may be quite unfair: some adolescent males are very careful drivers, and some mature women drive their minivans as if they were F-16s. But nobody can deny that the insurance companies are right on average.

Another strategy is for people who are good prospects to somehow *signal* their private information. **Signaling** involves taking some action that wouldn't be worth taking unless they were indeed good prospects. Reputable used-car dealers often offer warranties—promises to repair any problems with the cars they sell that arise within a given amount of time. This isn't just a way of insuring their customers against possible expenses; it's a way of credibly showing that they are not selling lemons. As a result, more sales occur and dealers can command higher prices for their used cars.

Finally, in the face of adverse selection, it can be very valuable to establish a good **reputation:** a used-car dealership will often advertise how long it has been in business to show that it has continued to satisfy its customers. As a result, new customers will be willing to purchase cars and to pay more for that dealer's cars.

Moral Hazard

In the late 1970s, New York and other major cities experienced an epidemic of suspicious fires—fires that appeared to be deliberately set. Some of the fires were probably started by teenagers on a lark, others by gang members struggling over turf. But investigators eventually became aware of patterns in a number of the fires. Particular landlords who owned several buildings seemed to have an unusually large number of their buildings burn down. Although it was difficult to prove, police had few doubts that most of these fire-prone landlords were hiring professional arsonists to torch their own properties.

Why burn your own buildings? These buildings were typically in declining neighborhoods, where rising crime and middle-class flight had led to a decline in property values. But the insurance policies on the buildings were written to compensate owners based on historical property values, and so would pay the owner of a destroyed building more than the building was worth in the current market. For an unscrupulous landlord who knew the right people, this presented a profitable opportunity.

The arson epidemic became less severe during the 1980s, partly because insurance companies began making it difficult to over-insure properties and partly because a boom in real estate values made many previously arson-threatened buildings worth more unburned.

The arson episodes make it clear that it is a bad idea for insurance companies to let customers insure buildings for more than their value—it gives the customers some destructive incentives. You might think, however, that the incentive problem would go away as long as the insurance is no more than 100% of the value of what is being insured.

But, unfortunately, anything close to 100% insurance still distorts incentives—it induces policyholders to behave differently from how they would in the absence of insurance. The reason is that preventing fires requires effort and cost on the part of a building's owner. Fire alarms and sprinkler systems have to be kept in good repair, fire safety rules have to be strictly enforced, and so on. All of this takes time and money—time and money that the owner may not find worth spending if the insurance policy will provide close to full compensation for any losses.

Of course, the insurance company could specify in the policy that it won't pay if basic safety precautions have not been taken. But it isn't always easy to tell how careful a building's owner has been—the owner knows, but the insurance company does not.

The point is that the building's owner has private information about his or her own actions; the owner knows whether he or she has really taken all appropriate precautions.

As a result, the insurance company is likely to face greater claims than if it were able to determine exactly how much effort a building owner exerts to prevent a loss. The problem of distorted incentives arises when an individual has private information about his or her own actions but someone else bears the costs of a lack of care or effort. This is known as **moral hazard.**

To deal with moral hazard, it is necessary to give individuals with private information some personal stake in what happens, a stake that gives them a reason to exert effort even if others cannot verify that they have done so. Moral hazard is the reason salespeople in many stores receive a commission on sales: it's hard for managers to be sure how hard the salespeople are really working, and if they were paid only straight salary, they would not have an incentive to exert effort to make those sales. Similar logic explains why many stores and restaurants, even if they are part of national chains, are actually franchises, licensed outlets owned by the people who run them.

Insurance companies deal with moral hazard by requiring a **deductible:** they compensate for losses only above a certain amount, so that coverage is always less than 100%. The insurance on your car, for example, may pay for repairs only after the first $500 in loss. This means that a careless driver who gets into a fender-bender will end up paying $500 for repairs even if he is insured, which provides at least some incentive to be careful and reduces moral hazard.

In addition to reducing moral hazard, deductibles provide a partial solution to the problem of adverse selection. Your insurance premium often drops substantially if you are willing to accept a large deductible. This is an attractive option to people who know they are low-risk customers; it is less attractive to people who know they are high-risk— and so are likely to have an accident and end up paying the deductible. By offering a menu of policies with different premiums and deductibles, insurance companies can screen their customers, inducing them to sort themselves out on the basis of their private information.

As the example of deductibles suggests, moral hazard limits the ability of the economy to allocate risks efficiently. You generally can't get full (100%) insurance on your home or car, even though you would like to buy full insurance, and you bear the risk of large deductibles, even though you would prefer not to.

Moral hazard occurs when an individual knows more about his or her own actions than other people do. This leads to a distortion of incentives to take care or to exert effort when someone else bears the costs of the lack of care or effort.

A **deductible** is a sum specified in an insurance policy that the insured individuals must pay before being compensated for a claim; deductibles reduce *moral hazard.*

Module 43 Review

Solutions appear at the back of the book.

Check Your Understanding

1. Your car insurance premiums are lower if you have had no moving violations for several years. Explain how this feature tends to decrease the potential inefficiency caused by adverse selection.

2. A common feature of home construction contracts is that when it costs more to construct a building than was originally estimated, the contractor must absorb the additional cost. Explain how this feature reduces the problem of moral hazard but also forces the contractor to bear more risk than she would like.

3. True or false? Explain your answer, stating what concept analyzed in this module accounts for the feature.

   People with higher deductibles on their auto insurance
   a. generally drive more carefully.
   b. pay lower premiums.

Multiple-Choice Questions

1. Which of the following is true about private information?
    I. It has value.
    II. Everyone has access to it.
    III. It can distort economic decisions.
    a. I only
    b. II only
    c. III only
    d. I and III only
    e. I, II, and III

2. Due to adverse selection,
    a mutually beneficial trades go unexploited.
    b. people buy lemons rather than other fruit.
    c. sick people buy less insurance.
    d. private information is available to all.
    e. public information is available to no one.

3. When colleges use grade point averages to make admissions decisions, they are employing which strategy?
    a. signaling
    b. screening

c. profit maximization
d. marginal analysis
e. adverse selection

4. Moral hazard is the result of
    a. asymmetric information.
    b. signaling.
    c. toxic waste.
    d. adverse selection.
    e. public information.

5. A deductible is used by insurance companies to
    a. allow customers to pay for insurance premiums using payroll deduction.
    b. deal with moral hazard.
    c. make public information private.
    d. compensate policyholders fully for their losses.
    e. avoid all payments to policyholders.

Critical-Thinking Question

Individuals or corporations (for example home-buyers or banks) believe that the government will "bail them out" in the event that their decisions lead to a financial collapse. This is an example of what problem created by asymmetric information? How does this situation lead to inefficiency? What is a possible remedy for the problem?

What you will learn in this **Module:**

- Why economists use indifference curves to illustrate a person's preferences

- The importance of the marginal rate of substitution, the rate at which a consumer is just willing to substitute one good for another

- An alternative way of finding a consumer's optimal consumption bundle, using indifference curves and the budget line

Module 44
Indifference Curves and Consumer Choice

Mapping the Utility Function

Earlier we introduced the concept of a utility function, which determines a consumer's total utility, given his or her consumption bundle. Here we will extend the analysis by learning how to express total utility as a function of the consumption of two goods. In this way we will deepen our understanding of the trade-off involved when choosing the optimal consumption bundle and of how the optimal consumption bundle itself changes in response to changes in the prices of goods. In order to do that, we now turn to a different way of representing a consumer's utility function, based on the concept of *indifference curves*.

Indifference Curves

Ingrid is a consumer who buys only two goods: housing, measured by the number of rooms in her house or apartment, and restaurant meals. How can we represent her utility function in a way that takes account of her consumption of both goods?

One way is to draw a three-dimensional picture. Figure 44.1 on the next page shows a three-dimensional "utility hill." The distance along the horizontal axis measures the quantity of housing Ingrid consumes in terms of the number of rooms; the distance along the vertical axis measures the number of restaurant meals she consumes. The altitude or height of the hill at each point is indicated by a contour line, along which the height of the hill is constant. For example, point *A*, which corresponds to a consumption bundle of 3 rooms and 30 restaurant meals, lies on the contour line labeled 450. So the total utility Ingrid receives from consuming 3 rooms and 30 restaurant meals is 450 utils.

A three-dimensional picture like Figure 44.1 helps us think about the relationship between consumption bundles and total utility. But anyone who has ever used a topographical map to plan a hiking trip knows that it is possible to represent a three-dimensional surface in only two dimensions. A topographical map doesn't

figure 44.1

Ingrid's Utility Function

The three-dimensional hill shows how Ingrid's total utility depends on her consumption of housing and restaurant meals. Point *A* corresponds to consumption of 3 rooms and 30 restaurant meals. That consumption bundle yields Ingrid 450 utils, corresponding to the height of the hill at point *A*. The lines running around the hill are contour lines, along which the height is constant. So every point on a given contour line generates the same level of utility.

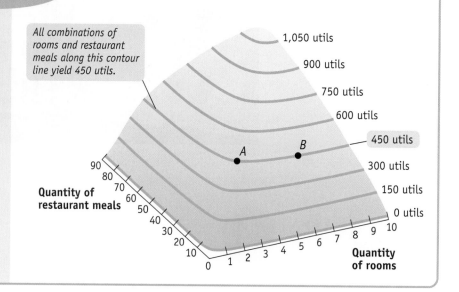

All combinations of rooms and restaurant meals along this contour line yield 450 utils.

offer a three-dimensional view of the terrain; instead, it conveys information about altitude solely through the use of contour lines.

The same principle can be applied to the representation of a utility function. In Figure 44.2, Ingrid's consumption of rooms is measured on the horizontal axis and her consumption of restaurant meals on the vertical axis. The curve here corresponds to the contour line in Figure 44.1, drawn at a total utility of 450 utils. This curve shows all the consumption bundles that yield a total utility of 450 utils. One point on that contour line is *A*, a consumption bundle consisting of 3 rooms and 30 restaurant meals. Another point on that contour line is *B*, a consumption bundle consisting of 6 rooms but only 15 restaurant meals. Because *B* lies on the same contour line, it yields Ingrid

figure 44.2

An Indifference Curve

An indifference curve is a contour line along which total utility is constant. In this case, we show all the consumption bundles that yield Ingrid 450 utils. Consumption bundle *A*, consisting of 3 rooms and 30 restaurant meals, yields the same total utility as bundle *B*, consisting of 6 rooms and 15 restaurant meals. That is, Ingrid is indifferent between bundle *A* and bundle *B*.

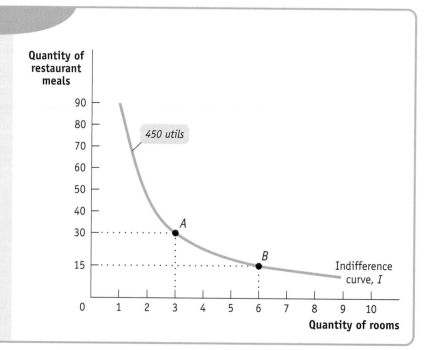

the same total utility—450 utils—as *A*. We say that Ingrid is *indifferent* between *A* and *B*: because bundles *A* and *B* yield the same total utility level, Ingrid is equally well off with either bundle.

A contour line that maps consumption bundles yielding the same amount of total utility is known as an **indifference curve.** An individual is always indifferent between any two bundles that lie on the same indifference curve. For a given consumer, there is an indifference curve corresponding to each possible level of total utility. For example, the indifference curve in Figure 44.2 shows consumption bundles that yield Ingrid 450 utils; different indifference curves would show consumption bundles that yield Ingrid 400 utils, 500 utils, and so on.

A collection of indifference curves that represents a given consumer's entire utility function, with each indifference curve corresponding to a different level of total utility, is known as an **indifference curve map.** Figure 44.3 shows three indifference curves—I_1, I_2, and I_3—from Ingrid's indifference curve map, as well as several consumption bundles, *A, B, C,* and *D*. The accompanying table lists each bundle, its composition of rooms and restaurant meals, and the total utility it yields. Because bundles *A* and *B* generate the same number of utils, 450, they lie on the same indifference curve, I_2.

Although Ingrid is indifferent between *A* and *B*, she is certainly not indifferent between *A* and *C*: as you can see from the table, *C* generates only 391 utils, a lower total utility than *A* or *B*. So Ingrid prefers consumption bundles *A* and *B* to bundle *C*. This is represented by the fact that *C* is on indifference curve I_1, and I_1 lies below I_2. Bundle *D*, though, generates 519 utils, a higher total utility than *A* and *B*. It is on I_3, an indifference curve that lies above I_2. Clearly, Ingrid prefers *D* to either *A* or *B*. And, even more strongly, she prefers *D* to *C*.

Section 9 Appendix

An **indifference curve** is a line that shows all the consumption bundles that yield the same amount of total utility for an individual.

The entire utility function of an individual can be represented by an **indifference curve map,** a collection of indifference curves in which each curve corresponds to a different total utility level.

figure 44.3 An Indifference Curve Map

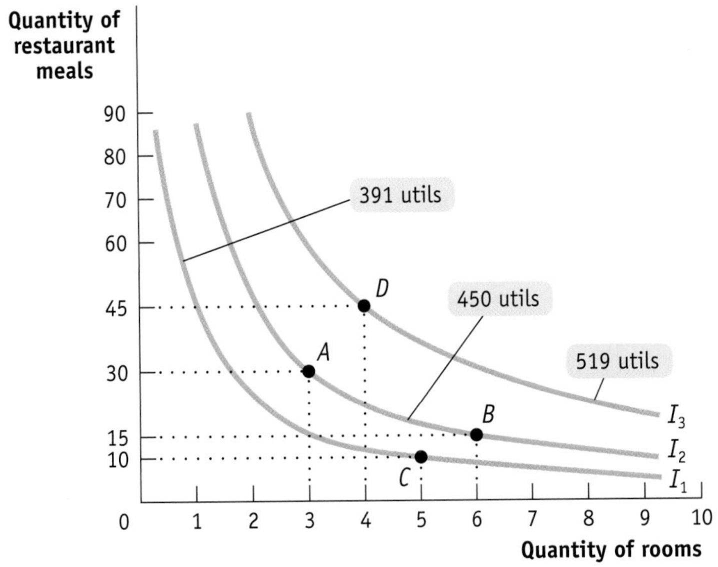

Consumption bundle	Quantity of rooms	Quantity of meals	Total utility (utils)
A	3	30	450
B	6	15	450
C	5	10	391
D	4	45	519

The utility function can be represented in greater detail by increasing the number of indifference curves drawn, each corresponding to a different level of total utility. In this figure bundle *C* lies on an indifference curve corresponding to a total utility of 391 utils. As in Figure 44.2, bundles *A* and *B* lie on an indifference curve corresponding to a total utility of 450 utils. Bundle *D* lies on an indifference curve corresponding to a total utility of 519 utils. Ingrid prefers any bundle on I_2 to any bundle on I_1, and she prefers any bundle on I_3 to any bundle on I_2.

Are Utils Useful?

In the table that accompanies Figure 44.3, we give the number of utils achieved on each of the indifference curves shown in the figure. But is this information actually needed?

The answer is no. As you will see shortly, the indifference curve map tells us all we need to know in order to find a consumer's optimal consumption bundle. That is, it's important that Ingrid has higher total utility along indifference curve I_2 than she does along I_1, but it doesn't matter *how much higher* her total utility is. In other words, we don't have to measure utils in order to understand how consumers make choices.

Economists say that consumer theory requires an *ordinal* measure of utility—one that ranks consumption bundles in terms of desirability—so that we can say that bundle X is better than bundle Y. The theory does not, however, require *cardinal* utility, which actually assigns a specific number to the total utility yielded by each bundle.

So why introduce the concept of utils at all? The answer is that it is much easier to understand the basis of rational choice by using the concept of measurable utility.

Properties of Indifference Curves

No two individuals have the same indifference curve map because no two individuals have the same preferences. But economists believe that, regardless of the person, every indifference curve map has two general properties. These are illustrated in panel (a) of Figure 44.4.

  a. *Indifference curves never cross.* Suppose that we tried to draw an indifference curve map like the one depicted in the left diagram in panel (a), in which two indifference curves cross at *A*. What is the total utility at *A*? Is it 100 utils or 200 utils? Indifference curves cannot cross because each consumption bundle must correspond to one unique total utility level—not, as shown at *A,* two different total utility levels.

  b. *The farther out an indifference curve lies—the farther it is from the origin—the higher the level of total utility it indicates.* The reason, illustrated in the right diagram in panel (a), is that we assume that more is better—we consider only the consumption bundles for which the consumer is not satiated. Bundle *B*, on the outer indifference curve, contains more of both goods than bundle *A* on the inner indifference curve. So *B*, because it generates a higher total utility level (200 utils), lies on a higher indifference curve than *A*.

  Furthermore, economists believe that, for most goods, consumers' indifference curve maps also have two additional properties. They are illustrated in panel (b) of Figure 44.4:

  c. *Indifference curves slope downward.* Here, too, the reason is that more is better. The left diagram in panel (b) shows four consumption bundles on the same indifference curve: *W, X, Y,* and *Z*. By definition, these consumption bundles yield the same level of total utility. But as you move along the curve to the right, from *W* to *Z*, the quantity of rooms consumed increases. The only way a person can consume more rooms without gaining utility is by giving up some restaurant meals. So the indifference curve must slope downward.

  d. *Indifference curves have a convex shape.* The right diagram in panel (b) shows that the slope of each indifference curve changes as you move down the curve to the right: the curve gets flatter. If you move up an indifference curve to the left, the curve gets steeper. So the indifference curve is steeper at *A* than it is at *B*. When this occurs, we say that an indifference curve has a *convex* shape—it is bowed-in toward the origin. This feature arises from diminishing marginal utility. Recall that when a consumer has diminishing marginal utility, consumption of another unit of a good generates a smaller increase in total utility than the previous unit consumed. Next we will examine in detail how diminishing marginal utility gives rise to convex-shaped indifference curves.

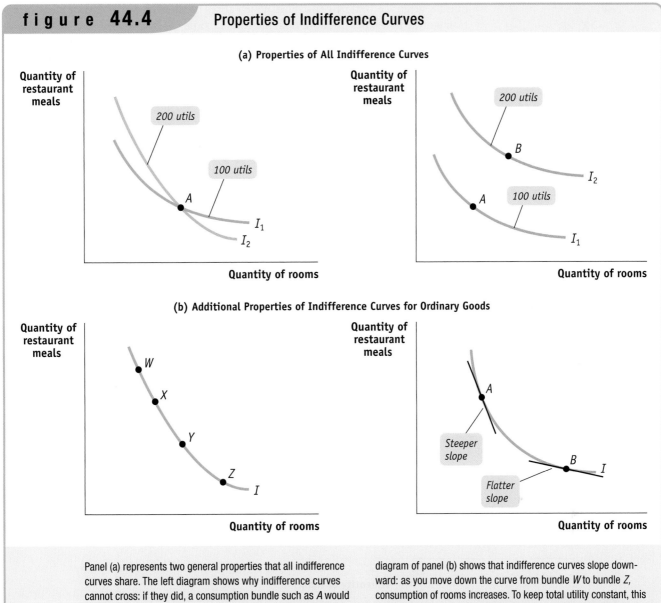

figure 44.4 Properties of Indifference Curves

(a) Properties of All Indifference Curves

Quantity of restaurant meals (vertical axis, left diagram)

200 utils
100 utils
A
I_1
I_2

Quantity of rooms (horizontal axis, left diagram)

Quantity of restaurant meals (vertical axis, right diagram)

200 utils
B
I_2
A
100 utils
I_1

Quantity of rooms (horizontal axis, right diagram)

(b) Additional Properties of Indifference Curves for Ordinary Goods

Quantity of restaurant meals (vertical axis, left diagram)

W
X
Y
Z
I

Quantity of rooms (horizontal axis, left diagram)

Quantity of restaurant meals (vertical axis, right diagram)

A
Steeper slope
B
I
Flatter slope

Quantity of rooms (horizontal axis, right diagram)

Panel (a) represents two general properties that all indifference curves share. The left diagram shows why indifference curves cannot cross: if they did, a consumption bundle such as A would yield both 100 and 200 utils, a contradiction. The right diagram of panel (a) shows that indifference curves that are farther out yield higher total utility: bundle B, which contains more of both goods than bundle A, yields higher total utility. Panel (b) depicts two additional properties of indifference curves for ordinary goods. The left diagram of panel (b) shows that indifference curves slope downward: as you move down the curve from bundle W to bundle Z, consumption of rooms increases. To keep total utility constant, this must be offset by a reduction in quantity of restaurant meals. The right diagram of panel (b) shows a convex-shaped indifference curve. The slope of the indifference curve gets flatter as you move down the curve to the right, a feature arising from diminishing marginal utility.

Goods that satisfy all four properties of indifference curve maps are called *ordinary goods*. The vast majority of goods in any consumer's utility function fall into this category. Below we will define ordinary goods more precisely and see the key role that diminishing marginal utility plays for them.

Indifference Curves and Consumer Choice

Above we used indifference curves to represent the preferences of Ingrid, whose consumption bundles consist of rooms and restaurant meals. Our next step is to show how to use Ingrid's indifference curve map to find her utility-maximizing consumption bundle, given her budget constraint, which arises because she must choose a consumption bundle that costs no more than her total income.

It's important to understand how our analysis here relates to what we did in the module "Utility Maximization." We are not offering a new theory of consumer behavior in this module—consumers are assumed to maximize total utility as before. In particular, we know that consumers will follow the *optimal consumption rule*: the optimal consumption bundle lies on the budget line, and the marginal utility per dollar is the same for every good in the bundle.

But as we'll see shortly, we can derive this optimal consumer behavior in a somewhat different way—a way that yields deeper insights into consumer choice.

The Marginal Rate of Substitution

The first element of our approach is a new concept, the *marginal rate of substitution*. The essence of this concept is illustrated in Figure 44.5.

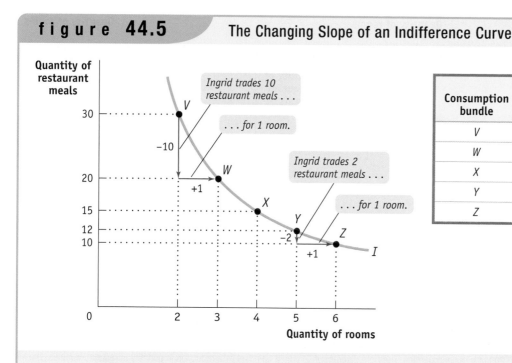

figure 44.5   The Changing Slope of an Indifference Curve

Consumption bundle	Quantity of rooms	Quantity of restaurant meals
V	2	30
W	3	20
X	4	15
Y	5	12
Z	6	10

This indifference curve is downward sloping and convex, implying that restaurant meals and rooms are ordinary goods for Ingrid. As Ingrid moves down her indifference curve from V to Z, she trades reduced consumption of restaurant meals for increased consumption of housing. However, the terms of that trade-off change. As she moves from V to W, she is willing to give up 10 restaurant meals in return for 1 more room. As her consumption of rooms rises and her consumption of restaurant meals falls, she is willing to give up fewer restaurant meals in return for each additional room. The flattening of the slope as you move from left to right arises from diminishing marginal utility.

We have just seen that for most goods, consumers' indifference curves are downward sloping and convex. Figure 44.5 shows such an indifference curve. The points labeled *V, W, X, Y,* and *Z* all lie on this indifference curve—that is, they represent consumption bundles that yield Ingrid the same level of total utility. The table accompanying the figure shows the components of each of the bundles. As we move along the indifference curve from *V* to *Z*, Ingrid's consumption of housing steadily increases from 2 rooms to 6 rooms, her consumption of restaurant meals steadily decreases from 30 meals to 10 meals, and her total utility is kept constant. As we move down the indifference curve, then, Ingrid is trading more of one good for less of the other, with the *terms* of that trade-off—the ratio of additional rooms consumed to restaurant meals sacrificed—chosen to keep her total utility constant.

Notice that the quantity of restaurant meals that Ingrid is willing to give up in return for an additional room changes along the indifference curve. As we move from *V* to *W*, housing consumption rises from 2 to 3 rooms and restaurant meal consumption falls from 30 to 20—a trade-off of 10 restaurant meals for 1 additional room. But as we move from *Y* to *Z*, housing consumption rises from 5 to 6 rooms and restaurant meal consumption falls from 12 to 10, a trade-off of only 2 restaurant meals for an additional room.

To put it in terms of slope, the slope of the indifference curve between *V* and *W* is −10: the change in restaurant meal consumption, −10, divided by the change in housing consumption, 1. Similarly, the slope of the indifference curve between *Y* and *Z* is −2. So the indifference curve gets flatter as we move down it to the right—that is, it has a convex shape, one of the four properties of an indifference curve for ordinary goods.

Why does the trade-off change in this way? Let's think about it intuitively and then work through it more carefully. When Ingrid moves down her indifference curve, whether from *V* to *W* or from *Y* to *Z*, she gains utility from her additional consumption of housing but loses an equal amount of utility from her reduced consumption of restaurant meals. But at each step, the initial position from which Ingrid begins is different. At *V*, Ingrid consumes only a small quantity of rooms; because of diminishing marginal utility, her marginal utility per room at that point is high. At *V*, then, an additional room adds a lot to Ingrid's total utility. But at *V* she already consumes a large quantity of restaurant meals, so her marginal utility of restaurant meals is low at that point. This means that it takes a large reduction in her quantity of restaurant meals consumed to offset the increased utility she gets from the extra room of housing.

At *Y*, in contrast, Ingrid consumes a much larger quantity of rooms and a much smaller quantity of restaurant meals than at *V*. This means that an additional room adds fewer utils, and a restaurant meal forgone costs more utils, than at *V*. So Ingrid is willing to give up fewer restaurant meals in return for another room of housing at *Y* (where she gives up 2 meals for 1 room) than she is at *V* (where she gives up 10 meals for 1 room).

Now let's express the same idea—that the trade-off Ingrid is willing to make depends on where she is starting from—by using a little math. We do this by examining how the slope of the indifference curve changes as we move down it. Moving down the indifference curve—reducing restaurant meal consumption and increasing housing consumption—will produce two opposing effects on Ingrid's total utility: lower restaurant meal consumption will reduce her total utility, but higher housing consumption will raise her total utility. And since we are moving down the indifference curve, these two effects must exactly cancel out:

Along the indifference curve:

(44-1) (Change in total utility due to lower restaurant meal consumption) +
(Change in total utility due to higher housing consumption) = 0

or, rearranging terms,

Along the indifference curve:

(44-2) −(Change in total utility due to lower restaurant meal consumption) =
(Change in total utility due to higher housing consumption)

Let's now focus on what happens as we move only a short distance down the indifference curve, trading off a small increase in housing consumption in place of a small decrease in restaurant meal consumption. Following our notation from before, let's use MU_R and MU_M to represent the marginal utility of rooms and restaurant meals, respectively, and Q_R and Q_M to represent the changes in room and meal consumption, respectively. In general, the change in total utility caused by a small change in consumption of a good is equal to the change in consumption multiplied by the *marginal utility* of that good. This means that we can calculate the change in Ingrid's total utility generated by a change in her consumption bundle using the following equations:

(44-3) Change in total utility due to a change in restaurant meal consumption
$$= MU_M \times Q_M$$

and

(44-4) Change in total utility due to a change in housing consumption
$$= MU_R \times Q_R$$

So we can write Equation 44-2 in symbols as:

Along the indifference curve:

(44-5) $-MU_M \times Q_M = MU_R \times Q_R$

Note that the left-hand side of Equation 44-5 has a negative sign; it represents the loss in total utility from decreased restaurant meal consumption. This must equal the gain in total utility from increased room consumption, represented by the right-hand side of the equation.

What we want to know is how this translates into the slope of the indifference curve. To find the slope, we divide both sides of Equation 44-5 by Q_R, and again by $-MU_M$, in order to get the Q_M, Q_R terms on one side and the MU_R, MU_M terms on the other. This results in:

(44-6) *Along the indifference curve:* $\frac{\Delta Q_M}{\Delta Q_R} = -\frac{MU_R}{MU_M}$

The left-hand side of Equation 44-6 is the slope of the indifference curve; it is the rate at which Ingrid is willing to trade rooms (the good on the horizontal axis) for restaurant meals (the good on the vertical axis) without changing her total utility level. The right-hand side of Equation 44-6 is the negative of the ratio of the marginal utility of rooms to the marginal utility of restaurant meals—that is, the ratio of what she gains from one more room to what she gains from one more meal, with a negative sign in front.

Putting all this together, Equation 44-6 shows that, along the indifference curve, the quantity of restaurant meals Ingrid is willing to give up in return for a room, $\frac{\Delta Q_M}{\Delta Q_R}$, is exactly equal to the negative of the ratio of the marginal utility of a room to that of a meal, $-\frac{MU_R}{MU_M}$. Only when this condition is met will her total utility level remain constant as she consumes more rooms and fewer restaurant meals.

Economists have a special name for the ratio of the marginal utilities found in the right-hand side of Equation 44-6: it is called the **marginal rate of substitution,** or **MRS,** of rooms (the good on the horizontal axis) in place of restaurant meals (the good on the vertical axis). That's because as we slide down Ingrid's indifference curve, we are substituting more rooms for fewer restaurant meals in her consumption bundle. As we'll see shortly, the marginal rate of substitution plays an important role in finding the optimal consumption bundle.

Recall that indifference curves get flatter as you move down them to the right. The reason, as we've just discussed, is diminishing marginal utility: as Ingrid consumes more housing and fewer restaurant meals, her marginal utility from housing falls and her marginal utility from restaurant meals rises. So her marginal rate of substitution, which is equal to the negative of the slope of her indifference curve, falls as she moves down the indifference curve.

The flattening of indifference curves as you slide down them to the right—which reflects the same logic as the principle of diminishing marginal utility—is known as the principle of **diminishing marginal rate of substitution.** It says that an individual who consumes only a little bit of good A and a lot of good B will be willing to trade off a lot of good B in return for one more unit of good A, and an individual who already consumes a lot of good A and not much of good B will be less willing to make that trade-off.

We can illustrate this point by referring back to Figure 44.5. At point V, a bundle with a high proportion of restaurant meals to rooms, Ingrid is willing to forgo 10 restaurant meals in return for 1 room. But at point Y, a bundle with a low proportion of restaurant meals to rooms, she is willing to forgo only 2 restaurant meals in return for 1 room.

From this example we can see that, in Ingrid's utility function, rooms and restaurant meals possess the two additional properties that characterize ordinary goods. Ingrid requires additional rooms to compensate her for the loss of a meal, and vice versa; so her indifference curves for these two goods slope downward. And her indifference curves are convex: the slope of her indifference curve—*the negative of* the marginal rate of substitution—becomes flatter as we move down it. In fact, an indifference curve is convex only when it has a diminishing marginal rate of substitution—these two conditions are equivalent.

With this information, we can define **ordinary goods,** which account for the great majority of goods in any consumer's utility function. A pair of goods are ordinary goods in a consumer's utility function if they possess two properties: the consumer requires more of one good to compensate for less of the other, and the consumer experiences a diminishing marginal rate of substitution when substituting one good for the other.

Next we will see how to determine Ingrid's optimal consumption bundle using indifference curves.

The principle of **diminishing marginal rate of substitution** states that the more of good R a person consumes in proportion to good M, the less M he or she is willing to substitute for another unit of R.

Two goods, R and M, are **ordinary goods** in a consumer's utility function when (1) the consumer requires additional units of R to compensate for fewer units of M, and vice versa; and (2) the consumer experiences a diminishing marginal rate of substitution when substituting one good for another.

The Tangency Condition

Now let's put some of Ingrid's indifference curves on the same diagram as her budget line to illustrate an alternative way of representing her optimal consumption choice. Figure 44.6 shows Ingrid's budget line, BL, when her income is $2,400 per month,

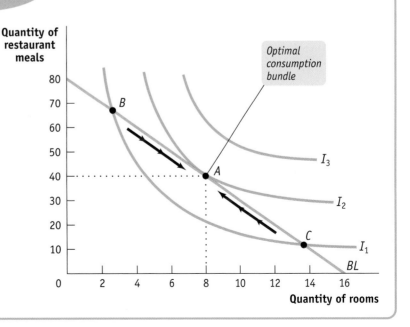

figure 44.6

The Optimal Consumption Bundle

The budget line, BL, shows Ingrid's possible consumption bundles, given an income of $2,400 per month, when rooms cost $150 per month and restaurant meals cost $30 each. I_1, I_2, and I_3 are indifference curves. Consumption bundles such as B and C are not optimal because Ingrid can move to a higher indifference curve. The optimal consumption bundle is A, where the budget line is just tangent to the highest possible indifference curve.

housing costs $150 per room each month, and restaurant meals cost $30 each. What is her optimal consumption bundle?

To answer this question, we show several of Ingrid's indifference curves: I_1, I_2, and I_3. Ingrid would like to achieve the total utility level represented by I_3, the highest of the three curves, but she cannot afford to because she is constrained by her income: no consumption bundle on her budget line yields that much total utility. But she shouldn't settle for the level of total utility generated by B, which lies on I_1: there are other bundles on her budget line, such as A, that clearly yield higher total utility than B.

In fact, A—a consumption bundle consisting of 8 rooms and 40 restaurant meals per month—is Ingrid's optimal consumption choice. The reason is that A lies on the highest indifference curve Ingrid can reach given her income.

At the optimal consumption bundle A, Ingrid's budget line *just touches* the relevant indifference curve—the budget line is *tangent* to the indifference curve. This **tangency condition** between the indifference curve and the budget line applies to the optimal consumption bundle when the indifference curves have the typical convex shape.

To see why, let's look more closely at how we know that a consumption bundle that *doesn't* satisfy the tangency condition can't be optimal. Reexamining Figure 44.6, we can see that consumption bundles B and C are both affordable because they lie on the budget line. However, neither is optimal. Both of them lie on the indifference curve I_1, which cuts through the budget line at both points. But because I_1 cuts through the budget line, Ingrid can do better: she can move down the budget line from B or up the budget line from C, as indicated by the arrows. In each case, this allows her to get onto a higher indifference curve, I_2, which increases her total utility.

Ingrid cannot, however, do any better than I_2: any other indifference curve either cuts through her budget line or doesn't touch it at all. And the bundle that allows her to achieve I_2 is, of course, her optimal consumption bundle.

The Slope of the Budget Line

Figure 44.6 shows us how to use a graph of the budget line and the indifference curves to find the optimal consumption bundle, the bundle at which the budget line and the indifference curve are tangent. But rather than rely on drawing graphs, we can determine the optimal consumption bundle by using a bit more math. As you can see from Figure 44.6, at A, the optimal consumption bundle, the budget line and the indifference curve have the same slope. Why? Because two curves can only be tangent to each other if they have the same slope at the point where they meet. Otherwise, they would cross each other at that point. And we know that if we are on an indifference curve that crosses the budget line (like I_1, in Figure 44.6), we can't be on the indifference curve that contains the optimal consumption bundle (like I_2).

So we can use information about the slopes of the budget line and the indifference curve to find the optimal consumption bundle. To do that, we must first analyze the slope of the budget line, a fairly straightforward task. We know that Ingrid will get the highest possible utility by spending all of her income and consuming a bundle on her budget line. So we can represent Ingrid's budget line, the consumption bundles available to her when she spends all of her income, with the equation:

(44-7) $(Q_R \times P_R) + (Q_M \times P_M) = N$

where N stands for Ingrid's income. To find the slope of the budget line, we divide its vertical intercept (where the budget line hits the vertical axis) by its horizontal intercept (where it hits the horizontal axis) and then add a negative sign. The vertical intercept is the point at which Ingrid spends all her income on restaurant meals and none on housing (that is, $Q_R = 0$). In that case the number of restaurant meals she consumes is:

(44-8) $Q_M = \dfrac{N}{P_M} = \$2,400/(\$30 \text{ per meal}) = 44 \text{ meals}$

$= \text{Vertical intercept of budget line}$

At the other extreme, Ingrid spends all her income on housing and none on restaurant meals (so that $Q_M = 0$). This means that at the horizontal intercept of the budget line, the number of rooms she consumes is:

The **relative price** of good R in terms of good M is equal to $\frac{P_R}{P_M}$, the rate at which R trades for M in the market.

(44-9) $Q_R = \dfrac{N}{P_R} = \dfrac{\$2,400}{(\$150 \text{ per room})} = 16 \text{ rooms}$

$\qquad\quad = \text{Horizontal intercept of budget line}$

Now we have the information needed to find the slope of the budget line. It is:

(44-10) $\text{Slope of budget line} = -\dfrac{(\text{Vertical intercept})}{(\text{Horizontal intercept})} = -\dfrac{\dfrac{N}{P_M}}{\dfrac{N}{P_R}} = -\dfrac{P_R}{P_M}$

Notice the negative sign in Equation 44-10; it's there because the budget line slopes downward. The quantity $\dfrac{P_R}{P_M}$ is known as the **relative price** of rooms in terms of restaurant meals, to distinguish it from an ordinary price in terms of dollars. Because buying one more room requires Ingrid to give up the quantity $\dfrac{P_R}{P_M}$ of restaurant meals, or 5 meals, we can interpret the relative price $\dfrac{P_R}{P_M}$ as the rate at which a room trades for restaurant meals in the market; it is the price—in terms of restaurant meals—Ingrid has to "pay" to get one more room.

Looking at this another way, the slope of the budget line—the negative of the relative price—tells us the opportunity cost of each good in terms of the other. The relative price illustrates the opportunity cost to an individual of consuming one more unit of one good in terms of how much of the other good in his or her consumption bundle must be forgone. This opportunity cost arises from the consumer's limited resources—his or her limited budget. It's useful to note that Equations 44-8, 44-9, and 44-10 give us all the information we need about what happens to the budget line when relative price or income changes. From Equations 44-8 and 44-9 we can see that a change in income, N, leads to a parallel shift of the budget line: both the vertical and horizontal intercepts will shift. That is, how far out the budget line is from the origin depends on the consumer's income. If a consumer's income rises, the budget line moves outward. If the consumer's income shrinks, the budget line shifts inward. In each case, the slope of the budget line stays the same because the relative price of one good in terms of the other does not change.

In contrast, a change in the relative price $\dfrac{P_R}{P_M}$ will lead to a change in the slope of the budget line.

Prices and the Marginal Rate of Substitution

Now we're ready to bring together the slope of the budget line and the slope of the indifference curve to find the optimal consumption bundle. From Equation 44-6, we know that the slope of the indifference curve at any point is equal to the negative of the marginal rate of substitution:

(44-11) $\text{Slope of indifference curve} = -\dfrac{MU_R}{MU_M}$

As we've already noted, at the optimal consumption bundle the slope of the budget line and the slope of the indifference curve are equal. We can write this formally by putting

Equations 44-10 and 44-11 together, which gives us the **relative price rule** for finding the optimal consumption bundle:

$$\textbf{(44-12)} \quad \textit{At the optimal consumption bundle: } -\frac{MU_R}{MU_M} = -\frac{P_R}{P_M}$$

or, *cancelling the negative signs,* $\dfrac{MU_R}{MU_M} = \dfrac{P_R}{P_M}$

That is, at the optimal consumption bundle, the marginal rate of substitution between any two goods is equal to the ratio of their prices. To put it in a more intuitive way, starting with Ingrid's optimal consumption bundle, the rate at which she would trade a room for more restaurant meals along her indifference curve, $\dfrac{MU_R}{MU_M}$, is equal to the rate at which rooms are traded for restaurant meals in the market, $\dfrac{P_R}{P_M}$.

What would happen if this equality did not hold? We can see by examining Figure 44.7. There, at point B, the slope of the indifference curve, $-\dfrac{MU_R}{MU_M}$, is greater in absolute value than the slope of the budget line, $-\dfrac{P_R}{P_M}$. This means that, at B, Ingrid values an additional room in place of meals *more* than it costs her to buy an additional room and forgo some meals. As a result, Ingrid would be better off moving down her budget line toward A, consuming more rooms and fewer restaurant meals—and because of that, B could not have been her optimal bundle! Likewise, at C, the slope of Ingrid's indifference curve is less in absolute value than the slope of the budget line. The implication is that, at C, Ingrid values additional meals in place of a room *more* than it costs her to buy additional meals and forgo a room. Again, Ingrid would be better off moving along her budget line—consuming more restaurant meals and fewer rooms—until she reaches A, her optimal consumption bundle.

But suppose we transform the last term of Equation 44-12 in the following way: divide both sides by P_R and multiply both sides by MU_M. Then the relative price rule becomes the optimal consumption rule:

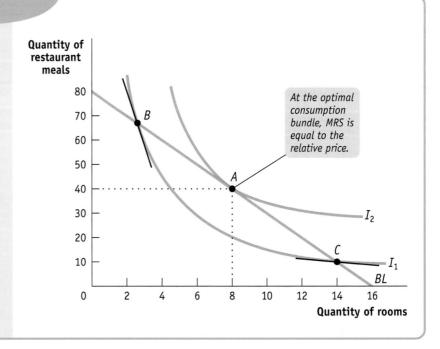

figure **44.7**

Understanding the Relative Price Rule

The *relative price* of rooms in terms of restaurant meals is equal to the negative of the slope of the budget line. The *marginal rate of substitution* of rooms for restaurant meals is equal to the negative of the slope of the indifference curve. The *relative price rule* says that at the optimal consumption bundle, the marginal rate of substitution must equal the relative price. This point can be demonstrated by considering what happens when the marginal rate of substitution is not equal to the relative price. At consumption bundle B, the marginal rate of substitution is larger than the relative price; Ingrid can increase her total utility by moving down her budget line, *BL*. At C, the marginal rate of substitution is smaller than the relative price, and Ingrid can increase her total utility by moving up the budget line. Only at A, where the relative price rule holds, is her total utility maximized, given her budget constraint.

At the optimal consumption bundle, MRS is equal to the relative price.

(44-13) *Optimal consumption rule:* $\dfrac{MU_R}{P_M} = \dfrac{MU_M}{P_M}$

So using either the optimal consumption rule or the relative price rule, we find the same optimal consumption bundle.

Preferences and Choices

Now that we have seen how to represent the optimal consumption choice in an indifference curve diagram, we can turn briefly to the relationship between consumer preferences and consumer choices.

When we say that two consumers have different preferences, we mean that they have different utility functions. This in turn means that they will have indifference curve maps with different shapes. And those different maps will translate into different consumption choices, even among consumers with the same income and who face the same prices.

To see this, suppose that Ingrid's friend Lars also consumes only housing and restaurant meals. However, Lars has a stronger preference for restaurant meals and a weaker preference for housing. This difference in preferences is shown in Figure 44.8,

---

figure 44.8

Differences in Preferences

Ingrid and Lars have different preferences, reflected in the different shapes of their indifference curve maps. So they will choose different consumption bundles even when they have the same possible choices. Each has an income of $2,400 per month and faces prices of $30 per meal and $150 per room. Panel (a) shows Ingrid's consumption choice: 8 rooms and 40 restaurant meals. Panel (b) shows Lars's choice: even though he has the same budget line, he consumes fewer rooms and more restaurant meals.

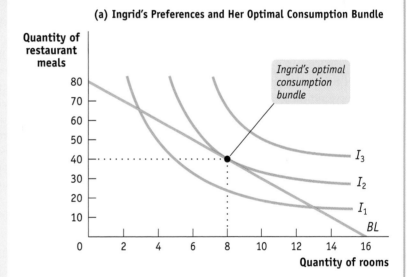

(a) Ingrid's Preferences and Her Optimal Consumption Bundle

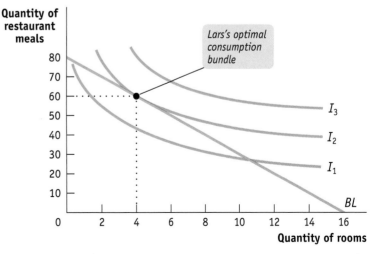

(b) Lars's Preferences and His Optimal Consumption Bundle

---

which shows *two* sets of indifference curves: panel (a) shows Ingrid's preferences and panel (b) shows Lars's preferences. Note the difference in their shapes.

Suppose, as before, that rooms cost $150 per month and restaurant meals cost $30. Let's also assume that both Ingrid and Lars have incomes of $2,400 per month, giving them identical budget lines. Nonetheless, because they have different preferences, they will make different consumption choices, as shown in Figure 44.8. Ingrid will choose 8 rooms and 40 restaurant meals; Lars will choose 4 rooms and 60 restaurant meals.

Module 44 Review

Solutions appear at the back of the book.

Check Your Understanding

1. The accompanying table shows Samantha's preferences for consumption bundles composed of chocolate kisses and licorice drops.

Consumption bundle	Quantity of chocolate kisses	Quantity of licorice drops	Total utility (utils)
A	1	3	6
B	2	3	10
C	3	1	6
D	2	1	4

   a. With chocolate kisses on the horizontal axis and licorice drops on the vertical axis, draw hypothetical indifference curves for Samantha and locate the bundles on the curves. Assume that both items are ordinary goods.
   b. Suppose you don't know the number of utils provided by each bundle. Assuming that more is better, predict Samantha's ranking of each of the four bundles to the extent possible. Explain your answer.

2. On the left diagram in panel (a) of Figure 44.4, draw a point *B* anywhere on the 200-util indifference curve and a point *C* anywhere on the 100-util indifference curve (but *not* at the same location as point *A*). By comparing the utils generated by bundles *A* and *B* and those generated by bundles *A* and *C*, explain why indifference curves cannot cross.

3. Lucinda and Kyle each consume 3 comic books and 6 video games. Lucinda's marginal rate of substitution of books for games is 2 and Kyle's is 5.
   a. For each person, find another consumption bundle that yields the same total utility as the current bundle. Who is less willing to trade games for books? In a diagram with books on the horizontal axis and games on the vertical axis, how would this be reflected in differences in the slopes of their indifference curves at their current consumption bundles?
   b. Find the relative price of books in terms of games at which Lucinda's current bundle is optimal. Is Kyle's bundle optimal given this relative price? If not, how should Kyle rearrange his consumption?

Multiple-Choice Questions

1. Which of the following is true along an individual's indifference curve for ordinary goods?
   a. The slope is constant.
   b. Total utility changes.
   c. The individual is indifferent between any two points.
   d. The slope is equal to the ratio of the prices of the consumption bundles.
   e. The individual doesn't care if utility is maximized.

2. Which of the following is/are true of indifference curves for ordinary goods?
   I. They cannot intersect.
   II. They have a negative slope.
   III. They are convex.

   a. I only
   b. II only
   c. III only
   d. I and II only
   e. I, II, and III

3. Moving from left to right along an indifference curve, which of the following increases?
   a. The marginal utility of the vertical axis good
   b. The marginal utility of the horizontal axis good
   c. The absolute value of the slope
   d. The marginal rate of substitution
   e. The demand for the vertical axis good

4. If the quantity of good X is measured on the horizontal axis and the quantity of good Y is measured on the vertical axis, the marginal rate of substitution is equal to

   a. $\dfrac{\Delta Q_X}{\Delta Q_Y}$.

   b. $\dfrac{MU_X}{MU_Y}$.

   c. $\dfrac{P_X}{P_Y}$.

   d. the ratio of the slope of the budget line and the slope of the indifference curve.

   e. 1 at the optimal level of consumption.

5. If the quantity of good X is again measured on the horizontal axis and the quantity of good Y is measured on the vertical axis, which of the following is true? The optimal consumption bundle is found where

   a. $\dfrac{MU_X}{MU_Y} = \dfrac{P_X}{P_Y}$.

   b. the slope of the indifference curve equals the slope of the budget line.

   c. the indifference curve is tangent to the budget line.

   d. $\dfrac{MU_X}{P_X} = \dfrac{MU_Y}{P_Y}$.

   e. all of the above are true.

Critical-Thinking Questions

Kathleen has $20 to spend on iPod song downloads and DVD rentals each week. The price of an iPod song download is $2 and the price of a DVD rental is $5.

a. Graph Kathleen's budget line.

b. Suppose all of Kathleen's indifference curves have the same shape and slope as the one in the following diagram. How many song downloads and DVD rentals will Kathleen purchase to maximize her utility? Explain.

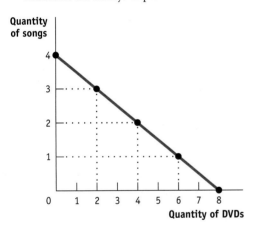

Pornchai Kittiwongsakul/AFP/Getty Images

Module 45
International Trade

In 2005 the average American ate 4.1 pounds of shrimp. Where's all that shrimp coming from? Mainly from Asia and Latin America. Local entrepreneurs have taken advantage of a favorable climate, cheap labor, and large coastal tracts to produce huge quantities of "farmed" shrimp raised in ponds, shipping their catch mainly to Japan and the United States.

Until now, we have analyzed the economy as if it were self-sufficient, as if the economy produces all the goods and services it consumes, and vice versa. This is, of course, true of the world economy as a whole. But it's not true of any individual country. Assuming self-sufficiency would have been far more accurate 40 years ago, when the United States exported only a small fraction of what it produced and imported only a small fraction of what it consumed. Since then, however, both U.S. imports and exports have grown much faster than the U.S. economy as a whole.

This module examines the economics of international trade. We start from the model of comparative advantage, which, as we saw in the module "Comparative Advantage and Trade," explains why there are gains from international trade. Some individuals, like U.S. shrimp producers, can be hurt by international trade. We'll examine the effects of policies, like the tariff on shrimp imports, that countries use to limit imports or promote exports, as well as how governments work together to overcome barriers to trade.

Comparative Advantage and International Trade

The United States buys shrimp—and many other goods and services—from other countries. At the same time, it sells many goods and services to other countries. Goods and services purchased from abroad are **imports;** goods and services sold abroad are **exports.**

Imports and exports have taken on an increasingly important role in the U.S. economy. Over the last 40 years, both imports into and exports from the United States have grown faster than the U.S. economy. Panel (a) of Figure 45.1 shows how the values of U.S. imports and exports have grown as a percentage of gross domestic product (GDP). Panel (b) shows imports and exports as a percentage of GDP for a number of countries. It shows that foreign trade is significantly more important for many other countries than it is for the United States. (Japan is the exception.)

Foreign trade isn't the only way countries interact economically. In the modern world, investors from one country often invest funds in another nation; many companies are multinational, with subsidiaries operating in several countries; and a growing

Goods and services purchased from other countries are **imports;** goods and services sold to other countries are **exports.**

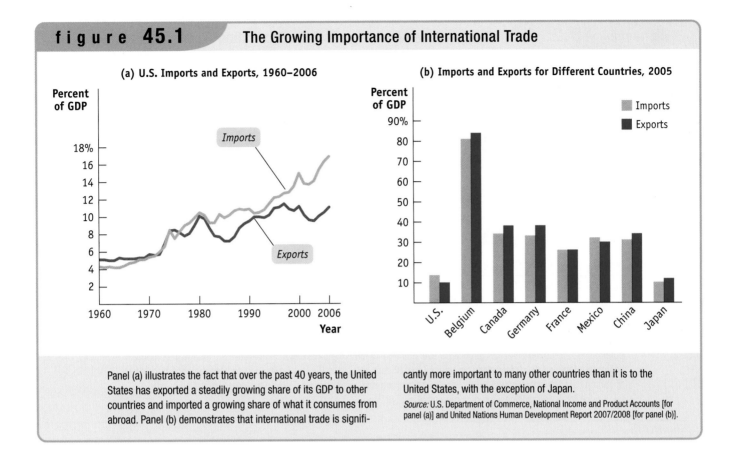

figure 45.1 The Growing Importance of International Trade

(a) U.S. Imports and Exports, 1960–2006

Percent of GDP

Imports
Exports

1960 1970 1980 1990 2000 2006
Year

(b) Imports and Exports for Different Countries, 2005

Percent of GDP

☐ Imports
■ Exports

U.S. Belgium Canada Germany France Mexico China Japan

Panel (a) illustrates the fact that over the past 40 years, the United States has exported a steadily growing share of its GDP to other countries and imported a growing share of what it consumes from abroad. Panel (b) demonstrates that international trade is signifi-cantly more important to many other countries than it is to the United States, with the exception of Japan.

Source: U.S. Department of Commerce, National Income and Product Accounts [for panel (a)] and United Nations Human Development Report 2007/2008 [for panel (b)].

number of individuals work in a country different from the one in which they were born. The growth of all these forms of economic linkages among countries is often called **globalization.**

In this module, however, we'll focus mainly on international trade. To understand why international trade occurs and why economists believe it is beneficial to the economy, we will first review the concept of comparative advantage.

Production Possibilities and Comparative Advantage, Revisited

To produce shrimp, any country must use resources—land, labor, capital, and so on—that could have been used to produce other things. The potential production of other goods a country must forgo to produce a ton of shrimp is the opportunity cost of that ton of shrimp.

It's a lot easier to produce shrimp in Vietnam, where the climate is nearly ideal and there's plenty of coastal land suitable for shellfish farming, than it is in the United States. Conversely, other goods are not produced as easily in Vietnam as in the United States. For example, Vietnam doesn't have the base of skilled workers and technological know-how that makes the United States so good at producing high-technology goods. So the opportunity cost of a ton of shrimp, in terms of other goods such as computers, is much less in Vietnam than it is in the United States.

So we say that Vietnam has a comparative advantage in producing shrimp. Let's repeat the definition of comparative advantage from the module "Comparative Advantage and Trade": *a country has a comparative advantage in producing a good or service if the opportunity cost of producing the good or service is lower for that country than for other countries.*

Figure 45.2 on the next page provides a hypothetical numerical example of comparative advantage in international trade. We assume that only two goods are produced

Globalization is the phenomenon of growing economic linkages among countries.

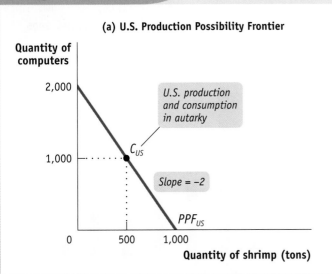

(a) U.S. Production Possibility Frontier

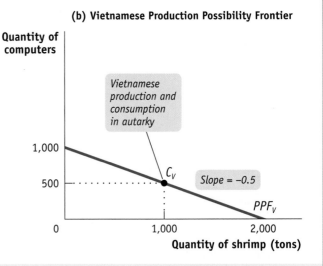

(b) Vietnamese Production Possibility Frontier

The U.S. opportunity cost of each ton of shrimp in terms of computers is 2: 2 computers must be forgone for every additional ton of shrimp produced. The Vietnamese opportunity cost of each ton of shrimp in terms of computers is 0.5: only 0.5 computer must be forgone for every additional ton of shrimp produced. So Vietnam has a comparative advantage in shrimp and the United States has a comparative advantage in computers. In autarky, C_{US} is the U.S. production and consumption bundle and C_V is the Vietnamese production and consumption bundle.

and consumed, shrimp and computers, and that there are only two countries in the world, the United States and Vietnam. The figure shows hypothetical production possibility frontiers for the United States and Vietnam. We simplify the model by assuming that the production possibility frontiers are straight lines. The straight-line shape implies that the opportunity cost of a ton of shrimp in terms of computers in each country is constant—it does not depend on how many units of each good the country produces. The analysis of international trade under the assumption that opportunity costs are constant is known as the **Ricardian model of international trade,** named after the English economist David Ricardo, who introduced this analysis in the early nineteenth century.

Table 45.1 presents the same information shown in Figure 45.2. We assume that the United States can produce 1,000 tons of shrimp if it produces no computers or 2,000 computers if it produces no shrimp. Because we measure shrimp output in tons, the slope of

table **45.1**

Production Possibilities

(a) United States	Production	
	One possibility	Another possibility
Quantity of shrimp (tons)	1,000	0
Quantity of computers	0	2,000
(b) Vietnam	**Production**	
	One possibility	Another possibility
Quantity of shrimp (tons)	2,000	0
Quantity of computers	0	1,000

The **Ricardian model of international trade** analyzes international trade under the assumption that opportunity costs are constant.

the production possibility frontier in panel (a) is −2,000/1,000, or −2: to produce an additional ton of shrimp, the United States must forgo the production of 2 computers.

Similarly, we assume that Vietnam can produce 2,000 tons of shrimp if it produces no computers or 1,000 computers if it produces no shrimp. The slope of the production possibility frontier in panel (b) is −1,000/2,000, or −0.5: to produce an additional ton of shrimp, Vietnam must forgo the production of 0.5 computer.

Economists use the term **autarky** to describe a situation in which a country does not trade with other countries. We assume that in autarky the United States would choose to produce and consume 500 tons of shrimp and 1,000 computers. This autarky production and consumption bundle is shown by point C_{US} in panel (a) of Figure 45.2. We also assume that in autarky Vietnam would choose to produce and consume 1,000 tons of shrimp and 500 computers, shown by point C_V in panel (b). The outcome in autarky is summarized in Table 45.2, where world production and consumption is the sum of U.S. and Vietnamese production and consumption.

Autarky is a situation in which a country does not trade with other countries.

table 45.2

Production and Consumption Under Autarky

(a) United States	Production	Consumption
Quantity of shrimp (tons)	500	500
Quantity of computers	1,000	1,000
(b) Vietnam	**Production**	**Consumption**
Quantity of shrimp (tons)	1,000	1,000
Quantity of computers	500	500
(c) World (United States and Vietnam)	**Production**	**Consumption**
Quantity of shrimp (tons)	1,500	1,500
Quantity of computers	1,500	1,500

If the countries trade with each other, they can do better than they can in autarky. In this example, Vietnam has a comparative advantage in the production of shrimp. That is, the opportunity cost of shrimp is lower in Vietnam than in the United States: 0.5 computer per ton of shrimp in Vietnam versus 2 computers per ton of shrimp in the United States. Conversely, the United States has a comparative advantage in the production of computers: to produce an additional computer, the United States must forgo the production of 0.5 ton of shrimp, but producing an additional computer in Vietnam requires forgoing the production of 2 tons of shrimp. International trade allows each country to specialize in producing the good in which it has a comparative advantage: computers in the United States, shrimp in Vietnam. As a result, each country is able to obtain the good in which it doesn't have a comparative advantage at a lower opportunity cost than if it produced the good itself. And that leads to gains for both when they trade.

The Gains from International Trade

Figure 45.3 on the next page illustrates how both countries gain from specialization and trade. Again, panel (a) represents the United States and panel (b) represents Vietnam. As a result of international trade, the United States produces at point Q_{US}: 2,000 computers but no shrimp. Vietnam produces at Q_V: 2,000 tons of shrimp but no computers. The new production choices are given in the second column of Table 45.3 on the next page.

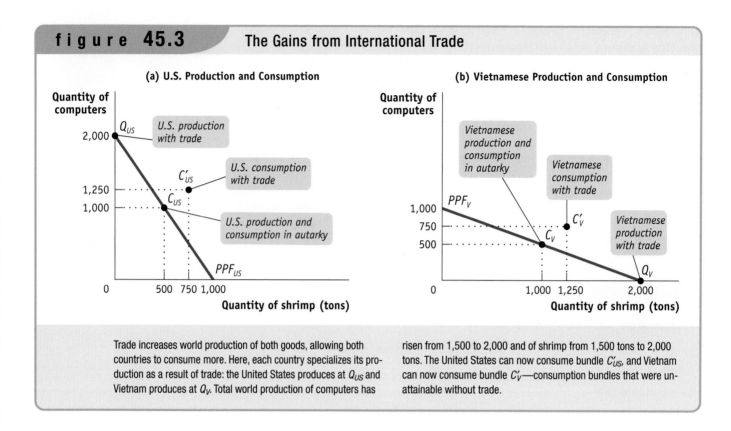

figure 45.3   The Gains from International Trade

(a) U.S. Production and Consumption

Quantity of computers

- Q_{US} — U.S. production with trade (2,000)
- C'_{US} — U.S. consumption with trade (1,250)
- C_{US} — U.S. production and consumption in autarky (1,000)
- PPF_{US}

Quantity of shrimp (tons): 500, 750, 1,000

(b) Vietnamese Production and Consumption

Quantity of computers

- PPF_V (1,000)
- C_V — Vietnamese production and consumption in autarky (500)
- C'_V — Vietnamese consumption with trade (750)
- Q_V — Vietnamese production with trade (2,000)

Quantity of shrimp (tons): 1,000, 1,250, 2,000

Trade increases world production of both goods, allowing both countries to consume more. Here, each country specializes its production as a result of trade: the United States produces at Q_{US} and Vietnam produces at Q_V. Total world production of computers has risen from 1,500 to 2,000 and of shrimp from 1,500 tons to 2,000 tons. The United States can now consume bundle C'_{US}, and Vietnam can now consume bundle C'_V—consumption bundles that were unattainable without trade.

By comparing Table 45.3 with Table 45.2, you can see that specialization increases total world production of *both* goods. In the absence of specialization, total world production consists of 1,500 computers and 1,500 tons of shrimp. After specialization, total world production rises to 2,000 computers and 2,000 tons of shrimp. These goods can now be traded, with the United States consuming shrimp produced in Vietnam and Vietnam consuming computers produced in the United States. The result is that each country can consume more of *both* goods than it did in autarky.

In addition to showing production under trade, Figure 45.3 shows one of many possible pairs of consumption bundles for the United States and Vietnam, which is also given in Table 45.3. In this example, the United States moves from its autarky consumption of 1,000 computers and 500 tons of shrimp, shown by C_{US}, to consump-

table 45.3

Production and Consumption After Specialization and Trade

(a) United States	Production	Consumption
Quantity of shrimp (tons)	500	750
Quantity of computers	2,000	1,250
(b) Vietnam	**Production**	**Consumption**
Quantity of shrimp (tons)	2,000	1,250
Quantity of computers	0	750
(c) World (United States and Vietnam)	**Production**	**Consumption**
Quantity of shrimp (tons)	2,000	2,000
Quantity of computers	2,000	2,000

tion after trade of 1,250 computers and 750 tons of shrimp, represented by C'_{US}. Vietnam moves from its autarky consumption of 500 computers and 1,000 tons of shrimp, shown by C_V, to consumption after trade of 750 computers and 1,250 tons of shrimp, shown by C'_V.

What makes this possible is the fact that with international trade countries are no longer required to consume the same bundle of goods they produce. Each country produces at one point (Q_{US} for the United States, Q_V for Vietnam) but consumes at a different point (C'_{US} for the United States, C'_V for Vietnam). The difference reflects imports and exports: the 750 tons of shrimp the United States consumes are imported from Vietnam; the 750 computers Vietnam consumes are imported from the United States.

In this example we have simply assumed the post-trade consumption bundles of the two countries. In fact, the consumption choices of a country reflect both the preferences of its residents and the *relative prices*—the prices of one good in terms of another—in international markets. Although we have not explicitly given the price of computers in terms of shrimp, that price is implicit in our example: Vietnam exports 750 tons of shrimp and receives 750 computers in return, so 1 ton of shrimp is traded for 1 computer. This tells us that the price of a computer on world markets must be equal to the price of 1 ton of shrimp in our example.

One requirement that the relative price must satisfy is that no country pays a relative price greater than its opportunity cost of obtaining the good in autarky. That is, the United States won't pay more than 2 computers for 1 ton of shrimp from Vietnam, and Vietnam won't pay more than 2 tons of shrimp for 1 computer from the United States. Once this requirement is satisfied, the actual relative price in international trade is determined by supply and demand—and we'll turn to supply and demand in international trade later in this module. However, first let's look more deeply into the nature of the gains from trade.

Comparative Advantage versus Absolute Advantage

It's easy to accept the idea that Vietnam has a comparative advantage in shrimp production: it has a tropical climate that's better suited to shrimp farming than that of the United States (even along the Gulf Coast), and it has a lot of usable coastal area. In other cases, however, it may be harder to understand why we import certain goods from abroad.

Consider, for example, U.S. trade with Bangladesh. We import a lot of clothing from Bangladesh—shirts, trousers, and so on. Yet there's nothing about the climate or resources of Bangladesh that makes it especially good at sewing shirts. In fact, it takes *fewer* hours of labor to produce a shirt in the United States than in Bangladesh.

Why, then, do we buy Bangladeshi shirts? Because the gains from trade depend on *comparative advantage,* not *absolute advantage.* Yes, it takes less labor to produce a shirt in the United States than in Bangladesh. That is, the productivity of Bangladeshi shirt workers is less than that of their U.S. counterparts. But what determines comparative advantage is not the amount of resources used to produce a good but the opportunity cost of that good—here, the quantity of other goods forgone in order to produce a shirt. And the opportunity cost of a shirt is lower in Bangladesh than in the United States.

Here's how it works: Bangladeshi workers have low productivity compared with U.S. workers in the shirt industry. But Bangladeshi workers have even lower productivity compared with U.S. workers in other industries. Because Bangladeshi labor productivity in industries other than shirt-making is very low, producing a shirt in Bangladesh, even though it takes a lot of labor, does not require forgoing the production of large quantities of other goods. In the United States, the opposite is true: very high productivity in other industries (such as high-technology goods) means that producing a shirt in the United States, even though it doesn't require much labor, requires sacrificing lots of other goods. So the opportunity cost of producing a shirt is less in Bangladesh than in the United States. Despite its lower labor productivity, Bangladesh has a comparative advantage in clothing production, although the United States has an absolute advantage.

Bangladesh's comparative advantage in clothing gets translated into an actual advantage on world markets through its wage rates. A country's wage rates, in general, reflect its labor productivity. In countries where labor is highly productive in many industries, employers are willing to pay high wages to attract workers, so competition among employers leads to an overall high wage rate. In countries where labor is less productive, competition for workers is less intense and wage rates are correspondingly lower.

There is a strong relationship between overall levels of productivity and wage rates around the world. Because Bangladesh has generally low productivity, it has a relatively low wage rate. Low wages, in turn, give Bangladesh a cost advantage in producing goods where its productivity is only moderately low, like shirts. As a result, it's cheaper to produce shirts in Bangladesh than in the United States.

The kind of trade that takes place between low-wage, low-productivity economies like Bangladesh and high-wage, high-productivity economies like the United States gives rise to two common misperceptions. One, the *pauper labor fallacy,* is the belief that when a country with high wages imports goods produced by workers who are paid low wages, this must hurt the standard of living of workers in the importing country. The other, the *sweatshop labor fallacy,* is the belief that trade must be bad for workers in poor exporting countries because those workers are paid very low wages by our standards. Both fallacies miss the nature of gains from trade: it's to the advantage of *both* countries if the poorer, lower-wage country exports goods in which it has a comparative advantage, even if its cost advantage in these goods depends on low wages. That is, both countries are able to achieve a higher standard of living through trade.

It's particularly important to understand that buying a shirt made by someone who makes only 30 cents an hour doesn't necessarily imply that you're taking advantage of that person. It depends on the alternatives. Because workers in poor countries have low productivity across the board, they are offered low wages whether they produce goods exported to America or goods sold in local markets. A job that looks terrible by rich-country standards can be a step up for someone in a poor country. And international trade that depends on low-wage exports can nonetheless raise a country's standard of living. Bangladesh, in particular, would be much poorer than it is—possibly its citizens would even be starving—if it weren't able to export clothing based on its low wage rates.

Sources of Comparative Advantage

International trade is driven by comparative advantage, but where does comparative advantage come from? Economists who study international trade have found three main sources of comparative advantage: international differences in *climate,* international differences in *factor endowments,* and international differences in *technology.*

Differences in Climate A key reason the opportunity cost of producing shrimp in Vietnam is less than in the United States is that shrimp need warm water—Vietnam has plenty of that, but America doesn't. In general, differences in climate play a significant role in international trade. Tropical countries export tropical products like coffee, sugar, bananas, and, these days, shrimp. Countries in the temperate zones export crops like wheat and corn. Some trade is even driven by the difference in seasons between the northern and southern hemispheres: winter deliveries of Chilean grapes and New Zealand apples have become commonplace in U.S. and European supermarkets.

Differences in Factor Endowments Canada is a major exporter of forest products—lumber and products derived from lumber, like pulp and paper—to the United States. These exports don't reflect the special skill of Canadian lumberjacks. Canada has a comparative advantage in forest products because its forested area is much greater compared to the size of its labor force than the ratio of forestland to the labor force in the United States.

Forestland, like labor and capital, is a *factor of production:* an input used to produce goods and services. (Recall that the factors of production are land, labor, capital, and entrepreneurship.) Due to history and geography, the mix of available factors of production differs among countries, providing an important source of comparative advantage. The relationship between comparative advantage and factor availability is found in an influential model of international trade, the *Heckscher–Ohlin model,* developed by two Swedish economists in the first half of the twentieth century.

A key concept in the model is *factor intensity.* Producers use different ratios of factors of production in the production of different goods. For example, oil refineries use much more capital per worker than clothing factories. Economists use the term **factor intensity** to describe this difference among goods: oil refining is capital-intensive, because it tends to use a high ratio of capital to labor, but clothing manufacture is labor-intensive, because it tends to use a high ratio of labor to capital.

According to the **Heckscher–Ohlin model,** *a country will have a comparative advantage in a good whose production is intensive in the factors that are abundantly available in that country compared to other countries.* So a country that has a relative abundance of capital will have a comparative advantage in capital-intensive industries such as oil refining, but a country that has a relative abundance of labor will have a comparative advantage in labor-intensive industries such as clothing production. The basic intuition behind this result is simple and based on opportunity cost. The opportunity cost of a given factor—the value that the factor would generate in alternative uses—is low for a country when it is relatively abundant in that factor. (For example, in rainy parts of the United States, the opportunity cost of water for residences is low because there is a plentiful supply for other uses, such as agriculture.) So the opportunity cost of producing goods that are intensive in the use of an abundantly available factor is also low.

The most dramatic example of the validity of the Heckscher-Ohlin model is world trade in clothing. Clothing production is a labor-intensive activity: it doesn't take much physical capital, nor does it require a lot of human capital in the form of highly educated workers. So you would expect labor-abundant countries such as China and Bangladesh to have a comparative advantage in clothing production. And they do.

That much international trade is the result of differences in factor endowments helps explain another fact: international specialization of production is often *incomplete.* That is, a country often maintains some domestic production of a good that it imports. A good example of this is the United States and oil. Saudi Arabia exports oil to the United States because Saudi Arabia has an abundant supply of oil relative to its other factors of production; the United States exports medical devices to Saudi Arabia because it has an abundant supply of expertise in medical technology relative to its other factors of production. But the United States also produces some oil domestically because the size of its domestic oil reserves makes it economical to do so. In our upcoming demand and supply analysis, we'll consider incomplete specialization by a country to be the norm. We should emphasize, however, that the fact that countries often incompletely specialize does not in any way change the conclusion that there are gains from trade.

Differences in Technology In the 1970s and 1980s, Japan became by far the world's largest exporter of automobiles, selling large numbers to the United States and the rest of the world. Japan's comparative advantage in automobiles wasn't the result of climate. Nor can it easily be attributed to differences in factor endowments: aside from a scarcity of land, Japan's mix of available factors is quite similar to that in other

The **factor intensity** of production of a good is a measure of which factor is used in relatively greater quantities than other factors in production.

According to the **Heckscher–Ohlin model,** a country has a comparative advantage in a good whose production is intensive in the factors that are abundantly available in that country.

Skill and Comparative Advantage

In 1953 U.S. workers were clearly better equipped with machinery than their counterparts in other countries. Most economists at the time thought that America's comparative advantage lay in capital-intensive goods. But Wassily Leontief made a surprising discovery: America's comparative advantage was something other than capital-intensive goods. In fact, goods that the United States exported were slightly less capital-intensive than goods the country imported. This discovery came to be known as the Leontief paradox, and it led to a sustained effort to make sense of U.S. trade patterns.

The main resolution of this paradox, it turns out, depends on the definition of *capital*. U.S. exports aren't intensive in *physical* capital—machines and buildings. Instead, they are *skill-intensive*—that is, they are intensive in *human* capital. U.S. exporting industries use a substantially higher ratio of highly educated workers to other workers than is found in U.S. industries that compete against imports. For example, one of America's biggest export sectors is aircraft; the aircraft industry employs large numbers of engineers and other people with graduate degrees relative to the number of manual laborers. Conversely, we import a lot of clothing, which is often produced by workers with little formal education.

In general, countries with highly educated workforces tend to export skill-intensive goods, while countries with less educated workforces tend to export goods whose production requires little skilled labor. The accompanying figure illustrates this point by comparing the goods the United States imports from Germany, a country with a highly educated labor force, to the goods the United States imports from Bangladesh, where about half of the adult population is still illiterate. In each country industries are ranked, first, according to how skill-intensive they are. Next, for each industry, we calculate its share of exports to the United States. This allows us to plot, for each country, various industries according to their skill intensity and their share of exports to the United States.

In the figure the horizontal axis shows a measure of the skill intensity of different industries, and the vertical axes show the share of U.S. imports in each industry coming from Germany (on the left) and Bangladesh (on the right). As you can see, each country's exports to the United States reflect its skill level. The curve representing Germany slopes upward: the more skill-intensive a German industry is, the higher its share of exports to the United States. In contrast, the curve representing Bangladesh slopes downward: the less skill-intensive a Bangladeshi industry is, the higher its share of exports to the United States.

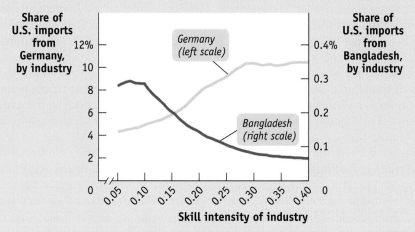

Source: John Romalis, "Factor Proportions and the Structure of Commodity Trade," *American Economic Review,* Vol. 94, No. 1, 2004.

advanced countries. Instead, Japan's comparative advantage in automobiles was based on the superior production techniques developed by that country's manufacturers, which allowed them to produce more cars with a given amount of labor and capital than their American or European counterparts.

Japan's comparative advantage in automobiles was a case of comparative advantage caused by differences in technology—the techniques used in production.

The causes of differences in technology are somewhat mysterious. Sometimes they seem to be based on knowledge accumulated through experience—for example, Switzerland's comparative advantage in watches reflects a long tradition of watchmaking. Sometimes they are the result of a set of innovations that for some reason occur in one country but not in others. Technological advantage, however, is often transitory. American auto manufacturers have now closed much of the gap in productivity with their Japanese competitors; Europe's aircraft industry has closed a similar gap with the U.S. aircraft industry. At any given point in time, however, differences in technology are a major source of comparative advantage.

Supply, Demand, and International Trade

Simple models of comparative advantage are helpful for understanding the fundamental causes of international trade. However, to analyze the effects of international trade at a more detailed level and to understand trade policy, it helps to return to the supply and demand model. We'll start by looking at the effects of imports on domestic producers and consumers, then turn to the effect of exports.

The Effects of Imports

Figure 45.4 shows the U.S. market for shrimp, ignoring international trade for a moment. It introduces a few new concepts: the *domestic demand curve;* the *domestic supply curve;* and the domestic, or autarky, price.

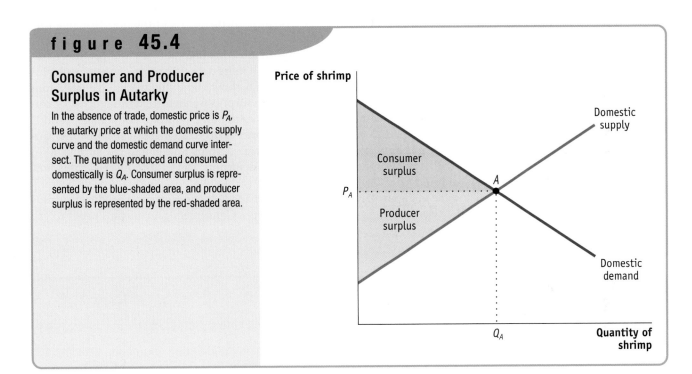

figure 45.4

Consumer and Producer Surplus in Autarky

In the absence of trade, domestic price is P_A, the autarky price at which the domestic supply curve and the domestic demand curve intersect. The quantity produced and consumed domestically is Q_A. Consumer surplus is represented by the blue-shaded area, and producer surplus is represented by the red-shaded area.

The **domestic demand curve** shows how the quantity of a good demanded by residents of a country depends on the price of that good. Why "domestic"? Because people living in other countries may demand the good, too. Once we introduce international trade, we need to distinguish between purchases of a good by domestic consumers and purchases by foreign consumers. So the domestic demand curve reflects only the demand of residents of our own country. Similarly, the **domestic supply curve** shows how the quantity of a good supplied by producers inside our own country depends on the price of that good. Once we introduce international trade, we need to distinguish between the supply of domestic producers and foreign supply—supply brought in from abroad.

In autarky, with no international trade in shrimp, the equilibrium in this market would be determined by the intersection of the domestic demand and domestic supply curves, point A. The equilibrium price of shrimp would be P_A, and the equilibrium quantity of shrimp produced and consumed would be Q_A. As always, both consumers and producers gain from the existence of the domestic market. In autarky, consumer surplus would be equal to the area of the blue-shaded triangle in Figure 45.4. Producer surplus would be equal to the area of the red-shaded triangle. And total surplus would be equal to the sum of these two shaded triangles.

The **domestic demand curve** shows how the quantity of a good demanded by domestic consumers depends on the price of that good.

The **domestic supply curve** shows how the quantity of a good supplied by domestic producers depends on the price of that good.

Now let's imagine opening up this market to imports. To do this, we must make an assumption about the supply of imports. The simplest assumption, which we will adopt here, is that unlimited quantities of shrimp can be purchased from abroad at a fixed price, known as the **world price** of shrimp. Figure 45.5 shows a situation in which the world price of shrimp, P_W, is lower than the price of shrimp that would prevail in the domestic market in autarky, P_A.

Given that the world price is below the domestic price of shrimp, it is profitable for importers to buy shrimp abroad and resell it domestically. The imported shrimp increases the supply of shrimp in the domestic market, driving down the domestic market price. Shrimp will continue to be imported until the domestic price falls to a level equal to the world price.

The result is shown in Figure 45.5. Because of imports, the domestic price of shrimp falls from P_A to P_W. The quantity of shrimp demanded by domestic consumers rises from Q_A to Q_D, and the quantity supplied by domestic producers falls from Q_A to Q_S. The difference between the domestic quantity demanded and the domestic quantity supplied, $Q_D - Q_S$, is filled by imports.

Now let's turn to the effects of imports on consumer surplus and producer surplus. Because imports of shrimp lead to a fall in its domestic price, consumer surplus rises and producer surplus falls. Figure 45.6 shows how this works. We label four areas: W, X, Y, and Z. The autarky consumer surplus we identified in Figure 45.4 corresponds to W, and the autarky producer surplus corresponds to the sum of X and Y. The fall in the domestic price to the world price leads to an increase in consumer surplus; it increases by X and Z, so that consumer surplus now equals the sum of W, X, and Z. At the same time, producers lose X in surplus, so that producer surplus now equals only Y.

The table in Figure 45.6 summarizes the changes in consumer and producer surplus when the shrimp market is opened to imports. Consumers gain surplus equal to the

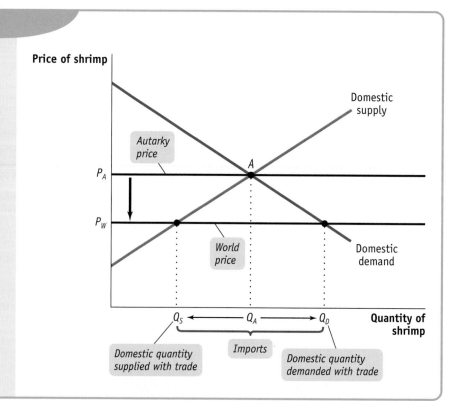

figure 45.5

The Domestic Market with Imports

Here the world price of shrimp, P_W, is below the autarky price, P_A. When the economy is opened to international trade, imports enter the domestic market, and the domestic price falls from the autarky price, P_A, to the world price, P_W. As the price falls, the domestic quantity demanded rises from Q_A to Q_D and the domestic quantity supplied falls from Q_A to Q_S. The difference between domestic quantity demanded and domestic quantity supplied at P_W, the quantity $Q_D - Q_S$, is filled by imports.

figure 45.6 — The Effects of Imports on Surplus

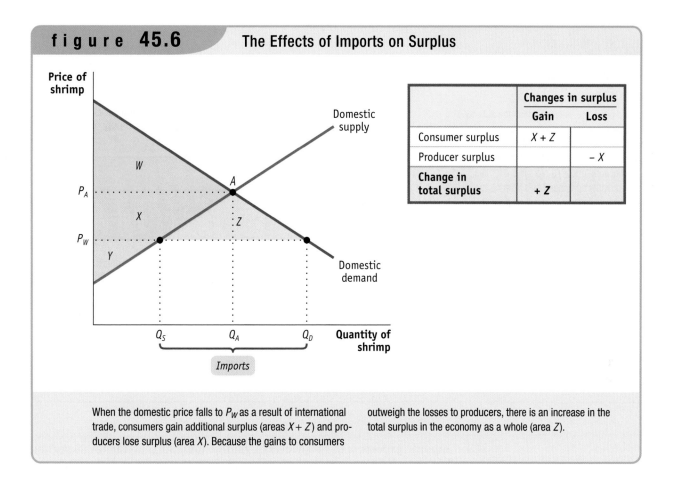

	Changes in surplus	
	Gain	**Loss**
Consumer surplus	$X + Z$	
Producer surplus		$- X$
Change in total surplus	**+ Z**	

When the domestic price falls to P_W as a result of international trade, consumers gain additional surplus (areas $X + Z$) and producers lose surplus (area X). Because the gains to consumers outweigh the losses to producers, there is an increase in the total surplus in the economy as a whole (area Z).

areas $X + Z$. Producers lose surplus equal to X. So the sum of producer and consumer surplus—the total surplus generated in the shrimp market—increases by Z. As a result of trade, consumers gain and producers lose, but the gain to consumers exceeds the loss to producers.

This is an important result. We have just shown that opening up a market to imports leads to a net gain in total surplus, which is what we should have expected given the proposition that there are gains from international trade. However, we have also learned that although the country as a whole gains, some groups—in this case, domestic shrimp producers—lose as a result of international trade. As we'll see shortly, the fact that international trade typically creates losers as well as winners is crucial for understanding the politics of trade policy.

We turn next to the case in which a country exports a good.

The Effects of Exports

Figure 45.7 on the next page shows the effects on a country when it exports a good, in this case computers. For this example, we assume that unlimited quantities of computers can be sold abroad at a given world price, P_W, which is higher than the price that would prevail in the domestic market in autarky, P_A.

The higher world price makes it profitable for exporters to buy computers domestically and sell them overseas. The purchases of domestic computers drive the domestic price up until it is equal to the world price. As a result, the quantity demanded by domestic consumers falls from Q_A to Q_D and the quantity supplied by domestic producers rises from Q_A to Q_S. This difference between domestic production and domestic consumption, $Q_S - Q_D$, is exported.

figure 45.7

The Domestic Market with Exports

Here the world price, P_W, is greater than the autarky price, P_A. When the economy is opened to international trade, some of the domestic supply is now exported. The domestic price rises from the autarky price, P_A, to the world price, P_W. As the price rises, the domestic quantity demanded falls from Q_A to Q_D and the domestic quantity supplied rises from Q_A to Q_S. The portion of domestic production that is not consumed domestically, $Q_S - Q_D$, is exported.

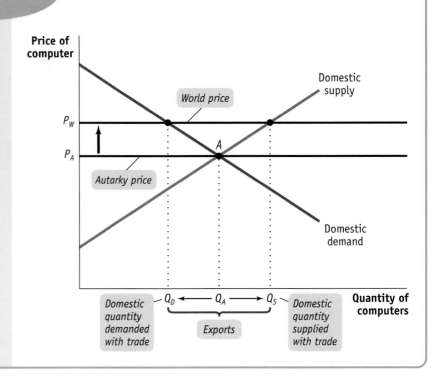

Like imports, exports lead to an overall gain in total surplus for the exporting country but also create losers as well as winners. Figure 45.8 shows the effects of computer exports on producer and consumer surplus. In the absence of trade, the price of computers would be P_A. Consumer surplus in the absence of trade is the sum of areas W and X, and producer surplus is area Y. As a result of trade, price rises from P_A to P_W, consumer surplus falls to W, and producer surplus rises to $Y + X + Z$. So producers gain $X + Z$, consumers lose X, and, as shown in the table accompanying the figure, the economy as a whole gains total surplus in the amount of Z.

We have learned, then, that imports of a particular good hurt domestic producers of that good but help domestic consumers, whereas exports of a particular good hurt domestic consumers but help domestic producers of that good. In each case, the gains are larger than the losses.

International Trade and Wages

So far we have focused on the effects of international trade on producers and consumers in a particular industry. For many purposes this is a very helpful approach. However, producers and consumers are not the only parts of society affected by trade—so are the owners of factors of production. In particular, the owners of labor, land, and capital employed in producing goods that are exported, or goods that compete with imported goods, can be deeply affected by trade. Moreover, the effects of trade aren't limited to just those industries that export or compete with imports because *factors of production can often move between industries*. So now we turn our attention to the long-run effects of international trade on income distribution—how a country's total income is allocated among its various factors of production.

To begin our analysis, consider the position of Maria, an accountant who currently works for the Crazy Cajun Shrimp Company, based in Louisiana. If the economy is opened up to imports of shrimp from Vietnam, the domestic shrimp industry will contract, and it will hire fewer accountants. But accounting is a profession with

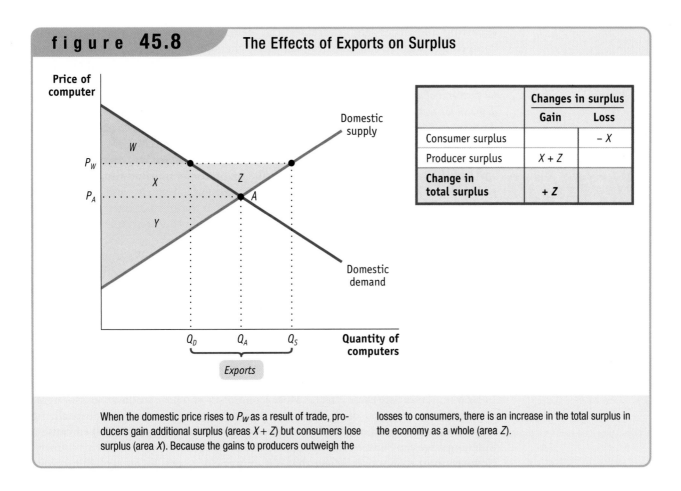

figure 45.8 The Effects of Exports on Surplus

	Changes in surplus	
	Gain	Loss
Consumer surplus		– X
Producer surplus	X + Z	
Change in total surplus	**+ Z**	

When the domestic price rises to P_W as a result of trade, producers gain additional surplus (areas $X + Z$) but consumers lose surplus (area X). Because the gains to producers outweigh the losses to consumers, there is an increase in the total surplus in the economy as a whole (area Z).

employment opportunities in many industries, and Maria might well find a better job in the computer industry, which expands as a result of international trade. So it may not be appropriate to think of her as a producer of shrimp who is hurt by competition from imported shrimp. Rather, we should think of her as an accountant who is affected by shrimp imports only to the extent that these imports change the wages of accountants in the economy as a whole.

The wage rate of accountants is a *factor price*—the price employers have to pay for the services of a factor of production. One key question about international trade is how it affects factor prices—not just narrowly defined factors of production like accountants, but broadly defined factors such as capital, unskilled labor, and college-educated labor.

Earlier in this chapter we described the Heckscher–Ohlin model of trade, which states that comparative advantage is determined by a country's factor endowment. This model also suggests how international trade affects factor prices in a country: compared to autarky, international trade tends to raise the prices of factors that are abundantly available and reduce the prices of factors that are scarce.

We won't work this out in detail, but the idea is intuitively simple. The prices of factors of production, like the prices of goods and services, are determined by supply and demand. If international trade increases the demand for a factor of production, that factor's price will rise; if international trade reduces the demand for a factor of production, that factor's price will fall. Now think of a country's industries as consisting of two kinds: **exporting industries,** which produce goods and services that are sold abroad, and **import-competing industries,** which produce goods and services that are also imported from abroad. Compared with autarky, international trade leads to higher production in exporting industries and lower production in import-competing industries. This indirectly increases the demand for the factors used by

Exporting industries produce goods and services that are sold abroad.

Import-competing industries produce goods and services that are also imported.

exporting industries and decreases the demand for factors used by import-competing industries. In addition, the Heckscher–Ohlin model says that a country tends to export goods that are intensive in its abundant factors and to import goods that are intensive in its scarce factors. So *international trade tends to increase the demand for factors that are abundant in our country compared with other countries, and to decrease the demand for factors that are scarce in our country compared with other countries.* As a result, *the prices of abundant factors tend to rise, and the prices of scarce factors tend to fall as international trade grows.* In other words, international trade tends to redistribute income toward a country's abundant factors and away from its less abundant factors.

The IRL at the end of the preceding discussion on comparative advantage and trade pointed out that U.S. exports tend to be human-capital-intensive and U.S. imports tend to be unskilled-labor-intensive. This suggests that the effect of international trade on U.S. factor markets is to raise the wage rate of highly educated American workers and reduce the wage rate of unskilled American workers.

This effect has been a source of much concern in recent years. Wage inequality—the gap between the wages of high-paid and low-paid workers—has increased substantially over the last 25 years. Some economists believe that growing international trade is an important factor in that trend. If international trade has the effects predicted by the Heckscher–Ohlin model, its growth raises the wages of highly educated American workers, who already have relatively high wages, and lowers the wages of less educated American workers, who already have relatively low wages. But keep in mind another phenomenon: trade reduces the income inequality *between* countries as poor countries improve their standard of living by exporting to rich countries.

How important are these effects? Most economists who have studied the issue agree that growing imports of labor-intensive products from newly industrializing economies, and the export of high-technology goods in return, have helped cause a widening wage gap between highly educated and less educated workers in this country. However, most economists believe that it is only one of several forces explaining growing wage inequality.

The Effects of Trade Protection

Ever since David Ricardo laid out the principle of comparative advantage in the early nineteenth century, most economists have advocated **free trade.** That is, they have argued that government policy should not attempt either to reduce or to increase the levels of exports and imports that occur naturally as a result of supply and demand. Despite the free-trade arguments of economists, however, many governments use taxes and other restrictions to limit imports. Much less frequently, governments offer subsidies to encourage exports. Policies that limit imports, usually with the goal of protecting domestic producers in import-competing industries from foreign competition, are known as **trade protection** or simply as **protection.**

Let's look at the two most common protectionist policies, *tariffs* and *import quotas,* then turn to the reasons governments follow these policies.

The Effects of a Tariff

A **tariff** is a form of excise tax, one that is levied only on sales of imported goods. For example, the U.S. government could declare that anyone bringing in shrimp from Vietnam must pay a tariff of $1,000 per ton. In the distant past, tariffs were an important source of government revenue because they were relatively easy to collect. But in the modern world, tariffs are usually intended to discourage imports and protect import-competing domestic producers rather than as a source of government revenue.

The tariff raises both the price received by domestic producers and the price paid by domestic consumers. Suppose, for example, that our country imports shrimp, and a ton of shrimp costs $2,000 on the world market. As we saw earlier, under free trade

An economy has **free trade** when the government does not attempt either to reduce or to increase the levels of exports and imports that occur naturally as a result of supply and demand.

Policies that limit imports are known as **trade protection** or simply as **protection.**

A **tariff** is a tax levied on imports.

the domestic price would also be $2,000. But if a tariff of $1,000 per ton is imposed, the domestic price will rise to $3,000, because it won't be profitable to import shrimp unless the price in the domestic market is high enough to compensate importers for the cost of paying the tariff.

Figure 45.9 illustrates the effects of a tariff on shrimp imports. As before, we assume that P_W is the world price of shrimp. Before the tariff is imposed, imports have driven the domestic price down to P_W, so that pre-tariff domestic production is Q_S, pre-tariff domestic consumption is Q_D, and pre-tariff imports are $Q_D - Q_S$.

figure 45.9

The Effect of a Tariff

A tariff raises the domestic price of the good from P_W to P_T. The domestic quantity demanded shrinks from Q_D to Q_{DT}, and the domestic quantity supplied increases from Q_S to Q_{ST}. As a result, imports—which had been $Q_D - Q_S$ before the tariff was imposed—shrink to $Q_{DT} - Q_{ST}$ after the tariff is imposed.

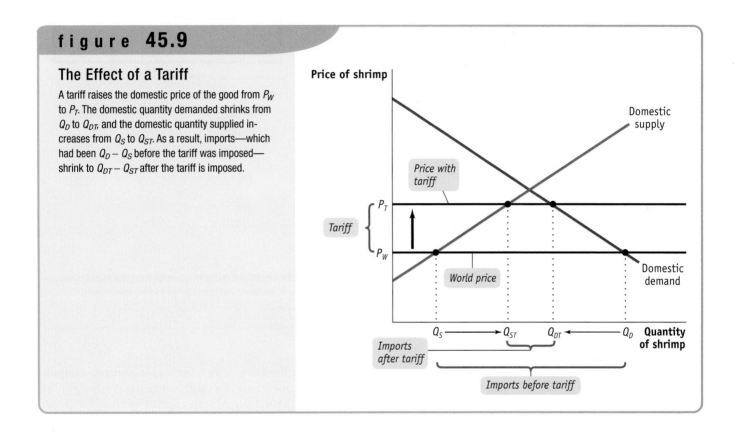

Now suppose that the government imposes a tariff on each ton of shrimp imported. As a consequence, it is no longer profitable to import shrimp unless the domestic price received by the importer is greater than or equal to the world price *plus* the tariff. So the domestic price rises to P_T, which is equal to the world price, P_W, plus the tariff. Domestic production rises to Q_{ST}, domestic consumption falls to Q_{DT}, and imports fall to $Q_{DT} - Q_{ST}$.

A tariff, then, raises domestic prices, leading to increased domestic production and reduced domestic consumption compared to the situation under free trade. Figure 45.10 on the next page shows the effects on surplus. There are three effects. First, the higher domestic price increases producer surplus, a gain equal to area *A*. Second, the higher domestic price reduces consumer surplus, a reduction equal to the sum of areas *A*, *B*, *C*, and *D*. Finally, the tariff yields revenue to the government. How much revenue? The government collects the tariff—which, remember, is equal to the difference between P_T and P_W on each of the $Q_{DT} - Q_{ST}$ tons of shrimp imported. So total revenue is $(P_T - P_W) \times (Q_{DT} - Q_{ST})$. This is equal to area *C*.

The welfare effects of a tariff are summarized in the table in Figure 45.10. Producers gain, consumers lose, and the government gains. But consumer losses are greater than the sum of producer and government gains, leading to a net reduction in total surplus equal to areas *B* + *D*.

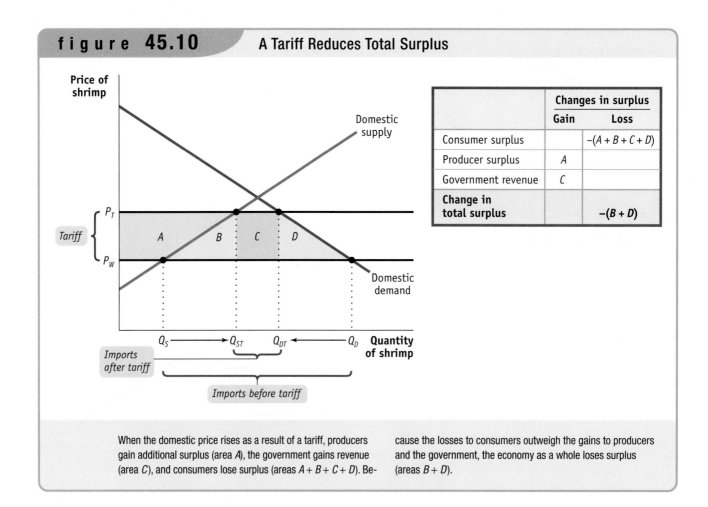

	Changes in surplus	
	Gain	**Loss**
Consumer surplus		$-(A + B + C + D)$
Producer surplus	A	
Government revenue	C	
Change in total surplus		$-(B + D)$

When the domestic price rises as a result of a tariff, producers gain additional surplus (area *A*), the government gains revenue (area *C*), and consumers lose surplus (areas *A* + *B* + *C* + *D*). Be- cause the losses to consumers outweigh the gains to producers and the government, the economy as a whole loses surplus (areas *B* + *D*).

An excise tax creates inefficiency, or deadweight loss, because it prevents mutually beneficial trades from occurring. The same is true of a tariff, where the deadweight loss imposed on society is equal to the loss in total surplus represented by areas $B + D$. Tariffs generate deadweight losses because they create inefficiencies in two ways. First, some mutually beneficial trades go unexploited: some consumers who are willing to pay more than the world price, P_W, do not purchase the good, even though P_W is the true cost of a unit of the good to the economy. The cost of this inefficiency is represented in Figure 45.10 by area D. Second, the economy's resources are wasted on inefficient production: some producers whose cost exceeds P_W produce the good, even though an additional unit of the good can be purchased abroad for P_W. The cost of this inefficiency is represented in Figure 45.10 by area B.

The Effects of an Import Quota

An **import quota,** another form of trade protection, is a legal limit on the quantity of a good that can be imported. For example, a U.S. import quota on Vietnamese shrimp might limit the quantity imported each year to 3 million tons. Import quotas are usually administered through licenses: a number of licenses are issued, each giving the license-holder the right to import a limited quantity of the good each year.

A quota on sales has the same effect as an excise tax, with one difference: the money that would otherwise have accrued to the government as tax revenue under an excise tax becomes license-holders' revenue under a quota—also known as quota rents. Similarly, an import quota has the same effect as a tariff, with one difference: the money that would otherwise have been government revenue becomes quota rents to license-holders. Look again at Figure 45.10. An import quota that limits imports to $Q_{DT} - Q_{ST}$

An **import quota** is a legal limit on the quantity of a good that can be imported.

will raise the domestic price of shrimp by the same amount as the tariff we considered previously. That is, it will raise the domestic price from P_W to P_T. However, area C will now represent quota rents rather than government revenue.

Who receives import licenses and so collects the quota rents? In the case of U.S. import protection, the answer may surprise you: the most important import licenses—mainly for clothing, to a lesser extent for sugar—are granted to foreign governments.

Because the quota rents for most U.S. import quotas go to foreigners, the cost to the nation of such quotas is larger than that of a comparable tariff (a tariff that leads to the same level of imports). In Figure 45.10 the net loss to the United States from such an import quota would be equal to areas $B + C + D$, the difference between consumer losses and producer gains.

The Political Economy of Trade Protection

We have seen that international trade produces mutual benefits to the countries that engage in it. We have also seen that tariffs and import quotas, although they produce winners as well as losers, reduce total surplus. Yet many countries continue to impose tariffs and import quotas as well as to enact other protectionist measures.

To understand why trade protection takes place, we will first look at some common justifications for protection. Then we will look at the politics of trade protection. Finally, we will look at an important feature of trade protection in today's world: tariffs and import quotas are the subject of international negotiation and are policed by international organizations.

Arguments for Trade Protection

Advocates for tariffs and import quotas offer a variety of arguments. Three common arguments are *national security, job creation,* and the *infant industry argument.*

The national security argument is based on the proposition that overseas sources of goods are vulnerable to disruption in times of international conflict; therefore, a country should protect domestic suppliers of crucial goods with the aim to be self-sufficient in those goods. In the 1960s, the United States—which had begun to import oil as domestic oil reserves ran low—had an import quota on oil, justified on national security grounds. Some people have argued that we should again have policies to discourage imports of oil, especially from the Middle East.

The job creation argument points to the additional jobs created in import-competing industries as a result of trade protection. Economists argue that these jobs are offset by the jobs lost elsewhere, such as industries that use imported inputs and now face higher input costs. But noneconomists don't always find this argument persuasive.

Finally, the infant industry argument, often raised in newly industrializing countries, holds that new industries require a temporary period of trade protection to get established. For example, in the 1950s many countries in Latin America imposed tariffs and import quotas on manufactured goods, in an effort to switch from their traditional role as exporters of raw materials to a new status as industrial countries. In theory, the argument for infant industry protection can be compelling, particularly in high-tech industries that increase a country's overall skill level. Reality, however, is more complicated: it is most often industries that are politically influential that gain protection. In addition, governments tend to be poor predictors of the best emerging technologies. Finally, it is often very difficult to wean an industry from protection when it should be mature enough to stand on its own.

The Politics of Trade Protection

In reality, much trade protection has little to do with the arguments just described. Instead, it reflects the political influence of import-competing producers.

We've seen that a tariff or import quota leads to gains for import-competing producers and losses for consumers. Producers, however, usually have much more influence over trade policy decisions. The producers who compete with imports of a particular good are usually a smaller, more cohesive group than the consumers of that good.

An example is trade protection for sugar: the United States has an import quota on sugar, which on average leads to a domestic price about twice the world price.

This quota is difficult to rationalize in terms of any economic argument. However, consumers rarely complain about the quota because they are unaware that it exists: because no individual consumer buys large amounts of sugar, the cost of the quota is only a few dollars per family each year, not enough to attract notice. But there are only a few thousand sugar growers in the United States. They are very aware of the benefits they receive from the quota and make sure that their representatives in Congress are also aware of their interest in the matter.

Given these political realities, it may seem surprising that trade is as free as it is. For example, the United States has low tariffs, and its import quotas are mainly confined to clothing and a few agricultural products. It would be nice to say that the main reason trade protection is so limited is that economists have convinced governments of the virtues of free trade. A more important reason, however, is the role of *international trade agreements*.

International Trade Agreements and the World Trade Organization

When a country engages in trade protection, it hurts two groups. We've already emphasized the adverse effect on domestic consumers, but protection also hurts foreign export industries. This means that countries care about each others' trade policies: the Canadian lumber industry has a strong interest in keeping U.S. tariffs on forest products low.

Because countries care about each others' trade policies, they engage in **international trade agreements:** treaties in which a country promises to engage in less trade protection against the exports of another country in return for a promise by the other country to do the same for its own exports. Most world trade is now governed by such agreements.

Some international trade agreements involve just two countries or a small group of countries. The United States, Canada, and Mexico are joined together by the **North American Free Trade Agreement,** or **NAFTA.** This agreement, signed in 1993, will eventually remove all barriers to trade among the three nations. In Europe, 27 nations are part of an even more comprehensive agreement, the **European Union** or **EU.** In NAFTA, the member countries set their own tariff rates against imports from other nonmember countries. The EU, however, is a *customs union:* tariffs are levied at the same rate on goods from outside the EU entering the union.

There are also global trade agreements covering most of the world. Such global agreements are overseen by the **World Trade Organization,** or **WTO,** an international organization composed of member countries, which plays two roles. First, it provides the framework for the massively complex negotiations involved in a major international trade agreement (the full text of the last major agreement, approved in 1994, was 24,000 pages long). Second, the WTO resolves disputes between its members. These

International trade agreements are treaties in which a country promises to engage in less trade protection against the exports of other countries in return for a promise by other countries to do the same for its own exports.

The **North American Free Trade Agreement,** or **NAFTA,** is a trade agreement among the United States, Canada, and Mexico.

The **European Union,** or **EU,** is a customs union among 27 European nations.

The **World Trade Organization,** or **WTO,** oversees international trade agreements and rules on disputes between countries over those agreements.

disputes typically arise when one country claims that another country's policies violate its previous agreements. Currently, the WTO has 151 member countries, accounting for the bulk of world trade.

Here are two examples that illustrate the WTO's role. First, in 1999 the WTO ruled that the European Union's import restrictions on bananas, which discriminate in favor of banana producers in former European colonies and against Central American banana producers, are in violation of international trade rules. The United States took the side of the Central American countries, and the dispute threatened to become a major source of conflict between the European Union and the United States. Europe is currently in the process of revising its system. A more recent example is the dispute between the United States and Brazil over American subsidies to its cotton farmers. These subsidies, in the amount of $3 to $4 billion a year, are illegal under WTO rules. Brazil argues that they artificially reduce the price of American cotton on world markets and hurt Brazilian cotton farmers. In 2005 the WTO ruled against the United States and in favor of Brazil, and the United States responded by cutting some export subsidies on cotton. However, in 2007, the WTO ruled that the United States had not done enough to fully comply, such as eliminating government loans to cotton farmers. At the time of writing, the United States has not yet replied to the WTO's ruling.

By the way, Vietnam and Thailand are both members of the WTO. Some students may wonder why, in that case, the rules don't prevent the United States from imposing tariffs on shrimp imports. The answer is that WTO rules do allow trade protection under certain circumstances. One circumstance is where the foreign competition is "unfair" under certain technical criteria. That's what the United States is alleging in the case of shrimp imports. Trade protection is also allowed as a temporary measure when a sudden surge of imports threatens to disrupt a domestic industry. The response to Chinese clothing exports, described in the IRL, is an important recent example.

The WTO is sometimes, with great exaggeration, described as a world government. In fact, it has no army, no police, and no direct enforcement power. The grain of truth in that description is that when a country joins the WTO, it agrees to accept the organization's judgments—and these judgments apply not only to tariffs and

in real life

Chinese Pants Explosion

From 1973 onwards, most world trade in clothing was regulated by a complex system of export and import quotas known as the Multifiber Agreement. However, in 1994 the members of the World Trade Organization agreed to end restrictions on the clothing trade over the next decade. At the end of 2004, the remaining restrictions were removed, with dramatic results: clothing exports from China, a huge country with vast reserves of cheap labor that had relatively small export quotas under the old system, exploded. Exports of clothing from China to the United States in January 2005 were more than twice their level a year earlier.

Chinese exports of cotton trousers were up more than 1,000%.

The Chinese pants explosion provided clear evidence of the extent to which quotas had previously been restricting trade. It also produced urgent demands for temporary protection from clothing producers in importing countries. Within a few months, both the United States and the European Union imposed new restrictions on China's clothing exports to counteract the flood.

Surprisingly, these new restrictions didn't violate WTO rules. When China joined the WTO in 2001, it agreed to what is known, in trade policy jargon, as a "safeguard mechanism": importing

countries were granted the right to impose temporary limits on Chinese clothing exports in the event of an import surge. And that's just what they did.

You shouldn't be too cynical about this failure to achieve complete free trade in clothing. World trade negotiations have always been based on the principle that half a loaf is better than none, that it's better to have an agreement that allows politically sensitive industries to retain some protection than to insist on free trade purity. In spite of the restrictions imposed on China, world trade in clothing is much freer now than it was just a few years ago.

import quotas but also to domestic policies that the organization considers trade protection disguised under another name. So in joining the WTO a country does give up some of its sovereignty.

New Challenges to Globalization

The forward march of globalization over the past century is generally considered a major political and economic success. Economists and policy makers alike have viewed growing world trade, in particular, as a good thing. We would be remiss, however, if we failed to acknowledge that many people are having second thoughts about globalization. To a large extent, these second thoughts reflect two concerns shared by many economists: worries about the effects of globalization on inequality and worries that new developments, in particular the growth in *offshore outsourcing*, are increasing economic insecurity.

Globalization and Inequality We've already mentioned the implications of international trade for factor prices, such as wages: when wealthy countries like the United States export skill-intensive products like aircraft while importing labor-intensive products like clothing, they can expect to see the wage gap between more educated and less educated domestic workers widen. Thirty years ago, this wasn't too much of a concern, because most of the goods wealthy countries imported from poorer countries were raw materials or goods where comparative advantage depended on climate. Today, however, many manufactured goods are imported from relatively poor countries, with a potentially much larger effect on the distribution of income.

Trade with China, in particular, raises concerns among labor groups trying to maintain wage levels in rich countries. Although China has experienced spectacular economic growth since the economic reforms that began in the late 1970s, it remains a poor, low-wage country: wages in Chinese manufacturing are estimated to be only about 3% of U.S. wages. Meanwhile, imports from China have soared. In 1983 less than 1% of U.S. imports came from China; by 2007, the figure was more than 16%. There's not much question that these surging imports from China put at least some downward pressure on the wages of less educated American workers.

Outsourcing Chinese exports to the United States overwhelmingly consist of labor-intensive manufactured goods. However, some U.S. workers have recently found themselves facing a new form of international competition. *Outsourcing*, in which a company hires another company to perform some task, such as running the corporate computer system, is a long-standing business practice. Until recently, however, outsourcing was normally done locally, with a company hiring another company in the same city or country. Now, modern telecommunications increasingly makes it possible to engage in **offshore outsourcing,** in which businesses hire people in another country to perform various tasks. The classic example is call centers: the person answering the phone when you call a company's 1-800 help line may well be in India, which has taken the lead in attracting offshore outsourcing. Offshore outsourcing has also spread to fields such as software design and even health care: the radiologist examining your X-rays, like the person giving you computer help, may be on another continent.

Although offshore outsourcing has come as a shock to some U.S. workers, such as programmers whose jobs have been outsourced to India, it's still relatively small compared with more traditional trade. Some economists have warned, however, that millions or even tens of millions of workers who have never thought they could face foreign competition for their jobs may face unpleasant surprises in the not-too-distant future.

Concerns about income distribution and outsourcing, as we've said, are shared by many economists. There is also, however, widespread opposition to globalization in general, particularly among college students. In 1999, an attempt to start a major round of trade negotiations failed in part because the WTO meeting, in Seattle, was

Offshore outsourcing takes place when businesses hire people in another country to perform various tasks.

disrupted by antiglobalization demonstrators. However, the more important reason for its failure was disagreement among the countries represented.

What motivates the antiglobalization movement? To some extent it's the sweatshop labor fallacy: it's easy to get outraged about the low wages paid to the person who made your shirt, and harder to appreciate how much worse off that person would be if denied the opportunity to sell goods in rich countries' markets. It's also true, however, that the movement represents a backlash against supporters of globalization who have oversold its benefits. Countries in Latin America, in particular, were promised that reducing their tariff rates would produce an economic takeoff; instead, they have experienced disappointing results. Some groups, such as poor farmers facing new competition from imported food, ended up worse off.

Angry protests regularly occur at annual meetings of the WTO.

Do these new challenges to globalization undermine the argument that international trade is a good thing? The great majority of economists would argue that the gains from reducing trade protection still exceed the losses. However, it has become more important than before to make sure that the gains from international trade are widely spread. And the politics of international trade is becoming increasingly difficult as the extent of trade has grown. It's important to realize, however, that trade negotiations have produced a world in which trade is remarkably free by historical standards.

M o d u l e 45 R e v i e w

Solutions appear at the back of the book.

Check Your Understanding

1. In the United States, the opportunity cost of 1 ton of corn is 50 bicycles. In China, the opportunity cost of 1 bicycle is 0.01 ton of corn.
   a. Determine the pattern of comparative advantage.
   b. In autarky, the United States can produce 200,000 bicycles if no corn is produced, and China can produce 3,000 tons of corn if no bicycles are produced. Draw each country's production possibility frontier assuming constant opportunity cost, with tons of corn on the vertical axis and bicycles on the horizontal axis.
   c. With trade, each country specializes its production. The United States consumes 1,000 tons of corn and 200,000 bicycles; China consumes 3,000 tons of corn and 100,000 bicycles. Indicate the production and consumption points on your diagrams, and use them to explain the gains from trade.

2. Suppose the world price of butter is $0.50 per pound and the domestic price in autarky is $1.00 per pound. Use a diagram similar to Figure 45-10 to show the following.
   a. If there is free trade, domestic butter producers want the government to impose a tariff of no less than $0.50 per pound.
   b. What happens if a tariff greater than $0.50 per pound is imposed?

3. Due to a strike by truckers, trade in food between the United States and Mexico is halted. In autarky, the price of Mexican grapes is lower than that of U.S. grapes. Using a diagram of the U.S. domestic demand curve and the U.S. domestic supply curve for grapes, explain the effect of these events on the following.
   a. U.S. grape consumers' surplus
   b. U.S. grape producers' surplus
   c. U.S. total surplus

Critical-Thinking Question

Over the years, the WTO has increasingly found itself adjudicating trade disputes that involve not just tariffs or quota restrictions but also restrictions based on quality, health, and environmental considerations. Why do you think this has occurred? What method would you, as a WTO official, use to decide whether a quality, health, or environmental restriction is in violation of a free-trade agreement?

Section 9 Review

Summary

The Economics of Information

1. **Private information** can cause inefficiency in the allocation of risk. One problem is **adverse selection,** the result of private information about the way things are. It creates the "lemons problem" in the used-car market because buyers will pay only a price that reflects the risk of purchasing a lemon (bad car), which encourages sellers of high-quality cars to drop out of the market. Adverse selection can be limited in several ways—through the **screening** of individuals, through **signaling** that people use to reveal their private information, and through the building of a **reputation.**

2. A related problem is **moral hazard:** individuals have private information about their actions, which distorts their incentives to exert effort or care when someone else bears the costs of that lack of effort or care. It limits the ability of markets to allocate risk efficiently. Insurance companies try to limit moral hazard by imposing **deductibles,** placing more risk on the insured.

Indifference Curves and Consumer Choice

3. Preferences can be represented by an **indifference curve map,** a series of **indifference curves.** Each curve shows all of the consumption bundles that yield a given level of total utility. Indifference curves have two general properties: they never cross and greater distance from the origin indicates higher total utility levels. The indifference curves of ordinary goods have two additional properties: they slope downward and are convex in shape.

4. The **marginal rate of substitution,** or **MRS,** of some good R in place of some good M—the rate at which a consumer is willing to substitute more R for less M—is equal to MU_R/MU_M and is also equal to the negative of the slope of the indifference curve when R is on the horizontal axis and M is on the vertical axis. Convex indifference curves get flatter as you move to the right along the horizontal axis and steeper as you move upward along the vertical axis because of *diminishing marginal utility:* a consumer requires more and more units of R to substitute for a forgone unit of M as the amount of R consumed rises relative to the amount of M consumed.

5. Most goods are **ordinary goods,** goods for which a consumer requires additional units of some other good as compensation for giving up some of the good, and for which there is a **diminishing marginal rate of substitution.**

6. A consumer maximizes utility by moving to the highest indifference curve his or her budget constraint allows. Using the **tangency condition,** the consumer chooses the bundle at which the indifference curve just touches the budget line. At this point, the **relative price** of R in terms of M, P_R/P_M (which is equal to the negative of the slope of the budget line when R is on the horizontal axis and M is on the vertical axis) is equal to the marginal rate of substitution of R in place of M, MU_R/MU_M (which is equal to the negative of the slope of the indifference curve). This gives us the **relative price rule:** at the optimal consumption bundle, the relative price is equal to the marginal rate of substitution. Rearranging this equation also gives us the optimal consumption rule. Two consumers faced with the same prices and income, but with different preferences and so different indifference curve maps, will make different consumption choices.

International Trade

7. International trade is of growing importance to the United States and of even greater importance to most other countries. International trade, like trade among individuals, arises from comparative advantage: the op-

portunity cost of producing an additional unit of a good is lower in some countries than in others. Goods and services purchased abroad are **imports;** those sold abroad are **exports.** Foreign trade, like other economic linkages between countries, has been growing rapidly, a phenomenon called **globalization.**

8. The **Ricardian model of international trade** assumes that opportunity costs are constant. It shows that there are gains from trade: two countries are better off with trade than in **autarky.**

9. In practice, comparative advantage reflects differences between countries in climate, factor endowments, and technology. The **Heckscher–Ohlin model** shows how differences in factor endowments determine comparative advantage: goods differ in **factor intensity,** and countries tend to export goods that are intensive in the factors they have in abundance.

10. The **domestic demand curve** and the **domestic supply curve** determine the price of a good in autarky. When international trade occurs, the domestic price is driven to equality with the **world price,** the price at which the good is bought and sold abroad.

11. If the world price is below the autarky price, a good is imported. This leads to an increase in consumer surplus, a fall in producer surplus, and a gain in total surplus. If the world price is above the autarky price, a good is exported. This leads to an increase in producer surplus, a fall in consumer surplus, and a gain in total surplus.

12. International trade leads to expansion in **exporting industries** and contraction in **import-competing industries.** This raises the domestic demand for abundant factors of production, reduces the demand for scarce factors, and so affects factor prices, such as wages.

13. Most economists advocate **free trade,** but in practice many governments engage in **trade protection.** The two most common forms of **protection** are tariffs and quotas. In rare occasions, export industries are subsidized.

14. A **tariff** is a tax levied on imports. It raises the domestic price above the world price, hurting consumers, benefiting domestic producers, and generating government revenue. As a result, total surplus falls. An **import quota** is a legal limit on the quantity of a good that can be imported. It has the same effects as a tariff, except that the revenue goes not to the government but to those who receive import licenses.

15. Although several popular arguments have been made in favor of trade protection, in practice the main reason for protection is probably political: import-competing industries are well organized and well informed about how they gain from trade protection, while consumers are unaware of the costs they pay. Still, U.S. trade is fairly free, mainly because of the role of **international trade agreements,** in which countries agree to reduce trade protection against each others' exports. The **North American Free Trade Agreement (NAFTA)** and the **European Union (EU)** cover a small number of countries. In contrast, the **World Trade Organization (WTO)** covers a much larger number of countries, accounting for the bulk of world trade. It oversees trade negotiations and adjudicates disputes among its members.

16. In the past few years, many concerns have been raised about the effects of globalization. One issue is the increase in income inequality due to the surge in imports from relatively poor countries over the past 20 years. Another concern is the increase in **offshore outsourcing,** as many jobs that were once considered safe from foreign competition have been moved abroad.

Key Terms

Private information, p. 426
Adverse selection, p. 427
Screening, p. 427
Signaling, p. 428
Reputation, p. 428
Moral hazard, p. 429
Deductible, p. 429
Indifference curve, p. 433
Indifference curve map, p. 433
Marginal rate of substitution (*MRS*), p. 438
Diminishing marginal rate of substitution, p. 439
Ordinary goods, p. 439
Tangency condition, p. 440

Relative price, p. 441
Relative price rule, p. 442
Imports, p. 446
Exports, p. 446
Globalization, p. 447
Ricardian model of international trade, p. 448
Autarky, p. 449
Factor intensity, p. 453
Heckscher–Ohlin model, p. 453
Domestic demand curve, p. 455
Domestic supply curve, p. 455
World price, p. 456
Exporting industries, p. 459

Import-competing industries, p. 459
Free trade, p. 460
Trade protection, p. 460
Protection, p. 460
Tariff, p. 460
Import quota, p. 462
International trade agreements, p. 464
North American Free Trade Agreement (NAFTA), p. 464
European Union (EU), p. 464
World Trade Organization (WTO), p. 464
Offshore outsourcing, p. 466

Problems

1. You are considering buying a second-hand Volkswagen. From reading car magazines, you know that half of all Volkswagens have problems of some kind (they are "lemons") and the other half run just fine (they are "plums"). If you knew that you were getting a plum, you would be willing to pay $10,000 for it: this is how much a plum is worth to you. You would also be willing to buy a lemon, but only if its price was no more than $4,000: this is how much a lemon is worth to you. And someone who owns a plum would be willing to sell it at any price above $8,000. Someone who owns a lemon would be willing to sell it for any price above $2,000.

   a. For now, suppose that you can immediately tell whether the car that you are being offered is a lemon or a plum. Suppose someone offers you a plum. Will there be trade?

   Now suppose that the seller has private information about the car she is selling: the seller knows whether she has a lemon or a plum. But when the seller offers you a Volkswagen, you do not know whether it is a lemon or a plum. So this is a situation of adverse selection.

   b. Since you do not know whether you are being offered a plum or a lemon, you base your decision on the expected value to you of a Volkswagen, assuming you are just as likely to buy a lemon as a plum. Calculate this expected value.

   c. Suppose, from driving the car, the seller knows she has a plum. However, you don't know whether this particular car is a lemon or a plum, so the most you are willing to pay is your expected value. Will there be trade?

2. You own a company that produces chairs, and you are thinking about hiring one more employee. Each chair produced gives you revenue of $10. There are two potential employees, Fred Ast and Sylvia Low. Fred is a fast worker who produces ten chairs per day, creating revenue for you of $100. Fred knows that he is fast and so will work for you only if you pay him more than $80 per day. Sylvia is a slow worker who produces only five chairs per day, creating revenue for you of $50. Sylvia knows that she is slow and so will work for you if you pay her more than $40 per day. Although Sylvia knows she is slow and Fred knows he is fast, you do not know who is fast and who is slow. So this is a situation of adverse selection.

   a. Since you do not know which type of worker you will get, you think about what the expected value of your revenue will be if you hire one of the two. What is that expected value?

   b. Suppose you offered to pay a daily wage equal to the expected revenue you calculated in part a. Whom would you be able to hire: Fred, or Sylvia, or both, or neither?

   c. If you knew whether a worker were fast or slow, which one would you prefer to hire and why? Can you devise a compensation scheme to guarantee that you employ only the type of worker you prefer?

3. For each of the following situations, draw a diagram containing three of Isabella's indifference curves.

   a. For Isabella, cars and tires are perfect complements, but in a ratio of 1:4; that is, for each car, Isabella wants exactly four tires. Be sure to label and number the axes of your diagram. Place tires on the horizontal axis and cars on the vertical axis.

   b. Isabella gets utility only from her caffeine intake. She can consume Valley Dew or cola, and Valley Dew contains twice as much caffeine as cola. Be sure to label and number the axes of your diagram. Place cola on the horizontal axis and Valley Dew on the vertical axis.

   c. Isabella gets utility from consuming two goods: leisure time and income. Both have diminishing marginal utility. Be sure to label the axes of your diagram. Place leisure on the horizontal axis and income on the vertical axis.

   d. Isabella can consume two goods: skis and bindings. For each ski she wants exactly one binding. Be sure to label and number the axes of your diagram. Place bindings on the horizontal axis and skis on the vertical axis.

   e. Isabella gets utility from consuming soda. But she gets no utility from consuming water: any more, or any less, water leaves her total utility level unchanged. Be sure to label the axes of your diagram. Place water on the horizontal axis and soda on the vertical axis.

4. Use the four properties of indifference curves for ordinary goods illustrated in Figure 44.4 to answer the following questions.

   a. Can you rank the following two bundles? If so, which property of indifference curves helps you rank them?

   Bundle A: 2 movie tickets and 3 cafeteria meals
   Bundle B: 4 movie tickets and 8 cafeteria meals

   b. Can you rank the following two bundles? If so, which property of indifference curves helps you rank them?

   Bundle A: 2 movie tickets and 3 cafeteria meals
   Bundle B: 4 movie tickets and 3 cafeteria meals

   c. Can you rank the following two bundles? If so, which property of indifference curves helps you rank them?

   Bundle A: 12 videos and 4 bags of chips
   Bundle B: 5 videos and 10 bags of chips

   d. Suppose you are indifferent between the following two bundles:

   Bundle A: 10 breakfasts and 4 dinners
   Bundle B: 4 breakfasts and 10 dinners

   Now compare bundle A and the following bundle:
   Bundle C: 7 breakfasts and 7 dinners

   Can you rank bundle A and bundle C? If so, which property of indifference curves helps you rank them? (*Hint:* It may help if you draw this, placing dinners on the horizontal axis and breakfasts on the vertical axis. And remember that breakfasts and dinners are ordinary goods.)

5. Assume Saudi Arabia and the United States face the production possibilities for oil and cars shown in the accompanying table.

Saudi Arabia		United States	
Quantity of oil (millions of barrels)	Quantity of cars (millions)	Quantity of oil (millions of barrels)	Quantity of cars (millions)
0	4	0	10.0
200	3	100	7.5
400	2	200	5.0
600	1	300	2.5
800	0	400	0

a. What is the opportunity cost of producing a car in Saudi Arabia? In the United States? What is the opportunity cost of producing a barrel of oil in Saudi Arabia? In the United States?

b. Which country has the comparative advantage in producing oil? In producing cars?

c. Suppose that in autarky, Saudi Arabia produces 200 million barrels of oil and 3 million cars; similarly, that the United States produces 300 million barrels of oil and 2.5 million cars. Without trade, can Saudi Arabia produce more oil *and* more cars? Without trade, can the United States produce more oil *and* more cars?

6. The accompanying table shows the U.S. domestic demand schedule and domestic supply schedule for oranges. Suppose that the world price of oranges is $0.30 per orange.

Price of orange	Quantity of oranges demanded (thousands)	Quantity of oranges supplied (thousands)
$1.00	2	11
0.90	4	10
0.80	6	9
0.70	8	8
0.60	10	7
0.50	12	6
0.40	14	5
0.30	16	4
0.20	18	3

a. Draw the U.S. domestic supply curve and domestic demand curve.

b. With free trade, how many oranges will the United States import or export?

Suppose that the U.S. government imposes a tariff on oranges of $0.20 per orange.

c. How many oranges will the United States import or export after introduction of the tariff?

d. In your diagram, shade the gain or loss to the economy as a whole from the introduction of this tariff.

7. The accompanying diagram illustrates the U.S. domestic demand curve and domestic supply curve for beef.

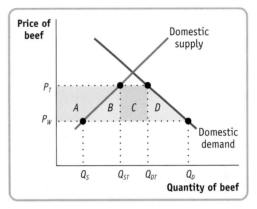

The world price of beef is P_W. The United States currently imposes an import tariff on beef, so the price of beef is P_T. Congress decides to eliminate the tariff. In terms of the areas marked in the diagram, answer the following questions.

a. What is the gain/loss in consumer surplus?

b. What is the gain/loss in producer surplus?

c. What is the gain/loss to the government?

d. What is the gain/loss to the economy as a whole?

>> Solutions to Module Review Questions

This section offers suggested answers to the Review Questions that appear at the end of each module.

Module 1
Check Your Understanding

1. Land, labor, capital, and entrepreneurship are the four categories of resources. Possible examples include fisheries (land), time spent working on a fishing boat (labor), fishing nets (capital), and the opening of a new seafood market (entrepreneurship).

2. **a.** time spent flipping burgers at a restaurant: labor
   b. a bulldozer: capital
   c. a river: land

3. **a.** Yes. The increased time spent commuting is a cost you will incur if you accept the new job. That additional time spent commuting—or equivalently, the benefit you would get from spending that time doing something else—is an opportunity cost of the new job.
   b. Yes. One of the benefits of the new job is that you will be making $50,000. But if you take the new job, you will have to give up your current job; that is, you have to give up your current salary of $45,000, so $45,000 is one of the opportunity costs of taking the new job.
   c. No. A more spacious office is an additional benefit of your new job and does not involve forgoing something else, so it is not an opportunity cost.

4. **a.** This is a normative statement because it stipulates what should be done. In addition, it may have no "right" answer. That is, should people be prevented from all dangerous personal behavior if they enjoy that behavior—like skydiving? Your answer will depend on your point of view.
   b. This is a positive statement because it is a description of fact.

Multiple-Choice Questions

1. d
2. d
3. b
4. b
5. a

Critical-Thinking Question

In positive economics there is a "right" or "wrong" answer. In normative economics there is not necessarily a "right" or "wrong" answer. There is more disagreement in normative economics because there is no "right" or "wrong" answer. Economists disagree because of (1) differences in values and (2) disagreements about models and about which simplifications are appropriate.

Module 2
Check Your Understanding

1. This illustrates the principle that one person's spending is another person's income. As oil companies increase their spending on labor by hiring more workers, or pay existing workers higher wages, those workers' incomes rise. In turn, these workers increase their consumer spending, which becomes income to restaurants and other consumer businesses.

Multiple-Choice Questions

1. b
2. c
3. c
4. d
5. e

Critical-Thinking Questions

Answer: The accompanying diagram illustrates the circular flow for Atlantis.

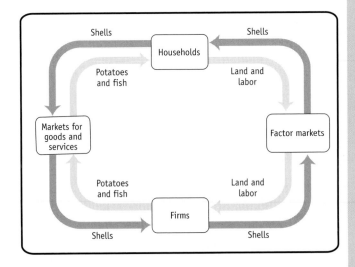

1. **a.** The flooding of the fields will destroy the potato crop. Destruction of the potato crop reduces the flow of goods from firms to households: fewer potatoes produced by firms now are sold to households. An implication, of

course, is that fewer cowry shells flow from households to firms as payment for the potatoes in the market for goods and services. Since firms now earn fewer shells, they have fewer shells to pay to households in the factor markets. As a result, the number of factors flowing from households to firms is also reduced.

b. The productive fishing season leads to greater quantity of fish produced by firms to flow to households. An implication is that more money flows from households to firms through the markets for goods and services. As a result, firms will want to buy more factors from households (the flow of shells from firms to households increases) and, in return, the flow of factors from households to firms increases.

c. Time spent at dancing festivals reduces the flow of labor from households to firms and therefore reduces the number of shells flowing from firms to households through the factor markets. In return, households now have fewer shells to buy goods with (the flow of shells from households to firms in the markets for goods and services is reduced), implying that fewer goods flow from firms to households.

Module 3

Check Your Understanding

1. a. False. An increase in the resources available to Tom for use in producing coconuts and fish changes his production possibility frontier by shifting it outward, because he can now produce more fish and coconuts than before. In the accompanying graph, the line labeled "Tom's original PPF" represents Tom's original production possibility frontier, and the line labeled "Tom's new PPF" represents the new production possibility frontier that results from an increase in resources available to Tom.

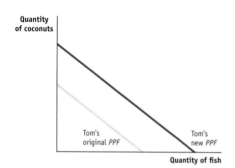

b. True. A technological change that allows Tom to catch more fish for any amount of coconuts gathered results in a change in his production possibility frontier. This is illustrated in the accompanying graph. The new production possibility frontier is represented by the line labeled "Tom's new PPF," and the original production possibility frontier is represented by the line labeled "Tom's original PPF." Since the maximum quantity of coconuts that Tom can gather is the same as before, the new production possibility frontier intersects the vertical axis at the same point as the old curve. But since the maximum possible quantity of fish is now greater than before, the

new curve intersects the horizontal axis to the right of the old curve.

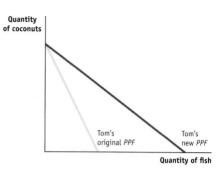

c. False. Production efficiency is achieved at points along a production possibility frontier, but every point inside a PPF is inefficient because more of either good could be produced without producing less of the other. Points outside the PPF are simply unobtainable.

Multiple-Choice Questions

1. c
2. d
3. d
4. e
5. a

Critical-Thinking Question

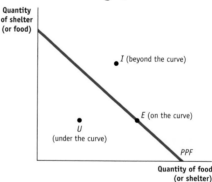

Module 4

Check Your Understanding

1. a. The United States has an absolute advantage in automobile production because it takes fewer Americans (6) to produce a car in one day than it takes Italians (8). The United States also has an absolute advantage in washing machine production because it takes fewer Americans (2) to produce a washing machine in one day than it takes Italians (3).

b. In Italy the opportunity cost of a washing machine in terms of an automobile is ⅜. In other words, ⅜ of a car can be produced with the same number of workers and in the same time it takes to produce 1 washing machine. In the United States the opportunity cost of a washing machine in terms of an automobile is $\frac{2}{6} = \frac{1}{3}$. In other words, $\frac{1}{3}$ of a car can be produced with the same number of workers and in the same time it takes to produce 1 washing machine. Since $\frac{1}{3} < \frac{3}{8}$, the United States has a comparative advantage in the production of washing machines: to produce a washing machine, only $\frac{1}{3}$ of a car must be given up in the United States but $\frac{3}{8}$ of a car must be given up in Italy. This means that Italy has a comparative advantage in automobiles. This can be checked as follows. The opportunity cost of an automobile in terms of a washing machine in Italy is $\frac{8}{3}$, equal to $2\frac{2}{3}$. In other words, $2\frac{2}{3}$ washing machines can be produced with the same number of workers and in the time it takes to produce 1 car in Italy. And the opportunity cost of an automobile in terms of a washing machine in the United States is $\frac{6}{2}$, equal to 3. In other words, 3 washing machines can be produced with the same number of workers and in the time it takes to produce 1 car in the United States.

   c. The greatest gains are realized when each country specializes in producing the good for which it has a comparative advantage. Therefore, based on this example, the United States should specialize in washing machines and Italy should specialize in automobiles.

2. At a trade of 1 fish for 1½ coconuts, Hank gives up less for a fish than he would if he were producing fish himself—that is, he gives up less than 2 coconuts for 1 fish. Likewise, Tom gives up less for a coconut than he would if he were producing coconuts himself—with trade, a coconut costs 1½ = $\frac{2}{3}$ of a fish, less than the $\frac{4}{3}$ of a fish he must give up if he does not trade.

Multiple-Choice Questions

1. a
2. a
3. a
4. d
5. d

Critical-Thinking Questions

a. Country A: opportunity cost of 1 bushel of wheat = 4 units of textiles
Country B: opportunity cost of 1 bushel of wheat = 6 units of textiles

b. Country A has an absolute advantage in the production of wheat (15 versus 10)

c. Country A: opportunity cost of 1 unit of textiles = ¼ bushel of wheat
Country B: opportunity cost of 1 unit of textiles = ⅙ bushel of wheat
Country B has the comparative advantage in textile production because it has a lower opportunity cost of producing textiles. (Alternate answer: Country B has the comparative advantage in the production of textiles because Country A has a comparative advantage in the production of wheat based on opportunity costs shown in part a.)

Appendix
Check Your Understanding

1. **a.** Panel (a) illustrates this relationship. The higher price of movies causes consumers to see fewer movies. The relationship is negative, and the slope is therefore negative. The price of movies is the independent variable, and the number of movies seen is the dependent variable. However, there is a convention in economics that, if price is a variable, it is measured on the vertical axis. So the quantity of movies is measured on the horizontal axis.

   b. Panel (c) illustrates this relationship. Since it is likely that firms would pay more to workers with more experience, then years of experience is the independent variable that would be shown on the horizontal axis, and the resulting income, the dependent variable, would be shown on the vertical axis. The slope is positive.

   c. Panel (d) illustrates this relationship. With the temperature on the horizontal axis as the independent variable, and the consumption of hot dogs on the vertical axis as the dependent variable, we see that there is no change in hot dog consumption regardless of the temperature. The slope is zero.

   d. Panel (c) illustrates this relationship. When the price of ice cream goes up, this causes consumers to choose a close alternative, frozen yogurt. The price of ice cream is the independent variable and the consumption of frozen yogurt is the dependent variable. However, there is a convention in economics that, if price is a variable, it is measured on the vertical axis. The quantity of frozen yogurt that consumers buy is on the horizontal axis. The slope is positive.

   e. Panel (d) illustrates this relationship. Because the intent is for diet books to influence the number of pounds lost, the number of diet books is the independent variable and belongs on the horizontal axis. The number of pounds lost is the dependent variable measured on the vertical axis. The absence of a discernable relationship between the number of diet books purchased and the weight loss of the average dieter results in a horizontal curve. The slope is zero.

   f. Panel (b) illustrates this relationship. Although price is the independent variable and salt consumption the dependent variable, by convention the price appears on the vertical axis and the quantity of salt on the horizontal axis. Since salt consumption does not change regardless of the price, the curve is a vertical line, and the slope is infinity.

2. **a.** The income tax rate is the independent variable and is measured on the horizontal axis. Income tax revenue is the dependent variable and is measured on the vertical axis.

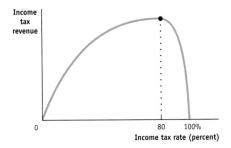

b. If the income tax rate is 0% (there is no tax), tax revenue is zero.

c. If the income tax rate is 100% (all of your income is taxed), you will have no income left after tax. Since people are unwilling to work if they receive no income after tax, no income will be earned. As a result, there is no income tax revenue.

d. For tax rates less than 80%, tax rate and tax revenue are positively related, so the Laffer curve has a positive slope. For tax rates higher than 80%, the relationship between tax rate and tax revenue is negative, so the Laffer curve has a negative slope. Therefore, the Laffer curve looks like the accompanying graph with a maximum point at a tax rate of 80%.

Module 5

Check Your Understanding

1. a. The quantity of umbrellas demanded is higher at any given price on a rainy day than on a dry day. This is a rightward *shift of* the demand curve, since at any given price the quantity demanded rises. This implies that any specific quantity can now be sold at a higher price.

b. The quantity of weekend calls demanded rises in response to a price reduction. This is a *movement along* the demand curve for weekend calls.

c. The demand for roses increases the week of Valentine's Day. This is a rightward *shift of* the demand curve.

d. The quantity of gasoline demanded falls in response to a rise in price. This is a *movement along* the demand curve.

Multiple-Choice Questions

1. e
2. a
3. c
4. d
5. a

Critical-Thinking Question

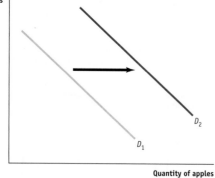

Module 6

Check Your Understanding

1. a. The quantity of houses supplied rises as a result of an increase in prices. This is a *movement along* the supply curve.

b. The quantity of strawberries supplied is higher at any given price. This is an *increase in* supply, which shifts the supply curve to the right.

c. The quantity of labor supplied is lower at any given wage. This is a *decrease in* supply, which shifts the supply curve leftward compared to the supply curve during school vacation. So, in order to attract workers, fast-food chains have to offer higher wages.

d. The quantity of labor supplied rises in response to a rise in wages. This is a *movement along* the supply curve.

e. The quantity of cabins supplied is higher at any given price. This is an *increase in* supply, which shifts the supply curve to the right.

2. a. This is an increase in supply, so the supply curve shifts rightward. At the original equilibrium price of the year before, the quantity of grapes supplied exceeds the quantity demanded, and the result is a surplus. The price of grapes will fall.

b. This is a decrease in demand, so the demand curve shifts leftward. At the original equilibrium price, the quantity of hotel rooms supplied exceeds the quantity demanded. The result is a surplus. The rates for hotel rooms will fall.

c. Demand increases, so the demand curve for second-hand snowblowers shifts rightward. At the original equilibrium price, the quantity of second-hand snowblowers demanded exceeds the quantity supplied. This is a case of shortage. The equilibrium price of second-hand snowblowers will rise.

Multiple-Choice Questions

1. d
2. d
3. c
4. b
5. d

Critical-Thinking Question

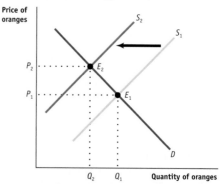

Module 7

Check Your Understanding

1. a. The decrease in the price of gasoline caused a rightward shift in the demand for large cars. As a result of the shift, the equilibrium price of large cars rose and the equilibrium quantity of large cars bought and sold also rose.

b. The technological innovation has caused a rightward shift in the supply of fresh paper made from recycled stock. As a result of this shift, the equilibrium price of fresh paper made from recycled stock has fallen and the equilibrium quantity bought and sold has risen.

c. The fall in the price of pay-per-view movies causes a leftward shift in the demand for movies at local movie theaters. As a result of this shift, the equilibrium price of movie tickets falls and the equilibrium number of people who go to the movies also falls.

2. Upon the announcement of the new chip, the demand curve for computers using the earlier chip shifts leftward (demand decreases), and the supply curve for these computers shifts rightward (supply increases).

a. If demand decreases relatively more than supply increases, then the equilibrium quantity falls, as shown here:

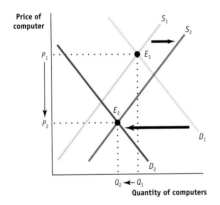

b. If supply increases relatively more than demand decreases, then the equilibrium quantity rises, as shown here:

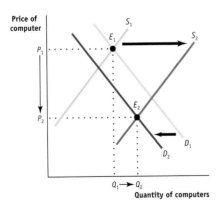

In both cases, the equilibrium price falls.

Multiple-Choice Questions

1. d
2. b
3. a
4. a
5. c

Critical-Thinking Question

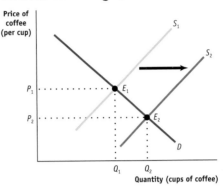

Module 8

Check Your Understanding

1.

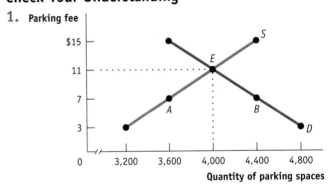

a. Fewer homeowners are willing to rent out their driveways because the price ceiling has reduced the payment they receive. This is an example of a fall in price leading to a fall in the quantity supplied. This is shown in the accompanying diagram by the movement from point *E* to point *A* along the supply curve, a reduction in quantity of 400 parking spaces.

b. The quantity demanded increases by 400 spaces as the price decreases. At a lower price, more fans are willing to drive and rent a parking space. It is shown in the diagram by the movement from point *E* to point *B* along the demand curve.

c. Under a price ceiling, the quantity demanded exceeds the quantity supplied; as a result, shortages arise. In this case, there will be a shortage of 800 parking spaces. It is shown by the horizontal distance between points *A* and *B*.

d. Price ceilings result in wasted resources. The additional time fans spend to guarantee a parking space is wasted time.

e. Price ceilings lead to the inefficient allocation of goods—here, the parking spaces—to consumers. If less serious fans with connections end up with the parking spaces, diehard fans have no place to park.

f. Price ceilings lead to black markets.

2. a. False. By lowering the price that producers receive, a price ceiling leads to a decrease in the quantity supplied.

b. True. A price ceiling leads to a lower quantity supplied than in an efficient, unregulated market. As a result, some people who would have been willing to pay the market price, and so would have gotten the good in an unregulated market, are unable to obtain it when a price ceiling is imposed.

c. True. Those producers who still sell the product now receive less for it and are therefore worse off. Other producers will no longer find it worthwhile to sell the product at all and so will also be made worse off.

3.

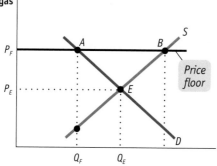

Price of gas

Quantity of gas

a. Some gas station owners will benefit from getting a higher price. Q_F indicates the sales made by these owners. But some will lose; there are those who make sales at the market equilibrium price of P_E but do not make sales at the regulated price of P_F. These missed sales are indicated on the graph by the fall in the quantity demanded along the demand curve, from point *E* to point *A*.

b. Those who buy gas at the higher price of P_F will probably receive better service; this is an example of *inefficiently high quality* caused by a price floor as gas station owners compete on quality rather than price. But opponents are correct to claim that consumers are generally worse off—those who buy at P_F would have been happy to buy at P_E, and many who were willing to buy at a price between P_E and P_F are now unwilling to buy. This is indicated on the graph by the fall in the quantity demanded along the demand curve, from point *E* to point *A*.

c. Proponents are wrong because consumers and some gas station owners are hurt by the price floor, which creates "missed opportunities"—desirable transactions

between consumers and station owners that never take place. Moreover, the inefficiency of wasted resources arises as consumers spend time and money driving to other states. The price floor also tempts people to engage in black market activity. With the price floor, only Q_F units are sold. But at prices between P_E and P_F, there are drivers who together want to buy more than Q_F and owners who are willing to sell to them, a situation likely to lead to illegal activity.

Multiple-Choice Questions

1. e
2. b
3. e
4. b
5. c

Critical-Thinking Question

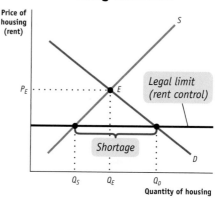

Module 9

Check Your Understanding

1. a. The price of a ride is $7 since the quantity demanded at this price is 6 million: $7 is the *demand price* of 6 million rides. This is represented by point *A* in the accompanying figure.

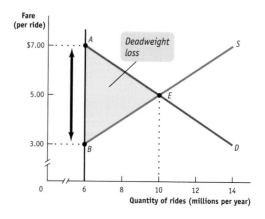

b. At 6 million rides, the supply price is $3 per ride, represented by point B in the figure. The wedge between the demand price of $7 per ride and the supply price of $3 per ride is the quota rent per ride, $4. This is represented in the figure above by the vertical distance between points A and B.

c. The quota discourages 4 million mutually beneficial transactions. The shaded triangle in the figure represents the deadweight loss.

d. At 9 million rides, the demand price is $5.50 per ride, indicated by point C in the figure on the next page, and the supply price is $4.50 per ride, indicated by point D. The quota rent is the difference between the demand price and the supply price: $1. The deadweight loss is represented by the shaded triangle in the figure. Compare that area to the figure above, and you can see that the deadweight loss is smaller when the quota is set at 9 million rides than when it is set at 6 million rides (illustrated above).

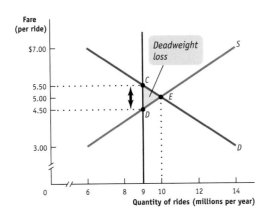

2.   The accompanying figure shows a decrease in demand by 4 million rides, represented by a leftward shift of the demand curve from D_1 to D_2: at any given price, the quantity demanded falls by 4 million rides. (For example, at a price of $5, the quantity demanded falls from 10 million to 6 million rides per year.) This eliminates the effect of a quota limit of 8 million rides. At point E_2, the new market equilibrium, the equilibrium quantity is equal to the quota limit; as a result, the quota has no effect on the market.

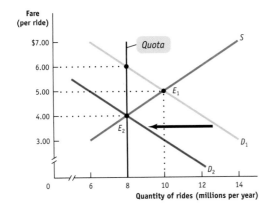

Multiple-Choice Questions

1. d
2. b
3. b
4. d
5. a

Critical-Thinking Question

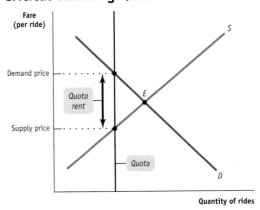

Module 10

Check Your Understanding

1. **a.** Since spending on orange juice is a small share of Clare's spending, the income effect from a rise in the price of orange juice is insignificant. Only the substitution effect, represented by the substitution of lemonade for orange juice, is significant.

   b. Since rent is a large share of Delia's expenditures, the increase in rent generates an income effect, making Delia feel poorer. Since housing is a normal good for Delia, the income and substitution effects move in the same direction, leading her to reduce her consumption of housing by moving to a smaller apartment.

   c. Since a meal ticket is a significant share of the students' living costs, an increase in its price will generate an income effect. Students respond to the price increase by eating more often in the cafeteria. So the substitution effect (which would induce them to eat in the cafeteria less often as they substitute restaurant meals in place of meals at the cafeteria) and the income effect (which would induce them to eat in the cafeteria more often because they are poorer) move in opposite directions. This happens because cafeteria meals are an inferior good. In fact, since the income effect outweighs the substitution effect (students eat in the cafeteria more as the price of meal tickets increases), cafeteria meals are a Giffen good.

2. By the midpoint method, the percent change in the price of strawberries is

$$\frac{\$1.00 - \$1.50}{(\$1.50 + \$1.00)/2} \times 100 = \frac{-\$0.50}{\$1.25} \times 100 = -40\%$$

Similarly, the percent change in the quantity of strawberries demanded is

$$\frac{200,000 - 100,000}{(100,000 + 200,000)/2} \times 100 = \frac{100,000}{150,000} \times 100 = 67\%$$

Dropping the minus sign, the price elasticity of demand using the midpoint method is 67%/40% = 1.7.

3. By the midpoint method, the percent change in the quantity of movie tickets demanded in going from 4,000 tickets to 5,000 tickets is

$$\frac{5,000 - 4,000}{(4,000 + 5,000)/2} \times 100 = \frac{1,000}{4,500} \times 100 = 22\%$$

Since the price elasticity of demand is 1 at the current consumption level, it will take a 22% reduction in the price of movie tickets to generate a 22% increase in quantity demanded.

4. Since price rises, we know that quantity demanded must fall. Given the current price of $0.50, a $0.05 increase in price represents a 10% change, using the method in Equation 10-2. So the price elasticity of demand is

$$\frac{\%\ \text{change in quantity demanded}}{10\%} = 1.2$$

so that the percent change in quantity demanded is 12%. A 12% decrease in quantity demanded represents 100,000 × 0.12, or 12,000 sandwiches.

Multiple-Choice Questions

1. d
2. c
3. b
4. e
5. c

Critical-Thinking Questions

a. The substitution effect will decrease the quantity demanded. As price increases, consumers will buy other goods instead.
b. The income effect will increase the quantity demanded. As price increases, real income decreases, so consumers will purchase more of the inferior good.
c. The substitution effect is larger than the income effect. If the income effect were larger than the substitution effect, more of the good would be purchased as the price increased, and the demand curve would be upward sloping.

Module 11

Check Your Understanding

1. a. Elastic demand. Consumers are highly responsive to changes in price. For a rise in price, the quantity effect (which tends to reduce total revenue) outweighs the price effect (which tends to increase total revenue). Overall, this leads to a fall in total revenue.
    b. Unit-elastic demand. Here the revenue lost to the fall in price is exactly equal to the revenue gained

from higher sales. The quantity effect exactly offsets the price effect.
    c. Inelastic demand. Consumers are relatively unresponsive to changes in price. For consumers to purchase a given percent more, the price must fall by an even greater percent. The price effect of a fall in price (which tends to reduce total revenue) outweighs the quantity effect (which tends to increase total revenue). As a result, total revenue decreases.
    d. Inelastic demand. Consumers are relatively unresponsive to price, so a given percent fall in output is accompanied by an even greater percent rise in price. The price effect of a rise in price (which tends to increase total revenue) outweighs the quantity effect (which tends to reduce total revenue). As a result, total revenue increases.

2. a. Once bitten by a venomous snake, the victim's demand for an antidote is very likely to be perfectly inelastic because there is no substitute and it is necessary for survival. The demand curve will be vertical at a quantity equal to the needed dose.
    b. Students' demand for blue pencils is likely to be perfectly elastic because there are readily available substitutes, such as yellow pencils. The demand curve will be horizontal at a price equal to that of non-blue pencils.

Multiple-Choice Questions

1. d
2. d
3. c
4. b
5. c

Critical-Thinking Questions

a.

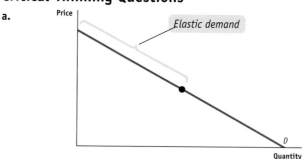

b. An increase in price will decrease total revenue because the negative quantity effect of the price increase is greater than the positive price effect of the price increase.

Module 12

Check Your Understanding

1. By the midpoint method, the percent increase in Chelsea's income is

$$\frac{\$18,000 - \$12,000}{(\$12,000 + \$18,000)/2} \times 100 = \frac{\$6,000}{\$15,000} \times 100 = 40\%$$

Similarly, the percent increase in her consumption of CDs is

$$\frac{40 - 10}{(10 + 40)/2} \times 100 = \frac{30}{25} \times 100 = 120\%$$

Chelsea's income elasticity of demand for CDs is therefore 120%/40% = 3.

2. The cross-price elasticity of demand is 5%/20% = 0.25. Since the cross-price elasticity of demand is positive, the two goods are substitutes.

3. By the midpoint method, the percent change in the number of hours of web-design services contracted is

$$\frac{500,000 - 300,000}{(300,000 + 500,000)/2} \times 100 = \frac{200,000}{400,000} \times 100 = 50\%$$

Similarly, the percent change in the price of web-design services is:

$$\frac{\$150 - \$100}{(\$100 + \$150)/2} \times 100 = \frac{\$50}{\$125} \times 100 = 40\%$$

The price elasticity of supply is 50%/40% = 1.25. Hence supply is elastic.

Multiple-Choice Questions

1. b
2. d
3. d
4. d
5. c

Critical-Thinking Questions

a. 40%/20% = 2
b. elastic
c.

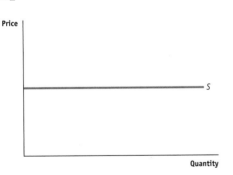

d. Inputs are readily available and can be shifted into/out of production at low cost.

Module 13

Check Your Understanding

1. A consumer buys each pepper if the price is less than (or just equal to) the consumer's willingness to pay for that pepper. The demand schedule is constructed by asking how many peppers will be demanded at any given price. The accompanying table illustrates the demand schedule.

Price of pepper	Quantity of peppers demanded	Quantity of peppers demanded by Casey	Quantity of peppers demanded by Josey
$0.90	1	1	0
0.80	2	1	1
0.70	3	2	1
0.60	4	2	2
0.50	5	3	2
0.40	6	3	3
0.30	8	4	4
0.20	8	4	4
0.10	8	4	4
0.00	8	4	4

When the price is $0.40, Casey's consumer surplus from the first pepper is $0.50, from his second pepper $0.30, from his third pepper $0.10, and he does not buy any more peppers. Casey's individual consumer surplus is therefore $0.90. Josey's consumer surplus from her first pepper is $0.40, from her second pepper $0.20, from her third pepper $0.00 (since the price is exactly equal to her willingness to pay, she buys the third pepper but receives no consumer surplus from it), and she does not buy any more peppers. Josey's individual consumer surplus is therefore $0.60. Total consumer surplus at a price of $0.40 is therefore $0.90 + $0.60 = $1.50.

2. A producer supplies each pepper if the price is greater than (or just equal to) the producer's cost of producing that pepper. The supply schedule is constructed by asking how many peppers will be supplied at any price. The accompanying table illustrates the supply schedule.

Price of pepper	Quantity of peppers supplied	Quantity of peppers supplied by Cara	Quantity of peppers supplied by Jamie
$0.90	8	4	4
0.80	7	4	3
0.70	7	4	3
0.60	6	4	2
0.50	5	3	2
0.40	4	3	1
0.30	3	2	1
0.20	2	2	0
0.10	2	2	0
0.00	0	0	0

When the price is $0.70, Cara's producer surplus from the first pepper is $0.60, from her second pepper $0.60, from her third pepper $0.30, from her fourth pepper $0.10, and she does not supply any more peppers. Cara's individual producer surplus is therefore $1.60. Jamie's producer surplus from his first pepper is $0.40, from his second pepper $0.20, from his third pepper $0.00 (since the price is exactly equal to his cost, he sells the third pepper but receives no producer surplus from it), and he does not supply any more peppers. Jamie's individual producer surplus is therefore $0.60. Total producer surplus at a price of $0.70 is therefore $1.60 + $0.60 = $2.20.

Multiple-Choice Questions

1. c
2. c
3. c
4. b
5. a

Critical-Thinking Question

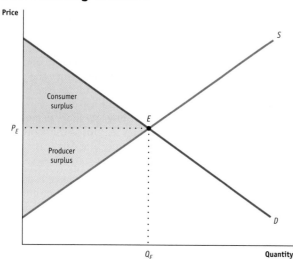

Module 14

Check Your Understanding

1. The quantity demanded equals the quantity supplied at a price of $0.50, the equilibrium price. At that price, a total quantity of five peppers will be bought and sold. Casey will buy three peppers and receive consumer surplus of $0.40 on his first, $0.20 on his second, and $0.00 on his third pepper. Josey will buy two peppers and receive consumer surplus of $0.30 on her first and $0.10 on her second pepper. Total consumer surplus is therefore $1.00. Cara will supply three peppers and receive producer surplus of $0.40 on her first, $0.40 on her second, and $0.10 on her third pepper. Jamie will supply two peppers and receive producer surplus of $0.20 on his first and $0.00 on his second pepper. Total producer surplus is therefore $1.10. Total surplus in this market is therefore $1.00 + $1.10 = $2.10.

2. The following figure shows that, after the introduction of the excise tax, the price paid by consumers rises to $1.20; the price received by producers falls to $0.90. Consumers bear $0.20 of the $0.30 tax per pound of butter; producers bear $0.10 of the tax. The tax drives a wedge of $0.30 between the price paid by consumers and the price received by producers. As a result, the quantity of butter sold is now 9 million pounds.

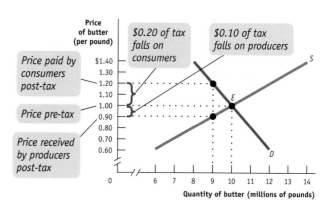

3. **a.** Without the excise tax, Zhang, Yves, Xavier, and Walter sell, and Ana, Bernice, Chizuko, and Dagmar buy one can of soda each, at $0.40 per can. So the quantity bought and sold is 4.
   b. With the excise tax, Zhang and Yves sell, and Ana and Bernice buy one can of soda each. So the quantity sold is 2.
   c. Without the excise tax, Ana's individual consumer surplus is $0.70 − $0.40 = $0.30, Bernice's is $0.60 − $0.40 = $0.20, Chizuko's is $0.50 − $0.40 = $0.10, and Dagmar's is $0.40 − $0.40 = $0.00. Total consumer surplus is $0.30 + $0.20 + $0.10 + $0.00 = $0.60. With the tax, Ana's individual consumer surplus is $0.70 − $0.60 = $0.10 and Bernice's is $0.60 − $0.60 = $0.00. Total consumer surplus post-tax is $0.10 + $0.00 = $0.10. So the total consumer surplus lost because of the tax is $0.60 − $0.10 = $0.50.
   d. Without the excise tax, Zhang's individual producer surplus is $0.40 − $0.10 = $0.30, Yves's is $0.40 − $0.20 = $0.20, Xavier's is $0.40 − $0.30 = $0.10, and Walter's is $0.40 − $0.40 = $0.00. Total producer surplus is $0.30 + $0.20 + $0.10 + $0.00 = $0.60. With the tax, Zhang's individual producer surplus is $0.20 − $0.10 = $0.10 and Yves's is $0.20 − $0.20 = $0.00. Total producer surplus post-tax is $0.10 + $0.00 = $0.10. So the total producer surplus lost because of the tax is $0.60 − $0.10 = $0.50.
   e. With the tax, two cans of soda are sold, so the government tax revenue from this excise tax is 2 × $0.40 = $0.80.
   f. Total surplus without the tax is $0.60 + $0.60 = $1.20. With the tax, total surplus is $0.10 + $0.10 = $0.20, and government tax revenue is $0.80. So deadweight loss from this excise tax is $1.20 − ($0.20 + $0.80) = $0.20.

Multiple-Choice Questions

1. c
2. e

3. b

4. d

5. c

Critical-Thinking Question

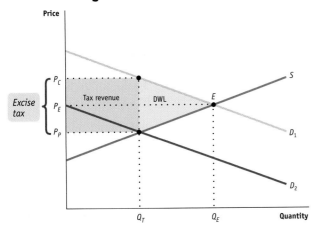

Module 15

Check Your Understanding

1. Consuming a unit that generates negative marginal utility leaves the consumer with lower total utility than not consuming that unit at all. A rational consumer, a consumer who maximizes utility, would not do that. For example, Figure 15.1 shows that Cassie receives 64 utils if she consumes 8 clams, but if she consumes a 9th clam, she loses a util, decreasing her total utility to only 63 utils. Whenever consuming a unit generates negative marginal utility, the consumer is made better off by not consuming that unit, even when that unit is free.

2. a. The accompanying table shows the consumer's consumption possibilities, bundles A through C. These consumption possibilities are plotted in the accompanying diagram, along with the consumer's budget line.

Consumption Bundle	Quantity of popcorn (buckets)	Quantity of movie tickets
A	0	2
B	2	1
C	4	0

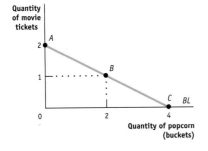

b. The accompanying table shows the consumer's consumption possibilities, A through D. These consumption possibilities are plotted in the accompanying diagram, along with the consumer's budget line.

Consumption Bundle	Quantity of underwear (pairs)	Quantity of socks (pairs)
A	0	6
B	1	4
C	2	2
D	3	0

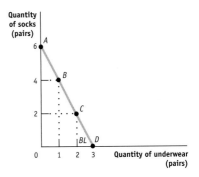

3. From Table 15.3 you can see that Sammy's marginal utility per dollar from increasing his consumption of clams from 3 to 4 pounds and his marginal utility per dollar from increasing his consumption of potatoes from 9 to 10 pounds are the same, 0.75 utils. But a consumption bundle consisting of 4 pounds of clams and 10 pounds of potatoes is not Sammy's optimal consumption bundle because it is not affordable given his income of $20; a bundle of 4 pounds of clams and 10 pounds of potatoes costs $4 × 4 + $2 × 10 = $36, $16 more than Sammy's income. This can be illustrated with Sammy's budget line from Figure 15.3: a bundle of 4 pounds of clams and 10 pounds of potatoes is represented by point X in the accompanying diagram, a point that lies outside Sammy's budget line. If you look at the horizontal axis of Figure 15.4, it is quite clear that there is no such thing in Sammy's consumption possibilities as a bundle consisting of 4 pounds of clams and 10 pounds of potatoes.

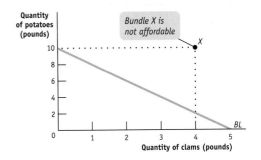

Multiple-Choice Questions

1. d
2. b
3. a
4. b
5. d

Critical-Thinking Questions

a.

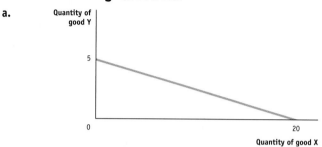

b. Yes, 100/$5 = 400/$20
c. Total utility will increase because marginal utility is positive, while marginal utility will decrease due to the principle of diminishing marginal utility.

Module 16

Check Your Understanding

1. a. Supplies are an explicit cost because they require an outlay of money.
   b. If the basement could be used in some other way that generates money, such as renting it to a student, then the implicit cost is that money forgone. Otherwise, the implicit cost is zero.
   c. Wages are an explicit cost.
   d. By using the van for their business, Karma and Don forgo the money they could have gained by selling it. So use of the van is an implicit cost.
   e. Karma's forgone wages from her job are an implicit cost.

2. a. Economic profit is zero, as explained by the following calculations:
   Implicit cost = $2,000 + $23,000 = $25,000
   Accounting profit = Total revenue − Explicit cost − Depreciation = $25,000
   Economic profit = Total revenue − Explicit cost − Depreciation − Implicit cost = Accounting profit − Implicit cost = $25,000 − $25,000 = $0.
   b. An economic profit of zero is considered a "normal profit." The resources devoted to this business could not earn more if used in the next best activity. This is just enough profit to keep you in this business with no regrets.

Multiple-Choice Questions

1. d
2. e
3. a
4. a
5. c

Critical-Thinking Questions

a. Total revenue = 2,000 × $2 = $4,000
b. Accounting profit = $4,000 − $400 − $100 = $3,500
c. Sunny would need to know the opportunity cost of her time.
d. In general, she would calculate her economic profit and operate if she makes at least normal profit (meaning zero economic profit). In Sunny's case, she earns $3,500 in accounting profit minus the $200 implicit cost of capital and the opportunity cost of her time. Because $3,500 − $200 = $3,300, she will make at least normal profit if the opportunity cost of her time is less than or equal to $3,300.

Module 17

Check Your Understanding

1. The profit-maximizing level of output is three units because marginal cost goes from being below marginal revenue at a quantity of three to being above marginal revenue at a quantity of four, thus passing through marginal revenue at the third unit.

2.

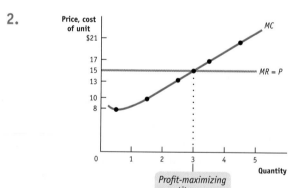

Multiple-Choice Questions

1. c
2. c
3. d
4. e
5. c

Critical-Thinking Question

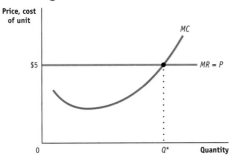

Module 18

Check Your Understanding

1. a. The fixed input is the 10-ton machine and the variable input is electricity.

b. As you can see from the declining numbers in the third column of the accompanying table, electricity does indeed exhibit diminishing returns: the marginal product of each additional kilowatt of electricity is less than that of the previous kilowatt.

Quantity of electricity (kilowatts)	Quantity of ice (pounds)	Marginal product of electricity (pounds per kilowatt)
0	0	
		1,000
1	1,000	
		800
2	1,800	
		600
3	2,400	
		400
4	2,800	

c. A 50% increase in the size of the fixed input means that Bernie now has a 15-ton machine, so the fixed input is now the 15-ton machine. Since it generates a 100% increase in output for any given amount of electricity, the quantity of output and the marginal product are now as shown in the accompanying table.

Quantity of electricity (kilowatts)	Quantity of ice (pounds)	Marginal product of electricity (pounds per kilowatt)
0	0	
		2,000
1	2,000	
		1,600
2	3,600	
		1,200
3	4,800	
		800
4	5,600	

Multiple-Choice Questions

1. d

2. e

3. a

4. b

5. a

Critical-Thinking Question

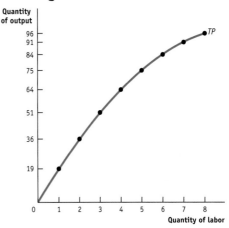

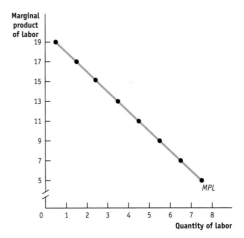

Module 19

Check Your Understanding

1. a. As shown in the accompanying table, the marginal cost for each pie is found by multiplying the marginal cost of the previous pie by 1.5. The variable cost for each output level is found by summing the marginal cost for all the pies produced to reach that output level. So, for example, the variable cost of three pies is $1.00 + $1.50 + $2.25 = $4.75. Average fixed cost for Q pies is calculated as $9.00/Q since fixed cost is $9.00. Average variable cost for Q pies is equal to the variable cost for the Q pies divided by Q; for example, the average variable cost of five pies is $13.19/5, or approximately $2.64. Finally, average total cost can be calculated in two equivalent ways: as TC/Q or as $AVC + AFC$.

Quantity of pies	Marginal cost of pie	Variable cost	Average fixed cost of pie	Average variable cost of pie	Average total cost of pie
0		$0.00	—	—	—
	$1.00				
1		1.00	$9.00	$1.00	$10.00
	1.50				
2		2.50	4.50	1.25	5.75
	2.25				
3		4.75	3.00	1.58	4.58
	3.38				
4		8.13	2.25	2.03	4.28
	5.06				
5		13.19	1.80	2.64	4.44
	7.59				
6		20.78	1.50	3.46	4.96

b. The spreading effect dominates the diminishing returns effect when average total cost is falling: the fall in *AFC* dominates the rise in *AVC* for pies 1 to 4. The diminishing returns effect dominates when average total cost is rising: the rise in *AVC* dominates the fall in *AFC* for pies 5 and 6.

c. Alicia's minimum-cost output is 4 pies; this generates the lowest average total cost, $4.28. When output is less than 4, the marginal cost of a pie is less than the average total cost of the pies already produced. So making an additional pie lowers average total cost. For example, the marginal cost of pie 3 is $2.25, whereas the average total cost of pies 1 and 2 is $5.75. So making pie 3 lowers average total cost to $4.58, equal to (2 × $5.75 + $2.25)/3. When output is more than 4, the marginal cost of a pie is greater than the average total cost of the pies already produced. Consequently, making an additional pie raises average total cost. So, although the marginal cost of pie 6 is $7.59, the average total cost of pies 1 through 5 is $4.44. Making pie 6 raises average total cost to $4.96, equal to (5 × $4.44 + $7.59)/6.

Multiple-Choice Questions
1. c
2. e
3. e
4. e
5. a

Critical-Thinking Question

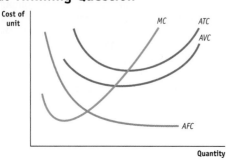

Module 20
Check Your Understanding

1. a. The accompanying table shows the average total cost of producing 12,000, 22,000, and 30,000 units for each of the three choices of fixed cost. For example, if the firm makes choice 1, the total cost of producing 12,000 units of output is $8,000 + 12,000 × $1.00 = $20,000. The average total cost of producing 12,000 units of output is therefore $20,000/12,000 = $1.67. The other average total costs are calculated similarly.

	12,000 units	22,000 units	30,000 units
Average total cost from choice 1	$1.67	$1.36	$1.27
Average total cost from choice 2	1.75	1.30	1.15
Average total cost from choice 3	2.25	1.34	1.05

So if the firm wanted to produce 12,000 units, it would make choice 1 because this gives it the lowest average total cost. If it wanted to produce 22,000 units, it would make choice 2. If it wanted to produce 30,000 units, it would make choice 3.

b. Having historically produced 12,000 units, the firm would have adopted choice 1. When producing 12,000 units, the firm would have had an average total cost of $1.67. When output jumps to 22,000 units, the firm cannot alter its choice of fixed cost in the short run, so its average total cost in the short run will be $1.36. In the long run, however, it will adopt choice 2, making its average total cost fall to $1.30.

c. If the firm believes that the increase in demand is temporary, it should not alter its fixed cost from choice 1 because choice 2 generates higher average total cost as soon as output falls back to its original quantity of 12,000 units: $1.75 versus $1.67.

2. a. This firm is likely to experience diseconomies of scale. As the firm takes on more projects, the costs of communication and coordination required to implement the expertise of the firm's owner are likely to increase.

b. This firm is likely to experience economies of scale. Because diamond mining requires a large initial setup cost for excavation equipment, long-run average total cost will fall as output increases.

Multiple-Choice Questions
1. a
2. e
3. e
4. d
5. e

Critical-Thinking Question

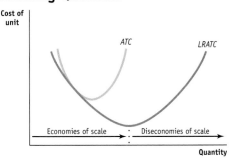

Module 21

Check Your Understanding

1. a. oligopoly
 b. perfect competition
 c. monopolistic competition
 d. monopoly

Multiple-Choice Questions

1. b
2. a
3. d
4. a
5. a

Critical-Thinking Question

a.

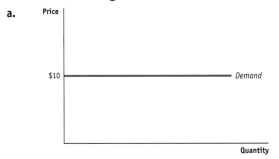

b. $10

Module 22

Check Your Understanding

1. a. The firm maximizes profit at a quantity of 4, because it is at that quantity that $MC = MR$.
 b. At a quantity of 4 the firm just breaks even. This is because at a quantity of 4, $P = ATC$, so the amount the firm takes in for each unit—the price—exactly equals the average total cost per unit.

2. The lowest price that would allow the firm to break even is $10, for the minimum average total cost is $500/50 = $10, and price must at least equal minimum average total cost in order for the firm to break even.

Multiple-Choice Questions

1. d
2. d
3. d
4. c
5. c

Critical-Thinking Questions

a.

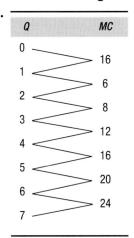

b. The profit-maximizing quantity is 4.
c. The firm's maximum profit is $TR - TC = (4 \times \$14) - \$56 = \$56 - \$56 = \$0$.

Module 23

Check Your Understanding

1.

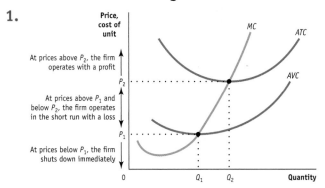

a. The firm should shut down immediately when price is less than minimum average variable cost, the shut-down price. In the accompanying diagram, this is optimal for prices in the range from 0 to P_1.
b. When the price is greater than the minimum average variable cost (the shut-down price) but less than the minimum average total cost (the break-even price), the firm should continue to operate in the short run even though it is making a loss. This is optimal for prices in the range from P_1 to P_2.
c. When the price exceeds the minimum average total cost (the break-even price), the firm makes a profit. This happens for prices in excess of P_2.

2. This is an example of a temporary shut-down by a firm when the market price lies below the shut-down price, the minimum average variable cost. The market price is the price of a lobster meal and the variable cost is the cost of the lobster, employee wages, and other expenses that increase as more meals are served. In this example, however, it is the average variable cost curve rather than the market price that shifts over time, due to seasonal changes in the cost of lobsters. Maine lobster shacks have relatively low average variable cost during the summer, when cheap Maine lobsters are available; during the rest of the year, their average variable cost is relatively high due to the high cost of imported lobsters. So the lobster shacks are open for business during the summer, when their minimum average variable cost lies below price; but they close during the rest of the year, when the price lies below their minimum average variable cost.

Multiple-Choice Questions

1. e

2. d

3. b

4. d

5. c

Critical-Thinking Questions

a. 6

b. $20 \times 6 = \$120$

c. $29.50 \times 6 = \$177$

d. $120 - \$177 = -\$57$ (or a loss of $57)

e. No, because $P < AVC$

Module 24

Check Your Understanding

1. a. A fall in the fixed cost of production generates a fall in the average total cost of production and, in the short run, an increase in each firm's profit at the current output level. So in the long run new firms will enter the industry. The increase in supply drives down price and profits. Once profits are driven back to zero, entry will cease.

b. An increase in wages generates an increase in the average variable and the average total cost of production at every output level. In the short run, firms incur losses at the current output level, and so in the long run some firms will exit the industry. (If the average variable cost rises sufficiently, some firms may even shut down in the short run.) As firms exit, supply decreases, price rises, and losses are reduced. Exit will cease once losses return to zero.

c. Price will rise as a result of the increased demand, leading to a short-run increase in profits at the current output level. In the long run, firms will enter the industry, generating an increase in supply, a fall in price, and a fall in profits. Once profits are driven back to zero, entry will cease.

d. The shortage of a key input causes that input's price to increase, resulting in an increase in average variable and average total cost for producers. Firms incur losses in the short run, and some firms will exit the industry in the long run. The fall in supply generates an increase in price and decreased losses. Exit will cease when the losses for remaining firms have returned to zero.

2. In the accompanying diagram, point X_{MKT} in panel (b), the intersection of S_1 and D_1, represents the long-run industry equilibrium before the change in consumer tastes. When tastes change, demand falls and the industry moves in the short run to point Y_{MKT} in panel (b), at the intersection of the new demand curve D_2 and S_1, the short-run supply curve representing the same number of egg producers as in the original equilibrium at point X_{MKT}. As the market price falls, each individual firm reacts by producing less—as shown in panel (a)—as long as the market price remains above the minimum average variable cost. If market price falls below minimum average variable cost, the firm would shut down immediately. At point Y_{MKT} the price of eggs is below minimum average total cost, creating losses for producers. This leads some firms to exit, which shifts the short-run industry supply curve leftward to S_2. A new long-run equilibrium is established at point Z_{MKT}. As this occurs, the market price rises again, and, as shown in panel (c), each remaining producer reacts by increasing output (here, from point Y to point Z). All remaining producers again make zero profits. The decrease in the quantity of eggs supplied in the industry comes entirely from

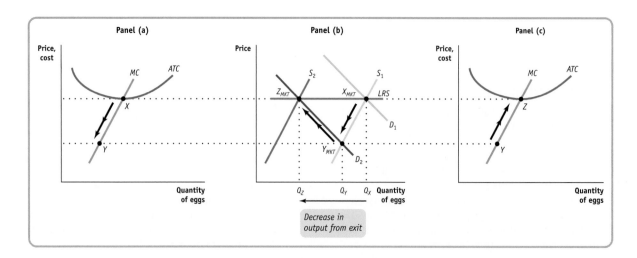

the exit of some producers from the industry. The long-run industry supply curve is the curve labeled *LRS* in panel (b).

Multiple-Choice Questions

1. d
2. b
3. a
4. e
5. b

Critical-Thinking Questions

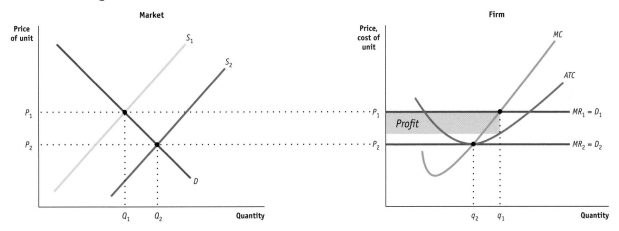

Module 25

Check Your Understanding

1. **a.** The demand schedule is found by determining the price at which each quantity would be demanded. This price is the average revenue, found at each output level by dividing the total revenue by the number of emeralds produced. For example, the price when 3 emeralds are produced is $252/3 = $84. The price at the various output levels is then used to construct the demand schedule in the accompanying table.
    b. The marginal revenue schedule is found by calculating the change in total revenue as output increases by one unit. For example, the marginal revenue generated by increasing output from 2 to 3 emeralds is ($252 − $186) = $66.
    c. The quantity effect component of marginal revenue is the additional revenue generated by selling one more unit of the good at the market price. For example, as shown in the accompanying table, at 3 emeralds, the market price is $84; so, when going from 2 to 3 emeralds the quantity effect is equal to $84.
    d. The price effect component of marginal revenue is the decline in total revenue caused by the fall in price when one more unit is sold. For example, as shown in the table, when only 2 emeralds are sold, each emerald sells at a price of $93. However, when Emerald, Inc. sells an additional emerald, the price must fall by $9 to $84. So the price effect component

in going from 2 to 3 emeralds is (−$9) × 2 = −$18. That's because 2 emeralds can only be sold at a price of $84 when 3 emeralds in total are sold, although they could have been sold at a price of $93 when only 2 in total were sold.

Quantity of emeralds demanded	Price of emerald	Total revenue	Marginal revenue	Quantity effect component	Price effect component
1	$100	$100			
			$86	$93	−$7
2	93	186			
			66	84	−18
3	84	252			
			28	70	−42
4	70	280			
			−30	50	−80
5	50	250			

e. In order to determine Emerald, Inc.'s profit-maximizing output level, you must know its marginal cost at each output level. Its profit-maximizing output level is the one at which marginal revenue is equal to marginal cost.

2. As the accompanying diagram shows, the marginal cost curve shifts upward to $400. The profit-maximizing price rises to $700 and quantity falls to 6. Profit falls from $3,200 to $300 × 6 = $1,800. The quantity a perfectly

competitive industry would produce decreases to 12, but profits remain unchanged at zero.

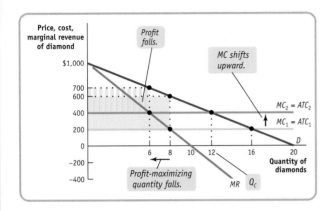

Multiple-Choice Questions

1. b
2. c
3. b
4. d
5. d

Critical-Thinking Question

a.

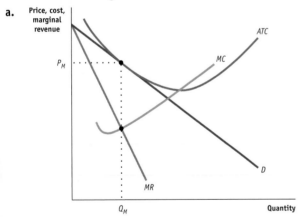

b. Yes, with the help of barriers to entry that keep competitors out.

Module 26

Check Your Understanding

1. **a.** Cable Internet service is a natural monopoly. So the government should intervene if it believes that the current price exceeds average total cost, which includes the cost of laying the cable. In this case it should impose a price ceiling equal to average total cost. If the price does not exceed average total cost, the government should do nothing.

b. The government should approve the merger only if it fosters competition by transferring some of the company's landing slots to another, competing airline.

2. **a.** False. Although some consumer surplus is indeed transformed into monopoly profit, this is not the source of inefficiency. As can be seen from Figure 26.1, panel (b), the inefficiency arises from the fact that some of the consumer surplus is transformed into deadweight loss (the yellow area), which is a complete loss not captured by consumers, producers, or anyone else.

b. True. If a monopolist sold to all customers willing to pay an amount greater than or equal to marginal cost, all mutually beneficial transactions would occur and there would be no deadweight loss.

3. As shown in the accompanying diagram, a "smart" profit–maximizing monopolist produces Q_M, the output level at which $MR = MC$. A monopolist who mistakenly believes that $P = MR$ produces the output level at which $P = MC$ (when, in fact, $P > MR$, and at the true profit-maximizing level of output, $P > MR = MC$). This misguided monopolist will produce the output level Q_C, where the demand curve crosses the marginal cost curve—the same output level that would be produced if the industry were perfectly competitive. It will charge the price P_C, which is equal to marginal cost, and make zero profit. The entire shaded area is equal to the consumer surplus, which is also equal to total surplus in this case (since the monopolist receives zero producer surplus). There is no deadweight loss because every consumer who is willing to pay as much as or more than marginal cost gets the good. A smart monopolist, however, will produce the output level Q_M and charge the price P_M. Profit for the smart monopolist is represented by the green area, consumer surplus corresponds to the blue area, and total surplus is equal to the sum of the green and blue areas. The yellow area is the deadweight loss generated by the monopolist.

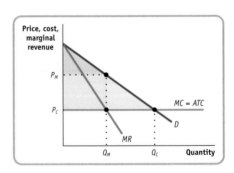

Multiple-Choice Questions

1. a
2. b
3. c
4. a
5. b

Critical-Thinking Questions

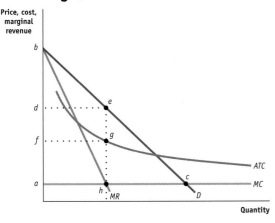

a. triangle *bca*
b. triangle *bed*
c. rectangle *degf*
d. triangle *ech*

Module 27

Check Your Understanding

1. a. False. The opposite is true. A price-discriminating monopolist will sell to some customers that would not find the product affordable if purchasing from a single-price monopolist—namely, customers with a high price elasticity of demand who are willing to pay only a relatively low price for the good.

   b. False. Although a price-discriminating monopolist does indeed capture more of the consumer surplus, less inefficiency is created: more mutually beneficial transactions occur because the monopolist makes more sales to customers with a low willingness to pay for the good.

   c. True. Under price discrimination consumers are charged prices that depend on their price elasticity of demand. A consumer with highly elastic demand will pay a lower price than a consumer with inelastic demand.

2. a. This is not a case of price discrimination because the product itself is different and all consumers, regardless of their price elasticities of demand, value the damaged merchandise less than undamaged merchandise. So the price must be lowered to sell the merchandise.

   b. This is a case of price discrimination. Senior citizens have a higher price elasticity of demand for restaurant meals (their demand for restaurant meals is more responsive to price changes) than other patrons. Restaurants lower the price to high-elasticity consumers (senior citizens). Consumers with low price elasticity of demand will pay the full price.

   c. This is a case of price discrimination. Consumers with a high price elasticity of demand will pay a lower price by collecting and using discount coupons. Consumers with a low price elasticity of demand will not use coupons.

   d. This is not a case of price discrimination; it is simply a case of supply and demand.

Multiple-Choice Questions

1. d
2. c
3. b
4. e
5. a

Critical-Thinking Question

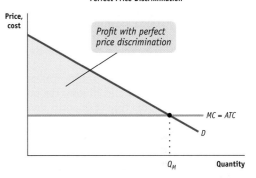

Consumer surplus is zero because each consumer is charged the maximum he or she is willing to pay.

Module 28

Check Your Understanding

1. a. This will decrease the likelihood that the firm will collude to restrict output. By increasing output, the firm will generate a negative price effect. But because the firm's current market share is small, the price effect will fall mostly on its rivals' revenues rather than on its own. At the same time, the firm will benefit from a positive quantity effect.

   b. This will decrease the likelihood that the firm will collude to restrict output. By acting noncooperatively and raising output, the firm will cause the price to fall. Because its rivals have higher costs, they will lose money at the lower price while the firm continues to make profits. So the firm may be able to drive its rivals out of business by increasing its output.

   c. This will increase the likelihood that the firm will collude. Because it is costly for consumers to switch products, the firm would have to lower its price substantially (with a commensurate increase in quantity) to induce consumers to switch to its product. So increasing output is likely to be unprofitable, given the large negative price effect.

   d. This will increase the likelihood that the firm will collude. It cannot increase sales because it is currently at maximum production capacity, making attempts to undercut rivals' prices as under the Bertrand model fruitless due to the inability to produce the output needed to steal the rivals' customers. This makes the option to cooperate in restricting output relatively attractive.

Multiple-Choice Questions

1. a
2. e
3. d
4. e
5. b

Critical-Thinking Questions

a. The first major reason is that cartels are illegal in the United States. The second major reason is that cartels set prices above marginal cost, which creates an incentive for each firm to cheat on the cartel agreement in order to make more profit. This incentive to cheat tends to cause cartels to fall apart.

b. Under the Cournot model, each firm treats the production of other firms as fixed and chooses the quantity that will maximize profit. This type of quantity competition results in relatively low production levels and positive economic profit. Under the Bertrand model, firms undercut the prices of their rivals until price equals marginal cost. This type of price competition results in normal profit (zero economic profit), as under perfect competition.

Module 29

Check Your Understanding

1. **a.** A Nash equilibrium is a set of actions from which neither side wants to deviate (change actions), given what the other is doing. Both sides building a missile is a Nash equilibrium because neither player wants to deviate from the decision to build a missile. To switch from building to not building a missile, given that the other player is building a missile, would result in a change from −10 to −20 utils. There is no other Nash equilibrium in this game because for any other set of actions, at least one side is not building a missile, and would be better off switching to building a missile.

   b. Their total payoff is greatest when neither side builds a missile, in which case their total payoff is 0 + 0 = 0.

   c. This outcome would require cooperation because each side sees itself as better off by building a missile. If Margaret builds a missile but Nikita does not, Margaret gets a payoff of +8, rather than the 0 she gets if she doesn't build a missile. Similarly, Nikita is better off if he builds a missile but Margaret doesn't: he gets a payoff of +8, rather than the 0 he gets if he doesn't build a missile. Indeed, both players have an incentive to build a missile regardless of what the other side does. So unless Nikita and Margaret are able to communicate in some way to enforce cooperation, they will act in their own individual interests and each will pursue its dominant strategy of building a missile.

2. **a.** Future entry by several new firms will increase competition and drive down industry profits. As a result, there is less future profit to protect by behaving cooperatively today. This makes each oligopolist more likely to behave noncooperatively today.

b. When it is very difficult for a firm to detect if another firm has raised output, it is very difficult to enforce cooperation by playing "tit for tat." So it is more likely that a firm will behave noncooperatively.

c. When firms have coexisted while maintaining high prices for a long time, each expects cooperation to continue. So the value of behaving cooperatively today is high, and it is likely that firms will engage in tacit collusion.

Multiple-Choice Questions

1. b
2. b
3. c
4. a
5. c

Critical-Thinking Question

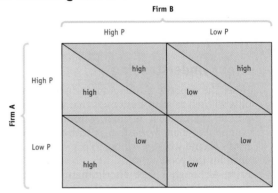

Module 30

Check Your Understanding

1. **a.** This is evidence of tacit collusion. Firms in the industry are able to tacitly collude by setting their prices according to the published "suggested" price of the largest firm in the industry. This is a form of price leadership.

   b. This is not evidence of tacit collusion. Considerable variation in market shares indicates that firms have been competing to capture each other's business.

   c. This is not evidence of tacit collusion. These features make it less likely that consumers will switch products in response to lower prices. So this is a way for firms to avoid any temptation to gain market share by lowering price. This is a form of product differentiation used to avoid direct competition.

   d. This is evidence of tacit collusion. In the guise of discussing sales targets, firms can create a cartel by designating quantities to be produced by each firm.

   e. This is evidence of tacit collusion. By raising prices together, each firm in the industry is refusing to undercut its rivals by leaving its price unchanged or lowering it. Because it could gain market share by doing so, refusing to do so supports the conclusion that there is tacit collusion.

Multiple-Choice Questions

1. d
2. d
3. c
4. e
5. a

Critical-Thinking Questions

a. A large number of firms: having more firms means there is less incentive for any firm to behave cooperatively.

b. Complex products/pricing schemes: keeping track of adherence to an agreement is more difficult.

c. Differences in interests: firms often have different views of their own interests and of what a fair agreement would entail.

d. Bargaining power of buyers: firms are less able to raise prices for buyers with significant bargaining power, which can result from size or access to many options.

Module 31

Check Your Understanding

1. a. An increase in fixed cost shifts the average total cost curve upward. In the short run, firms incur losses because price is below average total cost. In the long run, some firms will exit the industry, resulting in a rightward shift of the demand curves for those firms that remain, since each firm now serves a larger share of the market. Long-run equilibrium is reestablished when the demand curve for each remaining firm has shifted rightward to the point where it is tangent to the firm's new, higher average total cost curve. At this point each firm's price just equals its average total cost, and each firm makes zero profit.

b. A decrease in marginal cost shifts the average total cost curve and the marginal cost curve downward. In the short run, firms earn positive economic profit. In the long run new entrants are attracted into the industry by the profit. This results in a leftward shift of each existing firm's demand curve because each firm now has a smaller share of the market. Long-run equilibrium is reestablished when each firm's demand curve has shifted leftward to the point where it is tangent to the new, lower average total cost curve. At this point each firm's price just equals average total cost, and each firm makes zero profit.

2. If all the existing firms in the industry joined together to create a monopoly, they could achieve positive economic profit in the short run. But this would induce new firms to create new, differentiated products and then enter the industry and capture some of the profit. So, in the long run, thanks to the lack of barriers to entry, it would be impossible to maintain such a monopoly.

3. a. False. As illustrated in panel (b) of Figure 31.4, a monopolistically competitive firm sells its output at a price that exceeds marginal cost—unlike a perfectly competitive firm, which sells at a price equal to marginal cost. Not only does a monopolistically competitive firm maximize profit by charging more than marginal cost, but in long-run equilibrium, a price equal to marginal cost would be below average total cost and cause the firm to incur a loss.

b. True. Firms in a monopolistically competitive industry could achieve higher profit (*monopoly profit*) if they all joined together as a single firm with a single product. Because each of the smaller firms possesses excess capacity, a single firm producing a larger quantity would have a lower average total cost. The effect on consumers, however, is ambiguous. They would experience less choice. But if consolidation substantially reduced industry-wide average total cost and increases industry-wide output, consumers could experience lower prices with the monopoly.

c. True. Fads and fashions are promulgated by advertising and a desire for product differentiation, which are common in oligopolies and monopolistically competitive industries, but not in monopolies or perfectly competitive industries.

Multiple-Choice Questions

1. b
2. e
3. b
4. b
5. e

Critical-Thinking Question

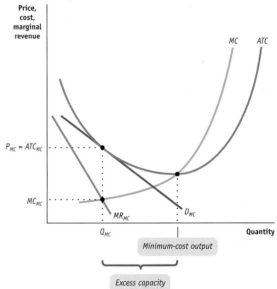

Module 32

Check Your Understanding

1. a. This type of advertising is likely to be useful because it provides new information on an important product.

b. This type of advertising is likely to be wasteful because it is focused on promoting Bayer aspirin over a rival's aspirin despite the two products being medically indistinguishable.

c. This is useful because the longevity of a business gives a potential customer information about its quality.

2. A successful brand name indicates a desirable attribute, such as quality, to a potential buyer. So, other things equal—such as price—a firm with a successful brand name will achieve higher sales than a rival with a comparable product but without a successful brand name. This is likely to deter new firms from entering an industry in which an existing firm has a successful brand name.

Multiple-Choice Questions

1. e
2. d
3. a
4. e
5. d

Critical-Thinking Question

Product differentiation is efficient when it conveys useful information to consumers and the marginal benefit of the product differentiation exceeds the marginal cost. It is not efficient from a societal standpoint if it does not convey useful information or other benefits worth more than the resources devoted to it. This is likely to be the case, for example, if it misleads consumers or creates undesirable market power.

Module 33

Check Your Understanding

1. Many college professors will depart for other lines of work if the government imposes a wage that is lower than the market wage. Fewer professors will result in fewer courses taught and therefore fewer college degrees produced. It will adversely affect sectors of the economy that depend directly on colleges, such as the local shopkeepers who sell goods and services to students and faculty, college textbook publishers, and so on. It will also adversely affect firms that use the "output" produced by colleges: new college graduates. Firms that need to hire new employees with college degrees will be hurt as a smaller supply results in a higher market wage for college graduates. Ultimately, the reduced supply of college-educated workers will result in a lower level of human capital in the entire economy relative to what it would have been without the policy. And this will hurt all sectors of the economy that depend on human capital. The sectors of the economy that might benefit are firms that compete with colleges in the hiring of would-be college professors. For example, accounting firms will find it easier to hire people who would otherwise have been professors of accounting, and publishers will find it easier to hire people who would otherwise have been professors of English (easier in the sense that the firms can recruit

would-be professors with a lower wage than before). In addition, workers who already have college degrees will benefit; they will command higher wages as the supply of college-educated workers falls.

2. **a.** The demand curve for labor shifts to the right.
   b. The demand curve for labor shifts to the left.

Multiple-Choice Questions

1. b
2. e
3. d
4. b
5. a

Critical-Thinking Questions

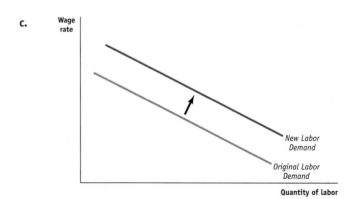

Module 34

Check your Understanding

1. a. This would increase the supply of land, shifting the supply curve to the right and leading to a new equilibrium at a lower rental rate and a higher quantity.

b. This would increase the marginal product of land and thus the value of the marginal product of land. The *VMP* curve for land would shift to the right, leading to a new equilibrium at a higher rental rate and a higher quantity.

2. When firms from different industries compete for the same land, an inter-industry land market develops and, other things being equal, each unit of land used by the various industries will rent for the same equilibrium rental rate, *R*. According to the marginal productivity theory of income distribution, *VMP* for land = *R* for the last unit of land rented. Because each industry rents until *VMP* for land = *R*, the last unit of land rented in each of these different industries will have the same value of the marginal product of land.

Multiple-Choice Questions

1. a
2. c
3. a
4. c
5. e

Critical-Thinking Question

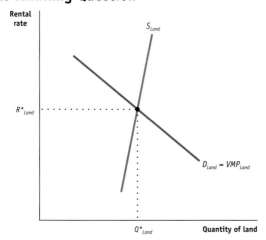

Module 35

Check Your Understanding

1. a. Clive is made worse off if, before the new law, he had preferred to work more than 35 hours per week. As a result of the law, he can no longer choose his preferred time allocation; he now consumes fewer goods and more leisure than he would like.

b. Clive's utility is unaffected by the law if, before the law, he had preferred to work 35 or fewer hours per week. The law has not changed his preferred time allocation.

c. Clive can never be made better off by a law that restricts the number of hours he can work. He can only be made worse off (case a) or equally as well off (case b).

2. The substitution effect would induce Clive to work fewer hours and consume more leisure after his wage rate falls—the fall in the wage rate means the price of an hour of leisure falls, leading Clive to consume more leisure. But a fall in his wage rate also generates a fall in Clive's income. The income effect of this is to induce Clive to consume less leisure and therefore work more hours, since he is now poorer and leisure is a normal good. If the income effect dominates the substitution effect, Clive will in the end work more hours than before.

Multiple-Choice Questions

1. d
2. a
3. e
4. c
5. d

Critical-Thinking Question

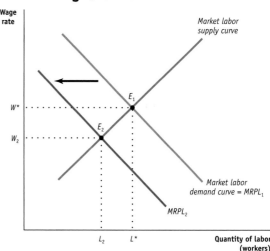

Module 36

Check Your Understanding

1. Yes, the firm is employing the cost-minimizing combination of inputs because the marginal product per dollar is equal for capital and labor: 500/$100 = 1,000/$200 = 5 units of output per dollar.

Multiple-Choice Questions

1. c
2. b
3. c
4. a
5. d

Critical-Thinking Questions

a. 20

b. 10/$10 = 1 pencil per dollar

c. The firm would hire 6 workers.

d. No. The marginal product per dollar spent on capital is 100/$50 = 2 pencils per dollar. Thus, the firm is not following the cost-minimization rule because the marginal product per dollar spent on labor (1) is less than the marginal product per dollar spent on capital (2).

Module 37

Check Your Understanding

1. a. False. Income disparities associated with gender, race, and ethnicity can be explained by the marginal productivity theory of income distribution, provided that differences in marginal productivity across people are correlated with gender, race, or ethnicity. One possible source for such correlation is past discrimination. Such discrimination can lower individuals' marginal productivity by, for example, preventing them from acquiring the human capital that would raise their productivity. Another possible source of the correlation is differences in work experience that are associated with gender, race, or ethnicity. For example, in jobs for which work experience or length of tenure is important, women may earn lower wages because on average more women than men take child-care-related absences from work.

b. True. Companies that discriminate when their competitors do not are likely to hire less able workers because they discriminate against more able workers who are considered to be of the wrong gender, race, ethnicity, or other characteristic. And with less able workers, such companies are likely to earn less profit than their competitors who don't discriminate.

c. Ambiguous. In general, workers who are paid less because they have less experience may or may not be the victims of discrimination. The answer depends on the reason for the lack of experience. If workers have less experience because they are young or have chosen to do something else rather than gain experience, then they are not victims of discrimination as long as the lower earnings are commensurate with the lower level of experience (as opposed, for example, to earning a lot less while having just a little less experience). But if workers lack experience because previous job discrimination prevented them from gaining experience, then they are indeed victims of discrimination when they are paid less.

Multiple-Choice Questions

1.   a

2.   a

3.   a

4.   b

5.   e

Critical-Thinking Questions

a. Market power—firms with market power can organize to pay lower wages than would result in a perfectly competitive labor market. Monopsonies pay less than the value of the marginal product of labor. And unions can organize to demand higher wages than would result in a perfectly competitive labor market.

b. Efficiency wages—some firms pay high wages to boost worker performance and encourage loyalty.

c. Discrimination—some firms pay workers differently solely on the basis of worker characteristics that do not affect marginal productivity.

Module 38

Check Your Understanding

1. a. This is an externality problem because the cost of wastewater runoff is imposed on the farms' neighbors with no compensation and no other way for the farms to internalize the cost.

b. Since the large poultry farmers do not take the external cost of their actions into account when making decisions about how much wastewater to generate, they will create more runoff than is socially optimal. They will produce runoff up to the point at which the marginal social benefit of an additional unit of runoff is zero; however, their neighbors experience a high, positive level of marginal social cost of runoff from this output level. So the quantity of wastewater runoff is inefficient: reducing runoff by one unit would reduce total social benefit by less than it would reduce total social cost.

c. At the socially optimal quantity of wastewater runoff, the marginal social benefit is equal to the marginal social cost. This quantity is lower than the quantity of wastewater runoff that would be created in the absence of government intervention or a private deal.

2. Yasmin's reasoning is not correct: allowing some late returns of books is likely to be socially optimal. Although you impose a marginal social cost on others every day that you are late in returning a book, there is some positive marginal social benefit to you of returning a book late—you get a longer period during which to use it for education and pleasure. If you need it for a book report, the additional benefit from another day might be large indeed.

The socially optimal number of days that a book is returned late is the number at which the marginal social benefit equals the marginal social cost. A fine so stiff that it prevents any late returns is likely to result in a situation in which people return books although the marginal social benefit of keeping them another day is greater than the marginal social cost—an inefficient outcome. In that case, allowing an overdue patron another day would increase total social benefit more than it would increase total social cost. So charging a moderate fine that reduces the number of days that books are returned late to the socially optimal number of days is appropriate.

Multiple-Choice Questions

1. a
2. a
3. d
4. b
5. d

Critical-Thinking Questions

a. The marginal social cost of pollution is the additional cost imposed on society by an additional unit of pollution.

b. The marginal social benefit of pollution is the additional benefit to society from an additional unit of pollution. Even when a firm could provide the same quantity of output without polluting as much, there is a benefit from polluting more because the firm can devote less money and resources to pollution avoidance.

c. The socially optimal level of pollution is that level at which the marginal social benefit of pollution equals the marginal social cost.

Module 39

Check Your Understanding

1. This is a misguided argument. Allowing polluters to sell emissions permits makes polluters face a cost of polluting: the opportunity cost of not being able to sell the permits that cover that pollution. If a polluter chooses not to reduce its emissions, it cannot sell its emissions permits. As a result, it forgoes the opportunity of making money from the sale of the permits. So, despite the fact that the polluter receives a monetary benefit from selling the permits, the scheme has the desired effect: to make polluters internalize the externality of their actions and reduce the total amount of pollution.

2. **a.** Planting trees imposes an external benefit: the marginal social benefit of planting trees is higher than the marginal private benefit to individual tree planters because many people (not just those who plant the trees) can enjoy the improved air quality and lower summer temperatures. The difference between the marginal social benefit and the marginal private benefit to individual tree planters is the marginal external benefit. A Pigouvian subsidy equal to the marginal external benefit could be placed on each tree planted in urban areas in order to increase the marginal private benefit to individual tree planters to the same level as the marginal social benefit.

   b. Water-saving toilets create an external benefit: the marginal private benefit to individual homeowners from replacing a traditional toilet with a water-saving toilet is almost zero because water is very inexpensive. But the marginal social benefit is large because fewer critical rivers and aquifers need to be pumped. The difference between the marginal social benefit and the marginal private benefit to individual homeowners is the marginal external benefit. A Pigouvian subsidy for installing water-

saving toilets equal to the marginal external benefit could bring the marginal private benefit to individual homeowners in line with the marginal social benefit.

   c. Disposing of old computer monitors imposes an external cost: the marginal private cost to those disposing of old computer monitors is lower than the marginal social cost, since environmental pollution is borne by people other than the person disposing of the monitor. The difference between the marginal social cost and the marginal private cost to those disposing of old computer monitors is the marginal external cost. A Pigouvian tax on the disposal of computer monitors equal to the marginal external cost, or a system of tradable permits for their disposal, could raise the marginal private cost to those disposing of old computer monitors up to the level of the marginal social cost.

Multiple-Choice Questions

1. a
2. d
3. c
4. a
5. a

Critical-Thinking Question

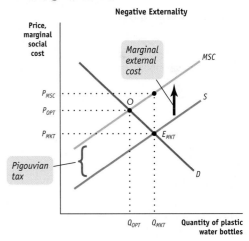

Module 40

Check Your Understanding

1. **a.** A public space is generally nonexcludable, but it may or may not be rival in consumption, depending on the level of congestion. For example, if you and I are the only users of a jogging path in the public park, then your use will not prevent my use—the path is nonrival in consumption. In this case the public space is a public good. But the space is rival in consumption if there are many people trying to use the jogging path at the same time or if my use of the public tennis court prevents your use of

the same court. In this case the public space becomes a common resource.

b. A cheese burrito is both excludable and rival in consumption. Hence it is a private good.

c. Information from a password-protected website is excludable but nonrival in consumption. So it is an artificially scarce good.

d. Publicly announced information about the path of an incoming hurricane is nonexcludable and nonrival in consumption, so it is a public good.

2. A private producer will supply only a good that is excludable; otherwise, the producer won't be able to charge a price for it that covers the cost of production. So a private producer would be willing to supply a cheese burrito and information from a password-protected website but unwilling to supply a public park or publicly announced information about an incoming hurricane.

Multiple-Choice Questions

1. a
2. b
3. e
4. d
5. e

Critical-Thinking Questions

a. Nonrival in consumption: the same unit of the good can be consumed by more than one person at the same time. Nonexcludable: suppliers of the good can't prevent people who don't pay from consuming the good.

b. The additional cost is zero. Public goods are nonrival, so the same unit can be provided to additional community members at no added cost.

Module 41

Check Your Understanding

1. a. This practice would be illegal because it constitutes a tying arrangement.

b. This practice would be illegal because it constitutes exclusive dealing.

c. This is legal because the merger does not lead to monopolization.

d. This practice would be illegal because it is a collusive agreement to restrain trade.

2. Wind energy is created by a natural monopoly, which means that marginal cost is below average total cost in the relevant range of production. (If fact, the marginal cost of wind energy is virtually zero, because the wind itself is free.) Thus, a requirement to charge a price equal to marginal cost would result in a price below average total cost and cause the firm to incur a loss. Only with subsidies could the firm survive with marginal cost pricing. If policymakers chose average cost pricing instead, the operator of the wind farm would make a normal profit and no subsidy would be necessary.

Multiple-Choice Questions

1. e
2. b
3. b
4. c
5. c

Critical-Thinking Question

Antitrust policy: prohibit practices that create monopolies and break up existing monopolies.
Public ownership: have government operate the monopoly with the goal of efficiency rather than profit.
Price regulation: restrict price to the lowest price that does not cause losses, which is the price at which the average total cost curve intersects the demand curve.

Module 42

Check Your Understanding

1. The poverty threshold is an absolute measure of poverty. It defines individuals as poor if their incomes fall below a level that is considered adequate to purchase the necessities of life, irrespective of how well other people are doing. And that measure is fixed: in 2009, for instance, it took $10,956 for an individual living alone to purchase the necessities of life, regardless of how well-off other Americans were. In particular, the poverty threshold is not adjusted for an increase in living standards: even if other Americans are becoming increasingly well-off over time, in real terms (that is, in terms of how many goods an individual at the poverty threshold can buy) the poverty threshold remains the same.

Multiple-Choice Questions

1. a
2. b
3. e
4. c
5. a

Critical-Thinking Question

(Answers to the first part of the question will differ.) Economics can add to our knowledge of the facts regarding trade-offs involved in implementing government programs to redistribute income. However, economics can't resolve differences in values and philosophies.

Module 43

Check Your Understanding

1. The inefficiency caused by adverse selection is that an insurance policy with a premium based on the average risk of all drivers will attract only an adverse selection

of bad drivers. Good (that is, safe) drivers will find this insurance premium too expensive and so will remain uninsured. This is inefficient. However, safe drivers are also those drivers who have had fewer moving violations for several years. Lowering premiums for only those drivers allows the insurance company to screen its customers and sell insurance to safe drivers, too. This means that at least some of the good drivers now are also insured, which decreases the inefficiency that arises from adverse selection. In a way, having no moving violations for several years is a way of building a reputation as a safe driver.

2. The moral hazard problem in home construction arises from private information about what the contractor does: whether she takes care to reduce the cost of construction or allows costs to increase. The homeowner cannot, or can only imperfectly, observe the cost-reduction efforts of the contractor. If the contractor were fully reimbursed for all costs incurred during construction, she would have no incentive to reduce costs. Making the contractor responsible for any additional costs above the original estimate means that she now has an incentive to keep costs low. However, this imposes risk on the contractor. For instance, if the weather is bad, home construction will take longer, and will be more costly, than if the weather had been good. Since the contractor pays for any additional costs (such as weather-induced delays) above the original estimate, she now faces risk that she cannot control.

3. **a.** True. Drivers with higher deductibles have more incentive to take care in their driving in order to avoid paying the deductible. This is a moral hazard phenomenon.
   b. True. Suppose you know that you are a safe driver. You have a choice of a policy with a high premium but a low deductible or one with a lower premium but a higher deductible. In this case, you would be more inclined to choose the cheap policy with the high deductible because you know that you will be unlikely to have to pay the deductible. When there is adverse selection, insurance companies use screening devices such as this to infer private information about how skillful people are as drivers.

Multiple-Choice Questions

1. d
2. a
3. b
4. a
5. b

Critical-Thinking Question

This is an example of moral hazard. The government bears the cost of any lack of care in the individual/corporate decisions. Distorted incentives lead the individual/corporation to make riskier decisions because, if a decision is bad, the cost falls on others. The individuals/corporations must be given a personal stake in the result of their decisions. This could be achieved by making the individuals/corporations repay at least some portion of the bailout cost.

Module 44

Check Your Understanding

1. **a.** As you can see from the accompanying diagram the four bundles are associated with three indifference curves: B on the 10-util indifference curve, A and C on the 6-util indifference curve, and D on the 4-util indifference curve.

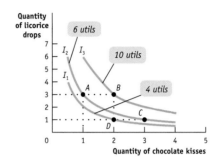

   b. From comparing the quantities of chocolate kisses and licorice drops, you can predict that Samantha will prefer B to A because B gives her one more chocolate kiss and the same number of licorice drops as A. Next, you can predict that she will prefer C to D because C gives her one more chocolate kiss and the same number of licorice drops as D. You can also predict that she prefers B to D because B gives her two more licorice drops and the same number of chocolate kisses as D. But without data about utils, you cannot predict how Samantha would rank A versus C or D because C and D have more chocolate kisses but fewer licorice drops than A. Nor can you rank B versus C, for the same reason.

2. Bundles A and B each generate 200 utils since they both lie on the 200-util indifference curve. Likewise, bundles A and C each generate 100 utils since they both lie on the 100-util indifference curve. But this implies that A generates 100 utils and also that A generates 200 utils. This is a contradiction and so cannot be true. Therefore, indifference curves cannot cross.

3. **a.** The marginal rate of substitution of books for games, MU_B/MU_G, is 2 for Lucinda and 5 for Kyle. This implies that Lucinda is willing to trade 1 more book for 2 fewer games and Kyle is willing to trade 1 more book for 5 fewer games. So starting from a bundle of 3 books and 6 games, Lucinda would be equally content with a bundle of 4 books and 4 games and Kyle would be equally content with a bundle of 4 books and 1 game. Lucinda finds it more difficult to trade games for books: she is willing to give up only 2 games for a book but Kyle is willing to give up 5 games for a book. If books are measured on the horizontal axis and games on the vertical axis, Kyle's indifference curve will be steeper than Lucinda's at the current consumption bundle.
   b. Lucinda's current consumption bundle is optimal if P_B/P_G, the relative price of books in terms of games, is 2. Kyle's current consumption bundle is not optimal at this relative price; his bundle would be optimal only if the relative price of books in terms of games were 5. Since, for

Kyle, $MU_B/MU_G = 5$, if $P_B/P_G = 2$, he should consume fewer games and more books to lower his MU_B/MU_G until it is equal to 2.

Multiple-Choice Questions

1. c
2. e
3. a
4. b
5. e

Critical-Thinking Question

a.

b. Kathleen would purchase 10 song downloads and 0 DVD rentals. We know that Kathleen wants to be on the highest indifference curve possible. We also know that there is no tangency point in this case because the indifference curve and the budget line are both straight lines with different slopes. Thus, the highest indifference curve that touches the budget line will touch it on one of the axes. Since the slope of the budget line is steeper than the slope of the indifference curve (−2.5 versus −0.5), the highest indifference curve that can be afforded, given the budget line, is at the point 10 songs and 0 DVD rentals.

Module 45

Check Your Understanding

1. **a.** To determine comparative advantage, we must compare the two countries' opportunity costs for a given good. Take the opportunity cost of 1 ton of corn in terms of bicycles. In China, the opportunity cost of 1 bicycle is 0.01 ton of corn; so the opportunity cost of 1 ton of corn is 1/0.01 bicycles = 100 bicycles. The United States has the comparative advantage in corn since its opportunity cost in terms of bicycles is 50, a smaller number. Similarly, the opportunity cost in the United States of 1 bicycle in terms of corn is 1/50 ton of corn = 0.02 ton of corn. This is greater than 0.01, the Chinese opportunity cost of 1 bicycle in terms of corn, implying that China has a comparative advantage in bicycles.
   b. Given that the United States can produce 200,000 bicycles if no corn is produced, it can produce 200,000 bicycles × 0.02 ton of corn/bicycle = 4,000 tons of corn when no bicycles are produced. Likewise, if China can

produce 3,000 tons of corn if no bicycles are produced, it can produce 3,000 tons of corn × 100 bicycles/ton of corn = 300,000 bicycles if no corn is produced. These points determine the vertical and horizontal intercepts of the U.S. and Chinese production possibility frontiers, as shown in the accompanying diagram.

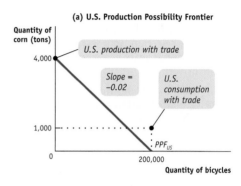

(a) U.S. Production Possibility Frontier

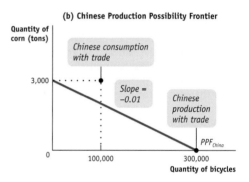

(b) Chinese Production Possibility Frontier

c. The diagram shows the production and consumption points of the two countries. Each country is clearly better off with international trade because each now consumes a bundle of the two goods that lies outside its own production possibility frontier, indicating that these bundles were unattainable in autarky.

2. In the accompanying diagram, P_A is the U.S. price of grapes in autarky and P_W is the world price of grapes under international trade. With trade, U.S. consumers pay a price of P_W for grapes and consume quantity Q_D, U.S. grape producers produce quantity Q_S, and the difference, $Q_D - Q_S$, represents imports of Mexican grapes. As a consequence of the strike by truckers, imports are halted, the price paid by American consumers rises to the autarky price, P_A, and U.S. consumption falls to the autarky quantity Q_A.

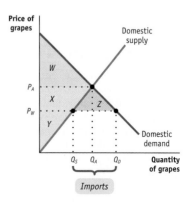

a. Before the strike, U.S. consumers enjoyed consumer surplus equal to areas $W + X + Z$. After the strike, their consumer surplus shrinks to W. So consumers are worse off, losing consumer surplus represented by $X + Z$.

b. Before the strike, U.S. producers had producer surplus equal to the area Y. After the strike, their producer surplus increases to $Y + X$. So U.S. producers are better off, gaining producer surplus represented by X.

c. U.S. total surplus falls as a result of the strike by an amount represented by area Z, the loss in consumer surplus that does not accrue to producers.

3. a. If the tariff is $0.50, the price paid by domestic consumers for a pound of imported butter is $0.50 + $0.50 = $1.00, the same price as a pound of domestic butter. Imported butter will no longer have a price advantage over domestic butter, imports will cease, and domestic producers will capture all the feasible sales to domestic consumers, selling amount Q_A in the accompanying figure. But if the tariff is less than $0.50—say, only $0.25—the price paid by domestic consumers for a pound of imported butter is $0.50 + $0.25 = $0.75, $0.25 cheaper than a pound of domestic butter. American butter producers will gain sales in the amount of $Q_2 - Q_1$ as a result of the $0.25 tariff. But this is smaller than the amount they would have gained under the $0.50 tariff, the amount $Q_A - Q_1$.

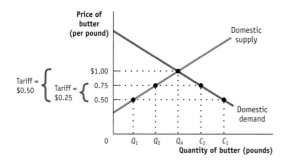

b. As long as the tariff is at least $0.50, increasing it more has no effect. At a tariff of $0.50, all imports are effectively blocked.

Critical-Thinking Question

Countries are often tempted to protect domestic industries by claiming that an import poses a quality, health, or environmental danger to domestic consumers. A WTO official should examine whether domestic producers are subject to the same stringency in the application of quality, health, or environmental regulations as foreign producers. If they are, then it is more likely that the regulations are for legitimate, non–trade protection purposes; if they are not, then it is more likely that the regulations are intended as trade protection measures.

Glossary

Italicized terms within definitions are key terms that are defined elsewhere in this glossary.

absolute advantage the advantage conferred by the ability to produce more of a good or service with a given amount of time and resources; not the same thing as *comparative advantage*. (p. 27)

accounting profit a business's revenue minus the *explicit cost* and depreciation. (p. 175)

administrative costs (of a tax) the *resources* used (which is a cost) by government to collect the tax, and by taxpayers to pay it, over and above the amount of the tax, as well as to evade it. (p. 152)

adverse selection occurs when an individual knows more about the way things are than other people do. Adverse selection problems can lead to market problems: private information leads buyers to expect hidden problems in items offered for sale, leading to low prices and the best items being kept off the market. (p. 783)

antitrust policy legislative and regulatory efforts undertaken by the government to prevent oligopolistic industries from becoming or behaving like *monopolies*. (p. 297)

artificially scarce good a good that is *excludable* but *nonrival in consumption*. (p. 395)

autarky a situation in which a country does not trade with other countries. (p. 449)

average cost pricing occurs when regulators set a monopoly's price equal to its average cost to prevent the firm from incurring a loss. (p. 401)

average fixed cost the *fixed cost* per unit of output. (p. 197)

average total cost *total cost* divided by quantity of output produced. Also referred to as *average cost*. (p. 196)

average variable cost the *variable cost* per unit of output. (p. 197)

barrier to entry something that prevents other firms from entering an industry. Crucial in protecting the profits of a *monopolist*. There are four types of barriers to entry: control over scarce *resources* or *inputs*, increasing returns to scale, technological superiority, and government-created barriers such as *licenses*. (p. 215)

black market a market in which goods or services are bought and sold illegally, either because it is illegal to sell them at all or because the prices charged are legally prohibited by a *price ceiling*. (p. 81)

brand name a name owned by a particular firm that distinguishes its products from those of other firms. (p. 316)

break-even price the market price at which a firm earns zero profits. (p. 236)

budget constraint the cost of a consumer's *consumption bundle* cannot exceed the consumer's income. (p. 158)

budget line all the *consumption bundles* available to a consumer who spends all of his or her income. (p. 158)

capital manufactured goods used to make other goods and services. (p. 3)

cartel an agreement among several producers to obey output restrictions in order to increase their joint profits. (p. 283)

change in demand a shift of the *demand curve*, which changes the quantity demanded at any given price. (p. 51)

change in supply a shift of the *supply curve*, which changes the quantity supplied at any given price. (p. 60)

circular-flow diagram a diagram that represents the transactions in an *economy* by two kinds of flows around a circle: flows of physical things such as goods or labor in one direction and flows of money to pay for these physical things in the opposite direction. (p. 12)

Coase theorem the proposition that even in the presence of *externalities* an *economy* can always reach an *efficient* solution as long as *transaction costs* are sufficiently low. (p. 372)

collusion cooperation among producers to limit production and raise prices so as to raise one another's profits. (p. 283)

command economy industry is publicly owned and a central authority makes production and consumption decisions. (p. 2)

common resource a *resource* that is *nonexcludable* and *rival in consumption*. (p. 393)

comparative advantage the advantage conferred if the *opportunity* cost of producing the good or service is lower for another producer. (p. 26)

compensating differentials wage differences across jobs that reflect the fact that some jobs are less pleasant or more dangerous than others. (p. 355)

competitive market a market in which there are many buyers and sellers of the same good or service, none of whom can influence the price at which the good or service is sold. (p. 48)

complements pairs of goods for which a rise in the price of one good leads to a decrease in the demand for the other good. (p. 53)

concentration ratios measure the percentage of industry sales accounted for by the "X" largest firms. (p. 217)

constant returns to scale long-run *average total cost* is constant as output increases. (p. 207)

consumer surplus a term often used to refer both to *individual consumer surplus* and to *total consumer surplus*. (p. 133)

consumption possibilities the set of all consumption bundles that are affordable, given a consumer's income and prevailing prices. (p. 158)

copyright the exclusive legal right of the creator of a literary or artistic work to profit from that work; like a *patent*, it is a temporary monopoly. (p. 216)

cost-minimization rule hire factors so that the marginal product per dollar spent on each factor is the same; a firm uses this rule to determine the cost-minimizing combination of inputs. (p. 352)

current account see *balance of payments on the current account*.

deadweight loss losses associated with quantities of *output* that are greater than or less than the efficient level, as can result from market intervention such as taxes, or from externalities such as pollution. (pp. 92, 150)

decreasing returns to scale long-run *average total cost* increases as output increases (also known as *diseconomies of scale*). (p. 207)

deductible a sum specified in an insurance policy that the insured individuals must pay before being compensated for a claim; deductibles reduce *moral hazard*. (p. 429)

demand curve a graphical representation of the *demand schedule,* showing the relationship between *quantity demanded* and price. (p. 49)

demand price the price of a given quantity at which consumers will demand that quantity. (p. 89)

demand schedule a list or table showing how much of a good or service consumers will want to buy at different prices. (p. 49)

derived demand for a factor results from (or is derived from) the demand for the output being produced. (p. 325)

diminishing marginal rate of substitution the principle that the more of one good that is consumed in proportion to another, the less of the second good the consumer is willing to substitute for another unit of the first good. (p. 439)

diminishing returns to an input the effect observed when an increase in the quantity of an *input,* while holding the levels of all other inputs fixed, leads to a decline in the *marginal product* of that input. (p. 189)

diseconomies of scale long-run average total cost increases as output increases. (p. 206)

domestic demand curve a *demand curve* that shows how the quantity of a good demanded by domestic consumers depends on the price of that good. (p. 455)

domestic supply curve a *supply curve* that shows how the quantity of a good supplied by domestic producers depends on the price of that good. (p. 455)

dominant strategy in *game theory,* an action that is a player's best action regardless of the action taken by the other player. (p. 290)

duopolist one of the two firms in a *duopoly.* (p. 282)

duopoly an *oligopoly* consisting of only two firms. (p. 282)

economic aggregates economic measures that summarize data across different markets for goods, services, workers, and assets. (p. 5)

economic profit a business's revenue minus the *opportunity cost* of *resources;* usually less than the *accounting profit.* (p. 176)

economics the study of scarcity and choice. (p. 2)

economies of scale long-run average total cost declines as output increases. (p. 206)

economy a system for coordinating a society's productive and consumptive activities. (p. 2)

efficiency-wage model a model in which some employers pay an above-equilibrium wage as an *incentive* for better performance. (p. 358)

elastic demand the *price elasticity* of demand is greater than 1. (p. 111)

emissions tax a tax that depends on the amount of pollution a firm produces. (p. 376)

employment the total number of people currently employed for pay in the *economy,* either full-time or part-time. (p. 12)

entrepreneurship the efforts of entrepreneurs in organizing resources for production, taking risks to create new enterprises, and innovating to develop new products and production processes. (p. 3)

environmental standards rules established by a government to protect the environment by specifying actions by producers and consumers. (p. 375)

equilibrium an economic situation in which no individual would be better off doing something different. (p. 66)

equilibrium price the price at which the market is in *equilibrium,* that is, the quantity of a good or service demanded equals the quantity of that good or service supplied; also referred to as the *market-clearing price.* (p. 66)

equilibrium quantity the quantity of a good or service bought and sold at the *equilibrium* (or *market-clearing*) *price.* (p. 66)

equilibrium value of the marginal product the additional value produced by the last unit of a factor employed in the *factor market* as a whole. (p. 356)

European Union (EU) a customs union among 27 European nations. (p. 464)

excess capacity when firms produce less than the output at which *average total cost* is minimized; characteristic of *monopolistically competitive* firms. (p. 309)

excise tax a tax on sales of a particular good or service. (p. 143)

excludable referring to a good, describes the case in which the suppli-

er can prevent those who do not pay from consuming the good. (p. 387)

explicit cost a cost that involves actually laying out money. (p. 174)

exporting industries industries that produce goods or services that are sold abroad. (p. 459)

exports goods and services sold to other countries. (p. 105)

external benefit an uncompensated benefit that an individual or firm confers on others; also known as *positive externalities.* (p. 371)

external cost an uncompensated cost that an individual or firm imposes on others; also known as *negative externalities.* (p. 370)

externalities *external costs* and *external benefits.* (p. 371)

factor distribution of income the division of total income among labor, land, and capital. (p. 325)

factor intensity the difference in the ratio of factors used to produce a good in various industries. For example, oil refining is capital-intensive compared to clothing manufacture because oil refiners use a higher ratio of capital to labor than do clothing producers. (p. 453)

factor markets where resources, especially capital and labor, are bought and sold. (p. 12)

firm an organization that produces goods and services for sale. (p. 12)

fixed cost cost that does not depend on the quantity of output produced. It is the cost of the fixed input. (p. 192)

fixed input an *input* whose quantity is fixed for a period of time and cannot be varied (for example, land). (p. 186)

free entry and exit describes an industry that potential producers can easily enter or current producers can leave. (p. 214)

free-rider problem when individuals have no *incentive* to pay for their own consumption of a good, they will take a "free ride" on anyone who does pay; a problem that with goods that are *nonexcludable.* (p. 389)

free trade *trade* that is unregulated by government *tariffs* or other artificial barriers; the levels of *exports* and *imports* occur naturally, as a result of supply and demand. (p. 460)

gains from trade An economic principle that states that by dividing tasks and trading, people can get more of what they want through *trade* than they could if they tried to be self-sufficient. (p. 23)

game theory the study of behavior in situations of *interdependence*. Used to explain the behavior of an *oligopoly*. (p. 288)

Gini coefficient a number summarizes a country's level of income inequality based on how unequally income is distributed across the quintiles. (p. 409)

globalization the phenomenom of growing economic linkages among countries. (p. 447)

Heckscher–Ohlin model a *model* of international trade in which a country has a *comparative advantage* in a good whose production is intensive in the factors that are abundantly available in that country. (p. 453)

Herfindahl–Hirschman Index, or HHI is the square of each firm's share of market sales summed over the industry. It gives a picture of the industry market structure. (p. 217)

household a person or a group of people who share income. (p. 12)

human capital the improvement in labor created by the education and knowledge embodied in the workforce. (p. 324)

implicit cost a cost that does not require the outlay of money; it is measured by the value, in dollar terms, of forgone benefits. (p. 174)

implicit cost of capital the *opportunity cost* of the capital used by a business; that is the income that could have been realized had the capital been used in the next best alternative way. (p. 176)

import quota a legal limit on the quantity of a good that can be imported. (p. 462)

imports goods and services purchased from other countries. (p. 105)

import-competing industries industries that produce goods or services that are also imported. (p. 459)

incentive anything that offers rewards to people who change their behavior. (p. 2)

income effect the change in the quantity of a good consumed that results from the change in a consumer's purchasing power due to the change in the price of the good. (p. 103)

income-elastic demand when the *income elasticity of demand* for a good is greater than 1. (p. 120)

income elasticity of demand the percent change in the quantity of a good demanded when a consumer's income changes divided by the percent change in the consumer's income. (p. 120)

income-inelastic demand when the *income elasticity of demand* for a good is positive but less than 1. (p. 120)

increasing returns to scale long-run *average total cost* declines as output increases (also referred to as *economies of scale*). (p. 206)

indifference curve a contour line showing all *consumption bundles* that yield the same amount of total utility for an individual. (p. 433)

indifference curve map a collection of *indifference curves* for a given individual that represents the individual's entire *utility function*; each curve corresponds to a different total *utility* level. (p. 433)

individual choice the decision by an individual of what to do, which necessarily involves a decision of what not to do. (p. 2)

individual consumer surplus the net gain to an individual buyer from the purchase of a good; equal to the difference between the buyer's *willingness to pay* and the price paid. (p. 129)

individual demand curve a graphical representation of the relationship between *quantity demanded* and price for an individual consumer. (p. 55)

individual labor supply curve a graphical representation showing how the quantity of labor supplied by an individual depends on that individual's wage rate. (p. 340)

individual producer surplus the net gain to an individual seller from selling a good; equal to the difference between the price received and the seller's *cost*. (p. 134)

individual supply curve a graphical representation of the relationship between *quantity supplied* and *price* for an individual producer. (p. 63)

industry supply curve a graphical representation that shows the relationship between the price of a good and the total output of the industry for that good. (p. 243)

inefficient allocation of sales among sellers a form of inefficiency in which sellers who would be willing to sell a good at the lowest price are not always those who actually manage to sell it; often the result of a *price floor*. (p. 84)

inefficient allocation to consumers a form of inefficiency in which people who want a good badly and are willing to pay a high price don't get it, and those who care relatively little about the good and are only willing to pay a low price do get it; often a result of a *price ceiling*. (p. 80)

inefficiently high quality a form of inefficiency in which sellers offer high-quality goods at a high price even though buyers would prefer a lower quality at a lower price; often the result of a *price floor*. (p. 85)

inefficiently low quality a form of inefficiency in which sellers offer low-quality goods at a low price even though buyers would prefer a higher quality at a higher price; often a result of a *price ceiling*. (p. 81)

inelastic demand when the *price elasticity of demand* is less than 1. (p. 111)

inferior good a good for which a rise in income decreases the demand for the good. (p. 54)

in-kind benefit a benefit given in the form of goods or services. (p. 412)

input a good or service used to produce another good or service. (p. 62)

interdependent the outcome (profit) of each firm depends on the actions of the other firms in the market. (p. 282)

international trade agreements treaties by which countries agree to lower *trade protections* against one another. (p. 464)

labor the effort of workers. (p. 3)

land all resources that come from nature, such as minerals, timber, and petroleum. (p. 3)

law of demand the principle that a higher price for a good or service, other things equal, leads people to demand a smaller quantity of that good or service. (p. 50)

law of supply other things being equal, the price and quantity supplied of a good are positively related. (p. 60)

leisure the time available for purposes other than earning money to buy marketed goods. (p. 340)

license gives its owner the right to supply a good or service. (p. 88)

long run the time period in which all inputs can be varied. (p. 186)

long-run average total cost curve a graphical representation showing the relationship between *output* and *average total cost* when *fixed cost* has been chosen to minimize average total cost for each level of output. (p. 205)

long-run industry supply curve a graphical representation that shows how *quantity supplied* responds to price once producers have had time to enter or exit the industry. (p. 247)

long-run market equilibrium an economic balance in which, given sufficient time for producers to enter or exit an industry, the *quantity supplied* equals the *quantity demanded*. (p. 246)

long-term reputation allows an individual to assure others that he or she isn't concealing adverse private information. (p. 784)

lump-sum taxes taxes that don't depend on the taxpayer's income. (p. 152)

macroeconomics the branch of *economics* that is concerned with the overall ups and downs in the *economy*. (p. 5)

marginal analysis the study of *marginal decisions*. (p. 3)

marginal cost curve a graphical representation showing how the cost of producing one more unit depends on the quantity that has already been produced. (p. 182)

marginal cost pricing occurs when regulators set a monopoly's price equal to its marginal cost to achieve efficiency. (p. 401)

marginal external benefit the addition to external benefits created by one more unit of the good. (p. 382)

marginal external cost the increase in external costs created by one more unit of a good. (p. 383)

marginal factor cost of labor (MFCL) the additional cost of hiring an additional worker. The marginal factor cost of land and the marginal factor cost of capital are equivalent concepts. (p. 344)

marginal private benefit the marginal benefit that accrues to consumers of a good, not including any external benefits. (p. 382)

marginal private cost the marginal cost of producing a good, not including any external costs. (p. 383)

marginal product the additional quantity of output produced by using one more unit of that *input*. (p. 187)

marginal productivity theory of income distribution every *factor of production* is paid its *equilibrium value of the marginal product*. (p. 336)

marginal rate of substitution (MRS) the ratio of the *marginal utility* of one good to the marginal utility of another. (p. 438)

marginal revenue the change in *total revenue* generated by an additional unit of output. (p. 181)

marginal revenue curve a graphical representation showing how *marginal revenue* varies as output varies. (p. 186)

marginal revenue product of labor (MRPL) equals the marginal product of labor times the marginal revenue received from selling the additional output. The marginal revenue product of land and the marginal revenue product of capital are equivalent concepts. (p. 344)

marginal social benefit of a good or activity the *marginal benefit* that accrues to consumers plus the marginal *external benefit*. (p. 382)

marginal social benefit of pollution the additional gain to society as a whole from an additional unit of pollution. (p. 368)

marginal social cost of a good or activity the *marginal cost* of production plus the marginal *external cost*. (p. 383)

marginal social cost of pollution the additional cost imposed on society as a whole by an additional unit of pollution. (p. 368)

marginal utility the change in total *utility* generated by consuming one additional unit of a good or service. (p. 157)

marginal utility curve a graphical representation showing how *marginal utility* depends on the quantity of a good or service consumed. (p. 157)

marginal utility per dollar the additional *utility* from spending one more dollar on a good or service. (p. 162)

market economy an *economy* in which decisions of individual producers and consumers largely determine what, how, and for whom to produce, with little government involvement in the decisions. (p. 2)

market share the fraction of the total industry output accounted for by a firm's output. (p. 213)

mean household income the average income across all households. (p. 409)

means-tested program a program in which benefits are available only to individuals or families whose incomes fall below a certain level. (p. 412)

median household income the income of the household lying in the middle of the *income distribution*. (p. 409)

microeconomics the branch of *economics* that studies how people make decisions and how those decisions interact. (p. 5)

midpoint method a technique for calculating the percent change in which changes in a variable are compared with the average, or midpoint, of the starting and final values. (p. 106)

minimum-cost output the quantity of output at which *average total cost* is lowest—the bottom of the U-*shaped average total cost curve*. (p. 199)

minimum wage a legal floor on the wage rate. The wage rate is the market price of labor. (p. 82)

model a simplified representation of a real situation that is used to better understand real-life situations. (p. 10)

monopolist a firm that is the only producer of a good that has no close substitutes. (p. 215)

monopolistic competition a market structure in which there are many competing firms in an industry, each firm sells a differentiated product, and there is *free entry into and exit from the industry* in the *long run*. (p. 219)

monopoly an industry controlled by a *monopolist*. (p. 215)

monopsonist a single buyer in a market. (p. 345)

monopsony a market in which there is only one buyer. (p. 345)

moral hazard the situation that can exist when an individual knows more about his or her own actions than other people do. This leads to a distortion of incentives to take care or to exert effort when someone else bears the costs of the lack of care or effort. (p. 429)

movement along the demand curve a change in the *quantity demanded* of a good that results from a change in the price of that good. (p. 51)

movement along the supply curve a change in the *quantity supplied* of a good that results from a change in the price of that good. (p. 60)

North American Free Trade Agreement (Nafta) a *trade* agreement among the United States, Canada, and Mexico. (p. 464)

Nash equilibrium in *game theory*, the *equilibrium* that results when all players choose the action that maximizes their *payoffs* given the actions of other players, ignoring the effect of that action on the *payoffs* of other players; also known as *noncooperative equilibrium*. (p. 290)

natural monopoly a *monopoly* that exists when *increasing returns to scale* provide a large cost advantage to having all output produced by a single firm. (p. 215)

natural rate hypothesis the hypothesis that the unemployment rate is stable in the long run at a particular natural rate. According to this hypothesis, attempts to lower the unemployment rate below the natural rate of unemployment will cause an ever-rising inflation rate. (p. 350)

negative income tax a government program that supplements the income of low-income working families. (p. 413)

network externality when the value of a good to an individual is greater when more people also use the good. (p. 384)

noncooperative behavior actions by firms that ignore the effects of those actions on the profits of other firms. (p. 284)

nonexcludable referring to a good, describes the case in which the supplier cannot prevent those who do not pay from consuming the good. (p. 387)

nonprice competition competition in areas other than price to increase sales, such as new product features and advertising; especially engaged in by firms that have a tacit understanding not to compete on price. (p. 300)

nonrival consumption referring to a good, describes the case in which the same unit can be consumed by more than one person at the same time. (p. 388)

normal good a good for which a rise in income increases the demand for that good—the "normal" case. (p. 53)

normal profit an economic profit equal to zero. It is an economic profit just high enough to keep a firm engaged in its current activity. (p. 178)

normative economics the branch of economic analysis that makes prescriptions about the way the *economy* should work. (p. 6)

offshore outsourcing the practice of businesses hiring people in another country to perform various tasks. (p. 466)

oligopolist a firm in an industry with only a small number of producers. (p. 217)

oligopoly an industry with only a small number of producers. (p. 217)

open-market operation a purchase or sale of U.S. Treasury bills by the Federal Reserve, undertaken to change the *monetary base*, which in turn changes the *money supply*. (p. 264)

opportunity cost the real cost of an item: what you must give up in order to get it. (p. 3)

optimal consumption bundle the *consumption bundle* that maximizes the consumer's total *utility* given his or her *budget constraint*. (p. 159)

optimal consumption rule when a consumer maximizes *utility*, the *marginal utility per dollar* spent must be the same for all goods and services in the *consumption bundle*. (p. 164)

optimal output rule profit is maximized by producing the quantity of output at which the *marginal revenue* of the last unit produced is equal to its *marginal cost*. (p. 181)

ordinary goods in a consumer's *utility function*, those for which additional units of one good are required to compensate for fewer units of another, and vice versa; and for which the consumer experiences a *diminishing marginal rate of substitution* when substituting one good in place of another. (p. 439)

other things equal assumption in the development of a model, the assumption that all relevant factors except the one under study remain unchanged. (p. 11)

output the quality of goods and services produced. (p. 12)

overuse the depletion of a *common resource* that occurs when individuals ignore the fact that their use depletes the amount of the resource remaining for others. (p. 393)

patent a temporary monopoly given by the government to an inventor for the use or sale of an invention. (p. 216)

payoff in *game theory*, the reward received by a player in a game (for example, the profit earned by an *oligopolist*). (p. 288)

payoff matrix in *game theory*, a diagram that shows how the *payoffs* to each of the participants in a two-player game depend on the actions of both; a tool in analyzing *interdependence*. (p. 288)

perfectly competitive industry an industry in which all producers are price-takers. (p. 213)

perfectly competitive market a market in which all market participants are price-takers. (p. 212)

perfectly elastic demand the case in which any price increase will cause the *quantity demanded* to drop to zero; the *demand curve* is a horizontal line. (p. 111

perfectly elastic supply the case in which even a tiny increase or reduction in the price will lead to very large changes in the *quantity supplied,* so that the *price elasticity of supply* is infinite; the perfectly elastic *supply curve* is a horizontal line. (p. 123)

perfectly inelastic demand the case in which the *quantity demanded* does not respond at all to changes in the price; the *demand curve* is a vertical line. (p. 110)

perfectly inelastic supply the case in which the *price elasticity of supply* is zero, so that changes in the price of the good have no effect on the *quantity supplied;* the perfectly inelastic *supply curve* is a vertical line. (p. 122)

perfect price discrimination a situation in which a monopolist charges each consumer his or her willingness to pay—the maximum that the consumer is willing to pay. (p. 271)

physical capital human-made goods such as buildings and machines used to produce other goods and services. (p. 324)

Pigouvian subsidy a payment designed to encourage activities that yield *external benefits*. (p. 382)

Pigouvian taxes taxes designed to reduce *external costs*. (p. 378)

positive economics the branch of economic analysis that describes the way the *economy* actually works. (p. 6)

poverty rate the percentage of the population with incomes below the *poverty threshold*. (p. 405)

poverty threshold the annual income below which a family is officially considered poor. (p. 405)

price ceiling the maximum price sellers are allowed to charge for a good or service; a form of *price control*. (p. 77)

price controls legal restrictions on how high or low a market price may go. (p. 77)

price discrimination charging different prices to different consumers for the same good. (p. 268)

price floor the minimum price buyers are required to pay for a good or service; a form of *price control*. (p. 77)

price elasticity of demand the ratio of the percent change in the *quantity demanded* to the percent change in the price as we move along the *demand curve* (dropping the minus sign). (p. 104)

price elasticity of supply a measure of the responsiveness of the quantity of a good supplied to the price of that good; the ratio of the percent change in the *quantity supplied* to the percent change in the price as we move along the *supply curve*. (p. 121)

price leadership a pattern of behavior in which one firm sets its price and other firms in the industry follow. (p. 300)

price regulation a limitation on the price that a *monopolist* is allowed to charge. (p. 263)

price-taking consumer a consumer whose actions have no effect on the market price of the good or service he or she buys. (p. 212)

price-taking firm a firm whose actions have no effect on the market price of the good or service it sells. (p. 212)

price-taking firm's optimal output rule the profit of a price-taking firm is maximized by producing the quantity of output at which the market price is equal to the *marginal cost* of the last unit produced. (p. 229)

price war a collapse of prices when *tacit collusion* breaks down. (p. 298)

principle of diminishing marginal utility the proposition that each successive unit of a good or service consumed adds less to total *utility* than does the previous unit. (p. 157)

principle of marginal analysis the proposition that the *optimal quantity* is the quantity at which *marginal benefit* is equal to *marginal cost*. (p. 181)

prisoners' dilemma a game based on two premises: (1) Each player has an incentive to choose an action that benefits itself at the other player's expense; and (2) When both players act in this way, both are worse off than if they had acted cooperatively. (p. 289)

private good a good that is both *excludable* and *rival in consumption*. (p. 426)

private information information that some people have that others do not. (p. 387)

producer surplus a term often used to refer to either *individual producer surplus* or to *total producer surplus*. (p. 139)

product differentiation the attempt by firms to convince buyers that their products are different from those of other firms in the industry. If firms can so convince buyers, they can charge a higher price. (p. 299)

production function the relationship between the quantity of *inputs* a firm uses and the quantity of output it produces. (p. 186)

production possibility frontier (PPF) illustrates the trade-offs facing an economy that produces only two goods; shows the maximum quantity of one good that can be produced for each possible quantity of the other good produced. (p. 16)

product markets where goods and services are bought and sold. (p. 12)

progressive tax a tax that takes a larger share of the income of high-income taxpayers than of low-income taxpayers. (p. 143)

property rights the rights of owners of valuable items, whether *resources* or goods, to dispose of those items as they choose. (p. 3)

proportional tax a tax that is the same percentage of the *tax base* regardless of the taxpayer's income or wealth. (p. 143)

protection policies that limit *imports*; an alternative term for *trade protection*. (p. 460)

public good a good that is both *nonexcludable* and *nonrival in consumption*. (p. 389)

public ownership when goods are supplied by the government or by a firm owned by the government to protect the interests of the consumer in response to *natural monopoly*. (p. 263)

quantity control (quota) an upper limit, set by the government, on the quantity of some good that can be bought or sold; also referred to as a *quota*. (p. 88)

quantity demanded the actual amount of a good or service consumers are willing to buy at some specific price. (p. 49)

quantity supplied the actual amount of a good or service producers are willing to sell at some specific price. (p. 59)

quota rent the earnings that accrue to the license-holder from ownership of the right to sell the good. (p. 91)

regressive tax a tax that takes a smaller share of the income of high-income taxpayers than of low-income taxpayers. (p. 143)

relative price the ratio of the price of one good to the price of another. (p. 441)

relative price rule at the *optimal consumption bundle*, the *marginal rate of substitution* of one good in place of another equal to their relative price. (p. 442)

rental rate the cost, explicit or implicit, of using a unit of either land or capital for a given period of time. (p. 335)

resource anything, such as land, labor, and capital, that can be used to produce something else; includes natural resources (from the physical environment) and human resources (labor, skill, intelligence). (p. 3)

Ricardian model of international trade a model that analyzes international *trade* under the assumption that *opportunity costs* are constant. (p. 448)

rival in consumption referring to a good, describes the case in which one unit cannot be consumed by more than one person at the same time. (p. 387)

scarce in short supply; a *resource* is scarce when there is not enough of the resource available to satisfy all the various ways a society wants to use it. (p. 3)

screening using observable information about people to make inferences about their *private information*; a way to reduce *adverse selection*. (p. 427)

shortage the insufficiency of a good or service that occurs when the *quantity demanded* exceeds the *quantity supplied*; shortages occur when the price is below the *equilibrium price*. (p. 68)

short run the time period in which at least one *input* is fixed. (p. 186)

short-run individual supply curve a graphical representation that shows how an individual producer's profit-maximizing output quantity depends on the market price, taking *fixed cost* as given. (p. 238)

short-run industry supply curve a graphical representation that shows how the *quantity supplied* by an industry depends on the market price, given a fixed number of producers. (p. 244)

short-run market equilibrium an economic balance that results when the *quantity supplied* equals the *quantity demanded*, taking the number of producers as given. (p. 245)

shut-down price the price at which a firm ceases production in the short run because the price has fallen below the minimum average variable *cost*. (p. 237)

signaling taking some action to establish credibility despite possessing *private information*; a way to reduce *adverse selection*. (p. 428)

single-price monopolist a *monopolist* that offers its product to all consumers at the same price. (p. 268)

socially optimal quantity of pollution the quantity of pollution that society would choose if all the costs and benefits of pollution were fully accounted for. (p. 369)

specialization a situation in which different people each engage in the different task that he or she is good at performing. (p. 23)

standardized product output of different producers regarded by consumers as the same good; also referred to as a *commodity*. (p. 213)

strategic behavior actions taken by a firm that attempt to influence the future behavior of other firms. (p. 291)

substitutes pairs of goods for which a rise in the price of one of the goods leads to an increase in the demand for the other good. (p. 53)

substitution effect the change in the quantity of a good demanded as the consumer substitutes the good that has become relatively cheaper for the good that has become relatively more expensive. (p. 102)

sunk cost a cost that has already been incurred and is nonrecoverable. (p. 207)

supply and demand model a model of how a *competitive market* works. (p. 48)

supply curve a graphical representation of the *supply schedule*, showing the relationship between *quantity supplied* and price. (p. 59)

supply price the price of a given quantity at which producers will supply that quantity. (p. 90)

supply schedule a list or table showing how much of a good or service producers will supply at different prices. (p. 59)

supply shock an event that shifts the *short-run aggregate supply curve*. A negative supply shock raises production costs and reduces the *quantity supplied* at any *aggregate price level*, shifting the curve leftward. A positive supply shock decreases production costs and increases the quantity supplied at any aggregate price level, shifting the curve rightward. (p. 192)

surplus the excess of a good or service that occurs when the *quantity supplied* exceeds the *quantity demanded*; surpluses occur when the price is above the *equilibrium price*. (p. 68)

tacit collusion cooperation among producers, without a formal agreement, to limit production and raise prices so as to raise one anothers' profits. (p. 293)

tangency condition on a graph of a consumer's *budget line* and available *indifference curves* of available *consumption bundles*, the point at which an indifference curve and the budget line just touch. When the indifference curves have the typical convex shape, this point determines the *optimal consumption bundle*. (p. 440)

tariff a tax levied on *imports*. (p. 460)

tax incidence the distribution of the tax burden. (p. 146)

technology the technical means for the production of goods and services. (p. 21)

technology spillover an *external benefit* that results when knowledge spreads among individuals and firms. (p. 382)

time allocation the decision about how many hours to spend on different activities, which leads to a decision about how much labor to supply. (p. 339)

tit for tat in *game theory*, a strategy that involves playing cooperatively at first, then doing whatever the other player did in the previous period. (p. 291)

total consumer surplus the sum of the *individual consumer surpluses* of all the buyers of a good in a market. (p. 129)

total cost the sum of the *fixed cost* and the *variable cost* of producing a quantity of output. (p. 192)

total cost curve a graphical representation of the *total cost*, showing how total cost depends on the quantity of output. (p. 193)

total producer surplus the sum of the *individual producer surpluses* of all the sellers of a good in a market. (p. 134)

total product curve a graphical representation of the *production function*, showing how the quantity of output depends on the quantity of the *variable input* for a given quantity of the *fixed input*. (p. 187)

total revenue the total value of sales of a good or service (the price of the good or service multiplied by the quantity sold). (p. 112)

total surplus the total net gain to consumers and producers from trading in a market; the sum of the *consumer surplus* and the *producer surplus*. (p. 143)

tradable emissions permits *licenses* to emit limited quantities of pollutants that can be bought and sold by polluters. (p. 378)

trade when individuals provide goods and services to others and receive goods and services in return. (p. 23)

trade protection policies that limit *imports*; also known simply as *protection*. (p. 460)

trade-off when you give up something in order to have something else. (p. 16)

unions organizations of workers that try to raise wages and improve working conditions for their members by bargaining collectively. (p. 357)

unit-elastic the price elasticity of demand is exactly 1. (p. 111)

U-shaped average total cost curve a distinctive graphical representation of the relationship between output and *average total cost;* the average total cost curve at first falls when output is low and then rises as output increases. (p. 197)

util a unit of utility. (p. 156)

utility (of a consumer) a measure of the satisfaction derived from consumption of goods and services. (p. 155)

value of the marginal product the value of the additional output generated by employing one more unit of a given factor, such as labor. (p. 328)

value of the marginal product curve a graphical representation showing how the *value of the marginal product* of a factor depends on the quantity of the factor employed. (p. 328)

variable cost a cost that depends on the quantity of output produced; the cost of the *variable input.* (p. 192)

variable input an *input* whose quantity the firm can vary at any time (for example, labor). (p. 186)

wasted resources a form of inefficiency in which people expend money, effort, and time to cope with the shortages caused by a *price ceiling.* (p. 80)

wealth (of a *household*) the value of accumulated savings. (p. 224)

wedge the difference between the *demand price* of the quantity transacted and the *supply price* of the quantity transacted for a good when the supply of the good is legally restricted. Often created by a *quota* or a tax. (p. 91)

willingness to pay the maximum price a consumer is prepared to pay for a good. (p. 127)

world price the price at which a good can be bought or sold abroad. (p. 457)

World Trade Organization (WTO) an international organization of member countries that oversees *international trade agreements* and rules on disputes between countries over those agreements. (p. 464)

zero-profit equilibrium an economic balance in which each firm makes zero profit at its profit-maximizing quantity. (p. 305)